The Amazing Secret History of Elmore James

The Amazing Secret History of Elmore James

by Steve Franz

Published by:
BlueSource Publications LLC • 8987 E Tanque Verde Rd #309-301 • Tucson, AZ 85749 • USA

Printed in the United States of America on acid-free paper by
Walsworth Publishing Company, Marceline, Missouri.

<u>Some material originally appeared in</u>:
Elmore James: Standing at the Crossroads
Unpublished Master's Thesis, 1994, University of Memphis,
Memphis, Tennessee and © 1994 by Stephen J. Franz
and
Elmore James: The Ultimate Guide to the Master of the Slide
Published by Primal Art, 1994, Saint Louis, Missouri and © 1994 by Stephen J. Franz.

ISBN-10: 0-9718038-1-1
ISBN-13: 978-0-9718038-1-7
Library of Congress Control Number: 2002090810

10 9 8 7 6 5 4 3 2

Printing history:
First edition, November 2002
Second printing, May 2008

(text = software version 1.5.6 / Discography = software version 1.7.8)

For information on purchasing additional copies, or for inquiries on distribution or quantity discounts, please contact us on the web at www.bluesourcepub.com

Although the author and publisher have exhaustively researched all sources to ensure the accuracy and completeness of the information contained in this book, we assume no responsibility for errors, inaccuracies, omissions, or any other inconsistency herein. Any perceived or imagined slights against people or organizations are unintentional.

Front Cover: Portrait of Elmore James taken from an 8 x 10 inch hand-colored original, courtesy Blues Unlimited. Date and original photographer unknown.

Back Cover: Photo by George Adins, courtesy Robert Sacré. "Cry For Me Baby" courtesy Bill Greensmith Collection.

The author is proud to be a supporter of Music Maker Relief Foundation. Please visit www.musicmaker.org to give your support to those who have given us so much in return.

For:

Cap'n Pete and Bob Pazderka,
and Mike, Simon, Marcel, and all the others

Thanks for everything

ELMORE JAMES

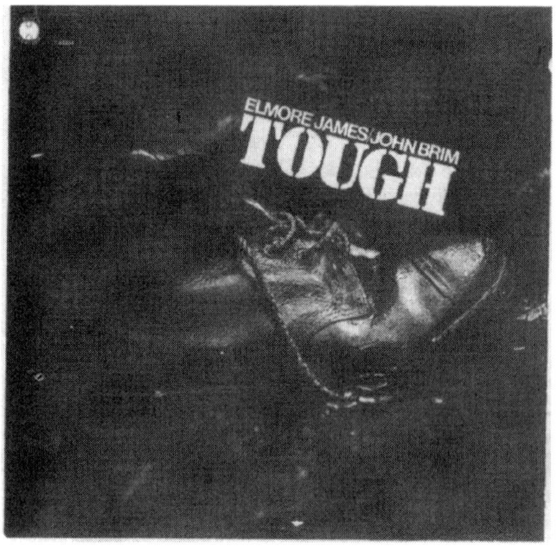

Blue Horizon (M)7-63204

Blue Horizon (S)7-66230
2 Records

Three albums in all, presenting a wide selection of this legendary singer and guitarists recorded work.

On "Tough" some of the tracks are handled by John Brim, while on "To Know A Man" you can even hear Mr. James talking! We've issued this double-album set just as it was recorded, false starts and all!

Historical value, and oh so together on. . . . . .

BLUE HORIZON
BLUE HORIZON RECORDS LTD
30 ST. GEORGE ST. LONDON W1

Send for a complete catalogue and do yourself a favour.

When these two Elmore James albums were released, in 1968 and 1969, respectively, they presented almost twenty tracks of completely new material. Vintage advertisement courtesy Alan Balfour Collection.

...maybe I should start

by confessing that I consider this man one of the all time great blues singers. His band is the epitome of its type....

—Simon Napier, from a review in Blues Unlimited 58

More years ago than I care to recall I was introduced to an album on the always-reliable Sue label... by someone who I knew by name only—Elmore James. What a revelation! Some of the most anguished and impassioned blues singing I had ever heard, together with the fiercest, almost violent guitar playing ever. I had to have more....

For years I struggled to learn how he did it (so, I imagine, did thousands of other budding guitarists). The slashing Elmore guitar style is now well known, of course, **but in 1965 it was a mystery** (in case you're interested, I gave up!)....

The second revelation was less pleasant. Elmore was dead. He had died a couple of years earlier of a heart attack. Thus we were deprived of a chance to see him in person and steal a few guitar licks, **and to this day he remains somewhat of a mystery,** with facts about him (and pictures) hard to find.

—Malcolm Jones, from the notes to "Let's Cut It" (Ace LP 192, 1987)

Foreword: January 1987

My 'formal' introduction to Elmore James came quite by accident, on one unusually warm—and memorable—January day in 1987. I had just transferred to Southern Illinois University-Edwardsville mid-semester, from the main Carbondale campus. At Edwardsville, the college administration had thoughtfully tucked away the art department across town in the defunct Wagner Electric facility—a conglomeration of dilapidated brick industrial buildings. With uptight and nosy college administrators miles away the atmosphere was much more relaxed than the typical graduate school environment, and it was not unusual for loud music to occasionally be played while students worked. On this particular day in January, a ceramics student, 'Wild' Bob Pazderka, was busy stoking a pottery kiln while he loudly enjoyed some blues. I was running an errand between buildings and happened to overhear the music. It sounded strangely familiar, kind of similar to the Elmore James song "Sunnyland" that I'd heard off the double LP *The Story of the Blues,* that Paul Oliver had produced years ago. I immediately forgot the errand and went over to hear more of the music. We introduced ourselves, and he pointed at the jambox and said, "Elmore James." It turns out he had recently broken up with his long-time girlfriend. A friend of his, upon hearing this, had simply handed him an Elmore James tape and told him, "Listen to plenty of this."

Well, that's what he was doing all right, and I found the music invigorating and mesmerizing, all at the same time. Just then there was a lull in our conversation, as the opening notes of "Standing at the Crossroads" broke out over the speakers. I was completely transfixed. I had heard music that rocked my soul before, but never anything quite like this. My whole being was so focused on the music emanating from the tiny speakers, that all activity, time, and motion in the surrounding world seemed to slow down or fade away, while the only thing that travelled through it was Elmore James, singing this song. I remember thinking to myself at the time that "Elmore was singing it like was the best goddamn song ever written." After the music finished I was speechless and found it difficult to tear myself away. "Maybe I could get a copy of that tape from you, Bob," I managed to suggest as I collected myself, starting to think about that errand I was supposed to run. "Sure," he said.

It took me almost a month to get a copy of that tape from Bob, and when I did I listened to it every day on my commute to school—both coming and going—for seven months straight.

By August 1987, I was the proud owner of my very first Elmore James vinyl album (in the mid-west at that time, you couldn't just waltz into a record store and expect to walk out with an Elmore James LP tucked under your arm). During my long commutes back and forth from school, I listened to my two

Elmore James albums every day. It began to dawn on me that all this might lead to, well, ...*something*. As to what, or where, I never would have imagined.

Advertisement from 15 July 1957 Billboard

Depending upon how you choose to interpret the events of history, it would be easy to say that Elmore James couldn't have picked a more inopportune moment in history to die than when he did. If he'd only lived a few months longer—maybe even just a few weeks longer—there'd probably be a different story to tell today. As far as the blues are concerned—a field where irony prevails just a little more often than should be allowed and normally surpasses any fictional contrivance one might conjure—the ironies that ebb and flow with the life and death of Elmore James, on some days, seem almost as big as Lake Michigan. For years after his death, his recordings remained maddeningly on the brink of widespread popularity—in spite of the fact that at one time he had shared (granted, separated by the better part of a decade)—a record label with the Beatles (Vee-Jay), and had almost shared one with Elvis Presley as well (Meteor). If it hadn't been for two French researchers, Jacques Demêtre and Marcel Chauvard, who sought him out at a Chicago nightclub and chatted with him while he was on break between sets, for instance, he would have never been interviewed. Two of his long-time band members, Johnny Jones and J.T. Brown, also died in the 1960s and they were never interviewed (although one researcher had a chance to meet one of them and passed it up). On another occasion, Belgian researcher Yannick Bruynoghe tried to interview Elmore when he had a chance to share a few beers with him, but monosyllabic responses were all Elmore provided. Boyd Gilmore, a childhood friend and musical colleague who probably could have filled in a few of the missing details about Elmore's early life, defied all efforts to be located before his (relatively speaking, of course) late death in 1976—in spite of intense worldwide interest to find and interview him. In 1965, one American record company issued an Elmore James LP, completely unaware that he was dead. No video of Elmore is known to exist.[1] Had he lived just a few more hours—long enough to play just one more performance—we might today have a few choice moments of him on film. Instead, the adoring fan who showed up the evening of 24 May 1963 at a Chicago club with his movie camera to capture some of the Broomduster on super 8mm had to go home empty-handed. Receiving some inoculations—possibly in preparation for a European tour—he died just days later and missed going on the tour by only a few months. Other blues musicians who lived at least into the mid-sixties had the opportunity to tour Europe and enjoy a wider audience they never knew they had, be interviewed by adoring fans, and in some cases jam and record with young modern rockers of the day. Not Elmore, though. Dead at the age of forty-five, he passed away just as the blues revival of the 1960s was gaining its tumultuous momentum. And if it hadn't been for the world's first blues magazine—a fairly obscure English publication at the time—there never would have been an obituary either.

[1] For more details on this topic, see Appendix One, "Elmore James—Myths and Folklore."

Of all my years of research and digging on Elmore James, the one thing I never did find—albeit, aside from the above mentioned one that appeared in the redoubtable *Blues Unlimited*[2]—was an obituary. God, how I searched. As a new ethnomusicology student in graduate school, it was one of my first assignments in "Bibliography & Research Methods." It seemed like such a simple thing—something so utterly taken for granted today that it hardly garners a passing thought in most people's minds: that the major events of our lives will be documented in a public place *somewhere*—birth, marriage, and death at the very least—something to clip out and put on the fridge, or something for someone else to dig up and find later. With a vast repository of newspapers available on microfilm, one might think it would be fairly easy to find a simple obituary for a human being that died in the second largest U.S. city in 1963. My first stop was kind of a long shot, I thought, but still worth a try: the *Chicago Tribune.* At the time, it seemed to make sense to look there, but I quickly found out the Memphis State University library was "missing" the *Tribune* for the days immediately following Elmore's death. It turned out that some time ago, they had temporarily let their subscription lapse to the microfilm service that was providing the *Tribune*—and so there was a large "gap" of a couple years in the library's *Tribune* collection (I had to order that particular reel of microfilm by inter-library loan, and when it arrived I discovered the lending library had sent the wrong reel). After other promising leads dried up or went nowhere, I decided that maybe I was taking the wrong tack. Perhaps the most logical place one might find an obituary for Elmore James, I presupposed, was *The Chicago Defender*. Published every Friday morning, it was the much heralded voice of the African-American community and was widely read in a multi-state area. Elmore died in Chicago on a Friday evening. Checking the paper for the following two weeks, I found absolutely nothing. Then the week after that, a grisly headline in huge type splashed across the top of the 14 June 1963 *Defender* announcing that Medgar Evers had been murdered. I checked the obituary column anyway—just to satisfy myself and make sure—but guessed accurately that I would find... nothing. With broad, sweeping issues facing the nation, it would seem that whatever attention there might have been on old Elmo at the time turned toward matters more vital and pressing than just the mere passage of a blues musician. Elmore James, it seemed, had just picked the wrong time to die, and in spite of reports of his well attended funeral, I still to this day have never found an obituary (published in the U.S. that is) for him.

I'm not one that ordinarily gets premonitions, but during the days and weeks that I was searching for Elmore's obituary, I began to get a funny feeling in my gut. Scouring for Elmore's obituary later proved to be prophetic—an odd kind of analogy for not only how research would progress throughout my entire thesis project, but how I would come to understand the saga of Elmore James.[3] How could someone who is widely acknowledged to be so outstanding and influential in his field—indeed, one of the primary architects of postwar Chicago blues—seem to be so utterly absent from the mainstream comings and goings of the last half of the twentieth century? How come the limelight never seemed to be right smack dab on Elmore—why was he always seemingly standing in the shadows, right next to it—always on the verge of widespread acclaim, but never getting a chance to claim it? It didn't—and still doesn't—make a whole lot of sense. On some level, I tried to chalk it up to the strange irony that seemed to haunt Elmore, chasing him like an ill, bitter Chicago wind. It sounded like a good a reason as any.

---

[2] It would be more accurate to say that *Blues Unlimited* was actually the world's first comprehensive *English-language* blues magazine. According to Bob Groom, *R&B Panorama*—a French-language periodical published in Brussels by Serge Tonneau—predated *Blues Unlimited* (Bob Groom, *The Blues Revival.* London: Studio Vista, 1971, 91-92).

[3] A friend and fellow student researching for his Ph. D., for instance, had a relatively easy time finding no less than eight obituaries for jazz guitarist Freddie Green. At the time, I was extremely jealous. Years passed, however, before I found out that Freddie Green died much later than Elmore did. In the obituary department, I guess that makes all the difference.

In 2003, the blues world will mark forty years since Elmore's death. It is hoped, then, that this book will belatedly help to rectify that ironic, yet puzzling state of affairs.

The story that follows was compiled painstakingly during a course of research that lasted almost fifteen years. In order to piece together Elmore's biography and the subsequent chapter on his legacy, I consulted well over 300 different blues recordings and almost 500 different books, articles, liner notes, interviews, newspaper items, record reviews, and advertisements. The book maintains a similar formatting to that which I was required to use for my thesis. Footnotes appear at the bottom of each page, rather than being collated in a separate section. I feel that this method of documentation is the least intrusive to the reader—if you want to look up a reference, you don't have to go thumbing through extra pages (I have also mined the footnotes with little nuggets and odd tidbits that didn't quite fit in the body of the text; those who choose to read them will hopefully feel rewarded). As far as musical sources are concerned, I have used the original, first known release of each song as a reference. Just as the work of authors is normally referenced based on the year of *publication* of their manuscript (and *not* the year of creation), so too, have I cited musical sources from their first known year of publication (on 78 or 45, or in the case of alternate takes and album-only tracks, by the year a song first appeared on LP). Although I realize this requires more research than just simply referencing songs by their recording date, I find this method preferable for several reasons. Chief amongst them is that, in the postwar era at least, recording dates are very often problematic and don't always reflect the reality in which the recordings were later issued—and sometimes, fixing a release date for a particular 78 or 45 is one of the few concrete facts that can be established about the recording. Additionally, the reader gets to discover the chronology in which Elmore's songs were originally issued—just as it happened all those years ago. The review of available literature and recordings—from chapter one—has been retained from my original thesis as well (and updated for this edition). Although some may find it a bit "academic," I feel that it provides a valuable historical framework for the reader. All new for this edition is an "epilogue" on the Broomdusters and a chapter on Elmore James' legacy—a further attempt to frame Elmore's influence in proper perspective. Also included are three appendices: the first, on popular Elmore "myths and legends;" the second, an updated version of my 1994 discography, *Elmore James: The Ultimate Guide to the Master of the Slide* (with a complete reprint of the original introduction, as well a new introduction for this book); and last, a "Cast of Characters" section that offers brief profiles of Elmore's family members, important musicians, and record labels mentioned in the book.

If you've read this far and never heard of Elmore James, well I think you're in for a treat. As I sat down that day in December 1994 in front of my thesis advisory committee to be grilled about my work, one of my professors patted the manuscript with his hand and said, "Obviously, the guy was great. How come I've never heard of him?" "Well," I smiled as I gathered my thoughts, "that's kind of a long story...."

Elmore James, broadcasting over WOPA radio station, while Homesick James looks on in the background. Photo by George Adins, courtesy Robert Sacré.

CHAPTER ONE

Introduction:

"So now we just listen..."

He was the king.

I've seen a lot of people play the slide. They tell me Robert Nighthawk was good but I never did meet him. Elmore is the best that I knew about. Tampa's slide was good but Elmore's was pretty, better'n anybody's compared. He could control his slide. He made it do what he wanted it to do. Oh, man. He have a slide sound like he ringin' a bell. Earl Hooker was good. He was damn good. But nobody slide like Elmo'. Homesick James and John Littlejohn come closer to him than anybody livin'.

–Robert Plunkett, from an interview in Living Blues 114

I cannot be overly objective about Elmore,

who has always made a stirring impression on my little mind. As a singer he is good, coming across with much in the feeling department. As a guitarist he is a good single-string player (often a neglected part); with the slide he is matchless. The whole combination formed a truly outstanding and original artist whose place on the postwar scene is fixed and very noticeable.

–Pete Lowry, from a review in Blues Unlimited 48

"...His time just had come like that"

On Friday night, 24 May 1963, at 1503 N. Wieland in Chicago, Illinois, at the residence of "Homesick" James Williamson, Elmore James suffered his final heart attack and passed from this life. He was forty-five years old. His mother Leola Brooks gave the report to the Cook County authorities. Elmore would be buried the next week at the New Port Community Cemetery in Ebenezer, Mississippi, near where he had lived as a child.[4]

Elmore James had just started making a bit of a comeback in the Windy City. He had overcome a three year blacklisting from the Chicago Musicians Union and was debuting that week at Big Bill Hill's Copa Cabana club with Homesick James. On Friday afternoon, 24 May 1963, they were getting ready for that night's performance. Homesick relates:

> I laid down for a while so he say, "Wake up, old dude. Get up."....After that we ate. Then he went and taken a shower. Then he come back and went in the room to change clothes. He was right off the room where my wife was and I asked him, "Do you want me to bring you the tablets or something?" So he mumbled something. So my wife went to the door and she looked in there and he was just laying out on the bed, y'know, on his back. One hand across his chest. She ran to get me, y'know, I wasn't fully dressed, say, "Come here, come on James. Something wrong with Elmore." This was around 7:30 in the evening and this was May 24th 1963. My daughter tried to give him artificial respiration but she wasn't able to succeed, and wasn't nobody, because his time just had come like that.[5]

What Elmore James left behind was a legacy of about one hundred recorded sides, thirty-three issued singles, one Long Play (LP) record album, a conspicuous blues/rhythm & blues performance career, an admiring group of fans and fellow musicians, and a few expired relationships with the opposite sex. Elmore was survived by his mother, grandmother, an uncle, and a handful of kids.[6] When one considers his two previous heart attacks, a penchant for smoking and excessive drinking, plus playing clubs, roadhouses and juke joints for over twenty-five years, it was probably a miracle that Elmore lived to be forty-five.

---

[4] Elmore James, Coroner's Certificate of Death. State of Illinois: State File number 63-609-2744, 1963; Patrick LeBlanc, telephone interview by Steve Franz, 7 June 1996; and Jeff Hannusch, "Elmore James Grave Marker to Be Dedicated." *Goldmine* 325 (8 January 1993): 7.

[5] Mike Rowe, *Chicago Breakdown.* London: Eddison Press Ltd., 1973, 205.

[6] Mike Leadbitter and Chris Robinson, "Lazy Bill Called Me Homesick (I Wasn't Though)(Part 3)." *Blues Unlimited* 86 (November 1971): 9; and Patrick LeBlanc, telephone interview by Steve Franz, 11 January 1995.

As a guitarist, Elmore James combined traditional Mississippi slide (sometimes called "bottleneck") guitar elements with modern, single-note style guitar solos. As a musician and bandleader, James displayed a formidable talent for innovation in a modern postwar blues band setting, and when coupled with James' natural bandleading talent and his profound understanding of rhythm, created a unique, readily identifiable sound. As an artist, James' massive, authoritative vocal capabilities coupled with introverted, existentialist lyrics have forever endeared him to a group of fans that consider him akin to a god. Other people claim that hearing Elmore James' music for the first time—even if it was only one song—was a life-changing experience for them; and comments ranging from "no one has ever been better" and "the greatest of all bluesmen" are fairly typical of the reverence of devotees. Indeed, it has been said by scholar Barry Pearson that James' performances were imbued with a certain shamanistic aura, that "Elmore's strength lay in his ability to 'move' or 'touch' his audience in such a way as to border on, or even surpass, religious hysteria."[7]

It is not just Elmore's fans, however, that rush to heap praise on him. Legendary Rhythm & Blues disk jockey Jimmy "Early" Bird told writer Joe McEwan that his "favorite singer was Elmore James, because he was the most intense and sincere in expressing himself [about] the trials and tribulations of his people."[8] Slide guitarist J.B. Hutto said that James "...was about the best [slide guitar] player I ever knew. Out of all I've heard, I mean Elmo was really, he was the BEST," he asserted to researchers Jim O'Neal and Amy van Singel.[9] "Now I wish I could sit down and play guitar like Elmore," said bluesman Arthur "Big Boy" Crudup. "To tell you the truth, I met a whole lot of people playin' guitar and could really play 'most anythin' you wanted, but I have never run into another man could play a bottleneck like Elmore plays it. That's the truth! Once I tried to play like that, bottleneck, but I was makin' chords peoples had never heard before, so I give it up. Elmore told me he had been playing in the same style for thirty-three years. At the bottleneck.... [No] man or person gonna pick it up in a few years and think he gonna do it like Elmore, 'cause they can't do it."[10] "Elmore James is, to me, one of the three or four most influential artists in my own thinking," said veteran St. Louis bluesman and postwar blues expert Leroy Pierson. "Obviously, the guy's impact on guitar was enormous, and not just in the black community in those days, but continues to be enormous today.... [But] to me the greatest strength of Elmore James was the declamatory, fierce style of singing... to me, probably the greatest singer of the postwar era."[11]

"Nobody knew what had happened..."

Most of what we know about Elmore James today had to be compiled meticulously piece by piece. In many cases, usable data come literally one sentence or phrase at a time. "We were explorers in an uncharted land," wrote Peter Guralnick regarding the efforts of early blues researchers. He comments further that "literally no facts were known" about many of the blues artists during that time: "We never

[7] Barry Pearson, "The Late Great Elmore James." *Keystone Folklore Quarterly* Vol. 17, No. 4 (Winter 1972): 162-163; Tom Hyslop, personal communication with Steve Franz. 16 June 1994; and Don Skoller, personal communication with Steve Franz. 22 August 1994.

[8] Joe McEwan, "Jimmy 'Early' Bird." *Blues Unlimited* 83 (July 1971): 5.

[9] Jim O'Neal and Amy van Singel, "J.B. Hutto." *Blues Unlimited* 71 (April 1970): 18.

[10] Mike Leadbitter, "Big Boy Crudup, Part 2." *Blues Unlimited* 76 (October 1970): 18.

[11] Leroy Pierson, personal interview by Steve Franz. St. Louis, Missouri, 27 March 1990.

imagined we would see any of these shadowy figures from our mythology. We never dreamt that [many blues artists]... would be rediscovered."[12] A tale Chris Strachwitz related a few years ago about some efforts in the late 1950s to find and interview Sam "Lightnin'" Hopkins evokes the mood of the times Guralnick spoke about: "Nobody knew where Lightnin' was from. [A] magazine in France... said 'He may be from Mississippi,' but then somebody said, 'No, maybe he's from Texas.' But nobody... [had] the sense to call up Herald Records or Modern or somebody and ask, 'Hey, where's this guy from?'... it didn't dawn on us."[13] Bobby Robinson, the famous Harlem record producer, had just as much difficulty locating Elmore James: "... I got curious, I didn't know if he's dead or what had happened, I started to enquire about him. And again back in Mississippi, I started to trace and nobody knew what had happened to Elmore James, he'd just gone."[14]

Bias on the part of researchers in the late 1950s and early 1960s—against contemporary blues artists like James—led many pioneering blues researchers to virtually ignore Elmore's efforts entirely during the period he was a working musician. Pierson relates accordingly:

> If you're Sam Charters, for instance, writing the first scholarly works on blues in the mid to late fifties, you have to realize that in those days that music was on the radio—the music we're talking about—Elmore James and Muddy Waters and Howlin' Wolf. So, it's very easy to have disdain for what's current. The same way many of us or our contemporaries may have disdain for what's on the radio now.[15]

This is corroborated by Guralnick's statements about the early blues researchers: "...as far as we were concerned, there were no contemporary blues singers.... We couldn't be bothered with such corruptions of style as amplification and popularity; we cavalierly dismissed Howlin' Wolf and Muddy Waters, as Charters had in his book."[16] Charters indeed had dismissed many of the current blues artists, save for Lightnin' Hopkins, whom he proclaimed to be "perhaps the last of the great blues singers" in his 1959 book *The Country Blues.*[17] This was rather unfortunate, especially in view of the scarcity of available information on Elmore James today. While early blues researchers were "cavalierly dismissing" James, Johnny Jones and J.T. Brown, two key members of the Broomdusters (Elmore's highly praised ensemble from the 1950s), passed away without ever being interviewed.

Consequently, very little information about Elmore James is known to have been published prior to his death.[18] Two French researchers and journalists, blues enthusiasts Jacques Demêtre and Marcel Chauvard, conducted the only known interview with him. This occurred during their legendary trip to the United States in 1959, while they were in Chicago. They published details of their trip—including their little chat with Elmore—in a series of articles entitled "Voyage au Pays du Blues" for the French magazine *Jazz Hot* between December 1959 and May 1960. Later, the series was translated into English, Spanish, Polish, and Yugoslavian.[19] This information was utilized again for a one and a half page biography published in a British periodical in October 1963; this was later revised and re-published in May 1965.[20] Other primary

---

12 Peter Guralnick, *Feel Like Going Home.* New York: Outerbridge & Dienstfrey, 1971, 23.

13 John Broven, "I Found Lightnin' Hopkins!" *Juke Blues* 31 (Summer 1994): 23.

14 John Broven, "Bobby's Happy House of Hits, part 2." *Juke Blues* 16 (Summer 1989): 12.

15 Pierson, personal interview, 27 March 1990.

16 Guralnick, 23.

17 Samuel Charters, *The Country Blues.* New York: Rinehart & Company, Inc., 1959, 254.

18 Robert Ford, *A Blues Bibliography: The International Literature of an Afro-American Music Genre.* Kent, England: Paul Pelletier, 1999, 321-324.

19 Sebastian Danchin, "Introduction," 8, 20. In Jacques Demêtre and Marcel Chauvard, *Land of the Blues.* Levallois-Perret, France: CLARB/Soul Bag, 1994. Note: The english language version originally appeared in the British publication *Jazz Journal*, in September 1960.

sources (from when Elmore was still living) consist solely of: recollections from people who knew him; some press coverage from the rhythm & blues industry trade magazines; about two dozen photographs; his 78 and 45 rpm singles;[21] files and notes from the American Federation of Musicians Local 208 in Chicago (which was utilized by Scott Dirks to create a fascinating article, for the April 2002 issue of *Living Blues* magazine, about Elmore's troubles with the union);[22] and some rather incomplete session files from most of the seven record companies for which he recorded (one of them, Trumpet Records, *did* keep satisfactorily complete documents including contracts, exact recording session dates, and a taped telephone conversation between Elmore and the label owner).[23]

Elmore in Perspective, Part 1: A Brief Overview of Elmore James in Print

Starting in the late 1950s and on into the mid 1960s, a steady trickle of information on Elmore James began to be published, primarily in specialty magazines, booklets, and liner notes. Many of these were either short, paragraph-length biographies (often courtesy of Messrs. Demêtre and Chauvard),[24] early discographical attempts,[25] record reviews and critiques,[26] or minor updates and corrections sent in by the magazine's readers.[27] In 1966, James Meredith published an intriguing recollection of an Elmore performance six years earlier in a Jackson, Mississippi, nightclub,[28] while three discographies (from 1963, 1965, and 1968) attempted to put some semblance of order to the details of James' recording sessions.[29] By

20 Big Joe Williams, Bob Koester, Marcel Chauvard, et al., "The Story of Elmore James." *Blues Unlimited* 5 (October 1963): 3-4; and Jacques Demêtre, Marcel Chauvard, and Bob Koester, "Elmore James." *Collectors Classics* 7 (May 1965): 3-4.

21 Note: The 1961 Crown LP *Blues After Hours* was composed entirely of previously issued Elmore James singles.

22 Scott Dirks, "Elmore James and the Musicians Union." *Living Blues* 162 (April 2002): 40-45.

23 "*'Do You Need a Good Artist?'* Elmore James's Phone Call to Lillian McMurry," *Living Blues* 67 (1986): 28; see also Marc Ryan, *Trumpet Records: An Illustrated History with Discography,* listed below.

24 Derek Coller, Jacques Demêtre, and Marcel Chauvard, "Elmore James." *Vintage Jazz Mart* 71 (January? 1960): 4; and Paul Oliver and Jacques Demêtre, "Chicago Blues Singers." *Jazz Monthly* Vol. 6, No. 2 (April 1960): 12-13.

25 Anthony Rotante, "Elmore James." *Vintage Jazz Mart* 68 (October 1959): 4, 34; Michel Vogler, "Elmore James Discography." *Jazz Statistics* 18 (1960): 3-4; Michel Vogler, "Elmore James Discography." *Jazz Statistics* 22 (June 1961): 3; and Wolfie Baum, "Elmore James Discography." *Jazz Statistics* 24 (December 1961): 8.

26 Yannick Bruynoghe, "Chicago: Home of the Blues," 67-76. In Sinclair Traill and Gerald Lascelles, eds., *Just Jazz No. 2.* London: Peter Davies, 1958; Barry Hansen, "Blues In Review." *Record Research* 33 (March 1961): 14; C.R. Wayland, "Robert Johnson and Standards in Blues Criticism." *Jazz Journal* Vol. 16 No. 4 (April 1963): 25-26; and Guy Stevens, "Elmore James: Classic Blues Singer." *Jazz Beat* 11 (November 1964): 13. Note: In the case of *Just Jazz No. 2,* Bruynoghe offers a unique—and rare—criticism of James live in performance at Sylvio's. From reading his short essay, however, one is left with the unmistakable impression that his favorite was Muddy Waters, and that he did not find Elmore James overly impressive, stating that it was "quite fascinating at times, but there was undoubtedly too much monotony in his repertoire and in the handling of some of his material." Just for the record, Bruynoghe spent more time describing the physical location and appearance of Sylvio's than he did on Elmore James (Bruynoghe, *Just Jazz No. 2,* 71-72).

27 Tony Standish, "Elmore James." *Vintage Jazz Mart* 70 (December 1959): 4;

28 James Meredith, *Three Years in Mississippi.* Bloomington, Indiana: Indiana University Press, 1966, 34-37. This recollection was reprinted as James Meredith, "Elmo' 1960: As A Negro Saw Him." *Blues Unlimited* 64 (July 1969): 8-9; and was translated into French in James Meredith, "Elmore Vu par un Noir." *Soul Bag* 94, (May/June 1983): 28.

the latter part of the 1960s, British researcher Mike Leadbitter—considered to be an early pioneer of Elmore James research—was starting to assemble and publish some biographical information on James.[30] A six-page article Leadbitter compiled and wrote in 1972 (utilizing fieldwork gathered by researcher Gayle Dean Wardlow) to this day is considered the cornerstone of biographical information on James.[31] Also in 1972, Barry Pearson published a scholarly paper on James in *Keystone Folklore Quarterly.* Unlike other articles which tend to focus on James' biography, Pearson instead focused on James the artist, and described in detail his musical and poetical styles, and his shaman-like role in the African-American community.[32] The following year, British researcher Mike Rowe used Elmore James as the showcase for the last chapter of his critically acclaimed history of Chicago blues, *Chicago Breakdown.* Although it relied on Leadbitter and Wardlow's article for background, Rowe did present some beneficial new information.[33] Leadbitter continued to research and write about Elmore James after the ground-breaking 1972 article—in short articles and liner notes.[34] Leadbitter's untimely death on Saturday, 16 November 1974 from meningitis was a tragic loss to the world of blues research.[35]

By far, *Blues Unlimited* magazine was, in the late 1960s and early 1970s, the leading source of information on Elmore James. Almost twenty articles, interviews, and news stories were published between 1969 and 1972 that added a great wealth of information to the James body of literature. Especially important were Bruce Bastin and Pete Lowry's investigation about James' stay in Atlanta in the mid 1950s,[36] and various interviews with Homesick James,[37] J.B. Hutto,[38] Joe and Jules Bihari,[39] and a

[29] Marcel Chauvard, Kurt Mohr, John Broven, et al., "Discography." *Blues Unlimited* 5 (October 1963): 4-6; John Broven, "Elmore James on Record." *Blues Unlimited* 5 (October 1963): 6-7; John Broven, Kurt Mohr, Mike Rowe, et al., "Discography." *Collectors Classics* 7 (May 1965): 4-6; and Mike Leadbitter and Neil Slaven, *Blues Records: 1943-1966.* London: Hanover Books, 1968, 159-161.

[30] Mike Leadbitter, "Elmore James." *R&B Scene* Vol.1, No. 5 (February 1965): 12, 16; Mike Leadbitter, *Delta Country Blues.* Bexhill-on-Sea, England: Blues Unlimited, 1968, 13-20; Mike Leadbitter, notes to Elmore James, *Something Inside of Me.* Bell LP 104, 1968; Mike Leadbitter, "Mike's Blues: Postwar Discography." *Blues Unlimited* 64 (July 1969): 15; Mike Leadbitter, notes to Elmore James, *To Know a Man.* Blue Horizon LP 7-66230, 1969; and Mike Leadbitter and John Broven, "Behind the Sun." *Blues Unlimited* 78 (December 1970): 4-8.

[31] Mike Leadbitter and Gayle Dean Wardlow, "Canton Mis'sippi Breakdown." *Blues Unlimited* 91 (May 1972): 5-10; and Gayle Dean Wardlow, telephone interview by Steve Franz, 27 November 1994.

[32] Pearson, 162-172.

[33] Rowe, *Chicago Breakdown,* 195-205.

[34] Mike Leadbitter, notes to Elmore James and Walter Horton, *Cotton Patch Hotfoots.* Polydor LP 2383200, 1973; Mike Leadbitter, "That Pinetop Man." *Blues Unlimited* 103 (August/September 1973): 7-8; Mike Leadbitter, "Canton, Mississippi Breakdown," 11-12. In the notes to *Genesis: The Beginnings of Rock Vol. 2.* Chess LP 6641.125, 1974; Mike Leadbitter, "Mike's Blues." *Blues Unlimited* 110 (October/November 1974): 19, 30; and Mike Leadbitter, "Mike's Blues." *Blues Unlimited* 111 (December 1974/January 1975): 5.

[35] Simon Napier, "Michael Andrew Leadbitter." *Blues Unlimited* 111 (December 1974/ January 1975): 3.
Note: In 1974, Mike Leadbitter was nearing completion on a *Delta Blues* book. After his death, *Living Blues* co-editor Jim O'Neal was to spearhead the completion and publication of the work, with the assistance of three additional co-authors (Bob Eagle, Steve LaVere, and Gayle Dean Wardlow). More than a quarter-century later, the manuscript remains unpublished. Bill Greensmith, who saw an early draft of the manuscript, called it "an impressive work for the time." Bill Greensmith, personal communication with Steve Franz. 27 December 2001. See also: Robert Pruter, "Famous Desk-Drawer Manuscripts, Part 2." *Juke Blues* 22 (Winter/Spring 1991): 26.

[36] Bruce Bastin and Pete Lowry. "Blues from the Southeast (Part 7)." *Blues Unlimited* 73 (June 1970): 4-5.

[37] Mike Leadbitter and Chris Robinson, "Lazy Bill Called Me Homesick (I Wasn't Though)." *Blues Unlimited* 84 (September 1971): 4-6; Mike Leadbitter and Chris Robinson, "Homesick James (Part 2)." *Blues Unlimited* 85 (October 1971): 7-10; and Leadbitter and Robinson, "Lazy Bill Called Me Homesick (I Wasn't Though)(Part 3)," 9-11.

[38] O'Neal and van Singel, 18-19.

[39] Gary Paulsen, "Jules Bihari!" *Blues Unlimited* 68 (December 1969): 13-14; Frank Scott and Gary Paulsen, "Joe and Jules Bihari! [Part 1]" *Blues Unlimited* 73 (June 1970): 9-12; Frank Scott and Gary Paulsen, "Joe and Jules Bihari! [Part 2]" *Blues Unlimited* 74 (July 1970): 11-13; and Frank Scott and Gary Paulsen, "Joe and Jules Bihari! [Part 3]" *Blues Unlimited* 75 (September 1970): 11.

history of Trumpet Records.[40] In 1971, Leadbitter compiled and edited *Nothing But the Blues,* a book comprised mostly of articles reprinted from the first fifty *Blues Unlimited* magazines. It offered rare, out-of-print (and in a few cases, previously unpublished) material not otherwise easily obtainable, and represented the work of over forty authors.[41] In 1983, *Blues Unlimited* marked their twentieth year of publication. They celebrated by reprinting Leadbitter and Wardlow's premier article on James.[42]

In 1970, *Living Blues* magazine (the United States' first blues periodical), started publication. Almost a dozen interviews with prominent blues artists and industry people that relate to James have been published there, and have proved quite invaluable. Of special importance was an interview with Big Joe Turner from 1972[43] and a 1982 piece on Bobby Robinson and Herb Abramson (a recording engineer that Robinson used).[44] Also indispensable was Jim O'Neal's interview with Lillian McMurry (of Trumpet Records) published in 1986,[45] a 1989 interview with Sam Myers that presented critical new information,[46] and interviews with Odie Payne and Robert Plunkett published in 1991 and 1994 respectively.[47] 1995 interviews with Junior Wells and Robert Jr. Lockwood were also helpful.[48]

Significant articles on James—or interviews with people who knew James—from sources other than *Living Blues* or *Blues Unlimited* have been sporadic, but important. In 1969, George Adins' recollection of a James performance from ten years earlier was published as part of the liner notes to the Kent album *The Legend of Elmore James.*[49] In 1972 *Record Exchanger* magazine published a three-part interview with Bobby Robinson, complete with discographies of Robinson's six record labels.[50] Six years later, Valerie Wilmer interviewed Robinson for a 1978 article in *Melody Maker,* a U.K. music trade magazine.[51] *Soul Bag* magazine, a French publication, devoted an entire issue to Elmore in 1983. It included a short James biography,[52] recollections from French and Belgian researchers who had seen him perform (including one from Jacques Demêtre again),[53] and a completely revised James discography.[54] 1984 witnessed *Goldmine*

40 Darryl Stolper, "It Was Very Rewarding: Trumpet Records History." *Blues Unlimited* 88 (January 1972): 4-6.

41 Mike Leadbitter, ed., *Nothing But the Blues.* London: Hanover Books, 1971. Note: this was also published in the U.S. by Oak Publications.

42 Mike Leadbitter and Gayle Dean Wardlow, "Canton Mis'sippi Breakdown." *Blues Unlimited* 144 (Spring 1983): 4-8.

43 Paul Clinco, "*Living Blues* Interview: Big Joe Turner." *Living Blues* 10 (Autumn 1972): 20-26.

44 Tom Pomposello, "The Bobby Robinson Tapes: Elmore James." *Living Blues* 54 (Autumn/Winter 1982): 9-11; and Jim O'Neal, "In Session with Elmore and Bobby Robinson: Herb Abramson." *Living Blues* 54 (Autumn/Winter 1982): 11.

45 Jim O'Neal, "*Living Blues* Interview: Lillian S. McMurry." *Living Blues* 67 (1986): 15-27.

46 Jim O'Neal and Peter Lee, "Sam Myers— Blowing it off the Top." *Living Blues* 85 (March/April 1989): 10-21.

47 Steve Cushing, "Odie Payne: An Inward Feeling of an Expression." *Living Blues* 96 (March/April 1991): 52-63; and John Anthony Brisbin, "Robert Plunkett: I Think I Had a Little Magic." *Living Blues* 114 (March/April 1994): 40-51.

48 Jim O'Neal, "Junior Wells: *Living Blues* Interview." *Living Blues* 119 (January/February 1995): 8-29; and Larry Hoffman, "Robert Lockwood, Jr.: *Living Blues* Interview." *Living Blues* 121 (May/June 1995): 12-29.

49 Bruce Bromberg, notes to Elmore James, *The Legend of Elmore James.* Kent LP 9001, 1969.

50 Art Turco, Sal Salzano, and Bob Turco, "Interview: Bobby Robinson. [Part 1]" *Record Exchanger* 10 (May 1972), 4-10; Art Turco, "Interview: Bobby Robinson. [Part 2]" *Record Exchanger* 11 (Fall 1972), 4-11; and Art Turco, "Interview: Bobby Robinson. [Part 3]" *Record Exchanger* 12 (Winter 1973), 4-11.

51 Valerie Wilmer, "Legend of the Back Streets." *Melody Maker* vol. 53 (18 November 1978): 47-48, 56.

52 Alan Balfour, "Elmore James Story." *Soul Bag* 94 (May/June 1983): 19-21.

53 Jacques Demêtre, "Rencontre avec Elmore James." Translated by Marty Champion. *Soul Bag* 94 (May/June 1983): 23-24; George Adins, "A la recherche du blues perdu." *Soul Bag* 94 (May/June 1983): 24-27; and Yannick Bruynoghe, "25 Years Ago." *Soul Bag* 94 (May/June 1983): 27-28.

54 Christian Besnier, "Elmore James/Discographie." *Soul Bag* 94 (May/June 1983): 12-15.

magazine publishing an article on Trumpet Records,[55] while in 1987 Nils Hanson published a Swedish article on James in the magazine *Jefferson.* It was a collection of vignettes from people who had either worked with Elmore (Odie Payne, Bobby Robinson) or had seen him live in performance (Meredith, Demêtre, Chauvard, and Adins).[56] In 1989, *Juke Blues* magazine (another British concern) published a two-part interview of Bobby Robinson, similar to the *Record Exchanger* and *Melody Maker* interviews.[57] 1992 found *Goldmine* issuing an article on James; as a bonus, it included a chronological listing of Elmore's 45s, LPs and CDs.[58] Also in 1992, two blues magazines reviewed the current state of Elmore's album reissues, the first appearing in *Blues Access,* and the latter, which also discussed historically important U.K. LP reissues as well, in British periodical *Blues & Rhythm.*[59] The same year Relic Records released two Elmore CDs, the second of which contained one of the first attempts to update Elmore's discography in almost a decade.[60] In 1993 *Il Blues,* an Italian periodical, published a short piece on James,[61] while the popular magazine *Guitar Player* issued an important interview with Homesick James the same year (his last published interview was over twenty years ago).[62] He was interviewed again the following year and the results were published in *Blues & Rhythm.*[63] Peter Doggett reviewed James' career and published a U.K. discography of his singles and LPs in a 1993 issue of *Record Collector* magazine.[64] In 1994 Gary Hearn produced a guide to Elmore James' Compact Disc releases,[65] and *Blues Revue Quarterly* published a ten-page James biography the same year.[66] Recently, *Juke Blues* magazine registered in with a profile of Elmore James in their ongoing "Blues Heritage Series."[67]

In the 1990s, research on Elmore James splintered into specialty groups, with scholars and researchers tending to focus on one aspect of James' career or one part of his life. Marc Ryan published a much anticipated, authoritative book on Trumpet Records in 1992, complete with a label discography.[68] Ray Topping, a dogged researcher working for Britain's Ace Records, has uncovered much new information on James' tenure as a Modern Records recording artist. In 1993 Topping also found and interviewed some of Elmore's former neighbors—from the 1930s and 1940s—still living in Canton, Mississippi.[69] New Jersey-

55 Vitrice McMurry and Almost Slim. "Mrs. Lillian McMurry's Story." *Goldmine* 103 (6 July 1984): 8-24.

56 Nils Hanson, "Elmore James Revisited." *Jefferson* 76 (Våren 1987): 2-9.

57 John Broven, "Bobby's Happy House of Hits, part 1." *Juke Blues* 15 (Spring 1989): 6-11; and Broven, "Bobby's Happy House of Hits, part 2," 10-15.

58 David Whiteis, "Elmore James: The Sky Is Crying." *Goldmine* 304 (20 March 1992): 18-24; and David Whiteis and Robert Pruter, "Elmore James Discography." *Goldmine* 304 (20 March 1992): 22-24.

59 Terry Hansen, "Elmore James' CD Legacy." *Blues Access* 9 (Spring 1992): 3-5; and Colin Mercer, "The Slide Is Crying." *Blues & Rhythm* 72 (September 1992): 12-15.

60 Steve Franz, "Elmore James Discography." In the notes to Elmore James, *Dust My Broom—The Best of Elmore James Part 2.* Relic CD 7040, 1992.

61 Antonio Lodetti, "Elmore James." *Il Blues* 43 (June 1993): 10-14.

62 Jas Obrecht, "The Ballad of Elmore & Homesick James." *Guitar Player* 285 (September 1993): 69-84.

63 Chris Millar and Mike Rainsford, "We Were Bad to the Bone!: Homesick James Interviewed." *Blues & Rhythm* 95 (January 1995): 4-8.

64 Peter Doggett, "Elmore James." *Record Collector* 161 (January 1993): 18-22.

65 Gary Hearn, *Elmore James & Sonny Boy Williamson on Compact Disc.* St. Neots, England: Limited Edition, 1994.

66 Ron Weinstock, "Elmore James—A BRQ Profile." *Blues Review Quarterly* 12 (Spring 1994): 24-33.

67 David Whiteis, "Elmore James, The Broomduster." *Juke Blues* 48 (Winter 2000/2001): 56-62.

68 Marc Ryan, *Trumpet Records: An Illustrated History with Discography.* Milford, New Hampshire: Big Nickel Publications, 1992.

69 Ray Topping, notes to Elmore James, *King of the Slide Guitar.* Ace LP 68, 1983; Cilla Huggins, "Dusting off Elmore!" *Juke Blues* 28 (Spring 1993): 18-19; Ray Topping, "Ramblin' from Town to Town," 10-17. In the notes to Elmore James, *The Classic Early Recordings 1951-1956.* Ace BOXCD 4, 1993; Ray Topping, "R.T. - On the Box!" 26-28. In the notes to Elmore James, *The Classic Early Recordings 1951-1956.* Ace BOXCD 4, 1993; Ray

based Relic Records' Walter Devenne and Donn Fileti have uncovered some data from James' recording days with Bobby Robinson.[70] They continued to interview the legendary record producer throughout the 1990s. Big Nickel Publications' Galen Gart has been issuing the highly acclaimed "First Pressings" series now for a number of years, compilations of rhythm & blues industry trade magazines of the years 1950 to 1958.[71] Gart has presented mountains of information to researchers that is simply indispensable. In February 1994, Primal Art published a monograph on James. A comprehensive update of the James discography was the focus of the work. Compiled from literally hundreds of sources, Elmore's original recordings were used to verify the accuracy of the discography.[72] At forty-eight pages, it was one of the longest known documents on Elmore James to date.

As unlikely as it may seem, new information on Elmore James continues to be published. George Paulus published a piece on Elmore's days in Belzoni in 1938, while William Donoghue presented some new information via an interview with Lillian McMurry—the first to be published in over a decade—in a 1997 *Blues & Rhythm* magazine.[73] In 1998, Gayle Dean Wardlow working with editor Edward Komara, published a book entitled *Chasin' that Devil Music: Searching for the Blues.* In it was an updated version of the classic Leadbitter-Wardlow piece "Canton, Mis'sippi Breakdown," with an addendum that addressed one of the more enduring myths of Elmore James—the circumstances under which he recorded his hit "Dust My Broom."[74]

Book-length biographies, which are very common in jazz and rock literature, have only recently started to be published in significant numbers in blues circles. Although some blues biographies were published in the 1960s and 1970s, they tended to be the exception rather than the rule. Traditionally preferring anthologies or surveys, publishers used to feel that a book devoted to one blues artist might be too risky to make a profit. Happily, this attitude is fading, as recent books on Willie Dixon, Leadbelly, Memphis Minnie, Muddy Waters, B.B. King, and Henry Townsend attest that the market for blues biographies has finally turned around.[75]

Topping, "Elmore James Discography," 29-33. In the notes to Elmore James, *The Classic Early Recordings 1951-1956.* Ace BOXCD 4, 1993; and Ray Topping, "Canton Mississippi Breakthrough 1993," 18-23. In the notes to Elmore James, *The Classic Early Recordings 1951-1956.* Ace BOXCD 4, 1993.

70 Donn Fileti, telephone interview by Steve Franz, 6 June 1992; and Walter Devenne, telephone interview by Steve Franz, 16 June 1992.

71 Galen Gart, comp. and ed., *First Pressings—The History of Rhythm & Blues Volume 3: 1953.* Milford, New Hampshire: Big Nickel Publications, 1989; Galen Gart, comp. and ed., *First Pressings—The History of Rhythm & Blues Volume 4: 1954.* Milford, New Hampshire: Big Nickel Publications, 1990; Galen Gart, comp. and ed., *First Pressings—The History of Rhythm & Blues, Volume 5: 1955.* Milford, New Hampshire: Big Nickel Publications, 1990; Galen Gart, comp. and ed., *First Pressings—The History of Rhythm & Blues, Volume 6: 1956.* Milford, New Hampshire: Big Nickel Publications, 1991; Galen Gart, comp. and ed., *First Pressings—The History of Rhythm & Blues, Volume 1: 1951.* Milford, New Hampshire: Big Nickel Publications, 1991; Galen Gart, comp. and ed., *First Pressings—The History of Rhythm & Blues Volume 2: 1952.* Milford, New Hampshire: Big Nickel Publications, 1992; Galen Gart, comp. and ed., *First Pressings—The History of Rhythm & Blues, Volume 7: 1957.* Milford, New Hampshire: Big Nickel Publications, 1993; Galen Gart, comp. and ed., *First Pressings—The History of Rhythm & Blues, Special 1950 Volume.* Milford, New Hampshire: Big Nickel Publications, 1993; and Galen Gart, comp. and ed., *First Pressings—The History of Rhythm & Blues, Volume 8: 1958.* Milford, New Hampshire: Big Nickel Publications, 1995.

72 Steve Franz, comp. and ed., *Elmore James: The Ultimate Guide to the Master of the Slide.* St. Louis: Primal Art, 1994.

73 George Paulus, "Belzoni Broomduster 1938." *Blues & Rhythm* 120 (June 1997): 4-5; and William Donoghue, "Did Elmore James Know He Was Recording 'Dust My Broom'?" *Blues & Rhythm* 125 (Christmas 1997): 10-11.

74 Gayle Dean Wardlow, *Chasin' that Devil Music: Searching for the Blues.* San Francisco: Miller Freeman Books, 1998, 159-169. For more details on this topic, see Appendix One, "Elmore James—Myths and Folklore."

75 Willie Dixon and Don Snowden, *I Am the Blues: The Willie Dixon Story.* London: Quartet Books, 1989; Charles Wolfe and Kip Lornell, *The Life and Legend of Leadbelly.* New York: Harper Collins, 1992; Paul Garon and Beth Garon, *Woman with Guitar: Memphis Minnie's Blues.* New York: Da Capo Press, 1992; Sandra B.

Elmore in Perspective, Part 2: A Brief Overview of Elmore James on Record

When Elmore James died in 1963, only half of what he had recorded had been released. At that time, his body of work was primarily obtainable only via 78 and 45 rpm singles. From his death until this year, three dozen 45s and over one hundred LPs and Compact Discs (CDs) have been issued. Altogether, James makes appearances on 90 singles and over 170 albums, with the latter number growing every year.[76]

After the initial enormous success of "Dust My Broom" (Trumpet 146) and "I Believe" (Meteor 5000) in the 1951 to 1953 time frame, James faded from the rhythm & blues charts. His singles continued to have strong showings over the next four years, and his releases were regularly reviewed by the trade press throughout his career. He was propelled back to popularity in 1960, when "The Sky Is Crying" (Fire 1016) hit the rhythm & blues charts and sold 600,000 copies. He again regained posthumous popularity in 1965, when "It Hurts Me Too" (Enjoy 2015) was released, selling 500,000 units.[77] Over the next two years almost two dozen James 45s were released. Two Sphere Sound LPs of Fire/Enjoy material were met with critical acclaim in 1965 and 1967, and they presented eight new tracks, plus the complete, unedited versions of two previously issued titles.[78] Overseas, Britain's Sue label issued two LPs that surveyed James' career—they also received critical acclaim.[79]

In the late 1960s, there was another flurry of activity regarding James' music. Two LPs from Great Britain's Blue Horizon label presented twenty-two previously unreleased James titles from the Chess vaults and Robinson's archives in 1968 and 1969 respectively.[80] Researchers Frank Scott and Bruce Bromberg were responsible, at the end of the decade, in opening the vaults of Modern Records. Two LPs and ten previously unissued Elmore James tracks resulted from their efforts.[81]

In the early 1970s two LPs presented three new titles of James material,[82] and no further developments were made with his catalog until 1983. That year, London-based Ace Records released a James album with nine previously unissued alternate takes.[83] Their efforts with the old Modern catalog continue to the present. In 1974 Bobby Robinson announced that his vaults contained two unissued sides by James. In spite of his plan to reactivate the Fire and Fury labels at that time, these sides were not released until fifteen years later, when Collectables Records (a Pennsylvania "budget" concern) finally issued them.[84] In 1992 Relic Records released two James CDs that received praise in blues circles. They

Tooze, *Muddy Waters: The Mojo Man.* Toronto: ECW Press, 1997; Sebastian Danchin, *'Blues Boy;' The Life and Music of B.B. King.* Jackson, Mississippi: University Press of Mississippi, 1998; and Henry Townsend, *A Blues Life,* as told to Bill Greensmith. Chicago: University of Illinois Press, 1999.

76 Franz, 32-37.

77 Joel Whitburn, *Top R&B Singles 1942-1988.* Menomonee Falls, Wisconsin: Record Research, Inc., 1988, 216; and "Bobby's Top Sellers." *Record Exchanger* 12 (Winter 1972): 11.

78 Franz, 33, 39; Elmore James, *The Sky Is Crying.* Sphere Sound LP 7002, 1965; and Elmore James, *I Need You.* Sphere Sound LP 7008, 1967.

79 Elmore James, *The Best of Elmore James.* Sue LP 918, 1965; and Elmore James, *Memorial Album.* Sue LP 927, 1965. Note: Sue also released four Elmore James singles in the mid-1960s. See Appendix Two, "Discography."

80 Elmore James and John Brim, *Tough.* Blue Horizon LP 7-63204, 1968; Elmore James, *To Know a Man.* Blue Horizon LP 7-66230, 1969; and Franz, 39.

81 Franz, 39; Elmore James, *The Legend of Elmore James.* Kent LP 9001, 1969; and Elmore James, *The Resurrection of Elmore James.* Kent LP 9010, 1969.

82 Franz, 40; Elmore James, *History of Elmore James.* Trip LP 8007, 1971; and Elmore James and Walter Horton, *Cotton Patch Hotfoots.* Polydor LP 2383200, 1973.

83 Franz, 40; and Elmore James, *King of the Slide Guitar.* Ace LP 68, 1983.

were interesting not only for the five unissued titles they contained, but Relic managed to find unedited masters of several sides that Robinson (or his colleagues) had previously edited for release.[85] Capricorn, a Time-Warner subsidiary, in 1992 issued a boxed-set that essentially duplicated Relic's efforts and served to bring mainstream media attention to James for the first time in over a quarter century.[86] Although highly touted by critics, the package did not present any previously unissued material. Finally, in October 1993, Ace released six new Modern titles as part of a three-CD survey of James' early career. Researched, compiled, and written by Topping, the long-awaited set was a significant event when issued in October, 1993.[87]

"...As far as Elmore is concerned"

Research and knowledge on Elmore James has come a long way since editors Simon Napier and Mike Leadbitter noted in the introduction to the May, 1965, edition of *Collectors Classics* that the four-page biography and discography they were publishing that month represented virtually "the total factual information available" on Elmore. They said at the time: "So altogether this booklet has used everything available and whilst there are a lot of gaps, it seems doubtful if they'll ever now be filled in as far as Elmore is concerned."[88] Had it not been for the persistent efforts of too few people and the dedicated work of researchers like Leadbitter, Napier, Wardlow and others, James might still be a mystery today. "Though few of us were ever lucky enough to hear him in person," wrote Mike Leadbitter in 1968, "his music and message lives on for all. Like many of his contemporaries, Elmore was found... just a little too late. So now we just listen and regret."[89]

---

84 "New York Blues News." *Living Blues* 18 (Autumn 1974): 38; Elmore James, *The Complete Fire and Enjoy Sessions, Part 4.* Collectables CD 5187, 1989; and Steve Franz, "Elmore James: The Complete Fire & Enjoy Sessions, Parts 1-4." *Rock & Roll Disc* Vol. 4, No. 9 (September 1990): 9-10.

85 Franz, 40; Elmore James, *Rollin' & Tumblin'—The Best of Elmore James.* Relic CD 7026, 1992; and Elmore James, *Dust My Broom—The Best of Elmore James Part 2.* Relic CD 7040, 1992.

86 Elmore James, *King of the Slide Guitar.* Capricorn CD 42006-2, 1992.

87 Franz, 40; and Elmore James, *The Classic Early Recordings 1951-1956.* Ace BOXCD 4, 1993.

88 Simon Napier and Mike Leadbitter, "Introduction." *Collectors Classics*7 (May 1965): 2.

89 Leadbitter, notes to *Something Inside of Me.*

CHAPTER TWO

1918-1952:
The Mississippi Years

Here's a guy with a real authentic kind of a sound, I call it a crying voice, he has a scream, an intensity to his voice **like no other blues singer I'd really heard.**

–Bobby Robinson, from an interview in Juke Blues 16

Elmore?

Elmore had some lungs like nobody else in the world.... and when he starts singing you'd hear him for **miles**, man, that guy had some lungs!

–Ike Turner, from an interview in Juke Blues 37

Bottleneck?

That's the reason I left mine alone, 'cause Robert Nighthawk and then Elmore James, that Earl Hooker and that [Houston] Stackhouse –well, when you get to them fellows, it wasn't no more bottleneckin'. 'Cause they was all of it. Yeah. So when I was around those fellows I kept mine in my pocket.

–Joe Willie Wilkins, from an interview in Living Blues 11

Homesick Called Me Cleanhead

"Elmore James," report Mike Leadbitter and Gayle Dean Wardlow, "was born Elmore Brooks at seven o'clock p.m. on January 27th 1918, the illegitimate son of Leola Brooks, a fifteen year old farm hand." The place was Richland, Mississippi, located in the southeastern corner of Holmes County, just about six miles north of Pickens.[90] According to the 1920 Census, Leola was one of seven children—the second oldest child of Wash and Sleata Brooks—with four brothers and two younger sisters. Curiously, Leola's age is given as fourteen (and not married), and there is no mention of a very young Elmore. It seems plausible to assume that for this auspicious occasion, the family decided to hide Leola's child while the Census was being taken. Whatever their reasoning might have been, we can only guess—perhaps the prospect of explaining Elmore's parentage to a government employee was more embarrassment than the family cared to face. In the end, Elmore James would not be among those counted for the 1920 Census. Wash Brooks, Elmore's grandfather, would die five years later at the age of fifty-two. According to his grave marker, he was the father of eleven children.[91]

James grew up on farms in central Madison and eastern Holmes Counties, (and possibly Yazoo County as well), all directly to the north of Jackson. Leadbitter and Wardlow depict the area as "a land of low, rolling hills with towns, kept alive by farming, or sawmill interests, nestling by the Big Black River." Leola and a man named Joe Willie "Frost" James—probably the father—moved in together, and Elmore adopted James' last name, keeping it throughout his life.[92] One of Elmore's first farming tasks was to help make sorghum molasses around Lexington or Durant in Holmes County. His formal education would be complete by the time he was ten, attending grammar school only through the 4th grade. When he wasn't in school or helping in the field, sometimes the young Elmo could be found down at the Ebenezer, Mississippi country store, whiling away his spare time singing songs on the front porch for the

[90] Leadbitter and Wardlow, 5. Note: There are actually three towns named "Richland" in Mississippi. One is located in Humphreys County (immediately to the west of Holmes County) and the other can be found in Rankin County (just southeast of Jackson). The Richland, Mississippi in Holmes County (where James was born), can be found on Mississippi state maps dating back as early as 1860. This is the present day location where State Routes 14 and 17 intersect, immediately west of Interstate 55.

Additional note: Elmore's mother, Leola Brooks, was also known to use the name "Leora" at times. See note in Appendix Three, "Cast of Characters."

[91] Patrick LeBlanc, personal communication with Steve Franz. 29 May 1996; and LeBlanc, telephone interview, 7 June 1996. 1920 Census data courtesy of the Estate of Elmore James.

[92] Leadbitter and Wardlow, 5.

passersby.[93]

By the age of twelve, Elmore had taken to a one-stringed instrument indigenous to some parts of Mississippi. Widely regarded as a children's instrument, scholar David Evans has documented many instances where proficiency of the "diddley bow" or "jitterbug" (as it is sometimes called) has led to mastery of the slide guitar later in adult life. Homesick James, a future colleague and a cousin—Homesick's father was related to James' family—remembered Elmore's first musical attempts: "Him and a guy by the name of Boyd Gilmore was tryin' to play. Elmore had a piece of wire tied up on a coffee can and a board—it had one string on it. He was tryin' to learn so hard...."[94] Homesick visited James in Pickens often and recalled, "We used to get out the house and string a piece of wire up and play it with a bottle, he'd do that then I'd do it with him."[95] Luckily, Elmore's parents did not hinder his early musical efforts—as was sometimes common with parents of future blues musicians. "No-one can remember just why the lively and mischievous little Elmo' wanted to play music," state Leadbitter and Wardlow, "but all his attempts were encouraged."[96]

James quickly graduated from the one-string instrument to a homemade guitar, described as a "lil ole two, three string box made out of a ole lard can."[97] Elmore's first efforts on a standard six-string guitar were probably shared with another musical cousin, Boyd Gilmore, whom Homesick recalled "had an old guitar."[98] Homesick himself had been playing the guitar since he was ten years old—largely self-taught—and he ran away from home to work on the streets for tips shortly after.[99] It seems likely that he was the catalyst that prompted James' further interest in the guitar: "See, I'm [several] years older'n Elmore," Homesick stated in a 1970 interview, "I started playin' guitar way before he did."[100] Jim O'Neal and Peter Lee attempted to verify Homesick's claim to have influenced Elmore in a 1989 interview with Sam Myers. Myers, who was a mutual associate of both musicians, wasn't very forthcoming one way or the other:

Q.: Did Elmore James ever say anything about how he learned guitar?
Myers: No, he never did.
Q.: Homesick James says he was playing that kind of slide guitar style before Elmore was?
Myers: He probably was.
Q.: Do you think Elmore picked any of it up from him?
Myers: I wouldn't know. Matter of fact, I never really heard him say. But I know when he was playing with Elmore, I never heard [Homesick] play lead guitar. [101]

"Elmore was a mischievous kid...." Homesick told Mike Leadbitter and Chris Robinson. "One time he

93 Ryan, *Trumpet Records,* 22; Elmore James, Notice of Separation from the U.S. Naval Service. Naval Service Record 8439732. LeFlore County, Mississippi, 31 December 1945; and Patrick LeBlanc, notes to *Masters of Blues—Tribute to Elmore James.* Icehouse CD P2 50569, 1996. Naval Service Record courtesy of the Estate of Elmore James.

94 Obrecht, "The Ballad of Elmore & Homesick James," 74-76; Leadbitter and Robinson, 4, 6; David Evans, "Afro-American One-Stringed Instruments." *Western Folklore* 29 (1970): 232-234; and David Evans, notes to *Bottleneck Blues.* Testament CD 5021, 1995.

95 Leadbitter and Robinson, 6.

96 Leadbitter and Wardlow, 5.

97 Ibid.

98 Obrecht, "The Ballad of Elmore & Homesick James," 76.

99 Sheldon Harris, *Blues Who's Who.* New Rochelle, New York: Arlington House, 1979, 574.

100 Leadbitter and Robinson, 6.

101 O'Neal and Lee, 11. Shortly after Elmore's death, Big Joe Williams offered this opinion in regards to his and Homesick's proficiency on guitar: "[Big Joe Williams] thinks that Homesick James will follow in the footsteps of Elmore James and feels that he has the ability to." John Broven, Mike Leadbitter, and Simon Napier, "The American Folk Blues Festival 1963: What They Said." *Blues Unlimited* 7 (December 1963): 7-9; reprinted in Leadbitter, *Nothing But the Blues,* 69.

almost cut his feet off with an axe, choppin' wood, and... L.J. [Grant, an acquaintance] got him to a doctor and got him all right, you know."[102] While they were living near Goodman, Mississippi, Homesick bestowed a lifelong nickname on James: "We used to call him Mr. Cleanhead (great fits of laughter). He got the name, see Elmore used to do a lot of funny things, he'd take off and cut his own hair... cut it all off his head, shave his head you know and I started calling him Mr. Cleanhead."[103]

Robert Earl

The realities of making a living were evidently hard for the small Mississippi family. Although they narrowly escaped the devastating 1927 Mississippi River flood—which displaced almost a million people from their homes and is estimated to have been, in sheer water volume alone, three times larger than the flood in 1993—another dilemma was fast approaching. The nation was on the brink of the Great Depression, and conditions were especially formidable to African-American sharecroppers like the James'. "They appear to have moved around constantly seeking better work," wrote Leadbitter and Wardlow. "Their son was already a man by Mississippi standards, doing his fair share in the fields."[104]

Floyd Jones, whose public debut as a musician occurred when he was only fifteen at a 4th of July baseball game in 1933, recalls, "I played at this ball game, and they had a dance that night over in the school building. At the time, we was working for sixty cents a day, farmin' and so on, and that particular day and night, I made seventeen dollars."[105] For Jones, that was about one month's pay. With incentives like that, it's easy to see why many a would-be musician gave up on the hard sharecropper's life. "Elmore never wanted to work in the field," recalled Leadie Dinkins, James' former neighbor,"I worked ten years on the Bee Lake plantation in Tchula, and we all got tired of the hard work...."[106] Homesick readily concurs. "With that hot sun out there in them fields, I wasn't goin' to stay out there and get baked, that's the reason I left home," he stated. "That's why I played the guitar! I wasn't goin' to stay out in that sun, that was tough."[107]

John Junior Gueston, who resided in Goodman in the 1930s, recalls seeing James with "a cheap six-string guitar," without a slide or bottleneck, playing with his "naked hand." He would play "Smokestack Lightning" or "Dust My Broom," and on Saturday nights played at "Mr. Victor Samples' place in Franklin."[108] Aside from Fred Chambers, who played both mandolin and guitar, James was the only other active musician in the area.[109]

The family didn't remain in Goodman for long, and by 1937 they moved north to the Delta, deciding on the Turner Brothers' Plantation at Belzoni. Leadbitter and Wardlow discovered:

---

102 Leadbitter and Robinson, 6.

103 Ibid.

104 Leadbitter and Wardlow, 5; and John Barry, *Rising Tide: The Great Mississippi Flood of 1927 and How It Changed America.* New York: Simon & Schuster, 1997, 16, 170, 171.

105 Robert Palmer, *Deep Blues.* New York: Viking, 1981, 119.

106 Topping, "Canton Mississippi Breakthrough," 22.

107 Leadbitter and Robinson, 5-6.

108 Leadbitter and Wardlow, 5-6.

109 Rowe, *Chicago Breakdown,* 195.

> They continued to move around fairly frequently, trying one plantation after another in the locality....While working for the Kincaid Plantation they adopted Robert Earl Holston—an orphan—as a brother for their son. Both boys were the same age and shared common interests; their friendship continued until Elmore's death. [110]

Robert's mother had died while giving birth to Idella, his younger sister. She was sent to live with her grandfather, one Mr. Keyes, while Robert came to live with Elmore's family.[111]

James evidently didn't need too much encouragement to drop farming in favor of more enticing activities. He developed a taste for moonshine whiskey "that was to last throughout his life," say Leadbitter and Wardlow.[112] Leadie Dinkins, who in the early 1990s was still living in Canton, Mississippi, told researcher Ray Topping that, "We all grew up on a plantation in Tchula. [Elmore James and Robert Earl] lived in the house next door to me. I used to make moonshine, and they would always come into my house for a drink!"[113] While they were at the Tchula plantation, local bluesman Ajan Wilson would become important to the inexperienced musicians. "He taught Elmore and Robert Earl to play guitar," stated Dinkins. "When they got good, they started performing at the Midnight Grill in Tchula."[114]

Blues musician David "Honeyboy" Edwards met James in Doddsville, Mississippi in 1937, playing an acoustic guitar. "He had a little old Stella, and he had that out in the country sound, that hollering, squalling sound," he stated:

> Elmore James was pretty good guitar picker when he wanted to, but he just loved to play that slide. He was playing mostly blues he'd made up and stuff like Texas Alexander and some Lonnie Johnson. He was getting a dollar a day driving a tractor on a plantation and he played on the weekends for a bootlegger named Grady Sharker [or Sharkey]. I'd hang around with him; we'd go fishing. Me and Elmore, we'd eat off the same plate. Elmore fooled around playing there for a long time.... [115]

But it wasn't always music that would occupy James' young mind. "Elmo was considered a lady's man, although he never acted rude around me," remembered Ruby LeFlore, who knew him at the time. "He was nice. Elmore was very talkative and friendly.... I do remember a lady saying she was gonna move out of Belzoni with Elmo to St. Louis, but I don't know that it ever happened."[116] Twenty dollars bought James his first nice guitar, a National, which he purchased from a pawnshop in Belzoni. He was slowly turning to the musician's life, "with the weekends becoming more important than the week."[117]

---

110 Leadbitter and Wardlow, 6.

111 Paulus, "Belzoni Broomduster 1938," 4.

112 Leadbitter and Wardlow, 6.

113 Topping, "Canton Mississippi Breakthrough," 22.

114 Ibid.

115 David Honeyboy Edwards, *The World Don't Owe Me Nothing,* as told to Janis Martinson and Michael Robert Frank. Chicago: Chicago Review Press, 1997, 113-114.

116 Paulus, "Belzoni Broomduster 1938," 5. It has previously been reported that around this time Elmore James met and married a woman named Josephine Harris. It turns out, according to research that Pat LeBlanc has uncovered, that the marriage of James and Harris was actually a *different* Elmore James, about ten years older, who also resided in Holmes County, Mississippi. LeBlanc, telephone interview, 7 June 1996.

117 Leadbitter and Wardlow, 6.

Robert and Sonny Boy

Elmore was honing his slide guitar style by listening to the records of Tampa Red and Kokomo Arnold, and performing when the chance allowed. It was around this time he met Alex (or Aleck) "Rice" Miller, better known as Sonny Boy Williamson #2. If one were to pick a few choice words to describe Williamson, those offered by Leadbitter and Wardlow might suffice—a "hard-drinking lecher, but a fine musician" is how they chose to describe him—and according to some interpretations of the man, that might be an accurate epitaph.[118] However, blues musician James Cotton, who when he was a kid lived with Williamson for a time, offered a slightly more insightful picture of Sonny Boy. "He was a good musician when he wanted to be. He couldn't talk it but he knew how to play it, and he knew when somebody else could play.... He did all the things that musicians do; made the music, chased the women, drank the whiskey," Cotton told Helen Doob Lazar in 1986. "He was pretty cool, he stayed out of trouble, except with Mattie his wife. She was always jumping on him (literally) but he wouldn't fight back, he'd just run. He was a big gambler and.... liked to shoot dice. Sometimes he'd get lucky, but mostly he'd lose more than he'd win. I've seen him with $1,000 in the morning and by the night he wouldn't have a dime."[119]

Williamson, who seemed to be the kind of man who couldn't be bothered with minor details, evidently was fond of claiming "I'm the only Sonny Boy; I'm THE Sonny Boy; there ain't no other one but me."[120] The fact that a man named John Lee "Sonny Boy" Williamson had made records starting in 1937 was only an inconvenience, and after that man's death in 1948 there was no one left to argue over who was first. It would ultimately be blues fans who would decide. Since Rice Miller did not release any records until three years after the first Sonny Boy's death, he came to be known as the second Sonny Boy, or Sonny Boy Williamson #2.[121]

Sunnyland Slim first met Williamson #2 in the mid-thirties and recalled that Sonny Boy, "...Came down around Caruthersville, Missouri, with a harp, playing it through an amplifier, and that was the first amplifier I had ever seen or heard, as they used a megaphone before then. At the Sportsman Hall, he had a car with speakers in it and was playing out in the street...."[122] Always known as a creative musician, Williamson became popular partly because of his unique harmonica sound, accomplished by dismantling the instrument and "slightly bending the reeds with a toothpick [to achieve] a loose, resonant effect." Williamson would be the key in getting James first on the radio and then on record.[123] The two soon became good friends.

Around the same time James may have also met legendary blues figure Robert Johnson. Whether he truly met Johnson—or if he just knew of the Delta blues wizard from his recordings—will probably never be satisfactorily proven. Robert Jr. Lockwood, who arguably knew Johnson as well as anyone could, tersely stated, "...all these artists today that claim to have run with Robert Johnson never ran with him—Robert Johnson never ran with anyone. They may have followed him," Lockwood added, "but he wasn't runnin' with anybody."[124] A differing image is offered by Calvin Frazier—who played second guitar with Johnson

118 Ibid.

119 Helen Doob Lazar, "*Living Blues* Interview: James Cotton." *Living Blues* 76 (1987): 23.

120 Paul Oliver, notes to Sonny Boy Williamson, *"The Original" Sonny Boy Williamson.* Blues Classics LP 9, 1965.

121 Ibid.; and Billy Altman, notes to Sonny Boy Williamson and Big Joe Williams, *Throw a Boogie Woogie.* RCA CD 9599-2, 1989.

122 Sunnyland Slim interview by Willie Dixon. In the notes to Sonny Boy Williamson, *The Real Folk Blues.* Chess LP 1503, 1966. Note: "harp" is slang for "harmonica."

123 Leadbitter and Wardlow, 6-7.

in Helena, Arkansas—of a bluesman willing to jam on a street corner with his fellow musicians. In fact, Johnson had even invited Frazier to go with him to an upcoming recording session![125]

As far as Elmore James' contact with Johnson is concerned, Homesick James' claim that "Sure, Elmore knowed Robert Johnson," isn't exactly brimming with detail; this is in sharp contrast to Sam Myers' statement that James never talked about Robert Johnson.[126] Sonny Boy Williamson—one who delighted in mythic heightening—told researcher Simon Napier, "Y'know, years back [James] used to play with Robert Johnson. He was as good as Johnson sure. But Robert he got the breaks. Elmore never liked that much."[127] Williamson undoubtedly meant, by that last statement, Johnson's 1937 debut on record. By the end of that October, Johnson had nine records out. It might have made a fellow musician slightly envious:

> Before his Mississippi and Arkansas audiences... Johnson could... garnish prestige merely by virtue of having recorded. "At that time one record was worth a dozen now," Johnny Shines said [in 1972]. "If a man made a record out there, he was a popular son of a gun... It's a thing unbelievable to most people: 'I have just met a man made records!'" [128]

Some of the most conclusive proof yet that Johnson and James knew each other comes from some anecdotal information offered by George Paulus, and a 1967 interview David Evans conducted with Houston Stackhouse. "Around 1967 I remember talking with local Chicago blues musicians who mentioned that Elmo, Robert Johnson, Floyd Jones and Sunnyland Slim all worked in the Delta together doing manual labor," Paulus stated. "Unfortunately," he adds with a hint of regret, "I spent more time looking for the yet undiscovered 78s by these artists instead of writing down their memories."[129] In addition to that intriguing bit of information, Stackhouse told Evans that Robert Johnson, Sonny Boy Williamson, and Elmore James were all playing together in the Delta, in the Greenwood area, around the time Johnson died in August 1938.[130] Elmore, however, would have only been twenty years old at the time.

Whether by personal acquaintance or by familiarization via phonograph records, Johnson's music was undeniably important to James. Traditionally, no one has disputed that Elmore borrowed from Robert Johnson—a famous guitar riff and a few songs—or did he? Maybe James simply borrowed some of the new guitar concepts that Johnson had adapted from piano techniques (and popularized by his records)? No one seems to dispute that James used Johnson's recordings of "Cross Road Blues" and "Rambling on My Mind" as the basis of his later versions of them. In blues circles, the authorship of "Dust My Broom" has been traditionally considered to be a moot point: Johnson was James' elder by more than six years, and Johnson was the first to commit the title to wax. Therefore, Johnson must be the originator—end of story.[131]

---

[124] Hoffman, 15.

[125] George Paulus, "Motor City Blues & Boogie." *Blues Unlimited* 85 (October 1971): 6. Note: Frazier was not able to go with Johnson to the recording session. According to George Paulus, "Some trouble ensued and one of Calvin's brothers was killed...Calvin ended up in a Memphis hospital after that and heard that Robert was poisoned." Ibid.

[126] Obrecht, "The Ballad of Elmore & Homesick James," 76; and O'Neal and Lee, 12.

[127] Simon Napier, notes to Elmore James, *Memorial Album.* Sue LP 927, 1965.

[128] Stephen Calt and Gayle Dean Wardlow, "Robert Johnson." *78 Quarterly* Vol. 1, No. 4 (1989): 48.

[129] Paulus, "Belzoni Broomduster 1938," 5.

[130] Houston Stackhouse, personal interview by David Evans. Crystal Springs, Mississippi, 3 September 1967. Note: In the October 1969 issue of *Blues Unlimited,* Tommy Lee Thompson (who knew Elmore personally) commented to researcher Gayle Dean Wardlow that, "[Elmore] used Bob's records." (Gayle Dean Wardlow, "Highway 80 Blues." *Blues Unlimited* 66 (October 1969): 12.)

[131] Robert Johnson, "Rambling on My Mind." Vocalion 03519, 1937; Robert Johnson, "Cross Road Blues." Vocalion 03519, 1937; and Robert Johnson, "I Believe I'll Dust My Broom." Vocalion 03475, 1937. Note: James' version of "Rambling on My Mind" was retitled "So Unkind" when released in 1968.

But some small threads of evidence make a plausible argument that it may have been the other way around. "They are reputed to have played together in Mississippi and it has even been suggested that Elmore taught Robert to play 'Dust My Broom,'" wrote Bob Groom in a 1976 article. "Whilst this seems rather too fanciful it is possible that there was some exchange of ideas between the two musicians, although Johnson was probably the more versatile musician...." Maddeningly, Groom does not elaborate on just exactly "who" or "where" it was that this idea was originally "suggested" (perhaps he was making an oblique reference to John Henry Barbee's 1965 Storyville LP, where Paul Oliver flatly states in the liner notes that "Dust My Broom" was a composition by Elmore James?)[132] Recent research gathered by the estate of Elmore James is also compelling. "Many state with a firm belief that Elmore James was solely responsible for the composition 'Dust My Broom,'" offered Patrick LeBlanc. "Elmo was singing that song out in the field and with his homemade guitar at house parties and fish fries when he was just ten years old, just a year or so after the flood in '27...." LeBlanc was told by a witness in Mississippi. "He put that song down when he was just a little boy...long before he made a record."[133] Gracie Oates, long-time resident of Ebenezer, Mississippi concurred further: "We didn't live that far apart," she told LeBlanc, referring to James. "In 1928, I think I was about seventeen then, he was playing his guitar and making them songs up himself. I remember him singing 'Dust My Broom' then. He wrote that song. He was singing it at house parties and on the store porch. There still some people down here that can tell you the same things I'm saying and more, about Elmore," Oates stated.[134] Ruby LeFlore, who saw James perform as a street musician more than a decade after Gracie Oates did echoes the above statements. "'Dust My Broom' was Elmo's trademark song, always," LaFlore told George Paulus. "I always put Elmore and 'Dust My Broom' together, it was always his song," she said. "He played lots of other songs, but...it was the song he was known for even back then [in 1938]. As soon as I heard the record of it years later I recognised Elmo immediately."[135]

Six or seven decades after the fact, it seems almost too late to be sure who first authored Elmore's most famous song. To focus on this issue, however, at the risk of ignoring Johnson's contribution to blues guitar would be to miss the point entirely. Specifically, Robert Johnson was important to James because of his one primary innovation and the two guitar techniques he helped popularize.

First, according to scholar Stephen Calt, was Johnson's innovation with moving bass figures, adopted primarily from boogie piano but simplified by Johnson. Johnson may have been inspired to do this via the work of Charley Patton—who seems to have been one the first blues guitarists to use moving bass figures on record—and Johnny Temple, whose 1935 recording "Lead Pencil Blues" is a concrete precursor to Johnson's use of the method. Elmore James would later use Johnson's bass guitar lines to give a steady thrust and solid rhythm to his guitar playing (as would many a Delta blues guitarist in the postwar era).[136]

Secondly, a technique that Johnson helped popularize was his reconfigured instrumental motif

---

132 Bob Groom, "Standing at the Crossroads: Robert Johnson's Recordings. [Part 1]" *Blues Unlimited* 118 (March/April 1976): 18; and Paul Oliver, *Blues Off the Record.* New York: Da Capo Press, 1984, 230.

Note: In all fairness, it should be pointed out that by the time *Screening the Blues* came out in 1968, Oliver had changed his tune about that, offering that "Dust My Broom" was a "traditional blues." See: Paul Oliver, *Screening the Blues: Aspects of the Blues Tradition.* New York: Da Capo Press, 1989 [reprint], 189; and also Oliver's entry on Elmore James in: Albert McCarthy, Alun Morgan, Paul Oliver, et al, *Jazz On Record: A Critical Guide to the First 50 Years 1917-1967.* London: Hanover Books, 1968, 151.

133 LeBlanc, personal communication, 29 May 1996.

134 LeBlanc, notes to *Masters of Blues—Tribute to Elmore James.*

135 Paulus, "Belzoni Broomduster 1938," 4.

136 Stephen Calt, notes to *The Roots of Robert Johnson.* Yazoo CD 1073, 1990 [reissue]; Johnny Temple, "Lead Pencil Blues." Vocalion 03068, 1936; and Robert Dixon, John Godrich, and Howard Rye, comps., *Blues and Gospel Records 1890-1943,* 4th Ed. Oxford: Clarendon Press, 1997, 906.

between verses; although most blues guitarists of the day would play a tonic chord as their "turnaround" Johnson's verses "ended on the dominant seventh."[137] Here again, Calt seems to imply that Johnson may have adopted this idea from boogie pianists as well, but it is much more likely that it was Tampa Red who was the inspiration in this case. Over a period of many years, Tampa Red can be heard to subtly yet consistently display the "turnaround" technique on slide guitar as far back as 1928—not only on his duets with pianists, but on his solo guitar work as well (Casey Bill Weldon was yet another slide guitarist who consistently displayed the "turnaround" technique on record prior to Johnson's use of it). Elmore James would use the "turnaround" extensively—adding drive by serving to propel the song along to the next verse rather than rest on the tonic chord between verses.[138]

Last was the "Dust My Broom" riff—Johnson's bottleneck figures at the twelfth fret of the guitar, played chordally as four sets of triplets and a truncated fifth set while the guitar was in open E tuning. This is the riff James polished and perfected and made famous as his readily identifiable slide-guitar signature.[139] Here also, it is possible to find ancestors to the "Dust My Broom" motif—maybe not always the entire well-known phrase, but certainly odd bits and pieces that make one wonder just how much time Robert Johnson spent soaking up guitar riffs and listening to blues 78s.

One such example dates from Halloween day, 1931, when Blind Willie McTell and Curley Weaver played guitar behind Ruth Mary Willis in Atlanta for OKeh. Although the record starts off as a fairly typical blues, by the second verse McTell can be heard to play repeated phrases, with a bottleneck, high on the neck of the guitar. Although no one would necessarily mistake it for the "Dust My Broom" riff (and one wouldn't want to be accused of reading too much into the performance, either), it is compelling enough to make one wonder if what they are hearing is a kernel of the idea starting to germinate.[140] The widely-popular pre-war artist Blind Boy Fuller also makes a strong entry in this category with his "Homesick and Lonesome Blues." As with the Willis/McTell/Weaver disc above, Fuller plays repeated phrases high on the neck of his guitar with a bottleneck, but in this case the "Broom" motif is quite striking and stands out very noticeably. Although recorded in late July 1935, Fuller's effort was not issued on 78 until just around or shortly before the same time that Johnson was getting ready to step into a studio.[141] Two more guitarists contributing to this list are B.K. Turner (a.k.a the "Black Ace"), and "Bukka" Washington White with recordings these artists made in 1937 (February and September, respectively). B.K. Turner's "Whiskey and Women" is interesting not only for its rhythmic patterns and the use of "Broom"-style slide figures high on the neck of the guitar, but also because of his unique approach to bottleneck guitar—in this case, with his national steel guitar placed flat on his lap, plucking the strings with finger picks, and employing a small bottle to slide up and down the neck—a technique he learned from Shreveport, Louisiana resident Oscar "Buddy" Woods (Turner himself was from Texas). Another interesting footnote to this recording is that it was used in the soundtrack to *The Blood of Jesus,* a feature film directed by Spencer Williams in 1941.[142]

137 Calt, notes to *The Roots of Robert Johnson.*

138 Ibid.; Papa Too Sweet, "Big Fat Mama." OKeh 8651, 1929; Tampa Red, *The Guitar Wizard.* Columbia/Legacy CD 53235, 1994; Casey Bill Weldon, "What's the Matter with My Milk Cow?" Vocalion 03078, 1936; and Dixon, Godrich, and Rye, 703, 1003. Note: the reader is referred to Tampa Red's Columbia/Legacy compact disc (which samples a cross-section of titles from 1928 to 1934 with piano duet as well as Tampa playing solo guitar), and Casey Bill Weldon's recording sessions from 25 March 1935 and 31 October 1935 as well.

139 Calt, notes to *The Roots of Robert Johnson.*

140 Ruth Mary Willis, "Low Down Blues." OKeh 8921, 1931; Dixon, Godrich, and Rye, 1046-1047; Wayne Smith, personal communication with Steve Franz. 3 January 2001; and Wayne Smith, personal communication with Steve Franz. 26 January 2001.

141 Blind Boy Fuller, "Homesick and Lonesome Blues." Vocalion 03234, 1936.

142 B.K. Turner, "Whiskey and Women." Decca 7340, 1938; Paul Oliver, *Conversation with the Blues,* 2nd ed. Cambridge: Cambridge University Press, 1997, 52, 53; and Dixon, Godrich, and Rye, 932. Note: Flourishes of the "Dust My Broom" riff can also be heard in Turner's "Lowing Heifer" (Decca 7387, 1938).

Bukka White's recording "Pinebluff Arkansas" did not meet with a fate quite as glamorous as inclusion in a movie; it was, instead, the lesser known flip side to his famous "Shake 'Em On Down." This piece starts off with strong slide guitar currents running through it that are vaguely reminiscent of the "Dust My Broom" idea. By the time Turner's and White's records were issued, however, Robert Johnson already had a handful of records out on the market. By the fall of 1938, John Henry Barbee and Calvin Frazier had both recorded "Dust My Broom" styled guitar pieces—Barbee for Vocalion (it was never issued as a 78) and Frazier for the Library of Congress.[143] Although possibly influenced by Johnson, these pieces themselves could be considered precursors for how the "Broom" riff would come to sound in the postwar years—more stylized, and with greater attention to timing and phrasing.

Although Johnson's influence has been vast, it should be noted that he was as much a product of his environment as any blues musician is (meaning that it is, after all, possible to prove that he didn't just develop these ideas out of thin air or from an accidental blow to the head). Johnson's real forte may not have necessarily lain in his having been the first to incorporate advanced ideas into several blues records, but perhaps more appropriately have been his ability to amalgamate and then crystallize the nascent ideas he was exposed to in the course of being a blues musician in the 1930s. As scholar David Evans perfectly encapsulated: "Robert Johnson's famous 1936 and 1937 recordings summarized much of what had happened in Mississippi blues until then and outlined many future directions of the music among Mississippians who would migrate to Chicago...."[144] Johnson himself wouldn't be a part of that migration. After his infamous death in 1938, it would be his music that would make *that* move.

Blasting Out the Message

By the late 1930s, Elmore James was finding more work as a musician. In the Belzoni area Jake Thomas and Percy Simpson ran the popular juke-joints; they paid two or three dollars plus tips, food and drinks, for one night's work. Holston, James' step-brother, would supply rhythm guitar backing. "[James] would sing 'Dust My Broom' and 'Black Mattie'...." an unidentified witness told Leadbitter and Wardlow. "He played mostly around plantations, but sometimes, late in the evenin' [he would] play out of the back of a truck or go 'cross the tracks to the juke-houses...play all night, drinkin' moonshine!"[145] Reverend Johnny Williams, who saw Elmore and Sonny Boy during the 1938 Christmas season at the Harlem in Belzoni, said Elmore "used a slide but he didn't use it all the way through." He told interviewer Sandy Sutherland, "the onliest thing I ever heard him use a slide on was 'Dust My Broom.' Y'know, believe it or not, he was playin' and singin' that then."[146] Eddie Taylor, who would record with James some twenty years later, also

[143] Bukka White, "Pinebluff Arkansas." Vocalion 03711, 1937; John Henry Barbee, "You'll Work Down To Me Someday." From the album *Giants of Country Blues – Vol. 1 (1927-1938).* Wolf CD 107, [no date]; Calvin Frazier, "Highway 51." From the album *This Old World's in a Tangle.* Laurie CD 7001, 1993; and Dixon, Godrich, and Rye, 39, 273-274.

Note: Frazier's "Highway 51," along with several of his other Library of Congress sides, were in such horrible shape they were almost not reissued on compact disc, for fear that the fidelity was just too bad. The recordings are of an importance historically, however, that makes us grateful to have them at all. See: Julie Anne Schwartz, "Did a Rhinoceros Step On These Acetates?" In the notes to Calvin Frazier, *This Old World's in a Tangle.* Laurie CD 7001, 1993.

[144] David Evans, notes to Johnnie Temple, *Complete Recorded Works in Chronological Order Vol. 1.* Document CD 5238, 1994.

[145] Leadbitter and Wardlow, 6.

saw him perform around this time, but wasn't very impressed, saying, "I first saw Elmore back in... Belzoni, but didn't think he was very good....," adding that, "I didn't pay no attention too much because I didn't like his style." These statements, in turn, caused researcher Mike Rowe to theorize that "from all accounts [James] was a slow learner."[147]

And learning is just exactly what he was doing. Mrs. Ruby LeFlore, who was friends with Holston's younger sister, remembered what it was like to see Elmore and Robert Earl playing in Belzoni on a typical weekend day during the 1938 to 1939 time frame. "Saturday was the big day when most people came to town to shop and that is when they played regularly. Robert and Elmo knew where the people could see and hear them and that's where they set up," she told aficionado George Paulus. "Usually they played music in front of a store or just a bit out in the street. They may have played in town during the week but I never really went in to town much during the week:"

> Well that's where Elmo and Robert played in the black section [of town; i.e., "cross the tracks'] in front of the stores.... There was also an area where carnivals would set up when they came to town and they both played there also. When the carnival came to town they would play for even more people....
>
> ....It might start with ten or twenty people and sometimes as many as fifty or more, the guys passed a hat or tin round for tips. The crowd was mixed, white folks and black folks. Some store owners came out, the store owners where all white of course, but yes, everyone seemed to enjoy Elmo and Robert playing.[148]

Sometimes Sonny Boy Williamson would join them, or compete on an opposite corner. A trick well-known to blues musicians, splitting up and playing opposite street corners could often result in each musician earning more than they ordinarily would have by playing together all day. After all, if passing one hat around was good, passing *two* hats around was even better:

> ...Elmo and Robert were on this side of the block and Sonny Boy Williamson was on the other corner. They would have duels with each other to see who could grab the listeners.... Usually Sonny Boy would have a guitar player with him. Sometimes Robert Earl would play with him. There were times when Sonny Boy joined with Elmore too.... People around town knew Sonny Boy, he was looked at by the people as the more professional singer-performer. [149]

They would usually start in the late morning and play all day. Ruby's curfew of nine o'clock didn't allow her to witness any after-hours activity, though. "Actually I wasn't really allowed to hang around town with blues singers or be standing around watching them sing," LeFlore recalled. "I had to sneak around you know."[150] Here, LeFlore speaks of a reality that is confirmed by many who grew up in Mississippi wanting to hear the blues. Dee Henderson, the award-winning host of the long-running *Cap'n Pete's Blues Cruise* radio show on WEVL in Memphis, would agree. "'The blues back then,' he says, 'Older people would tell you that was the devil's music—it was bad for ya—and you had to have a strong mind to keep it in your mind like I did.' The only alternative was gospel music: 'That's what was happening—blues or gospel.'"[151]

Playing in nearby towns—within fifty miles of Belzoni, became a real possibility for James and Holston during this time, as Holston acted as chauffeur for his grandfather and could borrow the car

[146] Sandy Sutherland, "Uncle Johnny Now Rev. Williams." *Blues Unlimited* 100 (April 1973): 19.

[147] Eddie Taylor and Frank Scott, notes to Eddie Taylor, *I Feel So Bad.* Advent LP 2802, 1972; and Rowe, *Chicago Breakdown*, 197. Note: Advent LP 2802 has been reissued in the U.S. as Hightone CD 8027, 1991.

[148] Paulus, "Belzoni Broomduster 1938," 4.

[149] Ibid., 4-5.

[150] Ibid., 4.

[151] Steve Franz, "Cap'n Pete: Blues from the Beginning." WEVL FM 90 *Program Guide* (May 1988): 1.

occasionally. "So we took [the] car out to other small towns. I remember goin' to Midnight and Louise and travelling down on Highway 49W," recalled Ruby LeFlore. "Elmo and Robert did pretty much the same thing there:"

> Find a place 'cross the tracks and start playing for the people in town. They both seemed to know the places where they would be allowed to play on the corners. In these towns I don't remember any white folks comin' to see them play. Their playing in these towns was restricted to black crowds, they passed the hat and can around as usual and always did well and were well liked by the crowds. Both guys were always happy with what they took in for their playing either in Belzoni or in other little towns.[152]

Playing on the street was good, real-life experience. Soon, James would team up with Lexington, Mississippi, guitarist Peter Brown, and it wouldn't be too long before his thoughts would turn towards forming a band. By 1938 the sound of traditional acoustic blues was changing. Juke boxes enjoyed their first widespread popularity and hit the streets with a vengeance that year. Along with them came the amplifier, which afforded many blues guitarists the opportunity to finally be heard above the noisy din of bar patrons—and everything else sometimes. "...There weren't many microphones and no amplification for the other instruments," wrote Justin O'Brien in *Living Blues* magazine. "Although you could order an electric guitar and a small amp from the mail order catalogues, other electronic equipment was scarce. The electric guitar, in its early years, would sometimes drown out singers, piano players, and harp men."[153] Even so, it was an effective crowd-drawing technique. "The first time I ever saw him was in Missouri in a little joint," pianist Eddie Boyd recalled about Sonny Boy Williamson. "So Sonny Boy took the juke box; I never seen this did before and somehow hooked up his microphone—and then he started playing his harp through the juke box. I guess that cat drew two hundred people around that joint that night."[154] By 1939 James was playing for [catfish] suppers at the Daybreak Plantation, often joined by Williamson, who came in from Greenville, Mississippi, or Cairo, Illinois, where he had a radio show on WEBQ.[155]

Elmore was ready to form his own band. He enrolled saxophonist Precious White, trumpeter Tutney Moore, and drummer "Frock" O'Dell, while his step-brother Holston continued on rhythm guitar. James bought himself a "cheap pickup and amplifier" to "blast out their message." There were numerous places to play: The Harlem Theatre, with locations in Belzoni and Hollandale; Hubert Gaston's Peacock Inn, also in Belzoni; not to mention a juke-joint "out of Goodman run by Big Boy McCray." An unknown witness told Leadbitter and Wardlow, "He had little dances at his house—Elmo' would play for him." Sometimes Sonny Boy Williamson would come in and the band would back him up, or Sonny Boy and Elmore might go over to Clarksdale to play at Muddy Waters' roadhouse at Stovall Plantation. Engagements would pick up for the musicians after the crops started coming in. "Wintertime we just [partied] all weekend," Robert Earl recalled, "no work to do, cotton all picked."[156] Johnny Shines echoed the sentiment and elaborated on the sharecropper economy to Pete Welding, and told him how it affected the itinerant musician at that time: "It was a seasonal thing, playing. In the fall it was better than at other times of the year. That was because of the harvest season, cotton picking, corn pulling and so on like that. There was more money

152 Paulus, "Belzoni Broomduster 1938," 5.

153 Justin O'Brien, "All Around Man: Lee Jackson (Part Two)." *Living Blues* 34 (September/ October 1977): 14; Leadbitter and Wardlow, 6; and Pierson, personal interview, 27 March 1990.

154 Heikki Lehtonen, "Crawl?....Nobody Makes Me!" *Blues Unlimited* 87 (December 1971): 10.

155 Leadbitter and Wardlow, 6; and Ryan, *Trumpet Records,* 13.

156 Leadbitter and Wardlow, 6; and Jim O'Neal and Amy O'Neal, "Muddy Waters." *Living Blues* 64 (March/April 1985): 17, 19.

around then." He continued:

> In the spring of the year there wasn't much of anything because the people were trying to get themselves straightened out.... Along about June and July things would begin to pick up to where you could get hold of some money. September, October, November and up through December and sometimes January, that's when you really had to get it. Didn't make no difference what kind of hustle you had to do, you HAD to get it right through then. Those were the big months, that's when the money was floating around.[157]

Aside from the gigs, James adopted another winter hobby, namely, rambling—"hoboin' mostly," but he would usually be back in a fortnight's time. Leadie Dinkins also recalls that he "would just take off with his guitar and move from town to town"[158] Among James' destinations were probably the towns of Schlater, Mississippi and Helena, Arkansas. In Schlater, Elmore met and eventually married a woman named Minnie Mae (James never "officially" received a divorce from her as long as he lived). In Helena, the attraction was undoubtedly Sonny Boy Williamson, who by 1942 was broadcasting *King Biscuit Time* over KFFA. Drummer Peck Curtis was a regular on Williamson's show and recalled to David Evans that "Elmore James and Sonny Boy was working together [in 1942]. They were working out of Indianola, Mississippi, advertising for a furniture company."[159] Curtis would often substitute for Williamson when he was absent from his duties at Helena-based KFFA, and told Evans that Williamson and James were among the top blues attractions in the area. "There wasn't nobody else but Elmore and Sonny Boy during that time," he mentioned. He noted that James' repertoire in 1942 included the familiar "Dust My Broom" and "Crossroads" and told Evans that, "Of course, he originated that song from Robert Johnson."[160]

Elmore's marriage and budding musical career were abruptly put on hold, though. He was drafted by the U.S. Naval Reserve on Saturday, 24 July 1943, and was inducted at Hattiesburg, Mississippi, exactly one week later. According to his Navy records, he had been living at Route 2, in Tchula, Mississippi, located in western Holmes County, and had been working for Mr. R.C. Calhoun's farm (in nearby Thornton) for the last seven months. He trained at the Great Lakes Naval Base in Illinois, located some thirty miles north of downtown Chicago, and was later transferred to Shoemaker, California (near Oakland), where he was shipped off to the Pacific—taking his guitar with him. He was stationed for a time in Guadalcanal and ultimately participated in the invasion of Guam. He achieved the rank of coxswain, and was later honored with the World War II Victory Medal and the Asiatic-Pacific Campaign Medal. On Wednesday, 28 November 1945, James was honorably discharged at Memphis, Tennessee. According to his discharge paper, he was headed for Route 1, in Schlater, Mississippi, to seek employment.[161]

---

157 Pete Welding, "Ramblin' Johnny Shines." *Living Blues* 22 (July/August 1975): 29.

158 Leadbitter and Wardlow, 6; and Topping, "Canton Mississippi Breakthrough," 22.

159 David Evans, "Peck Curtis: Interview." *Blues Unlimited* 69 (January 1970): 11-12; Leadbitter and Wardlow, 7; and LeBlanc, telephone interview, 11 January 1995.

160 Evans, "Peck Curtis: Interview," 12.

161 Leadbitter and Wardlow, 7; James, Notice of Separation from the U.S. Naval Service; Clayton Love, personal interview by Steve Franz. St. Louis, Missouri, 16 February 2002; and LeBlanc, telephone interview, 11 January 1995. Naval Service Record courtesy of the Estate of Elmore James. Note: According to Elmore's Naval Service Record, another of his assignments (immediately following the Guadalcanal entry), was listed simply as "Lion Six." Whether this was a sea-going vessel or a naval base is not clear.

Additional Note: Clayton Love, who also served in the Navy in World War II and was stationed at Shoemaker, California (almost a year after Elmore had been there), remembered going out on the weekends to enjoy the local nightspots and take in whatever rhythm and blues shows they might happen to find, but that he wasn't there very long (i.e., a few weeks, perhaps) before he shipped out. It seems very likely indeed that Elmore would have been exposed to same type of entertainment during his weekends at Shoemaker, however few they might have been (Love, personal interview, 16 February 2002).

"Aw, that place was really rockin'!"

By the end of 1945, James returned to Mississippi, only to learn his parents had separated and headed north. He didn't stay in Schlater long and soon relocated to Canton, perhaps after he heard his step-brother was running a business there.[162] "Robert Earl... set up his own radio repair shop [in Canton]. Elmore would sometimes be there helping out," recalled Leadie Dinkins, who knew the two step-brothers when they lived in Canton.[163] They both courted one Anita Powell, but it was Holston who received her hand in marriage. While in Canton, James performed at the Rainbow Inn, the King Lumber Company saw mill—he would play for the workers on the weekends, amongst various drinking and gambling activities—and the Club Bizarre. "Aw, that place was really rockin'!" remembered Dinkins.[164] Every now and then Elmore would travel north to Helena to see Sonny Boy Williamson or Peck Curtis. While in Canton in 1946, James' heart condition was discovered. He was treated for it at a nearby Jackson hospital.[165]

During Elmore's tenure with Holston at the radio repair shop, another aspect of his musical career took shape. James was already playing with an amplified acoustic guitar and was crystallizing the basics of his unusual slide approach. But it was here that he began to work out the ideas for an acoustic guitar amplification system that would guarantee a unique sound. Inspiration for customizing his gear may have come from Big Joe Williams, who added three strings to his guitar in order to achieve the sound he wanted; Sonny Boy, who tinkered with the harmonicas he used (discussed earlier); or Robert Johnson who, before he died, had added another first string to his National guitar (according to research presented by Stephen Calt and Gayle Dean Wardlow).[166]

Using parts from the shop and two D'Armond pickups (manufactured by Rowe Industries of Ohio), Elmore's recently gained knowledge of electronics and a soldering gun would be put to good use altering the guitar pick-ups to suit his needs.

In the sound hole, he placed a D'Armond five-pole pickup upside down—to over-emphasize the amplification of the guitar's treble strings. Ordinarily, a pick-up would have six poles, but Elmore James aficionado Brennan Totten explains:

> D'Armond brilliantly realized years ago that with metal or nickel-based strings, for some reason the B-string [the 2nd string] is always louder, no matter what you try to do. It's compensated on most pickups, and on that one they compensated by not bringing the pole all the way through the plastic. There is a pole under there, but it's cut short and covered by plastic. [167]

This pick-up had its own volume control and a characteristic "meaty" tone. This one pick-up by itself, however was not substantial enough. As musician Snooky Pryor explained, "Durin' that time guitars didn't have nothin' but a little old pick-up in the hole of the guitar called the D'Armond pick-up. You couldn't hardly hear it outside the room."[168] Elmore clearly knew this to be true, because by the bridge he placed another D'Armond pick-up commonly used by jazz guitarists, which offered additional volume and tone control. The second pick-up was placed where the guitar would sound bright and stiff. The two pick-

162 Rowe, *Chicago Breakdown*, 197; and LeBlanc, telephone interview, 11 January 1995.

163 Topping, "Canton Mississippi Breakthrough," 22.

164 Ibid.

165 Leadbitter and Wardlow, 7.

166 Leadbitter and Wardlow, 7; and Calt and Wardlow, 48.

167 Brennan Totten, telephone interview by Steve Franz, 22 July 1989.

168 Ibid.; and John Anthony Brisbin, "Pryor Arrangements." *Blues Access* 36 (Winter 1999): 54.

ups were wired in series, with the result being James' unique and unduplicated guitar sound. "He's obviously... given this some thought, and has set up a system whereby he can produce from an acoustic guitar just about any tone known to man on an electric [solid-body guitar]. It's really ingenious," stated Totten. "I find it hard to believe he threw this together for the hell of it. I think he worked it out over a period of time. There's an economy of thought involved in that—it's such a simple thing, and nobody would do that today."[169] Although it should be noted that Elmore was pictured with several different guitars over the years, he must have been particularly proud of that one—it was boldly emblazoned with the initials "EJ" in one corner, near the neck, visible to bar patrons and photographers alike.

"The peoples bought a lot of Talaho..."

James didn't stay in Canton long. 1947 saw him rooming at Henry Flowers' boarding house in Belzoni, Mississippi, and working on the Silver Creek Plantation. He gave a try at another marriage, to one Georgianna Crump. Soon after, he started to pick up the pieces of his musical career by making the occasional appearance on *King Biscuit Time* with Sonny Boy Williamson in Helena and holding a regular gig at Cornelius Horton's Webber's Inn, a local barrelhouse.[170] Houston Stackhouse, who worked with Williamson starting in 1946, recalls a typical altercation between Williamson and James: "Him and Elmo James was workin' together, and he beat Elmo James out of fifty dollars or somethin'. Elmo cracked him 'cross the head with his mike stand. Knocked a hole in his head."[171] Hard-headed Williamson was doubtless no worse for the wear. On another occasion, James, Williamson, and Stackhouse were playing in Helena: "I got to whippin' that guitar so bad that night. I was pretty swift with my hands then," Stackhouse told Jim O'Neal. " I got to playin' somethin' so good [Elmore] give me a ten dollar bill. 'Put this in your pocket, boy. God dog, you're playin' that thing.'"[172]

Williamson also moved in at Henry Flowers' place, after James. He had a new job advertising Talaho—described as "a locally manufactured patent medicine with a high alcohol content"—seven days a week for O.J. Turner's Drug Store.[173] The set-up was a little unusual: since Belzoni wouldn't have its own radio station for another ten years, the show was prerecorded at Turner's Drug Store and aired later from WAZF in Yazoo City or WJPR (possibly WGVM) in Greenville. The format was standard enough: blues and popular tunes Monday through Saturday and spirituals on Sunday. Sonny Boy Williamson amicably invited James to join him on a sporadic basis. With Williamson's inventive lyrics, unique harmonica approach, and James' "then novel guitar style," the show was a hit.[174] Robert Plunkett (who would later become James' drummer) was a regular listener and described Sonny Boy Williamson's uncanny marketing genius:

[169] Totten, telephone interview, 22 July 1989. The setup that Totten refers to can be clearly seen in a number of photographs. In particular, Totten was looking at the cover of Elmore James' *The Original Meteor and Flair Sides* (Ace LP 112, 1984) when he reached his conclusions. An almost identical photograph was used on the cover of *The Classic Early Recordings 1951-1956* box set (issued on Ace in the U.K., on P-Vine in Japan, and on Flair/Virgin in the U.S.), which also clearly shows this configuration.

[170] Leadbitter and Wardlow, 7.

[171] Jim O'Neal, *"Living Blues* Interview: Houston Stackhouse." *Living Blues* 17 (Summer 1974): 33.

[172] Ibid.

[173] Palmer, 206; and Leadbitter and Wardlow, 7.

[174] Leadbitter and Wardlow, 7; and Ryan, *Trumpet Records*, 13.

> [Elmore and Sonny Boy] started to broadcast out of a drug store in Belzoni..., advertisin' some kind of medicine called Talaho. Supposed to... make you feel good and all that stuff. It wasn't nothin' but Sonny Boy made up a good song about it. The little song went over good and the peoples bought a lot of Talaho. Every day at twelve o'clock, we'd listen to him. Elmore was playin' guitar. I don't know who they had on drums....
>
> One day, come a little shower of rain and we couldn't pick cotton. So my dad took me in to Belzoni to see 'em. That was at ten or 11 in the morning. Peoples gathered up in the drug store. Elmore and Sonny Boy were in back playin'. They had a crowd. I listened for a little while and oooh, I liked that so much. Elmore was gettin' down with that guitar. Sonny Boy was blowin' and poppin' his fingers and singin'. For the first time, I thought about bein' a musician. On the way back home, I said, "Daddy,... I'm gonna play with them guys one day." [175]

Appearing on the Talaho show with Sonny Boy Williamson was good exposure for James. It established "Dust My Broom" and his name in the Delta, and he was performing more than ever in Mississippi, Arkansas, and sometimes even Louisiana. It was around this time that a teenage J.B. Lenoir was delighted at getting a chance to sit in with Sonny Boy and Elmore, when they were playing down on Rampart Street in New Orleans, at the New York Inn. Other gigs in 1948 afforded Elmore the chance to meet and/or play with such bluesmen as the legendary Tommy Johnson (Gertrude Jordan, who operated a local café, was Johnson's sister-in-law and a mutual acquaintance of both men); Johnny Temple, whose substantial recording career was just coming to an end; and guitarists Charley Booker and Boyd Gilmore.[176] In Booker's case, he had also known Gilmore as a kid (as did Elmore), Booker's uncle had once played with the legendary Charley Patton, and by 1948 Booker was a proficient slide guitarist, who "could play in the style of Elmore James," according to one witness.[177] Arthur "Big Boy" Crudup was also among this group of noteworthy musicians. "I knowed Elmore in '48," Crudup recalled to Mike Leadbitter in 1970. "On Friday nights and on Saturdays we would play for dances, in the country on the plantations. Just me, Elmo and Sonny Boy. We would get ten dollars and all you could drink and eat. If a man had a club, and he hired us, then we would get thirty or forty dollars. Split between us."[178] One event in Arkansas stayed with Crudup a long time:

> This white woman in Little Rock, she liked [Sonny Boy Williamson]. And he was in her house taking it easy—he had his shoes off. He'd taken his shirt off and a white man came by. Sonny Boy, he left there runnin'! Me and Elmo was goin' back home [after a performance] in my old car and we ain't seen Sonny Boy. Elmo was sayin' 'Where is Sonny Boy' and I was sayin' 'Man, I don't know.' My radiator was leakin' and I stop by a ditch to get a little water. Sonny Boy call, 'Motherfucker, open the trunk and let me get in!' He was hidin' in the ditch there! So I took him home to Belzoni and he never did go to Little Rock again.[179]

At times, Williamson's, shenanigans must have seemed endless. "...It's some people come to Tunica once, wanted to kill him. [Sonny Boy] had done got 100 or $200 to play for 'em that Christmas, him and Elmo James.... That guy come down there with his gun to kill him, but he wasn't there. Gonna kill him about his money," Houston Stackhouse recalled for Jim O'Neal. "Say he done give him $200 for to play there that Christmas, guarantee money. Christmas come, Sonny Boy ain't showed up. When I went in that

175 Brisbin, "Robert Plunkett," 42.

176 Leadbitter and Wardlow, 7; John Broven, "J.B. Lenoir: Yet Another Forgotten Artist." *Blues Unlimited* 15 (September 1964): 5; and Gertrude Jordan, personal interview by David Evans. Jackson, Mississippi, 8 September 1966.

177 Gayle Wardlow, "Greenville Smokin'." *Blues Unlimited* 99 (February/March1973): 12.

178 Mike Leadbitter, "Big Boy Crudup." *Blues Unlimited* 75 (September 1970): 18.

179 Ibid.

night to Helena I walked in that crap house there. There's Sonny Boy standin' around up there. I said, 'Man, you [scoundrel], you! That man was lookin' for you to kill you today.' 'What Man?' I said, 'That man over there what you got that $200 from, was gon' play and didn't show up.' 'Oh man, I didn't get that money. Elmo James got that money.' [But] you know it had to be him got it, 'cause Elmo didn't get it."[180]

While he was still riding high from the success of the Talaho radio show, Williamson was lured in 1949 by Hadacol—yet another questionable patent elixir—to KWEM in West Memphis, Arkansas. When asked what was in the stuff, Hadacol's inventor, Louisiana State Senator Dudley Joseph LeBlanc, reportedly told Murray Nash (southern division chief for Mercury Records at the time) that, "...There was enough alcohol to make people feel good and enough laxative for a good movement." That, plus a handful of the B vitamins thrown in for good measure didn't hurt, either.[181] LeBlanc had money to burn on advertising, using the ploy as a tax dodge. Hadacol's 1949 sales easily topped two million, and LeBlanc was quickly trying to make disappear the company's $400,000 in profits so he wouldn't have to pay any taxes.[182] Pinetop Perkins told Mike Leadbitter that Williamson "ran off with Elmo to [West] Memphis to do this Hadacol thing," which more or less brought about the end of Sonny Boy's on again-off again appearances on the *King Biscuit Time* program, and the ad hoc group of musicians that had grown up around it. LeBlanc may have prompted Sonny Boy to be generous with his resources, as drummer Willie Nix remembered that Williamson invited artists such as B.B. King, Little Milton Campbell, and Floyd Jones all to appear on his KWEM radio show as well.[183] To KFFA, who had lost their star, it didn't seem to matter. Even without Sonny Boy, the *King Biscuit Time* radio show would still be broadcast—every weekday during the lunch hour—almost continuously into the next century.[184]

Nelson Street Blues

Around this time, Elmore James met Willie Love, another of Sonny Boy Williamson's musical friends. Love had been playing professionally at least since 1938, when he had first appeared as a member of the Silver Kings—a band led by drummer Barber Parker out of Tunica. After working solo in the Indianola area for a while, Love settled in Greenville, where he met Williamson. Guest spots on Williamson's *King Biscuit Time* followed, as did recognition in the Delta region. Love, a senior to James by more than a decade, was later recalled as "the best piano player in this town. A little more uptown...a little more classy."[185] Soon, James was a member of Love's group the Aces. The band consisted of Frock O'Dell on drums, Little Bill Wallace, a guitarist/bassist from Leland, James on guitar, with Love taking the piano and vocal chores. The band was stationed in Greenville, where Love had a radio spot on WGVM, sponsored by local merchants, with Eddie Williams as the host disk jockey.[186] Love's future guitarist Little Milton

180 O'Neal, *"Living Blues* Interview: Houston Stackhouse," 33.

181 Colin Escott, with George Merritt and William MacEwen, *Hank Williams: The Biography.* Boston: Little, Brown and Company, 1994, 169; Ray Astbury, "Drink That Hadacol." *Blues & Rhythm* 53 (July 1990): 4; and Leadbitter and Wardlow, 7.

182 Astbury, 4; and Ryan, *Trumpet Records,* 65.

183 Jim O'Neal, "Willie Nix: The Memphis Blues Boy in Mississippi." *Living Blues* 43 (Summer 1979): 11; and Leadbitter, "That Pinetop Man," 8.

184 Hank Harvey, "Growing Up With the Blues." *Living Blues* 71 (1986): 28; and Byron Foulger, "King Biscuit Name in Jeopardy." *Blues & Rhythm* 152 (September 2000): 20.

185 Mike Leadbitter, "Nelson Street Blues." *Blues Unlimited* 104 (October/November 1973): 13.

recalled a typical radio show:

> [Willie Love] bought his own time. And he was a little more business about it.... He would solicit the local merchants, around their stores... and he'd do those commercials, and that's where he got his money from. So he made a profit.... You could go in and buy you an hour. Maybe a hour cost you, heck,... ten or twenty dollars or less.... Lot of times, while his show was on I'd... go in, 'cause a lot of time wouldn't nobody show up but him, he'd just sit down and play the piano and sing. Sometime I'd go in and help him out.[187]

When he wasn't over with Love in Greenville, Elmore could be found driving a tractor during the day over at the Peetie Plantation, located near Doddsville, Mississippi, in eastern Sunflower County. Sometimes he would hook up with David "Honeyboy" Edwards, and they would play for people like Grady Sharker, who Edwards recalled was "a big whiskey maker there."[188] While Elmore was probably happy to be performing quite a bit locally and make an occasional appearance on Love's radio show, by now the idea must have at least crossed his mind about making a record or two. "He never talked about a desire to make records in my company," stated Ruby LeFlore, who had known James during his street-performing days in Belzoni. "I knew Elmo was ambitious, he wanted to play other places," she added, "I can tell you that Elmo took his music very seriously."[189] Leadbitter and Wardlow suggest (with the advantage that hindsight brings) that he may have felt that his best opportunity lay with Sonny Boy Williamson and not the ill-fated Willie Love. Love would record just twenty titles for Trumpet Records and enjoy his greatest success with "Nelson Street Blues," essentially a travelogue of downtown Greenville.[190] "The radio station in Greenville... wore out at least twenty copies playing ['Nelson Street Blues'] so much," recalled producer Lillian McMurry.[191] Love, however, kept ignoring doctors' and friends' admonitions about his constant drinking, and would be dead before the end of the 1953 summer. Kidney failure (in conjunction with uremic poisoning), plus a "cerebral vascular accident" on Saturday, 1 August ultimately led to terminal bronchiopneumonia. He died on Wednesday, 19 August 1953 at the age of forty-six.[192]

So, in 1950 James once again headed off to Arkansas to be near Williamson—but he didn't stay for long. Sonny Boy was on the move again, and a hard man to track down. On Wednesday, 14 June 1950, Williamson signed a two-year recording contract with Stan Lewis, who was busy running an important one stop record outlet in Shreveport, Louisiana, and producing talent for the Specialty, Chess, and Imperial labels.[193] "Studio time at KWKH," Leadbitter offered, "as long as one recorded after midnight when the station had closed down, was fifteen bucks an hour, and Stan [was] determined to make use of those cheap facilities."[194] For some unexplained reason, Lewis wasn't able to hold onto Williamson long enough to get him in the studio. "Sonny Boy didn't stay long enough to book dates," Joe Willie Wilkins told Fred Davis.

186 Leadbitter and Wardlow, 7-8; and Ryan, *Trumpet Records*, 14.

187 Jim O'Neal and Patty Johnson, "Little Milton: *Living Blues* Interview." *Living Blues* 114 (March/April 1994), 27.

188 Tony Burke and Norman Darwen, "'Who May Your Regular Be?'" *Blues & Rhythm* 156 (February 2001): 7-8.

189 Paulus, "Belzoni Broomduster 1938," 5.

190 Leadbitter and Wardlow, 7-8; Willie Love, "Nelson Street Blues." Trumpet 175, 1952; and Ryan, *Trumpet Records*, 64, 83, 84, et al.

191 O'Neal, "Lillian S. McMurry," 19.

192 Marc Ryan, notes to Sonny Boy Williamson/Willie Love, *Clownin' with the World.* Acoustic Archives CD 700, 1989; Leadbitter, "Nelson Street Blues," 13; and O'Neal, "Lillian S. McMurry," 19.

193 Leadbitter and Wardlow, 8; Mike Leadbitter, "Serving the South." *Blues Unlimited* 105 (December 1973/ January 1974): 6; and Mike Leadbitter, "Mike's Blues." *Blues Unlimited* 102 (June 1973): 20. Leadbitter adds: "A one-stop is a place where big buyers like retailers or jukebox operators need make only 'one stop' to find all the lines they're after, rather than travel miles visiting one [record] distributor after another."

194 Leadbitter, "Serving the South," 6.

"You couldn't tell what he was going to do next." Absolutely nothing came of the contract, and Williamson left town, last seen headed in the direction of Texarkana.[195]

Other opportunities, though, were soon to come Sonny Boy's way. Hearing that his harmonica playing friend might be making records for a new label in Jackson, Mississippi, James decided the best course of action was to stay nearby. He moved in at 331 Railroad Avenue in Canton, about twenty miles from the capital, and worked at Holston's radio repair shop. While in Canton, James and his step-brother still played gigs, such as performing for Mr. Beginning Brown on opening night at his Crossroads Grocery and Bar-B-Que, just outside of Canton. James would stay in touch with the owner through the years, as Mr. Brown told researcher Ray Topping that "Elmore always played at his cafe when he came to town."[196]

Eyesight to the Blind

By December 1950, Mississippi native Lillian McMurry was, along with her husband Willard, running a furniture store, a record shop, a new company—Diamond Record Co., Inc., and its new record label, Trumpet Records—in Jackson, Mississippi. She knew of Sonny Boy Williamson primarily by word of mouth and searched the Delta for him.[197] She managed to locate his wife, Mattie Williamson, in the back room of a make-shift Belzoni juke joint. "So I asked if he wanted to make some records and [Mattie] said, 'Yes,'" McMurry recalled to Jim O'Neal. "We made arrangements for [Sonny Boy] to call and then come to Jackson, sign the contract and do the recording."[198] Accompanying Williamson on the resulting Thursday, 4 January 1951, date were pianist Willie Love, Joe Willie Wilkins and Elmore James on guitars, and drummer Joe Dyson. Six of the eight titles from the session remain unissued (the masters to those have probably been lost or destroyed). "Eyesight to the Blind" and "Crazy about You Baby," however, were slated for release as Trumpet 129 around February or March. Sadly, only a few hundred copies of the single were shipped to McMurry's Record Mart before the master disc was consumed in a Chicago warehouse fire. Rather than remaster the single from one of the intact 78 rpm copies, McMurry instead had Williamson re-cut the titles—this time without James on guitar. When re-issued, "Eyesight to the Blind" was a big hit for the fledgling label.[199]

Sonny Boy Williamson and Elmore James were back in the studio on Tuesday, 10 July 1951, at Scott Radio Service, located at 128 North Gallatin Street in Jackson (also the location of the 4 January session). Joined by Henry Reed on bass and drummer Joe Dyson, the foursome re-cut six titles from the previous session and added two new numbers to the roster. After the session was over, McMurry wasn't satisfied. Rather than issue a performance that did not meet her rigid criteria, she scheduled a remake of all eight sides for Sunday, 5 August, at Scott Radio Service.[200]

On Wednesday 25 July, just ten days before the next Sonny Boy session, James was back at Scott Radio Service to accompany Willie Love on "Everybody's Fishing" and "My Own Boogie." Tenor saxophonist

195 Fred Davis, "Joe Willie Wilkins," 144. In Mike Leadbitter, ed., *Nothing But the Blues.* London: Hanover Books, 1971; and Leadbitter, "Mike's Blues." *Blues Unlimited* 102: 20.

196 Topping, "Canton Mississippi Breakthrough," 23; Leadbitter and Wardlow, 8; and McMurry and Slim, 14.

197 Ryan, *Trumpet Records,* 3, 13; and Palmer, 212.

198 O'Neal, "Lillian S. McMurry," 16.

199 Ryan, *Trumpet Records,* 15, 17, 82; and Franz, 6, 7, 34.

200 Ryan, *Trumpet Records,* 14, 20; and Franz, 6.

Otis Green joined in for the latter title, and guitarist Joe Willie Wilkins and probably drummer Alex Wallace rounded out the group. Satisfied this time, McMurry released the sides as Trumpet 147 later that December.[201]

"...Now my friends can get my room"

A few days before the 5 August session, Sonny Boy and Elmore stopped in at McMurry's store, the Record Mart, to audition a version of his trademark song, "Dust My Broom." Marc Ryan reports:

> She was pleasantly shocked to hear Elmore roar out the vocal; he had always been quiet and shy in her presence, having endeared himself with helpings of his exquisite fried chicken after sessions.... Now suddenly the diffident Elmore was delivering an impassioned bottleneck blues, with Sonny Boy riffing in perfect synch alongside him. Lillian enthusiastically offered an exclusive recording contract to Elmore, which he signed on 4th August....[202]

Fortuitously for Elmore James, McMurry had heard neither of the two previous recordings of the song—Robert Johnson's from almost fifteen years previous and Arthur "Big Boy" Crudup's from 1949. She patently refused to record unoriginal material, in part due to copyright and ownership problems. "I didn't even know until a few years ago that he didn't write 'Dust My Broom,'" stated McMurry over thirty years after the fact.[203] Had she been aware of the "borrowed" composition, it is probable that Trumpet 146 would never have been issued; without the success of "Dust My Broom" to boost James' popularity, he very well might have been forced to eke out a career on the periphery of the postwar blues industry. Instead, McMurry added Elmore James to the end of the roster for the 5 August Sonny Boy Williamson session. On Saturday, 4 August, Elmore and Sonny Boy went over to the studio at Scott Radio Service along with McMurry's brother Milton, in order to practice their tunes and get ready for recording the next day. "...So they rehearsed, and got it all supposedly together for the session," McMurry told William Donoghue. "Then they jumped up and all went fishing together. Sonny and Elmore and Milton!"[204]

On Sunday, 5 August 1951, Sonny Boy Williamson started off the recording session with his eight scheduled titles. Whatever magic had failed to materialize at the previous two sessions coalesced this time. "Do It if You Wanta" and "Cool, Cool Blues" were paired for release on Trumpet 139 in September; "Stop Crying" and "Come On Back Home" made up the sides for 140; "I Cross My Heart" and "West Memphis Blues"—an autobiographical number about a house fire—were released in November as Trumpet 144; and the upbeat "Pontiac Blues" became Trumpet 145, backed with the holiday-oriented "Sonny Boy's Christmas Blues." Complementing the singing and harp playing were the twin guitars of James and Wilkins (who had recorded together twice previously), Love on piano, bassist Leonard Ware, and possibly Frock O'Dell on drums.[205]

Lillian McMurry described to William Donoghue exactly what it was like to hold recording sessions at Scott Radio Service (where Trumpet sessions were held at this time). "...He had this little studio about ten

201 Franz, 6, 34.

202 Ryan, *Trumpet Records,* 22.

203 McMurry and Slim, 14; Ryan, *Trumpet Records,* 21-22; and Arthur "Big Boy" Crudup, "Dust My Broom." RCA Victor 50-0074, 1949.

204 Donoghue, "Did Elmore James Know He Was Recording....," 11; Ryan, *Trumpet Records,* 22; and Franz, 7.

205 Sonny Boy Williamson, *King Biscuit Time.* Arhoolie CD 310, 1989; and Franz, 7, 34.

by twelve [feet], just could get a piano on one end of it and then they had a glass in front of there. Outside the glass was one... old recording machine," McMurry related. "There was one microphone in the room...., hand signals when to start, and you had to get [the musicians] all lined up and hear what the sound was like before you started cutting anything."[206] That "old machine" that McMurry remembered was proprietor Ivan M. Scott's "Sonic Disc" recording machine. With this process, master takes were recorded direct to an acetate master, without using any audio tape (in 1951 tape was a relatively new and unproven recording technique, not yet in common usage).[207] Marc Ryan described the Sonic Disc as:

> ...a direct-to-disc technology developed by a small company in Freeport, New York. It had none of the advantages of the still-new tape recorder, and its deficiencies were the more apparent, the larger the band. The Sonic process did yield recordings with a very warm and deep mid-range, and on small combo recordings of three or four instruments, it served well. [208]

Once a final take was accomplished, a metal "mother" could be made from the precious acetate, and no editing was possible. "[When] they messed up, made errors or bad takes, we just had to put it in the garbage can," McMurry recalled. "Sometimes 120 takes. I think the most we ever did was about 160!"[209]

Ironically, "Dust My Broom" turned out to be the only Trumpet side issued by Elmore James as a lead vocalist. "Elmore was supposed to have been getting another side to record," commented McMurry years later, "but he just couldn't come up with it.... He couldn't even cut another song for the back of his record."[210] Previous attempts by researchers to "explain away" the mystery of James' lone Trumpet side have piqued the kind and honest McMurry. Rumors have persisted to this day, offering the theory that James was extremely nervous and thought it was only a rehearsal "while McMurry surreptitiously ran a tape," as one scholar inaccurately reported.[211] "That's a damn lie!" McMurry stated in a 1984 interview. "That made me so mad it spoiled my Christmas.... A ten-minute phone call could have straightened the whole thing out."[212] As Ryan further illustrates, what possible motivation could there be for McMurry to "trick" an artist into recording a song, when just the day before that artist had signed an exclusive recording contract?[213]

Perhaps McMurry's last ditch effort to provide James with the opportunity to record a follow-up may have been one of the intents of a Monday, 22 October 1951, Memphis session at the WHBQ Radio Studios. Jesse "Tiny" Kennedy recorded "Have You Heard About the Farmer's Daughter?" that day—supposedly with James playing lead guitar (the two other titles from that session have yet to be found). McMurry does recall sending Kennedy and James to Memphis to record, and it seems plausible that maybe McMurry was hoping they would return to Jackson with a track for the reverse of "Dust My Broom." After waiting for over two months for a flip side, she finally decided to go ahead with the release in October. It was paired with "Catfish Blues"—credited to Elmo James but really a pseudonymous performance by Bobo Thomas (McMurry naturally got James' permission before the release).[214]

206 Donoghue, "Did Elmore James Know He Was Recording....," 11.

207 Marc Ryan, telephone interview by Steve Franz, 2 November 1992; and Bob Koester, personal interview by Steve Franz. Chicago, Illinois, 20 November 1989.

208 Ryan, *Trumpet Records,* 14.

209 O'Neal, "Lillian S. McMurry," 20; and Ryan, telephone interview, 2 November 1992.

210 O'Neal, "Lillian S. McMurry," 20; and Leadbitter and Broven, 4.

211 Palmer, 214.

212 McMurry and Slim, 14.

213 Ryan, telephone interview, 2 November 1992. Note: For a complete discussion and historical analysis of this topic, see Appendix One, "Elmore James—Myths and Folklore."

It was around this time that Sonny Boy and Elmore enlisted the services of pianist Johnny "Big Moose" Walker to augment their ensemble. Having heard him play over the radio, Sonny Boy stopped by his house in Greenville to see if he was available. "Well, I was out working in the fields at that time," Walker told Tony Burke and Chris Smith. "So Sonny Boy came out there and said, 'You J.W. Walker?' And I told him I was and he said we need a piano player for tonight:"

> So I had to tell him I couldn't come 'cos I was working and needed the money. Sonny Boy told me: "If you come with us you can make a lot of money! $300 dollars!", something like that, at that time that was a lot of money.... So I told Sonny Boy, "I gotta tell ya, I can only play in... two keys, that's G and C." And Sonny Boy said, "That's the onliest [ones] we can play in!" So I joined him and the first time we played together the first thing he hit on was in A! So I had to play in A that night and every night they played in a different key! Eventually they played in every key and I learned it from there! [215]

Walker also told Burke and Smith that the three musicians started thinking about a sideline business. "See, we drank so much, Sonny Boy, Elmore James and I that there was nobody in the world that had the money to drink like we drank! So we decided to make our own!" Walker fondly recalled. "It got so that other people started enjoying it too, so we started to make whiskey and we set up a still in the woods. We would always keep a gallon or two stashed down in a hole in the woods. The [authorities] came one or two times but that didn't stop us."[216]

On Tuesday, 4 December 1951, Elmore James joined Sonny Boy Williamson once again in a recording studio, although unlike their other sessions, this one wouldn't be held at Scott Radio Service. Lillian McMurry had chosen, after securing the on-location engineering services of Bill Holford, to hold a marathon recording session in Jackson, which would occur over the first four days of December, 1951. "Determined to beat the onus of the Sonic Disc process once and for all," noted Marc Ryan, "Lillian decided to call nearly all of her contracted talent for new sessions. Everyone was alerted, [and] material was auditioned and discussed...."[217] Activities commenced on Saturday, 1 December 1951, at the Musician's Union Hall in Jackson with recordings by Willie Love (accompanied by Little Milton on guitar), and guitarist Lonnie Holmes (with Johnny "Big Moose" Walker holding down the piano bench). After some heated tempers flared over the "whites only" policies at the Union Hall, McMurry relocated all the equipment and musicians to the Cedars of Lebanon Club, where recording resumed on Monday, 3 December. Big Joe Williams chimed in with six consummate Delta blues performances, the Southern Sons Quartette recorded some gospel numbers, and finally, Sonny Boy Williamson took center stage for six titles. Not satisfied with the sound the bass player was making during rehearsal, McMurry instead called Cliff Givens, bass vocalist with the Southern Sons, to come back and sing the bass lines for Sonny Boy's session. The trick worked surprisingly well, judging by the enormous success of the first title recorded, "Mighty Long Time." Compared to Sonny Boy's previous recordings, it was unique and atypical—a solo acoustic piece, save for Givens' memorable "imitation" bass behind Williamson's simple, yet eloquent harmonica phrasing (the echo was added later)—which Marc Ryan aptly described as "one of the most achingly lonesome pieces of music ever committed to tape."[218] After waxing "Nine Below Zero," which would become the platter-mate to "Mighty Long Time," Elmore James joined the group for the last four

[214] Marc Ryan, telephone interview by Steve Franz, 7 June 1992; Rowe, *Chicago Breakdown,* 198; and Franz, 7.

[215] Tony Burke and Chris Smith, "Moonshine and the Moose." *Blues & Rhythm* 69 (May 1992): 13.

[216] Ibid.

[217] Ryan, Trumpet Records, 27.

[218] Ibid., 28-30, 85; Sonny Boy Williamson, "Mighty Long Time." Trumpet 166, 1952; and Various Artists, *Delta Blues—1951.* Acoustic Archives CD 702, 1990.

titles of the session. "Too Close Together" would later be used on one side of Trumpet 212, while "She Brought Life Back to the Dead" was another of Sonny Boy's clever paeans to a woman with supernatural powers. Two other titles with James on guitar, "Stop Now Baby" and "Mr. Down Child," would be paired for issue as Trumpet 168—the latter piece bearing alleged associations to Robert Johnson, but never recorded by him. When "Nine Below Zero" and "Mighty Long Time" were issued, circa April/May 1952, the record would go on to become a full-fledged two-sided hit for Sonny Boy. Even though it is not listed as an "official" *Billboard* R&B chart hit, this record would become the biggest seller in Trumpet's history, eventually racking up sales of over 60,000 copies.[219]

In the meantime, life was about to change for Elmore James. His first record, Trumpet 146, had arrived at the McMurry's Record Mart fresh from the pressing plant, on Tuesday, 27 November 1951. By Saturday, 12 January 1952, "Dust My Broom" had charted in Dallas at #6. Producer Bobby Robinson vividly remembers when he first heard "Dust My Broom" one morning in 1952, while he was routinely sampling new releases that came into his Harlem, New York, record store:

> ...I ran across a record by an unknown artist on a label that I had never heard of.... From the moment I started to play the record, I forgot about the other samples. I played it over and over on my loudspeaker. Suddenly the record shop filled with people wanting to buy the record. I told them that it was my one and only copy and not for sale at any price. This was my introduction to Elmore James and I have never been so moved by any singer before or since that memorable day. [220]

"As an anthem to a lonely sort of independence, the song had few equals," suggested Marc Ryan.[221] With just a sparse accompaniment of Williamson's harmonica, a stand up bass and drums, Elmore's mellifluous slide guitar figures floated around the lyrics and gave the record an undeniable warmth and immediacy:

> I'm gonna get up in the mornin', I believe I'll dust my broom,[222]
> I'm gonna get up in the mornin', I believe I'll dust my broom,
> I'll quit the best gal I'm lovin', now my friends can get my room.
>
> I'm gonna write a letter, telephone every town I know,
> I'm gonna write a letter, I'll telephone every town I know,
> If I don't find her in West Helena, she's in East Monroe I know.
>
> I don't want no woman, want every downtown man she meet,
> I don't want no woman, want every downtown man she meet,
> Man, she's a no good doney,[223] they shouldn't 'low her on the street.

---

219 Ryan, Trumpet Records, 30; Rowe, *Chicago Breakdown,* 143; Sonny Boy Williamson, *King Biscuit Time;* Alan Balfour, et al., "Sonny Boy Williamson Discography." *Soul Bag* 134 (Spring 1994): 13; Dick Lillard, "The Cash Box Charts, Part 2." *Blues & Rhythm* 81 (August 1993): 11; and Whitburn, 447.

220 Bobby Robinson, notes to Elmore James, *History of Elmore James.* Trip LP 8007, 1971; Ryan, 2 November 1992; and Ryan, *Trumpet Records,* 101. Note: Historically, it has been assumed that Trumpet 146 was only issued as a 78 rpm single. For a discussion on the possibility of Trumpet 146 also having been issued in the 45 rpm format, see Appendix One, "Elmore James—Myths and Folklore."

221 Ryan, *Trumpet Records,* 23.

222 "... dust my broom," i.e., to leave. From Stephen Calt, "The Idioms of Robert Johnson." *78 Quarterly* Vol. 1, No. 4 (1989): 56.

223 Ibid. Calt says that "doney" (sometimes "donay" or "donie") is "A black and Southern white variation of *dona,* a 19th century slang term for woman... [deriving] from respectful Italian, Spanish, or Portuguese terms for 'lady....' Although Son House defined 'donie' as 'a no-good woman,' it had no pejorative implication."

I believe, I believe my time ain't long,
I believe, I believe my time ain't long,
I've got to leave my baby, and break up my happy home. [224]

Part of the success of "Dust My Broom" was an intangible element present somewhere in the grooves of the record, lurking just beneath the surface, awaiting to be discovered by the listener. Maybe one of the enduring qualities that made "Dust My Broom" such a popular record was the "must be muddied" dictate that McMurry spoke of to Mike Rowe. "McMurry applied a rule of thumb judgement..." Rowe reported, "saying her blues records 'must be muddied.' She felt it was the muddy sound that made them popular."[225] While this was probably just an inherent side-effect of the Sonic Disc process which McMurry had employed, the result was quite endearing. If there ever was a list of blues records that seemed to reflect the physical geographical environs from which they emanated, "Dust My Broom" would surely be near the top of that list. Indeed, the earthy feel idiosyncratic to many of the early Trumpet 78s makes one wonder if they weren't manufactured from the very soil of Mississippi itself, the rich warmness so undeniably present in those records.

Another aspect of early Trumpet 78s never discussed publicly, was the fact that they were slightly speeded up for release. Typically, an Elmore James song with four verses and two solos would last about three minutes, whereas "Dust My Broom" clocked in at just under two and three-quarters. Two advantages are inherent with this trick: shorter records were more likely to be picked for radio airplay by disk jockeys, and speeding up the record picked up the tempo a bit. Although I admit to skepticism upon first hearing this theory, I was convinced after someone played an early Sonny Boy Williamson song at a slightly slower speed. Suddenly the harmonica sounded distinctly in concert pitch—brought into focus—and the tempo a more relaxed, and believably typical, medium pace.[226] Whether it was a dictate from McMurry, a technique known to Ivan Scott (after all, he *was* in the "radio service" business), or a flaw of 78s mastered with the Sonic Disc process, it is unknown what led to the early Trumpet singles being released this way. It did, however, lend a them a unique, anomalous character that has long been prized by listeners.

Over the next four months, "Dust My Broom" reached the top ten in Pueblo and Denver, Colorado; Oxford, Mississippi; Oakland and Los Angeles, California; Monroe and New Orleans, Louisiana; Somerset, Kentucky; and Chicago, Illinois. Lee Jackson, who resided in Chicago when "Dust My Broom" hit, recalled in a 1977 interview, "It was hot, man. Every record store you go into was spinnin' it. You were hearin' it, too. All the record vendors had it."[227] Sid Talmadge, a Los Angeles record distributor, told *Billboard* in March 1952 that he was "running into a nice deserved streak of luck, with Elmo James coming up a winner via his Trumpet [disk]."[228] "Dust My Broom" eventually peaked at #9 on the *Billboard* rhythm & blues charts in early April 1952, and sold almost 50,000 copies—one of Trumpet's top sellers.[229]

For James, the song would come to characterize his career, to both good and ill effect. While it gave him a readily identifiable trademark—always a positive thing if one is competing for nickels in the jukebox, and trying to distinguish yourself to the blues-buying public—it would appear that he came to be somewhat irritated by it later in life. Listeners would request the song constantly, and some critics would

[224] Elmore James, "Dust My Broom." Trumpet 146, 1951; and Franz, 7.

[225] Mike Leadbitter, "Notes." *Blues Unlimited* 88 (January 1972): 6. Note: these notes are an addendum by Mike Leadbitter to Darryl Stolper's article on Trumpet Records, in *Blues Unlimited* 88.

[226] Jobie Kilzer, personal interview by Steve Franz. Memphis, Tennessee, 20 January 1991.

[227] O'Brien, 15; Ryan, 2 November 1992; and Ryan, *Trumpet Records,* 101-102.

[228] Gart, *First Pressings—1952,* 32; and Topping, "Ramblin' from Town to Town," 11.

[229] Whitburn, 216; and Marc Ryan, personal interview by Steve Franz. Memphis, Tennessee, 3 July 1990.

later (incorrectly) postulate that he was capable of playing little else. Nevertheless, the record—with James' famous guitar riff—would prove to be widely influential.

In the immediate months following its release, Snooky Pryor's "Going Back on the Road" would be one the first records on the market to "mimic" this sound. Author Mike Rowe stated that Pryor's record was "...Interesting for its use of the 'Dust My Broom' theme with Moody Jones imitating the traditional slide patterns but picking with only his fingers."[230] A careful listening reveals that the "Dust My Broom" patterns—at least in the intro—are actually played by pianist Sunnyland Slim! Only later, after Pryor has begun singing, does Jones chime in with some tasty James-inspired guitar licks. With solid support from Jones and Sunnyland, Pryor wraps up his fast-paced side, copying James' ending solo as well. It's fairly obvious that the musicians were inspired to come up with something that sounded like Elmore's hit record. Pryor was in a Chicago studio recording his song on Monday, 28 April 1952—the very same week "Dust My Broom" was cresting at #9 on the *Cash Box* regional Chicago charts![231]

"My favorite blues singer..."

"Dust My Broom" naturally created interest with record label owners such as Leonard Chess from Chicago, Bob Shad of Mercury Records, Gotham Records' Harry Finfer, and a California-based effort, Modern Records, Inc. All four of the labels—and possibly some others—wanted to sign James with their stable, but they would have to wait. With the royalty money coming in, Elmore purchased a car, continued to perform at the clubs, and took it easy in Canton when he could. McMurry kept leaning on Sonny Boy Williamson, urging him to persuade James back into the studio for another Trumpet session.[232]

Bob Shad was one of the first producers to jump on the "Dust My Broom" bandwagon. Rather than try to lure Elmore James to Mercury, he made another move instead. He signed Sunnyland Slim and Robert Jr. Lockwood to the label, and announced the addition to Mercury's roster sometime in December 1951.[233] In the studio, he prodded Lockwood. "Bobby Shad...insisted that I do 'Dust My Broom.' It was me and Sunnyland," Lockwood recalled, "and [drummer] Alfred [Wallace]:"

> And I'll bet you ten times [Shad] asked me, he said "Did Elmore [James] write it?" I say, "No. Robert Johnson wrote 'Dust My Broom.'" He said, "Well, hell! If he didn't write it, goddamn it, why can't you play it?" I say, "Elmore James done recorded 'Dust My Broom' on Trumpet label," and I say "now Lillian McMurry got it copyrighted—but it ain't none of hers!" I say, "Well, okay. I'll record it." [234]

"And Mercury hold me responsible for it right now!" he insists, indicating there has been some kind of ongoing problem due to the fact that Lockwood is listed as the writer on the original Mercury release.[235]

Either Shad had a good ear for upcoming R&B hit records, or he had advance knowledge of Trumpet 146. As a completely unknown artist to both *Cash Box* and *The Billboard*, James' very first record failed to

230 Rowe, *Chicago Breakdown*, 101.

231 Snooky Pryor, "Going Back on the Road." J.O.B. 115, 1952; Ryan, *Trumpet Records*, 102; and Mike Leadbitter, Leslie Fancourt, and Paul Pelletier, *Blues Records 1943-1970*, vol. 2, L-Z. London: Record Information Services, 1994, 389.

232 Leadbitter and Wardlow, 8; and Ryan, *Trumpet Records*, 41-42.

233 Gart, *First Pressings—1951*, 121.

234 Hoffman, 24.

235 Ibid.; and Robert Jr. Lockwood, "Dust My Broom." Mercury 8260, 1951.

be reviewed when it was released in late November 1951. Additionally, "Dust My Broom" didn't chart until mid-January the following year, so Shad would have had to have been mindfully looking for it. Or plausibly, the Chicago-based Shad was familiar with the Windy City outfit that pressed McMurry's 78s, and he knew of it via that channel. Regardless, Shad had Lockwood in the studio even as James' version was still warm off the presses. Lockwood's strident, uptempo waxing of "Dust My Broom" was released as Mercury 8260 in the final hours of 1951, and sank from sight after that.[236]

Modern Records, it turned out, was the label that prevailed in snagging Elmore James. His next recording session would be for them, but not without some tribulation for the independent California label. "My favorite blues singer," says Jules Bihari, part owner of Modern Records with his three brothers, "was probably Elmore James. I ran all over Mississippi looking for him because I heard he was great.... he wasn't playing in Canton...." Bihari continues, "We went to his house and he wasn't there. We went out in the country and didn't find him there."[237] Jules' brother Joe picks up the story from here:

> We finally tracked Elmore down at a radio repair shop in Canton. A funny thing happened on that trip. I was driving a big Cadillac convertible, and we needed to check into a hotel. I said to Ike [Turner] 'You drive and I'll get in back'. We checked into a hotel [in Jackson], and the clerk at the desk said 'Ah, your chauffeur sir, we can take care of him'... and they put him into a room right next to me!.... Later we drove out to a nightclub, and that's where I first recorded Elmore James. [238]

The Biharis managed to get one session with James in the can before McMurry caught wind of the illicit proceedings. Although he was under exclusive contract to McMurry, Elmore probably felt as if his ship had finally come in. For years he had played with Willie Love and Sonny Boy Williamson on their radio shows, but James had never had a show of his own. He also recorded with Love and Williamson and had watched the subsequent singles be released by McMurry, while he waited for his turn. Now, a record company from Los Angeles—Beverly Hills, to be exact—wanted to record Elmore James. Elmore was, it seems, very willing to cooperate.[239]

The Biharis' trips south—to search for and record talent—in the early 1950s are the stuff of legend today. Ike Turner, Modern Records talent scout, describes a typical field session with them. "Modern would come down [to Mississippi] every month or so to record the talent I'd found," stated Turner. "If we couldn't get to a studio in Memphis or use a radio station, we'd give somebody a bottle of whiskey to let us use their living room to record in."[240] Usually, the Biharis would give the artist being recorded thirty dollars and their own pint. "They had a fabulous time," recalled Tamara Shad, whose father, Bob Shad, made several trips south with Joe Bihari. "They were both crazy for music—two lunatics out on the road." However, "It was very dangerous at the time," she added, "The police were always running them in, they didn't want them bothering black people...."[241] For his trouble in rounding up talent for them, the Biharis gave the twenty year-old Turner the use of a car and a salary of $100 a week; as Turner says, "That was a lot of money for a kid."[242]

---

236 Ryan, *Trumpet Records,* 101, 103; Gart, *First Pressings—1951,* 131; and Whitburn, 262.

237 Scott and Paulsen, "Joe and Jules Bihari! [Part 2]," 11.

238 Topping, "Ramblin' from Town to Town," 12.

239 Ryan, *Trumpet Records,* 32; and Galen Gart, *The American Record Label Directory and Dating Guide, 1940-1959.* Milford, New Hampshire: Big Nickel Publications, 1989, 146.

240 Terry Perkins, "We Like Ike." *The Riverfront Times* (24 June 1992): 32.

241 Norman Darwen and Tamara Shad, "Bob Shad – The Record Man: The *Sittin' In With* Story." *Blues & Rhythm* 100 (June/July 1995): 17; and Kerry Kudlacek and Dave Sax, "The Ike Turner Blues Story." *Blues Unlimited* 57 (November 1968): 5.

Elmore James' first Modern session was most likely executed at the Club Bizarre, in Canton, starting Friday night, 25th January, and going on into Saturday morning, 26th January, 1952. The Biharis were travelling with their trusty Magnecord tape recorder and hooked the machine up through the Club Bizarre's P.A. system. The Magnecord was Joe Bihari's "favorite thing to use on the road and it had four inputs for mikes," Ray Topping reported. "That was the first mobile one, where the earlier tape machines were too big and clumsy to take out."[243] In cases where large groups were recorded, Bihari could fashion an "extra" input by splicing two mikes together, and would move the musicians closer or further away from the microphones to balance the sound. Such was the fast-paced life on the road. "Crazy the way you had to do it," Joe Bihari offered, "But it worked.... If you listen to those recordings today, now that they've been filtered through all the modern equipment, they're fabulously good.... There is an old saying," he noted, "You can spend hundreds of thousands of dollars in the studio and get nothing and you can spend one hundred dollars in your garage and get a hit."[244]

The session, which featured Ike Turner's solid piano behind Elmore's stentorian guitar, lasted into the wee hours of the night and produced several raucous sides. The free-wheeling instrumental "Hawaiian Boogie" was notable for its busy, spirited slide guitar runs, and "Rock My Baby Right," and "Hand in Hand" were both later used as noisy flip sides to Flair singles. At least four more sides were recorded during the session—some with a saxophonist who must have wandered in half-way through—but most of these have been lost or were altered later with overdubbing.[245] From the completed master tapes, a very tired Joe Bihari chose the Smokey Hogg influenced "Long Tall Woman," and "Please Find My Baby"—a tune Elmore probably adapted from Tommy McClennan's "My Baby's Gone"—to be released as Elmore James' first Modern single.[246] Jules Bihari, who returned to Los Angeles about a week after the session, probably took the tapes with him to process them for release. "They were given Modern Music matrix numbers and test lacquers were cut" reported Ray Topping, but the disk never made it to the pressing plant. Joe Bihari's prize—his new Elmore James single—was stopped dead in its tracks by Lillian McMurry, who was about to take legal action. The disk was shelved indefinitely; "Please Find My Baby" was held up for release almost two full years in the ensuing legal battle, and this particular recording of "Long Tall Woman" wouldn't be issued for another forty years.[247]

Word had reached Lillian McMurry by Monday morning, 28 January, that Elmore James (and several other Trumpet artists under exclusive contracts) had recorded for Modern Records over the weekend. That day McMurry filed a temporary restraining order to get the Biharis—who were finished in Canton and had

242 Ike Turner with Nigel Cawthorne, *Takin' Back My Name.* London: Virgin Books, 1999, 50.

243 Huggins, 19; Topping, notes to *King of the Slide Guitar;* Marc Ryan, telephone interview by Steve Franz, 28 June 1994; Mark Harris, "Mark's Blues No. 2." *Pickin' the Blues* 25 (1984): 5, 7; and Steve Franz, *Elmore James: Standing at the Crossroads.* Master's Thesis, The University of Memphis, 1994, 149-150. Note: unless otherwise stated, in this book all further references to Franz refer to *Elmore James: The Ultimate Guide to the Master of the Slide.*

244 Turner with Cawthorne, 49-50.

245 Topping, "Ramblin' from Town to Town," 12; Huggins, 18; Elmore James, "Hawaiian Boogie." Modern Oldies 49, 1968 [also known as "Hawaiian Boogie #1"]; Elmore James, "Rock My Baby Right." Flair 1048, 1954; Elmore James, "Hand in Hand." Flair 1031, 1954; and Franz, 8.

Note: Included among these "lost" tapes was another recording of "Dust My Broom." According to an article in *Blues Unlimited* 57, the Biharis ended up having to fork it over to Lillian McMurry as part of their court settlement with her. (Kudlacek and Sax, 6.) McMurry undoubtedly destroyed the tape.

246 Topping, "Ramblin' from Town to Town," 12; Elmore James, "Long Tall Woman." From the album Elmore James, *The Classic Early Recordings 1951-1956.* Ace BOXCD 4, 1993; Elmore James, "Please Find My Baby." Flair 1022, 1953; Tommy McClennan, "My Baby's Gone." Bluebird B8669, 1941; and Andrew "Smokey" Hogg, "Long Tall Mama." Modern 20-574, 1948.

247 Topping, "Ramblin' from Town to Town," 12; Ryan, *Trumpet Records,* 32-33; Scott and Paulsen, "Joe and Jules Bihari! [Part 2]," 11; Gart, *First Pressings—1952,* 11; and Franz, 32, 40.

gone on to Greenville—to stop. She was told tales about how the Biharis had driven Elmore around Canton in their Cadillac (evidently, Elmore warranted more than just the standard issue pint of whiskey and thirty dollars), and that he insisted everyone in town call him *Mister* James. She had even lent him money against his royalties! All that, plus the strain of the broken contract was just too much.[248] "Some people," McMurry told Jim O'Neal, "would lie and were unfaithful; we just washed them out." She added, "[Elmore James has] recorded for everybody in the country—nobody'd ever keep him under contract. You know, some people have no ethics and think scruples are something you eat."[249]

McMurry's troubles with James are further outlined by a cancelled check, written by her on 8 January 1952 to Elmore James, with a memo stating "for drums." It seems that whatever drums Elmore might have rented or purchased, he probably used them for his session with Modern![250]

North to Chicago

In the spring of 1952 Elmore packed his bags and headed north to Chicago. "Look, I had to leave [Jackson]. You don't know like me. I had to leave there," is all he would ever tell Lillian McMurry about why he left:

> **Lillian McMurry**: Oh. Well, Elmo, you know you... just took the first opportunity that went your way.
> **Elmore James**: I know it. I had to—....
> **LM**: You had to leave Jackson?
> **EJ**: Yes, ma'am.
> **LM**: Well, uh, how come?
> **EJ**: I can explain to you. I'll explain to you.
> **LM**: But, well, Elmo, you could have told me. You know that you could have told me why you had to leave if you had to leave for some reason and could have reported to me.
> **EJ**: It was a good reason. I say, and it *was* a good a reason. [251]

Except for the above phone call he made to McMurry in the fall of 1955, she would never hear from Elmore James again—except his recordings, which she describes as all sounding like "Dust My Broom." Perhaps McMurry feels that his real talent lay in the culinary arts. She particularly misses his cooking, and especially his fried chicken—"the best I ever had," McMurry said.[252]

McMurry's achievements through Trumpet Records should be considered nothing short of extraordinary. Producing blues records is assuredly not the easiest business in the world—especially in a cutthroat industry usually dominated by men—but to produce a product of such inveterate and high consistent quality (as Trumpet blues 78s tend to be) is truly remarkable. "We had a lot of hits and were the fifth biggest independent label in the country," McMurry told Darryl Stolper. "We just couldn't collect from the distributors... they'd declare bankruptcy owing us a lot of money."[253] If it weren't enough to face lawsuits, wayward recording artists, and uncollectible debts, McMurry had to suffer outright

248 Ryan, *Trumpet Records*, 31-32; and McMurry and Slim, 14.

249 O'Neal, "Lillian S. McMurry," 19, 21.

250 Anonymous [Name withheld by request], personal interview by Steve Franz. Helena, Arkansas, 12 October 1990.

251 "Elmore James's Phone Call to Lillian McMurry," 28.

252 Ibid.; and McMurry and Slim, 14.

253 Stolper, 6.

discrimination—not just the local, homespun Mississippi variety—but on a national level from the American Federation of Musicians (run by the iron-fisted James C. Petrillo), as well. "We started recording at the union hall and the white musicians in [Jackson] got mad because I was recording black musicians," McMurry told Jim O'Neal. "They didn't even have a black musicians' union here. We had to send Sonny Boy to New Orleans [later on]... and put him in their union. Even though there was no black union here, the white union wouldn't allow any black musicians to join. I tried to start a union record company but Petrillo wouldn't let me if it had anything at all to do with any of the stockholders in a non-union company."[254] Trumpet was finally forced to cease operations in 1956. In spite of the mountains of hassles and obstacles, McMurry always seemed able to maintain a positive perspective about this segment of her life over the years. "It was very rewarding," she remarked to Darryl Stolper, "not monetarily, mind you, but to your soul."[255]

Updates on Trumpet and the McMurry's appeared from time to time in blues magazines. In 1966, David Evans announced in *Blues Unlimited* that the entire mint stock of Trumpet Records (about 30,000 45s and 78s) was for sale—approximately $1,500, plus shipping, could've taken the whole lot. Another item from 1972 noted that "Mrs. McMurry is selling her furniture store in Jackson—and moving to Alaska for real! If nobody'll give a good price for the Trumpet 78s she'll throw them in the Pearl River!"[256] But, evidently, a move North was not in the cards for McMurry. She was inducted into the Blues Hall of Fame in the fall of 1998. On Thursday, 18 March 1999, Lillian McMurry died of a massive heart attack. Sonny Boy Williamson had once, on one particularly memorable occasion back in 1953, immortalized her phone number by including it in a song he recorded for Trumpet. At the time of her death, Lillian McMurry still lived in Jackson, Mississippi, and still had the same phone number.[257]

Although Elmore James would return to his native Mississippi in later years, it wouldn't quite be the same. His session with Sonny Boy Williamson, on Tuesday, 4 December 1951, was the last time the two musicians ever recorded together. Although Williamson would make guest appearances with Elmore's band on and off over the years, after their migration to Chicago, they would eventually split up to lead two separate ensembles. On their August and December Trumpet sessions, Elmore and Sonny Boy had created an extraordinary kind of music that no amount of words could really ever describe. "These performances," writes Marc Ryan, "mixed downhome elements with swing rhythms and Delta tonalities for a fascinating glimpse of the blues in one of its unique, momentary transitional phases. Never again would a blues band make a record that sounded quite like this."[258]

Elmore James landed in the Windy City a few months after his Canton recordings. During the next eleven years, his indelible musical stamp would galvanize the sound of Chicago blues for a generation.

---

254 O'Neal, "Lillian S. McMurry," 22.

255 Stolper, 6.

256 David Evans, "Trumpet Records for Sale!" *Blues Unlimited* 39 (December 1966): 21; and "News." *Blues Unlimited* 94 (September 1972): 17. Note: McMurry finally disposed of her last batch of mint Trumpet stock in March 1989, when Marc Ryan was putting together his Trumpet series for the Acoustic Archives label—almost a quarter century after David Evans' initial report in *Blues Unlimited* (see Marc Ryan, "Tracing the Trumpet Masters." *Blues & Rhythm* 48 (Christmas 1989): 5.)

257 Bill Donoghue, "Obituaries: Lillian McMurry." *Blues & Rhythm* 139 (May 1999): 20-21; and Sonny Boy Williamson, "309." From the album Sonny Boy Williamson and Willie Love, *Clownin' with the World.* Acoustic Archives CD 700, 1989.

258 Ryan, *Trumpet Records,* 20.

CHAPTER THREE

Elmore James and the Broomdusters

I tried to play like Muddy Waters but couldn't.... He was too heavy for me. He was a blues master. That wasn't me. And the only people that could hang with 'em was cats like Little Walter and Elmore James, you know, guys that could do his thing. There was no room for a new cat like me doing something different.

–Bo Diddley, from an interview in Living Blues 77

He's one of the only postwar bluesmen that uses horns regularly on his records that they don't offend me. I'm not a big fan of horns in my down-home blues records. But, Elmore is a different kettle of fish. When Elmore used horns, they **were** down-home.

–Leroy Pierson, from a 1990 interview with the author

I never could develop the art of doing it. I'd always press too hard and it would hit the frets you know and you'd hear that, where other guys like Earl Hooker, Elmore James, they had this thing down. They had perfected it to a point where they would never hit the frets. They'd just barely touch the strings. I never could do that.

–Little Milton, talking about trying to play slide guitar, from an interview in Living Blues 18

"Yeah, I heard a LOT of them Elmores"

When Elmore James came to Chicago, he was already a veteran musician. He had been performing for at least fifteen years in Mississippi and had already participated in six recording sessions.

James landed in Chicago sometime in the spring of 1952. Lee Jackson, who had known Elmore from a decade ago, played regularly at the Tuxedo Lounge at 31st and Indiana. He remembered a string of Elmore James impostors coming in and asking to perform with the band. Jackson hadn't seen James in a while and wasn't sure if he'd be able to recognize him right away. Instead, he did the next best thing. He would give the man claiming to be Elmore James a guitar and a chance to sit in with the band. "I'd give him the guitar and right away I could tell it wasn't Elmore. All he have to do is strum a few chords and you know it wasn't Elmore:"[259]

> One night this guy comes into the bar with his cap on sideways, you know. And this is Elmore. And he must have stopped up the front of the bar first and talked to Johnny [the owner]. He came back there and said, "What do you say, man!" And grabbed my hand and I said, "Hey, how you doin'." Well, I didn't let on, but I didn't really recall him.... He says, "I'm Elmore." And I said to myself, "Yeah, I heard a LOT of them Elmores." He said "What about playin' one?" And I said, "Well, we're fixin' to come down now, and when we come back up I'll call you." ....When I went back, I announced Elmore, and the people just screamed. They're lookin' all around, you know, "Where's he at?" And he came up and takes a guitar, and man, he started on "Dust My Broom." I'm telling you, the house just cracked up. And I went around to the tables sayin', "HEY, man! THAT'S Elmore James!" [260]

James evidently had just gotten into town and didn't have a place to stay yet. According to Jackson, Elmore was looking for his uncle Mac Willie James first and work as a musician second. By that May, James was living on the South side, as a telegram sent by Lillian McMurry on Thursday, 22 May, reveals his address to be 738 East 46th Street. In the note, McMurry appears earnest and straightforward about what she had to say to him. "I know that Shad and Finfer are trying to get you to cut records for them," she wrote. "Don't give in or you will be responsible and we will know." For a tag line, she added "Hurry home." The missive seemed to have little effect on Elmore, though. On Monday, 2 June, he joined the musicians' union in Chicago. Later that summer Elmore found his uncle Mac Willie James at 4714 South Evans and moved in with him and fellow boarder Howlin' Wolf. "Hurrying home" is evidently what Elmore *wasn't* going to do.[261]

[259] O'Brien, 14-15.

[260] Ibid., 15.

He didn't have too much trouble landing a gig—Elmore's first steady Chicago club job was at Chuck's, located at Damen and Madison, with drummer Kansas City Red. Pianist "Little" Johnny Jones and drummer Odie Payne and joined forces with Elmore a short time later. "Well, we joined Elmore at the same time—Johnny Jones and I," Payne recalled to Steve Cushing. "Elmore came from... Mississippi ..., and he was lookin' for a band. Well, he was hot then, see, 'cause he had just made 'Dust My Broom.' And he came to [Chicago] and then that's where I and Johnny Jones joined him and played with him...." Sonny Boy Williamson joined the group on and off for a while, until he could get something of his own going.[262]

Odie and Johnny, up until the time they hooked up with Elmore, had been gainfully employed providing support to Tampa Red for the last few years—both in the studio and at the nightclubs. Payne, a native of Chicago, became familiar with Tampa Red's music when "Let Me Play With Your Poodle" was an R&B hit (during the last few days of 1942). As was common at the time, a local shop broadcast the record over their storefront speaker, trying to lure customers (and their cash) to come inside and buy the hits of the day. "I would stand there and just laugh and laugh and laugh, because of the words," Payne told Cushing. "Now this was Tampa Red. I was a late teenager, never knowin' nothin' about the man. But, I tell people, it's funny, about three years later [after serving a stint in the Army] I wind up workin' with the man—my first tavern engagement—I wind up workin' with Tampa Red."[263]

Johnny Jones was just one in a long string of top pianists who had backed up Tampa Red during his twenty year career. The list—which reads like a "who's who" of blues pianists—included "Georgia" Tom Dorsey, Black Bob, Blind John Davis, and Big Maceo Merriweather. Jones (who incidentally was also proficient on the harmonica) was born into a talented musical family in Jackson, Mississippi; he probably made the journey north sometime during 1945 with fellow musician "Baby Face" Leroy Foster. Foster went on to become an important drummer and electric guitarist in the early days of postwar Windy City blues, while Johnny—whom his wife Letha claimed arrived in Chicago already a professional musician—eventually went off to play with Tampa Red (after Tampa made him join the musicians' union in 1947), and spark a few early Muddy Waters records. Jones took over the piano bench from Merriweather after a stroke robbed this keyboard giant of his supreme talents. Merriweather seemed to accept it graciously; he not only took Johnny under his tutelage, but also endearingly referred to him as his "son," and introduced Jones to his future wife, Letha. In 1949, Muddy Waters, Leroy Foster, and Johnny Jones were all summoned for an Aristocrat recording session. Muddy's beautiful "Screaming and Crying" and Johnny's "Big Town Playboy" were among the outstanding results, representing a high-water mark of the era. "Big Town Playboy"—one of the few tunes Jones recorded that does not appear to have been derivative—finally became something of a standard after Eddie Taylor recorded a version of it for Vee-Jay in 1955. By all appearances, Jones seemed to embrace life and live it at a fast pace. After a long courtship, he married Letha on Tuesday, 15 April 1952, and was in the studio less than a week later to offer piano support for another Tampa Red recording session.[264]

261 Ibid., 14-15; Rowe, *Chicago Breakdown,* 198; Ryan, *Trumpet Records,* 41; and Topping, "Ramblin' from Town to Town," 12.

262 Cushing, 59; and Rowe, *Chicago Breakdown,* 198.

263 Ibid., 56-57; and Whitburn, 401.

264 Bob Eagle, "Big Town Playboy: Johnnie Jones." *Living Blues* 12 (Spring 1973): 28; Dixon, Godrich, and Rye, 881-891; Leadbitter, Fancourt, and Pelletier, 285, 565-567, 575; Welding, 31; Cushing, 58; Mike Leadbitter and Neil Slaven, *Blues Records 1943-1970, A Selective Discography,* vol. 1, A-K. London: Record Information Services, 1987, 739; Mike Paikos, *Rhythm & Blues Covers and Re-Recordings.* Moraga, California: [no publisher], 1998, 24; Muddy Waters, "Screaming and Crying," Aristocrat 406, 1950; and Johnny Jones, "Big Town Playboy." Aristocrat 405, 1950. Note: original Aristocrat label credit was to "Little Johnny–Muddy Waters." New evidence has also come to light that Johnny and Muddy were paired to back up Big Maceo for an April, 1949 recording session with Specialty Records (previously, the guitarist had been identified as Tampa Red).

With Payne and Jones, Elmore had firm musical backing for support. Boyd Atkins—who doubled on bass and saxophone—joined the new group for a while, but, soon after, J.T. Brown became Elmore's regular tenor saxophone player. "Brown was a colorful figure, remembered by other musicians as a drinker, gambler and carouser, with an apparent fondness for nicknames," wrote Jim O'Neal in 1978. "Many fellow bluesman regarded his strong, swaggering delivery and bleating tone with both admiration and a kind of comic delight—J.T.'s saxophone became, in local blues parlance, 'The Nanny Goat Horn.'"[265] No one recalls exactly when Brown arrived in Chicago, although he is known to have previously spent time in a travelling minstrel show (Louis Jordan was once a fellow member), worked in Memphis with Lee Jackson and Little Buddy Doyle, and later, lived in the Missouri Bootheel area, performing, at times, with either pianist Eddie Boyd or a local trio. By 1945, Brown had worked his way to Chicago, and could be heard playing saxophone on other people's blues records. He finally got to do a 78 of his own in 1950, recorded for the Harlem label with Grant "Mr. Blues" Jones. The following year, he used his connections to get a session with the new United/States operation. "I had been knowin' Brown for a long time," Leonard Allen (a former tailor, and one of the partners in United/States) told Jim O'Neal. "I knew Brown when we worked in the tailor business years ago. I don't know how he started playin' music 'cause when I knew him he wasn't no musician." It was a fortuitous move for Brown and the new company. His "Windy City Boogie" probably brought the label its first real cash flow, and on the strength of that one disc, Brown put together an outfit and started touring. Somewhere along the way, he was introduced to Elmore (possibly through their mutual acquaintance of Lee Jackson), and joined forces with the Broomdusters.[266]

James was cranking up his Chicago performances. By Saturday, 4 October 1952, the 708 Club at 708 E. 47th was running an advertisement in the *Chicago Defender* announcing: "Don't Miss This Treat/Tues. and Thurs./The Man Who Recorded 'DUST MY BROOM'/ELMORE JAMES and HIS TRIO" and at the bottom of the ad "Open Late, 4 to 5 am." It turned out to be his regular gig for months, and starting in November, the 708 Club added Wednesday in addition to the Tuesday and Thursday night shows. By November, Elmore added weekend appearances at Sylvio's to his performance roster. Operated by Sylvio Corroza (or Carozzo) at 2254 W. Lake, Elmore would have a relationship with the club, on and off, for more than half a decade. When Sylvio's advertisements first came out in the *Chicago Defender* that November, they unabashedly billed Elmore as "The Greatest Blues Sensation."[267]

Elmer James

Earlier that summer, however, James may have been surprised to hear himself play guitar—probably without his consent—on a Boyd Gilmore Modern single. The Biharis had recorded several titles by Gilmore, including "All in My Dreams," on 23 January 1952 during the ill-fated Mississippi trip. Joe Bihari,

---

265 Jim O'Neal, notes to J.T. Brown, *Windy City Boogie.* Pearl LP 9, 1978; and Cushing, 59.

266 O'Neal, notes to *Windy City Boogie;* Jim O'Neal and Amy O'Neal, *"Living Blues* Interview: Eddie Boyd, Part 2." *Living Blues* 36 (January/February 1978): 16; and Leadbitter and Slaven, *Blues Records 1943-1970*, 177-179. Note: Earl Phillips recalled, during a 1986 panel discussion with other Chicago blues drummers, coming to the Windy City in 1940. Not long after his arrival, Phillips worked part-time for the railroad, and recalled meeting J.T. Brown "out on the job." Phillips was not, unfortunately, any more specific than that (Steve Cushing and Justin O'Brien, "Behind the Beat of the Blues." *Living Blues* 96 (March/April 1991): 18). Scott Dirks' research has also uncovered the fact that J.T. Brown first joined the Local 208 Chicago musicians' union in December 1944.

267 *The Chicago Defender* [Advertisement], (4 October 1952): 23; *The Chicago Defender* [Advertisement], (1 November 1952): 19; *The Chicago Defender* [Advertisement], (15 November 1952): 17; and Dirks, 42-44.

who had already released one Gilmore single earlier that March, really wanted to release something on Elmore, who was still popular from "Dust My Broom." Indeed, James could use another single on the market about now. Bihari was prevented from doing so, however, due to the pending litigation with Diamond Record Company and Elmore's Trumpet contract (which had not yet expired). The Biharis had two unissued Gilmore titles they could release. Although they weren't very impressed with Gilmore—who played (in comparison to Elmore) using a rougher, but looser and more relaxed approach—as far as the Biharis were concerned, might just make an adequate substitute Elmore until the business with McMurry was finished. Joe Bihari, evidently, was the one who decided to spruce up a second Gilmore single, "All in My Dreams," with Elmore James' guitar. He accomplished this simply by splicing Elmore's guitar solos from "Please Find My Baby" (recorded at the January 1952 session) onto the Gilmore title. In late June the Biharis issued the doctored Gilmore single as Modern 872, to a strong showing in Memphis.[268] As Ray Topping observes, "At the time no-one would have known, when the Boyd Gilmore came out on 78. In 1952 this sort of thing was really innovative, because they were doing splicing and overdubbing at such an early stage of tape recording."[269]

Lillian McMurry was also experimenting with a surrogate Elmore James, but with a slightly different approach than the Biharis. Arthur "Big Boy" Crudup, the popular RCA Victor recording artist, came by McMurry's Jackson, Mississippi, store one day in late August 1952, with Sonny Boy Williamson. "He said he needed some money and wanted to record," McMurry recalled.[270] Crudup had been a staple of RCA Victor's blues catalog for the past eleven years, and McMurry wasn't entirely convinced by Crudup's assurances that he was now officially ex-RCA Victor material. Seizing the moment, McMurry came up with a plan. She offered Crudup a flat fee to record two titles and would purchase all the extant rights as well. Crudup probably didn't care one way or the other and told McMurry, "You can put anybody's name on [the record] you want to."[271] As Marc Ryan explains:

> Sensing a certain similarity between Crudup's work and that of Elmore James, Lillian reasoned that perhaps the time-honored subterfuge of a like-sounding pseudonym for Big Boy —say, *Elmer* James —would enable Trumpet to at last issue a follow-up to "Dust My Broom." ....It was a somewhat desperate ploy, but one that was not without promise.... [272]

McMurry issued the two "Elmer James" titles as Trumpet 186 shortly before Christmas 1952—the very same week RCA Victor released their latest "Big Boy" Crudup single! Unfortunately, McMurry was just a little too late, and in a matter of days the real Elmore James would have his answer record to "Dust My Broom" busting out coast to coast.[273]

---

268 Leadbitter and Slaven, *Blues Records 1943-1970,* 461-462; Gart, *First Pressings—1952,* 30-31, 61; Huggins, 18-19; Topping, notes to *King of the Slide Guitar;* Topping, "Ramblin' from Town to Town," 12; and Boyd Gilmore, "All in My Dreams." Modern 872, 1952.

269 Huggins, 19.

270 O'Neal, "Lillian S. McMurry," 24; and Ryan, *Trumpet Records,* 42.

271 Ibid.

272 Ryan, *Trumpet Records,* 42.

273 Ibid., 43; and Gart, *First Pressings—1952,* 125, 135. Note: Crudup's Elmer James titles were later reissued as Sarg 186, in 1961.

A Potent String Background

By the Fall of 1952, Joe Bihari had worked up a plan for safely releasing some Elmore James material, in an effort to cash in on the success of "Dust My Broom"—a plan that would generate sales without risking an additional lawsuit from McMurry. It had been almost a year since "Dust My Broom" was issued, and one year can be almost an eternity in the music industry.

In 1952 Lester Bihari was a Memphis resident, working promotions and scouting talent for his brothers, who ran Modern Records. "Although he was a brother," Ray Topping reported, "they didn't want him as part of the company."[274] Instead, Joe Bihari gave his brother Lester a pile of master tapes to help him start his own label, Meteor. According to researcher Frank Scott, "It wasn't strictly a Modern subsidiary, but was strongly affiliated to it by family ties and the fact that Joe's material was sometimes used."[275] To the Biharis, it all probably seemed perfect. Sam Phillips had just started his own record label, Sun, in Memphis. Up until recently, Phillips had provided Modern with material by B.B. King, Joe Hill Louis, and Howlin' Wolf—that is, until the Biharis' relationship with Phillips had soured (Phillips had sold tapes by Howlin' Wolf and Rosco Gordon to both Modern *and* Chess). The Biharis probably figured that a little friendly competition with their old supplier might be good for business.[276]

So, Lester set up shop in Memphis at 1746 Chelsea and prepared the details of launching a new business. Joe Bihari quietly recorded Elmore James in Chicago—far away from Mrs. McMurry. "I think [Joe] was still probably edgy about whether Elmore would go back to Trumpet," suggested Topping, but James "definitely wanted to hang around with Joe rather than Mrs. McMurry."[277]

Bihari got Elmore and his newly formed ensemble—actually Tampa Red's regular group featuring Johnny Jones on piano, Odie Payne on drums, and Ransom Knowling on bass—into Universal Studios probably on Saturday, 22 November. They recorded eight titles that day, with Elmore taking the lead on four sides and saxophonist J.T. Brown taking the lead on four more. Bihari then sent the tapes to his brother Lester in Memphis. Joe Bihari knew that Lester could issue whatever he wanted by Elmore James safely, because Lester's new label, Meteor, was not a *true* Modern subsidiary. Since Joe Bihari was not financially involved with the company in any way, he probably could not be implicated by McMurry in their on-going lawsuit. What made the arrangement doubly safe was the fact that James' contract with Trumpet had expired. Consequently, Joe had wasted no time signing Elmore to a one-year "Agreement for Personal Services" contract plus an additional two-year option, with a publishing deal set up through Modern. Their agreement was signed on Tuesday, 5 August 1952, exactly one day after Elmore's Trumpet contract expired.[278]

Meteor Records was publicly announced that fall to the trade press. "Les Bihari hits the markets shortly with a new recording company called Meteor," reported *The Billboard* in November 1952:

---

274 Huggins, 18.

275 Ibid.; and Scott and Paulsen, "Joe and Jules Bihari! [Part 2]," 11.

276 Colin Escott and Martin Hawkins, *Sun Records: The Brief History of the Legendary Record Label.* New York: Quick Fox, 1980, 17-20.

277 Huggins, 18; and Gart, *The American Record Label Directory,* 143.

278 Ryan, *Trumpet Records,* 22, 32-33; Dirks, 42; Franz, 9; Huggins, 18; and LeBlanc, personal communication, 29 May 1996. Note: according to one interview I read, McMurry claimed to have renewed her option on Elmore's contract before it expired. As for the length of time on the option, McMurry did not say.

Headquarters will be in Memphis, close to the pressing plant of Buster Williams. Label cut its first session a few days ago. Four sides were made in the record time of twenty-two minutes. Only using four people, Bihari comes up with two sides in real down home blues fashion, while his other two sides are hot and fast horn items. With distribution already set on a national scale, and the use of a Memphis plant plus a West Coast presser, the man's in business....[279]

The "twenty-two minutes" part later turned out to be untrue: "I told Joe [Bihari] about that," Ray Topping recalled, "and he said it was bullshit; he said it took Elmore twenty-two minutes to get a song together, let alone get four sides down! It was just Lester's blurb; he used to like thinking up stories like that, to exaggerate things...." A couple weeks later, a 13 December 1952 press release announced that "Lester Bihari... is branching out on his own with a new R&B label, Meteor. Bihari... has signed Elmo James, ex-Trumpet warbler, whose first release is 'I Believe' and 'I Held My Baby Last Night,' and Bep Brown's 'Round House Boogie' and 'Kickin' the Blues Around.'"[280] *Cash Box* reviewed the disc, giving it high marks for their "Award O' The Week":

James' manner of delivery has that certain something that lifts his material out of the ordinary class. His treatment of "I Believe"... is excitingly presented against a potent string background and we look for this side of wax to create a commotion. The under lid, "I Held My Baby Last Night"... James treats to a haunting vocal.... but final effort just falls short of the upper etching, and we go all out for the top deck. [281]

Over the years, scholars and critics alike have shown a tendency to widely misunderstand the importance of "I Believe;" a common theme is an attempt to pigeonhole it as just one of many amplified versions of "Dust My Broom." Actually, it was nothing less than Elmore's cleverly crafted answer record to "Dust My Broom" (if one listens closely, "I Believe" picks up the story line from where "Dust My Broom" left off), and almost five decades after its initial release, still quite an amazing record in its own right. Just as James' recordings with Sonny Boy Williamson in 1951 had been transitional, so was this. "I Believe" is one of the earlier recorded examples of a full five piece Chicago blues ensemble with electric guitar, heavy rhythm and horns, and, as such, is a prototypical record. It helped set the mold for how a 1950s Chicago blues band would be defined not only for that decade, but in the years to come as well.[282]

Like a train pulling out of a station, "I Believe" starts off with Elmore and J.T. riffing in synch, while the rest of the band slowly comes in as the introduction finishes. By the time James starts singing, the rhythm section is practically bulletproof, propelled by drummer Odie Payne, bassist Ransom Knowling,

279 Gart, *First Pressings—1952,* 120.

280 Huggins, 18; and "Lester Bihari Sets New Meteor Label." *The Billboard* (20 December 1952): 25. Note: "Bep Brown" is a pseudonym for J.T. Brown.

281 Topping, "Ramblin' from Town to Town," 15.

282 Just to set the record straight, it is important to remember that according to a number of reports, Muddy Waters was already making amplified sounds like these in the Chicago nightclubs at the time "I Believe" came out as a record. Thanks in part, however, to a superstitious Leonard Chess—who was loathe to change his hit record-making formula that featured Muddy in a stripped-down setting—a formula Chess had been milking since 1948—the world would not get to hear a Muddy Waters record with this kind of heavily amplified sound and full band until around 1953. "Gone to Main Street," recorded 17 September 1952 and released as Chess 1526 the same month Elmore was in the studio cutting "I Believe" with the Broomdusters, is perhaps the apex of Muddy's small ensemble sound during the 1951/1952 time period. "Mad Love" (a.k.a. "I Want You to Love Me"), recorded 24 September 1953, was Muddy's first session to feature Otis Spann on piano, and is a good, early example of the Muddy Waters full-blown band sound. It was released as Chess 1550 in October 1953. The flip side to "Mad Love," interestingly enough, featured a "Dust My Broom"-styled rocker, "Blow Wind Blow."

J.B. Lenoir was yet another early practitioner of the full five-piece Chicago blues band lead by a heavily amplified electric guitar. His song "The Mojo" is a particularly explosive example. It was recorded for the J.O.B. label on 12 January 1953, and released in May of that same year.

and Johnny Jones' solid-as-granite piano. The artistry, power, and electricity flow together effortlessly, building in intensity towards the end of the record. The proceedings are lent an extra, added tension due to the slide guitar tuning Elmore employed. Rather than tune the guitar to concert pitch and play blue notes with the bottleneck, he uses a traditional Mississippi approach that incorporates the "blue note" right into the guitar tuning—in this case, as he was using open E/open D tuning, via the use of a noticeably flattened third string on his guitar (one can hear blues guitarist Sam Collins employing just such a technique as early as 1927). During the last verse of "I Believe," the intensity is at an apogee while James dramatically sings:

> I believe, I believe my time ain't long,
> I believe, I believe my time ain't long,
> Dust my broom this mornin', I know I treat my baby wrong. [283]

After Elmore's verse is concluded he takes a potent solo—egged on by enthusiastic cheers from the band—and ends the record with the listener practically breathless. The flip side of the record, "I Held My Baby Last Night," was one of Elmore's first efforts at a slow-tempo, expressive blues—a formula he would use effectively on more than a dozen titles (his 1960 hit "The Sky Is Crying" being the most notable example).[284]

"...The interplay between them was as if they had played together all their lives," Mike Rowe commented.[285] Indeed, it seems true. Even Muddy Waters' top-drawer ensemble of pianist Otis Spann, rhythm guitarist Jimmy Rogers, harmonica ace Little Walter Jacobs, bassist Willie Dixon, and drummer Fred Below—considered to be one of the finer Chicago postwar blues bands—would have difficulty matching Elmore's crack outfit. "The Broomdusters rocked harder than any other Chicago blues band," Robert Palmer commented, "their music still sounded contemporary when copied by white rock groups twenty-five years after 'Dust My Broom' was an R&B hit."[286] It's also important to recall, as did Leroy Pierson, that the group of musicians Elmore picked out—especially Johnny Jones and Odie Payne—had already displayed quite a knack for working with slide guitar players (they both had worked for Tampa Red). This might explain part of the reason behind the musical rapport on "I Believe," but there's more to the story than that.

Elmore James and Tampa Red shared the slide technique, it is true. Both musicians also displayed an unusual tendency with their linear, single note slide guitar solos—some of the most developed slide work in Chicago. Tampa Red's slide guitar style is distinctively unique, given the time period and the geographical location where he grew up. The antecedents to his style were possibly like the work of Louisville, Kentucky, slide guitarist Sylvester Weaver and few other proponents of the day. As Leroy Pierson explains, "Virtually all bluesmen are products of their environment, in the sense that these sounds they make are sounds that they are imitating...."[287]

283 Elmore James, "I Believe." Meteor 5000, 1952; and Pete Whelan, "Sam Collins and the Gennett Madness." In the notes to *14 Rare Country Blues by Sam Collins & 2 Surprises by King Solomon Hill, Vintage 1927-1931.* Origin Jazz Library LP 10, c. 1965.

Note: A good, basic introduction to blue notes can be found in Eric Kriss' one-page article on the subject in *Living Blues* magazine. Kriss explains, for instance, that the two primary blue notes and the three secondary blue notes correspond directly to the pentatonic (i.e., five-tone) African scale; how the usage of the African scale/blue notes have been translated for usage on the Western twelve-note scale; how blue notes can be used to add harmonic tension to a performance; and a chart that illustrates how blue notes in the tonic chord translate into primary and secondary blue notes in the dominant and subdominant chords. See: Eric Kriss, "Blues Notes." *Living Blues* 21 (May/June 1975): 12.

284 Elmore James, "I Held My Baby Last Night." Meteor 5000, 1952.

285 Rowe, *Chicago Breakdown*, 198.

286 Palmer, 215.

> Tampa Red, coming from the area of the country that he came from and ending up playing the style of music that he played, it's odd. Tampa Red should have been a fast alternating thumb-picker. It's not odd that he plays slide. But that whole northern Florida, southern Georgia area is sort of known for... fast picking. So his... delicate, slow, deliberate playing is odd.... Tampa Red is really the first, what I would call, modern bottleneck stylist.
>
> See, most bottleneck players like Charley Patton or Fred McDowell, they play fill runs with the bottleneck. They're not really playing thought out linear leads with the bottleneck—it's just fill runs that are rhythmically exciting. That's not to denigrate them.... But Tampa Red, coming up with that deliberate linear one note styling—when he comes up the neck, he comes up with one note. When I come up the neck, I come up with a full chord like somebody from Mississippi. If it was Barbeque Bob [from Atlanta], he'd be coming up with a full chord.... For the time period, Tampa Red's *way* ahead of his time.[288]

This also made Tampa Red an immensely influential guitarist of the pre-war era. "I liked the Tampa style," recalled Muddy Waters. "Tampa made some of the best records that I can even think of."[289]

Elmore James, unlike Tampa Red, was from Mississippi, and his basic guitar style was steeped with the tradition of that region. James played traditional Mississippi (chordal approach) slide guitar style, driven rhythmically by the alternating, moving bass figures played with the thumb (inspired by Robert Johnson, discussed earlier in the text). But this is where Elmore leaves off from his Mississippi counterparts. James didn't use the slide to play fill runs; he used it to play 12-bar, thought-out, linear single-note guitar solos, inspired by the playing of Tampa Red. Unlike Tampa Red, however, James played with the rhythmic drive of someone from Mississippi (Tampa Red didn't use his thumb to keep the beat going; he relied on his pianists to do that). When James combined these two guitar styles—traditional Mississippi and modern solo style—he created something unique, and it made him a memorable—perhaps even a visionary—postwar guitarist.[290]

If it could be argued that there is a missing link between the Elmore James sound of the 1950s and the sounds of an earlier generation such as Kokomo Arnold, Tampa Red, and Robert Johnson, then it would have to be guitarist Robert Nighthawk. Taught by the equally legendary, but under-recorded Houston Stackhouse (who, in turn, had learned from Tommy Johnson, who was his neighbor), Nighthawk became an important, and influential bridge between the 1930s acoustic blues and the 1950's Chicago tough urban-electric sound. Although he was found to be somewhat taciturn by interviewers after he was "rediscovered" in 1964, Nighthawk evidently had a history of freely sharing his knowledge and skills on the slide guitar with his fellow musicians. "I've heard it said Nighthawk was one of the first to switch to electric guitar in the early forties, and adopting it to a bottleneck technique that is reputed to be one of the most influential, and very likely one of the smoothest," reported Don Kent in 1967. "He taught Earl Hooker how to play, supposedly taught a lot to Elmore James and imparted somewhat to Muddy Waters, who, in return for the favor, got Nighthawk the [1948] Aristocrat session."[291] Upon resuming his recording career, a look into Nighthawk's catalog between the years of 1948 and 1952 reveals an obvious indebtedness to Tampa Red. As Norman Darwen comments, "Nighthawk's own biggest influence, certainly by [this] time... was Tampa Red, whose clean smooth slide playing was a world away from the dirty downhome whine of Muddy's bottleneck," Darwen offered in the liner notes to a compact disc collection of Nighthawk's earliest

287 Pierson, personal interview, 27 March 1990; and Richard Spottswood, notes to *The Slide Guitar—Bottles, Knives & Steel.* Columbia CD 46218, 1990.

288 Pierson, personal interview, 27 March 1990.

289 O'Neal and O'Neal, 26.

290 Pierson, personal interview, 27 March 1990.

291 Don Kent, "A Note on Robert Nighthawk." *Blues Unlimited* 42 (March/April 1967): 8.

postwar sides. "It wasn't just Tampa's sound that he appropriated either; his two biggest hits... are both reworkings of songs Tampa recorded. However, these versions couldn't be confused with the originals as Nighthawk's undeniably amplified guitar (it was sometimes difficult to tell if Tampa was using an electric instrument) has a much tougher timbre and there is a rather doomy approach...."[292] Nighthawk's 1950 recording of "Six Three O," for example, illustrates our point here very well—it readily exhibits Tampa Red's impact on Nighthawk, but in and of itself is a mature example of the kind of amplified sounds that Elmore would be making just three short years later with his first Meteor release.[293]

On Thursday, 8 January 1953, Elmore and his band appeared before the musicians union Local 208 board of directors, along with Sylvio Corroza, who had filed a complaint against him. According to research collected by Scott Dirks, it was the first in what would become a long list of appearances before a board who, by all accounts, ruled over professional musical activities in the Chicago-land area "with an iron fist." James was not meeting the terms of their two-month agreement, Corroza complained, indicating that he had contracted for the band to appear on Fridays, Saturdays and Sundays at his lounge, but Elmore and the group had failed to appear on four separate occasions. Additionally, Corroza had filed a separate contract for Christmas and New Years appearances, but had found out only hours before the Christmas show (from J.T. Brown) that James was not going to appear, and had an engagement to play in East Chicago, Indiana, instead. Elmore offered the following explanations:

> ...On November 7th he sent a substitute orchestra which Mr. Corroza refused. On November 22nd he couldn't work because he had to make a recording session. He could not remember the reason for the orchestra's failure to appear on December 13th, but on December 21st he stated that he and the orchestra attended a relative's funeral in Benton Harbor, Michigan.
>
> Under questioning by the Board, it developed that on all of the dates in question James played outside engagements....
>
> The Board explained to James and the orchestra that the provisions of their contract must be enforced. The Board also explained to James that under no conditions can he accept engagements that conflict with his appearance at Sylvio's Lounge on Fridays, Saturdays, and Sundays.[294]

Elmore was fined $50 dollars, which the board order to be paid within ten days, or he would be "erased" (i.e., not allowed to play music until the fine had been paid). In addition, taxes of $3.20 and $5.12 were also levied because of the 13 December and the Christmas "no shows," which Elmore paid in two installments; $15 dollars on Thursday, 22 January 1953, and the balance, $43.32, on Tuesday, 10 February 1953.[295]

Regardless of the disciplinary action from the local union, things were moving quickly for Elmore at the national level. By Saturday, 17 January 1953, "I Believe" had made its debut on *The Billboard* charts, attaining the number five position in Chicago, with an additional note that the record was "Very strong in the South. Good action in New York and Philadelphia. Strong in St. Louis and beginning to build on Coast." Seven days later it was a "Territorial Tip" in New York and made strong showings in Atlanta, Newark, Dallas-Fort Worth, Los Angeles, and the San Francisco bay area. Thanks to coincidence, or perhaps the brilliant strategy of the Biharis, Elmore's "I Believe" was issued on the market simultaneously

[292] Norman Darwen, notes to Robert Nighthawk and Forest City Joe, *Black Angel Blues.* Charly CD RED 29, 1991; and Leadbitter, Fancourt, and Pelletier, 309-310.

[293] Robert Nighthawk, "Six Three O." Aristocrat 413, 1950; and Leadbitter, Fancourt, and Pelletier, 310. Note: when issued on 78 in 1950, the original label credit simply listed the artist(s) as "Nighthawks."

[294] Dirks, 41-42.

[295] Ibid. Note: Some of the information in regards to the fines Elmore paid to the Chicago musicians union are taken from his union file; courtesy of Pat LeBlanc and the Estate of Elmore James.

Additional note: Curiously, Scott Dirks' research into the minutes kept by the Local 208 board of directors does not indicate whether or not they had anything to say about Elmore recording on 22 November 1952 for Joe Bihari, for which, evidently, no formal paperwork was filed.

with another song called "I Believe,"—the insipid pop ballad, which was enjoying popular chart success at that time. Every week, *The Billboard* highlighted the top ten popular tunes in the nation with their "Honor Roll of Hits" page. For every week that "I Believe" (the pop song) appeared on that list, Elmore's name would appear in tiny print, under "Other Records: E. James, Meteor 5000." Perhaps it helped Lester sell a few extra platters, however, anyone who had ever heard the two songs would not likely confuse them. Although the official record reflects that "I Believe" debuted on the R&B charts on Valentine's Day, stayed there for three weeks and peaked at the ninth position, the truth is that "I Believe" was still cracking regional charts in early April. One of its last appearances was in Philadelphia, where it reached the number one position on Saturday, 4 April 1953.[296]

A photograph that Big Bill Broonzy took around this same time (possibly) shows Elmore James, Sonny Boy Williamson, Little Walter, and Tommy McClennan (yes, *Tommy McClennan*—just about one decade after his last recording session) walking down a Chicago sidewalk, looking kind of like they've just been handed the key to the city—laughing, joking, and having a good time. Elmore appears to be striding confidently, wearing a porkpie hat pushed down low over his forehead. With a hit record and newly found popularity in Chicago, it must have seemed to him, for a time, that he was on top of the world.[297]

Almost immediately, "I Believe" spawned imitators from all stripes. B.B. King's "Please Love Me" was recorded for RPM the same month "I Believe" hit the streets (but was held back for release some six months—possibly an attempt by the Biharis to first let "I Believe" run its course). It carried the "Dust My Broom" riff to fabulous new heights, thanks to its advance to the summit of the R&B charts for three weeks. All told, "Please Love Me" charted almost four months, from late June to mid-October, 1953. Never again would King have an R&B hit record that would spend this many weeks at the number one slot (It also inadvertently started a trend. Today, when blues guitarists play the "Broom" riff, they largely tend to play it without using a slide, just as B.B. King does here).[298] James Williamson was another musician, in the weeks following the release of "I Believe," to record a song in an Elmore-styled vein, which he did on Friday, 23 January 1953 for Chance Records. With straightforward support from pianist Lazy Bill Lucas, "Homesick" had a nice relaxed feel, and was rounded out with Williamson's distinct bottleneck figures. More importantly, the record bestowed a lifelong moniker on the performer, better known since then as Homesick James.[299] Memphis one-man-band sensation Joe Hill Louis was another artist who took a stab at Elmore's signature riff. He recorded "Jealous Man" for Henry Stone's Rockin' label sometime in early 1953. Released circa September, the record went nowhere, but was an interesting addition to Louis' repertoire nonetheless. One of Louis' label-mates at Rockin' was guitarist Earl Hooker, who in April 1953 recorded "Alley Corn," an instrumental which loosely based it patterns on the Elmore James theme. The tune never saw release as a Rockin' single, however, and remained unissued until 1998.[300]

Meteor released its second Elmore James single in April 1953. "Baby, What's Wrong" had been

296 "Territorial Best Sellers." *The Billboard* (17 January 1953): 44, 56; Huggins, 18; Topping, "Ramblin' from Town to Town," 13-14; Gart, *First Pressings—1953,* 10-11, 26; "Honor Roll of Hits." *The Billboard* (11 April 1953): 20; Whitburn, 216; and "Territorial Best Sellers." *The Billboard* (11 April 1953): 40.

297 Yannick Bruynoghe, "In Chicago with Big Bill & Friends: Chicago Scrapbook Excerpts." *Living Blues* 55 (Winter 1982/83): 12.

298 B.B. King, "Please Love Me." RPM 386, 1953; Whitburn, 238-240; and Leslie Fancourt, *B.B. King, Albert & Freddy, A Discography.* Kent, England: Retrack Books, 1993, 5. Note: King's first R&B hit record, "Three O'Clock Blues," had spent five weeks at number one.

299 Homesick James Williamson, "Homesick." Chance 1131, 1953; and Leadbitter, Fancourt, and Pelletier, 755.

300 Leroy Pierson, notes to *Downhome Delta Blues 1949-1952.* Nighthawk LP 109, 1980; Joe Hill Louis, "Jealous Man." Rockin' 517, 1953 (note: original label credit was given as Johnny Lewis); Earl Hooker, "Alley Corn." From the album *Rockin' the Blues.* Rockin' CD 5502-2, 1998; and Leadbitter and Slaven, *Blues Records 1943-1970,* 574.

recorded the same day as "I Believe," and included some amazing instrumental interplay between Elmore and J.T. Brown. Using the beginning and ending solos to showcase his incredible guitar talent (and throwing in a few T-Bone Walker licks for extra spice), James then provides Brown ample room for an atmospheric saxophone solo in the middle of the disc. Elmore was probably well aware of the value of having Brown in his ensemble; just as Leonard Allen—a record label owner that Brown had previously recorded for—succinctly commented, "J.T. Brown sold, that honking he did."[301]

When released, the writers' credits on both sides of Meteor 5003 read "James-Taub." Curiosity got the better of researchers Frank Scott and Gary Paulsen when they were interviewing Jules Bihari years later: "Who was J. Taub? (composer listed on many releases). Well, you're looking at him!! The name comes from my mother," although Bihari added, "As far as actual earnings went, it didn't mean anything."[302] Being on the receiving end of such practices, however, wasn't so much fun. Richard Berry—James' upcoming label-mate at Flair—offered this opinion: "I could almost at any given time go to Joe [Bihari] and ask for an advance and get it," he stated. But the convenience was not without cost. "Modern was collecting my royalties and keeping me ignorant. When I finally asked them, 'What's this Josea shit?' the Biharis told me the distributors would promote my records more if they saw that name on it!"[303] Meteor 5003 was the first in a long series of Modern releases—almost three dozen in all—that found Elmore James sharing writers' credit with "Josea," "Ling," or "Taub," each one a pseudonym for a brother Bihari (Joe, Saul, and Jules respectively).[304]

That May, Lester Bihari prepared to release a third Elmore James Meteor single. The plan was once again to use material his brother Joe had given him. A small stack of master tapes were sent to Los Angeles for overdubbing; included in the shipment were some titles by Elmore James and some by fellow Meteor artist Joe Hill Louis. The master tape to Elmore's "Please Find My Baby" (recorded the previous January by Joe, and used for the Boyd Gilmore single) was overdubbed with bass and drums, and assigned a Meteor matrix number. "Hawaiian Boogie" (from the same session), designated for the flip, was given the same treatment. But Joe Bihari had recently been in the studio with James and had a fresh stack of master tapes. Ultimately, the plans for Elmore's third Meteor single were abandoned, and he was switched to Joe's new endeavor, the Flair label.[305] A 6 May 1953 press release made the changes official:

---

301 Robert Pruter and Jim O'Neal, "Leonard Allen and the United/States Story, Part 1." *Living Blues* 92 (July/August 1990): 38; Elmore James, "Baby, What's Wrong." Meteor 5003, 1953; and Franz, 9, 32.

Note: One of the stranger entries in regards to Elmore's brief tenure while at Meteor Records was a curious advertisement that appeared in the R&B trade press. Gotham Records—one of the labels that had wanted to sign Elmore but lost out—placed an advertisement for Elmore James' "Sinful Women" (the flip side of "Baby, What's Wrong"), evidently intending to issue the title as Gotham 519 sometime circa the Spring of 1953 (my best guess). Although Gotham 519 eventually went to Doug Quattlebaum's "Lizzie Lou" instead of Elmore, it does raise some interesting questions. Did Lester Bihari set up this deal? Was he willing to do it because he needed the cash? Did Joe Bihari put a stop to it because he was about to sign Elmore over to his Flair label? Did Gotham have a connection in the industry the Biharis didn't know about? Also interesting to mull over: Elmore's "I Believe" was the number 1 R&B record in Philadelphia for the week of 4 April 1953, the city where Gotham Records was headquartered. Whatever the case may have been, Gotham must have been fairly sure the deal was going to go down if they had already started advertising it. This item thanks to Bruce Bastin, who found it among the Gotham files, and to Chris Smith, who wrote about it. (Chris Smith, notes to *East Coast Blues.* Krazy Kat LP 824, 1988).

302 Scott and Paulsen, "Joe and Jules Bihari! (Part 3)," 11; and Franz, 41.

303 Dave Marsh, *Louie Louie.* New York: Hyperion, 1993, 29.

304 Franz, 41, 42. Note: The reader may be amused to know that "Josea" "Taub" and "Ling" are the sort of gift that just keeps on giving—even into the 21st century. At the *All Music Guide* website, under the entry for Joe Hill Louis (who also recorded for Modern), it states that this artist "performed songs by Jules Taub and Sam Ling"! The only reply I can muster for that bit of asininity is that those "songwriters" "Taub" and "Ling" sure wrote a whole lot of bloody good blues songs, eh? You know—come to think of it—I think they wrote some songs for John Lee Hooker and B.B. King, too....

305 Joe Hill Louis, *Gotta Boogie Baby.* P-Vine Club CD 22002, 1995; Huggins, 18; and Franz, 8, 11.

> Flair records, a division of Modern Records which heretofore waxed...only country and western tunes, this week entered the rhythm and blues field with release of two platters featuring Elmore James and Little Johnny Jones.
>
> The releases also mark the departure of Joe Bihari from Modern to devote full time to Flair in his capacity as president and a.&r. chief. Bihari takes James with him, whom he had under personal contract. James previously recorded for... Meteor Records. [306]

After the enormous success of "I Believe" that year, "I think Joe and Jules Bihari decided they had to have this man on *their* label now, completely," Topping said.[307]

Although Lester Bihari may not have felt it at the time, it was the beginning of a slow end for Meteor Records. By the time the label had reached two dozen issues, Meteor was almost exclusively a rockabilly label—no doubt an effort to capitalize on the success Sun was having with that genre. Bud Deckleman's 1954 hillbilly offering "Daydreamin'" was Meteor's only other "hit." Due to lack of distribution, it did not chart nationally (Before his Meteor session could begin, Deckleman, a mechanic, had to fix Lester's tape recorders!). "Lester Bihari was a nice feller, he gave me a couple of nice suits and he was going to record me," David "Honeyboy" Edwards told Tony Burke and Norman Darwen, "but he had never got his equipment stuff in there like he wanted."[308] Without the continued success of a major artist to bring in steady sales, the label, plain and simple, was just cash-starved. This is reflected in the fact that by 1958—Meteor's last year of operation—they had averaged only eight releases a year. Lester just seemed to lack the natural business finesse of his brothers. A 1953 Meteor advertisement said "Please don't send any more orders on:—'I BELIEVE' by Elmore James and 'ROUND HOUSE BOOGIE' by Bep Brown—we're trying to fill the ones we have."[309] "Some guy came over to [Lester's] studio to record," Jules Bihari remembered in an interview. "Lester told him 'I think Sam Phillips can do a better job for you than I can. Why don't you go over to see Sam?' As it turned out the guy who wanted to record was Elvis Presley!"[310]

"It was a magnificent studio"

Just a week and a half prior to recording "I Believe," Chess Records added the name Elmore James to their roster of artists. Chess was the heavyweight independent Chicago label, and was home to such blues stalwarts as Little Walter Jacobs, Muddy Waters and Howlin' Wolf. According to research collected by Pat LeBlanc and the Estate of Elmore James, Leonard Chess offered a contract, which James signed and accepted on Wednesday, 12 November 1952. The agreement called for him to record a total of sixteen sides in a two year period. It was a deliberate, yet curious move, especially when one considers his recent fine and chastisement from the local union, and that he was barely three months into his three year contract with Joe Bihari. Perhaps it was his way of taking no chances, now that his professional career was fully underway in the Windy City.[311]

On 3 January 1953, *The Billboard* issued a review of "I Believe," giving it high marks. On 10 January

[306] Gart, *First Pressings—1953*, 49.

[307] Huggins, 18.

[308] Burke and Darwen, 8; and Escott and Hawkins, 46, 81.

[309] Topping, "Ramblin' from Town to Town," 14; and Gart, *The American Record Label Directory*, 143.

[310] Scott and Paulsen, "Joe and Jules Bihari! [Part 2]," 11.

[311] LeBlanc, personal communication, 29 May 1996; and Dirks, 42.

1953, *The Billboard* noted that "I Believe" was "building well in Chicago, Tennessee and Cincinnati. Heavy demand in New York. Top dealer pick this week." Exactly one week later, on Saturday 17 January 1953, Chess had Elmore James in the studio, making the first installment of his contract. He would record five titles that day.[312]

Len Chess' standard practice in the days before he had his own studio was to rent the Universal Recording Studios for sessions. It was the favored studio in town for many years, and visiting producers like Joe Bihari would use it too. "Joe said that he liked recording Elmore in Chicago most of all because he used the Universal Studios there," remembered Topping. "He said it was a magnificent studio... and [that] they had the best sound there...."[313] Malcolm Chisholm and Bruce Swedien were two engineers/mixers who worked at Universal during its 1950s hey-day, and they recalled what made it special. "Bill Putnam, the legendary engineer and inventor who operated Universal, had built all the consoles and microphone pre-amps himself, and they sounded just incredible!" noted Swedien.[314] Putnam became a sought-after engineer after his enormous success with the Harmonicats' "Peg o' My Heart" in 1947 (which Putnam issued on his own label). Author Kim Field stated that this "was... one of the first uses of an echo chamber on a recording session," and thanks in part to Putnam's ingenuity, "Peg o' My Heart" spent a full half-year on *The Billboard* charts (holding the number one position for two months), through the years selling an astounding twenty million-plus copies.[315] "Bill Putnam *made* the Harmonicats," Al Fiore, one of the original Harmonicats, said. "People couldn't believe what they were hearing. He was our genius, and he was the man who made the money for us."[316] For years afterward, record producers searching for that elusive magic formula for a hit record would beat a path to Putnam's door, and they included men like Joe Bihari and Leonard Chess. "'Peg' made Bill Putnam the biggest engineer in the country," Don Les, another Harmonicat related.[317] Malcolm Chisholm would concur: "You could look in *Billboard* during the mid-50's and, on a regular basis, three to five of the Top Ten hits would have been recorded in Chicago at Universal," he offered.[318]

Located originally in the Civic Opera Building, Universal enjoyed facilities at East Ontario in the early '50s, and then at 46 East Walton after 1957. Universal had three studio rooms, and Putnam himself usually mixed top-name sessions in the large Studio A with artists like Duke Ellington and Count Basie. "For the most part, I cut the blues sessions in Studio B, the small room. It was a little too small...." said Chisholm.[319] On blues sessions, Chisholm said "We didn't run a safety machine or 'back up' tape recorder at that time—and certainly not on a low-budget blues session. If you got a bad reel of tape, well, you just lost whatever music had been recorded that day. But that didn't happen often...."[320] By the late '50s, Universal was

312 "Reviews of This Week's New Records." *The Billboard* (3 January 1953): 24; "This Week's Best Buys." *The Billboard* (10 January 1953): 26; and Franz, 10.

313 Huggins, 18.

314 Bruce Swedien interview by Diana Reid Haig. In the notes to *The Cobra Records Story.* Capricorn CD 42012-2, 1993, 13.

315 Kim Field, *Harmonicas, Harps, and Heavy Breathers.* New York: Cooper Square Press, 2000, 63-64; and Joel Whitburn, *A Century of Pop Music.* Menomonee Falls, Wisconsin: Record Research, Inc., 1999, 66. Note: unless otherwise stated, in this book all further references to Whitburn refer to *Top R&B Singles 1942-1988.*

316 Field, 64.

317 Ibid., 65.

318 Malcolm Chisholm interview by Diana Reid Haig. In the notes to *The Cobra Records Story.* Capricorn CD 42012-2, 1993, 12. Note: Bill Putnam would later go on to be a top engineer and studio designer in Los Angeles, in the words of Dick Shurman, "a true unsung hero!" (Dick Shurman, personal communication with Steve Franz. 29 November 2001)

319 Chisholm, 12-13; and Swedien, 13-14. Note: Studio C, the smallest room, was used primarily to record narration.

"beginning to experiment with three-track recording, stereo recording and over-dubbing," Swedien remembers, "but all blues sessions would probably have been done in mono."[321]

For the Chess date, Elmore used the same musicians he had in November. With a different producer and record label, the five sides recorded that day had a completely different sound to them than the Meteor date two months earlier—even though both sessions were held at Universal Studios. Elmore's guitar was less raw and displayed a much more balanced tonal quality, while J.T. Brown's creative tenor saxophone work was featured very prominently in the mix. The first item recorded, "Country Boogie," was essentially "Baby, What's Wrong" without the words, with Elmore giving Brown and pianist Johnny Jones ample room for solos, while "My Best Friend" was a slow blues that owed a debt to T-Bone Walker's "Goodbye Blues" (which had been the flip side to one of Walker's 1948 R&B chart hits, "Long Skirt Baby Blues").[322] Two "Dust My Broom"-style tunes were also recorded. One of them was the smoldering, laid-back rocker "I See My Baby," loosely based on Elmore's "Hand in Hand" that he had recorded the previous January. It came complete with a nice guitar solo and this memorable coupling:

> Well, can you remember baby when you lay down 'cross my bed,
> Well, can you remember baby when you lay down 'cross my bed,
> Now, I hope you remember darling, every word that you have said. [323]

The other one was the terrific, swinging "She Just Won't Do Right," the final installment in Elmore's own series of "answer records" that began with "Dust My Broom" and continued with Meteor 5000. The intro begins with Elmore (once again, featuring his blue note-tuned guitar) and J.T. soloing together, blasting off in high gear. He picks up the story where "I Believe" left off:

> Well I've dust my broom, to give my friends a chance,
> Well I've dust my broom, just to give my friends a chance,
> But early the next mornin', I wanted my baby's romance.
>
> Well it's early in the mornin', I believe I'll go back home,
> Now it's early in the mornin', I believe I'll go back home,
> I'm gonna quit my runnin' around, And never no more to roam.

By the end of the song, however, Elmore's mind is made up:

> I stayed away from my baby, just as long as I could,
> I stayed away..., stayed as long as I could,
> Now I've got my suitcase all packed, and this time I'm going for good.[324]

The other notable item produced at the session was "Whose Muddy Shoes," probably inspired by Big Bill Broonzy's "You Do Me Any Old Way."[325] By this time—the last number to be recorded that day—the

320 Chisholm, 13.

321 Swedien, 13.

322 Elmore James, "Country Boogie." Checker 777, 1953; Elmore James, "My Best Friend." From the album Elmore James and John Brim, *Tough.* Blue Horizon LP 7-63204, 1968; T-Bone Walker, "Goodbye Blues." Black & White 123, 1948; Whitburn, 429, Leadbitter, Fancourt, and Pelletier, 659; and Franz, 9-10.

323 Elmore James, "I See My Baby." From the album Elmore James and John Brim, *Tough.* Blue Horizon LP 7-63204, 1968.

324 Elmore James, "She Just Won't Do Right." Checker 777, 1953.

325 Elmore James, "Whose Muddy Shoes." From the album Elmore James and John Brim, *Tough.* Blue Horizon LP 7-63204, 1968; and Big Bill Broonzy, "You Do Me Any Old Way." American Record Company 7-06-64, 1937.

band members are tight and the playing for the day is at a zenith. J.T. Brown works his smoky saxophone off James' smooth guitar, backed by the solid rhythm of Jones' piano and Odie Payne's drumming. It seems that Chess may have seriously considered "Whose Muddy Shoes" as the flip side for Checker 777. It was only a momentary consideration, however, and the tune was shelved for fifteen years. That distinction, instead, would go to "She Just Won't Do Right," which was picked to become the B-side to "Country Boogie." These sides, issued as Checker 777 in early August 1953, didn't last too long. Possibly because of pressure from Joe Bihari, the single was withdrawn from the market.[326]

The Broom Dusters

Before the Checker release was on the market, Joe Bihari had been in the studio, recording new material on Elmore James and Johnny Jones. The session was held at Universal Studios on Wednesday, 1 April 1953, and as with the previous two sessions, the same group of musicians was present. "Joe had tabs on [Elmore]," Ray Topping recalled, "because Joe knew exactly when to go to Chicago—so Elmore must have had telephone numbers and addresses for Joe to keep in contact with him."[327] The last two sessions had witnessed Elmore's ensemble cutting some solid numbers, but this time they would manage to top themselves with an outstanding studio performance. Although the phrase may be somewhat over-used, this truly was a working group of musicians.

Johnny Jones started off the session with "Sweet Little Woman" and "I May Be Wrong." "Sweet Little Woman," Jones' joyfully off-color treatment of the old standard "The Dozens" featured his innate sense of humor and another great solo by J.T. Brown, while "I May Be Wrong" was an update of the 1937 Count Basie Decca recording "Boogie Woogie" (featuring Jimmy Rushing on vocals; Roy Milton also recorded it twice as "Milton's Boogie"—a top five R&B hit version for the Juke Box label in 1945, and in 1946 for the eponymous Roy Milton imprint). After Johnny had finished, Elmore took the lead and recorded four sides in all: two powerful "Dust My Broom" styled numbers, the incredible instrumental "Hawaiian Boogie," and the more ordinary (by comparison only), "Can't Stop Lovin." Bihari chose the fast rocker "Early in the Morning" to be paired with "Hawaiian Boogie" as Flair 1011. When issued, the label read "Elmore James and the Broom Dusters," a sobriquet that would be used on many of James' discs.[328]

Two reviews of "Early in the Morning" were positive enough. *Cash Box* called the side "a strong middle tempo southern blues that should get powerful juke box action," while *Billboard* said that the record offered "plenty of quality in the vocal, with typical guitar backing. Beat is strongly marked. Watch it."[329]

Note: The American Record Company issued 78s on a mixture of imprints, including the Banner, Melotone, Oriole, Perfect, and Romeo labels. Beginning in September 1935, their numbering system was setup so that a particular 78 would carry the same issue number on each of their five different record labels. It is accepted practice to refer to issues by the American Record Company (more commonly, "A.R.C.," or just "ARC") under the "ARC" umbrella (rather than list each of the five different labels for each 78 issue). Dixon, Godrich, and Rye, xxxii-xxxiii, xlviii, 277.

326 Broven, Mohr, Rowe, et al., 5; Rowe, *Chicago Breakdown,* 200; and "Rhythm and Blues Tattler" [Advertisement]. *The Billboard* (8 August 1953): 36.

327 Huggins, 18; and Franz, 11.

328 Rowe, *Chicago Breakdown,* 201; Little Johnny Jones, "Sweet Little Woman." Flair 1010, 1953; Elmore James, "Early in the Morning." Flair 1011, 1953; Paikos, 32; and Whitburn, 292. Note: "Broom Dusters" is also commonly used as one word, i.e., "Broomdusters."

329 "Rhythm & Blues Record Reviews." *The Billboard* (13 June 1953): 22; and Les Moss, personal

On the flip side was the instrumental, "Hawaiian Boogie." Although Bihari had recorded a rough-and-tumble version of "Hawaiian Boogie" during the January 1952 session, this updated, second recording of the tune with James' Broomdusters sparkled with the precision of a well-oiled machine. "The small group of Johnny Jones, J.T. Brown and Odie Payne was the perfect vehicle for Elmore's artistry," wrote Mike Rowe in 1987, "as can be seen... from the fantastic 'Hawaiian Boogie,' an instrumental of such excitement, drive and intricacy that it is probably unequalled in postwar blues recording."[330] Leroy Pierson echoed Rowe's comment, saying "To me, 'Hawaiian Boogie' is the ultimate postwar instrumental. Every person in the band seems to know what the other person's doing before they do it."[331] Elmore kicks off "Hawaiian Boogie" with a rocket blast from his guitar. A split second later, J.T. Brown and Odie Payne fall in behind like a 20-Mule Team, while Elmore imperturbably produces devastating slide-guitar runs without even breaking a sweat. Johnny Jones pounds the piano in perfect accompaniment, his right hand replying to James' phrasing and his left hand propelling him forward. Elmore's solo during the first eighteen measures may very well be some of his finest recorded guitar work. There is not a wasted moment, not one misspent note for the entire record. James, as was typical of his early recordings with the Broomdusters, gives solo time to both Jones and Brown, themselves equally formidable musicians.[332]

As is often the case with blues records of this caliber, it has rarely been covered by other musicians. Three who tried it were Jeremy Spencer, Homesick James, and Hound Dog Taylor. In the company of Fleetwood Mac, Spencer cut a high-energy version, complete with saxes, for Blue Horizon in April 1968. Homesick's rendering, recorded for the Bea & Baby label in December 1971 with Sunnyland Slim, rambles along pleasantly as an informal jam, but lacks the punch of the original. Hound Dog Taylor's offering, from his second Alligator album, is branded with his driving boogie sound; like most of his recordings from this era, it is good, basic stripped-down blues, satisfying even if it does lack a certain technical proficiency.[333] Hearing these against Elmore's unduplicatable original, however, makes it clear that it is not just

communication with Steve Franz, 11 December 1992.

330 Mike Rowe, "Let's Cut It." *Blues Unlimited* 148/149 (Winter 1987): 27.

331 Pierson, personal interview, 27 March 1990.

332 Elmore James, "Hawaiian Boogie." Flair 1011, 1953. Note: This is sometimes referred to as "Hawaiian Boogie (No. 2)."

333 Fleetwood Mac, "Evenin' Boogie." From the album Fleetwood Mac, *Mr. Wonderful.* Blue Horizon LP 7-63205, 1968; Homesick James Williamson, "Homesick Sunnyland Special." From the album *Meat & Gravy from Cadillac Baby—Hits that Missed Vol. 2.* Red Lightnin' LP 0020, 1978; and Hound Dog Taylor, "Hawaiian Boogie." From the album Hound Dog Taylor and the Houserockers, *Natural Boogie.* Alligator LP 4704, 1974.

Note: During a 1971 interview Homesick James claimed to have not only authored "Hawaiian Boogie" but also to have recorded it before Elmore cut his version for Flair. Homesick told his interviewers the following story:

> *See I did them in ah, '53, all those unissued numbers, and you know "Williamson Shuffle," do you know what that is? That's "Hawaiian Boogie." I wrote "Hawaiian Boogie," I made it before Elmore, and they wouldn't let me do it, no they let me record it and they was late gettin' it out and about three weeks later... well me and Elmore was racin' with each other to get it out, and I'd say, I bet I make it before you do. Then Elmore got it out first.... and mine was never issued.* (Leadbitter and Robinson, "Lazy Bill Called Me Homesick (I Wasn't Though)(Part 3)," 9).

It turns out that Homesick was having a little fun with his interviewers. They couldn't have known it at the time, because in 1971: a) the title Homesick refers to had not yet been released to the general public, and b) the exact recording date of "Williamson Shuffle" had not been determined either (as Homesick related, it was thought to be sometime in 1953). Homesick's vintage waxings for Chance Records were finally made available via a rare 1977 LP (on the Japanese P-Vine label) and as part of a 1997 two disc set entitled *Chicago Blues—The Chance Era.* It turns out that not only was "Williamson Shuffle" recorded on 11 August 1953—more than two full months after "Hawaiian Boogie" was issued—but it's not even the same tune! (Leadbitter and Slaven, *Blues Records: 1943-1966,* 359; Keith Briggs, notes to *Chicago Blues—The Chance Era.* Charly CD 146-2, 1997; and Homesick James Williamson, "Williamson Shuffle." From the album Homesick James, *Chance Vintage Blues/R&B Crops Vol. 2.* P-Vine LP 706, 1977).

crackerjack guitar playing that makes a good blues record. It requires the kind of omniscient support the Broomdusters gave Elmore, and it comes across on their very best records—such as this one—just what an amazing amalgam of musicians they were.

In August 1953, Bihari released the final two numbers from the April 1953 session, the rumba-based "Can't Stop Lovin" and the thunderous "Make a Little Love," a song which Elmore had adapted from Howlin' Wolf's "Riding in the Moonlight," but revamped to showcase his signature guitar work. Maybe James and Bihari had a little chuckle in the studio over Big Boy Crudup's "Make a Little Love with Me" that Trumpet had issued under the name "Elmer James," and decided that it might be fun to get back at them a little by turning up the heat and have Elmore record his very own explosive version. "Make a Little Love" is indeed one of James' finest recorded examples of what a powerful sound he could put into the "Dust My Broom" riff. Still, in spite of the heavy guitar amplification, Elmore manages to get a full tonal quality out of the instrument. The companion release to "Make a Little Love" was a tune called "Can't Stop Lovin," a theme that James would rework several times in his career—re-recording the song twice and once as an instrumental—that borrowed musically from B.B. King's then-current top five R&B chart hit, "Woke Up This Morning."[334]

Regrettably, the master tapes from this session have all been lost, except that of "Hawaiian Boogie." "When they did a session on Elmore James," Ray Topping said, "they often spliced out the take that was going to be used for the single, or the 78, and put it on a fresh reel and the issued take was sent to the factory for processing. Somehow in Modern's plant the tapes got lost in the factory and never got sent back to the tape library...."[335] This problem was exacerbated by Modern's frequent relocating, and evidently many of the tapes were lost in transit between factory and headquarters. When "Hawaiian Boogie" was finally issued from the original master for the first time on album, the stunning sound belied the fact that the tape was thirty-four years old. It was a testament not only to the artistry of the Broomdusters at one of their recorded peaks, but of the beautiful, brilliant and crisp sound that made Chicago's Universal Studios famous.[336]

"And he taken the record and throwed it on the floor"

Elmore James' dates at the 708 Club and Sylvio's continued for some time. On Monday, 8 June 1953, he was recruited along with Johnny Jones and Odie Payne to participate in a "Junior" Wells[337] recording session, held at Universal Studios. Also present were bassist Willie Dixon, with brothers Louis and David Myers lending additional guitar support.[338]

334 Elmore James, "Make a Little Love." Flair 1014, 1953; Howlin' Wolf, "Riding in the Moonlight." RPM 333, 1951; Arthur "Big Boy" Crudup (as Elmer James), "Make a Little Love with Me." Trumpet 186, 1952; Elmore James, "Can't Stop Lovin." Flair 1014, 1953; B.B. King, "Woke Up This Morning." RPM 380, 1953; Whitburn, 238; and Franz, 18, 22, 30.

335 Huggins, 19; and Ted Carroll, personal communication with Steve Franz. 13 November 1992.

336 Huggins, 19. Note: The album this refers to is *"Let's Cut It" The Very Best of Elmore James.* Ace CD 192, 1987.

337 Born Amos Wells Blakemore, 9 December 1934, Memphis, TN; died 15 January 1998, Chicago, IL. Note: 1935 has also been given for year of birth.

338 Franz, 12. Note: It has also been suggested that Fred Below played on this session as well, switching off for several numbers with Payne during the session. Admittedly, this does not make a *whole* lot of sense. As proof, one current theory points to the drummer's use of sticks on some numbers and brushes on others. While the "two drummers" theory cannot be ruled out entirely, it seems much more likely that it was just one drummer—Odie Payne—switching off between his sticks and brushes, thereby serving to confuse discographers over the years.

Wells was recording for States Records, one of two labels owned by the United Record Company—a Chicago concern Leonard Allen founded in 1951 with partner Lewis Simpkins—headquartered at 5052 Cottage Grove Avenue. A tailor by trade, Allen was convinced by Simpkins (who had previous experience with the Premium and Miracle labels) to provide the start-up costs for the company. With bassist Willie Dixon as one of the label's A&R men, some serious blues talent was funneled through United's door.[339]

Wells recorded six titles with James, Jones, and Payne, and as far as debut recording sessions go, his talent shone through like fine crystal sparkling in the afternoon sunlight, indicating that a promising career might be in store for the young harmonica player. Allen issued "Cut That Out" and the instrumental "Eagle Rock" as States 122 in late July 1953, and apparently the coupling sold enough for him to consider issuing two more sides. "Hoodoo Man" and "Junior's Wail" were released as States 134 the following March. "Hoodoo Man," a classic Chicago blues featuring James' patented slide guitar, was spotted as a "Territorial Tip" in St. Louis the following month. With the company's poor management, however, the disc only broke even. Whenever United had a moderate seller, Allen would use the proceeds to generously shower disk jockeys with cash, prostitutes, dozens of free records (which they could sell for supplemental income) drinks and dinner out.[340] It was a plan that sometimes backfired, however. Junior Wells recalled, in a 1994 interview with Jim O'Neal, a not so amusing story involving himself, label head Leonard Allen, and Chicago disk jockey Al Benson. Allen and Wells had gone down to Benson's office with a copy of "Hoodoo Man," but unbeknownst to Wells, Allen had slipped twenty-five dollars inside the record sleeve before handing it to Benson. "I just remember that they taken me over to Al Benson..., he had his office here on 47th right off of King Drive—it was South Park then. And he taken the record and throwed it on the floor and stomped it," Wells recalled. "And he took the twenty-five dollars and it throwed it back to [Allen], took the record, throwed it on the floor and stomped it, and said, 'Now clean that shit up and get out of my office.'" The event so traumatized the young Wells that he wanted to block the song, and its memory, from his mind altogether (although Bob Koester would successfully wheedle him into recording it again, more than a decade later, for Delmark). "Tomorrow Night," released in December 1954, was the last Junior Wells/Elmore James side to be issued by States, and seemed to sink without a trace.[341]

In 1957, United Records would be put out of business, and Allen was faced with paying an $18,000 debt by himself (his partner Simpkins died in May 1953). If that weren't enough of a sting, one of Allen's employees—a family relation—had been skimming cash from the company's coffers. "We tried to be a major [label] and we were a small record company," Allen recalled before he died. "People thought we had a lot of money. Shit, we ain't never had a whole lot of money." In spite of the senseless squandering, Allen ostensibly was fair to his recording musicians, as he paid union scale for all his sessions.[342]

In 1975, Delmark Records' Bob Koester saved United/States from almost certain obscurity by purchasing the label's stock of master tapes and putting Jim O'Neal in charge of implementing an LP reissue program. In 1977, Delmark reissued almost all of the Wells/James session on the acclaimed album

339 Gart, *The American Record Label Directory*, 210; and Pruter and O'Neal, "United/States Story, Part 1," 37.

340 Bob Koester, notes to Junior Wells, *Blues Hit Big Town*. Delmark LP 640, 1977; "Rhythm and Blues Tattler" [Advertisement]. *The Billboard* (18 July 1953): 57; Junior Wells, "Hoodoo Man." States 134, 1954; Gart, *First Pressings—1954*, 44; Pruter and O'Neal, "United/States Story, Part 1," 39-40; Robert Pruter and Jim O'Neal, "Leonard Allen and the United/States Story, Part 2." *Living Blues* 93 (September/October 1990): 35-36; Robert Pruter and Jim O'Neal, "Leonard Allen and the United/States Story, Part 3." *Living Blues* 95 (January/February 1991): 41; and Franz, 12, 34.

Note: According to *Blues Records*, States 134 was also issued using the titles "Hodo Man" and "Somebody Hoodooed the Hoodoo Man" (Leadbitter and Slaven, *Blues Records: 1943-1966*, 344).

341 O'Neal, "Junior Wells: *Living Blues* Interview," 22; and Franz, 34.

342 Pruter and O'Neal, "United/States Story, Part 3," 41, 43; and Pruter and O'Neal, "United/States Story, Part 1," 37.

Blues Hit Big Town, preserving a very memorable moment of the recorded history of Chicago blues. As with the master tape of "Hawaiian Boogie," Wells' States sides are testimony to the brilliant high-fidelity sound Universal Studios was producing in the early 1950s, even though the tapes had languished in Leonard Allen's attic for many years! As Bob Koester later told the readers of *Blues Unlimited*, it was all thanks to the "recording wizardry of Bill Putnam," adding that, "We did nothing to the old United/States tapes made in the '50s but intersplice leader and mail them off to Wakefield Mfg. Co., our pressing plant, where they were mastered on state-of-the-art equipment.... The quality on the tapes has withstood [the test of time] all these years...." Toward the end of his life, United/States founder Leonard Allen returned to the tailoring business to supplement his small government income. He died on Tuesday, 16 July 1985, in Chicago.[343]

Make My Dreams Come True

Joe Bihari was back in the Windy City during August 1953 to record Elmore and the Broomdusters. After meeting with disk jockey Alan Freed in Las Vegas, Bihari headed towards Lake Michigan to cut sides with James, B.B. King, and later, John Lee Hooker in Detroit. After that, it was down to Texas to sign new talent, and then back to California to process the tapes he'd recorded. Although a session with Johnny Jones was also scheduled (probably with James in Chicago), the date was either cancelled at the last minute or all the tapes from it have been lost.[344]

Bihari was probably anxious to get more James material in the can. Elmore's Checker release had just come out on the market, and immediately before Bihari's trip commenced, James could be heard playing guitar on Junior Wells' States release. Although he had just issued Elmore's new Flair single, "Make a Little Love," Bihari was faced with the reality that James could currently be heard on three releases at once—and only one of them was Modern's material![345]

Once again the Broomdusters were in familiar surroundings. The session was held at Universal Studios, and saxophonist Boyd Atkins was added to the usual line-up of Johnny Jones on piano, Odie Payne on drums, Ransom Knowling on bass, and J.T. Brown on tenor saxophone. James only managed to record three titles that day, as all three required numerous takes before they were in satisfactory condition for release.[346]

Elmore started off the session with "Make My Dreams Come True," a reworking of a tune he had recorded for Chess seven months previously. One can imagine Bihari sitting down with James before the session to ask him *what else* had he recorded for Chess that he didn't know about and making a decision to have a go at re-recording one of the titles. Seven takes in all were required for "Make My Dreams Come True," transforming the tune from the leisurely-paced tepid blues he had recorded for Chess into an exciting "Dust My Broom" style rocker. With two horns riffing in synch to Elmore's buoyant guitar and

343 Bob Koester, "Putnam the Record Straight." *Blues Unlimited* 137/138 (Spring 1980): 25; "Chicago Blues News." *Living Blues* 22 (July/August 1975): 15; Pruter and O'Neal, "United/States Story, Part 1," 37-38; and Franz, 12, 37.

344 Topping, "Ramblin' from Town to Town," 13; Gart, *First Pressings—1953*, 69; and Leadbitter and Slaven, *Blues Records 1943-1970*, 739.

345 Gart, *First Pressings—1953*, 69-71; and Franz, 32, 34.

346 Franz, 13. Note: A union recording session at this time would usually be four songs scheduled to be recorded in three hours' time.

backing by the unshakable rhythm of Jones, Knowling and Payne, James came up with a great side, complete with lyrics that featured an uncharacteristically upbeat (for Elmore anyway) sentiment:

I'm in love with the woman, she in love with my best friend,
Yes, I'm love with the woman, she's in love with my best friend,
Well, now the way she treat me, we gotta start all over again.

I got a fine lookin' woman, she live way 'cross town,
Oh, I got a fine lookin' woman, an' she live way 'cross town,
Well, when I'm with my baby, I don't want no one else around.

Oh, I love my babe, I tell the world I do,
Oh, I love my baby, an' I tell the world I do,
Well a little of your lovin', darlin', can make my dreams come true.[347]

The next tune recorded, "Strange Kinda' Feeling" started out as a cross between Sister Rosetta Tharpe's swinging gospel foot-tapper "Strange Things Happening Every Day" and Jesse "Tiny" Kennedy's "Strange Kind of Feeling." On the latter, James had played guitar behind Kennedy's blues shouting of the tune in a 1951 Memphis session for Trumpet. The take was scrapped, however—a victim of Lillian McMurry's rigid standards—and instead she had Kennedy re-record the title in September 1952 with a new group of musicians. Kennedy's re-cut version of "Strange Kind of Feeling" was on the market before Christmas, 1952, and James drew upon it in the making of his own version of the song. Elmore recorded six takes of "Strange Kinda' Feeling" in all, changing the lyrics slightly each time and transforming it to a fast-tempo jump blues—so fast, in fact, that the producer told the Broomdusters to slow it down.[348] "Dark and Dreary," the last tune of the day, featured sympathetic horns to spotlight Elmore's fluid guitar work and a more introverted demeanor:

Well, the road seem dark and dreary, but I travel down that way,
Well, the road seem dark and dreary, but I travel down that way
Well, my baby left me, she just come back home today. [349]

Joe Bihari went back to Los Angeles apparently a happy man. Utilizing these fresh tapes with the virtually untapped Canton masters, he had enough material on James for three more singles, and he wouldn't be back to Chicago for another Elmore session until the following year.[350]

---

347 Elmore James, "Make My Dreams Come True." Flair 1031, 1954; Franz, 10, 13; and Elmore James, "My Best Friend."

348 Elmore James, "Strange Kinda' Feeling." Flair 1022, 1953; Ryan, *Trumpet Records,* 88; Gart, *First Pressings—1952,* 135; Sister Rosetta Tharpe, "Strange Things Happening Every Day." Decca 8669, 1945; Jesse "Tiny" Kennedy, "Strange Kind of Feeling." Trumpet 187, 1952; and Franz, 7, 13. Note: the progression of all six takes can be heard on the box set Elmore James, *The Classic Early Recordings 1951-1956.* Ace BOX CD 4, 1993.

349 Elmore James, "Dark and Dreary." Flair 1048, 1954.

350 Topping, "Ramblin' from Town to Town," 13; and Franz, 13, 15, 32.

"They was lookin' to get a real funky guitar"

Two months later, with Bihari safely in Los Angeles, James recorded for another label. On Wednesday, 7 October 1953, blues shouter Big Joe Turner was in Chicago to record four titles. Turner, recording for New York City-based Atlantic Records at the time, stated in a 1972 interview, "Well, the people I was workin' for... they knowed Elmo.... I had met him before and he lived in Chicago, and I was playin' some dates in Chicago, so that's where the company recorded me at. So they was lookin' around to get us a real funky guitar, so they come up with Elmo.... I think that's the only record we ever made with him. I think he made that session...."[351] According to Jerry Wexler, a partner in Atlantic Records, it was Phil and Leonard Chess who set up studio time at Universal and booked James and Jones as backing musicians. "Even though Phil and Leonard Chess are our main competition, they're also our friends," wrote Wexler. "They've arranged this session for us, recruiting Elmore James... and pianist Little Johnny Jones to back up Big Joe. Leonard and Phil come by that night...." Wexler recalled a revealing exchange between Atlantic vice-president Ahmet Ertegun and Leonard Chess:

> "I have an agreement with Muddy Waters," Leonard says that night. "'Muddy,' I tell him, 'when your stuff... stops selling, you can come over to my house and do the gardening.'"
> "Funny, but I got a different kind of deal with Turner," Ahmet says as Big Joe is getting ready to sing. "If his records don't sell, I can be *his* chauffeur." [352]

Atlantic released three of the four titles from the session. "TV Mama" was paired with "Oke-She-Moke-She-Pop" for release as Atlantic 1016 in December 1953. The idea for "TV Mama," a long-time favorite of blues fans, came easily to Turner. "I heard the 'The Last of the Red Hot Mamas' on the radio one time, or T.V.," he told interviewer Paul Clinco, "and she was mentionin' somethin' about the T.V. with the big wide screen, so I just made me a song about it."[353] "Oke-She-Moke-She-Pop" was, says Wexler, "Joe's version of 'Nov Shmoz Kapop,' the syndicated comic strip about the little hitchhiker."[354] Turner's shouting vocals coupled with James' hot slide guitar and Jones' piano coalesced nicely, and "TV Mama" easily became hit material for Atlantic. It debuted on the rhythm & blues charts on Saturday, 23 January 1954, where it stayed for almost two months and attained a top position of number six. A third title from the date, "Ti-Ri-Lee," was released as the less famous B-side to Atlantic 1053. The A-side, "Flip Flop and Fly" (an early rock 'n' roll prototype) featured the guitar work of another artist when released in March 1955.[355]

On Monday, 9 November 1953, Atlantic was in Chicago again, this time to record Elmore's pianist Johnny Jones as session leader. As was the case for the Big Joe Turner date, Atlantic probably rented Universal Studios. Although Jones was well represented as an accompanist on many conspicuous Chicago blues records, Johnny rarely recorded as a leader. His total commercial output consisted of just three singles released during his lifetime—one single each for Aristocrat, Flair, and Atlantic, another posthumous 45 released by Jim O'Neal in 1980, plus one other song, "Early in the Morning," that was credited to Tampa Red, but actually featured Jones on lead vocals.[356]

351 Clinco, 22; Gart, *The American Record Label Directory*, 15; and Franz, 14. Note: Atlantic probably knew James via his records, not personally.

352 Jerry Wexler and David Ritz, *Rhythm and the Blues*. New York: Alfred A. Knopf, 1993, 100-101.

353 Clinco, 22; Big Joe Turner, "TV Mama." Atlantic 1016, 1953; Big Joe Turner, "Oke-She-Moke-She-Pop." Atlantic 1016, 1953; and Franz, 34.

354 Wexler and Ritz, 101.

355 Whitburn, 419; and Franz, 14, 34.

Atlantic recorded four titles featuring Johnny's impish vocals and distinguished piano work and backing from a core-group of Broomdusters—Elmore on guitar, J.T. Brown on tenor saxophone, and Odie Payne on drums. Eventually chosen for release the following November were two "borrowed" numbers, "Hoy Hoy" and "Doin' the Best I Can." The latter was a warm, enjoyable cover of Harmon Ray's 1949 Decca recording "Working Man" (a.k.a. "Up the Line," on which, coincidentally, J.T. Brown had played saxophone; it was a tune originally associated with Peetie Wheatstraw), and featured a few sublime moments when Johnny's piano ever so gracefully intersected with J.T.'s saxophone during another of his smoky solos. On the other side was "Hoy Hoy," a close reading of Roy Milton's 1948 jump-blues top five R&B hit "Hop, Skip and Jump." Here, Jones manages a nice update with solid backing from the Broomdusters and Elmore playing a straight acoustic guitar without a slide (although a much faster alternate take features Elmore on electric guitar, which suggests a bit of experimentation went on during the session to find the "right" sound).[357] All of these titles seem fairly ordinary, however, when compared to the resplendent "Chicago Blues," which Atlantic shelved for nineteen years. It is the only extant recording of Elmore playing an acoustic slide guitar, and had this fine side been issued at the time, it would have probably inspired producers to record more examples of James in this riveting fashion. Why Atlantic would choose to issue derivative material instead of this exceptional (and seemingly) original composition for Jones' solitary Atlantic single is anyone's guess. Green Bay, Wisconsin guitarist Billy Flynn, accompanied by the Smoke Daddy Band, recorded a version of the song for the Easy Baby label in May 1999. Their waxing, complete with Flynn's creamy slide licks and a vintage 1950s sound, was a convincing study of Jones' original composition rendered faithful to the Elmore tradition—one of the few times this Jones classic has ever been covered.[358]

Elmore James' appearances at Sylvio's continued into the fall of 1953, occasionally with Sonny Boy Williamson sitting in with the group. The week after Thanksgiving, Jones was recruited by Al Benson's small Parrot label for an Albert King session, with rhythm support from John Brim and Willie Dixon. The very next day, Jones was back in the studio again, this time with Odie Payne, Ransom Knowling and Walter Horton to back up Tampa Red for his last RCA Victor session. Since 1949, Tampa Red had cut three dozen sides with Johnny and Odie, and it seems appropriate that they would be present for one last go 'round with the old "Guitar Wizard." "Big Stars Falling Blues" somehow seems befitting as a swan song to Tampa Red's remarkable career—and another indicator of subtle changes and gradual shifts in the blues and rhythm & blues record markets—it was the only title from the session to see immediate issue.[359] In a

356 Mark Harris, "Little Johnny Jones Discography." *Pickin' the Blues* 4 (April/May 1982): 8-9; Leadbitter, Fancourt, and Pelletier, 566; and Franz, 14. Note: "Early in the Morning" was issued as Victor 22-0123 under Tampa Red's name, although Jones was the lead vocalist.

357 Roy Milton, "Hop, Skip and Jump." Specialty 314, 1948; Whitburn, 292; Harmon Ray, "Working Man." Decca 48107, 1949; Leadbitter, Fancourt, and Pelletier, 394; Dixon, Godrich, and Rye, 1008-1009; Little Johnny Jones, "Hoy Hoy." Atlantic 1045, 1954; Little Johnny Jones, "Doin' the Best I Can." Atlantic 1045, 1954; Little Johnny Jones, "Hoy Hoy" [alternate take]. From the album *Blues Piano—Chicago, Plus.* Atlantic LP 7227, 1972; and Franz, 14, 34.

Note: "Hoy Hoy" was also covered by Lorrie and Larry Collins—a.k.a., the Collins Kids—a rockabilly duo (Collins Kids, "Hoy Hoy." Columbia 41087, 1958). According to Ray Topping, "Hoy Hoy" was also covered by rockabilly artist Clyde Stacy for the Candlelight label (c. 1956 or 1957). Bob McGrath's *R&B Indies* also lists Clyde Stacy doing "Hoy Hoy" for the Argyle label (a Los Angeles concern) in 1959. Whether that is a reissue of the Candlelight title or a different recording is not known.

Pop Quiz: Quick! What do the Collins Kids and Robert Johnson have in common? Give up? The answer is Don Law—he signed the Collins Kids to Columbia Records *and* he recorded Robert Johnson. Wow! Isn't that amazing?

358 Little Johnny Jones, "Chicago Blues." From the album *Blues Piano—Chicago, Plus.* Atlantic LP 7227, 1972; and The Smoke Daddy Band featuring Billy Flynn, "Chicago Blues." From the album *The Smoke Daddy Band featuring Billy Flynn.* Easy Baby CD 400, 2000.

359 Cushing, 59; *The Chicago Defender* [Advertisement], (1 October 1953). Reprinted in the notes to Elmore

symbolic sense, Tampa's last session with Johnny Jones and Odie Payne represented a "passing of the torch," if you will, from one generation of blues musicians to the next. "Soon after Tampa Red's world fell apart," wrote Alan Balfour. "His wife died, his drinking got worse and he suffered a nervous breakdown which led him to be institutionalized.... In 1960 [he] was coaxed into recording two albums... but his physical and psychological state was such that his 'guitar wizardry' was no longer in evidence...." Tampa Red somehow managed to "hang in there" during two more long decades—scraping by on social security, the odd royalty check or two and, during the last few years of his life, with his "constant companion" Effie Tolbert. The end finally came on Thursday, 19 March 1981. He was seventy-seven.[360]

A week or so after the Tampa Red session took place, Joe Bihari issued Elmore's next Flair single, "Strange Kinda' Feeling." On the flip side was "Please Find My Baby," a tune that Modern had attempted to release—including this issue—on four separate occasions. It must have made Joe Bihari slightly smug to finally see the release, as it had been one of the first recordings he'd made with Elmore two January's ago. It also signalled the imminent end of the lawsuit between Lillian McMurry and Modern Records. In February 1954, a U.S. District Court finally put an end to the legal bandying, finding for McMurry and awarding her $2,500—a meager sum compared to the one million she had originally sought. The Biharis didn't seem to care. They had cleverly made their wives the principal officers of Modern Records back in 1948, freeing themselves to operate the business as they wished and without concern for such matters as recording artists who had exclusive contracts to other labels. After all, they had Elmore James now, and that's probably all they had wanted from the start.[361]

"And that needle was just danglin' on 100"

Elmore's club work continued on into 1954, and the band was still working at Sylvio's on the weekends. Drummer Odie Payne recalls the toll it started to take on James:

> People requested "Dust My Broom" most of the time. And after you do it about two or three times, somebody comes up, "Do it again. I'll pay you." "I'm sorry, dear," he would say, "Look..." he would be very insulting. I could almost go through the bandstand the way he could insult people. He say, "I don't want your money. I got enough money to burn you." But, maybe, the way the man was talkin' could've been because, he drank some, too. What he did, he did well. Ladies loved it. But he had a temper. He would let loose some words through the microphone.... I would just have to hang my head.... [He] didn't bite his tongue. But to me it was sort of unbelievable that a man would do this.[362]

One thing was sure—the drinking was always very heavy when it came to Elmore and Johnny. "...I went down to Sylvio's to see [Elmore James]," blues harmonica player Billy Boy Arnold recalled, "And they used to have cocktail parties and they'd pull three tables together, put tablecloths on it, set 'bout five or six fifths of whiskey on it and this was for all the musicians, nobody else, y'know, the musicians and their girlfriends or their wives. And I would be right there at the cocktail party every Sunday."[363] "[Gin] was

James, *The Classic Early Recordings 1951-1956.* Ace BOXCD 4, 1993; Gart, *The American Record Label Directory,* 163; Fancourt, *B.B. King, Albert & Freddy,* 39; and Leadbitter, Fancourt, and Pelletier, 566-567.

360 Alan Balfour, notes to Tampa Red, *Complete Recorded Works in Chronological Order, Vol. 15.* Document CD 5215, 1993; and Jim O'Neal, notes to Tampa Red, Guitar Wizard. RCA Bluebird LP 2-5501, 1975.

361 Ryan, *Trumpet Records,* 32-33; and Franz, 8, 11, 34.

362 Cushing, 59; and *The Chicago Defender* [Advertisement], (16 January 1954). Reprinted in the notes to Elmore James, *The Classic Early Recordings 1951-1956.* Ace BOXCD 4, 1993.

Johnny Jones' favorite drink," Odie Payne remembered. "And he'd do the first couple of numbers and he'd say 'Wait a minute, Odie, wait a minute. Got to get me a drink.' He'd drink down this gin.... He says 'Look at my hands now. Now I'm ready.' Well, his hands would be steady as a rock. I guess, before then his hands would be shaky."[364] While James and Jones seemed to relish in the "high life," it evidently did not hold sway over Payne. "...I was always the black sheep in the band. I was a loner, I didn't associate. After we take a break," he told Steve Cushing, "I just go in the corner with my book or music.... I just didn't mix with the guys, because they was smokin' and drinkin' and I wasn't.... When a person wanted to get me a drink, they said, 'What do you want?' I said, 'Orange juice.' They look at me twice. 'Orange juice?' A lot of times they would refuse to buy it. They would rather buy me something stronger. I said, 'No, that's all right.'"[365]

Sleepy Otis Hunt, who played harmonica with James and the Broomdusters for a brief stint in the early 1950s, recalled for John Anthony Brisbin an amusing story about being on the road with the band around this time:

> We went on the road to Atlanta, Georgia, with Elmore [and Johnny]. We had a station wagon and Elmore starts drivin'. Now I been a scared guy all my life, never liked no fast drivin'. Johnny knowed it too. And boy that Elmore was just layin' on 100 [m.p.h.] but I didn't know it. Johnny said, "Well, look at the speedometer." And that needle was just danglin' on 100. I said, "God dog!" He said, "You know, the doctor don't even allow Elmore to walk to the second floor. He got a bad heart." Man, I just fell out. Elmore'd get down to 98 and go right on back up to 100. I said, "Good God Almighty, Johnny. Tell him to ease up!" He said, "You tell him."[366]

"Johnny Jones. God dog! I loved that boy as good as I did my brother," Hunt fondly remembered. "He was so funny. He made me cry and laugh.... Oh, he'd say things and do things just to get me excited. Then we both laugh till we cry."[367]

In early March 1954, Joe Bihari released two more Elmore titles as Flair 1031. The new issue, "Make My Dreams Come True," attracted some attention and received some nice reviews. The 6 March 1954 issue of *The Billboard* was optimistic about the record: "Elmore James shouts his romantic pleas in a manner sure to create attention. A good strong performance, with [an]... infectious beat in the backing, this could earn some loot."[368] The Saturday, 20 March 1954 review in *Cash Box* echoed *The Billboard's* comments: "James rides herd on this moving beat and comes up with a sock side. Could make a strong dent in the market."[369] A cursory glance at the "Territorial Best Sellers" lists for the weeks immediately following, however, indicates that it did not.

On Monday, 10 May 1954, Bihari was in Chicago for his next James session.[370] This time, guitarist Ike Turner was recruited—the first of only two instances where Modern would use a second guitar on an Elmore session. Jones and Payne were also present, and the horn section was flushed out with tenor sax man Raymond Hill and two anonymous alto and baritone saxophonists. The session, held at Universal

363 Mike Rowe, "'I Was Really Dedicated'—An Interview with Billy Boy Arnold, Part 2." *Blues Unlimited* 127 (November/December 1977): 11.

364 Cushing, 61.

365 Ibid., 60-61.

366 John Anthony Brisbin, "The Lost American Bluesmen." *Living Blues* 134 (July/August 1997): 32.

367 Ibid.

368 "Rhythm & Blues Record Reviews." *The Billboard* (6 March 1954): 102.

369 Rowe, *Chicago Breakdown*, 200; Gart, *First Pressings—1954*, 30; and Franz, 32.

370 Patrick LeBlanc, telephone interview by Steve Franz, 21 February 1995.

Studios again, turned into a real workout. The first two songs took about twenty different takes between the two of them, and by the time Elmore had recorded the third title and started on the fourth, he had run out of steam. After the aborted fourth take of "I Got a Strange Baby," the producer called it quits on Elmore's vocals for the day and recorded it instead as a scorching instrumental with Ike Turner on lead guitar.[371]

Also from this session came the very likeable, swinging "Where Can My Baby Be." Although issue-worthy, it was a gem that the Biharis instead chose to keep in the can (perhaps due to a little guitar distortion at the beginning of the take). While the horns riff away pleasantly in the background, Elmore shouts out the vocal: "...Every time I fall in love," he sings, "you know the jinx will fall on me." He continues:

> Oh, I'm so blue this mornin', I can't even go to work,
> Oh, I'm so blue this mornin', I can't even go to work,
> Now the woman I love done left me, and you know my feelings hurt.[372]

Very big at the time of this session was Guitar Slim's "The Things That I Used to Do" on Specialty. The record had charted in mid-January 1954, peaked at the number one position for an astounding fourteen weeks, and stayed on the charts the better part of five months. According to Ray Topping, "Bihari wanted Elmore to cut something in this vein," and James and Turner combined their thoughts.[373] They decided to borrow the basic themes of Tampa Red's lovely, buoyant 1944 recording "Sure Enough I Do," but to update it à la Guitar Slim's meandering but melodic electric guitar. The result, "Sho Nuff I Do," was a beautiful job featuring responsive horns, an Ike and Elmore twin-guitar solo, a vocal that featured James' declamatory style to a theatrical level, and a lilting melody with an affecting minor chord change. It's a pure rhythm & blues record, and Elmore sings with thick emotion:

> One mornin', one mornin', when I come in,
> I found my baby—she was makin' friends,
> Oh, but I love her, oh yes, I love her,
> Sho 'nuff I do.
>
> The first time I saw her, on a Friday night,
> Oh, I found her, she was tryin' to fight,
> Yes, but I love her, oh yes, I love her,
> Sho 'nuff I do.
>
> I saw her in the mornin', 'bout the break o' day,
> I told her I love her, and she want to run away,
> Oh yes I love her, oh yes, I love her,
> Sho 'nuff I do.

---

371 Elmore James, "Canton, Mississippi Breakdown." From the album Elmore James, *The Legend of Elmore James.* Kent LP 9001, 1969; and Franz, 15, 17.

372 Elmore James, "Where Can My Baby Be." From the album Elmore James, *The Legend of Elmore James.* Kent LP 9001, 1969.

373 Topping, "Ramblin' from Town to Town," 14; and Whitburn, 176.

Oh, I gotta leave you, oh baby,
Yes I gotta leave you—please don't make me stay,
I gotta leave you baby, because you won't change your way. [374]

Bihari declined this take (probably the eleventh), however, in favor of a less cohesive earlier take. When the two are played side by side, it's hard to understand why Bihari chose the released version over this take, one of the most sublime and moving of Elmore's songs.[375]

By the last week of May, Joe Bihari had released "Sho Nuff I Do" and "1839 Blues" as Flair 1039. This latter tune has roused the curiosity of many an Elmore fan over the years, due to the odd spoken introduction it contains:

Hey Joe! You know I'm a young man this night,
But you know I ain't seen my baby since 1839,
I gotta find her...." [376]

He then launches into another tale of a relationship gone wrong, sung with his trademark declamatory voice and surprising guitar support from Ike Turner. Many people have offered their opinion over the years about just what exactly Elmore meant by the "1839" idea. Author Paul Garon, in his book *Blues and the Poetic Spirit,* quoted from this song during a discussion of humor in the blues, and on at least one occasion that I know of, it was the subject of an amusing exchange of "letters to the editor" in a popular blues magazine. To one reader, it meant what it seemed to mean on the surface—that he just hadn't seen his baby in a good long time; to another, they thought it was a reference to military time—1839 meaning 6:39 p.m. to those of us not in the army—and have cited Elmore's Navy background to support their theory. Yet another idea has been advanced that Elmore literally meant what he sung, and for that to be true, Elmore would undoubtedly *have* to be a vampire in order for him to have not seen his baby for the better part of 115 years.[377]

Although Elmore didn't match Guitar Slim's success with these two sides, it was a strong pairing nonetheless. Three months later "Sho Nuff I Do" was still receiving action in New Orleans. In 1958, Texas artist Smokey Hogg would revive this theme when he recorded "Sure 'Nuff" for the Ebb label, clearly relying upon Elmore's version of the song as a jumping off point. Sometime in August 1954, Bihari also released "Dark and Dreary" as Flair 1048 (recorded at the August 1953 session). Although a gorgeous side by James, the issue was a new low for the Bihari brothers. Their usual ploy was to list writers' credits as "James-Josea" or "Josea-James" on most of Elmore's Flair releases. This issue went one step further, however, and simply left off the "James" part for both titles on Flair 1048, all the credit going to "Josea."[378]

---

374 Elmore James, "Sho Nuff I Do" [alternate take]. From the album Elmore James, *Original Folk Blues.* Kent LP 522, 1964; Guitar Slim, "The Things That I Used to Do." Specialty 482, 1953; Tampa Red, "Sure Enough I Do." Bluebird 34-0731, 1945; and Topping, "Ramblin' from Town to Town," 14.

375 Elmore James, "Sho Nuff I Do." Flair 1039, 1954; and Franz, 15.

376 Elmore James, "1839 Blues." Flair 1039, 1954.

377 Paul Garon, *Blues and the Poetic Spirit.* New York: Da Capo Press, 1979 [reprint], 85. Note: The exchange of "Letters to the Editor" occurred in *Blues & Rhythm* 75 and 77 (January and March 1993, respectively).

378 Smokey Hogg, "Sure 'Nuff." Ebb 127, 1958; Gart, *First Pressings—1954,* 46, 56, 87; and Franz, 13, 32, 41.

California Slickers

In June 1954, Modern Records was putting the finishing touches on their new $15,000 studio complex at 9317 W. Washington Boulevard in Culver City, California. A press release issued the previous month filled in the details:

> The brothers Bihari—Saul, Joe and Jules—will effect a consolidation of their disk facilities within a month, with the scheduled completion of recording studios and office space adjacent to Joe Bihari's Cadet Record Pressing Company in Culver City....
>
> New construction will total 5,000 square feet, with the recording studio to be equipped with Ampex tape machines, Altec Lansing sound systems and an RCA mixing panel. [379]

Elmore was invited out to the new studio by Joe Bihari that summer, and a session was arranged with the Maxwell Davis Orchestra, a working Los Angeles band present on many Modern sessions. Oddly, no formal paperwork was filed on Elmore's session. One plausible theory might be that Joe Bihari didn't feel like executing a union contract on James and illicitly snuck his Broomduster behind the back of the union by recording him after-hours, perhaps at the tail end of someone else's session. This may have been done concurrently with a two-day B.B. King/Maxwell Davis session held on Wednesday 18 August and Thursday 19 August 1954, one of two times Joe Bihari and Maxwell Davis' ensemble were present at the same time in the Modern studios that summer.[380]

Elmore recorded six titles with agreeable, consistent backing from Davis' Orchestra. The core of Davis' group included the solid rhythm section of bassist Ralph Hamilton, drummer Jesse Sailes and jazz/stride/boogie pianist Willard McDaniel. Unlike the Chicago sessions, which usually featured James' guitar at a conspicuous level, for this date the instrument was slightly down in the mix. Even so, the singing couldn't be better, and the song-writing was starting to reach an impressive level. There were also updates of old standards—one was an interpretation of John Lee "Sonny Boy" Williamson's 1938 recording of "Sunny Land," and Davis' sparse arrangement without the brass section was clever and noteworthy. "Standing at the Crossroads" was an update of Robert Johnson's similarly named Vocalion title, with a minor update to the lyrics and a climactic finish with Elmore's voice cracking melodramatically. "No Love in My Heart" was a musical theme and variation of "Can't Stop Lovin," but borrowed more obviously from the guitar riff and melody of B.B. King's "Woke Up This Morning," with Elmore offering a fresh set of lyrics.[381]

Elmore's talent as a songwriter was really starting to show through. On "Happy Home" James uses his "Dust My Broom" riff with a stop-time syncopation to underscore a sermonizing vocal:

> If you ever sad and lonesome, broken hearted too,
> Take my word, good people, something wrong with you.

---

379 Gart, *First Pressings—1954,* 47-48; and Gart, *The American Record Label Directory,* 146.

380 B.B. King, American Federation of Musicians Local Number 47 contract 1761: 18 August 1954; Maxwell Davis, American Federation of Musicians Local Number 47 contract 1525: 16 July 1954; Carmen Fanzone, personal interview by Steve Franz. Hollywood, California, 15 November 1993; Topping, "Ramblin' from Town to Town," 15; and Franz, 2, 16.

381 Sonny Boy Williamson, "Sunny Land." Bluebird B7500, 1938; Elmore James, "Sunny Land." Flair 1057, 1954; Ray Topping, notes to B.B. King, *Do the Boogie!* Ace CD 916, 1988; Franz, 16; Elmore James, "Standing at the Crossroads." Flair 1057, 1954; Robert Johnson, "Cross Road Blues;" Elmore James, "No Love in My Heart." Flair 1069, 1955; and B.B. King, "Woke Up This Morning."

That's why I'm worried, worried about my happy home,
Now if you get that feeling baby, you know something goin' on wrong.

Well I've often sat and wondered, what could a good man do?
I've been so good to you, woman, now what's wrong with you? [382]

"The Way You Treat Me" was also another indicator that things had not always gone well at home for Elmore. Here, he borrows an idea—as well as a few lines—from Brownie McGhee's "Evil, But Kindhearted" to use for the basic concept, and adds a few lyrics to better fit his own situation:

Well, when I lived in a small town, you were so nice to me,
When I lived in a small town, baby, you were so nice to me,
I brought you to Chicago, you don't do nothin' but walk the street. [383]

Elmore was soon back in Chicago, and Bihari had enough material for three singles—enough to last well into the new year. "Standing at the Crossroads" was the first single to be released from the session, and would be on the market by the end of October, 1954. Meanwhile, there was some activity back in the Windy City. J.T. Brown had a single out on Chicago's J.O.B. label in July (without the Broomdusters); and in September, Meteor scraped their vaults and released Brown's "Dumb Woman Blues," backed with "Saxony Boogie," recorded at James' initial November 1952 session with Jones, Payne, and Knowling.[384]

The person making the most commotion was surely a young slide guitarist enamored of James' style, who had just released a rough and ready single on the Chance label. Entitled "Combination Boogie," it was performed by ex-Georgia resident Joseph Benjamin Hutto, but the label simply read "J.B. and His Hawks." Mike Rowe appropriately described the group: "J.B. blew upon the Chicago scene with one of the noisiest and toughest bands ever. Singing in the fierce, declamatory style of his idol, Elmore, and backed by the heavily amplified guitar of Joe Custom, the crude harp of George Mayweather and the elemental percussion of Maxwell Street's Porkchop, they sounded ready to devour anything in sight!"[385] Hutto evidently had followed James from club to club, in places like Sylvio's, Ray's Lounge on Damen, and another club on Madison, trying to learn some techniques as best he could. Hutto later recalled to researchers Jim O'Neal and Amy van Singel how nice James had been about the whole thing:

I followed [James] just about everywhere he went. I started at Sylvio's. We had drinks together and he was telling me a little about how to use the bar [i.e., bottleneck], where to use it at, what type of bar I should get, how I should handle it.... And he was one of the guys... that don't mind explainin' things to you, questions that you asked him about music. He was really a type of guy what would take time out and sit down and explain things to you.... He was really, if you call a teacher that would be my teacher. He was the man I asked, he was the man that showed me different things and told me about the music. [386]

---

382 Elmore James, "Happy Home." Flair 1069, 1955.

383 Elmore James, "The Way You Treat Me." Flair 1062, 1955; and Brownie McGhee, "Evil, But Kindhearted." Alert 409, c. 1947. Note: Ike Turner (using the pseudonym "Lover Boy") recorded a song for the RPM label in 1954 entitled "The Way You Used to Treat Me." It has nothing in common with this recording by Elmore James. See: Ike Turner, "The Way You Used to Treat Me." RPM 409, 1954.

384 Leadbitter and Slaven, *Blues Records 1943-1970,* 178; Gart, *First Pressings—1954,* 75, 78; and Franz, 9, 16, 32, 34.

385 Rowe, *Chicago Breakdown,* 114-115; Gart, *First Pressings—1954,* 54; and J.B. Hutto, "Combination Boogie." Chance 1155, 1954. Note: Some discographies have incorrectly listed the issue number as 1153.

386 O'Neal and van Singel, 18.

If playing in the clubs was starting to wear on Elmore's nerves, it was also evidently starting to effect the whole group. James and pianist Johnny Jones would frequently quarrel before each night's performance, and of course, the drinking was always very heavy. This didn't sit too well with drummer Odie Payne, who was starting to get sick of it all. "After two years and a half with Elmore, I quit because he had a temper," he recalled to Steve Cushing. "Course we got to it a couple times. Not real bad, but still in all... and then his rapport with people was very unmusicianlike. You sit there, people payin' to see you, and you're entertainin'. And the man might insult the whole crowd. I would get so embarrassed."[387] By the end of 1954 the Broomdusters were on the skids, and Elmore headed back to Jackson, Mississippi, for a while.[388]

Slide Guitar in the Crescent City

Back in Jackson, Elmore met a woman known simply as Janice, and the two were soon married. "Standing at the Crossroads," his recent Flair single, grabbed the attention of Otis Ealey, a booking agent in Atlanta, Georgia. Ealey was so impressed with the single that he sent for James to come to Atlanta. This Elmore did, with wife Janice in tow. The two set up house at 384 Pine Street, where they lived for slightly more than half a year. When he was in town, the two helped operate the Lithonia Country Club (located on Atlanta's far east side), or Janice would look after it while her husband was on the road, passing her time with Willie Mabon's wife, whom she befriended. Ealey had already booked Howlin' Wolf, Muddy Waters, and John Lee Hooker to the area and took over the chores as Elmore's booking agent and new manager for the next two years.[389]

There were dates at movie theaters, army PX's, and various performances in and around Atlanta. Ealey recalls that James travelled with a four or five piece ensemble, usually a local pick-up band that would consist of Fats Jackson, Atlanta's preeminent rhythm & blues saxophonist, and at times a pianist remembered as "Tignor." Occasionally Johnny Jones or Sonny Boy Williamson would also sit in with Elmore, which is not unusual when one considers Ealey booked James as far north as Chicago. On one of these Windy City engagements, Chuck Berry—visiting from St. Louis with friend Ralph Burris on a Friday in early May 1955—first saw Elmore James: "Starting on 47th Street and Calumet, we hit most of the blues joints... that had live music. I saw Howlin' Wolf and Elmore James for the first time on 47th Street, a tour I'll never lose memory of. I didn't want to leave the place where Elmore James was performing but Ralph had seen these artists before and insisted that we try other places."[390]

Bastin and Lowry discovered from Ealey that James "seldom kept the same band together for more than a month or two," noting that "this didn't bother Elmore much and he was always able to get men to work with him. He was easy to get on with, likeable and good to have around. Otis said he didn't bother people and seldom bothered about rehearsals," although Elmore may have felt them to be superfluous, as Ealey commented that while in Atlanta James "worked... a good deal, and not surprisingly worked very steadily."[391]

---

387 Cushing, 60; and Rowe, *Chicago Breakdown*, 201.

388 Leadbitter and Wardlow, 9.

389 Ibid.; and Bastin and Lowry, 4-5.

390 Chuck Berry, *The Autobiography*. New York: Harmony Books, 1987, 97; Bastin and Lowry, 4-5; and Huggins, 19. Note: Bastin and Lowry note that "Tignor" is spelled phonetically.

Ealey also took care of Elmore's publicity, printing a few thousand photographs of James holding a solid body electric guitar, and others featuring James with wife Janice. Bastin and Lowry, writing their report in 1970, describe another item Ealey made that piqued their curiosity:

> [The photographs] were publicity handouts, as were the short films with soundtracks made of the... wait a minute. SHORT FILMS WITH SOUNDTRACKS made of the band and sent on ahead to theatres so that they could have a preview of the band.... and the tapes of Elmore which he had. All these had unaccountably vanished since his move... years back....Don't put too much faith in those films turning up, but [it is fun to think] of what MIGHT have been. [392]

But the agreeable times in Atlanta only turned out to be short-lived, and after six or seven months James and his wife had an altercation. The two separated, and James went back to Jackson, Mississippi, where he temporarily worked as a disk jockey.[393]

Joe Bihari arranged to rendezvous with him that summer in New Orleans, 180 miles to the south, for a fresh recording session. Bihari would have considered Jackson for the date, but according to Topping he favored the New Orleans location because "there was nothing really in Jackson good enough." The date was held at J & M Studios, Cosimo Matassa's legendary operation that was a fountain of many New Orleans rhythm & blues hits in the 1950s.[394] The musicians backing James on this fine session were long thought to be unknown, until recently when Ray Topping made a fortuitous discovery:

> Sometime during the early 60s Modern Records started to cannibalise their old session tapes in search of material for their Crown album series.... I have found many old tape boxes whose reels were re-used for later projects. One example is a B.B. King album master ready for production as a Crown LP. Beneath the new stickers relating to this B.B. King LP I found the original annotation for the 'Dust My Blues' session at Cosimo's in New Orleans. [395]

Topping also noted that the self-same reel had previously been employed for a Shirley & Lee session, but Matassa had erased it for use at the James date![396]

Enlisted for the session was Matassa's top-notch house band, consisting of pianist Edward Frank, bassist Frank Fields, and drummer Earl Palmer who led the ensemble. It was Elmore's first Modern session in three years that had not featured some kind of horn section, but even so, the backing he received from the group was absolutely solid and easily rivalled the Broomdusters on a good day. Fields' heavily pounding bass suggests he may have been playing an electric solid body instrument, and Palmer's drumming added a firm Crescent City beat to the proceedings. James' emotions about his recent break-up seem to show through in one form or another in every song he recorded that day, as his lyrical mood is overly pessimistic and the guitar playing is mostly savage and ferocious. "I Was a Fool" seems to best sum up how he must have felt at the time, as James plays some barbarous slide licks and sings, practically shouting:

---

391 Bastin and Lowry, 4.

392 Ibid., 5. Note: For further discussion of the Otis Ealey/Elmore James film footage, please see Appendix One, "Elmore James—Myths and Folklore."

393 Ibid., 4-5; Huggins, 19; "Elmore James's Phone Call to Lillian McMurry," 28; and Topping, "Ramblin' from Town to Town," 15.

394 Huggins, 19; Franz, 16; and Steve Franz, "About the Recordings." In the notes to Elmore James, *The Sky Is Crying: The History of Elmore James.* Rhino CD 71190, 1993.

395 Topping, "R.T. - On the Box!" 26. Note: "Yes, Ray showed me this tape box," wrote Dick Shurman, "Reels cost less than one dollar then." (Shurman, personal communication, 29 November 2001)

396 Huggins, 19.

Well, I was fool [to] believe what you said,
Yes, I was a fool to believe what you said,
Yes, I'm goin' back home, I wish that I was dead.

Oh, I was a fool, baby, to leave you yesterday,
Yes, I was a fool to leave you yesterday,
I gotta find me a woman, yes, I'll change my way. [397]

This was released as the flip side to Flair 1074, the A-side of which was "Dust My Blues," an arresting update of his Trumpet record with slightly different lyrics. On sale by the first week of August, this would tend to negate Bihari's claims that the session was held during a trip he made later in the month for a publicity visit (on Thursday, 11 August 1955, to honor local disk jockey Okey Dokey). Even if Bihari had held the session with James before making the presentation on the eleventh, this would still not have given enough time to hold the session, make masters, print the labels, press the record, mail it out to reviewers, and have it reviewed before the rhythm & blues trade magazines went to press for the Saturday, 6 August 1955, edition. Records could sometimes be rushed for release if need be, noted Carmen Fanzone of the Los Angeles musicians union, thereby avoiding the usual five to eight week lag time between date of recording and date of issue. It seems more likely that the session took place sometime in late June 1955, with Joe Bihari's lack of record-keeping, the passage of time, and his participation in a few hundred recording sessions blurring the specifics on this particular date.[398]

Lillian McMurry was none too happy when "Dust My Blues" appeared on the market and couldn't help but notice an inescapable similarity between it and the version James had recorded for her four years earlier:

Lillian McMurry: Well, you know that I leased out "Dust My Broom" to another label and re-released it.
Elmore James: Is that right?
LM: Yeah, this fellow leased it from me and so it's out again on the market; and the Biharis... you recorded a number for them just like it called "Dust My Blues." "Dust My Blues," which is exact same music and you know we had the music on that, don't you?
EJ: That's right.
LM: And yet they claim they got "Dust My Blues" see, which is just exactly like "Dust My Broom" only it says "Dust My Blues."
EJ: It's the same music.
LM: It's the same music, isn't it?
EJ: That's right.
LM: That's just what I said.
EJ: It is the same music.
LM: Well, that's been copyrighted, you know, ever since 1951, Elmo. You knew... you remember when I copyrighted the thing?
EJ: Sure do, right there in the store when the man wrote it.
LM: Um-hum. That's what I call high-powered stealing. Just stealing.[399]

Now that there was a record "just exactly like 'Dust My Broom'" on the market, McMurry may have felt it appropriate to reissue James' original version in an effort to capitalize on her big seller one last time.

[397] Elmore James, "I Was a Fool." Flair 1074, 1955; Topping, "Ramblin' from Town to Town," 15; and Franz, 8-11, 13, 15-16.

[398] Fanzone, personal interview, 15 November 1993; Elmore James, "Dust My Blues." Flair 1074, 1955; Gart, *First Pressings—1955,* 94, 99; Topping, "Ramblin' from Town to Town," 15; Huggins, 19; and Franz, 2.

[399] "Elmore James's Phone Call to Lillian McMurry," 28.

McMurry had leased the disc to Johnny Vincent's newly formed Ace label, based in Jackson, Mississippi, which had only been formally announced at the same time "Dust My Blues" had been released. Vincent retitled the disc "I Believe My Time Ain't Long" when it was released as Ace 508 in early September 1955.[400]

Exactly two months later, Flair released their last record. James' "Good Bye" recorded at the New Orleans date, was used for the label's swan song. "[It's] almost as if Joe knew that Flair was going to be discontinued," said Ray Topping.[401] Flair was a victim of changes in the rhythm and blues record market, partly brought about by the efforts of the young St. Louisan who had seen James perform in Chicago only seven months earlier. In August 1955, Chuck Berry's Chess single "Maybellene" was a smash success on the rhythm & blues and pop charts. It held the number one position on the former for eleven weeks and attained a peak position of number five on the latter, not relinquishing its grip on the charts until that Thanksgiving. It signalled the impending big-beat trend of rock and roll. "A good blues single usually sold around 10,000 copies and a big rhythm and blues hit might go into the hundreds of thousands," noted Robert Christgau, "but 'Maybellene' probably moved a million [copies], even if Chess never sponsored the audit to prove it."[402] Ray Topping reported that "B.B. King was the only blues artist who was selling [for Modern Records] by '55 and by '56 it had gone completely rock 'n' roll. The sales had really dropped in down home blues of any sort. So [the Bihari brothers] decided to drop Flair... and just keep Modern and RPM as their two labels."[403]

"Good Bye," with its sonorous slide guitar passages and the addition of a vocal group, Elmore's preaching-style vocals and references to Seymour Simons and Gerald Marks' jazz standard "All of Me" thrown in for spice (popularized by Billie Holiday's 1941 OKeh recording), made for a very likeable side. Researcher/author Peter Guralnick was moved to call the record "amazing," noting that it "brings to mind an improbable combination of Robert Johnson, Tampa Red, and Solomon Burke."[404] The vocal group cooing in the background may have been the Four Speeds—with whom Elmore had recently been working—or perhaps Joe Bihari had the master tape overdubbed at a later date in Los Angeles. The flip side to Flair 1079 was a robust update of Leroy Carr's standard "Blues Before Sunrise," with Elmore's fierce slide guitar and gospel-tinged melismatic vocals a little out of place when one considers the contemplative, subdued nature of Carr's original, a piano duet with guitarist Scrapper Blackwell.[405]

Sometime in early November 1955, Elmore left Jackson for Chicago semi-permanently, evidently taking Otis Ealey's station-wagon with him. Ealey ultimately had to send for it, and Elmore's ex-wife Janice ended up putting their furniture in storage. The Biharis had sent James a new contract, probably in preparation for switching him from the now-defunct Flair to the Modern label, one of their main concerns.[406] Elmore filled Lillian McMurry in on the details in his last conversation with her, a telephone call he made in the fall of 1955:

---

400 Ibid.; Gart, *First Pressings—1955,* 95, 99, 109; and Franz, 32.

401 Huggins, 19; Gart, *First Pressings—1955,* 129; and Gart, *The American Record Label Directory,* 85.

402 Robert Christgau, "Chuck Berry," 60. In Jim Miller, ed., *The Rolling Stone Illustrated History of Rock & Roll.* New York: Rolling Stone Press, 1976; Huggins, 19; and Whitburn, 41.

403 Huggins, 19.

404 Peter Guralnick, *Searching for Robert Johnson.* New York: Obelisk/E.P. Dutton, 1989, 81; Elmore James, "Good Bye." Flair 1079, 1955; and Martin Williams, "The Recordings," 25. In the notes to *The Smithsonian Collection of Classic Jazz.* Smithsonian/Columbia Special Products LP 11891, 1973.

405 "Elmore James's Phone Call to Lillian McMurry," 28; Elmore James, "Blues Before Sunrise." Flair 1079, 1955; Leroy Carr, "Blues Before Sunrise." Vocalion 02657, 1934; Dixon, Godrich, and Rye, 142; and Franz, 16.

406 Bastin and Lowry, 5; *The Chicago Defender* [Advertisement], (19 November 1955): 18; and Huggins, 19.

Elmore James: Hello, Mrs. McMurry?... How are you doin'?
Lillian McMurry: I'm gettin' along fine.
EJ: You are? Well, I wished I could say that.
LM: What's your trouble, Elmo?
EJ: Oh, nothing. Ah, what you got now?
LM: What have I got?
EJ: Do you need a good artist?
LM: Why? Who's free?
EJ: Me!
LM: You're not off of Modern.
EJ: I am, too.
LM: Have you got a written release?
EJ: I sho' haven't but my contract up. They sent me a contract and I haven't signed it. They sent me two sets.
LM: Oh. Well, Elmo, you know you didn't stand hitched before.... Do you think you'd stand hitched, Elmo?
EJ: Sure. Just look how long I been with this company and, of course, they are nice to me. [407]

Otis Ealey didn't seem to be too upset at the inconvenience James had caused, only wishing perhaps that the times he and Janice had shared in Georgia didn't have to end on such a sour note. Even so, Ealey continued to book James when he could up until 1961, and still held high regard for him nine years later, when Bastin and Lowry interviewed him, saying Elmore "was the greatest he'd ever heard."[408]

Wild about You

Back in Chicago, James resumed his club dates at Sylvio's with Johnny Jones, and by December 1955, was performing there five nights a week. Homesick James was lodging with Jones and his wife Letha at 1636 S. Springfield, and was performing at the Johnson Lounge with Big Bill Broonzy, not far from Sylvio's. When they weren't working, Jones and Homesick James used to sit around drinking and play old records by Big Bill, Tampa Red, and pianist Big Maceo Merriweather. Whether it was Jones, or James' uncle Mac Willie James, someone reintroduced Homesick James to his childhood friend Elmore James, and they occasionally would sit in on each other's performances when one of them couldn't find work. "See, I had my Dusters and Elmore would play with me, if he didn't have no work," Homesick James recalled in a 1970 interview, "See he would play one place and I would be playin' across the street... and he'd come over and play with me and I would go and play with him, but the owner he stopped that 'cause everybody would, you know follow us."[409]

Elmore James and his slightly revamped Broomdusters congregated for their last Modern recording session at Universal Studios on Wednesday 4 January 1956. Accompanying James that day were pianist Jones, on rhythm guitar Eddie Taylor, and on tenor saxes Raymond Hill and possibly J.T. Brown. Also enlisted for the date was James' former drummer Odie Payne, and a pleasant, although unknown, bassist.

They recorded the standard four tunes, starting with "So Mean to Me," a catchy jump blues style

407 "Elmore James's Phone Call to Lillian McMurry," 28.

408 Bastin and Lowry, 4-5.

409 Leadbitter and Robinson. "Homesick James, part 2," 9; Rowe, *Chicago Breakdown*, 200-201; and *The Chicago Defender* [Advertisement], (26 November 1955): 28.

number with plenty of hot guitar and a surprise ending, with outstanding support from Payne. Bihari chose not to release it at the time, however, and kept the title under wraps until 1969. Also shelved for more than a decade was the driving instrumental "Elmo's Shuffle," with its undulating bass foundation and flashy horns providing James another opportunity to showcase his slide guitar talent. As usual, Elmore gives plenty of time for solos from his fellow musicians.[410]

Another title recorded that day was "Wild about You," which required a staggering twenty-two takes before it was in suitable condition for release. The side used James' classic "Dust My Broom" riff and possessed an ebullience that made it an extremely enjoyable record. James' ululant guitar playing was just magnificent, effortlessly going through the ropes on his patented bottleneck licks with some solid horn support and a lyrical mood displaying James' unusual brand of upbeat pessimism:

> Well, I'm wild about you, baby, and you just won't treat me right,
> Well, I'm wild about you, baby, you just won't treat me right,
> You leave me early in the morning, and you don't come home 'til night.
>
> Well, I'm walking and I'm cryin', talkin' all in my sleep,
> Yes, I'm walking and I'm talking, talkin' all in my sleep,
> Well, I'm thinkin' about my baby, stoppin' every man she meet.[411]

Out of the twenty-two takes of "Wild about You," six were usable. Joe Bihari decided on the last take to be used for release on Modern the following month. Its companion side was "Long Tall Woman," a re-recording of a title that Joe Bihari had originally slated for release as James' first Modern single four years ago. Vastly superior to the older version, it shows how far James had progressed musically and personally in the last forty-eight months. In the 1956 recording, James is obviously much more sure of himself and his abilities in a recording session setting and is very comfortable with his slide guitar playing, where before it had seemed strained and tense. Rather than lyrics about his hometown in Canton, Mississippi, there are instead references to California—even if they were borrowed from Smokey Hogg's 1948 Modern single, "Long Tall Mama."[412]

After "Wild about You" was issued in February 1956, the Bihari brothers dropped James from their roster. "Joe decided to put 'Wild about You' on Modern," recalled Ray Topping. "It obviously didn't sell like the earlier records, so they didn't renew his contract after that. It wasn't worth concentrating on him any more."[413] Modern's axing of James is a reminder, over forty years after the fact, that Joe Bihari did not make records with Elmore James for the sheer nobility of it; Modern was in business to sell records, and the

---

410 Elmore James, "So Mean to Me." From the album Elmore James, *The Legend of Elmore James.* Kent LP 9001, 1969; Elmore James, "Elmo's Shuffle." From the album Elmore James, *The Resurrection of Elmore James.* Kent LP 9010, 1969; and Franz, 17, 39.

411 Elmore James, "Wild about You." Modern 983, 1956. Curiously, this exuberant little piece of Broomdusting has become rather a rarity. Since its original release four and a half decades ago, this particular track has only been reissued twice. An alternate take in the form of a lackadaisical cousin—a fine slice of Elmore in its own right, but an earlier and slower take, however—has been reissued many times. Unfortunately, well-meaning record companies keep getting the two different takes confused. The alternate take has been reissued so many times—but wrongly identified as the original single version—so often that the problem now seems to be reaching pandemic proportions. Listeners eager to hear the two different versions side-by-side can find both of them on *The Classic Early Recordings 1951-1956* three CD box set. And now, as a public service to Elmore fans and record companies everywhere, repeat after me: "The slow version (it's over three minutes long) is the alternate take; the fast version (it's just barely 2 and a half minutes) is the take issued on Modern 983." Thank you, and I hope I've been able to clear this up once and for all.

412 Huggins, 18; Elmore James, "Long Tall Woman." From the album *The Classic Early Recordings 1951-1956;* Elmore James, "Long Tall Woman." Modern 983, 1956; Franz, 8, 17, 32; and Hogg, "Long Tall Mama."

413 Huggins, 19.

Biharis probably felt that in 1956 James was no longer capable of sustaining the sales they required to operate at a profit. It's also interesting to note that four years later, when James would grace the rhythm & blues charts in a big way, Modern almost immediately changed their tune about the Broomduster and issued eight James singles between 1960 and 1969, one of which was leased to Britain's Sue label. Four LPs worth of material were also eked out of the Modern vaults over the same time span, which were duplicated and repackaged on twelve different occasions over the span of two continents.[414]

Obviously the relationship between Elmore James and Joe Bihari had been a strained one to some degree. Richard Berry offers a valuable "second opinion" into the Modern operation. "I think they did business on the scale that everybody else was doing on," Berry recalled. "They treated their artists with a little bit more humanity than some of the other record companies did." However:

> ...[Berry] received no performance royalties, no songwriting royalties, and many of his songs had been published with co-writer credit, and royalty money, assigned to the Biharis. You don't get rich [as a working musician] at fifty bucks a night, but after a while, it became clear that if the singers and musicians weren't getting rich, *someone* was.... "We were all young and ignorant. We didn't have a lawyer, never had a manager, didn't know that as minors [in Berry's case] our money was supposed to go through the courts and go into a fund until we were twenty-one," Richard told [Steve] Propes. "I didn't know anything about BMI [which collects money for broadcast performances, *if* the songwriter is registered with it] until Maxwell Davis told me about it in 1955." [415]

So, a kind of awkward balance evolved over time between Elmore James and Joe Bihari—such as James recording for three different record labels in 1953 while under contract to Modern, and Joe splicing Elmore's guitar onto the Boyd Gilmore single and listing writer's credits on James' releases as "Josea."

To be fair, however, it must be said that when Bihari first met Elmore he was able to recognize his talent, work hard with it and produce James with a keen eye and an experienced ear. "Joe was the producer, engineer and A&R man all in one. Even in Chicago he did his own engineering," Ray Topping related. "I've got great admiration for what Joe did. You don't get those classic records if there's a bum sitting behind the tape recorder. You can tell he worked bloody hard."[416] Surely unknowable to James and Bihari at the time was that their studio work together would produce thirty-four sides—nineteen of which featured Elmore's deftly chosen Broomdusters—that any other artist or blues band would have difficulty matching in terms of quality and musicianship. Elmore's arrival in Chicago was now a matter of record, so to speak. Five decades later these sides still stand as prime examples of the postwar peak of the recorded history of Chicago blues.[417]

---

[414] Franz, 2, 32-33, 35, 38.

[415] Marsh, 28-29.

[416] Huggins, 18; Ray Topping, "The Legend," 9. In the notes to Elmore James, *The Classic Early Recordings 1951-1956.* Ace BOXCD 4, 1993; and Franz, 8, 10, 12, 14, 41-42.

[417] Franz, 32, 34.

Elmore James, 1959, Chicago. Photo by Jacques Demêtre, courtesy Blues Unlimited.

CHAPTER FOUR

Elmore in the Post-Modern Years

Elmore James will always remain the **most exciting and dramatic** blues singer and guitarist that I've ever had a chance to see perform in the flesh.

—George Adins, on seeing Elmore James live in person

All was ready for the grand ritual of pure blues. What do I say? What words can I use to describe this?

—Jacques Demêtre, from Soul Bag 94

Paul Oliver, who heard Elmore at a West Roosevelt strip club in 1960, described him as "tall, emaciated and suffering from asthma, had poor eyesight and **looked older than his years.**"

from "The Story of Elmore James" in Blues Unlimited 5

"We used to keep Letha woke all night"

"1956 was a steady year of short tours [and] Sylvio's..." wrote Leadbitter and Wardlow about Elmore's activities that year.[418] Sylvio's seems to have been relieved to have James back from the southeast, as an all-star birthday bash was held (a few days early) for "The 'Old Man' Broom Duster" on Wednesday, 18 January 1956. Celebrating with Elmore that night were Howlin' Wolf, Sunnyland Slim, the Red Devil Trio, and one Big Bill "Bromzie." Placards proudly claimed it as "the biggest 'BIRTHDAY PARTY' that ever hit the Middle West."[419]

Back at the Local 208 union hall, however, there was a tiny bit of fallout over some of the details of Elmore's big birthday party, when Howlin' Wolf filed a complaint against Elmore James; they both appeared before the board on Thursday, 2 February 1956. According to the minutes kept by the union's board of directors, it seems that Elmore had asked Howlin' Wolf's drummer if the band could play the date, but forgot to ask the Wolf himself. Thinking it was a done deal, Elmore put Wolf's name on the flyers he had printed up. Evidently, the drummer hadn't mentioned it to Wolf either:

> On the night of the affair, Wolf stated that his girlfriend called him and asked him why he wasn't at [Sylvio's] because it was jumping. He got in his car and drove to the place and everybody was asking him when he was going to play which he did not. Wolf stated that he thought it was worth $25 for using his name.
>
> Elmore James admitted that he was wrong and stated that the admission at the door was 75 cents and the drinks were on the house. He stated that he paid the musicians that played (his own band) and paid the tax for them. He said he lost $18 on the promotion.
>
> On motion, the Board ruled that Elmore James must pay the Howlin' Wolf $25 for publicizing his name for his birthday party....[420]

In the end, there were probably no hard feelings, though. Sometime afterwards, guitarist Mighty Joe Young blew into town from Shreveport, Louisiana. Both Howlin' Wolf and Elmore James helped him get established in his new surroundings by welcoming the new-comer to sit in with their groups.[421]

418 Leadbitter and Wardlow, 9.

419 Advertisement courtesy of the collection of Yannick Bruynoghe. Reprinted in Jim O'Neal, "Big Bill: Opening the Door to the Blues." *Living Blues* 55 (Winter 1982/83): 5.

420 Dirks, 43.

421 Dick Shurman, "Voo Doo Dust." *Blues Unlimited* 107 (April/May 1974): 5.

Six weeks later, Elmore James was back in front of the union's board of directors, but this time with Odie Payne. Payne had filed a complaint against Elmore after being unceremoniously fired on Friday night, 2 March 1956, from Sylvio's. As a result, Payne called the union to have his name put on the "available" list so that he could find other work. Hiring Payne had probably been a stop-gap measure on Elmore's part upon returning to Chicago the previous November, until the two could either settle their differences or Elmore could find another drummer. When questioned by the union's board of directors, Elmore stated that, "...He liked Odie Payne's work as he had played [with] him for months before. He objected, however, to his surly and important attitude and accused Payne of putting in extra cute licks on the drums which broke the steady rhythm that he required for blues." After debating the matter at length with the two musicians, the board ruled in Elmore's favor, and dismissed Payne's claim.[422] It was a likely signal that Payne's days occupying the drummer's stool in Elmore's band had come to a close. On only two other known occasions would Payne once again join up with Elmore—during recording sessions in 1957 and 1959, for Mel London and Bobby Robinson, respectively.

As far as the Broomdusters were concerned, there was rarely a dull moment when they were playing and touring. By all accounts, Johnny Jones was the extrovert of the group: "With pure admiration in his voice," said Rowe, "Johnny Shines says, 'he was *terrible!*'"[423] "Dressed immaculately and with his hair and mustache perfectly groomed," reported Bruce Iglauer, "[Jones] would open the shows singing his favorite risque classics, 'The Dirty Dozens' and 'Love Her with a Feeling.'" Billy Boy Arnold recalled to Iglauer that Jones practically lived at Sylvio's for a while. "Most nights Sylvio's had three bands, and Johnny would play with all of them!" he remarked. "He didn't sit there like a lot of piano players and just play—he rocked with the rhythm, he bounced. He used to sing [the off-color] 'Dirty Mother For Ya' and that would just crack the house up! Johnny and Elmore had Sylvio's sewed up five nights a week!"[424]

Occasionally, the piano playing didn't stop with the end of the last show at Sylvio's, either. "I used to get off work and stay at [Johnny Jones'] house like I was home," Johnny "Big Moose" Walker told John Anthony Brisbin, "We used to keep Letha woke all night," he admitted. One of them, and then the other, would alternate all night on Johnny's piano bench in the front room, sometimes until dawn. "We used to be playin' all night long.... It'd be up in the day and we'd still be playin' piano," Walker recalled.[425] "When is y'all gonna get drunk and go to sleep," a frustrated Letha—who worked in a factory during the day—would call out to the two of them. "If we keep playin' piano," Walker would retort, "we ain't never gonna get drunk" (indicating that perhaps the lyrics to Johnny's Aristocrat single, "Big Town Playboy" were more than just a little autobiographical?).[426]

But Jones, by no means, had the market cornered in impish behavior. Oliver Sain, who came to Chicago in the mid 1950s and played with Elmore James at places like the 708 Club and Sylvio's, recalled that sometimes he would put down his guitar, and using a long microphone chord, walk around behind the bar and sing from there (whether Elmore served drinks while singing, Sain does not recall). Frequently, Sylvio's would have a "battle of the bands" with Elmore's Broomdusters facing off with Muddy Waters' group, giving the young, multi-talented Sain a chance to catch up on his sleep, dozing in the corner until it was Elmore's turn to take the stage again.[427] When he was on tour, Elmore would periodically leave the

422 Dirks, 43.

423 Rowe, *Chicago Breakdown*, 201.

424 Bruce Iglauer, notes to Johnny Jones, *Johnnie Jones with Billy Boy Arnold.* Alligator LP 4717, 1979.

425 John Anthony Brisbin, "Big Moose Walker: Playin' All Night Long." *Living Blues* 105 (September/October 1992): 40.

426 Ibid.; and Eagle, 29.

427 Oliver Sain, personal interview by Steve Franz. St. Louis, Missouri, 16 February 2002.

band stranded, coming back to Chicago with the proceeds from the previous night's performance, or might pawn his friends' possessions if he was short on cash (a curious habit of more than one slide guitarist that I know of). On one occasion, after working in the southwest United States and Mexico, Elmore and Johnny ran into some trouble at a Texas gambling house, and lost all their money. Jones' wife Letha wired his fare to him, "but Elmore had to pawn his guitar to get back to Chicago," reported researcher Bob Eagle.[428] "Elmore, he'd pawn everythin' he could get his hands on," Homesick James told Mike Leadbitter and Chris Robinson. "And if he get somethin' that belonged to you, if he knowed you, he'd pawn that too.... All musicians will do that," theorized Homesick James, assuming the role of a person who countenanced his share of malfeasance by blues musicians over the years.[429]

"Elmore and Johnny used to just have a fight every night," he told Mike Rowe. "That was the whole point. If they didn't get in no argument there wouldn't be no band, y'know. After they get to... yakkin' each other then the band would get lively. Everybody be in there—whole big party, yessir!" Sometimes, however, the fighting was serious. While they were playing in Maryland Heights, Missouri, at Bolton Oak Grove for several thousand people, a fight started that allegedly resulted in several deaths. Sharing the stage that evening were an unseasoned Tina Turner and a startled Etta James.[430] Touring the south was different in the mid fifties. "Homesick recounts one potentially dangerous incident," says Rowe, "which, trivial and amusing though it was, serves as an eloquent reminder of the times:"

> Homesick and Elmore were in the back of the station-wagon drinking when they pulled into a gas-station. As he filled up the white pump-attendant, staring at the band's motif which was painted across the side of the van, said, "That Broom-Dusters sure looks funny." Homesick, thinking it was one of the band mimicking the white accent, poked his head up and asked, "Who the hell said that?" When he saw the pump-attendant he quickly ducked down and didn't dare raise his head again until they were twenty miles out of town. [431]

When they weren't on tour, the Broomdusters kept up the club dates in Chicago, at times with the help of Sam Myers, a young harmonica player. Myers recalls that J.T. Brown was quite a popular crowd pleaser. "Other than Louis Jordan, I never heard anybody blow a tone out of a saxophone like J.T. Brown," he said. "His horn style was almost like Sonny Boy Williamson's deal with the harmonica. Sometimes it would sound like he was laughing when he played, and the audience loved him."[432] Sylvio's continued to book the Broomdusters regularly, and Elmore supplemented his income with dates at the Key Largo, Alex Club, Charlie's Lounge, and other west side haunts.[433]

On one occasion, however, an opportunity to make a few extra bucks almost cost Elmore his long-running gig at Sylvio's. On Sunday, 29 April 1956, Elmore, Eddie Taylor, and Sonny Boy Williamson had all headed a few miles north up to Evanston, Illinois, where they played at the Swedish Hall for fifty dollars, and then split the money three ways. Normally, that might have been the end of the story, but it turns out that playing the Evanston performance had made Elmore late for his regular appearance at

428 Eagle, 29; and Rowe, *Chicago Breakdown*, 205.

429 Leadbitter and Robinson, "Homesick James, part 2," 7; and Rowe, *Chicago Breakdown*, 205.

430 Rowe, *Chicago Breakdown*, 201-202; and O'Neal and O'Neal, 23-24.
Note: At one time—to further illustrate this point—the gang violence in East St. Louis was so bad that Ike Turner and his band members carried firearms to their gigs. Later, Turner and everyone in his band received "special deputy sheriff badges" that enabled them to legally carry the guns. See: Turner with Cawthorne, 64-65.

431 Rowe, *Chicago Breakdown*, 202.

432 Sam Myers, "Comments from Sam Myers." In the notes to Elmore James, *King of the Slide Guitar*. Capricorn CD 42006-2, 1992; and Leadbitter and Wardlow, 9.

433 Rowe, *Chicago Breakdown*, 202-203.

Sylvio's. Sylvio subsequently filed a complaint, and was ready to fire Elmore over it, as well as Sonny Boy, who had been playing with him for a couple weeks, but without a contract. Sylvio complained that Elmore "had not worked with him and that he appeared to be doing everything to jeopardize his business." Upon being questioned, Elmore showed the board a set of contracts for the Swedish Hall performance, but they were found to be "incomplete." While the board ultimately ruled in Sylvio's favor and fined Elmore (as well as docking his pay and giving it to Boyd Atkins and Jesse Fowler—the only two musicians who had showed up at Sylvio's on time that Sunday night), it seems that at some point Elmore and Sylvio must have patched things up—either that, or Elmore was good at begging to have his old job back—as indicated by his long-term presence at the club throughout 1956 and 1957, and continuing on into 1958.[434]

Elmore appeared before the union one more time in 1956, when he was questioned by the board on Thursday, 16 August 1956. Having played a performance at the Grand Terrace, the directors charged Elmore with not filing a contract on time prior to the engagement, and using a pianist, Johnny Jones, that failed to have a current union membership (as one Mr. Brown, the union's representative, had found out when he checked Jones' card); no doubt this was all exacerbated when Elmore failed to show up twice to discuss the matter with the union's directors. This time, however, Elmore had satisfactory explanations for everything: the contract had been given to someone else to mail, but they had not mailed it in a timely manner; he thought Jones' dues were paid up because Jones had told him they were (Jones had, in fact, told someone at the union to deduct his dues from another performance he had played, but they had obviously not done so), and when Mr. Brown had confiscated Jones' card, Elmore had come down to the office and paid $17.25 to keep Jones' membership current; as for his absence twice previous, the notices had not arrived in time for him to make either meeting. In an unusual display of leniency towards the Broomduster, the board rescinded the fines totalling $15 for his two earlier no-shows, and gave him a slap on the wrist by explaining that he was responsible for checking each band member's union card and to see to it personally that the contract made it to the union office on time. Having cleared that up, Elmore wouldn't appear before the union's board of directors again for a year and a half.[435]

Also by 1956, Big Bill Hill—a Chicago disk jockey remembered for "breaking" many important rhythm & blues records of the 1950s—had started his famous live broadcasts over WOPA radio. Muddy Waters recalled that Hill had the night shift, and "he was on all the twenty-four hours, looked like, you know."[436] According to Jimmy Dawkins, the live nightclub broadcasts started from the smaller clubs, with Hill eventually obtaining a steady broadcast out of Sylvio's: "One night he'd feature Muddy [Waters], [Little] Walter and Jimmy Rogers with their bands and another he'd bring on Wolf, J.B. Lenoir and Elmo'. Then they really had a downhome sound!"[437] "The first live broadcast of blues, on a Sunday, that was mine," Hill asserted in an early 1970s article. "I had 'em standing in line....when it was open, you couldn't get in there [Sylvio's]."[438] Bobby Robinson describes a meeting with Hill several years later, when he was on a promotional visit from New York City for his current release "Fannie Mae," and what must have been a typical evening on one of Hill's shows. "He had a dry cleaning plant on Chicago's west side, and he broadcast from the window of his business. He played a lot of blues so I went over there that night," Robinson said. "Someone had cued me in to take him a bottle of House of Lords scotch:"

---

[434] Dirks, 43.

[435] Ibid., 44.

[436] O'Neal and O'Neal, 39; and Jimmy Dawkins, "Big Bill Hill's Story." *Blues Unlimited* 70 (February/March 1970): 18.

[437] Dawkins, 18.

[438] Big Bill Hill, "Chicago Blues Radio: Big Bill Hill." *Living Blues* 7 (Winter 1971/72): 14.

> So I walked in with my bottle of scotch and introduced myself. He whipped out a couple of glasses and I brought out a copy of Fannie Mae. He... listened to it and said, "oh, we'll dig this new record." So he put it on and said, "ladies and gentlemen, sitting here is an old friend of mine, Bobby Robinson." He had never seen me before, "came all the way from New York out here to see me, everybody comes to see Big Bill Hill, we're just sitting here like two bugs in a rug, too cool to move." He had a lot of sayings like that. "He brought me a smash hit record by a new artist... named Buster Brown like the shoes, I'll tell you what we'll do, we're going to play it a few times... and let us know what you think of it." He had about eight phones, and he played that record twelve times in a row. He was drinking his scotch and he'd say, "that sounds good, let's hear it again." I thought this guy was going to get fired. The next morning I had orders for 5,000 records. Chicago went crazy for it. [439]

Robinson's story—although cute—serves to remind us of the power disk jockeys wielded at the time, in making or breaking a hit record; Hill, evidently, was no exception.

If 1956 had been a slow year for Elmore recording-wise, 1957 was surely going to be better. Just as winter was ending and with spring beginning, Elmore would soon be taking his "downhome sound" back into the recording studio. Chicago impresario Mel London had started a new record label, and he was looking for talent.[440]

Three Guitars and an Amp

Melvin R. London, the Windy City businessman behind such record labels as Profile, Age, All Points, Mel and Mel-Lon, began operations of his very first effort, Chief Records, in 1957. In March of that year, twenty-five year-old London was noted in the rhythm & blues trade press, which said "United Distrib's Mel London turned into a triple threat man with Chief's 'Man from the Island.' London penned the Calypso number, published it, and owns the label, not to mention he's the distributor's promotion man, too." One minor point the news story forgot to mention was that London was also the artist featured on the record![441] Researcher/writer Neil Slaven noted that London was just one among "the ranks of a small band of Chicago entrepreneurs that over the previous decade had taken on, with varying degrees of intent and success, the larger record companies.... The releases on their labels rarely reached double figures, even though individual records met with considerable success." London set up Chief's offices at 1510 W. Thirteenth St. in Chicago, and by April the label was showing solid signs of life.[442]

Elmore gathered an expanded group of Broomdusters together for a session with London on Friday, 12 April 1957, with Johnny Jones on piano and J.T. Brown on tenor sax. Also present were Elmore's former drummer Odie Payne, bass guitarist Homesick James (his first recording session with James), and possibly guitarist Eddie Taylor rounding out the rhythm section. Guitarist Wayne Bennett was also present for two titles recorded that day, the first of which was "The 12 Year Old Boy." Bennett really "made" the side, committing to tape some scorching lead guitar on a peculiar song that supposedly London had drafted, or that at least bore a similar name, "Nel Rondon," under the writer's credits (London would later claim

---

439 Turco, "Interview: Bobby Robinson. [Part 2]," 11.

440 Rowe, *Chicago Breakdown*, 203; and Leadbitter and Wardlow, 9.

441 Gart, *First Pressings—1957*, 39, 59; and Jim O'Neal, "Obituaries: Mel London." *Living Blues* 22 (July/August 1975): 4.

442 Neil Slaven, notes to *Chicago Calling*. Charly LP 1135, 1986; Gart, *The American Record Label Directory*, 43; and Gart, *First Pressings—1957*, 55.

authorship to two other songs James recorded for Chief):[443]

> I feel bad, I feel terrible, I'm just as sad as I can be,
> I feel bad, I feel terrible, I'm just as sad as I can be,
> I let a boy twelve years old take my baby away from me.
>
> He used to hang aroun' my crib[444] until late into the night,
> He used to hang aroun' my crib until late into the night,
> Well, I never dreamed that my baby and that boy could be so tight. [445]

The next side recorded was the exciting "Coming Home." It featured Elmore's feral vocals, screaming bottleneck glissandos, a withering "Dust My Broom" guitar riff, and Payne's fulminating drum beats, which appear intent on taking the skins off his instrument. I have often wondered—given that Elmore's guitar is so loud here—if he was actually playing an electric guitar at all; it sounds more like he's playing some form of tuned air raid siren, and that it just *happened* to sound like an electric guitar once they got the sound captured on tape. A persistent legend has it that James, Homesick, and Taylor were all miked off only one guitar amp (three guitars, one amplifier, no waiting), adding to the oddity of the recording. Elmore's guitar, aided by its unique amplification, however, easily surges above Taylor's and Homesick James' rhythmic din.[446]

"The 12 Year Old Boy" and "Coming Home" were paired for issue as Chief's second release sometime in May 1957. In Chicago "The 12 Year Old Boy" seemed to be the favored side, and it received an above average review: "Elmore James wails a slow beat down home blues with an authentic styling that makes it southern market wax. Instrumentation by the Broom Dusters typically in the deep south vein." The record had scarcely been released, however, before it was announced that Vee-Jay records, a heavier-weight independent Chicago label, would be handling national distribution. By the end of July Vee-Jay had reissued the single on its own label, where it had a much better chance on a national scale.[447]

The next Chief recording from the James session was "It Hurts Me Too," which had seen release at least twice before by its author, Tampa Red (*not* Mel London, who was listed as the writer of Elmore's version). Although the side received the typical firm support from Jones and Brown, James' version seems slightly stilted when compared to Tampa Red's smooth, lilting 1941 recording. Still, the tune was a favorite among Elmore fans and received another above average review when released in July 1957: "Elmore James wails a slow, mellow blues for the southern market. Melodic effort the James friends will like. Easy on the ears wax."[448] The side initially inspired two other blues artists to record versions of their own. The first was recorded by Buster Brown for Bobby Robinson's Fire label and was a little closer in spirit to Tampa Red's 1949 number nine R&B hit version. A second rendering executed in 1961 by Junior Wells was a little more

443 Rowe, *Chicago Breakdown,* 203; and Franz, 18, 42. Recording date information from Elmore James' Chicago musicians union file; courtesy of Pat LeBlanc and the Estate of Elmore James. Note: An alternate school of thought has also suggested Willie Johnson as the guitarist on "The 12 Year Old Boy."

444 Usually, slang for "dwelling," but can also connote a "nightclub," or in African-American usage mean "a place for sex." Jonathon Green, *The Slang Thesaurus.* London: Penguin Books, 1988 [reprint], 13, 20; and Robert Chapman, ed. *American Slang.* New York: Perennial Library, 1987 [reprint], 88.

445 Elmore James, "The 12 Year Old Boy." Chief 7001, 1957.

446 Elmore James, "Coming Home." Chief 7001, 1957; and Rowe, *Chicago Breakdown,* 203.

447 Moss, personal communication, 11 December 1992; Gart, *First Pressings—1957,* 69; Franz, 32; and Steve Franz, comp., "Dating Guide to Vee-Jay Records numbers 240 through 270." unpublished manuscript, 1994.

448 Moss, personal communication, 11 December 1992; Elmore James, "It Hurts Me Too." Chief 7004, 1957; Tampa Red, "It Hurts Me Too." Bluebird B8635, 1941; Tampa Red, "When Things Go Wrong with You." RCA Victor 22-0035, 1949; and Franz, 32, 42.

soulful and borrowed more obviously from Elmore's Chief reading.[449]

The flip to "It Hurts Me Too" was surely the most bizarre instrumental James ever recorded, "Elmore's Contribution to Jazz." Although the tune was borrowed from his Flair single "Can't Stop Lovin" less the lyrics, the music was much, much noisier. Paul Garon appropriately described the effort as "a frantic instrumental cha-cha-cha," noting that "Johnny Jones seems to pound the keyboard to pieces, while James's assaultive guitar seizes endless choruses in maniacal abandon. One can almost hear the whole band take a breath when it is all over."[450] Vee-Jay again scooped up the two sides for reissue, and the disc was shipped from the pressing plant sometime in mid-October, 1957. Vee-Jay's general manager Ewart Abner expressed enthusiasm for its outlook: "Amidst all the furore in rock 'n' roll records," noted a November 1957 news item, "Abner [is very] excited about his latest blues package, Elmore James' 'It Hurts Me Too,' Billy Boy [Arnold's] 'Prisoner's Plea,' and Gene Allison's 'You Can Make It If You Try.'"[451]

Mel London had recorded five titles at his initial session with Elmore James earlier that spring. "Knocking at Your Door," which also featured Bennett's searing lead guitar, became the fifth song of the session that did not see immediate issue on single that year, as London had no further James material to pair it with for release. Instead, he shelved the tune for another thirty-six months and set about a more immediate task—organizing his next session with Elmore. Suddenly, London had something else to worry about other than just the minor session details, as James went into the hospital after suffering a second heart attack. After his release, Elmore worked a little at Sylvio's—instead of being the headline act, he worked the door. It was only for a short while, however, and soon he resumed his performing schedule.[452]

Arthur Williams, a harmonica player now residing in St. Louis, Missouri, recalled sitting in with Elmore at the Happy Home around this time, and described his set up to a T: "He had a big ol' [guitar] layin' across his lap," Williams observed—with the initials "EJ" inscribed in one corner and his trademark D'Armond pickup in the sound hole. For his vocals, Elmore had two mike stands with goosenecks set up on either side of him, with a bullet mike in each one pointed right at his face. Not too surprisingly, he said, Elmore played very loudly. While Williams can't recall the specific purpose of the two vocal mikes (one plausible theory is that one speaker was placed where Elmore could hear it, and perhaps the other was placed at the opposite end of the bar), he does remember Elmore egging him on to blow his harp real hard, but due to Elmore's unusual setup it was mostly futile, saying, "You couldn't really hear anything over Elmore's guitar." Williams also couldn't help but notice that Elmore was taking medication while on stage, possibly something like nitroglycerin tablets, and remembers that the doctors had evidently warned Elmore that he should either stop singing or stop playing guitar, but not to continue doing both. "Well, you know he wasn't going to pay that no mind," offered Williams.[453]

Just as Chief's previous James single was starting to wane, London called Elmore back to the studio, probably in the fall. Out of all the sidemen used from the previous session, only J.T. Brown and Eddie Taylor were called back. Added to the roster were bassist Willie Dixon, drummer Fred Below, and guitarist Syl Johnson, who had previously recorded with Billy Boy Arnold and had joined Junior Wells for his first

449 Buster Brown, "When Things Go Wrong." From the album Buster Brown, *The New King of the Blues.* Fire LP 102, 1960; Tampa Red, "When Things Go Wrong with You;" Whitburn, 401; Junior Wells, "It Hurts Me Too." Chief 7035, 1961; and Leadbitter, Fancourt, and Pelletier, 697.

450 Paul Garon, "Postwar Chicago and the North," 203. In Paul Oliver, ed., *The Blackwell Guide to Blues Records.* Cambridge, Massachusetts: Basil Blackwell Inc., 1989; Elmore James, "Elmore's Contribution to Jazz." Chief 7004, 1957; and James, "Can't Stop Lovin."

451 Gart, *First Pressings—1957,* 147; Gart, *The American Record Label Directory,* 233; Franz, 32; and Franz, "Dating Guide to Vee-Jay Records numbers 240 through 270."

452 Rowe, *Chicago Breakdown,* 202-203; O'Neal and Lee, 19; and Dick Shurman, notes to Elmore James, *The Last Session.* Relic LP 1021, 1989; and Franz, 18-19, 32.

453 Arthur Williams, personal interview by Steve Franz. St. Louis, Missouri, 9 February 2002.

Chief session. Johnson was given the opportunity to play lead guitar for the session, augmenting "Cry for Me Baby" and "Take Me Where You Go" with his prowess. It was Elmore's only session where he failed to play the guitar, at this occasion preferring to let Johnson and Taylor handle those chores.[454]

The titles were released as Chief 7006 in December, 1957. Almost simultaneously, Vee-Jay again reissued the material on their label as well, offering it for sale before Christmas. This time the reviews were even more positive than before. On "Cry for Me Baby" it was noted that "James handles the infectious material in good style. It has the qualities necessary for a good selling record." "Take Me Where You Go" scored slightly lower marks, the review noting that "James rocks with a middle beat jump blues and again handles it like the pro he is."[455]

Although Elmore's two Chief sessions produced seven sides that could all arguably be called remarkable in one aspect or another, "Cry for Me Baby" seems to stand above the others for its setting in a minor key and a strikingly dark mood. Johnson's wandering lead guitar line was quite effective, and Fred Below's agile drumming coupled with Willie Dixon's reputation for some of the finest bass playing in Chicago gave the record a firm underpinning:

> Almost every night I cry myself to sleep,
> Everybody else is so happy, an' I just weep, weep, weep,
> Lord, these tears, tears, tears, why won't they let me be?
> Lord, I wish just once you would cry for me.
>
> Why do I remember? How could I forget?
> I wake up every mornin', my pillow soakin' wet,
> From these tears, tears, tears, why won't they let me be?
> Lord, I wish just once you would cry for me. [456]

Chief was just a small label, and by early 1960 it had managed to survive on a very meager schedule of just twelve releases. Even so, over the years to come London made sure that the material he recorded with Elmore saw the widest dispersion possible. "Cry for Me Baby" was issued as a single on six different occasions, and the inclusion of "Coming Home" on a 1960 Vee-Jay anthology LP made it the first of Elmore's songs to be issued in the long play format. Other titles were issued on 45s and albums at home and abroad, and ultimately, compact discs when Vee-Jay was (briefly) reorganized in 1992.[457]

Elmore's commitments to Chief faded after 1957, and London went on to embrace other endeavors. After problems with the I.R.S. supposedly brought about Chief's untimely demise, London started up again with the ephemeral Profile label and the slightly more durable Age Records. By early 1963, London had forged a partnership with Paul Glass, operator of All States Distributing. This led to the formation of U.S.A. Records, with London assuming an indeterminate role, possibly that of producer. London obliged the new company by reissuing "Cry for Me Baby" sometime during the last couple months of 1965. By the end of the decade, though, London was seemingly back to where he was before he started Chief, with a job

---

[454] Leadbitter and Slaven, *Blues Records 1943-1970,* 44; Leadbitter, Fancourt, and Pelletier, 696; Dick Shurman, personal communication with Steve Franz, 4 July 2001; Robert Pruter, "The Syl Johnson Story." *Living Blues* 122 (July/August 1995): 24; and Franz, 18-19.

[455] Moss, personal communication, 11 December 1992; Franz, 32; and Franz, "Dating Guide to Vee-Jay Records numbers 240 through 270."

[456] Elmore James, "Cry for Me Baby." Chief 7006, 1957.

[457] Gart, *The American Record Label Directory,* 43; Steve Franz, comp., "Dating Guide to Chief Records numbers 7000 through 7022." unpublished manuscript, 1994; Various Artists, *The Blues.* Vee-Jay LP 1020, 1960; "Vee-Jay Stars Celebrate Rebirth of Their Music." *Rhythm & Blues Foundation News* Vol. 2 (January 1993): 4; and Franz, 1, 18-19, 32-33, 35, 37.

as a "Promotional Shipping Clerk" for United Record Distributors. Neil Slaven noted that London "most of the time drove a delivery truck. He was by no means bitter about his situation and retained fond memories of the artists he'd recorded and the records he'd made."[458]

A news blurb from July 1971 noted that London was running Kinnarra Distributors, and with the assistance of Cary Baker was planning to tap into the Chief, Age and Mel-Lon vaults (such as they were) to produce reissue LPs on the Chicago Spirits label. Not long after that announcement, London paired his two biggest Elmore James successes on one single, with "It Hurts Me Too" and "Cry for Me Baby" becoming Mel 7011 circa late 1971 or 1972. London may have been inspired to offer that reissue based on Carey Bell's cover version of "Cry for Me Baby," which appeared on a 1970 Delmark album. Guitarist Eddie Taylor—who had played on the original version—was in the studio to accompany Bell for his rendering entitled "I Cry So Much." A blues harp player by trade, Bell enjoys the obscure distinction of being one of the few people to have ever recorded a version of this durable James classic.[459]

In Autumn 1972, a news item once again reported London's intent to release old Chief and Age material (on Jewel Records this time), but the story noted, sadly, that "London no longer has the original tapes or masters, however, and needs clean, unscratched records to tape from. Mel offers to return the records and provide free copies of the eventual LP's to anyone who sends *any* Chief or Age 45s or 78s to him...."[460] "Hell, I never thought there'd be a call for that stuff," London said in 1973, explaining his whimsical attitude toward record keeping and proper tape storage.[461] While a 1965 LP on the British Sue label, *Elmore James Memorial Album,* had been successful in collecting all seven of James' Chief titles for an overseas audience, it wasn't until 1972 when Cobblestone, a subsidiary of Buddah Records, became the first album in the United States to do so, on the LP *South Side Blues* (this was later reissued by Muse Records as an LP and a CD). By the fall of 1974, London was back at his old job, working at United Distributors as a shipping clerk. It was probably his last job. Mel London died of cancer on Friday, 16 May 1975, at West Side Veteran's Hospital in Chicago. He was forty-three.[462]

"I got plenty of money"

As 1957 came to a close and 1958 began, Elmore was performing at Sylvio's. A Belgian blues and jazz enthusiast and his wife, Yannick and Margo Bruynoghe, were visiting Chicago during the last days of 1957, and Big Bill Broonzy (whom the Bruynoghes had previously met) proudly took the couple around to numerous blues clubs to see the cream of the practicing crop of Chicago's blues talent. "I really wanted to see Chicago—the Chicago that I didn't know," recalled Bruynoghe a quarter of a century later, "to see Big Bill again at his place, and above all to meet all the blues singers of whom he had spoken about."[463]

458 Slaven, notes to *Chicago Calling;* O'Neal, "Obituaries: Mel London," 4; Neil Paterson, "Mel London," 51. In Mike Leadbitter, ed., *Nothing But the Blues.* London: Hanover Books, 1971; and Franz, 33.

459 "News." *Blues Unlimited* 83 (July 1971): 18; Carey Bell, "I Cry So Much." From the album Carey Bell, *Carey Bell's Blues Harp.* Delmark LP 622, 1970; Jim DeKoster, "Records." *Living Blues* 3 (Autumn 1970): 28-29; and Franz, 33.

460 "Blues News." *Living Blues* 10 (Autumn 1972): 40.

461 Jim O'Neal and Cary Baker, "Chicago Blues Label Guide." *Living Blues* 12 (Spring 1973): 8; and O'Neal, "Obituaries: Mel London," 21.

462 "News." *Blues Unlimited* 109 (August/September 1974): 20; O'Neal, "Obituaries: Mel London," 4; and Franz, 18-19, et al.

463 Yannick Bruynoghe, "25 Years Ago." Translated by Marty Champion. *Soul Bag* 94 (May/June 1983): 27;

Broonzy took the Bruynoghes to see Howlin' Wolf first at the 708 Club, and then on to other artists such as Little Walter, Muddy Waters, Jimmy Rogers, Otis Rush, Magic Sam, Eddie Boyd, and Elmore James at places like Smitty's Corner, Sylvio's and the 708 Club.[464] Of the 708 Club, Bruynoghe said that "It was not a club, but a sort of large café, very popular with the public [and] without swank," saving his praise for Sylvio's, which he said was "a *real* club, much more spectacular, with a very warm ambience."[465]

At Sylvio's, Bruynoghe snapped a photo of Elmore singing, without his guitar. He attempted to interview James during his several visits to the club, but Elmore was taciturn, evidently still slowly recuperating from his recent hospital stay: "He did not speak a lot. We had had the occasion to have a few beers together at the bar, but he spoke in monosyllables. He gave me a little biographical information, well known now, nothing interesting or confidential."[466] Although Bruynoghe's meeting with Elmore did not in particular seem very productive, it did hold significance on another level. As Jim O'Neal mentions, the Bruynoghes' visit to Chicago paved the way for other European blues researchers, who would traverse the Atlantic in the months and years to come, in search of the artists whose names appeared on the records they loved.[467]

Once again, though, union troubles were headed Elmore's way. On Thursday, 2 January 1958, drummer Junior Blackman appeared before the union's board of directors. Four days previous, the union's president—one Mr. Gray—had gone into Sylvio's Lounge and found Blackman, a non-union musician, "sitting in" with Elmore's band (according to the union's strict rules, this practice was forbidden). When questioned, Blackman made up a story about belonging to a local chapter of the union down in Louisiana, but Mr. Gray saw through it easily. Making matters worse, Blackman then went down to the union office the following day to join up, but "falsified important questions in [his] application." Now the union wanted to see Blackman, and they wanted to know the truth. Under questioning, Blackman admitted that he had lied about everything, and that the $56 he had brought with him, that he was going to use to join the union, had been borrowed from a friend. Blackman also stated that he had been in town since June, and had "participated in jamming" several times down at Sylvio's with Elmore James and Muddy Waters. While the board agreed to let Blackman join the union, he was denied playing with either artist for six months, and when the board met two weeks later, they wanted to see Elmore and Muddy.[468]

As scheduled, on Thursday, 16 January 1958, Elmore James appeared before the board. He stated:

> ...Raymond Scott was his regular drummer but after he played the first set he got off the stand and told him to use Blackman. Elmore tried to persuade him to finish the week to no avail.
>
> Scott went home. Elmore stated that he was on the spot with a job to play and no drummer. He had no choice but to accept the services of Blackman whom he thought was member of the Federation. It did not dawn upon him that he was not affiliated with any Local until President Gray made an investigation Sunday night, December 29, 1957. He did not permit Blackman to finish the job after President Gray told Blackman to cease playing.[469]

O'Neal, "Big Bill: Opening the Door to the Blues," 4-5; and Bruynoghe, "In Chicago with Big Bill & Friends: Chicago Scrapbook Excerpts," 7-16.

464 Bruynoghe, "In Chicago with Big Bill & Friends: Chicago Scrapbook Excerpts," 7-16; and Bruynoghe, "25 Years Ago," 28.

465 Bruynoghe, "25 Years Ago," 28.

466 Bruynoghe, "25 Years Ago," 28; and Bruynoghe, "In Chicago with Big Bill & Friends: Chicago Scrapbook Excerpts," 12.

467 O'Neal, "Big Bill: Opening the Door to the Blues," 4.

468 Dirks, 41, 44.

469 Ibid., 44-45.

The board fined Elmore $100, to "be held in abeyance for six months pending the future conduct of James as a member of Local 208."[470] The fact that the President had come down to Sylvio's to investigate personally was undoubtedly a sign that the union was watching Elmore carefully. Now, it seems, a clear message was being sent: "Don't screw up." Oddly, Elmore's union file (i.e., his "balance sheet" that was a permanent record of his debits and credits, with membership dues, taxes, and fines all duly recorded), makes no mention whatsoever of the $100 assessment—whether or not it was levied and finally paid, or ultimately rescinded. The only fine that was registered in his account for that year was on 3 January 1958, which was a "tax fine" of $5; Elmore paid it off two weeks later, and finished out the year with no further incidents or union board meetings.[471]

A story Willie Dixon remembered in his autobiography gives us another insight into the man Elmore was. Dixon recalls that sometime in mid-1958, he and Memphis Slim found themselves temporarily fed up with Chicago and decided to go to New York in an effort to secure better work. They were travelling in Dixon's antediluvian Plymouth and had just about twenty-five dollars between the two of them. They got as far as Cleveland before the alternator gave up the ghost. Dixon thought they should set out on foot and try to find blues artist Robert Jr. Lockwood, who had recently relocated there from Chicago. "We were walking down the street when all of the sudden, Slim said 'Man, do you hear some music?'" Dixon recalled, "We started listening and sure enough, we could hear Sonny Boy Williamson just hollerin' like mad. We were about two blocks from where they was playing at this little club...."[472]

> We went down there and there was Sonny Boy, Elmore James and Robert Junior. I was so glad to hear them.... after a while, Slim just walked onstage right up to the piano and moved somebody off it. He started playing and everybody started to hollering and going on.
>
> When the intermission came.... Robert Jr. called up some guy... and this fellow came over there with a battery and generator and fixed it. Elmore was a bragger who always pretended like he was in much better shape than he was and making more money than anybody. He said, "I got plenty of money. What do you guys need?" He gave us twenty dollars apiece, we filled the gas tank up and went on....[473]

As 1958 wore on, James toured with Williamson some more, going to various north and mid-west venues in St. Louis, Detroit and Gary, Indiana. But soon Elmore's thoughts turned towards Mississippi again, and later that year he headed south to Jackson. There he worked as a disk jockey at WRBC and stayed for the rest of the year, with no record contract pending, and into part of 1959, possibly through the summer. But, as he would later tell Bobby Robinson, "I have a daughter that lives here in Chicago and they got hold of my daughter, found out where I was and insisted that I come [back] to Chicago to do a few gigs."[474]

Upon returning to Chicago, James needed a drummer to flush out his band. Robert Plunkett, who had seen Elmore and Sonny Boy play in Belzoni years previously, had moved with his family to Chicago in the late 1940s, when he was a teenager. It wasn't too long after that that Tampa Red would hold Plunkett's interest (just as it had with drummer Odie Payne before him). By hanging around Tampa's gigs, he got the chance to chat with both Tampa and Johnny Jones on a frequent basis, and would sometimes give the car-

470 Ibid., 45.

471 Elmore James' Chicago musicians union file; courtesy of Pat LeBlanc and the Estate of Elmore James; and Dirks, 45.

472 Dixon and Snowden, 116-117.

473 Ibid., 117.

474 Broven, "Bobby's Happy House of Hits, part 2," 12; Leadbitter and Wardlow, 9; Rowe, *Chicago Breakdown*, 204, and Williams, Koester, Chauvard, et al., "The Story of Elmore James," 3.

less Jones a ride to the club. Through the years, Plunkett eventually met Homesick James, who in turn, later introduced Plunkett to Elmore James. After a successful "live" audition in front of the crowd at the Tay May Club (where Elmore was sitting in for a night with Magic Sam), Plunkett became Elmore's drummer in 1959.[475] He soon learned that Elmore had something particular in mind that he expected of his drummers:

> Elmore, he had a style for his drummer. That's what he wanted all the time, just boom-boom-boom. I didn't want to do that. See, I was a more fancier drummer than his.... previous drummer was....
> "Boy," he said, "You got to do it like this. Don't get me wrong but when you put that little beat in there, you make me sound like somebody else. I don't sound like Elmore." I started to think. The fancier drummin' sure would make him sound different and he wanna sound like he always sound. All his records sound alike and that's what he wanted. Finally, I said, "You're right." Then I started to get into it. [476]

Plunkett was part of Elmore's band that included, at this time, J.T. Brown and Homesick James (with Johnny Jones no doubt holding down the fort for three shifts, like he usually did, at some other venue). "We travelled all over the South and West," Plunkett told John Anthony Brisbin. "And people loved him. We played big clubs, barn-like dances. We did a lot of work in Jackson, Mississippi, Iowa too, all around through there and... part of Illinois. We'd go to St. Louis and stay for two months. Big clubs, nice clubs, loaded up with people all night."[477] Sometimes, they would play on a bill that included artists like Little Milton, Albert King, or Muddy Waters.

Plunkett also found that in the band, there was a subtle dynamic between Elmore and Homesick, almost like members of a family. On one occasion, while playing in Goodman, Mississippi at Tillman Branch's club, Homesick upbraided Elmore for getting drunk and disorderly. "He got drunk out there and started hollerin' at me," Plunkett related to Brisbin. "Homesick told him, said, 'It ain't him. It's you. You the one drunk. You fuckin' up.'"[478] Plunkett also noticed this about Elmore, that, "He would listen at Homesick for some reason. I saw him one time try to go off on Homesick. Homesick told him, 'Wait a minute. You know who you're talkin' to?' And he just quiet down. I don't know why but he would listen to Homesick."[479]

Homesick evidently was the member of the band that assumed some mantle of responsibility, not only doing his part to keep the unit together, but also looking out for Plunkett. "Homesick was like my father. I don't know why he did it but he just took it upon himself to look out for me," Plunkett related to Brisbin. "If it don't be for Homesick, I'd probably-a been a big whiskey drinker:"

> Homesick... said, "Don't give that kid no whiskey." Elmore say, "I ain't give him nothin'. Hell, he can get it hisself." He'd say, "Get it if you want it." But Homesick wouldn't let me. He said, "The kid gonna eat breakfast every mornin' and drink a glass of milk." He told Elmore, "If you wanna kill yourself on that whiskey, you go ahead."[480]

"Homesick wouldn't even let me stay with Elmore. He kept me all the time," Plunkett added. "Sometimes he'd leave me and go where Elmore'd be and they would drink some but I didn't get a chance to get the

475 Brisbin, "Robert Plunkett," 42, 45.
476 Ibid., 45.
477 Ibid., 45-46.
478 Ibid., 46.
479 Ibid.
480 Ibid.

whiskey."[481]

One day, after Plunkett had been Elmore's drummer for a while, he got the chance to fulfill a promise he made to his father back in Mississippi. He took Elmore by his parents house and asked his father, "'Daddy, you know this guy?' He looked up, said, 'Nah! Who is that?'" Plunkett told Brisbin. "I said, 'It's Elmore James.' He leaped up, shoutin', 'Boy, you always said you was gonna find Elmore and play with him!'"[482]

As we shall soon find out, Elmore's return to Chicago was fortuitous for more than one reason. His recording activity, during 1959 and 1960, would be a creative zenith for Elmore artistically. But before that would happen, he would be visited by two French blues enthusiasts, who were busy spending their 1959 summer vacation in the most unusual manner. They weren't coming to America to see the Grand Canyon, Niagara Falls, or Disneyland; their itinerary included stops in Harlem, the Detroit ghetto, and the south and west sides of Chicago—a long pilgrimage from the other side of the Atlantic in search of the blues. As the days were getting shorter and the leaves were starting to think about changing color, one of their stops would be on the west side of Chicago to see Elmore James.

"A magical blues universe"

From Thursday, 10 September to Saturday, 10 October 1959, Jacques Demêtre and Marcel Chauvard spent their own money and used their vacation time to come to the United States and see the "land of the blues," as Demêtre puts it. They stopped first in New York, then Detroit, and worked their way over to the Windy City before having to return to New York for their flight home. Toward the end of their Chicago visit, they would get to see Elmore James.[483] Their first attempt to watch him perform was on Madison Street. As they would soon find out, trying to see Elmore James live in person would turn into a strange saga in and of itself. "Later on in the evening," Demêtre and Chauvard continue, "We rode the 'El' with drummer Cassell Burrow. 'Would you like to come with me? I intend to sit in with Elmore James.' Thrilled by the prospect of meeting one of the greatest modern blues guitarists, we followed our guide to Madison Street on the west side of Chicago."[484] "Stick by me," Burrow cautioned. "The club where Elmore plays is at the other end of this block:"

> It was half-past ten when we got there, and as we drew near we could hear the sound of an electric guitar. We went into the Globetrotter's Lounge, a smoky room packed with people who were all listening very attentively to a band of three musicians: a female drummer, a guitarist and a harmonica player.
>
> "Is that Elmore James," we asked Cassell.
>
> "No, Elmore is at another club down the street. This is the Globetrotters with Johnnie Mae [Dunson] on drums, Gene Dennis on harp and Sunnyland Charles on guitar."
>
> Johnnie Mae sang a few blues.... She had a powerful voice which recalled Memphis Minnie.
>
> After a few beers, we left the place. We could hear the music of another blues band next door, a room called the Moonlight Inn. Three people performed on a stage:

---

481 Ibid.

482 Ibid., 42.

483 Demêtre, 23; and Danchin, 16, 18, 20.

484 Jacques Demêtre and Marcel Chauvard, *Land of the Blues.* Levallois-Perret, France: CLARB/Soul Bag, 1994, 134.

> "Elmore James?"
> "Not yet," Cassell answered.
> The band, with Little Sonny Cooper on harmonica and vocals, Eugene Williams on guitar and Hayes Wingfield on drums, was well worth hearing.[485]

"After a few more drinks," Demêtre and Chauvard continue, "we left for the Seeley Club, where we were welcomed by a huge black policeman, on duty outside the door. This time the room was smaller but people were dancing:"

> The band consisted of an electric piano..., guitar and drums.
> "It must be Elmore James this time."
> "No, this is Eddie Taylor!" Cassell answered.
> The band was truly excellent, with Eddie Taylor... on guitar, pianist-singer Elmore "Junior" Williams and drummer Bobby Davis.
> As in the two previous clubs, they all were young musicians from the South who played traditional black popular music with great enthusiasm. Cassell sat in with them and sang a blues in the style of Eddie Vinson....
> The audience danced, completely taken up by the music, and we were fascinated. With all the alcohol we had drunk so far, everything seemed unreal and we were sailing on a magic ocean of electric guitar playing.
> "What about Elmore James?" we still found the strength to ask between two blues songs.
> "Let's go find him," said Cassell.
> At last, we arrived at the right club; we waited outside as Cassell went in to look for him. [486]

"Too late," Burrow told them, "It's two-thirty already. Elmore has finished playing but he'll be out in a minute."[487] Demêtre says that he and Chauvard were anxious to interview and photograph James, and noted that "Elmore James seemed to us... relatively old... and carried his fifty years fully (note: Elmore would have actually been forty-one years old at the time). Without a doubt, the imprint of an agitated and tumultuous life of singing the blues had passed upon his face."[488] The next day, it turned out, Elmore would be playing at Charlie's Lounge. "Come and see me tomorrow, 1811 West Roosevelt Road," he offered.[489]

The next day, Sunnyland Slim drove Demêtre and Chauvard over to Charlie's Lounge. "The place was rougher than any of the ones we had visited so far," they commented.[490] Entering the club, they found James, Homesick James, and drummer Henry "Sneaky Joe" Harris ready to play. Sunnyland Slim got up on stage and sat in on piano:

> All was ready for the grand ritual of pure blues. What do I say? What words can I use to describe this? How to put the music on this paper—bluesy, one-hundred percent.... From the public's side, exclusively black except for the two of us, it was a party. A great festival... Elmore James was, at the instant, a shaman, and had a precise role—to exorcise their misery and to make them forget their troubles.
> It was during this time, while he was singing and playing that exclamations of encouragement came from the public without stop. "Yes, you is right, man!", "Talk to me!" and others "That's the truth!", forming like a choir, sustaining... his presentation....[491]

---

485 Ibid., 134, 136.

486 Ibid., 136, 138.

487 Ibid., 138.

488 Demêtre, 23, and Rowe, *Chicago Breakdown*, 217.

489 Demêtre and Chauvard, 138.

490 Ibid., 140.

"The band sounded rather wild," Demêtre and Chauvard noted, "but their music was very beautiful. Elmore sang just like a preacher, using many gospel effects. He accompanied himself magnificently on his electric guitar, a small metal slide on the little finger of his left hand. His stunning 'Hawaiian' style reminded us of Robert Johnson and Kokomo Arnold. Next to him, Sunnyland Slim played a mean boogie-woogie accompaniment on the piano."[492]

During intermission, Demêtre and Chauvard got a chance to sit with James for a while. "He gave himself readily to our interview," noted Demêtre later, "and confirmed for us that his source of inspiration was Robert Johnson and the 'Gospel' ....But all the time speaking to us... he kept a very closed and almost boorish attitude, which contrasted with his other personality, more expansive and cordial."[493] "Sunnyland Slim left," Demêtre and Chauvard wrote, "but we stayed on to enjoy the music of the Elmore James band. Elmore excelled on medium-fast blues, and he was really swinging."[494] Demêtre comments further:

> On the stage he was very content with himself to sing and to play without saying a word to the public, without ever smiling nor saying hello, without demanding anything....
>
> After the intermission, the music began again, more beautiful, and plunged us into a magical blues universe. Like people who had a spell cast over them, we listened in the shadows....
>
> Our musical euphoria was at it's peak when...a frightening transvestite couple took the stage and began to execute suggestive mimicks and to deliver a true strip-tease.... This seemed to please the other spectators, because *these* two seemed to visibly appreciate this type of exhibition and even began to agitate and vociferate, while we were beginning to feel ill at ease.
>
> The contrast between the beauty of his musical phrases and the horror of the visual spectacle was very marked. We realized more and more that it was urgent to leave. [495]

The owner of the club managed to hail a passing bus for Demêtre and Chauvard. On their way out the door, some of the patrons became argumentative towards the French enthusiasts, shouting at them "What'd you come to do at our place—photograph our blues singers?"[496] As the bus pulled away from the club and the west side, Demêtre and Chauvard probably had no idea that the occasion of their visit was the last time Elmore James would ever be interviewed by blues researchers. Demêtre and Chauvard later used their findings to help compile the earliest attempts at Elmore's biography.

Just a couple weeks later, yet another fan of the old Broomduster would make a pilgrimage—inadvertently, this time—to see Elmore James. It wasn't a blues enthusiast from overseas. He was the owner of a record label in New York City, and he had been looking for Elmore for such a long time, that he didn't even know he was still looking for him.[497]

---

491 Demêtre, 23-24.

492 Demêtre and Chauvard, 140.

493 Demêtre, 24.

494 Demêtre and Chauvard, 140.

495 Demêtre, 24.

496 Ibid.

497 Note: Interestingly, Demêtre and Chauvard also met with Bobby Robinson during their month-long stay in the United States. Reading their text, however, it becomes clear that they saw Bobby Robinson during the very first part of their trip, before they had had the chance to go to Chicago and see Elmore James. Demêtre and Chauvard, 32.

The Sky Is Crying

Robinson's now legendary Windy City encounter with Elmore James in early November 1959 was a bona fide stroke of fortuitous luck and pure happenstance, seemingly arranged by the will and force of nature. Robinson was in Chicago for a promotional visit and was not actively searching for James any longer, although he had tried to locate him in Mississippi a few years previously. As the 1950s were coming to a close, Elmore James was probably about the last thing on Bobby Robinson's mind.[498]

Robinson was no stranger to the music business, having already developed and operated such labels as Robin, Red Robin, Whirlin Disc, Fury, and now Fire. They had all had their start with Robinson and in particular grew out of the day-to-day operations of his Harlem record store, which, in turn, had been partly bankrolled with $14,000 Robinson had won in the Irish Sweepstakes. After World War II, he had been looking for a business to open, and after trying his luck with a shoeshine parlor, eventually hit upon the idea of opening a record shop. "Since I liked music I thought it would be a good idea to open a record store," the pragmatic Robinson recalled.[499] He also was fortunate in that he possessed a truly *primo* location. "...Strategically located between the Apollo Theater and Frank's, one of the large Harlem restaurants, ...this meant that every artist who appeared at the Apollo had to pass the store on their way to eat," Valerie Wilmer noted in a 1978 article on Robinson. "As time went by, they started to stop in the store to check on their record sales and find out what was going on. The word soon spread: 'Whenever you're in New York, stop in and see Bobby....'"[500] "In a short while things started to jump, and after about a year... everyone started to come to me for advice," Robinson remembered:

> The A&R men would come from Decca and [the Bihari] guys would come in from the west coast, and they would stop in to see me... and get advice. The Mesner fellows from Los Angeles and the Chess Brothers from Chicago were in here about once a month, and everybody started coming in.
>
> I was [selling a lot of records for them] and that's what drew their attention. Somehow I got to be an authority, I don't know how. [501]

Robinson recalls that many people would stop by with demos, asking him to listen critically and suggest additions to the arrangements, or to judge the quality of their product before it was released. "Ahmet Ertegun from Atlantic would come and I'd work with them night after night. It was when they were just getting started, 1948," Robinson remembered. "So it got to the point where so many people came in to see me during the course of the week that it took up a lot of my time. I thought, well, if I'm such an authority on records I'll go into the business myself. I knew nothing about it, not the first thing."[502]

Robinson started his first label in November 1951, and went on to record some of the finest rhythm & blues and vocal group talent in the 1950s. Robinson evidently had a natural talent for producing, and after eight years in the record business he had numerous hits and several gold records to his credit. "Bobby Robinson was a great producer," recalled Sam Myers. "First he'd go in the control room talking to the

---

498 Turco, "Interview: Bobby Robinson. [Part 2]," 11; Turco, "Interview: Bobby Robinson. [Part 3]," 4; and Bobby Robinson, "Comments from Bobby Robinson." In the notes to Elmore James, *King of the Slide Guitar.* Capricorn CD 42006-2, 1992.

499 Turco, Salzano, and Turco, 5; Turco, "Interview: Bobby Robinson. [Part 2]," 11; Gart, *The American Record Label Directory,* 85, 90, 179, 187, 242; and Pete Welding, "An Interview with Skip Layne." *Blues Unlimited* 92 (June 1972): 6.

500 Wilmer, 47.

501 Turco, Salzano, and Turco, 5.

502 Ibid.

engineer, then he'd come out and work with the band. He has an amazing memory. I've seen Bobby listen through a lot of tapes—maybe 500 or 600 songs, all by different people. One song will lock into his mind... and he'll remember that song even after hundreds of others have gone by." Myers adds, "Also, regardless of what Bobby wanted as a producer, he always tried to make us feel comfortable."[503]

During the first week of November 1959, Robinson was in Chicago promoting "Fannie Mae," his ninth release on Fire Records, a label he had started earlier that fall in New York City. Robinson had been to see Big Bill Hill to plug the issue, and after parting company with the genial Hill, Robinson went out around to the Windy City nightclubs looking for talent, and whatever else interesting he could find in the way of music.

> So we were cruising down the street there on the west side, and I'm looking, I told the guy to drive slow because every time I see a little club I want to see if there's any name.... So we were going down and on the right side there was a big white cardboard sign like a black eyebrow pencil, black marker chalked in... 'Elmore James here tonight...' So I said, "Hold it, stop the car!" [504]

Robinson entered the packed club not knowing what Elmore James looked like, never having seen a picture of him. Since the band was on intermission, Robinson couldn't be sure which one was James. "A guy was sitting in the corner with a mike tied onto the stand with a silk stocking. I was sitting at the bar wondering if it was Elmore James. When he started to play the guitar I knew it was him."[505] After the set was over, Robinson introduced himself, and later J.T. Brown stopped by, bringing his tenor sax with him to sit in with the group. Robinson offered to buy drinks for the musicians, and talked with James into the night. Elmore told him, "Well, I had a heart attack [a couple] years ago, I just quit, I been down in Mississippi fishing and rabbit hunting and whatnot, down on the farm...." Robinson asked James the magical question, "What are you doing recording-wise?" To which Elmore answered "No, nothing."[506]

Robinson didn't waste any time arranging a rehearsal and a recording session. In J.T. Brown's apartment building, where Elmore was staying, there was a large room and a piano, which served nicely for a rehearsal the next afternoon. Robinson was anxious to coax some new material out of James for a record: "I said, 'Elmore, to do the things you did before is fine, I'd like to do those also but I would like to come up with something new for the first record.' I said, 'Have you got any kind of new song?', he said, 'No, I haven't been doing anything,'" Robinson recalled. They sat down together to see what they could come up with, and Robinson noted "'Boy, it sure is raining out there,' [and James] said, 'Yeah, it looks as if the sky is crying.'"[507] Robinson liked the metaphor, and he and James worked it into a song, having the group rehearse it about a dozen times before Robinson felt it was in a suitable condition. Elmore also rehearsed a couple of older tunes with the group, which Robinson said was no problem for the group of veteran Broomdusters. Satisfied, Robinson arranged for studio time later that evening at an undisclosed downtown location.[508]

Present for the session, which probably occurred on either Tuesday, 3 November, or Wednesday, 4 November 1959, were Elmore on guitar and vocals, Homesick James on bass guitar, Johnny Jones on piano, J.T. Brown on tenor saxophone, Odie Payne on drums, and possibly Boyd Atkins playing the second tenor

503 Myers, "Comments from Sam Myers;" Turco, Salzano, and Turco, 5; and "Bobby's Top Sellers," 11.

504 Broven, "Bobby's Happy House of Hits, part 2," 12; and Turco, "Interview: Bobby Robinson. [Part 3]," 4.

505 Turco, "Interview: Bobby Robinson. [Part 3]," 4.

506 Broven, "Bobby's Happy House of Hits, part 2," 12.

507 Ibid.

508 Ibid.; and Turco, "Interview: Bobby Robinson. [Part 3]," 4.

saxophone. The first item recorded was a twangy, finger-snapping instrumental with a catchy tune, "Bobby's Rock." Another solid Broomdusting effort, it belied the fact that Elmore, Homesick, Johnny, J.T., and Odie hadn't been together in a recording studio for over two years. Elmore said that he had been performing the tune with the band, telling Robinson, "[it] gets a good reaction from the audience. They like to dance off it," adding that "It doesn't have any name but, if you like it, I'm going to call it 'Bobby's Rock.'"[509] It was a theme that would later be revived, quite effectively, by guitarists Earl Hooker, Freddy King, and John Littlejohn, among others. Hooker would quote from it during Ricky Allen's 1961 Age waxing of "You'd Better Be Sure," King for "King-A-Ling," recorded in September 1963 for the Federal imprint, and Littlejohn, most prominently, during his Arhoolie sessions in November 1968 (discussed later in the text).[510]

Next on the roster was the emotive dirge "The Sky Is Crying" (appropriately described by critic Dave Marsh as "spiritually ravaged") that would be the cornerstone of Elmore's popularity in the early 1960s:

> The sky is cryin', look at the tears roll down the street,
> The sky is cryin', look at the tears roll down the street,
> I'm wadin' in tears lookin' for my baby, and I wonder where can she be?
>
> I've got a bad feeling, my baby, my baby don't love me no mo',
> I've got a bad feeling, my baby don't love me no mo',
> Now the sky's been cryin', the tears rollin' down my door. [511]

As was the case with Elmore's most memorable recorded moments before this, "The Sky Is Crying" contained an enigmatic extra element that seemed to make the song greater than merely the sum of its parts. Maybe it was James' confidence, boosted by the familiarity of the Broomdusters, or as Robinson called them, Elmore's "home boys." Maybe it was a certain finesse that Robinson, now an experienced producer, knew how to draw out of James. Or maybe it was Elmore's lyrical slide guitar figures he used to punctuate the vocals, which were embellished with ever so slight dramatic pauses and ornamental touches of melisma. Perhaps it was an enigmatic guitar amplifier, possibly one that Elmore had outfitted in a unique way that gave him a special, transcendental guitar tone.[512] Possibly it could also have just been something more tangible, such as a recording studio technique. Present-day slide guitarist Ry Cooder reserved some of his highest praise for this session, saying about Elmore's guitar playing:

> His beautiful [slide guitar] sound is the greatest thing in the world, but only on the Chicago sides for Fire.... Even the Fire & Enjoy sides from New Orleans and New York sound [different]. He had something else he used on those. I don't think it was his [acoustic] Kay with a pickup, because there's no way a Kay with a pickup can sound like those Chicago sides.... It cannot. [513]

---

509 Robinson, "Comments from Bobby Robinson;" Elmore James, "Bobby's Rock." Fire 1011, 1959; and Franz, 20.
Note: For more information about the determination of a recording date for this session, please see "Introduction to the 2003 Edition" in Appendix Two, "Discography."

510 Ricky Allen, "You'd Better Be Sure." Age 29102, 1961; Freddy King, "King-A-Ling." Federal 12515, 1964; John Littlejohn, "Slidin' Home." From the album John Littlejohn, *John Littlejohn's Chicago Blues Stars.* Arhoolie LP 1043, 1969; and Leadbitter and Slaven, *Blues Records 1943-1970,* 30, 788.
Note: Freddy King also quoted the "Bobby's Rock" theme in his "Bossa Nova Blues," recorded November 1962. It was released by King as an LP-only track (Freddy King, "Bossa Nova Blues." From the album Freddy King, *Bossa Nova & Blues.* King LP 821, 1963; and Leadbitter and Slaven, *Blues Records 1943-1970,* 787).

511 Elmore James, "The Sky Is Crying." Fire 1016, 1960; and Dave Marsh with John Swenson, eds., *The Rolling Stone Record Guide.* New York: Random House, 1979, 437.

512 Obrecht, "The Ballad of Elmore & Homesick James," 72; and Broven, "Bobby's Happy House of Hits, part 2," 12.

513 Jas Obrecht, "Listening with Ry." *Guitar Player* (November 1992): 43.

According to Homesick James, the amplifier was a Gibson, "A big one. A GA-53, I think it was.... It's about two-and-a-half feet high, and could fit one ten and one twelve [inch] speaker in the cabinet." However, Homesick James feels the key to the mystery sound on "The Sky Is Crying" was not the guitar amplifier, and suggests, "That was a studio sound that people try to figure out. They'll never get that. The people [at the studio] knew how to operate that stereo sound into it. That's what that is. That's an echo sound."[514]

After "The Sky Is Crying," Robinson recorded three more numbers with James. "Dust My Broom" and "Held My Baby Last Night" were re-recordings of Elmore's earlier Trumpet and Meteor sides respectively, and lacked the verve that made "The Sky Is Crying" such an exceptional effort. Last was "Baby Please Set a Date," a tune which Homesick James claims to have authored but which had really originated a decade and a half earlier with Memphis Minnie, who recorded the earliest known version for Columbia Records. J.B. Lenoir would revive this theme six years later in his song "Louise," which he recorded for J.O.B. in 1951. But Bobby Robinson was never very happy with the version Elmore James recorded that day. "I tried to get him to sing it... and he was reading the words and it didn't come off. I had always had plans to go back and do it over."[515]

After the session, however, a very curious thing happened. Although Robinson was later to claim that "The Sky Is Crying" and "Bobby's Rock" were paired together for Elmore's first Fire release, that's not the way it actually happened.[516] "Bobby's Rock" was indeed released first—in late December, 1959—but for the flip side Robinson completely bypassed "The Sky Is Crying" and shelved it for another four months. Instead, he took a copy of Elmore's 1953 recording "Make My Dreams Come True," which Robinson discreetly dubbed off an old copy of Flair 1031, and used it as the underside of Fire 1011. Engineer Walter Devenne knows Robinson personally and has worked with much of Robinson's material in creating reissue packages. His theory is that Robinson initially must not have been very happy with the results of the Chicago session. In all fairness, notes Devenne, Robinson was careful to credit the publisher and author just exactly as they had appeared on the original Flair release. Perhaps the Bihari brothers owed Robinson a favor for all that "free advice" he had so generously shared all those years ago in his Harlem record shop. Credence is lent to Devenne's theory about Robinson's unhappiness, however, when one notes that Robinson didn't touch the re-recording of "Dust My Broom" for over five years, until it was slated for inclusion in a 1965 LP. Similarly, "Baby Please Set a Date" wasn't issued until 1967. It was a curious maneuver though—especially when one considers that just a few short months ago, Robinson was having monumental legal troubles over at Fury Records with Wilbert Harrison's "Kansas City" debacle.[517] Another, perhaps more simpler explanation might also be that Robinson just didn't have the time to devote his full attention on Elmore James—and what he perceived would be another "big hit"—right at that particular moment. What *was* taking up most of Robinson's free time that particular winter and spring of 1960 was Buster Brown's "Fannie Mae," an enormous million-selling-plus number one R&B hit that found a home on those charts for a full half-year; incredibly (for what was essentially a straight-ahead down-home blues record, that is), it was strong enough to become a Top 40 hit on the pop charts as well.[518] If this

514 Obrecht, "The Ballad of Elmore & Homesick James," 82.

515 Turco, "Interview: Bobby Robinson. [Part 3]," 11; Elmore James, "Dust My Broom." From the album Elmore James, *The Sky Is Crying.* Sphere Sound LP 7002, 1965; Elmore James, "Held My Baby Last Night." Fire 1016, 1960; Obrecht, "The Ballad of Elmore & Homesick James," 80; Garon and Garon, 48, 278, 292; Memphis Minnie, "Please Set a Date." Columbia 36895, 1945; J.B. Lenoir, "Louise." J.O.B. 1102, 1954; Leadbitter, Fancourt, and Pelletier, 38; and Franz, 20.

516 Robinson, "Comments from Bobby Robinson;" and Franz, 32.

517 Walter Devenne, telephone interview, 16 June 1992; Turco, Salzano, and Turco, 5; Turco, "Interview: Bobby Robinson. [Part 2]," 8,10; and Franz, 3, 13, 20, 32, 39.

518 Whitburn, 57; "Bobby's Top Sellers," 11; and Buster Brown, "Fannie Mae." Fire 1008, 1959.

latter scenario more correctly reflects the real course of events, however, one must wonder why Robinson has not been a bit more forthcoming about it over the years.

When released in March 1960, "The Sky Is Crying" brought Elmore James his first rhythm & blues chart action in seven years. It eventually peaked at number fifteen and stayed on the charts a solid five weeks. "[It] was an instant blues hit," recalled Robinson in 1982. "Right away it started to hit Chicago and it spread to Cleveland and it was the type of thing that went into markets that were previously not too big a blues market. But, every market it went in, it started to take off. Even in New York the record sold very good."[519] Possibly in exchange for the favor of having a hit record, Elmore helped Robinson scout out almost a dozen new blues artists in the Windy City. Of those who auditioned, only Willie "Chuck" Bradford and guitarist Mighty Joe Young would eventually have singles released on Robinson's Fire imprint.[520]

With an R&B hit record under his belt—his first in seven years—Elmore was off to a smashing start for the new year and the new decade. 1960, it seemed, might very well turn out to be Elmore James' year.

"That ain't Pinetop Perkins"

In December 1959, George Adins would add his name to the short list of blues devotees lucky enough to see Elmore James in his prime. "Elmore James will always remain the most exciting and dramatic blues singer and guitarist that I've ever had a chance to see perform in the flesh," remembered Adins.[521] It was Muddy Waters who had the pleasure of taking the Belgian blues aficionado over to Thelma's Lounge right around the time "Bobby's Rock" had been released. "On our way we listened to him on the radio as Big Bill Hill... was broadcasting direct from that place. I was burning to see Elmore James and before we even pushed open the door of the club, we could hear Elmore's violent guitar sound:"[522]

> Although the place was overcrowded, we managed to find a seat close to the bandstand and the blues came falling down on me as it had never done before. Watching Elmore sing and play, backed by a solid bluesband (Homesick James, J.T. Brown, Boyd Atkins and Sam Cassell) made me feel real fine. Wearing thick glasses, Elmore's face always had an expressive and dramatic look, especially when he was real gone on the slow blues. Singing with a strong and rough voice, he really didn't need a mike. On such slow blues as "I'm Worried" – "Make My Dreams Come True" – "It Hurts Me," his voice reached a climax and created a tension that was unmistakingly the down and out blues. Notwithstanding that raw voice, Elmore sang his blues with a particular feeling, an emotion and depth that showed his country background. His singing was... fed, reinforced by his own guitar accompaniment which was as rough, violent and expressive as was his voice. Using the bottleneck technique most of the time, Elmore really let his guitar sound as I had never heard a guitar sound before. You just couldn't sit still! You had to move.... [523]

Adins also described how Elmore would work with the crowd, noting at a west side Chicago performance at the Alex Club that, "...he always played for a dance audience and he made the people jump. 'Bobby's Rock' was at that time one of the favorite numbers with the crowd and Elmore used to play [it] for fifteen

519 Pomposello, 10; Whitburn, 216; and Franz, 32.

520 Shurman, 5; and Leadbitter and Slaven, *Blues Records 1943-1970*, 141.

521 Bromberg, notes to *The Legend of Elmore James.*

522 Ibid.

523 Ibid.

minutes and more. You just couldn't stand that hysteric sound coming down on you. The place was rocking, swinging!"[524]

As with Bruynoghe, and Demêtre and Chauvard before him, Adins found Elmore somewhat subdued. "I seldom saw Elmore smile on stage and as soon as he finished his set, he went behind the bar to get his liquor. Elmore really drank a lot, but never did his music suffer from it," he observed. "Elmore was no big talker and seemed to be rather withdrawn.... I believe something was worrying him all the time. When he was not playing he was drinking and vice versa."[525]

Robert Plunkett, Elmore's drummer, would concur with the foreign visitors' observations, and remembers vividly his increasingly sour mood around this time. "He drank all the time, anytime he could get it. He didn't want no food or no woman," he recalled. "He wanted some corn whiskey or scotch whiskey."[526] Playing in a club in St. Louis one night, Plunkett recollects that he and the other band members had been eyeing the attractive bartender:

> We was all talkin' about her, lookin' at her. So I looked over there and she called for me.... I went to the bar. She says, "Ask Elmore, can I go to the hotel with him tonight?" That broke my heart 'cause I wanted her to go with me. I go over to Elmore and I says, "Elmore, see that pretty lady behind the bar?" He squint. "Yeah, I see her." I said, "She wants to go to the hotel with you tonight." He say, "You tell that bitch she can send me a half a pint of scotch and she go to the hotel with you!" ...I said, "I can't tell her that." But I told her: "He say you can't go to the hotel with him but you can send him a half pint of scotch." She bought him a fifth but [to no avail].... [527]

"All the womens looked like they was crazy about Elmore," added Plunkett, "but he was the type of guy didn't give a damn about no woman. He'd say, 'Gimme some whiskey. You can have all the womens you want.'"[528]

It wasn't always that way, however. Plunkett remembers one incident when they were travelling, while not particularly funny at the time for Plunkett, got a big laugh out of Elmore. The police had evidently been looking for pianist Pinetop Perkins, and had been incorrectly tipped off that he played with Elmore's band:

> So [the police] come up in the hotel, man, and snatch me out of the bed, throw me on the floor, lockin' my hands behind me in handcuffs. Elmore run in: *"What's wrong! What's goin' on?"* Police say, "We got him now. We been lookin' for him for a long time." Elmore say, "Looking for *who*?" Said, "Pinetop Perkins." And he just bust out with the laughin'. I said, "Tell 'em! Tell 'em!" And they all laughin' now! They just standin' there laughin' and after awhile, he said, "That ain't Pinetop Perkins. That's Robert Plunkett." Then they get me up and brush me off. "So sorry, Mr. Plunkett." [529]

On Tuesday, 12 January 1960, Elmore James went down to the Local 208 union office, where he paid a variety of fees and taxes, in order to reinstate his union membership and pay back dues he still owed for 1958 and 1959. One month later, he dutifully came back and paid the remainder of the taxes he owed, plus made the first installment of that year's membership dues.[530] A week afterwards, on Thursday, 18 February

524 Ibid.

525 Ibid.

526 Brisbin, "Robert Plunkett," 46.

527 Ibid.

528 Ibid.

529 Ibid., 47.

530 Elmore James' Chicago musicians union file; courtesy of Pat LeBlanc and the Estate of Elmore James.

1960, Elmore appeared before the union's board of directors. This time, it was an infraction involving a minor dispute over an engagement he was to play in Gary, Indiana. During the board's regular biweekly meeting, Elmore told them that he had been called for the job by Jump Jackson, who, prior to the night of the show, had apparently arranged for him to receive an advance deposit of $80. Come that evening's performance, however, the band was not paid; out of the $350 they were supposed to receive, only Elmore had seen any money, and he told the board that he had already spent the $80 deposit money. He also told them that currently, his regular gig was at Mel's Hideaway Lounge, where he was making $90 a week. Upon discussion, the board informed Elmore that he was amiss in spending the deposit money (it was, no doubt, supposed to be deposited with the union first), and decided to fine Elmore one week's pay, of which $39 would go to Elmore's band members for the Gary performance, $48.60 would be eaten up in taxes, and the remainder, $2.40, would be returned to him.[531] It was the last time the Local 208's board of directors would show any kindness towards James.

The Sun Is Shining

Just as "The Sky Is Crying" was poised to make its ascent up the charts, Elmore, with the usual predictability, jumped ship and went to record for another label. Chess Records had once again managed to secure a recording date with James and may have even offered a contract. A session was arranged sometime in early April 1960, which would be the last time the Broomdusters would gather together in a studio setting.[532]

Present for the final Broomdusting were J.T. Brown on tenor sax, Johnny Jones on piano, Homesick James on second guitar, and Fred Below on drums. Elmore was in fine form for the session—still riding high from the previous November's successful studio venture—and was well in control of his voice and guitar. The first song recorded was a jumping "Dust My Broom" styled number, "I Can't Hold Out," that featured Dixon's trademark stop-time arrangement in each verse, hot slide guitar that sizzled like an arc welder's torch, and animated vocal flourishes from Elmore.[533] Willie Dixon had evidently written it a couple of years earlier while on tour (although Elmore would be listed as writer on the first release). "I was talking to [wife] Marie on the telephone, that's the reason I made that song," Dixon recalled, adding that Elmore had learned the song from him at Sylvio's, where Dixon used to play with the Broomdusters occasionally.[534] Guitar Crusher (a.k.a. Sidney Selby) was among the first, in 1962, to record a loosely based, chaotic cover version of this popular James standard, although it wouldn't be released until 1968.[535]

The next item recorded was "The Sun Is Shining," a powerful cousin of "The Sky Is Crying," coupled with a lyrical theme borrowed from a 1950 Peppermint Harris recording, "Raining in My Heart." It had been a number four R&B hit for the Texas guitarist in February 1950, and in retrospect, may have been responsible for planting the seed from which "The Sky Is Crying" later grew. Perforated with thick, stinging slide licks, "The Sun Is Shining" was a showcase for Elmore's dynamic vocals and his absorbing

531 Dirks, 45.

532 Obrecht, "The Ballad of Elmore & Homesick James," 80; and Franz, 21.

533 Elmore James, "I Can't Hold Out." Chess 1756, 1960; and Franz, 21. Note: It has also been offered that Henry "Sneaky Joe" Harris played drums on this session.

534 Dixon and Snowden, 115-116; and Franz, 21, 42.

535 Keith Tillman, "Current Singles." *Blues Unlimited 55* (July 1968): 22; Leadbitter and Slaven, *Blues Records 1943-1970,* 501; and Guitar Crusher, "I've Got to Know." T & S 102, 1968.

ability with preaching-style slow blues numbers.[536] Mike Rowe's comments here are pertinent: "Elmore's music had moved closer to that of the west side men. It was completely modern and up-to-the-minute blues but it also avoided all the pitfalls of the new school. With... Elmore's slide instead of the already overworked [B.B.] King-styled guitar, and untouched by rock 'n' roll or ballad influences, his music easily straddled the two styles."[537]

"I Can't Hold Out" and "The Sun Is Shining" made up the sides of one steamy blues 45 when it came back from the pressing plant in mid-to-late May, 1960. The quick processing time from recording date to production seems to indicate that Chess was trying to rush the release in order to ride the coattails of "The Sky Is Crying," which had already been released and would debut on the national rhythm & blues charts on Monday, 2 May 1960. Chess' hopes for the Elmore release are corroborated by the discovery that three different label configurations were printed, implying that the pressing went into several editions or had occurred in divergent locations. Ray Topping gave an explanation for this, noting that in those days, "When you've got a hit on your hands from coast to coast there's no way you're going to press in one place and try and ship all round the States. You allocate different pressing plants—one in the East Coast, one in the center and one in the West Coast if you're trying for a national hit...."[538] Apparently Chess was, but they wouldn't match Robinson's success with "The Sky Is Crying."

Chess also recorded two other titles at this session with James, the first being "Stormy Monday Blues," a muscular reading of T-Bone Walker's 1948 number five rhythm & blues hit (originally, "Stormy Monday Blues" had been a 1942 number one R&B hit recorded by Earl Hines and his Orchestra, featuring Billy Eckstine on vocals; it is possible that this was where Walker received a nugget of inspiration for his version). John Litweiler would later call Elmore's version of this classic blues number "the definitive performance of this too-often-performed standard."[539] The last side of the day was "Madison Blues," possibly inspired by one of the lesser dance crazes of the previous year called "The Madison." It was an energetic rocker with plenty of room for instrumental pyrotechnics, with Brown and one other saxophone player riffing buoyantly through the introduction, and later, James playing a full chordal stepped glissando descending down the neck of the guitar. The joyousness pervading the music brings to mind energetic stage acts such as James Brown, and one can almost imagine the Broomdusters in the studio dancing and swaying rhythmically to the beat.[540]

Even though it was the last time James, Brown, and Jones ever recorded together, the musicality between them was just as solid as it had been at their first session over seven years ago. Not only that, but

536 Peppermint Harris [r.n.: Harrison Nelson], "Raining in My Heart." Sittin' In With 543, 1950; Elmore James, "The Sun Is Shining." Chess 1756, 1960; Whitburn, 182; and Franz, 21.

Note: Two months after Peppermint Harris' version was a chart hit, Big Joe Turner recorded a song, "The Sun Is Shining," for Bayou (an Imperial subsidiary) that used some of the same lyrical themes. It was released in 1953 (Big Joe Turner, "The Sun Is Shining." Bayou 015, 1953). Although Jimmy Reed recorded a song for the Vee Jay label in 1957 entitled "The Sun Is Shining," it has nothing in common with this recording by Elmore James (See: Jimmy Reed, "The Sun Is Shining." Vee Jay 248, 1957). Likewise, this is the case for L.C. Green's similarly titled "When the Sun Is Shining," released on the Dot label in 1952.

537 Rowe, *Chicago Breakdown,* 204.

538 Huggins, 18; Whitburn, 216; Franz, 32; and Warren Cook, "Disc Dating." *Record Exchanger* 9 (March 1972): 23.

539 John Litweiler, "Elmore James/John Brim." *Down Beat* 36 (6 February 1969): 25; Elmore James, "Stormy Monday Blues." From the album Elmore James and John Brim, *Tough.* Blue Horizon LP 7-63204, 1968; T-Bone Walker, "Call it Stormy Monday." Black & White 122, 1947; Earl Hines and his Orchestra, "Stormy Monday Blues." Bluebird B11567, 1942; and Whitburn, 191, 429. Note: Among the first people to record a cover version of Walker's tune was Grant "Mr. Blues" Jones, for United in October 1952. At one time, Jones had recorded with J.T. Brown for the Harlem label, in 1950. See Paikos, 269; and Leadbitter and Slaven, *Blues Records 1943-1970,* 177, 738.

540 Elmore James, "Madison Blues." From the album Elmore James and John Brim, *Tough.* Blue Horizon LP 7-63204, 1968; and Franz, 21.

they had all progressed and grown together musically since then, so that the later recordings witnessed a team of musicians who by now where extremely comfortable with each other and knew what to anticipate in a studio setting. The Broomdusters had witnessed the issue of thirty-two titles spanning twenty-one singles and twelve additional items not released at the time (not including numerous alternate takes of some titles). The fact that the vast majority of the releases maintained an extraordinarily high level of artistry is simply attributable to what a brilliant match James, Jones, Brown (and Payne, too) were for each other on stage and in the studio. It truly was a natural composite of ability and sound, each member adding his special musical talent and sense of rhythm to the whole. By the time of their last session, Jones and Brown intimately understood and could subtly anticipate Elmore's movement and direction with the guitar, providing an unfailing backup not only to his work with the instrument but to his singing as well. They also seemed to understand, when it all was boiled down, that Elmores' intent was to move and to rock his audience. As Robert Palmer summarized, "...Elmore's [early] sides with Johnny Jones, along with the best fifties discs by Muddy [Waters], [Howlin'] Wolf, Sonny Boy [Williamson], Little Walter [Jacobs], Jimmy Rogers, Robert Nighthawk, and perhaps a few others, constitute the recorded pinnacle of Chicago blues."[541]

With "Madison Blues" the Broomdusters took leave of the stage, their task seemingly finished. Just a few days later, on Saturday, 16 April 1960, James was scheduled to give a live performance for one Willie B. Dodson at a location described only as a "Banking Hall." When Elmore failed to appear this time, he had apparently pissed off the wrong person, and the board wouldn't be interested in hearing any excuses. In short order, the union's board of directors would bring an abrupt and permanent end to Elmore's musical career in Chicago. The era of Elmore James and the Broomdusters was over.[542]

Something Inside of Me

On Thursday, 21 April 1960, the Local 208 board of directors convened their regularly scheduled meeting. Elmore James was brought in to explain why he had failed to appear for a performance the previous Saturday, 16 April. Additionally, the board wanted to know why it was that he had signed a contract for this performance two months ago, but had not filed the contract or the $35 deposit with the union:

> Elmore James stated that late Friday night his wife came to the club and told him that he had received a telegram notifying him of the death of one of his relatives. After the engagement he flew to New Orleans, attended the funeral Saturday, and returned to the club about 2:30 or 3:00 Sunday morning. He explained that he had contracted Sonny Boy Williamson to substitute for him.
>
> Elmore James was also asked why he negotiated with a person from a recording company in New York that did not have a license issued by the Federation....
>
> The Board explained to Elmore James that they were thoroughly disgusted with the manner in which he conducted his business, and that on too many occasions he had signed contracts and accepted deposits and then failed to appear on these engagements. Such actions on his part only gave the Local a bad reputation, and they advised that this conduct could not be condoned any further.[543]

541 Palmer, 215; Pearson, 171; and Franz, 9-11, 13-14, et al.

542 Elmore James' Chicago musicians union file; courtesy of Pat LeBlanc and the Estate of Elmore James; and Dirks, 45.

The board fined Elmore a total of $300—$100 for not making the deposit and filing the contract with his Local, $100 for not showing up at his Saturday engagement, and $100 for "negotiating with a record company that was not licensed by the American Federation of Musicians" (perhaps Bobby Robinson, unlike Joe Bihari or Leonard Chess evidently, may not have been aware of the proper palms that needed greasing in order to keep the union out of one's business?). On further motion, the board decided to "erase" (i.e., suspend) James for a period of one year, after which he was to come before the board and report his "musical activity" of the previous year. If they chose to reinstate him, he would not be allowed to play music in Chicago for an additional period of six months.[544]

In retrospect, the punishment seems harsh and severe, and the fact that a such small group of people could wield that much power over a person's musical and artistic career seems simply asinine by today's standards. It does seem plausible to consider that the Local 208 union, as a political entity that existed in the Windy City during the regime of the infamous Mayor Richard J. Daley, might be subject to the machinations—as were so many others—of his political whims and fancies. In the end, then, was Elmore just a bit player who got ground up in the wheels of that machine? Perhaps there's a much simpler explanation, too. Whatever the case may have been, it's hard to know for certain; what we do know is that Elmore—who had been instructed by the board to file the $35 deposit the following afternoon by one o'clock—did not. Instead, he came down to the union office exactly one week later and paid the two dollars in taxes he owed over the "Banking Hall" fiasco. The board waited one month before the $300 fine was officially registered as a debit against Elmore's union account. It would lay untouched—and unpaid—for some time to come.[545]

With the Chess date behind him and the union putting a stop to his musical activities in Chicago, James was back with Bobby Robinson again for a May 1960 session (which was probably held sometime during the week of 23 May). Homesick James remembered that their 1960 Ford Catalina was giving them problems in that blues-musicians-with-car-trouble-capital, Cleveland, Ohio. "We had problems with our station wagon one time... They repossessed it; they came and got it. Yeah. We got stranded."[546] Elmore had evidently gotten behind in his share of the payments, which he was splitting with Homesick James. "It was... a nice station wagon," Homesick James lamented. "It had 'Broomdusters' on the side of it."[547] Sam Myers picks up the rest of the story, who learned the details from pianist Big Moose Walker:

> And Moose said that they were all sitting up at this club playing. Whoever it was flew two guys from Chicago to where they were playing. And they [the repo men] did a nice thing. Sit... [the band's] stuff—clothing, luggage, and all on the inside of the club, and explained... what was going on. And they got the station wagon and went on.
>
> So when the band got tired, and they were getting ready to go on to the next gig, and went out, and there wasn't nothing but a empty space. Station wagon gone! (laughs) And Moose told Elmore about it. He said, "Man, you should report the thing stole!" So Elmore told 'em, "You run your mouth, but I'll run my business." And then everyone knew what was going on, (laughs) 'cause... [Elmore] wasn't raising no sand about it. [548]

---

543 Dirks, 45.

544 Ibid.

545 Elmore James' Chicago musicians union file; courtesy of Pat LeBlanc and the Estate of Elmore James.

546 Obrecht, "The Ballad of Elmore & Homesick James," 80; and Franz, 22.
Note: For more information about the determination of a recording date for this session, please see "Introduction to the 2003 Edition" in Appendix Two, "Discography."

547 Obrecht, "The Ballad of Elmore & Homesick James," 80.

548 O'Neal and Lee, 11.

In want of a mode of transportation, Elmore announced, "'I'm gonna call Bobby Robinson, and I'll see can we get a session.' Bobby agreed with it," Homesick told Jas Obrecht, "and we flew in from Cleveland, Ohio to New York, and that's where we recorded that 'Rollin and Tumblin' and [others]."[549] As was sometimes the case with Elmore, Big Moose was probably left to find his own way back to Chicago.

Possibly before even going into the studio, Robinson first and foremost had one important piece of business to take to care of, which was scheduled for Monday, 23 May 1960. Now that "The Sky Is Crying" was an R&B hit and receiving a lot of airplay, Elmore James would be properly registered with BMI (Broadcast Music, Inc.), for the purpose of collecting royalties for James, the author, and Fire Music (Robinson's publishing company) alike. The standard BMI contract that Elmore signed shows that four songs were registered—"Bobby's Rock," "Making My Dream Come True [*sic*]," "The Sky Is Crying," and "I Held My Baby Last Night." Elmore James was given one hundred percent writer credit for each song, with the publisher being listed as Fire Music for all four tunes (only slightly inaccurate, as the label for Fire 1011 actually states that "Make My Dreams Come True" was published by Flair Music, and the author—since it was a Bihari brothers' production—naturally, as "James-Josea"). The agreement was retroactive to 1 January 1960, and was scheduled to be terminated (unless renewed) on 31 December 1960. Elmore's address was given as 327 South Leavitt Street, Chicago 12, Illinois. Elmore's home phone number in Chicago was also listed (SEeley 3-4511), plus a New York business phone number (presumably in case BMI needed to get a hold of the publisher, Fire Music, or Robinson). For each "local" radio or TV broadcast performance that BMI tracked, Elmore James would receive one penny and Robinson's Fire Music would receive one penny. The ante was upped to a penny and a half when it came to "network" radio and TV broadcasts.[550]

Having dispensed with that piece of business, Robinson quickly arranged the details of the session. "I called Beltone [Studios] and told them, 'Whatever you have booked, cancel it. I want the whole night.' We began that session at eight o'clock in the evening and came out at eight o'clock in the morning," recalled Robinson in 1992. "When I brought Elmore into New York, he didn't know a soul but me. He just brought himself and his guitar, and we went right into the studio. No rehearsal, or anything."[551] Beltone, located in Manhattan at 31st and Fifth Avenue, would be the location for James' next two sessions with Robinson.[552]

Jimmy Spruill, who was present at the session, recalled that "Elmore brought two guitars to the session.... They were old guitars. I think one was an old Gibson, and he had that guitar set up to play slide."[553] Spruill added, "I played the rhythm guitar behind him on those sessions.... At that time, I was playing a Fender Stratocaster. Sometimes I would play just one part, and sometimes—if we overdubbed—I would play two parts. Sometimes Elmore would overdub too, but hardly ever. He [brought] his own songs, and we would work [them] up... on the spot."[554]

As Robinson indicated, it was an all night marathon session which produced ten titles. There were updates and re-recordings, the first being "Rollin and Tumblin," which was a masterful, almost polyrhythmic reading of the traditional Mississippi Delta standard, with a fabulous drumming contribution from Belton Evans. "I Can't Stop Lovin' You" was an update of his Flair title from seven years

549 Obrecht, "The Ballad of Elmore & Homesick James," 80.

550 Nadine Cohodas, *Spinning Blues Into Gold: The Chess Brothers and the Legendary Chess Records.* New York: St. Martin's Press, 2000, 77-80; and Walter Devenne, telephone interview, 16 June 1992; Elmore's contract with Broadcast Music, Inc. courtesy of Patrick LeBlanc and the Estate of Elmore James.

551 Robinson, "Comments from Bobby Robinson."

552 Franz, 22, 24; and Robinson, "Comments from Bobby Robinson."

553 Jimmy Spruill, "Comments from Jimmy Spruill." In the notes to Elmore James, *King of the Slide Guitar.* Capricorn CD 42006-2, 1992.

554 Spruill, "Comments from Jimmy Spruill."

before, and "Early One Morning" was an odd configuration of Elmore's "Dust My Broom" bottleneck guitar with the horn section playing the melody of "Fannie Mae" by Buster Brown. One other "Broom" styled number, "Fine Little Mama," was also recorded, but the titles which really stood out from the session were the powerful "Done Somebody Wrong," the tormented "I'm Worried," the unusual "Strange Angels," the sorrowful "I Need You," and his classic of angst and introspection, "Something Inside of Me."[555]

It was while Elmore had been in Cleveland that he had run into Eddie Kirkland—they were both staying at the same hotel—and Kirkland played Elmore a copy of his recent release on the Fortune label, "I Must Have Done Somebody Wrong." "That's a great song," Elmore told Kirkland. "Wanna cut it?" Kirkland offered, "Just give me the credit for it." "Yeah I'll give you the credit for it," Elmore replied, but as Kirkland later told interviewer Steve Gronda, "When the record come out I looked on the record—wrote by Elmore James, no mention of me!"[556] Authorship notwithstanding, Paul Garon described Elmore's version of "Done Somebody Wrong" as "one of his masterpieces, a power stop-time tune with slashing vocal and pile-driving guitar. James's ability to communicate such intense emotion with his abrasive groans and cries is a major sign of his splendor."[557] Jimmy Spruill's playing strongly added to the proceedings, as his patented "scratching" guitar style (sometimes described as a "chick-chick" sound) can readily be heard on the title. It was also another example of Elmore's ability to transform someone else's song by stamping it with a distinctiveness all his own—in this case, especially, by coupling Kirkland's verses with a fresh musical arrangement. The demeanor of the song easily lends itself to Elmore's persona—rather than offering extroverted tales of sexual prowess or hollow braggadocio, instead, the inward glance is preferred:

> Everything that happened, you know I am to blame,
> Everything is happened, you know I am to blame,
> I'm gonna find me a doctor, maybe my luck will change.
> Oh yeah.
>
> My mother told me these days would surely come,
> But I wouldn't listen to her, said, "I gotta have some fun," ah,
> I musta did somebody wrong,
> Ah, it's all my fault, I musta did somebody wrong.[558]

In the same vein, "I'm Worried" was another paradigmatic James offering, including a "Broom"-type bottleneck riff with a disquietingly eerie edge, troubled lyrics ("I'm worried, worried as a man can be/Worried about my baby, she gone away from me.../I hope some day, my baby love will return/If she don't come back to me, my whole life will go to ruin"), and Spruill providing a firm rhythmic scratching behind the top-notch horn section.[559] "Strange Angels" is interesting primarily for its lack of slide guitar

555 Elmore James, "Rollin and Tumblin." Fire 1024, 1960; Leroy Pierson, notes to *Lake Michigan Blues 1934-1941.* Nighthawk LP 105, 1980; Elmore James, "I Can't Stop Lovin' You." From the album Elmore James, *The Sky Is Crying.* Sphere Sound LP 7002, 1965; Garon, "Postwar Chicago and the North," 203-204; Elmore James, "Early One Morning." From the album Elmore James, *I Need You.* Sphere Sound LP 7008, 1967; Franz, 22; and Buster Brown, "Fannie Mae."

556 Steve Gronda and Bez Turner, "Eddie Kirkland Part 2: 'Eddie Kirk Is My Georgia Name.'" *Juke Blues* 5 (Summer 1986): 12.

557 Garon, "Postwar Chicago and the North," 203.

558 Elmore James, "Done Somebody Wrong." Fire 1031, 1960; Margey Peters, "Wild Jimmy Spruill: You Got to Move the Soul First." *Living Blues* 115 (June 1994): 32; and Eddie Kirkland, "I Must Have Done Somebody Wrong." Fortune 848, 1959.

559 Elmore James, "I'm Worried." Fire 1024, 1960.

playing and James sounding for three minutes more like a Texas blues artist than a traditional Mississippi one. According to Robert Plunkett, who was playing drums with him around this time, James often suffered complaints from fans who thought he was a one-trick pony: "...people think I can't play nothin' but the slide," he told Plunkett at one performance, who recalled that Elmore, "...took the slide off, put it in his pocket. I [thought to myself], 'He's gonna fuck up now.' 'Cause I didn't think he could play nothin' but slide either. The kid could play *guitar.* He was *good!* Yeah, he was really good."[560] Elmore's expansive-sounding guitar accompanied by thumping drums and bass with a full backing horn section underscores his odd lyric:

> Strange Angels, why do you treat me so mean?
> You's a strange angel, why do you treat me so mean?
> You're the meanest little girl that I most ever seen....
> I know I love you baby, but I don't know the reason why. [561]

"I Need You" is notable primarily for being Elmore's saddest, most heart-rending piece of recorded music. Elegant slide guitar motifs rich in tonality decorate Elmore's forlorn lyrics that are seemingly being wrenched out of his soul. His guitar, about a half a beat behind the rhythm, lends a hesitancy to the proceedings that makes it seem like just simply performing the song is almost too much to bear:

> You cheated on me, baby, all through the day,
> When I send for you, baby, you turn, you turn and go the other way,
> Yes, I need you, yes, I need you, both night and day.
>
> I send you money, baby, to come on home to me,
> You tell me, "Daddy, things ain't what they used to be,"
> I need you, baby, I love you, darlin', come on home to me. [562]

When originally released as a single in 1966, the song was mastered to fade out after the last verse above. Over twenty-five years later, Walter Devenne and Donn Fileti found the original unedited take of "I Need You." It contained this additional verse, where Elmore pleads with his partner:

> You want me, baby, say you're comin' right away,
> When I hear from you, baby, you done turn and gone the other way,
> I need you, baby, I want you, baby, come on home to me! [563]

"I Need You," like its musical cousin "Sho Nuff I Do" before it, had R&B hit-making potential written all over it. Richard Lillard, a disk jockey in Arlington, Virginia around the time "I Need You" was released, had this to share: "If you're wondering how Elmore James' recent sides sold well in Washington, here's the answer," went a report that Lillard sent to *Blues Unlimited.* "Lillard... says that a good friend of his, a Negro d-j for WOL Washington, was responsible. This guy 'broke' Elmore's 'I Need You' and was the primary factor in selling 23,000 copies to the Motown kids of D.C."[564] It was not enough, however, to get

[560] Brisbin, "Robert Plunkett," 46.

[561] Elmore James, "Strange Angels." From the album Elmore James, *I Need You.* Sphere Sound LP 7008, 1967. Note: Amos Easton (a.k.a. "Bumble Bee Slim") recorded a song for the Specialty label in 1951 entitled "Strange Angel." It appears to have very little in common with this recording by Elmore James. See: Amos Easton, "Strange Angel." Specialty 410, 1951.

[562] Elmore James, "I Need You." Sphere Sound 708, 1966.

[563] Elmore James, "I Need You Baby" [complete version]. From the album Elmore James, *Rollin' & Tumblin'—The Best of Elmore James.* Relic CD 7026, 1992; and Franz, 23, 40.

[564] "Blues News Coast-to-Coast." *Blues Unlimited* 36 (September 1966): 23.

the disc listed on the charts.

"Something Inside of Me," the last title from this session, is considered by many fans to be the consummate recorded example of Elmore's slide guitar talent combined with the existential, introverted lyrics he seemed to be focusing on now more than at any other stage of his career—in a sense, some might say, the magnum opus of his career. With laconic, haiku-like poetical phrases and Elmore's stately slide guitar, the song evokes a spine-tingling mood of extreme anomie and personal emptiness:

> There's something inside of me that just won't let me be,
> Something inside me that just won't let me be,
> My baby's gone and left me, and my heart's in misery.
>
> I wake up early in the mornin' in my bedroom all alone,
> I wake up early in the mornin' in my bedroom all alone,
> I don't find my baby, and I wonder, I wonder where she gone.
>
> My baby's gone, and I declare it's a cryin' shame,
> Yeah, you know, I declare it's a cryin' shame,
> Ever since she been gone, ah, you know, my life don't feel the same. [565]

Like a master who understands how to create and evoke a particular mood, James pours the entirety of his artistry into the recording. Drawing upon his decades of experience playing slide guitar, he offers dramatic trills up and down the neck one moment, and in the next he deftly scores magnificent single-note passages inspired by Tampa Red and Robert Nighthawk. At five minutes, it is Elmore's longest piece of recorded music, and it gives us the only real glimpse of what his guitar playing must have been like when he got a chance to "stretch out" and take the instrument through its paces. "Using the bottleneck technique most of the time, Elmore really let his guitar sound as I had never heard a guitar sound before," remembered George Adins about one of Elmore's live performances, "and when he gave free rein to his guitar, the people in the joint went crazy and some people ran to the bandstand throwing bills of one and five dollars at Elmore's feet."[566]

After the session Robinson had plenty of material to use for singles. The first two sides issued were "Rollin and Tumblin" and "I'm Worried," which became Fire 1024 in late July or early August 1960. The next pair was "Done Somebody Wrong" and "Fine Little Mama," which were issued as Fire 1031 just before the end of the year.[567]

After the New York session Homesick James accompanied his cousin back to Jackson, Mississippi, for a while, where they stayed with Johnny Temple at 905 Ann Banks. They hadn't been there too long before they were working again, enlisting Boyd Gilmore to help them play dances on Saturday nights. With the success of "The Sky Is Crying," work was seemingly easy to find. Sam Myers recalls playing with James at a variety of oddly named dives in Alabama, Louisiana, and around Jackson, including the Nagasaki; Club 400; Percy Simpson's place (where Elmore had played before); the Top-Hat in Laurel; the 3-D in Starkville; the Blue Light Club in Bovina; and Fats' Place in Leesburg. Even so, Elmore must have decided (or perhaps, been persuaded by his friends) that his best bet was to keep his options open—which he did by

[565] Elmore James, "Something Inside of Me." From the album Elmore James, *I Need You.* Sphere Sound LP 7008, 1967. Note: Ray Charles recorded a song, "Something Inside Me," for ABC. It has nothing in common with this recording by Elmore James. See: Ray Charles, "Something Inside Me." ABC 10901, 1967.

[566] Bromberg, notes to *The Legend of Elmore James;* and James, "Something Inside of Me."

[567] Franz, 32; and Steve Franz, comp., "Fire Records FM Series Numbering and Dating Guide." unpublished manuscript, 1994.

putting down a $125 installment on the $300 fine he owed the Local 208 in Chicago, and paying the remainder of his union dues for the year 1960 on Friday, 1 July 1960. At the end of the month, Elmore would participate in one major event in Maryland Heights, Missouri (a suburb of St. Louis). On Sunday, 31 July 1960, he was the headline act for the "St. Louis Blues Festival." Sharing the stage with the "Old Man Broomduster" were Howlin' Wolf and bandleader, trumpeter, and disk jockey E. Rodney Jones. After a couple of months staying with James in and around Jackson, however, Homesick James headed north. Elmore James may have felt comfortable in Jackson, but not Homesick James, and he left for Chicago.[568]

In the fall of 1960 James Meredith, an African-American college student attending classes in Jackson, often went to see James perform. His comments give us the only recorded vignette of a typical evening with Elmore in a Mississippi nightclub:

> This Saturday I got there around 1:30a.m., the best time to arrive because the band (two guitars and one drummer with a two-piece drum contraption) was just hitting its pace after the first intermission. The cooks and nursemaids who have to work in the white woman's kitchen and take care of the white man's baby are out on the town by this time. The white folks know that "Cookie" will leave the food on the table and the baby crying...if the boss ain't home by 1:00 a.m. on Saturday night. By 1:30 everybody has gotten high and fallen in the groove.
>
> When I drove up, I was lucky and found a parking place.... When I reached the door, it was blocked by too many people trying to get in. The heat and odor both hit me as I slid inside the door....
>
> The band leader, Elmo, loved to hear the crowd beg, and the audience knew that he had to be treated with tender care, because the least thing might upset him and he would refuse to play a note. But he was good at his trade....
>
> There was no dance floor as such; the dance floor was everywhere–in the aisles, between the tables, on the tables, or anywhere you could find a little space. It was the usual crowd. The dress ranges all the way from expensive furs and hundred-dollar dresses to loud, weary colors and maid uniforms. The men will wear anything from seventy-dollar shoes and three-hundred-dollar suits to four-colored shirts and purple trousers to musty, sweaty...overalls that they have worked in all week....
>
> About this time Elmo started one of his most popular numbers, "Dust My Broom." He had really gotten "his spirits on" and turned the picking over to his second guitarist, a quiet-looking young man. He was as good as the old pro himself. Elmo now dealt only with the mike, "I say raise your window, baby, I say raise your window, baby, and let me ease out real slow, I hear somebody knocking; it may be your husband, I don't know." At two o'clock in the morning on a Saturday night in Mississippi, after the people have worked hard all week long...this is the kind of music and singing that the poor Negroes want to hear. [569]

Standing at the Crossroads

Robinson sent for James, perhaps sometime in February or March, 1961, to come to New York for another session. "He went by train," recalled Homesick James, "'cause I was livin' in Chicago and he stopped off to ask me come on over with him, but I wouldn't go."[570]

Robinson had some fresh ideas for Elmore's second New York date: "I wanted to do a Big Band sound with Elmore James. There really weren't any Big Band blues things around at that time. It was a new idea. I

568 Leadbitter and Robinson. "Homesick James, part 2," 9-10; Rowe, *Chicago Breakdown,* 204; O'Neal and Lee, 12; Jim O'Neal, "I Once Was Lost, But Now I'm Found: The Blues Revival of the 1960s," 373. In Lawrence Cohn, ed., *Nothing But the Blues.* New York: Abbeville Press, 1993; and Elmore James' Chicago musicians union file; courtesy of Pat LeBlanc and the Estate of Elmore James.

569 Meredith, 34-37.

570 Leadbitter and Robinson, "Lazy Bill Called Me Homesick (I Wasn't Though)(Part 3)," 9.

handpicked the musicians and we did a session using baritone saxophone, two tenor saxophones, trumpet, alto horn, a trombone, a second guitar, bass and drums. This was completely foreign to Elmore," Robinson stated, uncharacteristically underestimating James' talents.[571] He had certainly recorded with horn sections previously (especially the Big Joe Turner and Maxwell Davis dates). Robinson's "handpicked" ensemble included Danny Moore on trumpet, George Coleman on tenor sax, Paul "Hucklebuck" Williams on baritone sax, possibly Dickie Harris on trombone, Johnny Acey on piano, Riff Ruffin on supporting guitar, Johnny Williams on drums, and an unidentified bass player.[572]

The session produced nine numbers and included the usual mix of classic tunes, re-recordings, and new material. "Stranger Blues" was a vigorous rendering of traditional blues themes à la James' sinewy slide guitar, while standards included Eddie Vinson's "Person to Person," and The Ravens' 1953 waxing (highlighted with Jimmy Ricks' lead vocal) "She's Got to Go." "So Unkind" was a smashing update of Robert Johnson's "Rambling on My Mind," where the listener finds Elmore so confident of his abilities that he can be heard to carry on a conversation while taking his guitar solo! "One Way Out" was another fast-rocking number that shares it origins with both Elmore James and Sonny Boy Williamson, as each recorded a version of it within months of the other. Although Williamson's rendering was the first to be issued, it was James who recorded the tune initially. The classic "Anna Lee" was Elmore's usual nod to important slide guitar antecedents—Tampa Red had originally recorded the tune in 1940, although Robert Nighthawk had helped to popularize it later that decade with a whining, electric version that hit number thirteen on the rhythm & blues charts.[573] The innocuous "My Kind of Woman" finds Elmore in a lighter-hearted mood for a change ("I don't want her too tall/I don't want her too big/It's a medium size woman that I really dig"),[574] while "Bleeding Heart" can easily compete among the greatest of Elmore's songs. "People, people, people," he sermonizes, "You know what it means to be left alone:"

> Understanding and a little lovin', a little love is all in the world I need,
> Understanding and a little lovin', baby, a little love is all in the world I need,
> Misunderstanding and a no-good woman, they both have caused my heart to bleed.
>
> Every mornin' the willows weep and moan for me,
> Every mornin' the willows weep and moan for me,
> The birds sing me a little song, my baby has caused my heart to bleed. [575]

Among those few to have recorded cover versions of this well-loved Elmore jewel are Jimi Hendrix and Eddie Taylor. Given Hendrix's reputation as a rock guitar deity, his version, recorded in New York in 1969, seems fairly direct and uncomplicated—strictly based on Elmore's original with a noticeably earthy, bluesy feel. Taylor's version, originally recorded in 1980 for the L+R label with Sunnyland Slim, Carey Bell, and

571 Robinson, "Comments from Bobby Robinson."

572 Franz, 14, 16, 24.

573 Elmore James, "Stranger Blues." Fire 1503, 1962; Eddie "Cleanhead" Vinson, "Person to Person." King 4582, 1952; The Ravens, "She's Got to Go." Mercury 70119, 1953; Robert Johnson, "Rambling on My Mind;" Elmore James, "So Unkind." From the album Elmore James, *Something Inside of Me.* Bell LP 104, 1968; Leslie Fancourt, *Chess Blues Discography,* 3rd ed. Kent, England: [no publisher], 1989, 50; Sonny Boy Williamson, "One Way Out." Checker 1003, 1961; Elmore James, "One Way Out." Sphere Sound 702, 1965; Tampa Red, "Annie Lou Blues." Bluebird B8654, 1941; Robert Nighthawk, "Annie Lee Blues." Aristocrat 2301, 1949; Elmore James, "Anna Lee." Fire 1503, 1962; Whitburn, 308; Dixon, Godrich, and Rye, 890; Franz, 24.

574 Elmore James, "My Kind of Woman." From the album Elmore James, *Something Inside of Me.* Bell LP 104, 1968.

575 Elmore James, "Bleeding Heart." Enjoy 2015, 1965. Note: Fats Domino recorded a song for the Imperial label in 1958 entitled "My Heart Is Bleeding." It has nothing in common with this recording by Elmore James. See: Fats Domino, "My Heart Is Bleeding." Imperial 5833, 1962.

Odie Payne on piano, harp, and drums respectively, was proficiently rendered and featured Taylor weaving bits and pieces of his slide guitar in and around Bell's spunky harp.[576]

The greatest song that Elmore James recorded at this session, however, was an update of "Standing at the Crossroads," a tune with which he had enjoyed limited success earlier on Flair and, of course, a number originally recorded by Robert Johnson. "Standing at the Crossroads" is quintessential James material and is the peak recorded example the "Dust My Broom" riff at its most potent, fever-pitched level. If there ever was a recorded moment where James really lets his guitar speak for itself, it would have to be during the solo, when his guitar almost seems to cry as he plays histrionic glissandos down the length of the instrument. The fierce vocals bring about Elmore's strange mix of heart-felt emotion, sorrow, and introspection:

> Well, I was standing at the cross road, and my baby's not around,
> Standin' at the cross road, and my baby's not aroun',
> Well, I began to wonder, is po' Elmo sinkin' down? [577]

"Standing at the Crossroads," however, is more than just another great Elmore James record—it is a three-minute epic masterpiece, and represents his final consummation of traditional Mississippi blues themes—not only in song material but also the slide guitar style as well—with his concepts of rhythm and amplification channeled through a fully supporting backing band. In this manner, James was free to play his instrument in the manner of modern postwar guitar soloists, while not having to worry about who was going to keep the rhythm going. As Mike Rowe said, "Elmore's position in the Chicago scene is important, for, while Muddy [Waters] updated Mississippi's blues for an early postwar audience, Elmore followed through the logical development and modernized them for all time."[578] "Standing at the Crossroads" is, to me, Elmore's most satisfying example of his ability to do just that.

After the session was over, Robinson recalled that he and James were very satisfied with the results. "Elmore loved playing with a bigger sound," he recalled. "He was elated because we had such a great session."[579] The first items to be issued from the date were "Stranger Blues" and "Anna Lee," which appeared on Robinson's newly initiated "Authentic Blues" series in the summer of 1962. As with the Chess release previously, Robinson must have had high hopes for the disc, as three different pressings of the single have been recovered. By an odd stroke of coincidence, the other blues artist featured in the series was James' old cohort, Arthur "Big Boy" Crudup.[580]

---

576 Eddie Taylor, "My Heart Is Bleeding." From the album *My Heart Is Bleeding.* Evidence CD 26054-2, 1994 [reissue]; and Jimi Hendrix, "Bleeding Heart." From the album *Jimi Hendrix: Blues.* MCA CD 11060, 1998.

577 Elmore James, "Standing at the Crossroads." From the album Elmore James, *The Sky Is Crying.* Sphere Sound LP 7002, 1965; Robert Johnson, "Cross Road Blues;" and Franz, 16.

578 Rowe, *Chicago Breakdown,* 205.

579 Robinson, "Comments from Bobby Robinson."

580 Turco, "Interview: Bobby Robinson. [Part 3]," 11; and Franz, 32.

A Candlelight Session at Cosimo's

After almost a year out of the Chicago scene and being comfortable in Jackson, Elmore let his payments to the Chicago musicians' union slip. As Homesick James recalled, "He wouldn't pay no union dues, so they banned him, but he could have played in Chicago. See he was nervous, so he [stayed in] Jackson." Not only did Elmore fail to renew his membership for 1961, but there was still the matter of the unpaid balance of $175 on his $300 fine (with fees and taxes, the total came to $183.25). From a strictly pragmatic standpoint, it must have seemed fairly ridiculous to cough up such a large chunk of money to the union, only to be told that, no, you couldn't play any engagements for six additional months. So, Elmore did nothing about it at all.[581]

His last encounter with the Chicago Local 208 union board of directors was on Thursday, 2 March 1961. As might be expected, it did not go very well:

> It was explained that Elmore James, who had been out of town for several months, returned to Chicago and immediately went to the Tay May club, 1400 West Roosevelt Road, and attempted to play without making any effort to clear some of his indebtedness to Local 208. He was not permitted to perform this engagement.
>
> James stated he had no way of paying this money unless he was permitted to work; and, he requested permission to go to work and have the management deduct so much per week until it is paid in full.
>
> Elmore James was told, in no uncertain terms, that he would not be able to play with or for any musicians in good standing until the total amount of $183.25 has been paid in full. [582]

While Elmore's idea of working off his fine certainly seemed practical enough, he had evidently crossed the board's path one too many times for them to even consider it as an option. Who it was that might have "ratted him out" to the union, we'll never know for sure. We can be certain of this, however—except for the last week of his life, it was Elmore's last documented appearance in Chicago.

In the summer of 1961, Bobby Robinson held his fourth recording session with Elmore James, this time in New Orleans at Cosimo Matassa's J & M Studios. "[They] were what I call 'candlelight' sessions," Sam Myers stated in a 1992 interview. "The studio didn't have any lights on in the office. They kept the lights down low, because they were dodging the union.... Back in New Orleans during that time, the union was very heavy." With Elmore's membership lapsed and his account at the Local 208 being in arrears, it could have caused problems had he been caught, not to mention the troubles it might have created for producer Robinson and studio-owner Matassa had it been discovered that the proceedings were non-union.[583]

By Myers' account, recording at Cosimo Matassa's New Orleans studio during the middle of summer was a sweltering proposition. "There was no air-conditioning running at the studio, because they didn't want the sound to bleed on the recordings," he recalled, "and the heat was rough:"

> So we'd be in there recording, with the door shut, no air-conditioning, and we'd work all night like that. But Cosmo figured out a clever way to get some air into the studio: he built a place in front of the building with big ventilation pipes and, every so often, they'd dump a mountain of ice into a hole in front of these pipes. It looked like a Mount Everest landslide. There were big, tall fans with their

---

581 Leadbitter and Robinson. "Homesick James, part 2," 9; Rowe, *Chicago Breakdown*, 204; Dirks, 45; and Elmore James' Chicago musicians union file; courtesy of Pat LeBlanc and the Estate of Elmore James.

582 Dirks, 45.

583 Myers, "Comments from Sam Myers;" Fanzone, personal interview, 15 November 1993; and Franz, 2.

> blades open blowing against that ice to get a breeze. The fans were far enough away from where we were that the sound wouldn't pick up. They would pipe that air into the studio, and it would get cooler then. We'd all lay on the floor between takes to really get a breeze. [584]

The group of musicians James had gathered together for the session was Mississippi's answer to the Broomdusters. "It was interesting," Robinson remembered, "because this time Elmore knew all the musicians, and I didn't! ....After the New York sessions, Elmore went back to Mississippi and formed a little combo like the one he'd had in Chicago...."[585] The ensemble included James, Myers on harmonica (for two titles), Johnny "Big Moose" Walker on piano, Sammy Lee Bully (or Bullie) on bass guitar, and "King" Mose Taylor on drums. Elmore started the evening off with their hottest number, "Shake Your Moneymaker," which was completed in just two takes, the first one being a false start. According to 1950s Chicago blues lore, drummer/vocalist James Bannister was the original author of a tune known as "Roll Your Moneymaker," but never recorded it. At one time Bannister had worked with both J.T. Brown and Magic Sam, which probably explains how the latter artist wound up playing guitar on the first known recording of the title—Chicago harp stylist Shakey Jake's 1958 version for the Artistic label—although credit for the memorable guitar motif probably goes neither to Bannister nor to Magic Sam, but to Mississippi John Hurt's 1928 OKeh recording, "Got the Blues Can't Be Satisfied." As for Elmore's link to the tune, it seems highly plausible to connect the dots through J.T. Brown back to the obscure Bannister, who recorded for Sun, Chess, and United before permanently leaving the blues world in the early 1960s in favor of the church.[586]

"Elmore really makes his guitar talk," offered John Broven about James' efforts on "Shake Your Moneymaker." Although solidly presented, the short fast-moving foot-tapper probably could have been run through its paces with a little more verve had the Chicago Broomdusters had the opportunity to work it over.[587] There is no trouble imagining, however, what a popular dance number this must have been in the clubs, when one considers James Meredith's comments: "This was a sure satisfier for this crowd. It had a fast sensuous beat and was loud and moving," he wrote. "Sometimes the band would play it for thirty minutes or longer without stopping, and the crowd would continue to beg for more when it was over. 'Shake your money maker, shake your money maker' was repeated over and over throughout the song, basically an instrumental number."[588]

The other significant result from the session was the second item on the roster, another tune associated with traditional Mississippi blues. As a theme, "Look on Yonder Wall" had first been recorded for Columbia Records shortly after the end of World War II by James "Beale Street" Clark as "Get Ready to Meet Your Man," although Jazz Gillum's version, recorded four months later for RCA Victor, would prove to be more widely known. During the next eight years, varying incarnations of the tune were offered by Arthur "Big Boy" Crudup, Boyd Gilmore, and Eddie Boyd, although in Gilmore's case the words were so badly slurred that "Look on Yonder Wall" came out "Just an Army Boy"—no doubt, when Gilmore recorded it in 1952, an attempt to fit the song to the then-current theme of the Korean War and avoid duplication with Crudup's recent release. Once again, it is tempting to connect the dots from Elmore back

584 Myers, "Comments from Sam Myers."

585 Robinson, "Comments from Bobby Robinson."

586 O'Neal and Lee, 19; Jim O'Neal, notes to Big Walter Horton and Alfred "Blues King" Harris, *Harmonica Blues Kings.* Pearl LP 12, 1986; Shakey Jake [r.n.: James Harris], "Roll Your Moneymaker." Artistic 1502, 1958; Leadbitter and Slaven, *Blues Records: 1943-1966,* 286; Mississippi John Hurt, "Got the Blues Can't Be Satisfied." OKeh 8724,1929; and Franz, 26-27.

587 Broven, "Elmore James on Record," 7; and Elmore James, "Shake Your Moneymaker." Fire 504, 1961.

588 Meredith, 35.

through J.T. Brown, who played clarinet on Clark's original version (a 1973 article in *Living Blues* also noted that at one time pianist Clark, along with his vocalist partner Homer Harris, had both worked with Elmore James and Johnny Jones in Chicago). Elmore's version, supported by Sam Myers' solid harmonica playing, has been another perennial favorite of Elmore's fans for years, and it initially inspired Duke recording artist Junior Parker to make his own rendering, which was released in 1963. Broven commented that Elmore's effort was "immensely satisfying from both musical and lyrical points of view. [The] harmonica player... combines very well with the rhythm group to provide Elmore with a first class setting."[589]

Next on the roster were two pieces with straight vocals (and no harmonica) from Sam Myers. "Angel Child" was an update of a tune Memphis Slim had recorded in 1948 for the Miracle label, while "Little Girl" was a surprising jump-styled dance number with a lively rhythm and slight pop music tinges. Afterwards, Elmore took the lead again for four more titles, but the the animation and bounce present during "Shake Your Moneymaker" and "Look on Yonder Wall" started to evaporate. Perhaps it was due to the heat, which Myers recalled was grinding.[590] Nothing else recorded at the session really measured up. "You Know You Done Me Wrong" seemed not quite fully developed, while "Mean Mistreatin' Mama" was a tepid run-through of a tune associated first with Leroy Carr and then Tampa Red, who had each recorded versions in 1934 (as had Josh White and Bumble Bee Slim). "Go Back Home Again" also featured Myers' harmonica talent and was mildly interesting, while "Sunnyland" was an update of James' previous Flair release, speeded up and married to the ubiquitous "Dust My Broom" riff. By the time Johnny "Big Moose" Walker finished off the session with a humorous piece, "Footrace to a Resting Place," everybody was probably relieved to call it quits for the night—in all, nine titles had been recorded (with some requiring multiple takes), six of them by Elmore.[591]

"Shake Your Moneymaker" and "Look on Yonder Wall" were initially the only sides to be issued from the session, which Robinson released as Fire 504 in late December, 1961. With their interestingly varied genealogies, both titles provide a compelling reminder (as does "Mean Mistreatin' Mama") that musical influences upon Elmore were much more diverse than many people might have previously thought. Over the years, "Shake Your Moneymaker" has proved to be quite a popular item, and it ties for first place along with "Cry for Me Baby" as the two James songs most often issued as a single. Revival blues bands of the 1960s were also fond of "Shake Your Moneymaker," and the song was used to showcase the talents of many budding rock-blues guitarists. Among others, Fleetwood Mac and The Paul Butterfield Blues Band recorded memorable, revved-up versions in the mid to late 1960s.[592]

---

589 Broven, "Elmore James on Record," 7; James "Beale Street" Clark, "Get Ready to Meet Your Man." Columbia 30005, 1945; Jazz Gillum, "Look on Yonder Wall." RCA Victor 20-1974, 1946; Arthur "Big Boy" Crudup, "Hand Me Down My Walking Cane." RCA Victor 22/50-0100, 1950; Boyd Gilmore, "Just an Army Boy." Modern 860, 1952; Eddie Boyd, "Nothing But Trouble." Chess 1561, 1954; Leadbitter and Slaven, *Blues Records 1943-1970,* 264, 461; Jim O'Neal, "Blues Questions and Answers." *Living Blues* 12 (Spring 1973): 37; Elmore James, "Look on Yonder Wall." Fire 504, 1961; and Junior Parker, "Yonder's Wall." Duke 367, 1963.

590 Various Artists, *N.Y. on Fire: Bobby's Harlem Rock Vol. 2.* P-Vine CD 5461, 1998; Memphis Slim, "Angel Child." Miracle 145, 1949; Franz, 26-27; and Myers, "Comments from Sam Myers."

591 Elmore James, "Mean Mistreatin' Mama." Enjoy 2020, 1965; Leroy Carr, "Mean Mistreater Mama." Vocalion 02657, 1934; Tampa Red, "Mean Mistreater Blues." Bluebird B5546, 1934; Elmore James, "You Know You Done Me Wrong." From the album Elmore James, *The Complete Fire and Enjoy Sessions, Part 4.* Collectables CD 5187, 1989; Dixon, Godrich, and Rye, 142, 234, 886-887, 1020; Elmore James, "Go Back Home Again." From the album Elmore James, *Rollin' & Tumblin'—The Best of Elmore James.* Relic CD 7026, 1992; Elmore James, "Sunnyland." From the album Elmore James, *To Know a Man.* Blue Horizon LP 7-66230, 1969; and Franz, 26-27.

592 The Paul Butterfield Blues Band, "Shake Your Money-Maker." From the album *Paul Butterfield Blues Band.* Elektra LP 7294, 1965; Fleetwood Mac, "Shake Your Money Maker." From the album, *Fleetwood Mac.* Blue Horizon LP 7-63200, 1968; Franz, 32-33; and Franz, "Fire Records FM Series Numbering and Dating Guide."

Elmore continued to stay busy in Jackson, rooming at Gertrude Jordan's house on Sage Street and performing at the clubs as often as four nights a week around the metro area, sometimes with guitarist Columbus Brooks accompanying—including one club owned by Will Stephenson and another called the Sunset Inn—and making what seemed to be a pleasant enough existence for himself. "Didn't neither one of us have a job working during the daytime," Myers stated. "Every morning we'd get up and decide what we were going to have for dinner that evening, and who was going to cook."[593] During the day James and Bill Sullivan (who owned Fat's Place where Elmore would occasionally play) might go hunting—trekking into the Mississippi woods on tractors to avoid the snakes—or they might go off by Leesburg, Mississippi, in Rankin County where the two of them had set up a still. "It's a whole lot of work that he knew to do," Myers remembered. "But he just never did do anything else but make whiskey.... He could get it different colors, ...red whiskey or either the clear kind." One of the things he would make out of his homebrew was an eggnog with a powerful kick. "And he went and got some nutmeg, and I think he put about a dozen eggs in the stuff. He even put ice cream in it," Myers told *Living Blues* magazine. "And he took a quart of that moonshine that he had made for Fats, and poured it... in there. I said, "Man, that stuff, bad as it is, won't do nothin' but just cook the rest of the stuff that you've got in there.' And he said, 'Aw, hell, man, the badder the whiskey is the better the eggnog it make!'" Myers adds, "Yeah, it tasted pretty good, though."[594]

On Elmore's regular night off, Thursday night, he would stop by the Gay Lady to see Sam Myers and his band play, and then would ask to sit in with them. "And he would tell them that he wasn't going to play the guitar—say he was going to let a youngster sounded a lot like the old man play. And he would just take the mike and sing," Myers recalled. "And then [Columbus] Brooks, he would play a lot of his stuff just like... [Elmore James]. When he would finish doing his numbers, he would say, 'If all of you all want to, just go on... outside and listen... and I bet you can't tell us apart!' They were just that close. And Elmore would get a lot of laughs from that."[595]

Reprise: Make My Dreams Come True

Just a couple weeks after Elmore James' forty-fifth birthday, Robinson once again summoned the Broomduster to come to New York and record. Over the years, Elmore had stayed in touch with Arthur Crudup, now living in Florida, and since the two of them were both artists on Fire's roster, Crudup evidently forwarded Elmore's current address to Robinson, who in turn arranged for the trip up to the Big Apple.[596]

The last two Elmore James recording sessions were held at A-1 Studios in New York City, on Wednesday, 13 February, and Thursday, 21 February 1963. Elmore made the trip in the company of Marshall Jones, who was presumably a band member or protégé of James. Jones recorded just two titles at the 13 February session—"Woke Up Happy" was thematically based on a 1947 Sonny Terry recording,

593 O'Neal and Lee, 10; Myers, "Comments from Sam Myers;" Gertrude Jordan, personal interview by David Evans. Jackson, Mississippi, 26 June 1989; and Jim O'Neal and Amy O'Neal, "Sam Myers in Jackson." *Living Blues* 3 (Autumn 1970): 19.

594 O'Neal and Lee, 10, 12; and "Back in Mississippi" [conversation]. From the album Elmore James, *To Know a Man.* Blue Horizon LP 7-66230, 1969.

595 O'Neal and Lee, 12.

596 Welding, "Skip Layne," 5.

while "You Can Do It If You Want To" seemed to be loosely centered around a piece that Arthur "Big Boy" Crudup had recorded in 1952. Jones' pair of sides remained unissued until 1993, when they were included in a box set retrospective of Fire/Fury material. Regrettably, Robinson's memory of Marshall Jones is so vague that he was not able to recall what instrument he played, noting that, "Marshall Jones was...one of two musicians that Elmore James brought to New York to record with him in... early '63.... [James played] the guitar backing up Marshall. We must have cut Marshall after Elmore was through recording one day at A-1 Studios. You can hear me giving Marshall instructions about the arrangement before the take begins. Although I liked his voice, I never released any material on this artist."[597]

The first of the two sessions on Wednesday the thirteenth did not yield anything extraordinary. Elmore's guitar had been tuned several steps below concert pitch and had a pronounced bass feel to it; he was backed by a sparse arrangement which included an efficient, no frills, bass and drums. Every song recorded at the date was a either a reworking or a re-recording of something he had done previously, such as "Look on Yonder Wall," "Dust My Broom," "Find My Kinda Woman," and "My Baby's Gone."[598] Not surprisingly, Robinson never used any of the material for singles, and Elmore's four tracks plus two alternate takes have become largely gratuitous album filler. In 1992, Walter Devenne and Donn Fileti discovered one of the original stereo master reels from this session, marked "Reel One of Two." "Reel two," said Devenne, "has not been found."[599]

On Thursday, 21 February 1963, Robinson held his last Elmore session, again at A-1 Studios in Manhattan. Herb Abramson was the engineer for the date, and presumably Marshall Jones was still accompanying Elmore, probably in the capacity of drummer or bass player. Abramson and Robinson each seem vague about the other personnel on the session. Robinson originally recalled, in 1969, that the piano player might be someone known as "Bushy Head," but by the early 1990s he had changed this story and

---

597 Bobby Robinson, "Comments from Bobby Robinson." In the notes to *The Fire/Fury Records Story.* Capricorn CD 42009-2, 1993; Various Artists, *The Fire/Fury Records Story.* Capricorn CD 42009-2, 1993; Sonny Terry, "Screamin' and Cryin' Blues." Capitol 40061, 1947; Arthur "Big Boy" Crudup, "Do It If You Want To." RCA Victor 20/47-4933, 1952, and Franz, 28-29, 40.

Note: There has been some degree of wondering and speculation over the last few years about Marshall Jones. In a 1994 issue of *Living Blues,* a story by Maureen Jung featured interviews with various Sacramento, California blues musicians, one of whom was a drummer, Marshall Jones. It is doubtful that this would be the same person that accompanied Elmore to this session, as this particular Marshall Jones moved from Louisiana to Sacramento in the 1950s (See Maureen Jung, "Sacramento Blues, Part One." *Living Blues* 114 (March/April 1994): 58, 60). In Eric LeBlanc's "Blues Dates" website, he lists one Marshall Jones who played piano and drums with Ike Turner and B.B. King, and who died on 18 August 1984 at the age of 41. Whether this could be the Marshall Jones who accompanied Elmore to New York City is not known, but is indeed a possibility. In November 2001, Marshall Jones was the subject of a thread at a postwar blues discussion group over the internet. Although no definite conclusions were drawn, writer/researcher Alan Balfour did report this intriguing entry, quoted from one of his personal research notebooks dating back to the early 1970s:

> *Marshall Jones? Slide guitar player? Poss. Chicago? May have recorded for Bobby Robinson in late 50s/early 60s. Perhaps a pseudonym for Homesick James.*

While readers are encouraged to draw their own conclusions (at least two other long-time blues writers/researchers were inclined to identify this person as Homesick James), the artist listed as Marshall Jones on *The Fire/Fury Records Story* just doesn't sound quite exactly like Homesick James (to this set of ears, anyway). As is frequently said in regards to cases such as this, unanswered questions remain (Alan Balfour, electronic communication with Steve Franz, 21 May 2002).

598 Elmore James, "Look on Yonder Wall." From the album Elmore James, *The Complete Fire and Enjoy Sessions, Part 4.* Collectables CD 5187, 1989; Elmore James, "Dust My Broom." From the album Elmore James, *Dust My Broom—The Best of Elmore James Part 2.* Relic CD 7040, 1992; Elmore James, "Find My Kinda Woman." From the album Elmore James, *History of Elmore James.* Trip LP 8007, 1971; and Elmore James, "My Baby's Gone." From the album Elmore James, *History of Elmore James.* Trip LP 8007, 1971.

Note: Although Elmore recorded a song called "My Baby's Gone" during the 25/26 January 1952 session, this version of "My Baby's Gone" is a re-recording of Flair 1022, "Please Find My Baby," with which it shares a similarity.

599 Devenne, telephone interview, 16 June 1992; and Franz, 28.

had decided that it was actually "Walking Willie" instead. Conventional blues wisdom had once agreed that "Bushy Head" was really Johnny "Big Moose" Walker, but in 1989 Dick Shurman resoundingly denounced the "Bushy Head"-Walker connection, returning the matter to the same vague plateau at which the discussion had started. Abramson does remember that James was accompanied to the studio by a fairly comely, heavy-set lady friend, but it has been determined that she was not the piano player either. Robinson evidently had plans to hold further sessions with "Bushy Head," but according to Abramson, "[Robinson] couldn't remember his name since then and nothing ever came about it. So it's really very vague as to who was in the band."[600]

By Robinson's and Abramson's accounts, the session was rather problematic. "It was kind of a thrown together session, wasn't planned as much, you know?" Robinson told blues researcher Dick Shurman. "I would say [James] was a little below peak performance, maybe it was because we didn't have any real exciting new material to work on, but he was in good voice and good form. I worked more closely with him on a lot of other sessions."[601] Abramson remembered that the first title slated to be recorded, "Hand in Hand," easily took up almost half of their session time: "Robinson didn't like the way Elmore did it, so he had him do it over and over again for about nine times. And about two hours of the session was gone by, and he still couldn't get it...." Abramson, an experienced studio engineer, had some tricks up his sleeve and asked Robinson if he wouldn't mind letting him work with James for a while. "I went out and conferred with Elmore," stated Abramson when Jim O'Neal interviewed him, "and I said 'Why don't you just do a set? Do about four numbers in a row.' Which he did, and then he did another set and he ended up doing a double album in that afternoon—one take of everything...you know, rather than trying to get some perfected arrangement idea going."[602]

Abramson's "set idea" really saved the session, which had been abortive up until now. James recorded thirteen more titles at the date, and it gives us a good idea of what Elmore's set list probably constituted those days. Most of the titles were re-recordings of earlier hits and songs strongly associated with James, such as "Dust My Broom," "It Hurts Me Too," "Twelve Year Old Boy," "I Believe," "I Can't Hold Out" (later retitled "Talk to Me Baby" for release) and a second version of "Bobby's Rock" entitled "Pickin' the Blues." There was also the obligatory nod to standards ("Everyday I Have the Blues" and The Ravens' "She's Got to Go"), as well as current items (B.B. King's "Got a Right to Love My Baby"). Also among the standards was "Up Jumped Elmore," which turned out to be an instrumental theme and variation of "Got My Mojo Working," a song which had previously been recorded on four occasions—twice by Muddy Waters, once by Louis Jordan, and once by its originator, Ann Cole. "It's a hell of an instrumental, and I recorded it as an instrumental because I couldn't remember the words," Robinson stated in regards to "Up Jumped Elmore." "I had left the words someplace when we went to the session. I had planned to record the instrumental part at that session and then go back and over-dub the words [at a later date]," he offered.[603]

Initially, Robinson did not issue any material from the session, as he was between record labels at the time. Fire Records had finally petered out the previous year, and Enjoy, although already started, had not quite picked up steam. With James having completed fourteen titles, the prospect of choosing something

600 O'Neal, "In Session with Elmore and Bobby Robinson: Herb Abramson," 11; Leadbitter, notes to *To Know a Man;* Robinson, "Comments from Bobby Robinson;" Shurman, notes to *The Last Session;* and Franz, 29.

601 Shurman, notes to *The Last Session.*

602 O'Neal, "In Session with Elmore and Bobby Robinson: Herb Abramson," 11; and Franz, 29.

603 Turco, "Interview: Bobby Robinson. [Part 3]," 11; B.B. King, "Got a Right to Love My Baby." Kent 333, 1960; Ann Cole, "Got My Mo-Jo Working (But it Just Won't Work on You)." Baton 237, 1957; Elmore James, "Pickin' the Blues." Enjoy 2015 [2nd pressing], 1965; Elmore James, "Up Jumped Elmore." Fury 2000, 1972; Shurman, notes to *The Last Session;* Paikos, 96; and Franz, 29-31.

appropriate for release must have at first seemed daunting. Robinson's knack for picking the hit proved trustworthy once again, however, and he released "It Hurts Me Too" sometime in early 1965 on Enjoy. It was another big seller for Robinson, and regrettably, a posthumous one for James. It reached number twenty-five on the rhythm & blues charts, where it stayed for eight weeks in the spring and early summer of 1965, and it made a momentary appearance at number 106 on the pop charts. The success immediately initiated three more Enjoy singles featuring James material over the course of a year. Two more songs from his last session were issued on Enjoy 2027, the first being "Dust My Broom," coupled with a pleasing remake of "Everyday I Have the Blues." Over the years James' Enjoy version of "It Hurts Me Too" has helped to greatly popularize Tampa Red's memorable song, inspiring re-recordings of it from such diverse artists as Junior Wells, Chuck Berry, John Mayall, Hound Dog Taylor, Calvin Leavy, and the Grateful Dead. In mid-1965, Danny Robinson (Bobby's brother) announced an ambitious plan to release at least eight more Elmore James singles on Enjoy. It would not come to pass, however, and there would be only one more issue on Enjoy following the "Dust My Broom" and "Everyday" coupling on 2027, before the label ground to an abrupt halt with number 2028 (a Sammy Taylor record). Nothing more ever came of the promised Elmore 45s.[604]

Some Elmore fans have been preoccupied and charmed by his last session over the years, but that is primarily due to the quick run-through of his biggest hits, the widespread availability and frequent reissue of the material, and the stereo mastering. The stereo masters from Robinson's two February 1963 Elmore James sessions are sadly the only ones he cut on James that survive today. According to Walter Devenne, Robinson paid close attention to the technical details at every session and inaugurated stereo recording on virtually all his sessions as early as 1958. At first, Robinson utilized a three-track master, a backup two-track stereo master, and a monaural safety take that would all roll at fifteen inches per second (a speed that uses a lot of tape but provides superlative sonic quality). "As early as 1958 he was recording in stereo," Devenne observed, "almost before anyone else did." By the time of Elmore's 1963 sessions, Robinson had dropped the three-track in favor of the more standard four-track and would still roll the stereo backup and mono safety take. Sadly, the four track masters to this session no longer exist, as some judicious mixing and remastering with today's equipment would assuredly restore some of the pep from the proceedings lost through poor microphone placement.[605]

Some things Elmore said during a tape recorded conversation with Bobby Robinson at the end of this session were quietly telling, though. Comments such as, "Can't think good as I used to, wait a while," and "Can he remember that? Try to make out you old as I am, huh?" were interesting choices of words from a slide guitarist who had just a couple weeks previous celebrated his forty-fifth birthday. The most remarkable thing, perhaps, about this 21 February 1963 session was one of the last pieces of music Elmore ever recorded, an update of his earlier Flair song "Make My Dreams Come True." It was the last time he would ever commit to tape the guitar riff that he had made famous over eleven years earlier with "Dust My Broom." After a tough, long day in the studio, the musicians finally seem to hit a kind of groove, while Elmore seems to relax a bit, his guitar sounding more confident and sure of itself. Elmore applies the

604 Turco, "Interview: Bobby Robinson. [Part 3]," 7; "Fire Discography," *Record Exchanger* 12 (Winter 1972): 12; "Enjoy Discography." *Record Exchanger* 12 (Winter 1972): 12; Whitburn, 216; Elmore James, "Everyday I Have the Blues." Enjoy 2027, 1965; Elmore James, "It Hurts Me Too." Enjoy 2015, 1965; Junior Wells, "It Hurts Me Too (When Things Go Wrong)." From the album *Chicago/The Blues/Today! Vol. 1.* Vanguard LP 9216, 1966; Chuck Berry, "It Hurts Me Too." Mercury 72748, 1967; John Mayall & the Bluesbreakers, "It Hurts Me Too." Decca (U.K.) 12621, 1967; Hound Dog Taylor, "It Hurts Me, Too." From the album Hound Dog Taylor and the Houserockers, *Hound Dog Taylor and the Houserockers.* Alligator LP 4701, 1971; Calvin Leavy, "It Hurts Me Too." Soul Beat 110, 1973; Franz, 29, 33; "Blues News." *Blues Unlimited 26* (October 1965): 19; and Ken Clee, *The Directory of American 45 R.P.M. Records, Volume 2.* Philadelphia: Stak-O-Wax, 1997, 485.

605 Devenne, telephone interview, 16 June 1992.

bottleneck to the guitar strings, and slides up the neck perfectly and effortlessly, singing with his still declamatory voice, not quite tarnished by smoke, drink, or the ravages of time, and for the last time declares:

> Well, I love my baby, I'll tell the world I do,
> Yes, I love my baby, I'll tell the world I do,
> Well now, a little of your lovin', baby, an' make my dreams come true. [606]

As for Bobby Robinson, he is still living in Harlem (as of this writing). During those years he was busy running record labels of his own, the practical Robinson never gave up his record shop where he gained his initial entry into the music business. "Even today while busily selling singles from the Top 40 Soul charts, [Robinson] will still slip the occasional blues record on to the deck in his shop," author and photojournalist Valerie Wilmer noted in 1978. "The authentic sounds of the South flood out over 125th Street, catching the imagination of older blacks who were reared on the music as well as that of youngsters who have never heard their roots so clearly spelt out."[607] At one time—when record industry fortune had smiled brightly on him—Robinson had had an office in downtown New York, complete with a prestigious Broadway address. It didn't feel right to Robinson, though. "I just somehow felt lost," he admitted to Wilmer. "I could be in a little dinky office in Harlem with the studios right there, the hamburgers and hotdogs cooking downstairs and the loud noises in the street, and it's a different kind of vibration."[608] Those Harlem vibrations seem to have suited Robinson's constitution perfectly. Even though sometime in the last decade he finally handed the reigns over to someone else to take care of the day to day sales and management, Robinson—even while pushing the age of eighty—would still come in to preside over his legendary record shop every Sunday.

It is interesting to note that Elmore's biggest successes—if you want to speak just in terms of raw sales figures—came about during his tenure with Robinson. Altogether, his two biggest 45s for Robinson, throughout the 1960s, would eventually rack up sales of well over a million units. This success was, in part, due to a simple and straightforward production philosophy Robinson possessed, which he shared with Valerie Wilmer. "What I try to do in producing records is to get the authentic qualities out of the artist and the music as near as possible and to hell with the trends," he told Wilmer in 1978. "If I can get the real thing, the real sounds and feeling, and we can project that on records, there are thousands of people out here that would relate to that."[609] Robinson wasn't wrong about that, and because of his perseverance, we have him to thank for what many fans have dubbed Elmore's greatest—possibly most influential, and certainly most varied—body of work. "Nobody can really adequately repay... Elmore James for the transcendent anguish of "Something Inside Me...." offered Steven Tracy in *Write Me a Few of Your Lines,* a hefty tome of blues articles and excerpts he edited into a book.[610] Well, maybe a good place to start would be to try thanking Bobby Robinson.

---

606 Elmore James, "Make My Dreams Come True." From the album Elmore James, *To Know a Man.* Blue Horizon LP 7-66230, 1969; and "Back in Mississippi" [conversation].

607 Wilmer, 48.

608 Ibid., 56.

609 Ibid., 48.

610 Steven Tracy, ed., *Write Me a Few of Your Lines: A Blues Reader.* Amherst, Massachusetts: University of Massachusetts Press, 1999, xv.

"The last time I saw Elmore..."

Back in Chicago, meanwhile, Elmore James was still in demand. There was talk of sessions with the new U.S.A. label and performances overseas—James evidently was slated to join the 1963 American Folk Blues Festival tour in Europe (sponsored by Lippmann and Rau). Most immediately, Big Bill Hill wanted to have Elmore on hand for the opening of his new Copa Cabana Club. Hill successfully intervened between James and the union, and after fixing up the mess, he sent for him. James moved in with Homesick James at 1503 N. Wieland. On Sunday, 19 May 1963, James, Homesick, and drummer Cassell Burrow headlined at the Copa and stopped off after their performance to see Howlin' Wolf, who was holding forth at James' old haunt, Sylvio's. Monday and Tuesday they continued the engagement at the Copa, and the next day, Wednesday, Elmore went to down to the Local 208 headquarters to pay his back dues for previous three years and make an installment on the fine he still owed, so that he could start legally on Friday, 24 May 1963. On Thursday or Friday afternoon James received some inoculations in preparation for going to Europe. Afterwards, he stopped to place a phone call to some friends in Jackson, Mississippi, to share the news about his upcoming departure.[611]

"The last time I saw Elmore was the night before he died," recalled James' friend and associate Robert Plunkett:

> I didn't even know he was back in town. I hadn't seen him in two, three months. I walked in [Big Bill Hill's] Copa Cabana on Roosevelt and Christiana. He was sittin' there talkin' to a couple of guys. I walked by him and went on in the back.... He came back there..., said "Don't you ever walk by me and don't speak to me. I ain't seen you in three month!" I said "Well, I don't wanna bother you when you talkin' to somebody." He say, "I don't care who I'm talkin' to. *Always* say somethin' to me." I say, "Okay, I'm sorry." He say, "We workin' tomorrow night, next door upstairs." ...And so I went on havin' fun. Then I went home. The next night I was gettin' dressed. I was almost dressed at about eight o'clock and I heard somebody call me. I went to the window. It was G.L. Crockett.... He yells up, "Robert! Robert! Elmore's dead." I yell down to him, "No, he ain't dead. I'm fixin' to go play with him now." He said, "No man. He just dropped dead." We went to the club and some of his people was there. And they told us, said, "Yeah. He just died. Just died."[612]

Waiting patiently for Elmore's arrival that night at the Copa Cabana Club was Chicago drummer Sam Lay, his Super 8 mm. movie camera in hand ready to take some footage of James in action. The thankless task of making the report to the coroner fell to James' mother, who had to face the even bleaker prospect of having to bury her son. Although an autopsy wasn't ordered, cause of death was inevitably as stated on the certificate, "organic heart disease." Several hundred people attended James' wake in Chicago, and Big Bill Hill footed the expense of shipping the body back to Mississippi for the funeral. Elmore James was buried in Ebenezer, Mississippi on Wednesday, 29 May 1963.[613]

611 Leadbitter and Wardlow, 10; Jordan, personal interview, 26 June 1989; Rowe, *Chicago Breakdown,* 204-205; and LeBlanc, telephone interview, 21 February 1995.

612 Brisbin, "Robert Plunkett," 47.

613 Topping, "Ramblin' from Town to Town," 17; James, Coroner's Certificate of Death; Jordan, personal interview, 26 June 1989; Leadbitter and Wardlow, 10; Williams, Koester, Chauvard, et al., "The Story of Elmore James," 4; and Hannusch, 7.

Note: According to Gertrude Jordan, in an interview conducted by David Evans, she feels that Elmore died due to the inoculations he received in preparation for the Europe tour. In another account of Elmore's death, it was offered that he simply forgot to take his heart medication that day. Jordan additionally recalled that Elmore may have suffered from adult-onset diabetes (a malady to which slide guitarists seem especially prone—don't ask me why, but it seems often to be the case), which would have served to greatly exacerbate any existing medical problems.

"So died one of the best loved of all the bluesmen," commented Mike Rowe. He was one of the key artists responsible for updating traditional Mississippi blues in postwar Chicago. Rowe added further that "The starkness of the Delta blues is always present in [James'] work; the ferocious and anguished vocals, the impassioned bottleneck guitar and the powerful surging rhythms remain as fresh today as they ever did."[614]

One of the first items ever to appear about Elmore James in a blues magazine would be his obituary, just weeks after he died. "Neil Paterson writes from Chicago of the death of the very popular Elmore James," noted the August 1963 edition of *Blues Unlimited* magazine. "A great loss to the blues world." In irony that befitted a blues musician, the magazine was published in England by a group of fans that, for the most part, had never met or seen Elmore and were separated significantly from him by socio-economic class and geography. They had only been introduced to the man via his 45s and 78s and had a handful of tales gathered from Demêtre and Chauvard's interview to go on, and little else. Paterson's four-line obituary was only the start of what would become intense interest in the man, his life, and music. Almost a year after he died, a tribute song was recorded in Elmore's honor, and released on the British Decca label. It was all merely the beginning of the legend of Elmore James.[615]

---

614 Rowe, *Chicago Breakdown*, 205.

615 Neil Paterson, "Obituary." *Blues Unlimited* 4 (August 1963): 9; Napier and Leadbitter, 2; and John Mayall & the Bluesbreakers, "Mr. James." Decca (U.K.) 11900, 1964.

CHAPTER FIVE

The Legend of Elmore James

Most of the blues singers, they've seen it happen, or it happened to them. The singer probably tried to tell somebody his problems but nobody would listen, because you got problems of your own. But if he sings it, somebody will listen.

In other words, the blues is nothing but a story being told. You know, you exaggerate with anything. But most of the time it would be real life. That just about sums it up. **It's a story being told to music.**

Like Charley Patton, he sings about the high waters. That's one a lot of them did, and they weren't lying either. It happened in '27 when Charley Patton wrote about it, and again in '37. The whole Delta was under water. So that's the way the blues is, **singing about life.**

That's why I never could understand why people used to be so against it. They said that blues music was the devil's music. They taught you it was bad for you. But you're only singing about life you see every day. Why go against something that you're looking at every day?

–Dee Henderson, a.k.a "Cap'n Pete,"

host of the award-winning radio show "Cap'n Pete's Blues Cruise," from a 1995 interview

"He lived as hard as he sang..."

"Supposedly he lived as hard as he sang," Barry Pearson said nine years after Elmore James' death, "and legends will probably project an image of a man burned out by the intensity he put into his work and the life style it implied."[616] To a large extent, unfortunately, the life style it *did* imply was a lot of heavy drinking. Sonny Boy Williamson, Willie Love and Elmore James, "all could turn a fifth upside down and kill it like that!" Lillian McMurry stated. She adds, "Any three or four of them, would be in a recording session, each one take a drink and the bottle would be empty. In two or three hours they wanted more. I always wondered how they drank and never showed it."[617] In West Memphis, Arkansas—a city second only to Las Vegas at the time for drinking, gambling and having a good time, Otis Spann (long-time pianist for Muddy Waters) and Elmore James were both known for being "the life of the party" when they were in town.[618] "I'm Elmore," he might announce to the crowd while lifting a drink in the air, "After me there won't be no more."[619] "He'd drink till he fall out. He'd get crazy too," Robert Plunkett recollected. "Shit, he'd get so high sometimes he couldn't play. He'd drink him a couple of half a pints till he'd go off every kind of way. A lot of people don't know it but I know it."[620] Legends die hard though, and consequently Elmore's life has lent itself very easily to attempts at romanticization through the years, especially when one takes into account lyrics like "I believe, I believe my time ain't long," and the life cut short by heart attack at an early age. Thus, James draws comparison to other legendary Mississippi blues artists such as Charley Patton and Robert Johnson, whose brilliant lives were also cut short but who left a highly regarded body of recordings with which to be remembered.

"No matter how much research is done in the future, no one will ever discover the secrets [people] like Elmore James carry in their souls," asserted Michael Bromberg in 1969. "And so it should be, for what good is a legend if all its mysteries have been revealed."[621] Fortunately, and it owes much to James' credit as an artist, Bromberg's statement has proven to be quite inaccurate through the years. Almost four decades since Elmore's death, and over thirty years since Bromberg's words were written, all the wealth of

616 Pearson, 163.

617 McMurry and Slim, 10, 12; and O'Neal, "Lillian S. McMurry," 19.

618 Mike Leadbitter and John Broven, "Behind The Sun—West Memphis." *Blues Unlimited* 79 (January 1971): 6.

619 Obrecht, "The Ballad of Elmore & Homesick James," 78.

620 Brisbin, "Robert Plunkett," 46.

621 Michael Bromberg, notes to Elmore James, *The Resurrection of Elmore James.* Kent LP 9010, 1969.

information and the widespread availability of Elmore's catalog have not tarnished his stature in the least. If anything, it has been increased. Neither refusing to wallow in sentimentality nor stooping to contrivance, Elmore's blues songs have an undeniably enduring quality to them. What Elmore James sang about was adult human relationships. Even his dance tunes such as "Shake Your Moneymaker" and "Madison Blues," in some manner still deal with the subject of human relationships.

But what is it, exactly, that makes the music of Elmore James so extraordinary, that makes it stand out above many of his contemporaries? I think it's two things, really, that make Elmore special—and for why he is so revered by his fans.

The first is more obvious, perhaps. Simply stated, Elmore's talent is immense. It kind of reminds me of what a rock critic once said of the Beatles. If you take the Beatles and break the group down into the four component parts of John, Paul, George, and Ringo, you wouldn't necessarily find, according to the thinking of this particular critic, four different "all-time-great superstar" rock musicians. On an individual basis, there have been more talented lead guitarists than George, more technically proficient drummers than Ringo, and better vocalists than John or Paul. But why this critic felt that they were possibly the world's greatest rock band was how each of their personally unique abilities combined and complemented with each other so perfectly that made the end product of the Beatles so very special. Their trump card? Surely it would be George Martin, their talented producer, rightly crowned "the fifth Beatle," and/or Brian Epstein, their astute manager.

Essentially, one could level a similar argument about Elmore James. Blues guitarists more gifted than Elmore—possibly, yes. Better songwriters than Elmore? Without a doubt. Better vocalists or bandleaders? Most assuredly. But what truly makes Elmore extraordinary is that he *was* a fabulous guitarist, *was* a talented songwriter and bandleader, and *was* a great vocalist—and while it is not uncommon for a blues artist to excel in one or two of these areas—and sometimes even three—Elmore excelled in each and every one of them. That kind of aptitude is rare, indeed, and in Elmore James, these talents were combined into a finished product where the whole adds up to way more than just the sum of its parts. This is one of the reasons his music has so effortlessly withstood scrutiny and the visages of time. Elmore was unequivocally and exceptionally talented. The proof of this is born out in his music. It leaps up at you out of the grooves, and grabs your attention. Elmore's trump card? That would unquestionably have to be the Broomdusters—and a series of good producers to work with, who understood him and his music.

The second part of what makes Elmore James extraordinary is much more difficult to grasp. It is the part of Elmore's music that is not immediately observable, but is undeniably present. It is the part of his music that can be felt by the soul, rather than be heard with the ears. On that unusually warm day in January, 1987, I felt it. The force of what I felt that day has stuck with me for all these years. Basically, I think it goes something like this.

"There could be no blues without the spiritual," opined the great Big Bill Broonzy.[622] With that little nugget of truth, Broonzy offered us an insight into a unique and instinctive knowledge of African-American musical traditions that many people, from that day to this, might still be arguing over. If this were a courtroom trial, Broonzy would have already dispensed with his closing arguments while the rest of us were still debating the jury selection. Indeed, it bears repeating: "There could be no blues without the spiritual." What was Big Bill hinting at? The way I interpret Broonzy's comment isn't so much a suggestion that the blues evolved from the spiritual and transcended that form of music as it developed, but rather, that there could be no blues without the spiritual (or it's modern-day heir, gospel) because the one simply cannot exist without the other—that is to say, *they are both different sides of the same coin.* In order for the

622 Studs Terkel, notes to Big Bill Broonzy and Washboard Sam, *Big Bill Broonzy and Washboard Sam.* Chess LP 1468, 1962.

blues to exist, so too must gospel. They are two halves of a whole, balancing one another out, very much in the classic Chinese philosophical sense of the Yin and the Yang. Big Bill understood this intrinsically.[623] "If the blues are viewed in the proper perspective, it is clear that their mood is very similar to the ethos of the spirituals," scholar James H. Cone offered in his book, *The Spirituals and the Blues.* "Indeed, I contend that the blues and the spirituals flow from the same bedrock of experience, and neither is an adequate interpretation of black life without the commentary of the other."[624] What Cone suggests is easily confirmed: the blues and African-American spiritual/gospel music all come from a common well; their shared roots and traditions inextricably bound. Vocal stylings, instrumentation, and sometimes the performers themselves have been common to both of these musical forms (and it would be easy to take the list further). As Harley Cokliss succinctly sums it up in the film *Chicago Blues:* "Blues and gospel speak the same language. The storefront church belongs to the same world as the tavern and club. It is the same sense of community; the same knowledge that the brother talking or singing up there knows what you feel."[625] There is, of course, one historical difference that has imbued and informed (however subtly or profoundly) much of the consequent dialogue and rhetoric between and about these two musical genres. "But the blues is about the troubles of this world," Cokliss states as he finishes his thought. "It doesn't offer solutions—it's a lament. Gospel *has* a solution—God is the answer."[626] Owing to jejune, over-used metaphors whose barbs have been dulled through the years, the labels of "profane" (or "the devil's music") for the blues and "sacred" for gospel are just too easy, too naive. More appropriately—and perhaps more accurately—we could boil it down this way. If gospel music is a celebration of a higher power—an affirmation that there is a supreme being, a guiding force that is "out there somewhere" in the universe—then by definition, the blues is the opposite of that. That is to say, the blues, in its most radical (i.e., root), primal form, asks the fundamental question "what if we are alone in the universe?" As a spokesperson or articulator for his or her community, one of the tasks the blues artist is charged with is that of allowing for the maintenance of skepticism within their community (according to Cone, this is a role that has been documented as far back as slavery times); this question then is just a natural extension of that role—especially when one considers gospel music's exuberant faith in an ordered, well-run and well-staffed universe—a naturally skeptical response to that ideology by the blues artist is definitely appropriate.[627] "Ain't no heaven and there ain't no burnin' hell," the great Son House unceremoniously offered in one of his 1930 recordings, adding, "Where I'm goin' when I die, ain't nobody tell."[628] Let us reflect on Son House's words as we take a deep breath and consider this for a moment: what if Son House is right? Indeed, what if there is no higher power "out there somewhere" who is in charge (and, I might add, keeping tabs on us like some kind of demented Santa Claus)? What if it is only us, here on this warm fleck of a rock we call planet Earth, circling around the sun in the vast, cold emptiness of outer space? Standing on the brink of the abyss and defiantly crying

---

623 Another great Big Bill Broonzy moment, as reported by Pete Seeger:

"No two people, not even the professors, have been able to agree completely on a definition of folk music. The Funk & Wagnalls *Dictionary of Folklore* lists many, which only partly overlap each other.

One definition says: 'A folk song must be old, carried on for generations by people who have had no contact with urban arts and influence. A folk song must show no trace of individual authorship.'

At the other end is the definition of the late Big Bill Broonzy, the blues singer. He was asked if a certain blues he sang was a folk song. 'It must be,' he replied. 'I never heard horses sing it.'" (Pete Seeger, *The Incompleat Folksinger.* New York: Simon and Schuster, 1972, 62.)

624 James H. Cone, *The Spirituals and the Blues: An Interpretation.* San Francisco: Harper & Row, 1972, 111.

625 Harley Cokliss, dir., *Chicago Blues.* Irit Films, 1970.

626 Ibid.

627 David Evans, "Blues." Memphis State University, Memphis, Tennessee, 5 September 1989; and Cone, 109-110.

628 Son House, "My Black Mama—Part 1." Paramount 13042, 1930.

out into the void, the blues acknowledges the possibility that there may be no one there to answer back. On one level, we can interpret this in a literal, intrinsic sense meaning that, yes, we actually *are* alone in the universe because nobody will ever be able to "get inside our heads" and truly know what it means to be us—to know us as we know ourselves, from within. But try taking a step back and looking at it from a much broader perspective, and many people may find it an absolutely terrifying prospect—too scary to think about for more than a few minutes at a time. Yet, some of the greatest and most enduring blues songs either hint at this possibility or speak to it directly—in one form or another. A few examples come to mind: Charley Booker's dark masterpiece "Walked All Night;" Leroy Carr's somber, heartfelt "Midnight Hour Blues;" Howlin' Wolf's eerie, ethereal "No Place to Go;" Robert Johnson's heart-rending "Love in Vain," or the frightening alone-ness immanently apparent in his "Cross Road Blues;" the bone-chilling nihilism in Little Walter's "Blue and Lonesome" (ironically, the last 45 of his career); Otis Rush's gut-wrenching classic of angst, "So Many Roads, So Many Trains;" the emptiness of Sonny Boy Williamson's tear-jerker "Mighty Long Time;" and Elmore James' introspective, gorgeously poetic "Something Inside of Me;"—they all speak to a common theme, a shared existentialist element—something that forms the irreducible marrow from which the blues are made.[629]

Topics such as these in blues songs are not necessarily meant to frighten, depress, or startle listeners as they are so much an attempt by the blues singer to come face to face with some of the deeper questions about the world we live in and what it means to be a human being. According to an article by Eddie S. Meadows entitled "African World View in Blues" (in the last issue of *Blues Unlimited* magazine), the concept of "Nommo" is presented and explained as one of the "aspects of African world view [that] can be found in the text of the blues." As Meadows relates, "Nommo" is the "Importance of participation and experience; and the belief that the universe moves in a rhythmical and cyclical fashion. The African concept of Nommo is said to be behind the African emphasis on verbal skill. Nommo is the 'magic power of the word,' through which persons actualize life and master life's contents." Meadows further elaborates:

> The concept of Nommo can also be used to explain Michael Haralambos's description of the psychological function of blues as one of "closure." He notes: "When a malady is labelled, a difficult experience classified, anxiety and tension are reduced because order is created out of disorder." The blues artist, then, is recognized by the black community for his/her ability to put into words those everyday things that baffle, anger, or move people. To sing about a trying event is, in many ways, a mastery over that event. According to underlying African world view, the use of art to conquer misery is not an escape, for vocalization of the event or object reaffirms its reality.[630]

In this sense, then, the blues tries to deal with some of the deeper mysteries that surround our lives by singing about them; perhaps one of the strongest—and perhaps most central—of the African retentions that can be found in the blues.

As was said earlier, Elmore James sang about human relationships. Another thing that his music

[629] Charley [a.k.a. Chris] Booker, "Walked All Night." From the album *Sun—The Roots of Rock, Volume 12: Union Avenue Breakdown.* Charly LP 30127, 1977. Leroy Carr, "Midnight Hour Blues." Vocalion 1703, 1932; Howlin' Wolf, "No Place to Go." Chess 1566, 1954; Robert Johnson, "Love in Vain." Vocalion 04630, 1939; Robert Johnson, "Cross Road Blues;" Little Walter [Jacobs], "Blue and Lonesome." Checker 1117, 1965; Otis Rush, "So Many Roads, So Many Trains." Chess 1751, 1960; Sonny Boy Williamson, "Mighty Long Time;" and James, "Something Inside of Me."

[630] Eddie S. Meadows, "African World View in Blues: A Prefatory Analysis." *Blues Unlimited* 148/149 (Winter 1987): 18. Here, Meadows is quoting Geneva Smitherman, *Talkin and Testifyin: The Language of Black America.* Boston: Houghton & Mifflin, 1977, 78; and Michael Haralambos, *Right On: From Blues to Soul in Black America.* New York: Drake Publishers, 1975, 59. Meadows also stated that, "Nommo was first discussed, to my knowledge, by Janheinz Jahn in *Muntu: An Outline of the New African Culture.* New York: Grove Press, 1961, 132-135."

consistently addresses is that of human suffering. These are the two central themes that we find in his music—that of human relationships and that of human suffering—and he channeled his creativity as an artist through these two subjects and into his music. During a time in which Elmore's contemporaries like Muddy Waters and Howlin' Wolf may have been content in commemorating their sexual prowess or animal magnetism, Elmore was singing about something else entirely: "I'm so blue this mornin', I can't even go to work;" or "It's all my fault, I musta did somebody wrong;" and "If you ever sad and lonesome, broken hearted too/Take my word, good people, something wrong with you;" or "Almost every night I cry myself to sleep/Everybody else is so happy, an' I just weep, weep, weep/Lord, these tears, tears, tears, why won't they let me be?" These are just but a few samples from his music; there are many more from which to chose. Again, James H. Cone's words are enlightening: "Without pain and suffering, and what that meant for black people in Mississippi, Tennessee, and Arkansas, there would have been no blues," he offered. "The blues are not art for art's sake, music for music's sake. They are a way of life, a life-style of the black community; and they came into being to give expression to black identity and the will for survival. Thus to seek to understand the blues apart from the suffering that created them is to misinterpret them and distort the very creativity that defines them."[631] Cone's statement is echoed in the words of Haralambos, as quoted by Meadows—to sing about something is, in a sense, to gain mastery over it; and when presented in the context of community, helps the community to do the same as well. It must have taken a toll on him, though. How is it possible to maintain that kind of intensity in your music—in the clubs and on record—without wanting *something* to help kill the pain at the end of the day? Perhaps what caused Elmore to drink so heavily, then, wasn't necessarily just merely from alcoholism, but maybe because he could find no other acceptable option for numbing a harsh pain in his life that just wouldn't go away.

Suffering is the great equalizer of the human race. Not one person on this planet, before they leave, will be exempted from its grasp. It's not too surprising, then, that we find songs such as "Something Inside of Me," "Bleeding Heart," "Sho Nuff I Do," and "The Sky Is Crying" as among the greatest in Elmore's catalog. Charles Shaar Murray, the John Lee Hooker biographer, had this to say about suffering and the blues: "If anything can truly be said to be the philosophical core of the blues," he wrote, "it is this: when you suffer, you can at least boogie, and when you boogiein', you ain't sufferin'. But, first, you got to face the fact that you're sufferin'. Once you've acknowledged your pain, you can get to dealing with it."[632] That is why, on the other end of Elmore's musical spectrum, we find such enduring rockers as "Hawaiian Boogie," "Make a Little Love," "I Believe," and "Standing at the Crossroads." And there's a perfectly good reason for all this. "Because we know that we have survived, that we have not been destroyed, and that we are more than the stripes on our backs" stated James H. Cone, "we can sing as a way of celebrating our being."[633] Indeed, can there be any more dynamic and joyful celebration of life than Elmore's "Hawaiian Boogie," for instance? At last, then, here is the real kicker about Elmore. If you wanted to know the secret that people like Elmore James carry in their souls, then here it is: In spite of the fact that we might be alone in the universe, and in spite of the fact that we suffer, what the blues teaches us about life is that it is still possible to dance—it is still possible to boogie and be joyous—it is still possible to celebrate life. What the music of Elmore James is about is the undeniable and inexpugnable spark of the human spirit—a spark that will not go out—that cannot be overcome by darkness.

Some of the greatest philosophers of the twentieth century—armed with pens or typewriters—at times, attempted to say as much. But Elmore didn't arm himself with a pen or typewriter—his weapon of

631 Cone, 123-124.

632 Charles Shaar Murray, *Boogie Man: The Adventures of John Lee Hooker in the American Twentieth Century.* New York: St. Martin's Press, 2000, 8.

633 Cone, 128.

choice was the electric guitar. Even though they might have been saying some of the same sorts of things, the philosophers—in contrast to Elmore—quickly devolve into a seething morass of whiners. Never could they have imagined a message this potent or powerful—as it was, set to music and electrically amplified. What Elmore had to say he said on his own terms, using his own traditions and set of rules. Not only that, but Elmore sang what he sang about eloquently, and in highly listenable increments of about three minutes at a time—a story with a solid rhythm and a driving beat that, if you wanted to, you could dance to it. At the verge of nothingness, his response isn't to wither or shrivel away, but to acknowledge it, deal with it, and then respond with a joyous, celebratory dance of life. In this regard, then, Elmore James didn't just *stand* on the brink of the abyss and cry out into the void, he *boogied* on it—and because he has done this for us, we, in turn, will never have to fear it ourselves. And if that doesn't rank as one of the most remarkable and amazing things that ever happened on this planet, then I honestly don't know what does.

The One Minute Elmore

In 1992, Jim O'Neal ran a contest in his occasional periodical, the *Stackhouse/Delta Record Mart Mail Order Catalogue and Rooster Blues Newsletter*. In it, O'Neal did a spoof of the then-current ongoing column in *Living Blues* magazine, called "Desert Island Discs." In this series, reviewers and contributors would write in to *Living Blues* and list their ten favorite blues albums of all time (or, as the name implies, the ones they would pick if they were going to be stranded on a desert island). In his newsletter, O'Neal one-upped *Living Blues* with his "Endless Loop Blues Contest," the premise being, "But suppose you couldn't take ten albums to the island with you. What if you had to listen to only one song, over and over again, ad infinitum?" The winning entry, picked by Jim himself (and Judy Dorsey, station manager of Memphis community radio station WEVL FM 90), was Charley Booker's "Walked All Night."[634] Although I admit Booker's waxing is definitely worthy of the highest accolades, the correct answer, in my opinion, should have been Elmore James' "I Believe" on Meteor 5000 (Although I have to admit that "Hawaiian Boogie" and "Standing at the Crossroads" are both close runners up). But just to go O'Neal one better—if only to prove that being a founding editor of *Living Blues* magazine doesn't necessarily also make you the king of unlikely hypothetical scenarios—what if instead of one song, you could only have one minute? The one minute I would choose would be the last one minute of "I Believe." There are few moments in recorded blues as defining as this one minute of audio—Elmore's declamatory, fierce vocals in which he sings about—as usual—something going on wrong somewhere; Johnny Jones, Odie Payne and J.T. Brown rocking away in the background, every single member of the group pounding out the rhythm, keeping the beat going as solid as a glacier and the playing as hot as fiery magma; to the final, triumphant shouts and cheers from the Broomdusters while James offers up his trademark, yet gloriously soaring, transcendent electric guitar solo, over Jones' crashing piano. Oh, that solo! Part grit and part valve grinding compound fused into 19,000 volts of electricity, the sound of Elmore's guitar climbs out of the grooves of the disc and ascends to a towering height until it is floating effortlessly over the Broomdusters somewhere off in the background. As far as the Broomdusters go, this is about as good as it gets, and truly inspired moments like these come along as rarely as do cool August days in Mississippi. For myself, this is how I will choose to remember Elmore James. For that one brief minute, all is right with the world. For one brief minute,

[634] Jim O'Neal, "The ENDLESS LOOP BLUES Contest: I Win." *Stackhouse/Delta Record Mart Mail Order Catalogue and Rooster Blues Newsletter* 5 (March 1992): 2.

there is nowhere else on earth better to be than where I am right now. For one brief minute, the Broomdusters are always flesh and blood, never gone, but still with us in the here and now—alive and vital. For that one minute, all is well, balance has been restored to the universe, and I am at peace. And just as quickly, the last notes from Elmore's electric guitar fade out and it's gone—the arm of the record player abruptly veering off into the return groove, and then silence (or, as is much more common in the age of digital, the CD player quietly advances to the next selection).

And that, my friends, is where we will leave Elmore James, with the sound of his guitar fading into nothingness. Fortunately for us, we are lucky—Elmore's music never has to be very far from our hearts, our souls, or our ears—it's a moment we can get back any time we want. As long as there are people who want to celebrate that moment—that inextinguishable spark of the human spirit—then, maybe—just maybe—the music of Elmore James will live forever.

Otis Ealey, Elmore's Atlanta manager, had this publicity photo made circa 1955. While the image has been seen many times with the bottom cropped off, this rare original version shows Ealey's name and address clearly visible in the lower right-hand corner. Courtesy Blues Unlimited.

Elmore James with an unknown admirer. Courtesy Blues Unlimited (date and photographer unknown).

Sonny Boy Williamson, early 1950s. "Eyesight To The Blind" helped get a fledgling Trumpet Records off the ground. The other three singles all feature Elmore's guitar work. Courtesy Blues Unlimited.

Tampa Red, "The Guitar Wizard," in a 1940s publicity shot. His advanced slide guitar playing is an often overlooked influence on Elmore James. Pianist Johnny Jones and drummer Odie Payne both played and recorded with Tampa Red in the late 1940s and early 1950s. Bill Greensmith Collection.

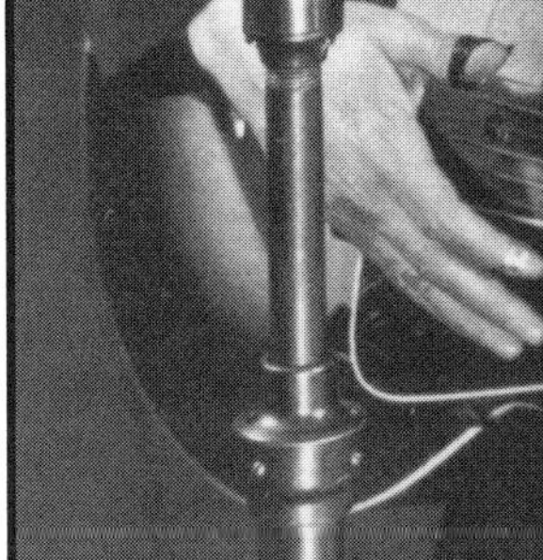

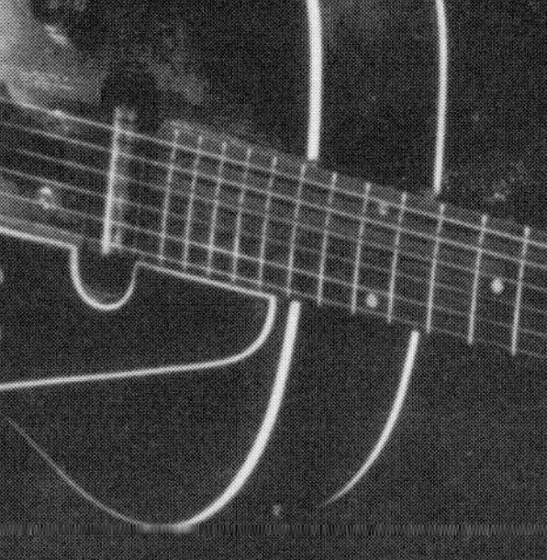

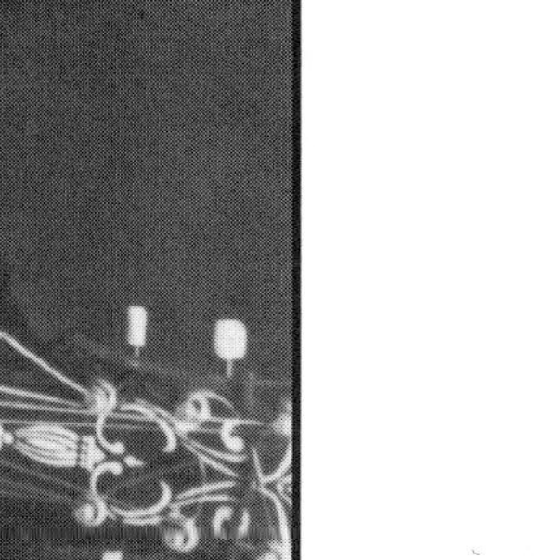

Robert Nighthawk, posing for an early 1960s publicity shot. His smooth, amplified slide technique was an important, influential bridge between the 1930s acoustic blues and the 1950s Chicago tough urban-electric sound. Earl Hooker, Elmore James, and Muddy Waters were among those with whom he shared his knowledge. Courtesy Blues Unlimited. "Annie Lee Blues" courtesy Bill Greensmith Collection.

Arthur "Big Boy" Crudup, 1940s. He was among the first of the Mississippi blues artists to feature an electric guitar on his records. Although Crudup never recorded with Elmore, they often had competing singles out at the same time, such as this 1962 Fire release. Bill Greensmith Collection.

Ike Turner, from a 1959 publicity shot. In the early fifties, Turner helped the Bihari brothers scout out talent, such as Elmore James, for their family of record labels. On "Please Find My Baby" (recorded at James' first session with the Biharis), Ike plays piano, while "1839 Blues" showcases some of Turner's guitar work. Bill Greensmith Collection.

Left to right: B.B. King, Big Bill Hill, Fontella Bass. Disk jockeys like Hill were influential in their ability to "make" or "break" a record. Hill's on-location broadcasts over Chicago radio station WOPA regularly featured Elmore James live in performance. Bill Greensmith Collection.

The man who sat behind the tape recorder for many of Elmore's great early records on Meteor, Flair, and Modern, Joe Bihari (left), posing with B.B. King (center) and disk jockey Hunter Hancock, on the cover of the 24 April 1954 issue of Cash Box magazine. Blues Unlimited/Bill Greensmith Collection.

A man with many record labels, Mel London (left), with one of his recording artists, Ricky Allen (center), and an unknown lady (right). In the spring of 1957, Elmore James helped get Chief Records—London's first venture into the record business—off the ground. Courtesy Blues Unlimited. "Cry For Me" courtesy Bill Greensmith Collection.

Chicago blues Mafioso, circa 1952 or 1953. From left to right: Walter Horton, Willie Nix, Patty Nix, J.T. Brown, unknown lady, Muddy Waters, and Jimmy Rogers. Blues Unlimited Collection.

From left to right: Boyd Atkins, S.P. Leary, Magic Sam, Letha Jones, Johnny Jones, Georgia Maghett, Odell Campbell. 18th & Michigan, 1959. Courtesy Letha Jones/ Blues Unlimited.

Putting extra cute licks on the drums. Odie Payne, c. 1967. Photo by Mike Rowe

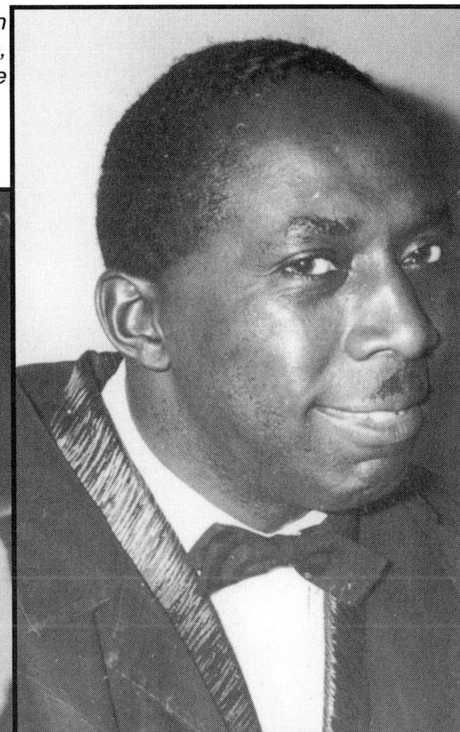

Magic Sam and Johnny Jones, clowning for the camera. Courtesy Letha Jones/Blues Unlimited.

Elmore and J.T. Brown, live in performance over WOPA, December 1959. Photo by George Adins, courtesy Robert Sacré.
Note the two microphones; the one on the right is for broadcasting, while the one on the left is for the house P.A. system.

Another of Adins' classic photos of Elmore and J.T. performing live over WOPA, December 1959. Photo by George Adins, courtesy Robert Sacré.

A tale of two photographs. This photo, taken by George Adins in December 1959 in Chicago, has commonly been seen with the bottom cropped off (right) because of the overexposure from Adins' flash bulb in the right corner of the original photo (above). It is reproduced in full here for the first time. From left to right: Homesick James, Elmore James, J.T. Brown, Boyd Atkins. Courtesy Robert Sacré (Note: the amplifier is a Magnatone with two speakers in the cabinet).

Elmore James, playing to a crowded bar; December 1959. Photo by George Adins, courtesy Robert Sacré.

Above: Behind the lens, George Adins. Given the general rarity of Elmore James photos, his images are an important part of the photographic record. Left: Elmore, J.T., and Homesick broadcasting over WOPA, while Big Bill Hill mans the controls (lower left corner). Photo by George Adins. Courtesy Robert Sacré.

Above: Elmore James, Sonny Boy Williamson, Tommy McClennan, and Little Walter, circa 1953, Chicago. Photo by Big Bill Broonzy, courtesy Margo and Yannick Bruynoghe Collection/ Living Blues. Right: Eddie Taylor and Floyd Jones. Eddie Taylor worked and recorded with Elmore James in Chicago, while Floyd Jones, along with Sunnyland Slim and Robert Johnson, reputedly worked together with Elmore in the 1930s, doing manual labor in the Mississippi Delta. Courtesy Blues Unlimited.

Eddie Taylor, London, 1974. Lurking in the background are, from left to right, Bruce Bastin, Frank Weston, and photographer Bill Greensmith.

John Littlejohn, Chicago, 1972. Photo by Bill Greensmith.

Hound Dog Taylor at the 1972 Ann Arbor Blues Festival. Photo by Bill Greensmith.

J.B. Hutto, London, 1972. Photo by Bill Greensmith.

Left to Right: Homesick James, Johnny Shines, Howlin' Wolf. 1972 Ann Arbor Blues Festival. Photo by Bill Greensmith. Advertisement from 28 March 1953 Billboard.

Hot in Memphis, Sizzling in New Orleans . . . No not the weather . . . it's

"HOME SICK"

by James Williamson

on Chance Records

1151 E. 47th. St. Chicago, Illinois
Phone: KEnwood 8-4813

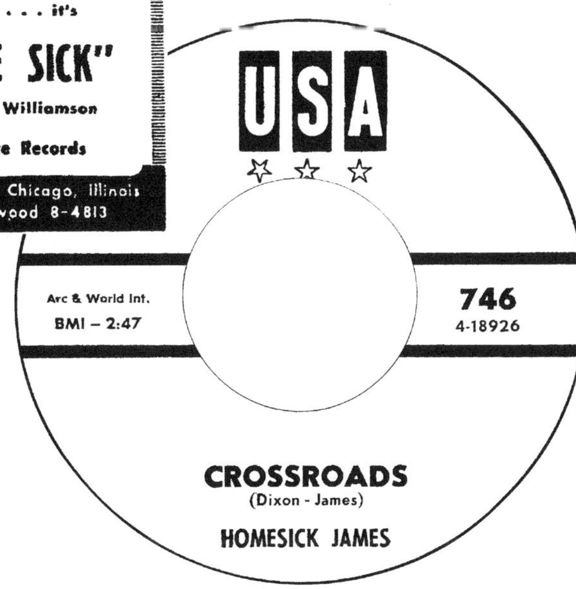

ODIE PAYNE Jr. and the BIG BAND

Bill Hill TV Group

DARLENE PAYNE

and the O. D. GIRLS

HARRY ROZELLE

(Mr. West Side) Singing and His Latest Recording and Others

SAX MALLARD ·

FAMOUS SAXOLOGIST

HENRY REED Trumpet

Sunday, July 19

3:00 P.M.

UNITED CHURCH of ALTGELD

13015 So. Ellis Avenue

Chicago, Illinois 60627

Ad from Blue Flame magazine, 1972.

NEWS BEHIND THE JAZZ SCENE

SONNY BOY

IN spite of Sonny Boy's attachment to London, it looks as though he'll really be going home after this. He's been persuaded that he should go home and see his wife before he gets involved in the red tape and paperwork of becoming a British citizen.

His desire to join us permanently seems more than just a passing whim, though whether he can face the daunting formalities and delays, even in that magnificent bowler, remains to be seen.

News item from Jazz Beat magazine, February 1964, courtesy Alan Balfour Collection. "Bloody Tears" courtesy Bill Greensmith Collection.

CHAPTER SIX

Whatever Happened to...

I'm sure that everybody's got this feeling about certain people– everybody knows people that they just have that feeling about them that they're

not going to be seventy years old, ever. *Not everybody makes it, you know.*

–Keith Richards, *said in regards to fellow Rolling Stone Brian Jones (from the documentary 25 x 5)*

Johnny, J.T., and Odie

"Unfortunately acclaim has come to Elmore James too late for any of us to do any more than honor his memory," offered Neil Slaven more than thirty years ago, adding, "Time never seems to have been on his side."[635] Sad to say, the same could more or less be said of the Broomdusters—Johnny Jones, J.T. Brown, and Odie Payne—as well. They were all still recruited for recording sessions (some more than others), with Johnny sparking some sessions with Howlin' Wolf, Eddie Taylor, and Hubert Sumlin; J.T. for several Chess dates; and Odie for 1963 and 1964 Chuck Berry sessions, as well as Magic Sam's notable *West Side Soul* LP. On Tuesday, 25 June 1963, Norman Dayron visited a Chicago club where Jones was performing, and with his tape recorder in tow made the only known live recording of Elmore James' pianist. Sixteen years later, the bulk of Dayron's tapes, which featured Jones in a primarily solo setting or joined by Billy Boy Arnold on some tunes, were finally issued on the Alligator label (and later reissued on compact disc).[636] Around this time, someone (possibly Johnny's wife Letha) snapped a photo of Johnny at home with fellow keyboard legend Otis Spann. Otis is seated at the piano while Johnny stands over him; Johnny is wearing a cowboy hat and Otis a sombrero (possibly a souvenir from the ill-fated trip to the border with Elmore?). The photo is troubling, though. If one looks closely at it, a few puffs of gray hair are visible peeking out from underneath the brim of Johnny's hat, and the photo, which shows Johnny's face in profile only, seems to make his appearance look like that of a grandfatherly piano legend more than anything, greatly belying his true age. Is it just a trick of the light, or is this the the corporeal evidence of a life lived at the speed of fast forward? Where is the dapper, handsome Johnny from just a few years ago?[637] In 1964, there was another recording session, this time for Carl Jones (no relation), and during a remake of Leroy Carr's "Prison Bound Blues," Johnny sang:

> Letha you will never see my smilin' face again,
> Letha you will never, baby, see my smilin' face again,
> But always remember your daddy have been your friend. [638]

---

635 Neil Slaven, notes to Elmore James and John Brim, *Tough.* Blue Horizon LP 7-63204, 1968.

636 Eagle, 29; Johnny Jones, *Johnnie Jones with Billy Boy Arnold.* Alligator LP 4717, 1979; and Iglauer, notes to *Johnnie Jones with Billy Boy Arnold.* Note: Some of these recordings were also issued in England on *Live at the Fickle Pickle* (Flyright LP 549, 1979).

637 Rowe, *Chicago Breakdown,* 144.

638 Little Johnny Jones, "Prison Bound Blues." Rooster Blues 23, 1980.

Afterwards, he was scheduled to tour Europe with Howlin' Wolf and Hubert Sumlin. He suddenly began losing weight, and couldn't make the tour because his lungs were now giving him trouble as well. By the time Wolf and Sumlin returned from their overseas tour, Little Johnny Jones was dead. He passed away exactly one week before Thanksgiving, on 19 November 1964, at the age of forty. He and his wife Letha never had any children.[639] "Yet another bluesman has vanished as silently as he appeared," Mike Leadbitter wrote in his January 1965 obituary. "In a Chicago full of guitarists and with comparatively few top rate pianists, the death of Little Johnny Jones is a great loss, as it is to us, who were never really given a chance to appreciate him."[640]

In the 1960's, J.T. Brown's name still came up once and a while—as a session musician here and there (both he and Jones had been recruited to play on a couple of Howlin' Wolf titles), and the occasional gig. There was a date for the Atomic-H label in 1959 or 1960 and three titles were waxed, but not released at the time. "My very first gig with J.T. was in August, 1963 when he called me about a job he had up in Grand Rapids, Michigan," guitarist Jimmy Dawkins remembered. "I will never forget that time because it was more like a death march than a playing engagement. We played in a very plush supper club. The band had to be very easy on stage and always on guard... because one might forget where he was and put in a few soulful licks.... We quit after two weeks," Dawkins stated. "After that we played many times together around Chicago. He was playing clubs, benefits, and social gatherings. Gypsies would call him to play their dances." At times, such was the life of a musician—whatever it took to pay the bills and keep some money in your pocket.[641]

After the Atomic-H session, J.T. Brown didn't record anything more under his own name for a decade, when a group of blues enthusiasts who called themselves Fleetwood Mac came over from England and recorded two LPs worth of material at the Chess studios in one day, Saturday, 4 January 1969. They were joined by the likes of Otis Spann, Honeyboy Edwards, and Walter Horton. J.T. Brown was also fortuitously called in for the session. One member of Fleetwood Mac in particular, Jeremy Spencer, was an amazingly capable Elmore James enthusiast and imitator who had spent years perfecting the technique, and had been dazzling British crowds with his skill for some time. Brown's set with Spencer was memorable if not brief, and for just about a half hour the unlikely pair of musicians generated some of the original magic present on Elmore's original recordings with the Broomdusters. A photograph snapped during the session shows a bemused J.T. shaking hands with Jeremy, and it's tempting to speculate what thoughts might have been running through his mind. Sadly, it proved to not only be the swan song of the blues-oriented Fleetwood Mac, but J.T. Brown's as well. On Saturday, 30 August 1969, Homesick James saw J.T. at a big Grant Park blues festival, in downtown Chicago. "I saw J.T. Brown and he didn't look good then," Homesick later remembered.[642] The next thing that appeared about J.T. was a one-paragraph item prepared by Mike Leadbitter in *Blues Unlimited* the following winter. It read:

---

639 Eagle, 29; and Iglauer, notes to *Johnnie Jones with Billy Boy Arnold.*

640 Mike Leadbitter, "Little Johnny Jones—An Obituary." *Blues Unlimited* 18 (January 1965): 18.

641 Jimmy Dawkins, notes to *Chicago Ain't Nothin' But a Blues Band.* Delmark LP 624, 1972; J.T. Brown, *Windy City Boogie.* Delmark CD 714, 1998; and Daniel Groslier, "J.T. Brown/Discographie." *Soul Bag* 94 (May/June 1983): 16.

642 Leadbitter and Robinson, "Lazy Bill Called Me Homesick (I Wasn't Though)(Part 3)," 11; Mick Fleetwood and Stephen Davis, *Fleetwood: My Life and Adventures with Fleetwood Mac.* New York: William Morrow & Co., 1990, 42-43, 68-69; and Fleetwood Mac, *Fleetwood Mac in Chicago 1969.* Sire/Warner Bros./Blue Horizon CD 9 45283-2, 1994 [reissue].

> J.T. Brown died in Chicago on the 24th of November [1969] at 2:30pm. He had recently undergone surgery. He passed away unknown. No-one had ever interviewed him. Best known for his rocking sax work with J.B. Lenoir and Elmore James, he leaves us a few obscure singles. Nobody seems interested in sax-playing bluesmen. Pity—for J.T. was a veteran on the Chicago scene.... They called him "Nature Boy", "Sax Man", "Bep", and "Big Boy" and he played some pretty wild stuff, and occasionally he sang. Goodbye, J.T.[643]

In December 1989, Dick Shurman noted that J.T. "was rumored to possess unissued tapes of Elmore." Whatever became of those tapes, and the nature of what they contained, is a complete mystery—by now, surely lost forever.[644]

Odie Payne, Elmore's drummer in the Broomdusters, and second only to Chicago blues drummer Fred Below, still remained active from the sixties onward. He recorded for Delmark, Chuck Berry, and for a Muddy Waters session. Payne invoked a number of trademark gestures, among them a terrific left hand and a strong right foot on the bass pedal—"so fast," S.P. Leary was moved to comment about Payne's foot, "it could simulate a roll;" and the use of the cowbell, which can be prominently heard on a number of Elmore James' recordings. The reason for the latter, he told a blues fan, was to get a response from the audience, and to know after the record came out what recording sessions he'd been on. Payne's talents weren't exclusive to the drum kit either; he was proficient on the piano as well, opening the 1981 American Folk Blues Festival in London, for instance, by performing "I Don't Know" on the ivories. In 1988, he recorded a solo album entitled *No, What Did She Say.* It turned out to be his last session. On Wednesday, 1 March 1989, Odie Payne passed away of bone cancer; he was sixty-two. Just two years after his death, Payne's extended interview with Steve Cushing appeared in the March/April 1991 issue of *Living Blues* magazine (number 96). He was the only original member of the Broomdusters to ever be interviewed at any great length.[645]

643 Mike Leadbitter, "J. T. Brown." Blues Unlimited 70 (February/March 1970): 14.

644 Dick Shurman, notes to *Cool Playing Blues.* Relic CD 7016, 1990. Note: J.T. wasn't the only person who supposedly held unissued tapes of Elmore. According to Mike Leadbitter and Simon Napier, in *Collectors Classics 7,* "A certain West Coast company and a disk jockey in Massachusetts also own unissued Elmore James material—will it ever see the light of day?" The "West Coast company" they refer to is obviously Modern Records, whose tapes are now owned by Ace Records in the U.K.—but who is the "Massachusetts d.j.?" Working on a tip from Jim O'Neal, I contacted Skippy White, former owner of the Bluestown and Silver Cross record labels, and present-day proprietor of a retail record store in Cambridge, Massachusetts. While White himself is not in possession of any such tapes, he feels fairly certain that this story might have been just a rumor, possibly originating with disk jockey Jimmy "Early" Bird. According to White, Bird was very heavily into Elmore James, wearing out copies of "It Hurts Me Too" on his radio show, and was, at one time, friendly with Bobby Robinson. Bird was also—according to White—the type of person that, when it came to storytelling, anyway, had somewhat of a fondness toward exaggeration or embellishment. (Napier and Leadbitter, 2; and Skippy White, telephone interview by Steve Franz. 6 September 2002).

As far as the original source of the "J.T. Brown possessing tapes of Elmore" rumor, the following may help shed some light on that. It was submitted by Frank Scott to a postwar blues discussion group over the internet:

> *I believe that I may have been the source of the info about J.T. Brown. I met him in a Chicago blues club in 1963 (I think) and was talking to him about Elmore since I knew he had played with him. I don't know how it came about but he mentioned to me words to the effect that he had a whole lot of tapes of Elmore that had never been issued—I don't remember his exact words. For all I know he may have just been trying to impress me—a white Englishman in a blues club in 1963 was still relatively uncommon. In those days I wasn't quite the fanatic I later became and so never tried to follow up on his comment.*
>
> *It certainly wouldn't be unreasonable to imagine that he had tapes since he worked with Elmore quite a bit and was certainly present at rehearsals, record sessions and club dates. I wonder what happened to the tapes (if they existed)?* (Frank Scott, electronic communication. 14 September 2002).

As much as we'd all like it to be otherwise, it looks like anyone who had big dreams of holding a copy of the *Lost Elmore Sessions* CD in their hands will, unfortunately, have to just keep doing that—dreaming.

645 Justin O'Brien, "Odie Payne." *Living Blues* 87 (July/August 1989): 30-34; Norman Darwen, "Hip Linkchain

Sonny Boy

In the early 1960s, Elmore's old partner from the Mississippi days, Sonny Boy Williamson, was still very much active. In regards to his remarkably colorful life, I can't add much that hasn't already been repeated numerous times, and tales and yarns of his entertaining antics have now passed into the realm of blues legend and folklore—although I do remember Willie Dixon's recollections of touring Europe with Sonny Boy as being particularly memorable (*Living Blues* 82, September/October 1988). Leonard and Phil Chess—when they could find the aging harmonica wizard—still held recording sessions with him, and even though the quality may not have been quite as consistently brilliant as it had been in the early and mid-'50s, there were still choice moments. "Help Me" and "Bring It on Home" stand out as high water marks of his career, as does the hilarious—and thinly veiled, autobiographical—"The Goat." When he was in Munich for the 1964 American Folk Blues Festival tour, a heartfelt and sincere Williamson charmed the crowd with a new composition entitled "I'm Trying to Make London My Home." But just as Lillian McMurry would end up *not* moving to Alaska, neither would Sonny Boy make a new permanent home for himself across the sea.[646]

Around the time Elmore died, drummer Robert Plunkett got to fulfill the other half of the promise he made his father, when Sonny Boy Williamson came into his life. "I worked with [Sonny Boy]... for about three years, Robert Plunkett told John Anthony Brisbin. "Crazy old man.... I had more fun with that cat. He liked me, used to call me Son. He would give me a drink out of his bottle when he wouldn't give nobody else one," Plunkett recalled. "Sonny Boy was a good musician too. He could sing well and blow a harmonica well.... He'll be a clown too, blow the harp with his nose. Sometimes, he'll have three harps. Got a little one in his mouth, one with his nose, and one outside his mouth."[647]

"This particular Sunday night when we got off, he called me over to the table where he was," Plunkett remembered. "This was in '65 after he'd been to Europe and come back dressed in that [funny] suit. He said, 'You don't work no day job now, do you?' I said, 'No.' He said, 'Could you meet me down here tomorrow at twelve o'clock?.... I want you to take me to the bus station.' I say, 'Where you goin'?' He say, 'I'm going home.' I say, 'Why you goin' home?' He say, 'I'm going home to die, motherfucker!'" Plunkett told him, "'Sonny, don't talk like that.' He said, 'You ask me, goddammit! I'm goin' home to die.' ....I say, 'You sick?' 'Hell no,' he said. 'I ain't sick. I'm just tired.' I thought about that man till I went to sleep:"

> In the mornin' I thought to myself, "I'm going over there but I know Sonny Boy wasn't serious. He ain't gonna be there." So I pulled... in front of the door at Curley's Place, twelve o'clock, and there was him sittin' in there at the table by hisself. I got out of the car, went on in, set down. He had a fifth of gin, two glasses. We sat together from twelve till two drinkin' that gin and talkin'. He said he never made much money but he had a lot of fun.... Finally, he looked at his watch and said, "Well, son, come on and take the old man to the bus station." I... carried him downtown on Lake Street to the bus station. Carried his stuff in. He gave me a big hug. When he got on the bus, he shook my hand, said, "I won't see you no more. Keep on playin' drums, boy. You a good drummer...." I'm sure I was the last person in Chicago that knew him who saw him. I was the last one. And he went home. [648]

When Williamson arrived in Helena, Arkansas, one of his first stops was to look up his friends at station

---

and Odie Payne." *Blues & Rhythm* 44 (May 1989): 17; and S.P. Leary, personal interview by Steve Franz. Chicago, Illinois, 19 November 1989.

646 Leadbitter, Fancourt, and Pelletier, 765.

647 Brisbin, "Robert Plunkett," 47.

648 Ibid., 47-48.

KFFA, where he was given his old spot performing on *King Biscuit Time.* "We wondered why he came back. He still had the bowler hat, attache case and two-tone suits he picked up in England," recalled Sonny Payne, long-time announcer for the *King Biscuit Time* radio program. "I asked him, 'Sonny Boy, why'd you come back?' He said, 'I just come home to die. I know I'm sick.'" Payne remembered that, "He looked bad. You name it, and he had it. But I asked him how come he knew he was going to die. He looked me right in the eye and said, 'We're just like elephants. We knows.'"[649]

He stayed in the Helena area for a month and a half or so in the spring of 1965. During that time, Chris Strachwitz of Arhoolie Records was on one of his field trips in the mid-south. He stopped by KFFA to record one of Williamson's *King Biscuit Time* radio shows, live in the studio, which he did by tying his one microphone onto Williamson's mike stand for the fifteen-minute performance. One day in late May 1965, a warm spring day, some friends got together to go fishing, and invited Sonny Boy to come along. "Sonny Boy's companions noticed that he didn't say much, just kept looking at his line and bobber in the water," journalist Hank Harvey noted. "The next day, Sonny Boy failed to show up for *King Biscuit Time.* Peck [Curtis] went the few blocks to his apartment above the Dreamland Cafe and found him dead in bed."[650] The man who had once theorized that, "You haven't got but one life to live so why sleep it away," passed quietly, silently, in his sleep, on Tuesday, 25 May 1965. Since Sonny Boy rarely ever spoke of his childhood (so far, his name has failed to turn up in the 1910 census, further complicating the issue), no one can really quite be sure how old he was when he died, but sixty-five—give or take five years or so—seems like a fairly good estimate.[651]

---

649 Harvey, 27.

650 Ibid.; and William Donoghue, *'Fessor Mojo's "Don't Start Me to Talkin."* Elliott & James Publishing: Seattle, 1997, 61-62.

651 Leadbitter and Broven, "Behind The Sun—West Memphis," 6; and Donoghue, *'Fessor Mojo's "Don't Start Me to Talkin,"* 10-11.

Homesick James, cool as a cucumber, caught in action, 1972, Chicago. Photo by Bill Greensmith.

CHAPTER SEVEN

The Legacy of Elmore James

It's been said before; when it comes to blues, bottleneck guitar is the garni du jour. They're all at it, steel or glass, aspirin bottle or knife, a sweeping St. Vitus dance up and down the fretboard. Some go for straightforward slash and burn with all the noise and commotion of a steamhammer, others daintily pick their way through an intricate web of syncopated slide work to draw their victims in. Each one achieves an individual voice, for that is the technique's unique propensity.

But no one plays slide guitar like Elmore James.

It ought to be so simple. A repetitive phrase that anyone can play, let alone sing in taunting parody. But no one... has yet been able to replicate the combination of instrument, amplification, and technique that produced the quintessential Elmore James sound. –Neil Slaven, from the notes to Elmore James, "Rollin' and Tumblin'" (Recall CD 231, 1999)

The best Sunday afternoon I remember [at Florence's] was when J.B. Hutto, back in town after a year's absence, performed with Hound Dog [Taylor] and band. "Pet Cream Man," "Old Oak Tree," "Hipshakin'" and more. It was superb–the best I've ever heard from the man, making everything since sound weak. **When he and Dog started work on Elmore James tunes**–two slides for the price of one in an old-fashioned cutting contest–we had boogie unlimited.

–Sandy Sutherland, "Blues for Florence" (Blues Unlimited 106)

"Dust My Broom" As a Regional Phenomenon

Over the years, the music of Elmore James has been imitated, emulated, and duplicated to great and varying degrees. While Elvis Presley is certainly the most renowned musician to have spawned a world-wide group of imitators, Elmore James has certainly had his fare share of them as well. Not only is Elmore possessed of an ardent group of admirers who are visibly impassioned about his music, but he is also uniquely possessed of a small legion of artists who have variously called themselves "Elmore James Jr.," or, more blatantly, just plain "Elmore James" when they felt like it, and even in one case that I know of, a white British guitarist who played Elmore's slide licks while wearing minstrel black face! The "Dust My Broom" riff has wended its way into rock & roll, country & western, zydeco, and that most ubiquitous symbol of popular culture—beer commercials.

Around the time Lillian McMurry released "Dust My Broom" on the unsuspecting world, however, an interesting phenomenon could be observed taking place in the mid-south. Namely, that Elmore James wasn't the only person making records with the "Dust My Broom" sound.[652] Aside from the previously discussed Robert Jr. Lockwood recording of "Dust My Broom" for Mercury (Lockwood had recorded a similar version of "Dust My Broom" for J.O.B. in March 1951, but it was not released at the time), Snooky Pryor's "Going Back on the Road," and Boyd Gilmore's "All in My Dreams" (with some of Elmore's guitar spliced in for good measure), our first three entries are all recordings made by the Bihari brothers during their legendary January 1952 field trip to the mid-south. First, we find Junior Brooks and his recording (made in Little Rock on Monday, 21 January) of "She's the Little Girl For Me" on Modern's RPM subsidiary striking a familiar chord. An interesting but rough-hewn slide guitarist (he was also known as "Crippled Red" evidently), Brooks died after making making just a handful of recordings for the Biharis, and consequently almost nothing is known of him. Although Dr. Ross suggested that he was from Grenada, Mississippi, it has also been reported that he was from the area around Pine Bluff, Arkansas.[653] Our next

[652] Note: Although it doesn't quite qualify for this survey, Little Willie Littlefield's recording of "Love Me Tonight" contains a certain prescience, lending it a distinct "harbinger of things to come" quality—it even shares a lyrical theme, loosely, with Elmore's "Make a Little Love"—that at least begs for "honorable mention" status. Recorded in October 1949 in Los Angeles, this title would not see release in any form for three and a half decades, when Ace Records (in England) salvaged it from the Modern vaults. This recording can be found on *Twenty Great Blues Recordings of the '50s and '60s, Vol. 2.* Cascade LP 1010, 1984 (Cascade, evidently, was Ace's 'budget' label).

[653] Mark Harris, "Mark's Blues No. 1." *Pickin' the Blues* 24 (May 1984): 8-11; Pierson, notes to *Downhome Delta Blues 1949-1952;* Junior Brooks, "She's the Little Girl for Me." RPM 343, 1952; and Steve Franz, notes to *Sounds Like "Dust My Broom:" Development and Transition of the Most Famous Guitar Riff in History, Volume 1 (1931-1953).* Compact disc (unissued), 2001. Note: Mark Harris lists a recording date of 21 January 1952 for the

entry in this survey comes from Houston Boines' "Relation Blues," with guitarist Charley Booker, pianist Ike Turner, and blues harpist Boines all pitching in to provide a pleasant "Broom"-type ruckus. Recorded in Greenville, Mississippi, on Wednesday, 23 January, Boines' title was released on the Bihari's short-lived Blues & Rhythm subsidiary the very next month (around the same time that they issued Junior Brooks' "She's the Little Girl for Me").[654] Recorded the very same day as Boines' title above, Boyd Gilmore's "Ramblin' on My Mind" represents yet another entry in our list of blues artists who recorded compositions in a similar vein to "Dust My Broom" around the time that Elmore did. Interesting not only because of the fact that Gilmore can be visibly heard to clear his throat during the opening bars of the song, we also find Ike Turner once again chiming in on the piano to help Gilmore flush out the "Broom" riffs. Although "Ramblin' on My Mind" is a tune closely associated with Robert Johnson, Gilmore distinguishes his version by adding a few lyric touches of his own, and by interjecting a guitar solo similar to that which Elmore played during the last few bars of his Trumpet side.[655] In the 1960s and 1970s, numerous blues musicians mentioned Gilmore's name while they were being interviewed for *Blues Unlimited* or *Living Blues,* offering comments like, "I'd just seen him a couple years ago in such and such a place." It was to no avail; an enigma until the end, Gilmore was always seemingly a few steps ahead of any blues researcher who might be looking for him. Indeed, Gilmore was so difficult to find that his obituary did not appear until 1980—almost four years after his death in Fresno, California.

Our next entry in this survey is more of an enigma than even Boyd Gilmore (and that's really saying something). "Where Have You Been So Long," recorded for Chicago's J.O.B. label, carries no information as to the artist or the recording date, although the recording quality would perhaps indicate more the early 1950s (as opposed to later that decade). Although there is strong circumstantial evidence that points to Gary, Indiana guitarist John Brim as the possible perpetrator behind this recording, the vocalist in the song just does not sound like Brim, and the remainder of the titles in the Brim opus do not show any further propensity to the slide guitar or in recording Elmore James-styled tunes. While Mike Rowe has suggested Robert Nighthawk and Johnny Young as possible identities for this "stunning slide guitarist" (as he described it), the timbre of the voice has a quality more similar to an Eddie Taylor, Baby Face Leroy, or Hudson Showers type. Since none of these vocalists really "match" the unidentified artist either (yeah, Nighthawk, *maybe...* if he had a clothespin on his nose), it begs the question that perhaps the vocalist and the slide guitarist are two different people? Obviously, further listening and input will be required to solve this mystery.[656]

Brooks title, but this is slightly problematic. According to his research, Drifting Slim (a.k.a Elmon Mickle), Sunny Blair, and Junior Brooks all recorded titles that day for Modern. Dirftin' Slim's titles were issued as Modern 849, but here's the rub—Modern 850 and 851 were already being featured in a Christmas advertisement by Modern in December 1951, and they were reviewed by the trade press during the last weeks of December (Modern 850 the week of 22 December 1952, and Modern 851 the next). If one subscribes to the theory that most record companies tend to issue records chronologically (some don't, but that's another story), then it becomes difficult to explain a 21 January 1952 recording date for Mickle's titles on Modern 849 (and Blair & Brooks' titles to some extent as well). I suspect this is why other discographies have traditionally listed a 1951 recording date for Brooks' sides on RPM 343. Even so, a 21 January 1952 recording date is not entirely unplausible. See Gart, *First Pressings—1951,* 125, 130.

654 Houston Boines, "Relation Blues." Blues & Rhythm 7001, 1952; Leadbitter & Slaven, *Blues Records 1943-1970,* 125; and Franz, notes to *Sounds Like "Dust My Broom."* Note: The artist credit on Blues & Rhythm 7001 was listed as Houston Baines.

655 Boyd Gilmore, "Ramblin' on My Mind." Modern 860, 1952; and Leadbitter & Slaven, *Blues Records 1943-1970,* 461.

656 Unknown, "Where Have You Been So Long." From the album *Blues Is Killin' Me.* Flyright CD 28, 1990; Leadbitter & Slaven, *Blues Records 1943-1970,* 149; Mike Rowe, notes to *Blues Is Killin' Me.* Flyright CD 28, 1990; and John & Grace Brim, *Gary Stomp—The (Almost) Complete Singles 1950-1956.* Compact disc (unissued), 2001.

Our next entries in the "Dust My Broom" survey come from Woodrow Adams, a slide guitarist that is the dictionary definition of "down home" if ever there was one. Born in Tchula, Mississippi, Adams, together with boyhood friend L.C. Green, learned to play guitar, and later on—after a move to Robinsonville in the 1940s—some tips on blowing a harmonica from Howlin' Wolf. In the 1950s, he had just two singles released, one for Checker and the other for Meteor. In all—including an unissued session from the Sun Records vaults—Adams recorded three "Broom"-type compositions in the 1950s. His "The Train Is Coming" suffers from an out of tune guitar (although Sylvester Hayes' harmonica is satisfyingly gritty), while his Checker side "She's Done Come and Gone," seems to suffer from a sound reminiscent of the band being recorded in a cave. His most "together" side is the piquant "Baby You Just Don't Know" on Meteor, thanks in part to guitar support from Joe Hill Louis. Although most discographies have placed this last title as having been recorded in 1955 (probably a guesstimate based on its 1955 release date), I have long suspected that it was actually recorded a couple of years earlier, perhaps by Sam Phillips or by Lester Bihari's brother Joe.[657] "With the latter-day success of men like Junior Kimbrough and CeDell Davis, it's safe to say that his ramshackle approach would find greater favor today," wrote a biographer for the *Sun Blues Box,* surmising appropriately that, "There's something endearing (if it isn't condescending to say so) about his subtly detuned guitar and wayward slide technique." In 1968, David Evans located and interviewed Adams, still playing and recording.[658]

Swinging over to Texas, our next artist in the survey is Melvin "Little Son" Jackson, with his Imperial label waxing of "I Wish to Go Home," recorded in Fort Worth, Texas in June 1952. With "Broom" quotes showing up in Jackson's guitar flourishes as well as the lyrics, Jackson proves beyond a reasonable doubt that Texas artists possessed more than just a passing familiarity with the Mississippi Delta blues songbook, borrowing pages from it when the mood struck them. Jackson recycled bits and pieces of the "Broom" riff in almost half a dozen other songs he recorded for Imperial; he is discussed further in the next section, "'Dust My Broom' Since Then, Part 1: Texas Pickers & Steel Sliders."[659]

Next on the list are three recordings made by Sam Phillips, all of which remained unissued at the time. Pat Hare, Willie Kizart, and David "Honeyboy" Edwards all recorded "Dust My Broom" style guitar pieces while at Sun. In Hare's and Kizart's cases, they were guitarists on recordings by Walter Bradford and Raymond Hill, respectively. Recorded in June 1952, Pat Hare's unmistakable distorted electric guitar behind vocalist Walter Bradford's "Love for my Baby" has all the makings for a tasty slice of down home blues. Here, Hare ably supplies an admirable "Broom" sound, played without a slide, and is careful to supply his own version of Elmore's classic ending solo as well, while Bradford leads the ensemble through a set of lyrics loosely based on the old "Take a Little Walk with Me" standard. Willie Kizart's "Broom"-ish sounding guitar on Raymond Hill's "My Baby Left Me" made me drop everything I was doing when I first heard it, racing over to hit the repeat button. "Wow! Check out the unissued Boyd Gilmore piece they dug up for the new *Sun Box*!" was my immediate and instinctive reaction (And who would blame me? With only a half-dozen or so titles in the Gilmore catalog, anything new would be cause for celebration). After my initial enthusiasm died down and I checked the session details, however, I discovered that it was

---

657 Woodrow Adams, "The Train Is Coming." From the album *Sun—The Roots of Rock, Vol. 12: Union Avenue Breakdown.* Charly LP 30127, 1977; Woodrow Adams, "She's Done Come and Gone." Checker 757, 1952; Woodrow Adams, "Baby You Just Don't Know." Meteor 5018, 1955; Mike Leadbitter, "A Jumpin' and a Shufflin'," 14. In the notes to *Genesis: The Beginnings of Rock Vol. 2.* Chess LP 6641.125, 1974; and Leadbitter & Slaven, *Blues Records 1943-1970,* 19.

658 Martin Hawkins, Colin Escott, et al., "The Blues In Memphis/Artists' Biographies," 17. In the notes to *Sun Records—The Blues Years 1950-1958.* Charly CDSUNBOX 7, 1996.

659 Melvin "Little Son" Jackson, "I Wish to Go Home." Imperial 5319, 1954; and Leadbitter & Slaven, *Blues Records 1943-1970,* 663.

actually Willie Kizart instead. Maybe so, but I'd be willing to bet a stack of dimes that if it wasn't Gilmore playing the guitar, that it's Kizart playing on equipment he borrowed from Boyd Gilmore for this October, 1952 session. Like the Bradford/Hare track above, Kizart works his way through the tune without the use of a slide, careful, as is Hare, to utilize Elmore's trademark ending solo during the song. To most readers, Kizart's name will be more memorable as the crackerjack "fuzz-tone" guitarist playing on Jackie Brenston's classic "Rocket 88" (which also, incidentally featured Hill on the tenor sax). Finally, David "Honeyboy" Edwards' heavily amped rendition of "Sweet Home Chicago" puts him in the company of such artists as Tommy McClennan, Walter Davis, and Jimmy McCracklin, who have all recorded versions of this durable Kokomo Arnold standard (and popularized by Robert Johnson's recording of it).[660] Still active at the the time this was being written, Edwards amazingly carries on a tradition dating back to the days when Robert Johnson was an active musician. With the help of Janis Martinson and Michael Robert Frank, Edwards published his autobiography, *The World Don't Owe Me Nothing,* in 1997.

Our next stop in this survey takes us to the west coast. In September 1952, the Los Angeles-based Swing Time label released a version of "Dust My Broom" by saxophonist Earl Brown, in the company of guitarist/bandleader Lowell Fulson and pianist Lloyd Glenn. Interestingly, Elmore James' seminal Trumpet waxing appears to have contributed very little for Brown's inspiration, the lyrics and jumping rhythm loosely reminiscent of Arthur "Big Boy" Crudup's 1949 RCA Victor recording. Even though Fulson had already scored a half-dozen R&B hits while at Swing Time, this pairing of Brown and Fulson appears to have made no dents in the market, and has been relegated to the status of "obscurity" ever since.[661]

Earl Hooker's first foray into a recording studio as a leader occurred on Wednesday, 26 November 1952, the day before Thanksgiving. Although the session was held in Florida, the material ended up in the hands of Cincinnati based King Records, where it met with a slightly odd fate. His waxing of "Shake 'Em Up" (a.k.a. "Poor Joe") was an engaging enough instrumental that strongly ran in the Elmore groove, but it would not be issued as a single at the time. In fact, it was not issued under Earl Hooker's name at all—this title and three others recorded at the same session were issued as part of his cousin's LP on the King label—yes, that's right—his cousin's album.[662] Just exactly how these four Earl Hooker titles came to constitute one-fourth of the 1961 LP *John Lee Hooker Sings Blues* is anybody's guess—and it wasn't like King didn't already have enough material on the Boogie Man to fill up both sides of an album (they did). It does

660 Walter Bradford, "Love for My Baby." From the album *Sun Records—The Blues Years 1950-1958.* Charly CDSUNBOX 7, 1996; Raymond Hill, "My Baby Left Me." From the album *Sun Records—The Blues Years 1950-1958.* Charly CDSUNBOX 7, 1996; David "Honeyboy" Edwards, "Sweet Home Chicago." From the album *Sun Records—The Blues Years 1950-1958.* Charly CDSUNBOX 7, 1996; Leadbitter & Slaven, *Blues Records 1943-1970,* 142, 389, 560; and Groom, "Standing at the Crossroads: Robert Johnson's Recordings [Part 1]," 19.

Note: Although Honeyboy Edwards was the first person to record a version of "Sweet Home Chicago" using an Elmore-styled riff, it is Detroit blues artist Bobo Jenkins who has the distinction of being the first person to have a single out on the market using this now time-tested formula. His recording "Baby Don't You Want to Go," cut for the Fortune label in 1956 (and released as Fortune 838 in the fall of 1957), was the first issued version of this blues standard to marry the Elmore James riff to the "Sweet Home Chicago" theme. During a 1954 recording for the Imperial label, "Sweet Old Chicago," Roosevelt Sykes' hot guitarist—both Ernest McLean and Walter Nelson have been suggested as possible suspects—does briefly quote the figure as well (Sykes' "Sweet Old Chicago" was released on the Imperial label in the spring of 1955). And where might Bobo Jenkins have gotten the idea from, you might ask, if Honeyboy Edwards' version was not released at the time? One possible source of inspiration may have been from seeing Elmore perform in Mississippi at Camp Anderson, when Jenkins was a teenager. (Bobo Jenkins, "Baby Don't You Want to Go." Fortune 838, 1957; Roosevelt Sykes, "Sweet Old Chicago." Imperial 5347, 1955; Paulus, "Motor City Blues & Boogie," 5; Leadbitter, Fancourt, and Pelletier, 558; Chris Smith, notes to Roosevelt Sykes, *Complete Recorded Works in Chronological Order, Vol. 10.* Document CD 6050, 1994; and Groom, "Standing at the Crossroads: Robert Johnson's Recordings [Part 1]," 19.)

661 Gart, *First Pressings—1952,* 96; Leadbitter and Slaven, *Blues Records 1943-1970,* 174; Whitburn, 161; and Earl Brown, "Dust My Broom." Swing Time 307, 1952; and Crudup, "Dust My Broom."

662 Earl Hooker, "Shake 'Em Up." From the album *John Lee Hooker Sings Blues.* King LP 727, 1961; and Leadbitter and Slaven, *Blues Records 1943-1970,* 574.

kind of make you wonder what unsuspecting people who bought the album thought, though, doesn't it?

Our last entry in the survey comes from Arkansas, another Bihari recording. Baby Face Turner's "Blue Serenade" was recorded on Sunday, 6 April 1952, in North Little Rock, and was released later that September on Modern. Turner was one of the group of musicians that worked with Junior Brooks, Sunny Blair, and Driftin' Slim (a.k.a. Elmon Mickle), a melange of talent that Leroy Pierson christened "one of the most exciting blues groups to record in the fifties." Of all the recordings in this survey, "Blue Serenade" is the one that intersects most loosely with Elmore, but intersect it does indeed, as the "Broom" theme keeps being repeated throughout the song, thanks in part again to Ike Turner, who provides keyboard support for the group. It could also be said that "Blue Serenade"—as well as Junior Brooks' "She's the Little Girl For Me"—is at the crux of this whole survey, speaking representatively, of blues musicians who recorded pieces of music that sounded similar to "Dust My Broom," and who recorded them at about the same time that Elmore did. Whether Turner's and Brooks' performances demonstrate an influence from "Dust My Broom"—which made consistent appearances on the *Cash Box* R&B charts between 12 January 1952 and 10 May 1952—is hard to say.[663] Specifically, where do regional styles and local traditions leave off and influence from phonograph records begin—or for that matter, influence from record company executives who are eager for an artist to mimic or imitate the sounds that are enjoying R&B chart success at that particular moment? This is a question that has been discussed many times in blues circles, and it seems that the answers are not easy. As far as Elmore is concerned, we have seen it go both ways, for instance, when Snooky Pryor recorded the obviously Elmore-ish "Going Back on the Road" in Chicago the same week that "Dust My Broom" was on the Chicago charts; and the other way around, years later when Elmore recorded "Sho Nuff I Do," which was brought about by Ike Turner's and Joe Bihari's idea that Elmore record something along the lines of Guitar Slim's "The Things That I Used to Do."

This also raises another question—namely, when Elmore recorded "Dust My Broom," was he borrowing from a traditional regional guitar style, one that had been developing in the mid-south for a couple of decades? Earlier in the text, antecedents and early recorded examples of the "Dust My Broom" riff from the 1930s were discussed; but would anyone disagree that the "Dust My Broom" riff that Robert Johnson played and the one that Elmore James played were different? Maybe not exactly *different*, but perhaps that their recordings in this vein show a refinement of the concept, a logical line of development of the idea (take, for instance, Calvin Frazier's 1938 recording of the "Broom" riff and sandwich it in between Robert Johnson and Elmore James, and I think you'll begin to see what I mean). In this case, then, "She's the Little Girl For Me" and "Blue Serenade" may not necessarily be evidence of influence from "Dust My Broom," but that these records as a group—along with the almost all of the examples in this survey—perhaps speak to evidence of a regional blues guitar style in the mid-south that happened to strongly emerge on record between 1951 and 1953. Further evidence of this is born out in the fact that of the the fourteen recordings surveyed above, one was recorded in Chicago, one was recorded in Fort Worth, Texas, one was recorded in Los Angeles, one in Florida (by Earl Hooker, long a fixture in mid-south blues at this time, up until his migration to Chicago later in the 1950s—where he had also incidentally lived as a child), and ten were recorded in the mid-south. If you include the Lockwood and Pryor tunes discussed earlier, including Lockwood's unreleased J.O.B. side, that would bring the number of titles recorded in Chicago up to four; note, however, that Lockwood and Pryor (like Hooker) were also former residents of the mid-south prior to moving north. Subtracting Earl Brown's Swing Time recording from our survey (since it has so very little to do with Elmore or the "Broom" theme), altogether then—including Boyd Gilmore's "All in My Dreams" and B.B. King's "Please Love Me," each discussed earlier, plus both the Lockwood titles—we

663 Baby Face Turner, "Blue Serenade." Modern 882, 1952; Pierson, notes to *Downhome Delta Blues 1949-1952;* Leadbitter, Fancourt, and Pelletier, 621; and Ryan, *Trumpet Records,* 101-102.

have a survey of eighteen "Dust My Broom"-styled recordings where sixteen of the performances (or the performers themselves) can be linked directly to the mid-south.

Whether or not Elmore's Trumpet recording of "Dust My Broom" was evidence of a larger regional phenomenon taking place at the time depends primarily on one's point of view, and will have to be a topic for additional reflection and discussion before any further conclusions are drawn. As time goes on, greater access is being made available to historical blues records, thanks to ongoing compact disc reissue programs by several key companies, and perhaps fresh insights will be found in analyzing more of these recordings from the 1930s, 1940s, and 1950s.

"Dust My Broom" Since Then, Part 1: Texas Pickers & Steel Sliders

When Elmore's "I Believe" exploded on the scene in the last waning moments of 1952, it transformed "Dust My Broom" from its country blues origins and catapulted it firmly into the territory of the urban landscape. Shortly afterward, B.B. King demonstrated that it was not necessary to use a slide to play Elmore's famous guitar riff, and since then, it could be said that the "Dust My Broom" riff has practically enjoyed a life of its own.

In Texas, guitarists have amply demonstrated that they are cognizant of Elmore James' music. In some instances, it is also interesting to note their approach to the topic—perhaps singularly unique among all the blues musicians that ever picked up an instrument and tried to play something that sounded like Elmore James.

In June 1953, just as B.B. King's "Please Love Me" was getting ready to make its big splash on the charts, Melvin "Little Son" Jackson, a country blues guitarist from Dallas, Texas, took a turn at the "Broom" riff with his "Thrill Me Baby." Originally from Tyler, Texas, Jackson moved to Dallas in the 1930s, served in the European theater in World War II and returned to Dallas, where he started his recording career in 1948, waxing for Bill Quinn's Gold Star outfit. In 1950, Jackson started an association with Imperial Records that lasted four years and would see Jackson record more than fifty titles for the label. Although Jackson can be heard to quote Elmore's famous guitar phrase in a handful of recordings—including "Black and Brown" from 1952, "How Long," "Losin' My Woman," and "Piggly Wiggly" from 1953, plus the previously discussed "I Wish to Go Home"—his most satisfying use of the riff is surely in the slide piece "Thrill Me Baby." Here, Jackson joins a long tradition of Texas guitarists that—to a lesser or greater extent—also played bottleneck, from Blind Lemon Jefferson and Blind Willie Johnson continuing on through B.K. Turner (a.k.a the "Black Ace") and Hop Wilson. Given the strictly chordal approach to "Thrill Me Baby," Jackson probably played this piece "Texas style," with the instrument positioned flat across his lap, and the resultant effect sounding faintly reminiscent of an amplified Hawaiian slack key guitarist. Coming back from a gig in Oklahoma one night, Jackson and his fellow band members were involved in a car accident that left him hospitalized for a broken collarbone and some other injuries. Afterwards, he decided to give up playing the blues in favor of church and a more settled existence. In July 1960, Arhoolie Records' Chris Strachwitz coaxed Jackson out of semi-retirement long enough to record him performing an album's worth of blues material.[664]

664 Melvin "Little Son" Jackson, "Thrill Me Baby." Imperial 5267, 1954; Melvin "Little Son" Jackson, *The*

"I am smiling like I'm happy, but you don't know how I feel," once sang Weldon "Juke Boy" Bonner during a January 1960 session for Goldband Records. "I feel like life is a cheater, and it gave me a dirty deal." Indeed, if someone ever decided to create a "blues musician who deserved a better break" hall of fame, then Bonner would probably be one of the first inductees. Another Texas artist with a creative and unique body of work to his credit, his story is an all-too-grim reminder that the life of the blues musician is frequently not glamorous, "cool," sexy, or financially rewarding. Virtually ignored in Houston, Bonner used to tell his long-time friend Roberto Gonzalez that he "had to go to Europe to earn $1,000 but he couldn't make $50 in his hometown."[665]

Variously dubbed a "poet" and the "one man trio," Bonner's large repertoire included everything from the obligatory tales of unrequited love to current-day political commentary, with classic blues standards and original compositions sandwiched in between, which Bonner sang while accompanying himself on the guitar and harmonica. Making his debut on Bob Geddins' Oakland-based Irma label in 1957, Bonner didn't record again until 1960, when he recorded in January, March, and December for the Goldband imprint in Lake Charles, Louisiana. For all of his session work on Irma and Goldband, Bonner would only see two singles issued as a result. "Every time I'd go through Lake Charles I'd get the same runaround you know," Bonner told Mike Leadbitter. "He'd say we've got the record working and it'll be out next week! Just hold on!" Eddie Shuler, Goldband's chief, inadvertently did Bonner the biggest favor of his entire career. He gave permission for eight of Bonner's recordings to be issued in 1966 on the Storyville label in Europe (tracks by Hop Wilson also appeared on the same LP), where his recordings were met with much greater enthusiasm than he was currently enjoying in the states. Among his fans were Mike Leadbitter (who visited Houston in May 1967, and met Bonner) and Simon Napier, the editors of *Blues Unlimited* magazine. It was a connection that would finally open a few doors for Bonner.[666]

Bonner didn't start recording prolifically until 1967 (his career had been sidetracked by an ulcer that ultimately claimed half of his stomach in a November 1963 operation). Some of the tapes were made by Bonner himself and sent to Europe in the hopes of promoting his career. On another occasion, the editors and readers of *Blues Unlimited* took up a collection so that Bonner could get a 45 made; when Arhoolie Records boss Chris Strachwitz heard the resulting record during a Texas field trip, he started recording Bonner himself — artistically speaking, it would be the apex of his career.[667]

A lot of Bonner's material, such as "No Place to Run" (January/February 1967), "Look Out Your Window" (December 1967), "Life Is a Nightmare" (from January 1968, a personal favorite), and "Regent Sound" (from November 1969, performed on a 12-string guitar), borrows from and easily melds into the basic structure of the "Broom" format. In a straight-ahead Elmore mode, Bonner recorded at least three versions of "Dust My Broom;" one of them (from December 1967) later found its way onto a Flyright compact disc. "How Well I Remember" (January/February 1967) also shows an obvious debt to the old Broomduster; his "Blues for Elmo," recorded in May 1969 for Arhoolie, unfortunately remains unissued. Perhaps Bonner's most successful marriage of an original set of lyrics to the "Broom" format was his

Complete Imperial Recordings. Capitol CD 31744, 1995; Leadbitter and Slaven, *Blues Records 1943-1970,* 662-664; and Chris Strachwitz, "Lil' Son Jackson," 187-189. In Mike Leadbitter, ed., *Nothing But the Blues.* London: Hanover Books, 1971.

665 Tom Moran, "Story of a Bluesman." *Living Blues* 38 (May/June 1978): 41 [reprint]; and Weldon "Juke Boy" Bonner, "Life Is a Dirty Deal." From the EP *More Downhome Blues.* Jan & Dil EP 451, 1966 (this was later reissued on *Juke Boy Bonner 1960-1967.* Flyright CD 38, 1991).

666 Mike Leadbitter, "An Interview with Juke Boy Bonner." *Blues Unlimited* 78 (December 1970): 18; Leadbitter and Slaven, *Blues Records 1943-1970,* 126-127; and Mike Leadbitter, "I Know Houston Can't Be Heaven," 168. In Mike Leadbitter, ed., *Nothing But the Blues.* London: Hanover Books, 1971.

667 Tony Burke, notes to Juke Boy Bonner, *Things Ain't Right—The 1969 London Sessions.* Sequel CD 209, 1992; and Leadbitter, "An Interview with Juke Boy Bonner," 18.

"Going Back to the Country (Where They Don't Burn the Buildings Down)," a commentary on the Texas Southern University riots of 1967. "I'm not too crazy about country livin', and it's really not my desire," he sings, "But if I move back in the sticks, I ain't got to worry about bein' killed by no sniper's fire."[668]

Passport troubles prevented Bonner from joining a 1968 overseas tour. Fortunately, this was all straightened out in time for him to join the American Folk Blues Festival entourage the following year; he would return to play Europe on several different occasions in the 1970s. But making a decent living from his music always seemed to elude Bonner—this, in spite of the fact that his name graced the bins of record shops from the U.K. to Japan, and his overseas performances. Roy Ames' Home Cooking label brought Bonner a tiny amount of success in 1975, but it was too little too late. Declining health throughout the 1970s was finally taking its toll on the once energetic performer. Robert Springer, who reviewed Bonner's February 1977 concert for *Blues Unlimited,* found his performance chaotic and repetitive, with Bonner drunk and not in possession of his full artistic faculties. Divorced, broke, suffering from ill health and evidently an embittered alcoholic, Bonner died alone in a ten by ten-foot rented room in Houston on Wednesday, 28 June 1978. "I've been sick," he told Houston Chronicle reporter Tom Moran the night of his last performance. "I haven't worked in 14 months, since I came back from Germany. Just unload a truck every now and then and pick up some aluminum cans, that's about all. No music jobs at all." "That's the story of a bluesman," his friend Roberto Gonzalez told Moran. "This great man, he just vanishes and nobody cares until he dies.... He died in his room, there with the rats and tons of music he had written. There are other people like him, bluesmen, that just died and vanished." Even though some of Bonner's children lived nearby, they were apparently not in a position to offer financial assistance. According to Lenora Preston, Bonner's sister, he opted to live in the small rented quarters because "he didn't want to be a burden on anybody." Officially, the cause of death was listed as cirrhosis of the liver. Bonner was forty-six.[669]

Continuing in the Texas tradition, L.C. "Good Rockin'" Robinson was another blues musician who fiddled around with the "Dust My Broom" riff. As a kid, he picked up some pointers on bottleneck blues guitar from his uncle Blind Willie Johnson, but Robinson later adopted the steel guitar as his sliding medium of choice, after being smitten in the 1930s by the playing of Leon McAuliffe, the renowned steel player with Bob Wills and his Texas Playboys. Once, when working in Temple, Texas, Clyde Barrow gave Robinson twenty-five dollars to sing "Sittin' On Top of the World" for he and his girlfriend Bonnie. After serving in World War II, Robinson headed out to Oakland to be near his musical brother, A.C. Robinson, and a four song session resulted for the Black & White label in 1945.[670] Record-wise, nothing else happened until the mid fifties, when L.C.'s path crossed with that of Bob Geddins, owner/operator of the bay area-based Rhythm label. Robinson's 1954 waxing "Why Don't You Write to Me" makes it clear that he was no stranger to the music of Elmore James—not hard to believe at all when one considers that in 1952 "Dust My Broom" had hit big on the west coast (in Oakland and Los Angeles both). Using a relaxed, easygoing approach, Robinson effectively demonstrates the adaptability of Elmore's slide licks to his steel instrument. 1959 brought about the end of the Robinson brothers' fifteen year musical partnership of performances around the bay area, when A.C. joined the church and gave up playing the blues; L.C. continued to gig

668 Juke Boy Bonner, *Juke Boy Bonner 1960-1967.* Flyright CD 38, 1991; Juke Boy Bonner, *Life Gave Me a Dirty Deal.* Arhoolie CD 375, 1992; Juke Boy Bonner, *Things Ain't Right—The 1969 London Sessions.* Sequel CD 209, 1992; Leadbitter and Slaven, *Blues Records 1943-1970,* 126-129; and Moran, 41.

669 Moran, 41; Ray Templeton, notes to Juke Boy Bonner, *Juke Boy Bonner 1960-1967.* Flyright CD 38, 1991; Robert Springer, "Juke Boy Bonner's (Last?) European Tour." *Blues Unlimited* 124 (March/June 1977): 32-33; and Burke, notes to *Things Ain't Right.*

670 Joel Selvin, notes to L.C. "Good Rockin'" Robinson, *Mojo in My Hand.* Arhoolie CD 453, 1996; and Leadbitter, Fancourt, and Pelletier, 421, 427.

without him. It wouldn't be until 1968 that Robinson would go inside a studio again, this time to record half an album on the World Pacific label. Chris Strachwitz finally caught up with Robinson in 1971, when he recorded him for his Arhoolie label.[671]

For Robinson's first Arhoolie session, members of the Muddy Waters blues band were employed, with Muddy supervising. Robinson's "Across the Bay Blues" was vaguely centered around Elmore's "The Sky Is Crying," while "L.C.'s Shuffle" showed off more of his tasty steel slide licks. "I've Got to Go," from Robinson's second Arhoolie date, was more obviously based on straight-ahead Elmore-styled material, which Robinson approached in an unhurried manner.[672] "Always did want to meet him," Robinson said in regards to Elmore James during a 1975 interview with Tom Mazzolini. "I love his style of playing. I wish I had his band behind me," he confessed. "A lot of people call me Elmore James because they don't know, just like they've never seen him. A guy gave me $20 one night, he said, 'I've always heard of you, Elmore, now I got a chance to see ya.' And I just kept playing like Elmore James and he never knew, he was drunk anyway. He said, 'You the best in the business!'"[673]

For the 1975 Thanksgiving holiday, Strachwitz arranged for a reunion of the two Robinson brothers over community radio station KPFA, where L.C. was recorded on the fiddle, his other instrument. L.C. died in Berkeley, California, the following September. *Mojo in My Hand,* on Arhoolie, is a most satisfying overview of his talents.[674]

Today, bluesman Sonny Rhodes carries on in the L.C. Robinson tradition. While it is probable that Hop Wilson's playing may have initially inspired him, after being transplanted from Texas to Oakland it would be Robinson who took the young Rhodes under his wing and showed him the rudiments of playing slide lap-style. It is still possible to hear Rhodes wail away on Elmore's famous riff, bringing the art of Texas-style slide guitar playing into the twenty-first century.[675]

Legendary rock 'n' roller Chuck Berry—although not from Texas—was another performer to play Elmore slide licks on a pedal steel guitar. His 1960 recording "Run Around" was his most convincing example of this, with the beginning of the song featuring Berry unrestrainedly hammering out the "Broom" riff, and finishing up the rest of the song with a heavy, Elmore-styled duple-rhythm beat. Chess later snuck the tune onto one of Berry's many albums, *New Juke Box Hits,* released in 1961. "Childhood Sweetheart," which finds Berry playing the Elmore riff B.B. King-style in a composed, undissembled manner (and backed by a vocal chorus), although more ordinary in comparison, was released by Chess as a single in September, 1959. Likewise was the case with "O Rangutang," a straight-ahead "Broom"-type instrumental that Chess consigned to the flip side of "Nadine," Berry's top 30 R&B hit from the spring of 1964.[676]

The Chuck Berry pedal steel slide work that will probably be most familiar to readers is his 1958 recording "Blues for Hawaiians" (and, perhaps, its cousin—a very similar piece entitled "Surfing Steel" (a.k.a. "Crying Steel") that was recorded in 1960). Here, Berry makes a musical bet that his audience won't be familiar with the original on which "Blues for Hawaiians" is based, the 1939 Decca recording "Floyd's

671 Selvin, notes to *Mojo in My Hand;* L.C. "Good Rockin'" Robinson, "Why Don't You Write to Me." Rhythm 1772, 1954; and Ryan, *Trumpet Records,* 101-102.

672 L.C. "Good Rockin'" Robinson, *Mojo in My Hand.* Arhoolie CD 453, 1996.

673 Tom Mazzolini, "*Living Blues* Interview: L.C. 'Good Rockin'' Robinson." *Living Blues* 22 (July/August 1975): 21.

674 Selvin, notes to *Mojo in My Hand;* and Robinson, *Mojo in My Hand.* Note: L.C. Robinson also recorded an LP for ABC-Bluesway, *House Cleanin' Blues* (LP 6082). It was released in 1974.

675 Robert Santelli, *The Big Book of Blues: A Biographical Encyclopedia.* New York: Penguin Books, 1993, 342-343.

676 Chuck Berry, "Run Around." From the album Chuck Berry, *New Juke Box Hits.* Chess LP 1456, 1961; Chuck Berry, "Childhood Sweetheart." Chess 1737, 1959; Leslie Fancourt, *Chess R & B Discography,* 2nd ed. Kent, England: [no publisher], 1991, 4, 5; and Whitburn, 42.

Guitar Blues," by Andy Kirk and His 12 Clouds of Joy. This piece was actually a showcase for steel player Floyd Smith, who seems to have recently discovered electricity, blasting and careening his way through a three minute musical odyssey that must have dimmed the lights in the surrounding neighborhood while Floyd was tearing his way through this performance (which could have just as easily been titled "Mr. Floyd's Wild Ride"). Although Berry isn't quite up to snuff compared to Smith's talent when it comes to steel playing, "Blues for Hawaiians" and "Surfing Steel" are delectable, pleasing additions to the Berry repertoire nonetheless. Both tunes were later used by Chess to flesh out a couple of Chuck's LPs, *Berry Is on Top* and *Chuck Berry on Stage* (overdubbed by Chess with fake audience noise to simulate a "live" recording), respectively.[677]

The foremost proponent of steel guitar playing in the blues world, hands down, was unquestionably Hop Wilson, a figure as obscure as Chuck Berry is famous, and whose fascinating recordings are all prized collectors items. Admittedly, I had never heard of Wilson until one day in 1993 when the Bullseye Blues CD *Houston Ghetto Blues* landed on my doorstep. Even from the first few notes of the disc, it became immediately apparent that Wilson possessed a unique and rare talent.

Born Hardy Leroy Wilson, Hop (or "Poppa" Hop) grew up in a large family in the town of Crockett, Texas, the county seat of Houston County, located some 100 miles north of the eponymous city. Although Wilson's first instrument was the harmonica, he switched to guitar before he was even a teenager. When he was twelve, his brother purchased a steel guitar for him from a pawn shop, and Hop became adept on that as well after a few years of practice. In the 1940s, Wilson moved to Houston, and after serving in Korea (where he was evidently injured), returned to the area to pursue life as a musician. In 1956 he teamed up with vocalist/drummer Ivory Lee Semien, and toured around parts of Texas and Louisiana. "Ivory Lee turned to home remodeling, carpentry and apartment management, while Hop collected his disability checks and stayed home writing loads of songs and concocting all sorts of things to wow his Friday, Saturday and Sunday night audiences with," wrote William Orten Carlton in *Living Blues* magazine.[678] In March 1958, the pair of musicians stopped by Eddie Shuler's Goldband studios in Lake Charles, Louisiana, evidently having been sent there by Steve Poncio, who was at the time a Houston music industry figure who wore many hats, including those of talent scout and record distributor.[679]

Wilson and Semien recorded a handful of titles at Shuler's studio in Lake Charles, including "Chicken Stuff" and "Rocking in the Cocanut Top," regarded by blues fans today with a status akin to that of the "instant classic." The latter tune, playing up to the theme implied by its title, had been overdubbed with various jungle sounds and animal noises. "Hop was a creative genius," offered Carlton, and had this to say about Wilson's playing on record and in the clubs: "Hop didn't sing the monkey noises in 'Rocking in the Cocanut Top,' he played them! I have never seen a man's hands move as fast as his! He had tremendous hand coordination and thus could play things on a steel guitar that very few others could even dream of. The night we heard him, he played these noises—fire engines, police sirens, trains, etc.—on the strings, all without gadgetry."[680] Mike Leadbitter, who in May, 1967, had the opportunity to see Hop Wilson play in

677 Andy Kirk and His 12 Clouds of Joy, "Floyd's Guitar Blues." Decca 2483, 1939; Chuck Berry, "Blues for Hawaiians." From the album Chuck Berry, *Berry Is on Top.* Chess LP 1435, 1959; Chuck Berry, "Surfing Steel" (a.k.a. "Crying Steel"). From the album Chuck Berry, *Chuck Berry on Stage.* Chess LP 1480, 1963; and Fancourt, *Chess R & B Discography,* 3, 5.

678 William Orten Carlton, "Hop Wilson." *Living Blues* 26 (March/April 1976): 8-9; and Leadbitter, *Nothing But the Blues,* 193-194.

679 Ray Topping, notes to Hop Wilson & His Buddies, *Steel Guitar Flash!* Ace CD 240, 1994; and Leadbitter, Fancourt, and Pelletier, 774-775.

680 Carlton, 9; and Hop Wilson, "Rocking in the Cocanut Top." Goldband 1246, 1973. Note: "Cocanut" is the spelling from the original label of the Goldband issue. Also, as a point of clarification: Wilson and Semien recorded two different versions of "Rocking in the Coconut Top" at these early sessions in 1958. One of these

person, also gave an enthusiastic report. As we pick up the story, Mike is in Houston, Texas, listening to Juke Boy Bonner; on one side of the street, Bonner is playing in one club, and the other side, Hop Wilson is in another:

> After two beers and some nips from my whiskey bottle we [crossed] the street to feel a wave of music hit us. As we scrambled for a seat, Hop... broke into "Chicken Stuff." I soon realized that no records can recreate the wild sound that this man produces. With his guitar across his knees and a steel in his left hand, Hop was turning loose some of the most chilly, wailing music I've heard, helped by a grinning [drummer named] "T" who kept up a rock steady drum beat. Hop is completely lost in his music when he plays, only raising his head to shout "Play!" to the drummer or to sometimes cast a brief smile at the audience who sit swaying and stomping round him. A version of "See That My Grave Is Kept Clean" nearly brought the house down; the audience, who by now had finished my whiskey, were yelling for more and urged the musicians on into "Don't Answer the Door." As I staggered out an hour later the strains of "Chicken Stuff" were beating in my ears again. I prayed fervently that this fantastic man should one day play in Europe and give everyone a chance to hear what I had.[681]

At least one more session for Goldband was held, but where Wilson's art really shined through was at an October 1960 session held at Houston's Audio Company of America studios (or simply "ACA" for short), where owner-engineer Bill Holford presided (Holford had also been recruited a number of times by Lillian McMurry for Trumpet Records sessions). This time, Wilson and Semien were recording material for a label that Semien had started himself, the aptly named Ivory Records. Holford recalled that Wilson was, "A quiet man... coming to his studio with his steel guitar all raggedy and stuck together with tape. He remembered they had problems with the electrics, Hop's steel guitar had pieces of wire hanging out and this gave them problems recording him."[682] To hear the results, though, you wouldn't notice it. A remake of "Chicken Stuff" was attempted, but the truly exemplary side had to be "My Woman Has a Black Cat Bone," showcasing Wilson at the very apogee of his ability.[683] With a wonderfully loose and relaxed feel, Hop slides his way across the steel guitar with a breathtaking adroitness that belies the inherent complexity in what he is playing. This recording was later chosen for issue as a single on Semien's new Ivory imprint.

In the strictly Elmore vein, Wilson gives a nod to the Broomduster with a few of his precious recordings. "Rockin' with Hop" (a.k.a. "Rockin' in the Jungle") from the very first session in March 1958, brings to mind images of Elmore James, which researcher Ray Topping described as a "real gem," and a "steel guitar masterpiece.... [that] displays all the intensity of Elmore James' best slide work, evoking his 'Hand in Hand' on Flair Records for sheer feeling and emotion."[684] "Be Careful with the Blues," recorded at a November 1961 session, saw release as an Ivory single and finds Wilson paying direct homage to Elmore with an instrumental that, throughout its two and half minute course, basically repeats a theme and variation on the "Broom" riff, Poppa Hop-style. When compiling tapes for the release of the album *Steel Guitar Flash!,* Topping came upon several unissued sides, one of them featuring Wilson playing an Elmore-styled riff behind an unidentified vocalist on "My Woman Done Quit Me" that dates from an

versions was released on the Trey label (a Goldband subsidiary, later purchased by Atlantic Records) circa 1959 and credited to King Ivory Lee. I think most people would agree the version later released on Goldband 1246, circa 1973, is far superior. Previously, a release date of 1977 has been stated for Goldband 1246. Given that Mike Leadbitter reviewed Goldband 1246 in the February/March 1974 issue of *Blues Unlimited,* this would tend to strongly indicate 1973 for year of release.

681 Leadbitter, "I Know Houston Can't Be Heaven," 169.

682 Topping, notes to *Steel Guitar Flash!;* Ryan, *Trumpet Records,* 27; Leadbitter, *Nothing But the Blues,* 194; and Leadbitter, Fancourt, and Pelletier, 775.

683 Hop Wilson, "My Woman Has a Black Cat Bone." Ivory 127, c. 1961.

684 Topping, notes to *Steel Guitar Flash!;* and Hop Wilson, *Steel Guitar Flash!* Ace CD 240, 1994.

October 1960 session.[685]

After a February 1962 session for Goldband, Wilson recorded nothing further. "Hop had a few chances to record for larger labels, but was very suspicious of doing business with people he did not know," wrote Joseph Lomax. "A few of Hop's tunes were issued on a pirated album in England in 1970. When Hop learned of this, he became more vehement in his opposition to doing further recording. Having his material stolen disgusted him so much that he quit playing altogether for a period of months."[686] In August 1974, Rob Hall and William Orten Carlton made the trip over to Hop's home turf, over by the Houston railroad yards, where they saw him perform at Hayes Lounge. Semien helped arrange a meeting of sorts, where Hop seemed amiable enough. "We had explained to Ivory that our motives were not to rip off anyone. Hop was expecting us, and said he trusted us but that 'I don't trust too many people. They're always after something.... Everyone wants something out of old Hop, and old Hop ain't gonna give no more,'" Carlton recalled. "We remarked that he could be a worldwide success, but his answer was that perhaps he could be, but then everyone would beat a path to his door and it was bad enough already."[687] Wilson invited Carlton and his friend to come back and stay with him the next time they were in town, but, "...Neither of us could go [the following] summer," Carlton later regretted. "We'd probably have found Hop on his deathbed." Exacerbated by ill health, respiratory infections, and substandard living conditions, Hop Wilson died on Wednesday, 27 August 1975, in the Houston Veterans Administration Hospital of anoxic encephalopathy. He was forty-eight. "Although his local celebrity would go on to influence the slide and steel work of Johnny Winter and Jimmie Vaughan,"observed journalist/rocker Cub Koda, "Hop took his tuning- and slide-technique secrets to his grave, passing them along to no one."[688] *Steel Guitar Flash!*, on Britain's Ace label, is a comprehensive retrospective of Hop Wilson's career.

"Dust My Broom" Since Then, Part 2: More from the Mid-South & the Mid-West

In this section, we will examine more of the "Dust My Broom" tradition, as practiced by first-rate Chicago blues artists, unknown and obscure—as well as famous—guitarists from Mississippi and Louisiana, to recordings made by rhythm and blues legends, from the mid-1950s to the 1980s.

Guitarist/vocalist "Little" Milton Campbell was another mid-south blues musician, who in the early 1950s, registered in with a couple versions of the "Dust My Broom" riff. Led by Ike Turner's typically solid piano, we find Milton lending modern, fuzz-toned guitar support for Houston Boines' December 1953 Sun recording "Carry My Business On." The tune wasn't released at the time—Little Milton later told Cilla Huggins that in spite of the fact that they worked all day and into part of the night in the studio, label owner/engineer Sam Phillips just wasn't satisfied with the results. "We were supposed to have gone back into the studio at a later date and re-do the stuff over again 'cause it was unfinished product see," Milton

685 Ibid.

686 Joseph Lomax, "Hop Wilson." *Living Blues* 26 (March/April 1976): 8.

687 Carlton, 8-9.

688 Cub Koda, notes to *Blues Masters, Vol. 18: More Slide Guitar Classics.* Rhino CD 75348, 1998.
Note: It has also been suggested that Hop Wilson was fifty-four, not forty-eight, at the time of his death. For those who are curious, "Anoxic encephalopathy" (anoxic meaning "absence of oxygen" and encephalopathy meaning "any of various diseases of the brain") is commonly a result of emphysema and/or chronic obstructive pulmonary disease.

told Huggins, "but we never got back." This was Boines' last recording session, and after many years, no one seemed to know of his whereabouts: "...We were trying to find him a few years ago 'cause he had some money coming in," Milton offered in 1982, "Nobody know,... I just lost track."[689] Boines' name, along with other artists such as Boyd Gilmore, will maddeningly remain as just another biographical "blip" on the blues radar screen.

Milton's other entry in the "Broom" department comes from his second Sun single, "If You Love Me." Milton's use of the theme is more gutsy than in the previous entry, which he plays B.B. King style—without using a slide. Careful listening reveals that once again Ike Turner lends a hand on the piano, helping to anchor the side with a firm support, although not quite as noticeably as he does with Boines' record. Since Milton worked with Willie Love and knew Elmore back in his Trumpet Records days, it seems possible that he may have picked up a few pointers from Elmore himself, in spite of the fact that "If You Love Me" shows an obvious influence from B.B. King's "Please Love Me."[690] Little Milton has continues to enjoy a long and successful recording/performing career that has spanned the better part of five decades now.

After playing piano support on many other "Dust My Broom" type records (including both Milton titles above), Ike Turner finally registers in with one of his very own on "All the Blues All the Time," an instrumental track that appeared on his one and only 1963 Crown LP, *Ike Turner Rocks the Blues.* At eight and a half minutes long, "All the Blues All the Time" is kind of an early attempt at "Hooked on Blues," with Turner—having now switched over to guitar—stringing together minute-and-a-half-long snippets of blues classics and standards by Little Junior Parker, B.B. King, John Lee Hooker, and Elmore James, among others. His version of B.B. King doing Elmore à la "Please Love Me" is remarkably right on the money, while his take on Elmore, a run through of "Canton, Mississippi Breakdown," is a worthwhile endeavor, if only to show that he can give the best of the best a run for their money when he feels like it. Although Ray Topping has suggested that Elmore doesn't actually play guitar on the original version of "Canton, Mississippi Breakdown" (recorded in Chicago on 5 April 1954), a side-by-side comparison with Ike's version of the tune in "All the Blues All the Time" (possibly recorded in Hollywood during a 24 April 1954 session for Modern Records), would indicate that this is definitely *not* the case.[691] A true survivor in his own right, Turner has had a tumultous career in the music business, and of late has released an autobiography (with Nigel Cawthorne's help) and a critically acclaimed "come back" album. A recent appearance on a TV documentary, where he casually pounded out the first few bars of "Rocket 88" on the piano with an aplomb that has changed little since its original recording five decades ago, proves that his remarkable talents are completely undiminished.

Over in Louisiana, meanwhile, we traverse from the territory of the renowned to that of the unknown once again. Ramblin' Hi Harris, in the company of two unidentified guitarists and a drummer, recorded "Early One Morning" probably as an audition for Jay Miller at his celebrated Crowley, Louisiana studios (located some twenty miles west of Lafayette). Whoever the guitarists were, one of them was clearly familiar with the music of Elmore James, playing the piece B.B. King style, but with a distinct, easy going Louisiana accent.[692] Unfortunately, a quick search for any biographical reference to Harris turned up zilch,

689 Cilla Huggins, "A Little More on Milton," Blues Unlimited 144 (Spring 1983): 32; and Houston Boines, "Carry My Business On." From the album *Sun Records—The Blues Years 1950-1958.* Charly CDSUNBOX 7, 1996.

690 "Little" Milton Campbell, "If You Love Me." Sun 200, 1954.

691 Ike Turner, "All the Blues All the Time." From the Album Ike Turner & the Kings of Rhythm, *Rocks the Blues.* P-Vine CD 3031/3032, 1993 [reissue]; Ike Turner, American Federation of Musicians Local Number 47 contract 1001: 24 April 1954; and Ray Topping, "Discography," 252. In Ike Turner with Nigel Cawthorne, *Takin' Back My Name.* London: Virgin Books, 1999.

and nothing further is known about this artist.

Material Jay Miller recorded was often slated for later release on the Excello label, with whom Miller had close ties. In other cases—like Ramblin' Hi Harris—musicians recorded auditions at Miller's studio, but sometimes didn't make the cut. In the case of Early Drane, neither was the case—he evidently recorded an album's worth of demo tapes in his living room and sent them directly to Excello head Ernie Young, in Nashville. Cub Koda picks up a few more details in the notes to *Blues Hangover/Excello Blues Rarities:* "Our most treasured find in exploring the Excello vaults come with the discovery of the audition tapes from January 1966 of one Early Drane from Eupora, Mississippi," wrote Koda almost thirty years after the fact. "Could this be the same 'Earl Draines' whose guitar graced early Willie Mabon and Big Boy Spires sessions in Chicago and also—as a member of the Blues Rockers—recorded the immortal 'Calling All Cows' for Excello back in 1955?" Koda doesn't come across with any definitive answers, but Drane left behind an interesting, albeit small, legacy nonetheless. His adaptation of "Look On Yonders Wall" is a souped-up Elmore James-styled "acoustic" version of the durable blues standard (with Drane straying from the traditional lyric line before the first verse is even finished), his manic slide playing recalling some of Kokomo Arnold's work.[693]

Like so many other blues musicians who landed in Chicago, Eddie Taylor's early life began in Mississippi, where he was born in Benoit, on 29 January 1923. It was seemingly a life steeped in the blues: Taylor's mother and Memphis Minnie had gone to school together, and she would sometimes babysit Eddie when he was still a toddler; he recalled seeing Charley Patton, Son House, and Robert Johnson in the area when he was just seven or eight. "I used to run away from home and follow musicians around on my bicycle," he remembered. "I'd come back home and then leave again, rambling around Mississippi, wherever there was guitars." When Taylor came upon a house party, sometimes he would crawl under the porch and fall asleep listening to the sounds of the blues (too young to be let in), and later on at home, would try to replicate what he had heard on his own guitar, a twelve-dollar Sears & Roebuck that his mother ordered for him when he was thirteen.[694]

Taylor left Mississippi in stages, first to Memphis in 1943 and then moving permanently to the Windy City in 1949. Although he is perhaps better known for his presence on many of Jimmy Reed's (with whom he had been friends since childhood) and John Lee Hooker's best recordings for Vee-Jay, he would infrequently record titles under his own name, some of which are outstanding. His debut on the Vee-Jay label occurred in 1955, but it wasn't until nine years later that Taylor showed off his Elmore James chops, in a 1964 session for the Vivid label, evidently a short-lived Vee-Jay subsidiary during the label's waning years. "Leave This Neighborhood" combined some of the best elements of Elmore's music in a short, two and half minute record, featuring Jimmy Reed blowing his trademark squeaky harp, Johnny Jones on piano (unfortunately, somewhat buried in the mix), and Hubert Sumlin backing on second guitar. Taylor squeezes in a few memorable lines while ably playing Elmore's classic guitar figures:

> I'm tired of everybody of telling me how to live my life,
> I'm tired of everybody of telling me how to live my life,
> I'm in love with this woman, and she goin' to be my wife.[695]

692 Leadbitter and Slaven, *Blues Records 1943-1970,* 527; and Ramblin' Hi Harris, "Early One Morning." From the album *Louisiana Swamp Blues.* Flyright CD 09, 1989.

693 Early Drane, "Look on Yonders Wall." From the album *Blues Hangover/Excello Blues Rarities.* Excello CD 2002, 1995; and Cub Koda, notes to *Blues Hangover/Excello Blues Rarities.* Excello CD 2002, 1995.

694 Taylor and Scott, notes to *I Feel So Bad.*

695 Ibid.; and Eddie Taylor, "Leave This Neighborhood." From the album Eddie Taylor, *Big Town Playboy.* P-Vine CD 5259, 1997; and Leadbitter, Fancourt, and Pelletier, 576.

Taylor recorded further in the 1970s and 1980s. In June 1972, Frank Scott recorded Taylor for an album (originally issued on Advent, later reissued on Hightone). Of this highly enjoyable set, Taylor's remake of the "Twelve Year Old Boy" and "Jackson Town"—the latter tune featuring him in rare form on the slide guitar—are particular standouts (this also begs the question that it may be Taylor who is the slide guitarist on Jimmy Reed's "Boogie in the Dark"—more on this later).[696] A 1997 collection on the Japanese P-Vine label, *Big Town Playboy,* contains all of Taylor's Vee-Jay and Vivid recordings, plus six other choice Vee-Jay tracks of Taylor backing John Lee Hooker, Elmore James, Floyd Jones, and Jimmy Reed. Prior to his death—on Christmas day, 1985—Taylor was interviewed on relatively few occasions, a real shame that a lot more of his stories and recollections weren't preserved for future generations of blues enthusiasts and researchers to enjoy.

Of all the bluesmen discussed so far, James "Son" Thomas deserves a special, personal mention. As was noted earlier by Malcolm Jones, over the years many people have "struggled to figure out how [Elmore] did it." At one time, I could have been lumped in that category of people struggling to figure it out too. Although I tried and tried—at that particular time, I had about as much technical information on Elmore's guitar playing as Malcolm Jones had had in 1965—it wasn't until I saw a short film clip of James "Son" Thomas playing an Elmore James slide riff on the guitar that the light bulb finally went off over my head and I said, "A ha! *That's* how Elmore did it!" As it turns out, Thomas came by his Elmore slide licks honestly. "I learned from my uncle [Joe Cooper]. He showed me two or three chords and he would charge me [a dollar] to play his guitar," Thomas later recalled. "The first electric guitar I played was Elmore James'. I was in my teen years, oh, this was about the middle-'40s," he stated.[697] "I wasn't allowed at nightclubs but I would slip out on a Saturday night, and Elmore James played all night long. That was north of Yazoo City on 49 East. I'd slip down there and play with Elmore and Sonny Boy Williams[on]," Thomas told scholar William Ferris. "Sonny Boy..., he didn't like me to play Elmore's guitar, but Elmore, he didn't care. He'd let me play as long as I'd want to, and Sonny Boy would set on the stage and roll his eyes."[698]

It's hard to imagine a more succinct—or vivid—profile of Thomas than the following paragraph about him, written by Brett Bonner:

> Born in Eden, Mississippi [about fifty miles south of Greenville] on October 14, 1926, James "Son" Thomas was a man who understood the blues from the inside out he didn't just sing them, he lived them. During his life, Son worked as a sharecropper and a grave digger, was shot by an ex-wife, was plagued by emphysema and epilepsy and was severely burned after falling onto a space heater. Through it all, he never became embittered, only wiser. After being "discovered" and recorded by William Ferris in 1968, Son went on to charm fans at blues festivals all over the world. He was featured in National Geographic and on Charles Kuralt's "On The Road" TV series, sang at the White House and even won international fame as a sculptor [....Human heads were his favorite subject, and he would use hair gathered from the local barber and teeth from the local dentist]. Son Thomas was a special man.[699]

Not too long after seeing him in the film clip, I was honored to get the chance to introduce Thomas for the 1990 Mid-South Music & Heritage Festival in Memphis. Unfortunately, it was a hectic day for me as an emcee, and I wished I'd had more of a chance to really sit down and enjoy his set. Rail thin, I remembered thinking that it looked like a stiff breeze might blow him over. Although Thomas died in 1993, he has

696 Eddie Taylor, *I Feel So Bad.* Advent LP 2802, 1972 (also reissued as Hightone CD 8027, 1991).

697 William Ferris, *Blues from the Delta.* New York: Da Capo Press, 1984 [reprint], 38; and Brett J. Bonner, notes to James "Son" Thomas, *Beefsteak Blues.* Evidence CD 26095-2, 1998.

698 Ferris, 39.

699 Bonner, notes to *Beefsteak Blues.*

fortunately left behind a bit of a recorded legacy for us to enjoy. You can hear his whining Elmore slide licks to good effect on two different versions of "Standing at the Crossroads." One is on *Beefsteak Blues,* a 1998 compact disc from the Evidence label (originally released on L+R in Germany, and featuring Bonner's notes), and the other on *Hard Times,* a recent French label issue from Black & Blue (which features more of Thomas' slide work on "It Hurts Me Too," performed distinctly in the Elmore fashion).[700]

As with James "Son" Thomas, Lonnie Pitchford also deserves a special mention. Born in rural Holmes County on 8 October 1955 into a large musical family, Lonnie's father farmed during the week and played guitar around the house and at neighborhood juke joints on weekends. His first experience with a musical instrument came when he just five or six, when he scrounged parts from around the house to make his own one-stringed diddley bow (sometimes also called a jitterbug). When he was barely a teenager, his oldest brother managed to purchase a guitar, and as Lonnie later recalled, "...All of us had to play that one guitar." By the time he was nineteen or twenty, Pitchford had a band that played blues and popular tunes at area clubs on weekend nights in Ebenezer, Canton, and Lexington, and on Sundays was part of a gospel group that sang in various local churches. He travelled around the mid-west doing a variety of odd jobs, but things really changed for him starting in the early 1970s, when he met Worth Long, who brought Lonnie's talent—and his handcrafted one-stringed instruments—to festival stages all around the country. Long also managed to arrange for Pitchford to meet and study with a variety of blues luminaries, including Robert Jr. Lockwood, Houston Stackhouse, Honeyboy Edwards, John Lee Hooker, Eugene Powell, Sam Chatmon, and several others.[701]

As might be expected, Pitchford's first appearance on record was a memorable one—it was a fantastic acoustic version of "Shake Your Money Maker" that German blues enthusiasts Siegfried "Ziggy" Christmann and Axel Küstner recorded in Lexington, Mississippi, on 21 October 1980, for their fourteen-volume *Living Country Blues* series on the L+R label (now reissued, in part, on a three CD set from Evidence). It was his "One String Boogie," however, that truly showcased his talent on the diddley bow. Recorded during the 1983 American Folk Blues Festival Tour, Pitchford gives a barn-burning tour de force performance that leaves no doubt in one's mind about why it is that he received standing ovations for his one-stringed performances all over the country.[702]

After having toured North America, Europe, and Australia, and making TV and film appearances, Pitchford finally recorded a full-length album of his own during the early 1990s, that eventually saw release in 1994 on the Rooster Blues label. *All Around Man* (the title track was inspired by a Bo Carter song), is a true delight, as Pitchford offers up a cross-section of his multi-instrumental skill on acoustic and electric slide guitar, more delectable one-stringed pieces (on one of them, he goes into some detail about how to make one), striking interpretations of two Robert Johnson tunes, and a surprising treat. As it turns out, living in and around the area of Elmore's old stomping grounds wasn't Pitchford's only connection to the old Broomduster—his former mother-in-law, Fannie Mae Smith, had at one time dated Elmore James, and recalled that Elmore used to sing a song for her sometimes. Entitled "Don't You Do That No More" on

700 James "Son" Thomas, *Beefsteak Blues.* Evidence CD 26095-2, 1998; and James "Son" Thomas, *Hard Times.* Black & Blue CD 440.2, 2000. Note: "Standing at the Crossroads" must have been a favorite of Thomas'. He first recorded the tune at his initial recording session in 1968; it was issued on the X-tra label, in England. According to William Ferris, Thomas acknowledged that his source for the song was Elmore James. Ferris, 93, 188-189.

701 Lonnie Pitchford, notes to *All Around Man;* Jim O'Neal and Patty Johnson, comps. Rooster Blues CD 2629, 1994.

702 Lonnie Pitchford, "Shake Your Money Maker." From the album *Living Country Blues: An Anthology.* Evidence CD 26105-2, 1999; Lonnie Pitchford, "One String Boogie." From the album *American Folk Blues Festival '83.* L+R CD 2063, 1984; Pitchford, notes to *All Around Man;* and Axel Küstner, notes to *Living Country Blues: An Anthology.* Evidence CD 26105-2, 1999.

Pitchford's CD, Elmore fans will immediately recognize the tune as "Bobby's Rock" but are not likely to recognize the words. As Lonnie explains, "...Elmore James used to sing that song for her, 'Don't You Do That No More.' I started playing the music one day, a instrumental song that Elmore James got out, and as soon as I started, she started singing that. Said, 'Elmore James used to sing that.' I said, 'What?!' And that's when I started doing it, doing the verses to it. But that was all the verses that she could remember. And she'd always sing just those verses. I think he never recorded it. Not the lyrics."[703]

Sadly, Pitchford's first full-length album would also, ironically, turn out to be his last. He died of AIDS on Sunday, 8 November 1998, at the age of forty-three. According to Dr. Ed Amos, expert locator of the final resting place of many a blues musician (and author of a recent book on the subject), Pitchford is buried just a few meters behind Elmore's grave, in the New Port Community Cemetery in Ebenezer, Mississippi. Lonnie Pitchford was interviewed in the November/ December 1990 issue of *Living Blues* magazine, and Robert Nicholson spent a chapter discussing him in his book *Mississippi: The Blues Today!* As of this writing, *All Around Man* is no longer in print, but will hopefully not remain so for much longer; it is unreservedly recommended. To hear more of Christmann and Küstner's recordings, dubbed "one the last great blues field recording trips," *Living Country Blues: An Anthology* is highly recommended (the set also includes Pitchford doing an exciting, primeval version of "Boogie Chillen" on his one-stringed instrument). The hefty booklet accompanying the set features Küstner's notes about their field trip, and artist profiles by Brett Bonner.[704]

"Dust My Broom" Since Then, Part 3: More from the 1950s

This section traces further developments of the "Dust My Broom" format in the mid to late 1950s, primarily among what could have been called, at the time, the promising "up and coming" young talent.

Alvin Smith (a.k.a. Al King) was born in Monroe, Louisiana in 1926, where he remained a resident until he was seventeen. The elders in his family did not particularly care for the blues, driving the point home by giving the young Al a beating after sneaking out to see Billie Holiday on one occasion, and another one when he was overheard singing some blues while feeding the family's chickens. As he would later sing about, he left Monroe in 1943, and later served in the military; afterwards he headed out to San Francisco to join the postwar boom in the big city. His first ventures in the music industry were actually in Los Angeles on the Recorded in Hollywood label, and later with the Savoys, a vocal group that had a successful record in 1953 on the Combo imprint—successful enough for the group to appear on a TV show, anyway. Unfortunately, the group split up while the record was still hot, and Al decided to try it is a solo.[705]

His next recording, on the Oakland-based Music City label, featured Smith singing a heartfelt piece about growing up, a sense of longing, and the passage of time. While a young Johnny Heartsman warms up the record with the familiar sounds of Elmore James, Smith speaks an introduction before he starts

703 Pitchford, notes to *All Around Man;* and Lonnie Pitchford, *All Around Man.* Rooster Blues CD 2629, 1994.

704 Brett Bonner, notes to *Living Country Blues: An Anthology.* Evidence CD 26105-2, 1999; and Robert Nicholson, *Mississippi: The Blues Today!* New York: Da Capo Press, 1999, 24.

705 Tony Collins, "'On My Way:' The Al King Story." *Juke Blues* 27 (Autumn 1992): 9; and Chris Biehler, notes to Al King, *Blues Master.* Forevermore CD 4601, 1996.

singing: "Oh, tell me the truth snaggle tooth, and then I'll rob you of all your youth." The record possessed an undeniable warmth, like a mug of hot tea on a chilly fall afternoon, with plain, yet candid lyrics:

> Left home in '43, and here it is 1954,
> Left home in '43 and here it is 1954,
> Well I'm going back home, I mean down in old East Monroe.

"It was very successful," Smith later told Tony Collins. Yet after "On My Way," Smith recorded little else in the "down home" blues vein, and this side will always remain as an endearing, enjoyable slice of fifties blues memorabilia (An interesting aside, not only did Elmore's "Dust My Broom" crack the *Cash Box* regional R&B charts in both Los Angeles and Oakland in 1952, it also hit number five in Monroe, Louisiana—Smith's old hometown—the week of 29 March 1952; Likewise, "I Believe" was a top-ten *Billboard* hit on the regional Los Angeles chart for six consecutive weeks in February and March, 1953). In the 1960s, Smith changed his name to Al King, and recorded further with Johnny Heartsman (for the Sahara label), and additionally for the Bihari brothers as the decade was coming to a close.[706]

When twenty-two year old Matthew T. "Guitar" Murphy became a member of Memphis Slim's band in 1952, it changed things for both musicians. Although Slim had previously worked with Robert Johnson and Big Bill Broonzy on separate occasions, a guitarist was something never regularly featured in his touring group up until that time. "There was two things I couldn't stand in those days," he recalled later. "I couldn't stand no damn guitar and harmonica. But Murphy was such a damn genius, man, 'til I had to use him. And after that I damn near had to have a guitar. I brought him from Memphis where he was playing with Tuff Green."[707] Murphy jumped at the chance to play with Memphis Slim, one of the blues musicians that had helped popularize the old Sparks Brothers' war horse "Everyday I Have the Blues" (Lowell Fulson was another), and who had already enjoyed a recording career dating back to 1940, with six R&B chart hits under his belt.[708]

While at United Records, Slim and Murphy recorded over thirty titles together. "Sassy Mae," dating from a March 1954 session, was Memphis Slim's tribute to a woman with supernatural powers, with Murphy rounding out the side with jazzy, calmly confident Elmore James runs. One of Slim's more satisfying efforts during his tenure at United, the record unfortunately failed to make any chart appearances. Slim and Murphy's association lasted for many years; in 1961 Slim's band, the "House Rockers," broke up and Slim moved to Paris permanently; Murphy would later go on to appear in the film *The Blues Brothers.* Incidentally, Matt can be heard providing the tasteful guitar backing behind Sonny Boy Williamson for my favorite "unplugged" version of the "The Sky Is Crying," dating from a November 1963 session held in Copenhagen (originally issued in Denmark on the Storyville label, later reissued on an Alligator Records compact disc). A forthcoming CD promised by Delmark will reissue the remaining Memphis Slim/Matt Murphy United titles.[709]

Another of the Chicago blues' "younger generation" that made a bow to Elmore James was

[706] Alvin Smith, "On My Way." Music City 744, 1954; Collins, 10, 13; and Ryan, *Trumpet Records,* 101.
Note: Incidentally, Alvin Smith's record is not the only Elmore-ish bay area blues disc Johnny Heartsman played on, either—he can also be heard lending bass support on Jimmy Wilson's appropriately entitled "Strangest Blues." Guitarist Lafayette Thomas presumably plays the leading Elmore figures, during which the band lays down an elementary Cuban-style rhythm in the background, creating a truly odd, yet interesting effect. It was recorded in 1954 and released on both the Rhythm and the Elko labels probably the same year (Jimmy Wilson, "Strangest Blues." Rhythm 1765, 1954; and Leadbitter, Fancourt, and Pelletier, 776).

[707] Jim O'Neal, notes to Memphis Slim, *Memphis Slim U.S.A.* Delmark CD 710, 1998 [reissue].

[708] Ibid.; Dixon, Godrich, and Rye, 154; and Whitburn, 286.

[709] Memphis Slim, "Sassy Mae." United 176, 1954; O'Neal, notes to *Memphis Slim U.S.A.;* Leadbitter, Fancourt, and Pelletier, 208-209, 762; and Whitburn, 286-287.

guitarist/vocalist Jody Williams. Born in Mobile, Alabama in 1935, by the time he was nineteen Williams was playing lead in Howlin' Wolf's band, and—in the company of fellow guitarist Hubert Sumlin—made appearances on a handful of Wolf's prime tracks as well (it has also been suggested that it is Williams and B.B. King playing guitar on Otis Spann's one and only vintage-era 45). At the ripe age of twenty, Williams made his debut as a vocalist for disk jockey Al Benson's Blue Lake label, a subsidiary of his respected Parrot imprint. On "Groan My Blues Away" Williams puts a slight twist on the Elmore James theme—half slide and half finger-picked—played in open E tuning in a breezy manner in descending, stepped-chordal arpeggios, riffing in unison with Harold Ashby's tenor sax. Unfortunately, Benson held back the title from release, and blues fans would have to wait for three and a half decades to get to hear Williams' only recording to feature him playing the slide guitar (All four of Williams' Blue Lake sides appear on the Relic Records album *Cool Playing Blues.* As a bonus, that same album features three previously unknown titles by J.T. Brown; just for the record, I'll repeat what Dick Shurman said in his liner notes: "No, Elmore isn't present!").[710]

After recording with Billy Boy Arnold, Bo Diddley, and Otis Rush (among others), Jody Williams gave up music in the mid-1960s for a career in electronics, a trade he learned in school on the GI Bill after having served in the Army. In the year 2000, Williams made a surprise appearance at Robert Jr. Lockwood's 85th birthday party in Chicago, and since then started playing once more, and recording. In the spring of 2002 his new CD, *Return of a Legend,* was issued to widespread critical acclaim. With only a few relatively obscure singles to his credit from the 1950s and 1960s, it is a most welcome addition to Williams' catalog.[711]

Morris Pejoe blew into the Windy City in 1951, when he was twenty-seven. Originally from Louisiana, Pejoe had been a violinist before spending some time in east Texas in the late forties, where he soaked up the guitar sounds of Clarence "Gatemouth" Brown, Lightnin' Hopkins, and T-Bone Walker. Pejoe made his first 78 for Checker the year after he came to Chicago, a remake of a Fats Domino tune that also featured Jody Williams on guitar and fellow Bayou State émigré Henry Gray on the eighty-eights. He recorded more for Chess the next year, had one session for United in December 1954 (held in producer Al Smith's basement, memorialized on the Delmark CD *Wrapped in My Baby*), and in May 1955, drifted over to Vee-Jay where he recorded enough material for one single.[712]

At United, Pejoe cut the Elmore-ish "Let's Get High"—two different takes were mastered by United, one featuring a jury-rigged stop-time arrangement—and at Vee-Jay, recorded "Hurt My Feelings," whose format was essentially drawn out of a similar well. Aided on both titles by Henry Gray's energetic piano, Pejoe seems to try to make the point that he, too, is a force to be reckoned with among the ranks of Chicago blues guitarists. While "Hurt My Feelings" is a more cohesive (and relaxed) effort for sure, there is something undeniably pleasant about the hard-driving and high-octane, slightly out-of-kilter, homemade feel of "Let's Get High."[713]

After these sessions, Pejoe would only record four more singles, one each for blues cult-favorites Abco and Atomic-H (where he again recorded "Let's Get High," this time utilizing a distinct rockabilly/western motif, but it was left unissued), and in the late sixties one 45 apiece for the unknown Kaytown and Friendly

710 Shurman, notes to *Cool Playing Blues;* Jody Williams, "Groan My Blues Away." From the album *Cool Playing Blues.* Relic CD 7016, 1990; and Leadbitter, Fancourt, and Pelletier, 516, 724,

711 Shurman, notes to *Cool Playing Blues;* Leadbitter, Fancourt, and Pelletier, 724-725, and Dick Shurman, "Dick Shurman's Chicago Scene." *Juke Blues* 47 (Summer 2000): 10.

712 Bill Dahl, notes to Morris Pejoe and Arthur "Big Boy" Spires, *Wrapped in My Baby.* Delmark CD 716, 1998; and Leadbitter, Fancourt, and Pelletier, 352-353.

713 Morris Pejoe, "Hurt My Feelings." Vee-Jay 148, 1955; Morris Pejoe, "Let's Get High." From the album Morris Pejoe and Arthur "Big Boy" Spires, *Wrapped in My Baby.* Delmark CD 716, 1998; and Leadbitter, Fancourt, and Pelletier, 353.

Five labels, with the latter featuring his partner "Little" Mary Lane on vocals. After Pejoe split with Lane (it was a long-running personal and musical relationship, evidently), he moved to Detroit in the early 1970s, where he died on Tuesday, 27 July 1982 at the age of fifty-eight.[714]

In 1989, Dee "Cap'n Pete" Henderson and I had the privilege of interviewing Bo Diddley when he appeared in Memphis, and later on that weekend got to see him in concert. Although I was already familiar with his records, it became apparent from his live show that, if he had wanted to, he could have easily grown up to be a helluva slide guitar player, as a large percentage of the material he played that night was based on a straight "open E" guitar tuning (earlier, he had told us his tuning was a secret (sure, whatever); but thinking about the "Bo Diddley" beat married to the sound of an Elmore James-type slide guitar left all sorts of "what ifs?" popping up in my head throughout the evening and the rest of the week). It is indeed true that over the years the music of Elmore James has crept into the music of Bo Diddley, it's just that, being his own man, Bo played it his way.

Two prime examples of this spring to mind, the frequently overlooked gem "Little Girl" from his very first session in March 1955, and "Blues Blues," from December 1958. While both songs retain the same fundamental structure of a heavy duple rhythm Elmore James-styled song ("Blues Blues" more so than "Little Girl"), Bo plays them in a manner that does not find him sliding (or fingering) his way up to the twelfth fret of the guitar to play the familiar four sets of triplets that constitute a proper "Broom" signature. To further cloud the issue, only the first verse and both solos in "Little Girl" retain the standard 12-bar format, all the rest of the verses have just eight. There has also been some contention over the years as to who actually played on "Little Girl." A variety of names have been tossed out—Otis Spann or Henry Gray on piano; Frank Kirkland or Clifton James on drums; and Lester Davenport or Billy Boy Arnold on harmonica—take your pick. Personnel details are also somewhat vague on "Blues Blues." One thing is certain, however—Jerome Green, the "Yo-Yo Ma of the maracas"—graces both sides with his inimitable talent.[715]

My all-time favorite Bo Diddley blues record, however, has to be "Live My Life," yet another of Bo's tunes that utilizes a basic Elmore James song structure. Having only been released on four different occasions on the North American continent, it is not one of Bo's better known sides, but certainly deserves to be. With an edgy, declamatory vocal, a classic blues lyric storyline, Jerome Green shaking the maracas like there's no tomorrow, and rock-crushing full-tilt guitar, Bo Diddley was rarely better at playing the blues than he is here (Chess evidently liked "Live My Life" so much that they rubbed out the vocal track, overdubbed some additional piano, and used the resulting "instrumental" as album filler for Bo's fourth LP, *In the Spotlight*).[716]

In his determination to seek a different sound, Bo Diddley created his own readily identifiable signature that is arguably just as recognizable—perhaps even more so—than the "Dust My Broom" riff. Now in his seventies, Bo Diddley is still going strong. Bo Diddley-ologist George R. White has devoted a substantial portion of his life to compiling a comprehensive discography of the musician's work, and has written a biography on Bo as well. In the United States, MCA/Chess has reissued a fair sum of Diddley's

714 Dahl, notes to *Wrapped in My Baby;* and Bob McGrath, *The R&B Indies.* West Vancouver, Canada: Eyeball Productions, 2000, 461; and Various Artists, *Chicago Ain't Nothin' But a Blues Band.* Delmark CD 624, 1999.

715 Bo Diddley, "Little Girl." From the album Bo Diddley, *Go Bo Diddley.* Checker LP 1436, 1959; Bo Diddley, "Blues Blues." From the album Bo Diddley, *Rare & Well Done.* MCA/Chess CD 9331, 1991; George R. White, *The Complete Bo Diddley Sessions.* Bradford, England: George R. White Publications, 1993, 13, 23-24; and Leadbitter and Slaven, *Blues Records: 1943-1966,* 19.

716 Bo Diddley, "Live My Life." From the album Bo Diddley, *In the Spotlight.* Checker LP 2976, 1960; and White, 28-29.

catalog from his Chess/Checker glory days; Two English labels, Ace and the Beat Goes On, have been reissuing material as well. With all the attention played on him with a discography, a biography, and reissue programs on two continents, it will hopefully now be possible, after all these years, to—once and for all—finally know Diddley.

Keepers of the Flame

While we have seen that lots of people played the "Dust My Broom" riff over the years, perhaps few people would disagree that nobody played it quite like Elmore did. At times, some people came close, and of those who did, Joe Carter, Hound Dog Taylor, John Littlejohn, J.B. Hutto, and Homesick James stand head and shoulders above the rest.

Joe Carter

As with Hop Wilson, the name Joe Carter may not exactly be a household word to some readers. Playing the Chicago clubs was Joe's thing, not recording. His name comes up in relatively few blues books, and other than a few stories retold by George Paulus in the liner notes to Carter's Barrelhouse LP, he evidently gave no interviews, either. With no known 45s, a handful of recordings scattered on a half-dozen or so anthologies, and only one full-length LP dating from 1976 (finally reissued in Japan in 1997), there's not much of Carter, or his recordings, to go around.[717]

I first came across the name of Joe Carter while I was doing research for my master's thesis. Looking up articles on Elmore James in a periodical guide to music literature, I got a number of hits for an "Elmore James Jr." On several occasions, when I had a bit of extra time, I wrote down the leads and followed them up later just out of sheer curiosity. Most of them led to either a review of a live performance Carter had recently given, or a review of Joe's 1976 Barrelhouse LP, *Mean & Evil Blues.* Long out of print by the time I was doing my research, it would be some time before I would get the chance to actually hear the down and out, gut-bucket blues of Joe Carter and His Chicago Broomdusters.

Joe Carter was born in Midland, Georgia, on 6 November 1927. When he was eleven, his parents furthered his interest in music by giving him a new "Stella" guitar as a Christmas present. Lee Willis, a local musician, introduced Joe to a few fundamental chord changes and a couple of different guitar tunings. Typically, Carter would play on the streets for change, and when he was a bit older, also at area juke joints and house parties. When family relatives invited him up for a visit to the Windy City in 1952, Joe eagerly welcomed the opportunity to travel. Also, he would finally get to see some of his favorite blues musicians in person, having previously only heard them on records.[718]

Upon arrival, Carter wasted no time heading over to the Club Zanzibar at 13th and Ashland to see Muddy Waters. When Muddy loaned him the money to buy his first electric guitar, Carter ended up

[717] Leadbitter and Slaven, *Blues Records 1943-1970,* 242; and George Paulus, notes to Joe Carter and His Chicago Broomdusters, *Mean & Evil Blues.* Barrelhouse LP 07, 1976.

Note: In 1966, an artist by the name of Joe Carter recorded a single for the Phoenixville, Pennsylvania-based B-J label. The titles were "Soul Before News" b/w "Just to Let You Know" (B-J 1001). This is almost certainly the soul singer Joe Lee Carter (a.k.a. Joe L. Carter or Joel Carter) that also had a single on the Detroit-based Clissac label in 1970 and the Memphis-based Hi label in 1971—*not* the Joe Carter we are discussing here (McGrath, 151, 259, 536; and Paulus, notes to *Mean & Evil Blues*).

[718] Paulus, notes to *Mean & Evil Blues.*

staying in Chicago full-time. The early fifties was a golden era for blues in Chicago, and he met no problems putting together a band: Joe on slide guitar and vocals, Otis "Big Smokey" Smothers on guitar and vocals, and Lester Davenport on harmonica (drummer Jimmy Malender might have joined the group a bit later). As Carter related it to George Paulus, "One had to have that harp. Every club, or what passed as a club, demanded a harp, but they went without a drummer if need be, as the money was at times small, the competition very tough, and two or three club dates might be played in one night." Connections to Elmore were plenty: Davenport's father, Neely, was a slide guitarist living in Tchula, Mississippi in the early to mid-forties; sometimes Elmore James would stop by and they would sit on the front porch and play together while a youthful Lester listened earnestly; once in Chicago, it was a neighbor, Homesick James, who took Davenport and his cousin Smokey Smothers under his wing, tutored them, and first let them get up on stage with him. Every once and a while, when Elmore James, Howlin' Wolf, or Muddy Waters would have a band member who was sick or couldn't make it for the evening, Joe (or one of his crew) might come and fill-in for the evening; that, evidently, was how Joe came to meet his other idol, Elmore James.[719]

During the late fifties, Cobra Records contacted Joe in regards to setting up a recording session—along with his regular band, it had been arranged for Freddy King to lend secondary fret assistance—but Carter declined. Making good money in the clubs, Joe felt he really didn't need the dough (and, possibly, the headaches that can sometimes be associated with such things). Joe played with a "who's who" of Chicago blues acts, including Junior Wells and Sonny Boy Williamson, but by 1965 the scene had deteriorated to the point that it was no longer possible to play music four nights a week and make a full-time living from it, so he took a sabbatical for five years.[720]

Starting in the 1970s, Joe was lured back into club work, regrouped a small band, and started playing again. On Friday, 3 July 1970, Dick Shurman recorded Joe at the Washburne Lounge, over on the west side of Chicago, with members of Willie Johnson's band lending rhythm support. In all, four titles were recorded, including a version of "Sweet Home Chicago;" the other three—"Pickin' the Blues," "I'm Worried," and "The Sky Is Crying"—were Elmore James songs. Apparently, this was Carter's debut recording date, but unfortunately, the titles were never issued. By the end of the year, Joe was back at the Washburne Lounge to hold down a regular gig, and in January 1971, guested for a couple tracks during a Hubert Sumlin recording session that Swiss producer Willy Leiser conducted.[721]

As the early 1970s progressed, magazines like *Living Blues,* headquartered in Chicago at that time, greatly helped to fuel interest in the local blues scene (not to mention national and international interest as well) by not only reviewing records, but also by printing an ongoing guide to who was playing where in the Windy City at any given time. It was possibly through this venue that Carter's path crossed with that of producer/researcher/writer/collector George Paulus', and resulted in the eleven titles that appeared on *Mean & Evil Blues* in 1976.

"This collection of songs is the type of blues you might be lucky enough to hear if you are in Chicago on a night when Joe's playing [in one of] the ghetto bars...," offered Paulus. "Just as the violence has not been taken off the streets, neither has the rough edge of his music."[722] Of the tunes collected on Carter's

719 Ibid.; Marcel Chauvard and Jacques Demêtre, "Smokey Smothers," 97. In Mike Leadbitter, ed., *Nothing But the Blues.* London: Hanover Books, 1971; and John Anthony Brisbin, "Lester Davenport: It's All About Havin' a Good Time." *Living Blues* 107 (February 1993): 21-22.

720 Paulus, notes to *Mean & Evil Blues.*

721 "Blues News." *Living Blues* 4 (Winter 1970/1971): 26; "Live Chicago Blues." *Living Blues* 4 (Winter 1970/1971): 24; Paulus, notes to *Mean & Evil Blues;* Leadbitter and Slaven, *Blues Records 1943-1970,* 242; and Shurman, personal communication, 29 November 2001.

722 Paulus, notes to *Mean & Evil Blues.*

debut album, he offers up a straight-ahead mixture of blues standards, Muddy Waters tunes, and Elmore James songs, with a simple, uneventful accompaniment of second guitar and drums from Walter "Big Red" Smith and Johnny Junious, respectively. A rough-edged, doomy tension is brought about by Joe's sulphuric slide playing and the use of a Shure "bullet" microphone for the vocals (so called because of its shape, this mike has long been favored by blues harmonica players for amplifying their instrument because it is easily cupped in one's hands; it can also be used for vocals, but changes the dynamics of the human voice somewhat. Elmore was once photographed by Demêtre and Chauvard using just such a mike for his vocals; you can also hear one-man-band sensation Joe Hill Louis playing his harp and singing into a bullet mike on many of his recordings); even though Paulus probably could have used a better quality microphone for the sessions, my guess is he chose this arrangement to more closely reflect an "authentic" club sound (by comparison, "Talk To Your Daughter," recorded with a similar line up of musicians in 1975—but with different equipment—is distinctly missing a lot of that "rough-edged, doomy feel" from the Barrelhouse LP). Covers of Elmore James songs included Joe singing an obligatory, standard-issue version of "Dust My Broom," a torturous "It Hurts Me Too," a phlegmatic rendition of "Shake Your Moneymaker" which just misses the mark of being taken at a jumping pace, and an Elmore classic that has rarely ever been covered, "I'm Worried." Here, the tormented demeanor of Elmore's original lyrics coupled with Joe's generally somber approach gel perfectly with the squall of his slide guitar, qualifying it to be a true highlight, and, by and large, my favorite track of the album.[723]

As was often the case, LPs like this one would help bring a wider audience—and acclaim—to the artist. André Hobus gave a glowing, enthusiastic review of Carter's January 1978 performance in Belgium that left the audience begging for more, and heaping praise on him for his "irresistible versions" of Elmore classics, particularly his rendering of "Anna Lee," which Hobus described as "pure joy, with long slide runs reminiscent of a Hawaiian guitar" that still managed to maintain a "knife-edged stinging" quality to them. After the show, Carter promised to be back next year, and he was; although judging by the comments of Karl Dallas—who reviewed Carter's first London concert for *Melody Maker* ("Elmore James Jr., 100 Club")—it was a seemingly lugubrious affair of tepid Elmore retreads that left Dallas largely unimpressed. In 1981, an appearance by an "Elmore James Jr." singing "Bad Feeling" on the *Genuine Mississippi Blues* LP (from the Jackson-based Ace Records), playing in the Elmore style—and with lyrics that could have easily been taken from a page in either Elmore's or Joe Carter's book—turned out to be a false alarm (that was actually Saint Louis' own Howlin' Wolf emulator, Big Bad Smitty, playing lead slide guitar behind Chicago singer Ernest Johnson). Carter continued performing through at least part of the 1980s, when a bout with throat cancer brought about his permanent retirement from music. Although his contributions to Elmore's legacy are not lengthy (his entire recorded output, for instance, would apparently fit nicely on one CD), they will not soon be forgotten, either.[724]

---

723 Joe Carter and His Chicago Broomdusters, *Mean & Evil Blues.* P-Vine CD 5202, 1997 [reissue]; and Joe Carter, "Talk To Your Daughter." From the album *Chicago Blues 2.* JSP CD 405, 1998.

724 André Hobus, "Joe Carter." *Blues Unlimited* 129 (March/April 1978): 33; Karl Dallas, "Elmore James Jr., 100 Club, London." *Melody Maker* vol. 54 (17 February 1979): 50; and Neil Slaven, notes to *John Vincent Presents Genuine Mississippi Blues... Plus: The Ace (MS) Blues Masters Vol. 4.* West Side CD 579, 1999.

Hound Dog Taylor

The name Hound Dog Taylor is one that will, perhaps, find many readers nodding and smiling. Best known for a series of albums he recorded for the Alligator label (it was, in fact, a Hound Dog Taylor LP with which Alligator got its start more than thirty years ago), Taylor has left an ingratiating, indelible stamp on the blues world. More than a quarter century since his death, Taylor is still sorely missed.

Born Theodore Roosevelt Taylor in Natchez, Mississippi, on 12 April (1915, 1916, or 1917—pick one), Taylor had to make a go of it on his own from age nine, when a mean step-father kicked him out of the house. As a kid, the six-fingered Taylor tried his hand at tinkling the ivories before deciding on guitar, learning on a homemade instrument fashioned out of a cigar box. In his late teens, he got his first "real" guitar from Sears & Roebuck, and starting around 1935, could be found playing in the Tchula area of Mississippi. Elmore James was a neighbor who was working on a nearby plantation; after they met, Elmore would prove to be Taylor's main influence. Through Elmore, Taylor also met Sonny Boy Williamson, and in the late 1930s played with them, and Robert Jr. Lockwood as well, at area juke joints and house parties. Supposedly, he even made a brief appearance on Sonny Boy's *King Biscuit Time,* but that all came to an end in the early 1940s, when false accusations involving a white woman forced him to hurriedly flee north. Throughout the forties and fifties he worked at various jobs in Chicago, including one at Ace Woodwork, making butterscotch in an ice cream factory, and hauling freight for the American Television Company—until 1957, that is, when he decided to pursue music full time. His recording debut would occur three years later, for Narvel "Cadillac Baby" Eatmon's Bea & Baby label.[725]

"Baby Is Coming Home" and "Take Five" were the sides of Taylor's first record, and proves right from the start that, first of all, he was indeed a disciple of the Elmore tradition, and secondly, more than ready to get into a good-time boogieing groove. Both tunes were original compositions, per se, and whereas "Baby Is Coming Home" retained a strict "Dust My Broom" format, "Take Five" was a short and fast slide guitar rocker with a basic, repeated theme; a little more than a decade later, he would record a rawer version for Alligator Records that would feature him in prime form.[726]

A couple years later, around 1962, "Christine" and "Alley Music" became the titles on Taylor's next 45, this time, for Carl Jones' Firma imprint (a part of his of C.J./Colt/Firma conglomeration of labels). More high-spirited partying was to be had on "Alley Music," which possibly may have been slated as a promo or theme song for Big Bill Hill's radio show (Hill appears to interject some enthusiastic salutations on the disc), while "Christine" is another Elmore-styled rocker with a dual existence—one version contains a plaintive vocal sung to a sweetheart, the other is an instrumental version—an instinctive and joyous celebration of the "Dust My Broom" riff that never fails to bring a smile to my face. This is good old-fashioned, straightforward party music, and even though the format may be unadorned, there is something about the latter version of "Christine" that makes it one of Taylor's most sincere, and satisfying, efforts.[727]

A five year hiatus would occur before Taylor set foot once again in a recording studio. This time it was for a major independent, Chess/Checker, with sessions supervised by Leonard's son Marshall. Although

725 Mike Leadbitter, "Hound Dog Taylor." *Blues Unlimited* 48 (November/December 1967): 21; Jim O'Neal and R.T. Cuniff, "Hound Dog Taylor." *Living Blues* 4 (Winter 1970/1971): 5; Wesley Race, "Hound Dog Taylor." *Blues Unlimited* 93 (July 1972): 16; and Leadbitter, Fancourt, and Pelletier, 576.

726 Hound Dog Taylor, "Take Five." Bea & Baby 112, c. 1960; and Hound Dog Taylor, "Baby Is Coming Home." Bea & Baby 112, c. 1960. Note: These titles were reissued on the compilation *Bea & Baby Records Presents: The Best of Chicago Blues.* Wolf CD 120.293 (year of issue unknown, c. mid 1990s).

727 Hound Dog Taylor, "Alley Music." Firma 626, c. 1962; Hound Dog Taylor, "Christine." Firma 626, c. 1962; and Hound Dog Taylor, "Christine" [instrumental version]. From the album *C.J.'s Roots of Chicago Blues, Vol. 1.* Blue Flame LP 101, c. 1970; and Leadbitter, Fancourt, and Pelletier, 576. Note: all of these titles, plus one bonus track, were reissued on the compilation *Chicago Blues from C.J. Records, Vol. 1.* Wolf CD 120.281, c. 1998.

"Watch Out" and "Down Home" were released as a single on Checker, the session—for lack of a better word—just failed to congeal. For many years I have listened to these sides, and I always keep coming back to the same conclusion—that perhaps Taylor just was not in top form that particular day, or that the chosen material did not showcase his talent in its best possible light. Adding insult to injury, Taylor's Checker single couldn't have been released at a worse time: it came out sometime in the fall of 1969—given that Chess had been sold to the General Recorded Tape Corporation earlier in the year, and with the death of patriarch Leonard Chess on Thursday, 16 October 1969—it was a period of massive upheavals for the company, and resultingly, Taylor's single went nowhere.[728]

Sadly, the trend started with Taylor's Checker 45 continued for the 1967 American Folk Blues Festival Tour. Mike Leadbitter was particularly harsh with his criticism of Taylor's live performance, accusing him of "hacking out songs which I can listen to any time by the real thing" (by which, I can only imagine, he was referring to a stack of Elmore James records he had at home). To be fair, though, Taylor's accompaniment on "The Sky Is Crying" (the only recording with Taylor on vocals to be issued on LP from the concert series that year)—even though it contained Odie Payne on drums and Little Walter on unamplified harp—just did not suit him. While Payne was his usual reliable self, the main detractors were the bassist—and most surprisingly—an atypically insensitive Little Walter on harp.[729]

In 1971, all that changed when Bruce Iglauer began recording Hound Dog Taylor for a brand new label he started just for the occasion, Alligator Records. "Alligator Records was created to make just one record," wrote Bruce Iglauer twenty years after the fact. "It was called *Hound Dog Taylor and the Houserockers* and it was cut in just two nights in the spring of 1971, with the band playing the same beat-up guitars through the same raggedy amps they used at Florence's [at the time, a famous blues spot in Chicago]. It was my first attempt to capture the sound and feel of the blues clubs on a record."[730] A glimpse of that "sound" and "feel" was captured by Jim O'Neal and R.T. Cuniff, in this memorable piece they wrote in the Winter 1970/1971 issue of *Living Blues* magazine:

> I can think of few experiences as exhilarating as a Sunday afternoon at Florence's on Chicago's south side, watching Hound Dog as he laughs, stomps, and flails away at his guitar, infecting everyone in the vicinity with a gleeful boogie disease. "Dog" can't play a verse without breaking into happy laughter, and it's a rare listener who isn't bopping with him all the way.
>
> And there's Taylor's great second guitarist, Brewer Phillips, flashing a toothy grin, kicking his leg up in the air and unleashing rapid, raucous riffs. Taylor and Phillips split up sometimes, but always come back together—a lot of musicians can't keep up with Hound Dog at all, and no one blends in like Phillips does. Behind them is drummer Ted Harvey, always chewing a wad of gum and yelling for another drink while he bashes both sticks on a battered snare drum.
>
> And clustered around the band are people—people who've seen Hound Dog a hundred times before but who are still amazed at the boogies and bottleneck blues; people standing, dancing, smiling, just looking and shaking their heads. Out of all the bluesmen in Chicago, only Hound Dog consistently gets such crowd responses.[731]

---

728 Various Artists, *Slidin'.* Charly CD RED 36, 1991; Cohodas, 295, 299; and Leadbitter, Fancourt, and Pelletier, 576. Note: There has been some debate as to whether Taylor's Checker single was actually issued or not. According to Norman Darwen, Taylor claimed it was only issued in California, for instance (Norman Darwen, notes to *Slidin'.* Charly CD RED 36, 1991).

729 Simon Napier and Mike Leadbitter, "The Sixth American Folk Blues Festival – 1967." *Blues Unlimited* 48 (November/December 1967): 20; and Hound Dog Taylor, "The Sky Is Crying." From the album *American Folk Blues Festival '67.* L+R CD 2070, 1990.

730 Bruce Iglauer, notes to *The Alligator Records 20th Anniversary Collection.* Alligator CD 105/106, 1991.

731 O'Neal and Cuniff, 4.

Between 1971 and 1982, Alligator released four Hound Dog Taylor & the Houserockers albums—the self-titled first LP, the second was *Natural Boogie*, a "live" album, *Beware of the Dog*, became the third (it was in the final phase of production as Taylor died), and a fourth one six years later, *Genuine Houserocking Music*. Each album is peppered with Elmore James songs: "Held My Baby Last Night," "Wild About You Baby," and "It Hurts Me Too" (which was molded closely after Elmore's Enjoy 45), were on the first album, while "Hawaiian Boogie," "Talk to My Baby," and "Roll Your Moneymaker" (a special Elmore-Shakey Jake-Magic Sam cross-bred version) were programmed on the second one. "Dust My Broom" and "The Sun Is Shining" were featured on the "live" third LP, with "Crossroads" and a studio version of "The Sun Is Shining" being selected for the fourth album. Although Elmore's slower material (like "Held My Baby Last Night" and "The Sun Is Shining") was in capable hands when it came to Taylor, arguably, the "Dog" was at his best when he was boogieing, and in keeping with that spirit, favorite highlights from the four albums include a churning, revved-up version of "Take Five" from the second album, and a superbly stunning rendition of "Crossroads"—drawn deeply from Elmore's classic reading of the Robert Johnson standard—that appeared on the fourth LP (if your stereo system has a "stereo/mono" button, set it for mono; for some reason, Taylor seems to sound much better in mono than he does in stereo). If one were to take Taylor's four LPs, however, and listen to them in order, they would undeniably find a certain amount of repetition sinking in by the time they had worked half way through the third album (Pete Welding's statements about Elmore—"he only knew three solos, but he knew them cold," and that "Elmore James' music was like homecooking—nothing fancy but damned good"—would have actually been much more accurate had they been applied to Hound Dog Taylor—it makes one question just exactly whose records were playing on Welding's turntable when he wrote those words). But Hound Dog and the Houserockers were such affable types, that, in a way, it doesn't really seem to matter just all *that* much. Generally, one could make a strong argument for *Natural Boogie* being Taylor's best overall album, offering the most satisfying balance of material.[732]

My favorite specific Taylor performance, though, is a version of "Wild About You Baby" that appeared on an obscure Fan Club issue, *Live at Joe's Place*. The disc features Taylor in live performance in 1972 at Cambridge, Massachusetts, in a free-spirited, rowdy demeanor that, in comparison, makes the mood of his third album seem more like a church supper. *Live at Joe's Place* is, I imagine, what it must have really been like to have seen Taylor in live performance (here, even Lieber & Stoller's "Kansas City" becomes a vehicle for Taylor to haul out the "Broom" riff). Out of the eleven titles on the disc, four are Elmore compositions. His five and a half minute version of "Wild About You Baby" is truly the pièce de résistance of his career. It is a flat out Elmore James-styled boogie that finds Taylor maniacal and unrelenting, until—just when you think maybe he's going to wrap up the side, he's off again, egged on by gleeful shouts from the band, repeating the "Broom" riff over and over and over again, not giving the audience a respite until the full five and half minutes have elapsed. It is a classic Hound Dog Taylor moment, and one that, I feel, ultimately reflects the absolute best of his artistry and his good-natured, good-time party music.[733]

---

732 Hound Dog Taylor and the Houserockers, *Hound Dog Taylor and the Houserockers.* Alligator LP 4701, 1971; Hound Dog Taylor and the Houserockers, *Natural Boogie.* Alligator LP 4704, 1974; Hound Dog Taylor and the Houserockers, *Beware of the Dog.* Alligator LP 4707, 1976; Hound Dog Taylor and the Houserockers, *Genuine Houserocking Music.* Alligator LP 4727, 1982; and Pete Welding, notes to Elmore James, Eddie Taylor, and Jimmy Reed, *South Side Blues.* Cobblestone LP 9001, 1972.

733 Hound Dog Taylor, *Live at Joe's Place.* Fan Club CD 100, 1992.

Note: Speaking of "live" Hound Dog Taylor, I was recently given the opportunity to see footage of him in performance at the 1973 Ann Arbor Blues Festival, and also for a short segment entitled "Reelin' In The Years" that was filmed in Denmark for the American Folk Blues Festival Tour in October, 1967.

After his first album, *Hound Dog Taylor and the Houserockers* was issued, things changed significantly for the three musicians. Instead of playing for $45 a night (that was $45 for the whole group, *not* $45 each person), they would play their special brand of rocking, raggedy blues for stadiums and festivals from Ann Arbor to Miami, for clubs in Ohio, New England, and the rest of the U.S, the Philharmonic in New York City, and even to points on the opposite side of the globe, in Australia and New Zealand. They appeared on national Canadian television (Taylor thanked the audience for their contribution of Canadian Club to the world), and no less a cultural icon than *Rolling Stone* did a piece on them.[734]

Hound Dog Taylor died of cancer on Wednesday, 17 December 1975, in Chicago. "When I die," he used to tell Bruce Iglauer, "don't have a funeral—have a party!" Thanks to the ongoing availability of his catalog, that party continues to this very day. In the last couple years, Iglauer has released a "tribute" album to Hound Dog Taylor, as well as *Deluxe Edition,* a compilation culled from his four original Alligator albums that features numerous photos, two "bonus" tracks, and a mini fold-out poster of Taylor posing with the family dog and his infamous "supercheap Japanese guitar." Bruce Iglauer's memorable profile of Hound Dog Taylor and the Houserockers, from the liner notes to *Genuine Houserocking Music,* is worth the price of admission alone.[735]

The Ann Arbor set is, at times, a bit like watching the best restored version of the film classic *Lost Horizon* (due to the interspersed still shots that were a result of the primeval video cameras frequent running out of tape, although, thankfully, the soundtrack is intact), but that does not mar in any way an opportunity to see the "Dog" completely in his natural element. The set, consisting of just seven numbers—"Sadie," three Elmore pieces, plus three instrumentals—ends abruptly during a Ted Harvey drum solo, but not before Taylor has completely enraptured his audience.

Starting off with "Held My Baby Last Night," the first thing that comes to mind is an instantaneous gut reaction—"Damn, sounds just like the records!"—a testimony to producer Bruce Iglauer's idea to capture Hound Dog Taylor "as is" in the studio, without fancy studio tricks or gimmicks. Hunched over his guitar while playing fiery, stinging slide lines, grinning from ear-to-ear for the camera, Taylor's ease and dexterity with his instrument exudes a casual elegance which belies the straight-ahead rawness of what he is playing. The second number is a lively, fast-paced instrumental that features lots of slide guitar, after which he breaks into the opening notes of "Wild About You Baby" with a marvelously irresistible Elmore-ish slide guitar explosion. This, in turn, causes the audience to become a massive sea of bobbing heads swaying in synch to the music, and later during the piece, Taylor takes a few moments to clown around a little on the guitar. After "Shake Your Moneymaker," Taylor begins a slow piece which segues into "Sadie." During his solo, he can be seen taking his left hand completely away from the guitar, only coming back to play just a note or two, before repeating the process all over again. The last two numbers are both instrumentals, one led by Brewer Phillips, during which things start to heat up a bit. It is Taylor in full party mode, and a rare opportunity to witness some of the magic with which he held audiences, night after night, for years.

The five and a half minutes of footage shot in 1967 during the American Folk Blues Festival tour, however, is a horse of a slightly different color. Somewhat restrained (even his hair is slicked back), Hound Dog performs "Wild About You," with a very good, tight sound, that is very much in the same vein as his Chess studio sides, recorded that same year. Little Walter backs him up on acoustic harp, synching with him very well and helping to provide a concordant solidity to the proceedings (in contrast to his mediocre performance on "The Sky Is Crying"). For the second number, Taylor is in a supporting role behind Koko Taylor for "Wang Dang Doodle," playing very nice, if undistinguished, simple and repeated phrases, while he and Walter—supported by bassist Dillard Crume and drummer Odie Payne—mesh very well once again. It is not without a certain degree of irony that one watches this short segment fade out, wishing there could be a little more of it, and knowing full well that within a few months, Walter would be gone—this footage being among the very few moments on film that we are grateful to have of the harmonica master. (My sincere thanks to Paul Vernon, Bill Greensmith, and Frank Awalt for making this footage available to me.)

734 Bruce Iglauer, notes to Hound Dog Taylor and the Houserockers, *Genuine Houserocking Music.* Alligator LP 4727, 1982.

735 Bruce Iglauer, notes to Hound Dog Taylor and the Houserockers, *Beware of the Dog.* Alligator LP 4707, 1976; and Iglauer, notes to *Genuine Houserocking Music.*

John Littlejohn

"John L. Funchess is the reincarnation of Elmore James!" boldly proclaimed Gary Paulsen in *Blues Unlimited,* after he and Chris Strachwitz heard Littlejohn perform at a west side Chicago club in 1968. "He is not just another Elmore imitator—he is Elmore. From the moment he put a slide on his finger we both knew what we were hearing."[736] Born on 16 April 1931[737] in either Scott, Hinds, or Washington Counties in Mississippi, John "Littlejohn" Funchess grew up in Jackson. His first encounter with a guitar was thanks to his father: "I never played guitar or seen one until my father won it in a crap game for fifty cents and brought it home," he recalled. "And before that I had a lil ole wire on the wall, tryin' to play that with a bottle on each end to hold it. That's where I first started tryin' to play the guitar...." While still a youngster, Littlejohn's father would sometimes take him along on his extracurricular weekend activities. "Well, there was a guy used to go round the frolics, places, with my dad and I was small and he would take me with him, you know. And the guy used to play all night, frolics. His name is Henry Morgan and I've another, a cousin, he [played] guitar too—his name is Milton Funchess. And between these two I started picking up little things. My mother she started givin' fish-fries and things like that and I started doin' the same thing they was doin'. Playin' at night."[738] Just barely a teenager, Littlejohn was learning quickly; during the day, his chores typically involved hauling water for people working in the fields, and also for his parents, who were working at a peach and pecan orchard/nursery. As with many other African-Americans living or growing up in Mississippi at the time, blues as well as country and western music were both enjoyed on the family radio at night. He remembers hearing Arthur "Big Boy" Crudup singing "My Mama Don't Allow Me" around the fall or winter of 1944, and later, Lightnin' Hopkins. One song in particular inspired him to advance past the one-stringed instrument he once had played as a youngster and into playing bottleneck-style guitar instead. "I heard a lot of western songs, hillbilly songs," Littlejohn told Shurman, "and I heard this 'Steel Guitar Rag' and all that and it took me in mind of using a slide. But at that time I didn't know what a slide was. I never had seen a slide!"[739]

After helping his brother deliver ice in Jackson and chopping cotton with a friend in Arkansas, Littlejohn recorded some material for Johnny Vincent in Jackson, at the time running his Champion label out of an address on Farish Street (just a block or so south of Trumpet Records' home quarters). Although details are a bit sketchy, Littlejohn evidently cut one or two sides for Vincent, the tape of which got destroyed in a fire. Consequently, Littlejohn's single was a "no go." Too bad, for if he had, he could have been label mates with that voice that had so enticed him over the radio, Arthur "Big Boy" Crudup, who had a 78 out on Champion—as by "Arthur 'Blues' Crump & his Guitar"—in 1952, the same year that Littlejohn's session had supposedly taken place.[740]

Afterwards, Littlejohn and his cotton-chopping companion went from the frying pan into the fire. A man passing out leaflets enticed them to try their hand at picking cherries in New York, but the work was horrible. Instead, a job driving a bulldozer in Rochester was a much better prospect, even though it didn't last too long (while he was there, Littlejohn apparently did *not* run into fellow blues guitarist and ex-Magnolia State resident Son House, also living in Rochester at the time). Eventually, Littlejohn caught a bus

736 Gary Paulsen, "The Re-incarnation of Elmore James." *Blues Unlimited* 63 (June 1969): 17.

737 Note: An alternate birth year of 1921 has also been suggested.

738 Dick Shurman, "Never Seen a Slide." *Blues Unlimited* 92 (June 1972): 12.

739 Ibid.; and Chris Strachwitz, notes to *John Littlejohn's Chicago Blues Stars.* Arhoolie LP 1043, 1969.

740 Strachwitz, notes to *John Littlejohn's Chicago Blues Stars;* Bill Rowe, "Johnny Littlejohn." *Career Discographies* 3 (September 1995): 30; and McGrath, 221.
Note: Remember Crudup's single for Trumpet that came out under the name "Elmer James?" That was also issued in 1952!

headed for Gary, Indiana, with talk of good pay in the steel mills luring him there. When he arrived, however, he had to settle for a lower paying job at a gas station instead, giving him all the impetus he needed to start saving some money for a guitar and an amp so he could start playing the blues professionally.[741]

Initially, Littlejohn worked with a group of musicians who were all playing in the Gary area that included Eddie Taylor and Jimmy Reed, along with husband and wife team John and Grace Brim. "The way it was, Jimmy was mostly on harp. He didn't play guitar too hot, and me and John Brim was playin' [guitar] and Eddie was playin' bass-guitar," Littlejohn recalled, with Grace sometimes singing, and taking care of the drummer's chores (although she could also play harmonica in a pinch). It was enough exposure to get Littlejohn on his feet, and not long after he left to form his own band—evidently, not even sticking around long enough to partake in either John Brim's Parrot session or Jimmy Reed's second studio date at Vee-Jay, both of which took place sometime during the month of December, 1953. With his own band, Littlejohn played gigs in and around Gary, Chicago Heights, Joliet (a gig that lasted quite some time), and Benton Harbor and Grand Rapids, Michigan. "We played blues," Littlejohn remembered. "Piney Brown's songs, Big Boy Crudup's and Elmo's....," although later, the set list was expanded to include hits of the day from Little Walter, Willie Mabon, Eddie Boyd, and others. Littlejohn's band included Tommy Moses Jr., who blew harp; Jesse Williams, who hailed from Canton, Mississippi (and probably played second guitar); and drummer Margaret Lamont. In Joliet, Littlejohn met up with guitarist Blue Smitty, who had had a single issued on the Chess label. After an accident prematurely brought about the unfortunate demise of his guitar and amplifier, Smitty sold him one of his, a Kay. "...I played with that 'cause I didn't have a lot of money to pay," he told Dick Shurman. "We was workin' seven nights a week," Littlejohn related, saying in regards to his band that, "We never did split up." Eventually, their busy schedule brought them to clubs and taverns on the south and west sides of Chicago, right smack in the middle of the Windy City's 1950s blues heyday. As the new decade dawned, Littlejohn made an association with Howlin' Wolf that would last, on and off, for five or six years. Whenever the Wolf and his lead guitarist Hubert Sumlin were on the skids, Wolf would call Littlejohn to fill in for two or three months while tempers cooled. "You got to know Wolf to really play with him. Play those licks. People that don't know him, they can't play [because] they.... scared of him," Littlejohn told Shurman, adding (somewhat) reassuringly, "But he only a common man!" Like a lot of Chicago blues artists, Littlejohn had to hold a day job, working as an auto mechanic for United Delco to insure a steady paycheck. "I've been a mechanic off and on for the last twenty years," he would tell author Anthony Connor and photographer Robert Neff in 1974. "I love to hear the motors run. This is my life: it's between music and grease," adding, "Girls—I don't worry about them. Money I don't worry about, because I know I ain't never going to have none."[742]

741 Strachwitz, notes to *John Littlejohn's Chicago Blues Stars;* and Harris, 247.

742 Shurman, "Never Seen a Slide," 12-14; Anthony Connor and Robert Neff, *The Blues: In Images and Interviews.* New York: Cooper Square Press, 1999 [reprint], 90; Leadbitter and Slaven, *Blues Records 1943-1970,* 149; and Leadbitter, Fancourt, and Pelletier, 399.

Note: The listing in *Blues Records* for Jimmy Reed's second recording session—possibly (or "poss" for short) 29/30 December 1953, and for which it is claimed that John Littlejohn plays second or third guitar—is somewhat problematic. The late discographer/journalist Bill Rowe, publisher of the short-lived *Career Discographies* magazine, in the September 1995 edition published a comprehensive overview of John Littlejohn's recording career (as the name *Career Discographies* implies, discographies of this type were Rowe's main focus). In an extended footnote, Rowe offered the following observation about Jimmy Reed's poss. 29/30 December 1953 Vee-Jay session. It read:

> *The identification of Johnny Littlejohn as the third (sic) guitarist on the above session was first mooted in the discography accompanying Charly's* The Vee-Jay Years *CD box set (CDREDBOX 9)(Fancourt, 1994). This assertion has been carried through to* Blues Records, Volume 2 *(Leadbitter, Fancourt, and Pelletier,*

From the time Littlejohn arrived in Gary, it would take well more than a decade to see his name on a round piece of vinyl. He told Dick Shurman how Leonard Chess had given him the run around: "Went down there about fifteen times and he told me I had to come back with somethin' different. I was too close to Wolf, too close to Muddy Waters. My harp blower was too close to Little Walter. He wanted me to do some B.B. King things. I come back with some B.B. King things and he said it was too close to T-Bone Walker. And I went with a slide, and he said it was too close to Elmore James."[743] His perseverance finally paid off, though, in the late 1960s. Tenor saxophonist Menard Rogers produced a session in August 1966 which resulted in Littlejohn waxing four tunes, including "What in the World" and "Kitty O" (with penmanship credits to Brook Benton and Clyde Otis on the latter title), each of which appeared on their own Margaret single. The flip sides to these two singles were "Can't Be Still" and "Johnny's Jive," respectively, with Rogers providing a spoken vocal and his tenor sax to each tune. After the Margaret 45s came out in 1968, "What in the World" b/w "Can't Be Still" were immediately picked up by Oscar "Bo Dud" Coleman to be reissued on his Terrell imprint; after that, the tapes apparently fell into the hands of Cadillac Baby, possibly to set up a distribution deal. "What in the World" was up-to-the-minute, typical late 1960s Chicago blues, with Littlejohn's guitar sounding bluesy and glints of J.B. Lenoir showing through in his lyrics.[744]

Further sessions produced by Willie Dixon and Oscar "Bo Dud" Coleman were held in 1968, with Littlejohn playing guitar behind James L. Smith on his A-1 Dud single, and cutting an additional two titles

> *1994). As no documentary evidence has yet been found to substantiate this, and as aural evidence suggests that there may be only two guitarists present, the session has been included here... for the purposes of aural comparison and discussion.* (Rowe, "Littlejohn," 30)

Furthermore, Littlejohn told Shurman in a 1970 interview that he hadn't recorded with Reed. "Me and Jimmy Reed and Eddie Taylor was playin' together, there was Grace Brim and John Brim.... I didn't cut anythin' with him, we just played together, on gigs. Actually, I first met him when he came out of the Navy. He was livin' way out in South Chicago and he used to come over in Gary and we used to play all night for six or seven dollars." While Littlejohn's statement is slightly confusing (on the surface, anyway), there can be no doubt that he is unequivocally referring to Jimmy Reed, who had served in the Navy (as far as I know, Brim did not). To further clarify the point, Littlejohn additionally told Shurman that, "Menard Rogers was the first person ever put me on tape. That was 'Kitty O' and 'What in the World,'" referring to his August 1966 Margaret session (Shurman, "Never Seen a Slide," 12, 14). While I have heard of blues musicians claiming to play or have been present at sessions that they were not (hell, if everyone who'd ever claimed to have been present at Elmore's "Dust My Broom" Trumpet session had indeed *actually* been there, then the 10 x 12 foot room where it was recorded would have been crammed full with dozens of observers, participants, and passersby), I know of few cases where it has been the other way around.

My best guesses are:

1) that Eddie Taylor is the person who plays slide guitar on Jimmy Reed's "Boogie in the Dark." Taylor not only grew up hearing famous Delta slide guitarists such as Son House, Charley Patton, and Robert Johnson, as his later work proves he was quite adept at playing slide—unfortunately, he just didn't do it that often (Taylor and Scott, notes to *I Feel So Bad*); and

2) That it is Jimmy Reed playing slide guitar on "Boogie in the Dark." According to Bob Koester, one night—strictly by chance—he happened to find a very drunk Jimmy Reed in the back room of an empty Chicago club just wailing away on the slide guitar. Figuring that he really should share this special moment with *someone,* he used the club's pay phone to call Paul Garon, and held the phone up so that Garon could hear what was transpiring. According to Koester, the skeptical Garon thought that his leg was being pulled. (Bob Koester, "Letters." *Juke Blues* 48 (Winter 2000/2001): 27)

743 Shurman, "Never Seen a Slide, " 13.

744 Rowe, "Littlejohn," 30, 41; McGrath, 756, 1140, 1146; and John Littlejohn, "What in the World." Margaret 997, 1968.

Note: According to the label shot for Littlejohn's Margaret single, distribution was by "Lynn's 1 Stop." This was most likely the Lynn's Record Shop on Nelson Street, in Greenville, Mississippi, that is referred to by Paulsen in his June 1969 *Blues Unlimited* article on Littlejohn. How one of Littlejohn's Margaret's singles eventually wound up on an anthology of recordings from Cadillac Baby's Bea & Baby label is anybody's guess (although Dick Shurman has noted that Menard Rogers was in the hospital for quite some time with T.B., and gave that reason as to why Rogers leased out the sides in the first place. Shurman, "Never Seen a Slide," 14).

each at June and October sessions, with Abb Locke on tenor sax and Lafayette Leake on piano. "Bloody Tears," a Dixon-penned tune that featured Littlejohn's forceful vocals, haunting lyrics, and an Elmore-styled slide riff, was lauded by Chicago blues chronicler Mike Rowe and also the subject of a very positive review by Jim O'Neal in the second issue of *Living Blues* magazine. "Probably John's best 45," O'Neal stated simply. The single was later picked up for reissue by the Weis label, which had the distinct advantage of being distributed by Stax Records, the famous Memphis operation. For Littlejohn's follow-up, another Dixon tune was chosen, "29 Ways;" although the effort was described as "excellent" by Mike Rowe, the record apparently failed to make few splashes beyond that, and was resigned to an obscure fate on Coleman's short-lived T.D.S. label.[745]

With Littlejohn's next recording session, he hit pay dirt. *John Littlejohn's Chicago Blues Stars* was arguably the finest album of his career, and a landmark of late 1960s Chicago blues, all thanks to Buddy Guy and Chris Strachwitz at Arhoolie Records. "Back in 1968, I told Buddy Guy... that I was interested in recording his favorite neglected giants of Chicago blues," offered Chris Strachwitz recently. "Buddy's prompt response was: Earl Hooker and John Littlejohn!" With the help of Willie Dixon, a John Littlejohn session was arranged at the legendary Universal Studios in Chicago for a November 1968 recording date. Songs included his two Margaret titles, "Kiddeo" and "What in the World You Gonna Do," an in-the-groove rocking J.B. Lenoir cover, "How Much More Long" (that came out later on the compact disc reissue), impeccably rendered blues standards like "Catfish Blues," and two Elmore classics, "Shake Your Money Maker" and "Slidin' Home," the latter piece a reworking of the "Bobby's Rock" theme. "Dream," a slow blues in the Elmore tradition of "I Held My Baby Last Night" and "The Sky Is Crying," featured more of Littlejohn's sure-footed vocals and incisive slide guitar with classic Elmore lyrics liberally tossed with a bit of fresh text to enliven the mix. On "Shake Your Money Maker," Littlejohn strikes a balance between down-and-dirty and mirthful, which I imagine that, played live in a club, would quite effectively whip the audience into a frenzy. Throughout the album Littlejohn's slide guitar is crisp and clean, and one can almost imagine that Elmore himself would be nodding with approval to hear Robert Pulliam's and Willie Young's riffing tenor saxes in the background during "Dream," or while Littlejohn takes "Shake Your Money Maker" through its paces. On "Slidin' Home," Littlejohn's playing is at its zenith. More than just a simple cover version of an Elmore tune, at four minutes in length Littlejohn has plenty of room to explore new territory and ample time to take this piece to new heights undreamed of in Elmore's original two-minute version. It is a truly inspired piece of slide guitar work, and through the years has been one of the most enduringly satisfying performances of his career.[746]

After the Arhoolie session, Littlejohn finally got the chance to record at Chess Records that he'd been chasing all those years. A standard four-song session, with Mighty Joe Young and band, was held in February 1969, with the first title recorded, "Keep on Running," the most obvious nod to the old Broomduster. In spite of Chess' reputation, though, Littlejohn's session fell flat compared to his work with Arhoolie just two and half months previous. Whereas Arhoolie had obviously attempted to provide the listener with a snapshot of what it might be like to hear Littlejohn play in a club on any given night, Littlejohn's Chess set possessed more of a modern soul-blues sound, the implied intent that, perhaps, this type of sound might have a better chance of becoming hit material. Still, Chess might have done well to pair "Keep on Running" b/w "I Had a Dream" (a re-waxing of the "Dream" that he had cut for Arhoolie) to make a strong, bluesy single that could have easily pleased the discriminating palates of blues critics and

745 Rowe, "Littlejohn," 30-31; Rowe, *Chicago Breakdown*, 207; Jim O'Neal, "45's." *Living Blues* 2 (Summer 1970): 34; and McGrath, 1140, 1236-1237.

746 Chris Strachwitz, notes to John Littlejohn, *Slidin' Home.* Arhoolie CD 9019, 2001; John Littlejohn, *John Littlejohn's Chicago Blues Stars.* Arhoolie LP 1043, 1969 [reissued as *Slidin' Home;* Arhoolie CD 9019, 2001]; and Rowe, "Littlejohn," 31.

reviewers at the time. It was not to happen though; as was mentioned earlier, 1969 was a year of drastic changes at the famous Windy City independent label—for instance, Chess had been sold to GRT just a couple weeks prior to Littlejohn's session—and in effect, Littlejohn was too late for his Chess session to really do him any good—Chess (or the new owners of Chess) just sat on his tapes. Only much later were the four titles issued, first on an obscure Blues Ball anthology LP in the United States, and later, finding their way onto LPs and CDs in England and Japan. To this day, only one of the titles, "She's Too Much," has ever been formally issued by MCA/Chess in their continuing reissue program.[747]

After Chess, Johnny Littlejohn paired up with Jimmy Rogers—the guitarist that had formerly held the "linchpin" seat in Muddy Waters' band—to make a half-dozen down-home styled recordings produced by Frank Scott in August 1970. According to Mike Rowe, Rogers decided to come out of musical retirement "after a clothing store in which he had an interest was burned down during the riots," and dubbed the pair of guitarists as "the most exciting prospect on Chicago's music scene." Of the titles that Littlejohn and Rogers recorded for Scott, "Mean Old World" was a Little Walter standard, while "Slidin'" was a bottleneck instrumental loosely centered around the venerable "Sitting on Top of the World" theme. "Dust My Broom," not released at the time, was a fairly rare treat for Littlejohn/Elmore fans, as Littlejohn tends to seldom indulge himself in straightforward "Broom"-type recordings such as this. Unfortunately, the team of Rogers and Littlejohn was brought to an abrupt end when the house they were both living in burned down, and Rogers split to live on the West Coast for a while.[748]

In 1973, Littlejohn recorded an album for Bluesway (an ABC subsidiary), and also made an appearance on the Bob Riedy Band's Rounder LP *Lake Michigan Ain't No River* (other guests included Johnny Young, Sam Lay, Carey Bell, and Jimmy Rogers). He performed three titles, including a high-test version of "Dust My Broom" that whetted the appetite of the listener just enough to leave them wanting a little more, and a clever remake of Lowell Fulson's "Reconsider Baby" that featured a musical arrangement borrowed straight from J.B. Lenoir's 1959 Shad single, "Lou Ella."[749]

Three years would pass before Littlejohn would record again. Live 1976 recordings, at Ma Bea's Lounge in Chicago, offered versions of "Dust My Broom" (somewhat lacking in the verve present for the Bob Riedy sessions), the "Twelve Years Old Boy," and a particularly milquetoast rendition of "Bobby's Rock." They later appeared on the MCM label in France, and on Storyville in Denmark. Recordings in Paris a few days before the 1978 Thanksgiving holiday—with Lafayette Leake and Fred Below—were later issued on the Black & Blue label, while a mid-May 1979 session at the Malaco studios in Jackson witnessed the reuniting of Littlejohn with Johnny Vincent. This time around a single actually did result from their efforts—"She's Nineteen Years Old" with "I Wanna Go Home" (which featured the perennial Sam Myers on harmonica) was later anthologized on Vincent's *Genuine Mississippi Blues* LP. The fall of 1980 paired Littlejohn with the reactivated 4 Brothers label in Chicago, while the following year saw John recording with Carey Bell in Tokyo at the Pit Inn, for a pleasing in-person set which included versions of his Margaret and Arhoolie sides, as well as a rousing send-up of "Bloody Tears." John was back in the studio again in 1983, helping out Valerie Wellington for a session at Chicago's Universal studios, and then was off

747 Various Artists, *Slidin';* Rowe, "Littlejohn," 31; and Cohodas, 294-295.

748 Rowe, *Chicago Breakdown,* 208; Rowe, "Littlejohn," 32; Various Artists, *Chicago Blues at Home.* Advent LP 2806, 1977 [also reissued as Testament CD 5028, 1995]; and John Littlejohn, "Dust My Broom." From the album *Bottleneck Blues.* Testament CD 5021, 1995.

749 Rowe, "Littlejohn," 32; John Littlejohn, "Dust My Broom." From the album, The Bob Riedy Chicago Blues Band, *Lake Michigan Ain't No River.* Rounder LP 2005, 1973; John Littlejohn, "Reconsider Baby." From the album, The Bob Riedy Chicago Blues Band, *Lake Michigan Ain't No River.* Rounder LP 2005, 1973; and J.B. Lenoir, "Lou Ella." Shad 5012, 1959.

to Paris for more recording dates with Buster Benton and Lafayette Leake. More activity in 1984 and 1985 resulted in an LP for the Rooster Blues label, *So-Called Friends,* with Eddie Taylor helping out on half of the titles. An intermission in recording activity occurred between 1985 and 1989, when he registered in with a few titles for Austria's Wolf label. Plagued with health problems for years, Littlejohn was slowly being worn down by heart attacks and kidney problems. An LP's worth of material that was recorded by JSP in 1992 became his last entry into the recording studio. Sometime afterwards, a major stroke left him mostly disabled. He died in Chicago, Illinois, on Tuesday, 1 February 1994. He was sixty-two.[750]

John Littlejohn will not only be remembered for his inspired interpretations of Elmore James classics, but will also be remembered as a great artist—and vocalist—in his own right. "Johnny's slide work was some of the finest of the post-Elmore James era...." offered David Whiteis in *Living Blues.* "He also played a not-insignificant role in keeping the timeless sounds of postwar Chicago blues gloriously alive during an era when some were trying to pronounce the genre dead."[751] For those who might be new to Littlejohn's music, *Slidin' Home* (recently reissued by Arhoolie, featuring the entire contents of his 1969 album plus three bonus tracks) is a highly recommended introduction.

J.B. Hutto

J.B. Hutto, from his recording debut in 1954, throughout the 1960s, 1970s, and until his death in 1983, continually was one of Elmore's most passionate disciples. Comments such as "one of the most exciting bands in Chicago today," (Mike Rowe, from 1966) and "just about everything he's ever done is worth listening to" (Bob Koester, from 1976) are typical of the accolades fans and critics have showered on him.[752] In Hutto's hands, Elmore's "Dust My Broom" riff evolved to new levels—thanks in part to his clever songwriting, which found him moving beyond ordinary tales of unrequited love, and onto to other topics such as substance abuse and economic downturns—that, when coupled with his rich, caramel-like voice and keenly developed slide guitar skill, became like old whiskey—while aging had mellowed the harshness ever so slightly, you still felt that powerful kick after it went down.

Joseph Benjamin "J.B." Hutto was born in Elko, South Carolina, on 29 April 1929 and grew up in Augusta, Georgia (1926 has also been offered as year of birth, and previous reports listing his birthplace as Georgia later proved to be incorrect). His father was a deacon in the church, and when he was growing up, Hutto was enlisted, along with his brothers and sisters, to sing in the family gospel group, the Golden Crown Gospel Singers. It was the blues, however, that truly held his interest: "I heard the blues... when I was young boy," he told Jim O'Neal and Amy van Singel, "and really, I always did like the blues." Every now and then, Hutto would sneak off to wherever there was a juke box, and listen to records by Big Joe Williams, John Lee "Sonny Boy" Williamson, Big Bill Broonzy, and others. With a father who was an upstanding church member, it wasn't necessarily the kind of behavior that would have been favored at home. "And I'd go in there and listen to 'em. I was supposed to [have] been a quartet singer, but I think I liked it there a little better," he remembered fondly.[753]

Even so, working in a gospel group constituted good, solid, musical experience, and over time, Hutto

750 Rowe, "Littlejohn," 32-36; John Littlejohn, *Dream.* Storyville CD 8034, 1995; John Littlejohn and Carey Bell, *The Blues Show! Live at Pit Inn.* Yupiteru LP 23-4004, 1982; and David Whiteis, "John Littlejohn." *Living Blues* 115 (June 1994): 60.

751 Whiteis, "John Littlejohn," 60-61.

752 Mike Rowe, "Mike Rowe's Review," 62, In Mike Leadbitter, ed., *Nothing But the Blues.* London: Hanover Books, 1971; and Dave Weld, "Interview with Bob Koester." *Living Blues* 30 (November/December 1976): 23.

753 O'Neal and van Singel, 18-19; Harris, 259; Rowe, *Chicago Breakdown,* 114; Dave Weld, "*Living Blues* Interview: J.B. Hutto." *Living Blues* 30 (November/December 1976): 17.

had the chance to try his hand at several different instruments before deciding upon the guitar: "Well, first of all I was a drummer, and I was a singer and a drummer, and I tried a little piano and that didn't work (laughs). So I went to try to play a guitar, so I picked a little on it," he later recalled.[754] When he moved to Chicago in 1949 (brought about due to the death of his father earlier that year), he had not yet picked up the bottleneck technique, but would start practicing shortly after his arrival. "I didn't know nothin' about no slide guitar till I got to Chicago," he told Dave Weld in a 1976 interview. It was blues musician Johnny Ferguson who gave Hutto his first musical entree into the blues mecca of the Windy City, as one of Ferguson's "Twisters." The group covered standard blues hits of the day; Ferguson played guitar, which he had set up to play in open E tuning, and Hutto was supposed to pitch in on vocals and drumming chores, but soon tired of the drumming part ("them drummers got too many pieces there. I couldn't get it together," he told Weld). "So I started fooling around with his guitar; take a break and I started messing with the chords, you know, to see what I could do," Hutto said. "That's really where I started from right there and I just kept goin', little by little." When not playing with Ferguson, Hutto would see artists like Muddy Waters and Little Walter in the clubs. Later, he saw Robert Nighthawk on a couple of different occasions, but it would primarily be Elmore who influenced his slide guitar work. Hutto was a patient observer and spent a lot of time following Elmore around from club to club, asking him for a few pointers on technical details, and hoping for a chance to sit in, if one should happen to arise. In his spare time Hutto started writing songs, too, preparing for a day that was soon to come.[755]

In 1954, J.B. put together his own group, and started playing at Red's Lounge, just a few doors down from the corner of Madison and Damen. Even before their recording debut, they sounded tough: George Mayweather on harmonica, Joe Custom on bass-guitar, and Eddie "Porkchop" Hines on drums and washboard, with Hutto fronting the group on vocals and guitar. According to his interview with Dave Weld, Hutto says that a representative from Chance Records somehow heard about the group (possibly Ewart Abner, General Manager for the label) and arranged for a session to be held at the Chess studios, probably circa February, 1954. Four numbers were cut at the first session, including "Combination Boogie," "Now She's Gone," "Pet Cream Man," and "Lovin' You." Each member of the band was given twenty dollars, and, as Hutto said later, "This guy come to me and started talking about a record, and I said, 'Yeah, I just finished up a session, you know.' So he says, 'What did you come up with?' And I said, 'We got twenty dollars apiece.' He said, 'Twenty dollars apiece!' And I said, 'Yeah, I thought I had some money.'" As it turned out, the man was Larry Dobey, a representative of the musicians' union, that—in this particular case—acted as an ombudsman to secure normal union pay, at scale, for each member of the group. Evidently, Hutto had already signed a multi-year contract with Chance, but after arrears were made to the group, nothing else really happened— "That's the only money that I ever really did get out of that record," Hutto told Weld.[756]

A positive review of Hutto's debut record on Chance 1155, "Combination Boogie," b/w "Now She's Gone," on 1 May 1954, is the only historical record of any note (other than the actual records themselves) indicating that Hutto had even set foot in a recording studio that year. As is sometimes the case, good,

---

754 O'Neal and van Singel, 18.

755 Weld, 15-17; and Rowe, *Chicago Breakdown*, 114.

756 Weld, 15-16; Rowe, *Chicago Breakdown*, 115; Gart, *The American Record Label Directory*, 41; and Robert Pruter, Armin Büttner, and Robert L. Campbell, "The Chance Label." http://hubcap.clemson.edu/~campber/chance.html, May 2002.

Note: In their lengthy research on the Chance label, Robert Pruter, Armin Büttner, and Robert L. Campbell have offered these notes in regards to J.B. Hutto's first Chance session: "According to Bob Koester, the original tape boxes indicated that the session was recorded by Joe Brown and sold to Chance, so J. B.'s debut was yet another J.O.B. product." Even so, this does not necessarily preclude the possibility that the session was recorded at Chess, as Hutto later recalled to Dave Weld. See: Pruter, Büttner, and Campbell, "The Chance Label."

deserving records don't always make a big splash in the markets. This one certainly didn't, but what was in the grooves was an altogether different story. Opening with a flurry of bottleneck trills from Hutto, one thing was definitely clear right from the start—that, just as his teacher Elmore James was prone to do, Hutto likewise incorporated a blue note into his open-E tuning by slightly lowering the pitch of the third string of his guitar. This, in turn, greatly helped to lend "Combination Boogie" its tough, biting sound—one might almost acquaint it to an undercurrent similar to the taste of bitter chicory root—that was a precursor to the direction urban Chicago blues would take in the late 1950s, after the music was in the hands of a younger generation of artists, such as Otis Rush, Buddy Guy, Magic Sam, and J.B. Hutto. An invigorating, but fairly straightforward outing, "Combination Boogie" did not feature any guitar pyrotechnics from Hutto, but rather a washboard solo from "Porkchop" and a harmonica passage from George Mayweather that immeasurably spiced up the side. Just before the song finishes, Hutto slides up the neck of his guitar, adding a final bit of window dressing—as if to show off just a bit what it was he had been busy practicing lately. The record was, in every aspect, a remarkable side stamped with a unique feel that only hinted at what was yet to come from this artist. The flip side, "Now She's Gone," was a tale of woe set to a brutal "stop time" beat currently in vogue at that time—thanks in part to Muddy Waters, who could be heard using the formula to good effect on "Mad Love" just a few months previous and "Hoochie Coochie Man" very early in 1954 (when Hutto's debut disc hit the market, "Hoochie Coochie Man" would, in fact, still be riding high on the R&B charts).[757]

Although not reviewed by the trade press, Hutto's next Chance single was released circa September 1954. "Lovin' You" contained a similar feel to "Combination Boogie," but with a bit more of a "Dust My Broom" slant to it. Its platter-mate, "Pet Cream Man," was, again, a different story. A smoldering, sexually-charged affair, its lyrics dated as far back as Texas Alexander, while the musical portion owed much to Walter Davis' 1938 recording "If You Only Understand" (a.k.a. "Pet Cream Blues;" Detroit harp blower Walter Mitchell also recorded a version of the song a decade later for the J-V-B label). An entertaining footnote from author/blues historian Mike Rowe has it that Chicago disk jockey Sam Evans wouldn't play Hutto's "Pet Cream Man," even though the Pet Milk company was the sponsor of his radio show![758]

Just over a month later, on Tuesday, 19 October 1954, a second session was arranged utilizing the same line up as before, except this time the ensemble was augmented by the addition of pianist Johnny Jones. In retrospect, it was a great idea, and helped to make Hutto's third, and final, Chance single one of his strongest efforts as well. In "Dim Lights" we find Hutto's first full-fledged use of the "Dust My Broom" format, which he coupled with classic blues imagery—shouted in a declamatory fashion—involving black cat bones, having one's baby leave them, and getting drunk in a dimly lit tavern (the rest of the lyrics are, admittedly, a bit harder to decipher). With Mayweather blowing some choice harp, the added piano of Johnny Jones, and a harsh, gritty urgency pervading the disc, it was absolutely a top-drawer effort. "Things Are So Slow" was an aptly-tempoed slow blues offering commentary about being laid off from work as a result of an economic recession, and finds Hutto joining a tradition in postwar Chicago blues including artists such as Floyd Jones, J.B. Lenoir, and John Brim, who also offered economic commentary in some of their songs (although the 1950s are typically thought of as an era of a "booming" economy in the United States, this was not always the case for working African-Americans). "Things are so slow, don't think I can make it anymore," he sings at one point, adding with resignation, "I had to tell my wife, she didn't

757 Hutto, "Combination Boogie;" J.B. Hutto, "Now She's Gone." Chance 1155, 1954; Gart, *First Pressings—1954*, 54; and Whitburn, 435. Note: the original labels simply gave credit to "J.B. and His Hawks."

758 Rowe, *Chicago Breakdown*, 115; J.B. Hutto, "Lovin' You." Chance 1160, 1954; J.B. Hutto, "Pet Cream Man." Chance 1160, 1954; and Leroy Pierson, notes to *Detroit Ghetto Blues 1948-1954*. Nighthawk LP 104, 1976.

fuss/finance took the car, we'll have to ride the bus." Only very infrequently would Hutto offer political or social commentary in his songs, but when he did—as in this case—he did so eloquently.[759]

"Dim Lights" and "Things Are So Slow" not only made up the sides of Hutto's last single—it was also the last record ever issued by Chance Records. Starting in 1955, the label appears to have fallen off the face of the musical world map, not to be heard from again. The five titles recorded at Hutto's second session were later sold to Vee-Jay (coincidentally, Ewart Abner just happened to be General Manager there, too), who remastered them very late in 1955, but never did anything with the material. They were probably lost forever sometime around 1966 when Vee-Jay went out of business—a short while later, in February 1967, their assets were sold at public auction—that is, save for one previously unreleased item, "Price of Love." Issued on an obscure album (of dubious legitimacy) sometime in the late 1970s, "Price of Love" is testimony, as is "Things Are So Slow," to Hutto's fast-growing songwriting skills. "You have a price on your love, and your heart is an empty shell," he sings to an untruthful lover; "You're just a crooked paradox darling, and you loathe it deep within." Partially based on a slowed down version of the "Broom" riff, "Price of Love" would have been worthy material for a fourth single—if either Chance or Vee-Jay had been around/seen fit to issue it.[760]

More than a decade would pass before Hutto would be in a recording studio again, this time, for a vastly different audience. In December 1965, author/producer Sam Charters was holding recording sessions in Chicago for a now-legendary series of three albums entitled *Chicago/The Blues/Today!* It was through this series of Vanguard LPs that I first encountered J.B. Hutto's music—as, I imagine, did so many others (who, also like myself, were not fortunate enough to have collected his three rare Chance singles). Over the years, Hutto's original band members Porkchop, Mayweather, and Custom had gone their own ways. In the meantime, J.B. had worked as an undertaker, quitting music after the club and house-party scene had just gotten too rough (the final straw, evidently, was when he lost his guitar—a woman in the audience broke it over her husband's head). In the intervening years since his last appearance in a recording studio, however, J.B.'s music had just gotten tougher and bolder, and his new group, consisting of Herman Hassell on bass and Frank Kirkland on drums, suited him just perfectly.[761]

"I had already recorded in most of the small studios in Chicago," wrote Sam Charters almost thirty-five years later, "but for these sessions I wanted to use the big RCA studio building that was built on pilings over the lake close to the Chicago Loop. The sound in the studio was good, but just as important for me was the history lingering in the space. It was the studio that had been used for the Chicago blues records on the old Bluebird label."[762] In retrospect, Charters was correct in his assessment of the space; it lent something distinct and special to the series of recordings that helped make the whole three volume set exceptional. Of Hutto's allotted five sides (each LP was split up this way in order to accommodate three different artists), two of them constituted revamped "Broom" riffs—the fast-paced "Going Ahead," and "Too Much Alcohol"—with the latter tune owing its heritage to John Lee "Sonny Boy" Williamson's 1947 recording, "Alcohol Blues" (which had most likely been recorded in that exact same room). Hutto's marriage of Williamson's tune to a heavy "Broom" beat is especially creative, and is a poignant example of

759 J.B. Hutto, "Dim Lights." Chance 1165, 1954; J.B. Hutto, "Things Are So Slow." Chance 1165, 1954; Leadbitter and Slaven, *Blues Records 1943-1970*, 650; and Pruter, Büttner, and Campbell, "The Chance Label."

760 J.B. Hutto, "Price of Love." From the album *Chicago Blues After Midnight 1952-1957*. Delta Swing LP 379, c. 1977 ("Price of Love" was also reissued on *Chicago Blues—The Chance Era*. Charly CD 146-2, 1997); Leadbitter and Slaven, *Blues Records 1943-1970*, 650; Gart, *The American Record Label Directory*, 233; and "Vee-Jay Records." *Blues Unlimited* 42 (March/April 1967): 24.

761 Weld, 18; Rowe, *Chicago Breakdown*, 194; Leadbitter and Slaven, *Blues Records 1943-1970*, 650.

762 Samuel Charters, "*Chicago/The Blues/Today!*: A Reminiscence," 21-22. In the notes to *Chicago/The Blues/Today!* Vanguard CD 172/74-2, 1999.

just how much things had changed in Chicago in slightly less than a generation. "Married Woman Blues," a longer, slow blues, was a tormented narrative involving the perils of loving the wrong woman, while "That's the Truth" featured more great bottlenecking and fiercely shouted lyrics from Hutto, over Herman Hassell's slithering bass lines.[763]

The real show stopper of the session—in fact, really, of the whole three album series (others will, undoubtedly, have their favorite moments as well)—was Hutto's incredible "Please Help." Philosophically speaking, Hutto's lyrics were straight out of Elmore's angst-ridden book, while musically, the piece boldly portrayed new directions that Elmore's slide guitar heritage might be heading. From the evidence of "Please Help," Hutto proves beyond any doubt that, in his capable hands, they were headed in all the right directions. Raw and freewheeling, his fluid slide lines spewing molten ingots of hot steel, "Please Help" had a dancing-too-close-to-the-edge-of-a-cliff quality about it that made it provocative and intoxicating. Toward the end of the side, Hutto brings the proceedings to a full rolling boil with his repeated vocal eruptions of "He'p!" and "Yeah, yeah, yeah, I need he'p," over and over again. "Please Help" was, as movie critics are sometimes moved to say, the performance of a lifetime. It was the climactic fulfillment of a promising talent that had begun more than a decade ago with his three Chance singles. A dramatic photo of J.B. Hutto in action, snapped by the prominent Chicago photographer Raeburn Flerlage in 1966 is, how I imagine, what Hutto might have looked like while performing "Please Help." Dynamic and intense, beads of sweat clearly visible on his forehead, the shot captures Hutto in his full, declamatory glory.[764]

Thanks to these five recordings—and to the wonders of high fidelity stereo as well—we are offered a clearer glimpse than ever into some of the finer details of Hutto's guitar technique. In "Married Woman Blues," "That's the Truth," and especially "Please Help," we find Hutto playing understated, meandering single-note lead lines, which he alternates with full-bore, blasting chordal assaults with his slide. In 1976, he told Dave Weld the following about his methods:

> **Hutto**: I... use a finger and thumb pick at all times. I use these two fingers right here on my right hand. I see a lot of people using the bar [i.e., slide] on their middle finger, but I use it on my little finger and these fingers I left free to walk up, you know to make my notes. That's one thing I learnt.
> **Weld**: How about your thumbpick—how do you use it
> **Hutto**: [Puts on thumbpick] I just put it like that and come down on the guitar. You see I'm playing with those two fingers.
> **Weld**: Oh, so you use the downstroke for the [thumb] pick and and the upstroke for the finger.
> **Hutto**: Right. There, that's where I learned my thing. People say now that I got my own style....[765]

After Hutto's Vanguard sessions, things picked up somewhat for him. He continued playing at Turner's Lounge (another classic photo of him in action was snapped by Mike Rowe at Turner's; it was later published in his book *Chicago Breakdown*), and, in June 1966, he recorded an album for Pete Welding's Testament label. Six months later, Hutto also started work on an LP for Delmark, but the project got sidetracked because of illness, and wouldn't be finished until further recordings were held in May and August of 1968. It was finally released in 1969, and "Hip Shakin'"—the only track on the LP featuring Hutto's old line up of Hassell on bass and Kirkland on drums—was easily the standout track of the album. Another story with a not-so-subtle sexual intrigue woven into the imagery, Hutto was, again, in fine form.

763 Sonny Boy Williamson, "Alcohol Blues." Victor 20-2893, 1948; and Various Artists, *Chicago/The Blues/Today!, Vol. 1.* Vanguard LP 9216, 1966.

764 Raeburn Flerlage, *Chicago Blues—As Seen from the Inside: The Photographs of Raeburn Flerlage.* Toronto: ECW Press, 2000, 121; and *Chicago/The Blues/Today!, Vol. 1.*

765 Weld, 17.

Hassell's thunderous bass playing nicely anchored Hutto's subtly underemphasized guitar (mostly a result of the wide-channel stereo separation employed by the album's engineer), and Kirkland's drumming, as was typical by now, offered the musical glue that held it all together.[766]

The same year that *Hawk Squat* was released, Hutto won the *Down Beat* magazine "International Critics Award for Rock-Pop-Blues group deserving of wider recognition." The following year, 1970, Hutto appeared on a local Chicago TV show, and was also featured in Harley Cokliss' film *Chicago Blues* (which aired on BBC-1 TV in 1971; it showed Hutto sporting his trademark *bon chapeau,* a ubiquitous part of his stage act from this point on). By 1972, Hutto had made his first visit to Europe. Some of his live London dates, circa February 1972, were recorded and later released under the Flyright imprint in the U.K. Delmark recorded another album, *Slidewinder,* in December 1972.[767]

In another sense, however, success seemed slow to reach Hutto's door. While his colleague Hound Dog Taylor would eventually see himself being written about in *Rolling Stone* magazine and playing the Philharmonic in New York City, those sorts of kudos would elude Hutto. In the late 1960s or early 1970s, Hutto came down with diabetes (a disease to which many slide guitarists seem oddly prone) and Frank Kirkland died, serving to break up the powerhouse trio of Hutto, Hassell and Kirkland once and for all. He also finally gave up playing at Turner's Lounge—ten to twelve dollars a night was just too little money, practically bordering on usury. "You know I worked for Turner, ooooh man, fifteen years or more and Turner never paid me up to no standard price like he should," Hutto told Dave Weld. "We kept them Friday and Saturday, we used to keep that joint, you know,... [but] we drank up the money before we got it. He wouldn't give it [i.e., give the band free drinks], you had to buy it. Charge you fifty cents coming in that door, too. Well, come to think of it, he wasn't a bad guy; we just didn't know what we was doin', you know. People see, they goin' to take advantage of that."[768]

Bob Koester, who recorded Hutto for two Delmark albums, could only stand by and watch as several unfortunate coincidences conspired against his artist's good fortune:

> There was a problem in Detroit when the union came in and we just couldn't play [a] job, had to turn around and come back. It may have been the non-union members in [Hutto's] band, it could have been the failure to file a contract in advance for the job. But I remember that was a heartbreaker, because it was an important club. It was a club that Paul Butterfield had turned into a blues club, and [James] Cotton and different blues bands were playing there.... And that hurt.
>
> There was a car breakdown on two occasions, on the way to DeKalb. He had a horrible breakdown; to kick off *Slidewinder* we had done J.B. Hutto T-shirts and found people who would wear them around [the] Ann Arbor blues festival. There was a hookup on the educational radio network and the record was out, and I think we even considered throwing some off the stage into the audience, but LPs are pretty dangerous. And J.B. didn't get to the concert; his car broke down, so he missed the radio shot and that affected things and it cost him his relationship with a booking agent.[769]

By the mid 1970s, Hutto's career appeared to finally get on track, and problems that had either plagued him or his band for years finally seemed to get ironed out. He was playing gigs on both coasts now, and returned to tour Europe as well, resulting in an album being recorded in Stockholm for the Amigo label, in February 1976. As Dave Weld observed, things just seemed to keep getting better for him. "J.B. Hutto's, a club near St. Louis, was named after him. European tours were more successful with each

766 J.B. Hutto, "Hip Shakin'." From the album J.B. Hutto & His Hawks, *Hawk Squat.* Delmark LP 617, 1969; and Leadbitter and Slaven, *Blues Records 1943-1970,* 650-651.

767 Harris, 260; and Weld, 24.

768 Weld, 16; Bob Koester and Sue Koester, notes to J.B. Hutto & His Hawks, Hawk Squat. Delmark LP 617, 1969; and Dave Weld, "J.B. Hutto." *Living Blues* 57 (Autumn 1983): 13.

769 Weld, "Interview with Bob Koester," *Living Blues* 23.

new visit. New York and East Coast dates were booked month after month, and new albums were recorded for Varrick (Rounder) and Black & Blue. J.B. was simply playing the best he ever had, and more people than ever were privileged to hear it." Fortunately, some of these performances were preserved for our later enjoyment, including a live set from 1977 at Sandy's Jazz Revival in Beverly, Massachusetts (featuring Hound Dog Taylor expatriates Brewer Phillips and Ted Harvey), *Live at the Shaboo Inn, Connecticut, 1979,* and *Keeper of the Flame,* which features seven live tracks from a July 1979, South Bend, Indiana performance. Over the course of his three decade-plus career, the sound of Elmore James never left his music, and the "Dust My Broom" riff was still offered up with an appropriate fierceness in Hutto's peerless fashion. One set staple, evidently, was a tune called "Sixteen Year Old Boy," a theme and variation on Elmore's "The 12 Year Old Boy," but with a theoretically more believable premise involving a high school-aged kid instead of the pre-teen schoolboy that Elmore had sung about. Other highlights include, from the live 1977 set, a six minute you've-got-to-hear-it-to-believe-it sledgehammer version of the 1940 Tampa Red ditty, "Don't You Lie To Me" (in comparing the two recordings, the phrase "Godzilla Meets Bambi" comes to mind), a fresh update of his classic "Dim Lights" (from the July 1979, South Bend date), and from the Shaboo Inn set, the smoking instrumental boogie "J.B.'s Stomp," and "I Don't Know Why," whereupon Hutto ruminates about the deleterious effects of alcohol, as opposed to the relative benign nature of marijuana.[770]

By the time the actor, Ronald Reagan, had been installed in the White House, photos appeared to show Hutto looking tired, and older than his years. While diabetes had been his main health complaint, he now was suffering from cancer as well—a tumor had been discovered on his lung, but because of his diabetes, Hutto refused any operation to remove it. By the spring of 1983, the cancer had spread to his hip, shoulder, and skull. "Gaunt and bald, he looked pretty bad," wrote Dave Weld about his visit in early June, 1983, to see J.B. in the hospital. "Yet he was lucid and coherent when I visited him at Cook County Hospital, where we enjoyed a few moments of music among the rows of cancer patients. His fingers flew in the air as I played guitar. He was fingering out the notes he knew so well, and probably adding more." Weld noted that, "The great pain didn't keep him from smiling," adding, "he was never one to frown very much anyway." Even from his hospital bed Hutto still had plans to return to Boston, where in the last couple years he had been playing extensively, but it was not to happen. A week after Weld's visit, J.B. Hutto died at his home, with Lulu Belle, his wife of thirty-three years nearby, in Harvey, Illinois, on Sunday, 12 June 1983. He was fifty-four.[771] The recently remastered, re-released 3 CD set *Chicago/The Blues/Today!* is a highly recommended jumping off point for exploring the career of J.B. Hutto (not to mention Chicago blues of the mid 1960s in general). His seven Chance recordings are collected on *Chicago Blues—The Chance Era,* a 1997 two-CD set from the Charly label.

---

770 Weld, "J.B. Hutto," 13; J.B. Hutto, *J.B. Hutto and the Houserockers Live 1977.* Wolf CD 120.289, 1991 [reissue of Baron LP 101, 1978]; J.B. Hutto, *J.B. Hutto and the New Hawks: Live at the Shaboo Inn, Conn., 1979.* Fan Club CD 085, 1991; and J.B. Hutto, *J.B. Hutto and the New Hawks: Keeper of the Flame.* Wolf CD 120.292, 1991.

771 Weld, "J.B. Hutto," 12-13; and Harris, 260.

Homesick James

If Elmore James could be thought of as the captain of the "Dust My Broom" ship, then our last artist in the survey, Homesick James Williamson, would certainly be considered his "first mate." At the age of eighty-or-ninety-something, he is a member of a small and elite club of blues musicians still playing today that were also active before World War II, and with a recording career that easily spans five decades, has a left a major legacy for us to examine and enjoy. A legacy that, at times, has been joyous, occasionally maddening, and other times quite brilliant; and while some of Homesick's recordings have not always lived up to their full potential, probably no one would argue with the moniker used on the title of one of his recent compact disc releases—*Chicago Slide Guitar Legend.*

It is incredible to think that Homesick's recorded debut occurred almost five decades ago. "Farmer's Blues" and "Lonesome Ole Train," which he recorded on 12 June 1952 with Lazy Bill Lucas on piano and Alfred Elkins on bass, were virtually anachronistic by the time they were released as Chance 1121, sometime in July 1952, when one compares them to what his Chicago blues guitarist colleagues were putting down in the studios at the time: Johnny Shines' scintillating masterpiece "Ramblin'" had been recorded in late April 1952; Blue Smitty's "Elgin Movements" was—for July 1952 anyway—absolutely years ahead of its time; and Jimmy Rogers and Muddy Waters had never sounded jauntier than they had with "The Last Time" and "Gone to Main Street," recorded in August and September of 1952, respectively. As Leroy Pierson noted, Homesick had adapted "Lonesome Ole Train" from Tommy Johnson's songbook, while "Farmer's Blues" was a staple of Lightnin' Hopkins, Smokey Hogg, and Lowell Fulson, among others. However, no Texas artist ever played the piece with a slide quite like Homesick does here, his slow and deliberate—but riveting—bottleneck performance marred only by the fact that he cuts off his guitar solo in mid-stream by shouting out "Gimme another one of them fish sammiches," and then comes in too early with the final verse. Homesick's now-legendary "unorthodox" bottleneck technique was not quite yet evident on "Farmer's Blues" (that was to come later), however, generic Elmore-like flourishes can definitely be heard throughout the piece as he periodically slides up the neck to play the familiar repeated phrases at the twelfth fret of the guitar. On the faster tempoed "Lonesome Ole Train," he takes a leaf from Kokomo Arnold's book by, this time, humming to himself throughout the song. Problems aside, Homesick's debut single was a fascinating entry into the world of postwar blues records, and as was previously said in regards to J.B. Hutto's first record, only hinted at what was yet to come.[772]

"We had another record out on Chance, in 1953," Homesick told Chris Millar in a 1994 interview, "that was the one that really got me a name, 'Homesick.'" Truer words were never spoken, as from that day to this James Williamson has been known as Homesick James ever since. Not only that, but it was also Homesick's first record to feature a fully implemented version of the "Dust My Broom" riff in a song, again, taken at a leisurely, relaxed tempo that seems to suit him well. This time around, Homesick's timing problems were not in evidence, perhaps aided by the stabilizing influence of Johnny Shines on second guitar, added especially just for this 23 January 1953 session. The record was on the market a month later,

772 Homesick James Williamson, "Farmer's Blues." Chance 1121, 1952; Homesick James Williamson. "Lonesome Ole Train." Chance 1121, 1952; Leadbitter, Fancourt, and Pelletier, 754; Leroy Pierson, notes to *Chicago Slickers 1948-1953.* Nighthawk LP 102, 1976; and Various Artists, *The Cream of Chicago Blues: The Guitarists, Vol. 1, 1946-1952.* Compact disc (unissued), 2001.

Note: Some confusion exists over which of the two takes of "Lonesome Ole Train" was selected for Chance 1121 (discographies vary). Using Nighthawk LP 102 (*Chicago Slickers 1948-1953*) as a cross reference to currently available compact disc issues, I have found that, possibly, Homesick's humming was overdubbed onto one of the two takes (perhaps the second take) for the version released as Chance 1121—either that, or the master tape to "Lonesome Ole Train" is missing-in-action (as is the master tape to "Homesick," from his second Chance single). It is also possible that the master tape was slowed down by a few seconds during mastering, as the issued version is approximately ten seconds longer than either of the two extant takes on CD.

receiving a favorable review at the end of February. An advertisement the following month claimed that it was "Hot in Memphis," and "Sizzling in New Orleans," but that was evidently just ad copy hype, as no further trace of "Homesick" appeared in the trade presses. In his lyrics, Homesick has a little fun with his listeners; on "The Woman I Love" (the flip side to "Homesick"), he claims that Georgia is his home state (in actuality, he was originally from Fayette County, Tennessee), and on "Homesick," well, the title of his 1970 interview with *Blues Unlimited* magazine pretty much says it all—"Lazy Bill Called Me Homesick (I Wasn't Though)."[773]

Chance held one final Homesick James session on 11 August 1953, but none of the five titles were ever issued as singles. Johnny Shines was dropped in favor of adding Snooky Pryor on harp, resulting in, perhaps, Homesick's most cohesive Chance session to date. It was just the first of many instances that would find the two musicians paired together in a recording studio. "Lonesome Blues," the first title recorded at the session, showed off more of Homesick's tasty "Dust My Broom" chops, with Pryor contributing some extra juicy amplified harp. Timing problems crept back in, however, as Homesick completely screws up his guitar solo to a fare-thee-well, compressing a standard twelve-bar solo into about six and a half or seven bars instead—a feat duplicated by few other blues musicians. "Late Hours at Midnight" offered yet more Elmore-styled sliding, just taken at a slower tempo than in "Lonesome Blues." Once again, Homesick seems to adapt much better to the relaxed pace, which appears to help minimize his timing problems. "Well, Homesick is a good slide player—or he would be if he played in time, let's put it that way," J.B. Hutto once offered in regards to his fellow Chance Records colleague. "Time means a whole lot in music. And Homesick has no time [laughs]. I've seen Floyd Jones sit up on the bandstand with Homesick and *sweat.* You got to jump in here and here and here. Homesick's all right by himself. When he can play like he wants to, he's a good guitarist, but put him with a band... [laughs]." The last piece recorded at the session, "Long Lonesome Day," was yet another go-round with the "Broom" theme, and with Pryor chugging away quite pleasurably in the background, held together nicely. The lyrics of the first verse—granted, even though they are a tad on the generic side—do bring to mind Sam Myers' 1960 Fury recording, "Sad, Sad Lonesome Day."[774]

In all, Homesick's series of recordings for Chance constituted sixteen different songs—fourteen of which have been issued in one form or another (some featuring alternate takes)—that, in retrospect, were representational of the kind of musical transitions happening in Chicago in the 1952 to 1953 time frame. As far as the traditional themes and motifs that helped inspire his core repertoire, Homesick had this to say to Jim O'Neal in 1976: "The Tommy Johnson that taught Homesick how to play ain't never made no record," he told Jim O'Neal in regards to his unrecorded mentor (i.e., *not* the famous Tommy Johnson, but some other guitarist from rural Tennessee who just happened to share the same name as the Victor and Paramount Records recording artist). "And the fact about it, don't nobody know who he is but me. He used to sing 'Lonesome Ole Train,' 'Homesick Blues,' and 'The Woman I Love,' too—all those tunes that I did later. He was a little older than I was. I was sixteen or seventeen years old, and I would sit around and listen and play right along with him, and we used to travel from one place to the other. That old man give me a head start with my guitar, I mean all the way." As far as singing the blues was concerned, Homesick's father may not have been too concerned one way or the other, because at one time he had played the snare

773 Millar and Rainsford, 8; Gart, *First Pressings—1953,* 20, 25; Leadbitter and Robinson, "Lazy Bill Called Me Homesick (I Wasn't Though)(Part 3)," 9; Leadbitter, Fancourt, and Pelletier, 755; Homesick James Williamson, "The Woman I Love." Chance 1131, 1953; and Williamson, "Homesick."

774 Homesick James, *Chicago Slide Guitar Legend.* Official CD 5253, 1998; Leadbitter, Fancourt, and Pelletier, 755; Dan Forte, "J.B. Hutto," 192. In Jas Obrecht, ed., *Rollin' and Tumblin': The Postwar Blues Guitarists.* San Francisco: Miller Freeman, 2000; and Sam Myers, "Sad, Sad Lonesome Day." Fury 1035, 1960.

drum in Othar Broadnax's Fife and Drum band, a local party/dance band that played in a radius including rural Fayette and Tipton Counties in Tennessee, and, on occasion, northern Mississippi as well. Homesick's mother, however, was none too happy. "Singin' don't even bother me 'cause that come natural. I was born like that," Homesick confessed to O'Neal. "My mother used to make me sing in the church... [and] never did want me to play blues, but I just went ahead on. She was a good guitar player and singer, too. But when I was growin' up, six or seven years old, she quit and went to the church. I imagine she said, 'I don't want my son to come up and catch me out here playin' around these juke joints and singin' the blues.'"[775]

Unfortunately, Homesick's next recording session is somewhat of an ongoing mystery. In the first (1968) edition of Leadbitter and Slaven's *Blues Records,* a coupling of "Johnnie Mae" and "Telephone Blues" was listed as having been recorded circa 1960 and issued on Atomic-H, a Chicago label belonging to the very entertaining figure of Rev. Houston. H. Harrington, an evangelist and ordained Methodist minister, inventor, and patent holder for such machines as the "Vertical Rising Jet Air Craft" and "The World's First Flying Submarine" (something that might be handy, for instance, in sneak attacks during a war, Harrington claimed). As it turned out, *Blues Records* was only partially correct. In 1972, Jim O'Neal offered that Homesick James was still under contract to Chance Records when his Atomic-H session took place—in Harrington's basement studio at 1651 S. Trumbell, Chicago, with Lazy Bill Lucas on piano and Sneaky Joe Harris on drums—putting the time frame of the recordings more like late 1953 or perhaps early 1954, not 1960. "At least one 78 from this session was issued on 'Atomic Records' under the name Jick and His Trio," wrote O'Neal in *Living Blues* magazine. "Nineteen years, several locations, and who knows how many records later, Rev. Harrington's enigmatic recording operation is still going, despite the lack of any real commercial success. Atomic (later Atomic-H) records have sold 'just enough for me to keep from quittin',' says Rev. Harrington. 'It's hard to give up once you get started.'"[776]

The whole story on Homesick's Atomic/Atomic-H single, however, wouldn't be revealed until 1976. That year, in the September/October issue of *Living Blues,* Bez Turner wrote in to the then-ongoing column "Questions & Answers" to share what little *was* known—it stated that the original listing in *Blues Records* (i.e., "Johnnie Mae" b/w "Telephone Blues") was erroneous and that the record didn't exist; also, it stated: "*Living Blues* is negotiating on Homesick's behalf to have his only *known* record on this label ("1954 Blues"/"Call Up My Baby," Atomic 1955, credited to Jick and His Trio) reissued on LP. Homesick remembers recording "Johnnie Mae" and other unissued tracks for Atomic (the H was added to the logo later), but no tapes of his sessions for the label have turned up." In spite of renewed activity at Atomic-H in 1972—four 45s from the label were reviewed in the Spring 1972 issue of *Living Blues,* and an anthology of Atomic-H material was issued on a Delmark LP the same year—Homesick's mythical Atomic pairing failed to make any appearances. In September 1999, Delmark reissued a greatly expanded version of the 1972 LP on compact disc; once again, Homesick James' single was not among the included tracks. Hopefully, this ultra-rare Homesick record (only one copy is known to exist) will finally manage to find its way onto a reissue album sometime soon, giving us a small glimpse into what Homesick's musical activities in the mid fifties might have sounded like.[777]

Eight years would pass before Homesick recorded on his own again. When he was ready, though, he burst forth with two revved up classics, the Memphis Minnie tune "Set a Date" (the flip side, "Can't Afford

---

775 Jim O'Neal, notes to Homesick James, *Goin' Back Home.* Trix LP 3315, 1976; and Bengt Olsson, notes to *On The Road Again: Country Blues 1969-1974.* Flyright CD 58, 1997.

776 Leadbitter and Slaven, *Blues Records: 1943-1966,* 359; Jim O'Neal, "Atomic Blues." *Living Blues* 9 (Summer 1972): 8; and Bez Turner, "Three Mexicans, A Hillbilly and a Polock." *Blues Unlimited* 141 (Autumn/Winter 1981): 6.

777 "Questions and Answers." *Living Blues* 29 (September/October 1976): 41; and Greensmith, personal communication, 27 December 2001.

to Do It," was yet another Memphis Minnie number) for Carl Jones' Colt imprint, and a Robert Johnson-inspired version of "Crossroads" for Lee Rothman's and Paul Glass' U.S.A. label. While both titles are indelibly marked with the Elmore sound, writer/producer Pete Welding couldn't help but notice, for the latter title, that the lyrics had been "borrowed" directly from the unissued alternate take of Robert Johnson's "Cross Road Blues"—the version that had first seen the light of day on the 1961 Columbia LP *King of the Delta Blues Singers.* As it turned out, there was no real mystery here—months before the U.S.A. session took place, George Mitchell (who would later author the book *Blow My Blues Away*), had given a copy of the Robert Johnson LP to Homesick James, who had learned the words from there. As Homesick told Pete Welding, "Well, I can play the Johnson way, the way I learned from the record, but I generally just do it by myself," adding (somewhat confusingly), "I suppose it would be possible to do it with a modern band, but since the changes are so irregular, the other musicians would have to be familiar with the way Robert Johnson played it. Then they could follow me" (actually, most readers would be inclined to think that Homesick's accompaniment on "Crossroads" of sax, piano, bass and drums did indeed constitute a "modern band").[778] Some evidence points to the session being torturous, as Willie Dixon can be heard patiently coaching Homesick in the studio about his guitar intro as the engineer rolls the tape for the twenty-seventh and twenty-eighth takes. In all, twenty-nine takes were required to get it "just right." The hard work paid off, though. "His U.S.A. recording of 'Crossroads' and 'My Baby's Sweet' was a fairly big Chicago blues hit," noted Pete Welding in February 1965, "and was directly responsible for his receiving a good bit of critical acclaim [and] widespread exposure...." Exposure that, I might add, was dispersed over two continents, as Homesick's Colt and U.S.A. 45s were each picked up for reissue in the U.K., in mid-1964, on the Sue label (no relation to Henry "Juggy" Murray's New York City-based Sue label). A young *Blues Unlimited* magazine enthusiastically reviewed Homesick's recordings, giving a plug for the U.S.A 45 on two different occasions—once after the original had come out, and again in a brief mention for its U.K. reissue in October, 1964.[779]

"Crossroads" was also Homesick's first known recording to feature his "unorthodox" slide guitar tuning—the easiest way to describe it is to say that he essentially plays in open E tuning, but with his guitar tuned five half-steps lower than concert pitch (to the key of B!), that tends to give a lax, resonant bassy feel to his six-stringed box. Oddly, none of Homesick's slide pieces he recorded for Chance had featured him employing such a tuning (two pieces, "Williamson Shuffle" and "12th Street Station," are in the key of B, but are played without a slide, and do not possess that extra deep bass feel). While Pete Welding has claimed that Homesick's unique tuning was due to the fact that, as a young kid, he learned the slide guitar unaided and without the help of outside influences (one noted exception was his mother, who Homesick remembers—before she quit playing blues and joined the church—used to play "John Henry" in the "knife style;" that is, with the guitar flat across her lap and using a pocket knife for a slide), one can only wonder why Homesick's most unusual tuning only made it's first appearance in 1962, and not somewhat earlier. While Welding also claims that no one else plays with such a tuning, the truth of the matter is that some of Casey Bill Weldon's recordings feature him playing slide guitar in the key of B. How Weldon arrived at that key is a complete mystery to me—I spent a considerable amount of time trying to figure out his tuning for a paper I once wrote on the slide guitar, and the farthest I ever got was to just

778 Pete Welding, "Homesick James Williamson." *Collectors Classics* 7 (May 1965): 8; Leadbitter, Fancourt, and Pelletier, 755; Homesick James Williamson, "Crossroads." U.S.A. 746, 1963; and Homesick James Williamson, "Set a Date," Colt 632, 1964.

779 Pete Welding, notes to Homesick James [Williamson], *Blues on the South Side.* Prestige LP 7388, 1965; Various Artists, *Willie Dixon: Working on the Blues Vol. 2/Chef Willie Cooks Up the Blues.* P-Vine CD 2347, 1992; and Mike Leadbitter and Mike Nicholls, "Current U.S. & British Singles." *Blues Unlimited* 16 (October 1964): 16.

make a couple of educated guesses. That small detail notwithstanding, any further comparison between Casey Bill Weldon and Homesick James might very well cause some readers to chuckle to themselves, as most similarities between the two musicians end once you get past their use of the slide and their (sometimes used) key signature. Just as a guess, maybe Homesick learned this uncommon tuning from his mentor, "Tommy Johnson," or maybe it was something he perfected while he was playing second guitar behind Elmore James. With Elmore's guitar tuned to E and Homesick's guitar lowered to the key of B (kind of similar to the idea of playing "cross harp" on the harmonica), this arrangement might aid a small trio of musicians by helping to add a missing "bass" element when it was just Elmore, Homesick and a drummer up on the stage playing those Chicago clubs. To further cloud the waters, we find Elmore, in his 13 February 1963 session for Bobby Robinson, playing "Find My Kind of Woman," "My Baby's Gone," and "Dust My Broom" in the very bassy-sounding key of C (two whole steps below E). How this may or may not relate to Homesick's unusual guitar tuning is not known, but is very interesting to make note of nonetheless.[780]

Another session in 1962, this time for drummer/bandleader/producer Armund "Jump" Jackson's Chicago-based La Salle imprint, rounded out Homesick's recording activity in 1962. It was the last documented pairing of pianist Lazy Bill Lucas backing Homesick James in a studio, before Bill moved to Minneapolis, circa 1964. While Homesick recorded almost enough material for an LP, the small handful of singles that La Salle ever issued did not feature any of his work. It seems, possibly, that these tapes may have met an untoward fate over the years, as a recent two-volume reissue package of La Salle recordings failed to turn up any titles by Homesick (in the reissue, it is mentioned that some of the tapes had deteriorated). Once again, we can only keep our fingers crossed that it's not too late for some of this material to surface, only hoping that if somebody has copies, they will deem to share it with us.[781]

Homesick's next entry into a recording studio occurred on 7 January 1964, to record an album for the Prestige label, produced by Sam Charters. It had been Homesick's U.S.A. 45 that had led Charters to Homesick, and it was an advantageous thing, too. The resulting LP, *Blues on the South Side*, would not only become a classic of 1960s Chicago blues (even the cover, sporting a quintessential Raeburn Flerlage black and white photo, was a classic "real estate period" album cover), but could easily stand as amongst the best recordings Homesick has ever made. For one thing, Charters managed to assemble a fine group of talent behind Homesick for these sessions, anchoring him in the studio with Lafayette Leake on piano, Clifton James on drums, and Eddie Taylor on bass. Problems with timing were at a bare minimum, and many of the tracks featured Homesick's unique sub-concert-pitch slide guitar tuning. Naturally, there were recordings of previous material—"Homesick's Blues" and "The Woman I'm Lovin'" were from his second Chance single, "Johnnie Mae" was unissued material dating from his first Chance session (no relation to the identically-titled song recorded by the Blues Rockers in 1955—with Lazy Bill Lucas on vocal and piano—and later released on Excello), while "Gotta Move" involved the usual nod to Elmore's song list. We also get three instrumentals this time, "Homesick's Shuffle" was full of romping good-time fun, as was "Working with Homesick," while "Crawlin'"—probably the weakest of the three instrumentals—was tapped, along with "The Woman I'm Lovin'," to be issued on a Bluesville single to promote the album. Three titles out of the twelve shared a similar musical theme. They were "Lonesome Road," "The Cloud Is Crying," and "Stones in My Passway." The first, "Lonesome Road," was a stunning remake of the Tommy Johnson standard "Big Road Blues," while "The Cloud Is Crying" was, according to Homesick, a more meteorologically correct take on Elmore's "The Sky Is Crying." Since learning a Robert Johnson piece had

780 Welding, "Homesick James Williamson," 7; and Elmore James, *The Last Sessions*. Relic CD 7097, 1995.

781 Harris, 342; and Leadbitter, Fancourt, and Pelletier, 755; and McGrath, 703.

worked so well for his U.S.A. 45, Homesick also learned one for this album—"Stones in My Passway" was another of Johnson's classics to be found on *King of the Delta Blues Singers,* only this time, unlike "Crossroads," it was a Johnson recording that had rarely ever been covered. For the lyrics, Homesick doesn't stray too far from Johnson's original set (the lyrical inspiration of which can be traced all the way back to an obscure couplet from the Old Testament book of Job). Musically, it is a galvanizing performance set in an unusual tempo, and Homesick is incomparable with his slide guitar. The piece appears to have that quality about it of not so much being sung by the artist, as it is being wrenched out of him. It is all at once terrifying and awe inspiring, extending way beyond the realm of merely a Johnson tune that has been set to amplification and a modern band, to something that justifiably stands all on its own as a high-water mark of 1960s Chicago blues, and of Homesick's recording career as well.[782]

Almost three months later, on 26 March 1964, Homesick was back in the studio again. Spivey Records, so named because of pre-war recording artist Victoria Spivey's involvement with the label, issued a remarkably chaotic—and yet fascinating—series of LPs that, by comparison, made Atomic-H Records look like a well-oiled, fine-tuned machine (or, perhaps, vice versa). Sometimes, amazing treasures could be found on these twelve inch slabs of vinyl, such as a rare performance featuring Willie Dixon playing solo acoustic guitar, the first recordings of Bob Dylan (or so was claimed, anyway, playing harmonica behind the person who "discovered" him, Big Joe Williams, at a 2 March 1962 New York City date), some of the last recordings of John Henry Barbee, St. Louis Jimmy, and Otis Spann, and also a handful of titles by Homesick James.[783]

All four of Homesick's Spivey recordings, in one way or another, were derivative performances. "I Got to Move" had recently been recorded at the Prestige sessions, while "Queen's Rock"—taken here mostly as a peppy instrumental with a few lyrics scattered here and there—had seen previous incarnation as "My Baby's Sweet" on the flip side of Homesick's U.S.A. 45. "Somebody's Been Talking" used the same melodic structure that "Lonesome Road"/"The Cloud Is Crying"/"Stones in My Passway" had on his Prestige album, with the intensity meter ranging just a notch or two below that of "Lonesome Road," and Homesick squeezing in some toothsome Elmore-styled sliding in a very ambivalent major/minor key signature. Lastly was Homesick's version of Elmore's classic "Can't Hold Out." In this extremely relaxed, informal setting, accompanied by the legendary Washboard Sam (whose last recordings had been made over a decade ago) and an unintrusive second guitarist, Evans Spencer, this is the type of setting in which Homesick so obviously excels. "Can't Hold Out" is prime Homesick, and one of the most satisfying Elmore-styled performances of his career, as he blithely chugs away on his deeply tuned guitar while ripping off "Broom" riff after "Broom" riff in an extended solo. Having Washboard Sam on the session—providing Homesick with a rock solid underpinning—was a stroke of inspiration (I'm inclined to think it is Willie Dixon who could be thanked for that), and it is a shame that, prior to Washboard Sam's death just two and half years later, more recording sessions of this nature were not arranged. As it is, Homesick's four Spivey recordings give us a glimpse of what it would probably be like to hear Homesick playing and singing in his living room with a couple of old friends nearby, and I, for one, am thankful for it.[784]

After the Spivey date, Homesick recorded a few sides, in August 1964, that appeared on the (now rare)

---

782 Homesick James [Williamson], *Blues on the South Side.* Prestige LP 7388, 1965; Welding, notes to *Blues on the South Side*; and Leadbitter & Slaven, *Blues Records 1943-1970,* 114.

783 Leadbitter & Slaven, *Blues Records 1943-1970,* 62, 348; and Leadbitter, Fancourt, and Pelletier, 452, 521-522, 730, 756.

784 Homesick James, *Chicago Slide Guitar Legend;* Homesick James, "Somebody's Been Talkin'." From the album *Encore for the Chicago Blues.* Spivey LP 1009, c. 1965/1966; and Homesick James, "I Got to Move." From the album *Spivey's Blues Cavalcade.* Spivey LP 1015, 1975; and Leadbitter, Fancourt, and Pelletier, 676.

British Decca LP, *South Side Chicago Blues.* Also appearing on the album were some particularly choice performances by Robert Nighthawk, Johnny Young, and Walter Horton. Homesick's recordings, "Crutch and Cane" and "Got to Move," were, once again, pieces that had also been performed by Elmore James—the former being a version of "Look on Yonder Wall" and the latter being yet another recording of the title he had just waxed for Prestige and Spivey. "Crutch and Cane" featured more of Homesick's booming Elmore-styled sliding, and was adeptly presented. An alternate take of "Crutch and Cane" along with two more titles recorded at the same session—which featured a cracker-jack line-up of Walter Horton on harmonica, Henry Gray on piano, Willie Dixon on bass, and Clifton James on drums—were later released on the obscure Sunnyland label in England.[785]

More than a year would pass before Homesick came back into the studio. When Sam Charters was in town, circa December 1965, to hold sessions for the *Chicago/The Blues/Today!* series, Homesick was one of the people he called up. Four titles later appeared on volume two of the three-volume series, and as had been the case with the Charters-produced LP *Blues on the South Side,* these recordings were expertly produced and captured Homesick at his top-notch best. Once again, an uncluttered accompaniment of Willie Dixon on bass and Fred Below on drums seemed to suit Homesick to a "T," and his slide guitar, well, quite literally had never sounded better. Two songs were Elmore retreads—a rompin' version of "Dust My Broom" that went down quite smoothly, and "So Mean to Me," which bore just a vague resemblance to the "So Mean to Me" that Elmore had recorded at his last Modern session in 1956, with Homesick freely substituting some of the lyrics at will. "Somebody's Been Talking" bore little musical similarity to the Spivey title of the same name, and was masterfully rendered. As for "Set a Date," with its playfully swooping Elmore-ish slide lines and lyrics touching on romantic anxiety, it may very well be Homesick captured at his finest moment. While his previous version of "Set a Date" on Colt had a clamorous, edgy feel of feel to it, this version finds Homesick under the dictionary definitions of both "cool" *and* "mellifluous." What was said in regards to J.B. Hutto's recordings for *Chicago/The Blues/Today!* could also be said of Homesick James': if this is the direction where Elmore's legacy was headed, then that heritage was in the most capable of hands, indeed.[786]

Yet, in spite of his stellar performance on *Chicago/The Blues/Today!,* for the remainder of the 1960s, Homesick wasn't so active musically, or in the studio. "I stopped playin', well I'll tell you," Homesick told Mike Leadbitter and Chris Robinson in 1970. "I don't work for nothin' right, I could get gigs for fifteen, twenty, twenty-five dollars a night, for two-three nights a week.... I don't work for that kind of money, I can't use it.... I couldn't afford to do it, I got a big family at home, and if I work three nights for seventy-five dollars a week I got to pay for clothes,... [and] what are my kids goin' to eat? Who's gonna pay the rent? You can't do that on seventy-five dollars." Here, Homesick speaks candidly of an economic reality that has stared many blues musicians in the face: the struggle to make a decent living from their music, for many, has been an almost unreachable goal—and artists who achieve success on a massive scale, like Muddy Waters, John Lee Hooker, or B.B. King, are few and far in between—and even they sometimes had to wait decades to see their perseverance and endless hard work pay off at a level with which one might live comfortably. Unfortunately, it is an issue that blues musicians in Chicago struggle with right to this very day. "When I first got to Chicago the work was good, for blues, up until 1960," Homesick continues, "but it

[785] Homesick James, *Chicago Slide Guitar Legend;* Leadbitter, Fancourt, and Pelletier, 756; and Robert Sacré, "An Interview with Henry Gray." *Crazy Music* 11 (Dec 1977): 31.
Note: Willie Mabon has also been given as the pianist on this session.

[786] Various Artists, *Chicago/The Blues/Today!, Vol. 2.* Vanguard LP 9217, 1966; and Leadbitter, Fancourt, and Pelletier, 756.
Note: At the time Homesick's recording of "Set a Date" was released on the above LP, the version Elmore had recorded for Bobby Robinson (in November 1959), had not yet been released.

ain't no good now.... I used to work five days a week and play seven nights a week. I used to play guitar every night till two o'clock and get home 'round three, three-thirty—get up and be on my job at seven-thirty, eight o'clock. I'd play till round two o'clock in the mornin' you know, and I was gettin' too old to do that...."[787]

A revival of recording activity in 1970 and 1971 was largely thanks to Willie Dixon: "...All the time he would let me know if anythin' came in [just] like I never been forgotten, you know," Homesick told Leadbitter and Robinson. "Like some big show come in, they say they want Homesick James, then he would put me on the show." While he was in Europe for a tour, sessions were held, in December 1970, for the French Black & Blue label; yet another version of the "Got to Move" theme and a version "Shake Your Money Maker" were among the titles offered up for posterity.[788] In December 1971, he joined with pianist Sunnyland Slim and drummer Willie Williams to record for the Bea & Baby label. Some of the results included nods to Elmore's song bag, including "My Baby's Gone," and an instrumental themed after "Hawaiian Boogie" entitled "Homesick Sunnyland Special." Typically in the Homesick fashion, though, he liberally interprets any original material strictly in his own terms, always resulting in a fresh twist on old themes. In 1973, Homesick had two albums issued, one with Snooky Pryor on the Caroline label, while *Ain't Sick No More,* produced by Al Smith for ABC's Bluesway subsidiary—even though it featured a distinguished line up of Pryor along with Dave Myers, Eddie Taylor, and Willie Smith—failed to find the cohesive stability and superior artistry that had made his sessions with Sam Charters for Prestige and Vanguard so special (in contrast, *Snooky Pryor and the Country Blues,* which sported another crackerjack line-up of backing musicians with Homesick prominently on slide guitar behind Pryor's vocals and harp—also produced by Al Smith—was a splendid effort solidly presented). In 1976, Pete Lowry issued a very pleasant acoustic set, *Goin' Back Home,* on his Trix label. Half recorded in Chicago and half recorded in Homesick's old home town of Somerville, Tennessee, the album featured more of Homesick's swell "Broom" riff bottlenecking. A rambling, six-plus-minute instrumental entitled "Homesick's Contribution to Jazz," however, had very little in common with the similarly titled "Elmore's Contribution to Jazz" that he and Elmore had recorded for Chief almost twenty years previous. "Texas Dust" presented a fresh twist on the oft-repeated "Dust My Broom" motif, and while the liner notes provided no real explanation on the change in title, perhaps it was Homesick's rendering of how he supposed a Texas guitarist might approach this blues standard (Any better ideas will be gratefully considered)? A photo on the back cover of the album shows a sprightly Homesick posing with his mother and father on the front porch of their Somerville, Tennessee home, looking quite good for someone in his sixties.[789]

A session with Snooky Pryor in Vienna, Austria, in October 1979, rounded out Homesick's recording activities for the 1970s. According to the liner notes by Paul Michael Sedlacek and Sam Burckhardt, the session was recorded "off the cuff" and no final editing of the tapes was deemed necessary, resulting in an easygoing, "live in the studio" album with Homesick and Snooky swapping vocal duties as they saw fit. Elmore material included Homesick's theme-and-variation on "Shake Your Money Maker" with lots of savory harp blowing from Snooky, and two other "Broom" styled compositions, "No More Lovin'" and the title track, "Sad and Lonesome." Once again, the combination of Homesick and Snooky is something that worked quite well, and is reflective of the kind of quality that could be found in their Chance sessions from

787 Leadbitter and Robinson, "Lazy Bill Called Me Homesick (I Wasn't Though)(Part 3)," 10.

788 Ibid.; 10-11; and Leadbitter, Fancourt, and Pelletier, 756.

789 Homesick James, "My Baby's Gone." From the album *Meat & Gravy from Cadillac Baby—"Records was cheap to make then," Vol. 1.* Red Lightnin' LP 0019, 1978; Jim O'Neal and Bill Greensmith, "Discography." In the notes to *Meat & Gravy from Cadillac Baby—"Records was cheap to make then," Vol. 1.* Red Lightnin' LP 0019, 1978; Homesick James, *Ain't Sick No More.* Bluesway LP 6071, 1973; Snooky Pryor, *Snooky Pryor and the Country Blues.* Today LP 1012, 1973; and Homesick James, *Goin' Back Home.* Trix LP 3315, 1976.

a quarter century ago.[790]

After the Wolf LP came out in 1980, nothing more was heard from Homesick in over a decade. In the April 1993 issue of *Blues & Rhythm* magazine, editor Tony Burke offered, "Did you ever think we would see another full album release by Homesick James? No? Neither did I." Burke was referring to *Sweet Home Tennessee,* Homesick's latest studio effort that had been issued by the Appaloosa label, and would mark a revival of activity for Homesick in the 1990s. "Reports... have indicated that Homesick was in a bad way and that he had moved back home to Tennessee to see his days out," noted Burke. To borrow from a famous phrase, however, obviously those reports were premature. Burke practically glowed over Homesick's latest effort, saying that, "'Gotta Move' [the opening track from the album] is perhaps the key to what Williamson's playing is all about, a smooth, purring slide workout lasting six minutes on which he really lets it flow."[791] Actually, the Homesick revival had begun back in August 1992, when Michael Robert Frank of the Chicago-based Earwig Records held some recording sessions, with Honeyboy Edwards guesting on three tracks. *Goin' Back in the Times* was the resulting album that saw issue in 1994. Also in 1994, *Billboard* magazine celebrated their 100th year of publication. In a special, memorabilia-choked issue, a full page ad presenting a portrait of Homesick smiling beatifically was an especially nice touch. An album of fresh Homesick material for Trix, *Got to Move,* made an appearance in 1995, while Appaloosa issued a second album, *Juanita,* in 1997 (later reissued on Evidence). Just a few weeks after *Juanita* came out, Priority issued *Words of Wisdom,* and one year later, Fedora responded with *The Last of the Broomdusters.* As the old saying goes, Homesick was obviously "trying to make hay while the sun was shining." 1998 also witnessed, in a European compact disc issue, the first ever attempt at providing an overview of Homesick's career from the 1952 to 1971 time span (excepting, of course, Homesick's missing Atomic single) on *Chicago Slide Guitar Legend,* from the Official label (the 1977 P-Vine LP, *Chance Vintage Blues/R&B Crops Vol. 2,* was exclusively devoted to anthologizing Homesick's rare and unissued Chance recordings; as a bonus, it also featured some of Homesick's pen and ink drawings on the front and back cover).[792]

"It is a fact like no other that these men do not live forever," once opined John Simmons in the liner notes to one of Big Joe Williams' Delmark LPs. At the age of either 88, 92, or 97 ("...He doesn't care to count his years publicly," noted Larry Hoffman, "he reminds me simply that '...everybody knows I've been around a long time.'"), Homesick is, sadly, one of the last of a diminishing breed. "All of 'em gone but me," he offered in regards to his old blues friends, but quickly added, "I'm still hangin' in there."[793] In 2001, Homesick James was part of a group, also consisting of Robert Jr. Lockwood, Henry Townsend, and Honeyboy Edwards, that was scheduled to play various places in the United States and Europe—in effect, a chance for festival-goers to see a capsule history of the blues presented on one stage in one afternoon. For those who had the once-in-a-lifetime chance to see them perform, I sure hope they enjoyed every minute.[794]

Homesick's rich legacy and memorable recordings, spanning the better part of fifty years, saw the "Dust My Broom" riff through to almost the end of the twentieth century (and perhaps into the twenty-first, if he has any new CDs come out soon). More than that, though, he has offered fresh perspectives on

790 Homesick James and Snooky Pryor, *Sad and Lonesome.* Wolf LP 120.409, 1980.

791 Tony Burke, "New Releases/Homesick James with the Hypnotics." *Blues & Rhythm* 78 (April 1993): 25.

792 Michael Erlewine, et al., eds. *All Music Guide to the Blues,* 2nd ed. San Francisco: Miller Freeman Books, 1999, 483-484. Note: Homesick's full page ad in the 100th Anniversary issue of *Billboard* magazine (dated 1 November 1994) can be found on page 195 of that issue.

793 Homesick James, *Goin' Back in the Times.* Earwig CD 4929, 1994.

794 John Simmons, notes to Big Joe Williams, *Nine String Guitar Blues.* Delmark CD 627, 1990 [reissue]; and Larry Hoffman, notes to Homesick James, *Goin' Back in the Times.* Earwig CD 4929, 1994.

old themes, re-casting and reworking classic motifs and impressing upon them his own unique and indelible sound. It is a legacy that won't soon be forgotten, and that—in its own right—proudly stands shoulder-to-shoulder with that of his cousin's, the Mississippi Broomduster, Elmore James.

Homesick's historic recordings for the Chance label (two compact discs, *Chicago Slide Guitar Legend* and *Chicago Blues—The Chance Era* present an almost identical track list), along with his recordings for *Chicago/The Blues/Today!* and his Prestige LP, *Blues on the South Side* (currently still in print on compact disc), are all highly recommended starting points for exploring the lengthy career of Homesick James Williamson. Unfortunately, the original, 78 rpm-release versions of "Lonesome Ole Train" and "Homesick" are only available on *Chicago Slickers 1948-1953* (Nighthawk LP 102) and *Chicago Blues—The Early 1950s* (Blues Classics LP 8), respectively, as the versions of these songs issued on CD (and on the 1977 P-Vine LP as well) are all alternate takes.

A Few Final Thoughts on "Dust My Broom"

When I chose the title for my master's thesis, I decided upon *Elmore James: Standing at the Crossroads* for a couple of different reasons. Not only has the title been a perennial favorite since that memorable day back in January, 1987, but I also feel that it perfectly summarizes and clarifies Elmore's role in blues history. In a way, one could view Elmore as a sort of blues equivalent to the Roman god Janus—with two faces looking in opposite directions—one face to the past, and blues history, the other face looking forward, to the present, and, ultimately, the future. In this sense, Elmore stands smack dab in the middle of one the most crucial intersections in blues history—where past blues traditions met with modern influences. While Elmore's music is indeed a harbinger of what would soon come, in the shape of rock and roll, and other offshoots (here, it is important to remember that until guitarists like T-Bone Walker, Arthur "Big Boy" Crudup, Muddy Waters, and Elmore James came along, the lead instrument in rock and roll/rhythm and blues had been the saxophone), but also incorporates the deeply held, archetypal musical traditions of the blues community that Elmore grew up with, and using that formidable framework, he used that tradition to fashion his own unique body of work.

Recently, I was reading Frederic Ramsey's classic *Been Here and Gone.* I came upon this following observation, which Ramsey made over the course of five different field trips to Alabama, Mississippi, and New Orleans during the years 1951 through 1957:

> The work songs were as old as work. In Africa, they had been carried around in the heads and in the muscles of the ancestors of [people like] Tom Huff [a person whom Ramsey had interviewed during one of his field trips and whose parents had both been slaves].
>
> The simplest songs caught the rhythm of work to be done: chopping wood, pulling ropes, cutting brush, tilling the soil. Like chants, they incorporated a call-and-response....
>
> Field calls grew up alongside work songs. They probably began as high, wordless chants sung in falsetto. The call was a variation of *la hoo hoo*, a gentle, whooping sound that nevertheless carried far. The response came back: *yehee, lahee.*
>
> During slavery, they were used for communication between squads in neighboring fields. Sometimes the call-and-response was followed by a brief exchange of information not meant for the master's ears: a slave had escaped, and the word passed from field to field.
>
> Later, just as the earliest religious music was bent to different expressions, the field call began to pass on stories of everyday life. Even when all the lines were carried by one singer, the older call-and-response could still be heard as rest or emphasis behind the story.[795]

According to the book *Bill Wyman's Blues Odyssey*, James "Son" Thomas is quoted as saying that "Dust My Broom" was "...an old field holler to tell everyone, except the people the hollerer didn't want to tell, that he was running away."[796] An old field holler, a cry, or a whine—each phrase has been used repeatedly to try to describe blues songs, the roots of the blues, or the slide guitar. In a sense then, maybe we could think of the "Dust My Broom" riff as just theme and variation on the ages-old call-and-response that Ramsey had observed. We could think of it using this structure (here, using Elmore's "Wild about You" as a musical example):

"A" LINE [ESTABLISHING THE THEME]:

MEASURE (or BAR):	**1**	**2**	**3**	**4**
	CALL ——————————————> I		RESPONSE ——————————> I	
[Well I'm] •	wild about you baby but you •	just won't treat me right	• *Dust My Broom riff* •	*End of Broom riff, and (descending) rhythmic couplet played on guitar. Singing typically begins on last beat of the 4th measure.* Well I'm...

"A" LINE, REPEATED [HELPS ADD TENSION AND DRAMA]:

MEASURE:	**5**	**6**	**7**	**8**
	CALL ——————————————> I		RESPONSE ——————————> I	
	wild about you baby but you •	just won't treat me right	• *Dust My Broom riff* •	*End of Broom riff, and (descending) rhythmic couplet played on guitar. Singing typically begins on last beat of the 4th measure.* You leave home...

795 Frederic Ramsey, Jr., *Been Here and Gone.* Athens, Georgia: University of Georgia Press, 2000 [reprint], 36, 38.

796 Bill Wyman with Richard Havers, *Bill Wyman's Blues Odyssey.* London: Dorling Kindersley, 2001, 339.

"B" LINE [CLOSURE]:

MEASURE:	9	10	11	12
	CALL ——————————————>|		RESPONSE ——————————>|	
	early in the morning but you •	don't come home till night •	*Descending figures leading to turnaround played on guitar. Call & Response pattern finished for these 12 measures. Singing typically begins on last beat of the 4th measure, or, a solo begins instead [helping to add further emphasis to what was just sung].*	

Additional notes: In a 12-bar guitar solo, the "Broom" riff will typically occur on the first, third, and seventh measures. Although a basic "Broom" riff is constituted of four sets of triplets and truncated (usually descending, but not always) fifth set, endless variations are possible by dropping individual notes or whole sets of triplets. Instead of triplets, notes might just be played as a sustain instead, again, changing or adding emphasis, as need be.

Within each individual line, a pattern of call-and-response can be observed if the words being sung are thought of as the "call" and the "Dust My Broom" riff coming in right behind it as the "response." In this capacity, the "Broom" theme serves to highlight or underscore what was just sung, as Ramsey stated, fitting his definition of call-and-response. In this sense, then, it is becomes not quite so important as to who it is that should be credited with creating the "Dust My Broom" riff—afterall, sliding up the neck of a blue-note tuned guitar to play repeated notes or phrases at the twelfth fret is an idea that goes back at least as far to 1927 (to Crying Sam Collins), if not further—as it is to understand that the concept originated out of blues tradition, and was fashioned out of that framework.

In the music of Elmore James, we find a modern blues artist in terms of his instrumentation, approach to the material, and even lyrics (one could say that Elmore was "post-modern" long before it was considered "cool" to be post-modern), and at the same time, the origins of his music owe so much to the rich legacy of blues traditions—some of them are so old, that they even date back to Africa—that "Standing at the Crossroads" is the most succinct, and apropos, description of Elmore's place in blues history that I can think of.

Elmore James (right), with unknown friend (left), taking it easy in Chicago.
Courtesy Oliver Davis and Jim O'Neal/BluEsoterica Archives & Productions.

Very special thanks are in order to Marc Ryan of Acoustic Archives and Dr. David Evans for their generosity in sharing their unpublished research material with me and especially Dr. David Evans' assistance by loaning his rare, original blues magazines that were an invaluable aid to research. Robert Ford at the University of Exeter and Graham Langley at the *British Institute of Jazz Studies* are both due rounds of applause for their kindhearted assistance with digging up long-forgotten and very rare copies of the earliest articles pertaining to Elmore James, which would have otherwise been quite impossible to find without their inestimable aid. I also give a most special thanks to Pat LeBlanc and the Estate of Elmore James—I'm glad I was able to share with them some of my research material, just as they were able to share some of their research material with me.

Additional special thanks to: Dick Shurman and Bill Greensmith for generously sharing thoughts and resources; Robert Sacré, Mike Rowe, Jim O'Neal, and *Living Blues* editor Scott Barretta for ideas and assistance with the photos; Dr. Wayne Smith—thanks for the moral support and the Blind Willie McTell discussions; Fred Rothwell and Bob Eagle, thanks for the old reviews and discography updates, respectively; Bob Hardy for more old *BU's;* plus special help from Victor Pearlin, John Tefteller, Gary Hearn, Robert Campbell, Brennan Totten, and the WEVL FM 90 crew, especially Dee "Cap'n Pete" Henderson and Dr. Ed Amos; and the "First Friday" guys—Frank, Bruce, the two Tony's, and Bill.

Last of all, the project would not have been complete without their generous assistance: Walter Devenne and Donn Fileti of Relic Records, Paul Mawhinney of Record Rama Sound Archives, Jim Spake and Judy Dorsey of WEVL-FM 90, Carmen Fanzone, Frank Scott, Wally Hall, Galen Gart, Gary Peterson, Patrick Milligan, Alan Balfour, Ron Edwards, Ed Doney, Chris Smith, Danny Crone, Sarah Richey, Mike Lang of Dreamland Palace, and finally, my wife, Deborah Dietz, whose patience and enthusiasm for the project was unfailing.

Birth and death date information has been checked for accuracy at Eric LeBlanc's Blues Dates: «www.bluesworld.com/bluesdates.html». Also most helpful was «www.allmusicguide.com».

Additionally, a special gratitude for the reference works of Mike Leadbitter, Neil Slaven, Leslie Fancourt, and Paul Pelletier, as well as Ken Clee, William R. Daniels, Robert Ford, Galen Gart, Paul Mawhinney, Bob McGrath, Jerry Osborne, Mike Paikos, and Joel Whitburn—without whose unrivaled work there would be nothing but an empty shelf where my blues and R&B discography/ bibliography reference library now sits. Thanks to each and every one of you.

Be sure to catch "Cap'n Pete's Blues Cruise" every Friday night from 9pm to Midnight (CST), at «www.wevl.org». Stone cold blues, brought to you by the man who knows them the best....

APPENDIX ONE

Elmore James—Myths and Folklore

Introduction

Ever since November 1964, when Guy Stevens wrote in *Jazz Beat* that, "Tragically, Elmore died of a heart attack during a recording session in Chicago last year,"[797] there's been a steady stream of garbled facts, half-truths, and outright lies wending and weaving their way into the fabric of the Elmore James legend—some of which have been so utterly taken for granted—that many people have become convinced that they are true. In this appendix, we look at three different pieces of Elmore James myth/folklore, and delve into some of the historical background and literature surrounding them, starting with the tale of Lillian McMurry, Elmore James, and the recording of "Dust My Broom."

Lillian McMurry, Elmore James, and "Dust My Broom"

The story that James was 'tricked' into recording "Dust My Broom" has been the hardest myth of the Elmore James legend to shake. I am always surprised—although I know I shouldn't be—when I still encounter this bit of misinformation in liner notes and articles (one recent example was found in the liner notes to an Elmore James CD dating from 1997—although it's just my opinion, I think the well-known author and discographer really should have double checked his references than to repeat this erroneous story yet one more time). It even happened on an Elmore James CD for which I was named "Research Director" and was asked to contribute some notes about how the recordings were made. Naturally, I was not allowed to see (let alone edit, for that matter) the *rest* of the liner notes—written by a very famous author—before the package had already hit the streets.

Vitrice McMurry and Almost Slim offered their theory about the origin of this yarn in a 1984 article in *Goldmine* magazine. They suspected the culprit of being a researcher who was trying to explain why it was that Elmore only ever had the one song on Trumpet—or for that matter, why he never made a follow-up record on Trumpet (the established practice when an artist has a hit record).[798]

William Donoghue was perhaps the first writer to base an entire article around this theme in his 1997 piece for *Blues & Rhythm* magazine entitled "Did Elmore James Know He Was Recording 'Dust My

797 Stevens, 13.

798 McMurry and Slim, 14.

Broom'?" Donoghue offers that the fallacy got its start with a Homesick James interview from *Blues Unlimited* 85, in 1971. In a nutshell, Homesick says that Elmore told him that McMurry had tricked him.[799]

Gayle Dean Wardlow and Edward Komara also examined this topic in the recent book *Chasin' that Devil Music.* In an extended footnote written by Komara, he cites an earlier example of Homesick's story, this time from May 1965. Komara is referring to this passage from *Collectors Classics* 7, page three:

> ["Dust My Broom"] became very popular in 1951 and was later reissued and retitled, coming out on Ace as "I believe my time ain't long." The reverse "Catfish Blues" isn't by Elmore at all, but features a mysterious artist "Q.S. Kiewny" [note: phonetic spelling]. It has been said that Elmore was so nervous at this session that Kiewny took over, but the whole thing is surrounded by a certain mystery. Homesick James for example says Elmore wasn't even aware that he was being recorded! [800]

Komara also noted that Wardlow believes Sonny Boy Williamson may have been another propagator of the "Elmo was hoodwinked" story. Williamson had toured Europe extensively in the early 1960s and was eagerly interviewed by blues fans there—who soaked up his stories and tall tales like sponges.[801] It is interesting to note, by way of comparison, that no mention of subterfuge is made in one of the earliest articles on Elmore James—"The Story of Elmore James" from *Blues Unlimited* 5 (October 1963). Coincidentally, that article was published just as Sonny Boy's first tour of Europe was starting. When John Broven published one of the earliest articles on Sonny Boy Williamson in *Blues Unlimited* 8 (January 1964), Broven wrote that Williamson said he had recorded with Elmore, but didn't elaborate much beyond that.[802]

Flash forward to December 1965, and *Blues Unlimited* 28. On page ten, we find the following article, entitled "Call The Doctor—Information Received," by Mike Leadbitter. A summary of bits and pieces of information offered during an interview with "Dr." Isaiah Ross, it stated the following:

> Next the real Elmore James record story! (Christ was Sonny Boy a liar!). Elmore and SBW were broadcasting together in Belzoni, Miss. and Elmore's most-played and requested number was "Dust My Broom". A 'talent scout' noticed this so he went down to the studio with recording equipment and when Elmore next did it, he taped it. The resultant master was sold to Trumpet who put it out with a 'local boy' singing and playing on the flip, but forgot to credit it to him. Anyway this *is* borne out with the other story that while Elmore was playing in one room, he was being recorded in another! [803]

Nice story—but again, just that. Judging by Leadbitter's comment—"Christ was Sonny Boy a liar!"—he must be referring to a Sonny Boy Williamson interview, published sometime between the Fall of 1963 (Sonny Boy's first appearance in Europe) and December 1965 (date of the above quote) that I was unable to locate among my research materials.

It wasn't until the October 1969 issue of *Blues Unlimited* that the questions surrounding the flip side to "Dust My Broom" were cleared up. That issue featured a Gayle Dean Wardlow interview of blues guitarist Tommy Lee Thompson, during which Wardlow would play various blues records for Thompson. At one point in the article it states, "Here Gayle plays the mysterious 'Catfish Blues' (Trumpet)."

799 Donoghue, "Did Elmore James Know He Was Recording....," 10; and Leadbitter and Robinson. "Homesick James, part 2," 9.

800 Demêtre, Chauvard, and Koester, 3. Note: *Collectors Classics* was published by *Blues Unlimited* magazine.

801 Wardlow, *Chasin' that Devil Music,* 166.

802 Williams, Koester, Chauvard, et al., "The Story of Elmore James," 3-4; and John Broven, "Sonny Boy Williamson." *Blues Unlimited* 8 (January 1964): 3-4. Note: Broven's article was reprinted in Leadbitter, *Nothing But the Blues,* 24-25.

803 Mike Leadbitter, "Call the Doctor—Information Received." *Blues Unlimited* 28 (December 1965): 10.

> That's Sonny Boy and Bobo! Call him Bobo. He was from Jackson. He was a Thomas—Bobo Thomas. He played guitar.... He went out there to record that record by himself (i.e.: under his own name), but she (Mrs. McMurry) wouldn't let him. So she, the Elmore James record, was on the other side and... Sonny Boy Williamson blowed the harmonica for them. [804]

Even so, there were still a lot of questions left to be answered. Mike Leadbitter, for his part, was still trying to figure out the mystery right up until the time of his death. In one of his last columns, he asked a few questions out loud in his "Mike's Blues" column:

> Over the years, we've had all sorts of confusing stories from the parties involved on why, when and where Modern first recorded Elmore. We also knew two facts: one, that Elmore just cut 'Broom' for Trumpet in 1951 and never returned, and two, that the man's contract with Meteor was announced in December 1952. But no one has explained why he never recorded for Trumpet again, though under contract, why Lillian McMurry was so sore at the Biharis over Elmore, and why it took him a year to get him in a studio again. The answer I'm sure, is [Boyd Gilmore's] 'All In My Dreams.'

Mike was definitely on the right track, but, at the time, was not privy to a few key details—namely, that Modern had indeed recorded Elmore while he was still under contract to Trumpet—hence McMurry's feeling of "soreness" at the Biharis. In 1974—which the above excerpt dates from—Leadbitter was consulting discographies that placed "Please Find My Baby" and "Hand In Hand" as having been recorded in 1954; he didn't know that they were actually recorded in January 1952, but he was beginning to suspect as much. His main clue to this was that Elmore's guitar part from "Please Find My Baby" had somehow found its way onto Boyd Gilmore's "All In My Dreams." (for more on that story, see chapter three). "All In My Dreams" was released as a single in June 1952; ergo, Leadbitter was beginning to rightly question the chronology of events in regards to Elmore, his Trumpet contract, and his first Modern session.[805]

For her part, Lillian McMurry's account about "Dust My Broom" never really changed much over the years. Essentially, she always said that Elmore only had the one song, and was supposed to work up material for the flip side but never got it together.[806] I spoke with McMurry briefly on the telephone once, and she simply said, "If you go down to see the [Trumpet Records] archive at Ole Miss, you will know the truth."[807] I don't think I was able to sufficiently convince her that I already believed her. The evidence in her favor, of course, is overwhelming. The signed contract the day before the recording; the thirty-five dollar check to Elmore against advance royalties (again, written the day before "Dust My Broom" was recorded); Elmore's later acknowledgement to Lillian that he was there with her when they wrote up the

---

804 Wardlow, "Highway 80 Blues," 12.

Note: In an interview with Dick Shurman, Billy Boy Arnold offered an "alternate" theory regarding "Catfish Blues." Arnold told him: "That's Guitar Slim playing 'Catfish Blues.' Elmore told me that himself, because I asked Elmore. I said that don't sound like you, and he said that's Guitar Slim." As Shurman added, "Admittedly Gayle Wardlow's search seems to be turning up consistent evidence contradicting this theory, but in view of Billy Boy's general credibility it should be taken into account." (Dick Shurman, "Billy Boy Arnold's Story," 71-72. In Mike Leadbitter, ed., *Nothing But the Blues.* London: Hanover Books, 1971). Interestingly, when Jim O'Neal interviewed McMurry in 1980 she recalled the artist's name on "Catfish Blues" as "Slim," and added that, "Slim could only sing just like he did on 'Catfish Blues' and that was it. It was just old-time unoriginal blues." (O'Neal, "Lillian S. McMurry," 20). It seems entirely possible to me that Elmore could have very well been telling Billy Boy Arnold the truth, just that the "Slim" Elmore was referring to was, perhaps, *not* the Eddie "Guitar Slim" Jones of rhythm and blues fame, but rather a local Jackson musician that just happened to use a like-sounding moniker for his nickname.

805 Leadbitter, "Mike's Blues." *Blues Unlimited* 110: 19, 30.

806 Stolper, 5-6; McMurry and Slim, 14; O'Neal, "Lillian S. McMurry," 20; and Lillian McMurry, personal interview by David Evans and Marc Ryan. Jackson, Mississippi, 13 March 1989.

807 Lillian McMurry, telephone interview by Steve Franz, 27 November 1994.

copyright paperwork to "Dust My Broom;" the fact that she gave Elmore a good couple months to work up another song; plus the use of a recording technique, which by its very nature, would have made any clandestine recording all but impossible—point to McMurry having done absolutely everything properly and in order. This in turn, completely corresponds with all the reports that Trumpet Records was a company that McMurry ran impeccably.

So, that would tend to bring the spotlight of blame back to, yes, that's right—our hero—old Elmore himself. I believe that Homesick was simply reporting what Elmore told him, which sounds like an attempt to save face if I ever heard one. You can imagine fellow musicians bugging him and fans asking him (as did Billy Boy Arnold) something to the effect of, "Hey man, how come that's not you singing on the other side of that record;" and Elmore, saving some face or just simply not wanting to discuss it at length, perhaps offering a reply like, "Oh man, I done made that record and didn't even know I was making it! Next thing you know it's a hit record coast to coast." Besides, it might have given Elmore a bit of a laugh to spin a yarn like this on occasion (rather than admit the truth, perhaps), and besides, what fellow blues musician *wouldn't* believe a story about getting screwed by a record company?[808]

To Lillian McMurry, it was no mystery about who was to blame for bringing the "Elmore was tricked" story to a vastly wider audience. She seemed to believe that that distinction rested squarely on the shoulders of Robert Palmer. "I did *not* surreptitiously record him, as... Robert Palmer said," McMurry emphatically told David Evans and Marc Ryan during a personal interview on 13 March 1989. "Robert Palmer never interviewed me, he never asked to see anything. He just sat down and wrote what he wanted to write."[809] If one was to attempt to "read between the lines" of what McMurry said about the debacle over the years, my guess is that it would perhaps be a comment on the difference between a blues musician's erroneous story from an interview that appeared in a relatively obscure English specialty magazine, versus a story that appeared in a book (stated flatly as bona fide fact) that anybody could find a copy of by just walking into their nearest bookstore. And who would blame her for thinking that (if indeed, that was what she was thinking)? Afterall, McMurry never talked (as far as this author is aware) of suing *Blues Unlimited* magazine—but she certainly considered it with Robert Palmer.[810]

Anyway, if there's a lesson to be learned from this myth spun out of control and repeated too many times, it would seem to prove a couple of old axioms. The first—if it's printed in black and white, it must be true; and the second—you guessed it—don't believe everything you read.[811]

---

808 Leadbitter and Robinson. "Homesick James, part 2," 9.

809 McMurry, personal interview, 13 March 1989.

810 McMurry and Slim, 14.

811 Update: The reader may be amused to know that this little bullshit story just won't die, and has now been brought forth to a whole new generation of readers thanks to a hefty (and I might add, lavishly produced and illustrated) blues book published in October 2001, written by a famous rock 'n' roller. Oh well—the very same book also got the details of J.B. Lenoir's death wrong, as well, so, chalk one up to human error, I guess—and the unending saga of contemporary musical myths.

Was Trumpet 146 Issued as a 45?

A question sure to be of interest to record collectors and Elmore fans everywhere—was Trumpet 146 ever issued as a 45 rpm single? The answer seems to be a flat-out "no," or an unqualified *maybe,* depending upon who you ask. Conventional blues wisdom has usually stipulated that Trumpet 146 was only issued in the 78 rpm format, end of story. Even with "Dust My Broom" racking up strong sales and its 'official' registry as an R&B chart hit in April 1952, it's reasonable enough to assume that a small, struggling company like Trumpet just might not have the budget to press up both 78s and 45s; especially when one considers industry reports indicating that the 45 format—especially in the R&B category—was slow to catch on in jukeboxes in the South at that time.[812]

Evidence of Trumpet 146 existing as a 45 is circumstantial at best. Paul Mawhinney, curator of the Record Rama Sound Archives in Pennsylvania, and editor of the hefty two volume *MusicMaster: The 45 RPM Record Directory,* lists Trumpet 146 as a 45 in its entry on Elmore James.[813] When I spoke with Mawhinney on the phone once, I asked him about that entry. He said it was another collector who had told him about the existence of Trumpet 146 as a 45, and based solely on that evidence, Mawhinney included it in his database (Mawhinney now requests that collectors sending information on 45s to be added to his database also submit label shots for his permanent files).

Ken Clee's massive *Directory of American 45 R.P.M. Records* also lists Trumpet 146 as having been issued as a 45, but then again, it indicates that *every* Trumpet release was issued as a 45—even all the way back to Trumpet's debut disc (Southern Sons Quartette on Trumpet 118, released circa November 1950). This seems unlikely, at best.[814]

Perhaps the most intriguing circumstantial evidence for Trumpet 146 being issued as a 45 comes from an advertisement in a November 1966 issue of *Blues Unlimited.* On page nineteen we find Fred Davis' auction/sale list of Trumpet 45s and 78s (only $2.50 each!). Although a 45 of Trumpet 146 is *not* among those listed, a 45 copy of Trumpet 144 *is* (Sonny Boy Williamson, "I Cross My Heart"). This could mean one of three things: a) that all Trumpet singles, as far back as 144 at least, were also issued as 45s; b) McMurry issued Sonny Boy Williamson's records in both formats because he was the label's biggest seller at that time, and it would be worth it to spend the extra cash at the pressing plant on his records (whether McMurry would have spent money pressing up two formats on a new and unproven artist, such as Elmore James, is not known); or, c) that McMurry took the records of her best-selling artists and had them re-pressed as 45s at a later date—i.e., after the 45 had demonstrated wide popularity among record buyers and on jukeboxes.

"By all rights, it should have been pressed on a 45 since it was a hit," offered long-time collector Victor Pearlin. "I have been collecting records for forty years," he adds, "and have never come across anyone who has ever said that they have seen a copy of it!" Another long-time collector, John Tefteller, concurs. "There

812 Gart, *First Pressings—1952,* 33, 35; and Whitburn, 216.

813 Paul Mawhinney, ed., *MusicMaster: The 45 RPM Record Directory, 1947-1982.* Artist Vol. Pittsburgh: Record Rama, 1983, 513; and Paul Mawhinney, ed., *MusicMaster. The 45 RPM Record Directory, 1947-1982.* Title Vol. Pittsburgh: Record Rama, 1983, 209.

814 Ken Clee, *The Directory of American 45 R.P.M. Records, Volume 4.* Philadelphia: Stak-O-Wax, 1997, 774-775.

Note: Just for the sake of argument, Clee's list of early releases on the Aladdin label—from 1945 and 1946—would indicate they were also issued on 45—even though the 45 format did not exist at the time! Although "45" is part of the title of Clee's work, he obviously means—in some of his label listings—a more generic approach to the term "45," meaning "released as a single." This minor disparity aside, Clee's work is an outstanding, invaluable resource.

is no 45 of Trumpet 146," he flatly asserts. "Lillian McMurry told me in 1983 when I spent the day with her that one was never pressed," he says. "Part of the reason was that Trumpet, as most all other small record companies of the day, would press the 78's first. Then, if there was enough sales and orders for the 78, a 45 would be pressed."[815]

If for some reason one ever were to surface—however unlikely that might seem—it could possibly turn out to be a "bootleg" reproduction (such as the reproductions of Flair 1011, Meteor 5003 and Checker 777 dating from the early 1970s), or if a legitimate issue, one of the rarer postwar blues records of all time. Even so, it's not likely that a 45 of Trumpet 146 would reveal anything not already discernible from a clean 78 copy, and in only one case that I know of did a Trumpet 45 play differently from its 78 counterpart (Sonny Boy Williamson's "She Brought Life Back to the Dead"). With nothing but the thinnest threads of circumstantial evidence to go on, it seems that we have to conclude, beyond a reasonable doubt, that a 45 of Trumpet 146 just does not exist. In the meantime, researchers or readers possessing an insatiable curiosity about early Trumpet releases may be able to find more clues by perusing the Trumpet Records files located in the Blues Archive at Ole Miss, in Oxford, Mississippi.

Elmore James on Film?

The curious reader might be inclined to ask if those promotional films that Otis Ealey took of Elmore James in 1955 ever *did* turn up (for background information, please see chapter three). Don't get your hopes up, but here's what I *do* know:

A) The following message was posted by one Eliot Williams of the University of Wisconsin Medical School to the internet-based Blues-L discussion group on 24 November 1995: "While we're on the subject of blues greats rarely seen on film, I think someone asked recently about Elmore James. I seem to remember (possibly during the recent PBS broadcast of the BBC rock documentary but I'm not sure) seeing a grainy film snippet of Elmore, apparently playing at full throttle but unfortunately without sound. Am I imagining this or does it exist?"[816]

B) During a telephone interview with Pat LeBlanc on 7 June 1996, he told this author, "I think it's [i.e., the footage] somewhere in Europe." LeBlanc elaborated by referring to a conversation he'd had with a man named Joel Berliner, who indicated that the Rolling Stones were interested in using the alleged footage in their *Voodoo Lounge* CD ROM. LeBlanc further told me that Berliner had evidently told him "I think we've found it [in Europe]," but as LeBlanc told me, "But that's all he said."[817]

Since that time, two interesting things have happened:

First, I have received a copy of the documentary *Rock & Roll* Williams refers to, and indeed episode five, "Crossroads," is devoted to blues. In it, there is blurry and grainy black & white footage of a band playing in a club. In this instance, Williams' use of the word "snippet" is generous. The entire length of the footage from start to finish is less than twelve seconds. In the footage, the camera pans across patrons in the club during the first half of the footage, and then focuses on the band while it's playing. The camera focuses on a saxophone player for a while before panning over to the guitarist. The guitarist—the last

[815] Victor Pearlin, electronic communication with Steve Franz. January 8, 2002; and John Tefteller, electronic communication with Steve Franz. January 8, 2002.

[816] Eliot Williams, electronic communication. 24 November 1995.

[817] LeBlanc, telephone interview, 7 June 1996.

member of the band to appear in the shot—can only be seen for a *few frames* (not even one whole entire second). The film is in such poor condition that it is virtually impossible to make out *who* it is, although in slow motion one can definitely see the hands of the guitarist move up and down (Unfortunately, the end credits shed no additional light in helping to identify the band, the guitarist, or the source of the footage). It is slightly difficult to imagine that Williams may have casually seen this footage on TV and recognized Elmore so quickly, as I had the benefit of viewing the footage frame-by-frame in slow motion over and over again and could not make a determination. It would have been easy enough to simply ask Robert Palmer about it, but unfortunately, he has since deceased.[818]

Second, there was a huge controversy over an alleged appearance in film by Robert Johnson. Had this actually been the case (it later turned out that the footage dated from a few years *after* Johnson's death), it would have ranked as one of the greatest blues discoveries of all time. With that in mind, if the Elmore James film really had been found and used by a group as notable as the Rolling Stones—or in a TV documentary aired in two continents—I think *maybe* I would have heard something about it. Stranger things have definitely happened though—just look at the recent release on the Flyright label of private recordings John Lee Hooker made more than fifty years ago, originally recorded by someone who used to live in Detroit, but moved to Czechoslovakia forty years ago!

Perhaps the last word on this subject belongs to researcher/author Paul Vernon. Judging by the title of his 1999 book, *African-American Blues, Rhythm and Blues, Gospel and Zydeco on Film and Video, 1926-1997,* Vernon is, perhaps, the world's premiere authority on the subject of blues artists appearing in film. Researched over the course of twenty years and extensively cross-referenced and indexed, an entry for Elmore James does not appear in Vernon's book (either as an artist or as an accompanist). Elmore fans will surely watch with keen interest as updates and corrections to Vernon's work become available.[819]

---

818 Alan Lewens and Karen Walsh, prods., *Rock & Roll—Episode 5: Crossroads.* WGBH/BBC, 1995.

819 Paul Vernon, *African-American Blues, Rhythm and Blues, Gospel and Zydeco on Film and Video, 1926-1997.* Brookfield, Vermont: Ashgate Publishing, 1999, ix, 139, 385. This book was also published in the U.K. by Ashgate Publishing at Aldershot, Hants, England.

Note: According to Bill Greensmith, "Lots of silent footage shot by drummer Sam Lay, mostly in Chicago, is coming out of the woodwork of both known and unknown/unidentifiable artists. Elmore is not known to exist on this footage." (Greensmith, personal communication, 27 December 2001)

APPENDIX TWO

DISCOGRAPHY

Note: This is the full text to the 1994 edition. Only minor edits have been made.

Introduction to the 1994 edition

"What are you going to do with that?" queried Frank Scott when I told him that I had been working on an update to the Elmore James Discography. "I dunno," I said, "maybe publish it." "Well, we all love Elmore," he objectively observed. So it would seem. Rocketing into the national spotlight with 1992's major label, big corporate, big-promotional-budget effort, it seems that after 40 years since "Dust My Broom" first cracked the R&B charts, Elmore had finally got his fifteen minutes of fame. And deservedly so. Behind the curtain of the Time-Warner media blitz, scholarly research on the Broomduster has reached the proverbial fever pitch of "Elmore's Contribution to Jazz." In the United States, Walter Devenne and others were spending countless hours painstakingly screening reels of tape from practically every New York studio Bobby Robinson ever set foot in. Marc Ryan published an anticipated, much-needed tome on Trumpet Records, complete with a label discography. Meanwhile in England, Ray Topping was working on finding every last scrap of Elmore audio he could find in the old Modern Records files. During all this excitement, Vee-Jay records quietly emerged from the dust and started reissuing CDs. Although Elmore passed away more than thirty years ago, it would seem there could be no better time for Elmore James than now. The 1990s have indeed witnessed the resurrection of Elmore James.

About The Recordings

Elmore James was active as a recording musician between 1951 and 1963. This was a period of time that witnessed great improvements in audio technology. By the time of Elmore's last session in 1963, multi-track taping— a principle still used today—had been around for a few years.

In 1951, though, audio tape was not a proven, time-tested recording method. So Elmore recorded his first single in the same manner that blues recordings had been made for decades—direct to an acetate master disc. Scott's Radio Service in Jackson, Mississippi was using the 'Sonic Disc' process on 5 August 1951 when "Dust My Broom" was waxed. Once a final take was in the can, a metal "mother" could be made from the precious acetate. "No editing was possible," commented Trumpet Records chronicler Marc Ryan, "so you had to have a perfect performance in order to have a record." Lillian McMurry, proprietor of Trumpet Records, was not in the habit of saving alternate takes, finding the "less-than-perfect" performances encumbering. Two sessions of Elmore James accompanying Sonny Boy Williamson in early 1951 were not up to McMurry's tough standards, and were subsequently destroyed.

Elmore's first session for Modern Records, Inc. happened during one of their legendary field trips through Mississippi. Modern's talent scout, Ike Turner, recalled in a 1992 interview "If we [Turner and Modern producer/executive Joe Bihari] couldn't get to a studio in Memphis or use a radio station, we'd give somebody a bottle of whiskey to let us use their living room to record in." In this instance, Modern rented space from a juke joint—probably the Club Bizarre in Canton—and hooked up a portable Magnecord tape recorder to the P.A. system. The Magnecord "was [Joe Bihari's] favourite thing to use on the road and it had four inputs for mikes," Modern votary Ray Topping said lately. "That was the first mobile one, where the earlier tape machines were too big and clumsy to take out."

When Elmore's exclusive contract with Trumpet supposedly came due in the Fall of 1952, Joe Bihari decided it was a good time to get Elmore back in the studio. Rather than risk the wrath of Mrs. McMurry again—who quickly found out about Elmore's first Modern date and filed a lawsuit—Bihari quietly held the session in Chicago. He then sent the tapes to his brother Lester, in Memphis, to help him start a new label. "Les Bihari hits the market shortly with a new recording company 'Meteor'" reported a November 1952 *Billboard* magazine. "The label cut its first sessions a few days ago. Four sides were made in the record time of 22 minutes only using four people." "I told Joe [Bihari] about that," Ray Topping recalled, "and he said it was bullshit; he said it took Elmore twenty-two minutes to get a song together.... Lester ... used to like thinking up stories like that, to exaggerate things...." After "I Believe" smashed the R&B markets in early 1953, "I think Joe and Jules Bihari decided they had to have this man on *their* label now, completely." Topping theorized. Subsequently, Elmore was switched to Joe's new endeavor, the Flair label (a subsidiary label of Modern).

Elmore's next seven sessions (including one for Chess Records) took place at Chicago's acclaimed Universal Recording Studios. Joe Bihari "said that he liked recording Elmore in Chicago most of all because he used the Universal Studios there," remembered Topping. "He said it was a magnificent studio...." Malcolm Chisholm and Bruce Swedien were two engineers/mixers who worked at Universal during its 1950s hey-day, and recalled recently what made it special. "Bill Putnam, the legendary engineer and inventor who operated Universal, had built all the consoles and microphone pre-amps himself, and they sounded just incredible!" noted Swedien. "You could look in *Billboard* during the mid-50's and, on a regular basis, three to five of the Top Ten hits would have been recorded in Chicago at Universal," offered Chisholm.

Located originally in the Civic Opera Building, Universal enjoyed facilities at East Ontario in the early '50s, and then at 46 East Walton after 1957. Universal had three studio rooms, and Putnam himself usually mixed top-name sessions in the large Studio A with artists like Duke Ellington and Count Basie. "For the most part, I cut the blues sessions in Studio B, the small room." said Chisholm. By the late '50s, Universal was "beginning to experiment with three-track recording, stereo recording and over-dubbing," Swedien remembers, "but all blues sessions would probably have been done in mono." Some of Elmore's greatest early sides, such as "Hawaiian Boogie", "Make A Little Love" and "Sho Nuff I Do" were blessed with the full, rich ambience that is characteristic of the Universal sound.

In June 1954, Modern Records was putting the finishing touches on their new 5000 square foot studio complex at 9317 W. Washington Boulevard, in Culver City, California (a suburb of Los Angeles). The new location was to be flushed out with "Ampex tape machines, Altec Lansing sound systems and an RCA mixing panel," the R&B trade press reported. Elmore visited the studio later that summer, and with members of the Maxwell Davis Orchestra in support, they cut six tough sides. Sadly, 9317 W. Washington was recently paved over, and a building no longer exists at that site any more. An exhaustive search of the Los Angeles musicians' union files indicates that Modern Records never filed any formal paperwork on the session—Elmore's only California studio date.

One small mystery is Elmore's Summer 1955 New Orleans session. Joe Bihari said that he recorded Elmore at J & M studios during a trip he made in August, 1955. The trip in reference was for a presentation the Biharis made to a New Orleans Dee-Jay on 11 August. The first single from this session, Flair 1074 ("Dust My Blues"/"I Was A Fool"), had already been *reviewed* in the R&B trade mags by 6 August. Although singles could be rushed for release in a pinch, it seems doubtful Bihari could have rushed it this fast.

For Elmore's last session with Modern, they returned in January 1956 to Universal Studios, Chicago, with a core group of Broomdusters backing. The Bihari's dropped Elmore as an artist after issuing the only single from the session—"Wild About You" (Modern 983). Although lack of sales is the common reason cited for the axing, that didn't stop Modern from issuing eight more 45s and four albums worth of Broomduster material during the 1960s. Modern Records changed headquarters many times during their tenure, and as a result the master tapes to almost a dozen singles have been lost from Elmore's early recording career.

Mel London, the Windy City entrepreneur behind such labels as Age, All Points, Mel and Mel-Lon began operations of his very first effort, Chief Records, in 1957. The 25 year old London had a knack for getting attention from the trade press that year, even though the label's first release—"Man From the Island" by Mel London—only received a rating of one-star ("fair"). His next release, by Elmore James ("The 12 Year Old Boy"/ "Coming Home"), generated considerably more attention (and a rating of three-stars, "very good"). Enough attention so that a big independent label like Vee-Jay Records took notice and struck a national distribution deal. Elmore had two sessions with London, and his work presented a raw, nightclub-edged tone that had not been present since his earliest Meteor and Flair sides. Before London died in May 1975, he too got a lot of mileage out of the Elmore material. "Cry For Me Baby" was released no less than six times as a 45 (on Chief, Vee-Jay, U.S.A., S&M, M-Pac, and Mel) and all seven Elmore sides for Chief have appeared on various albums and compilations. London's frequent reissuing may have also been the direct cause of how he wound up losing all of his Elmore master tapes, as was reported in a 1972 *Living Blues* news blurb.

Six of Elmore's last seven sessions were held for Bobby Robinson's New York based labels, Fire, Enjoy, and Fury. The first session was held in Chicago in November 1959 after Elmore and Robinson met by chance in a club. Although today the relationship has been much heralded by critics and the press, as well as resulting in some of Elmore's greatest platters, it seems that Robinson wasn't very happy with the initial results. For Elmore's first Fire release, Robinson used the twangy, rolling instrumental "Bobby's Rock" backed with "Make My Dreams Come True," which he dubbed off an old copy of Flair 1031. It wasn't until four months later that Fire 1016 was issued, and "The Sky Is Crying" brought Elmore his first R&B chart action of the 1960s. The two remaining titles from the session weren't released for another five years.

After a moonlight gig with Chess Records in April 1960, Elmore's next two sessions with Robinson were held in New York City at Beltone Studios. "When I brought Elmore into New York, he didn't know a soul but me," recalled Robinson in 1992. "He just brought himself and his guitar, and we went right into the studio.... I called Beltone and told them, 'Whatever you have booked, cancel it. I want the whole night.'

We began that session at eight o'clock in the evening and came out at eight o'clock in the morning."

Elmore's fourth Fire session, held at New Orleans' J & M Studios, was "what I call 'candlelight' sessions," Sam Myers stated in a late interview. "The studio didn't have any lights on in the office. They kept the lights down low, because they were dodging the union.... Back in New Orleans during that time, the union was very heavy." Elmore was the main dodger, having been blacklisted earlier that spring for non-payment of dues. "It was interesting," Robinson remembered, "because this time Elmore knew all the musicians, and I didn't! ....After the New York sessions, Elmore went back to Mississippi and formed a little combo like the one he'd had in Chicago...." With the engineering experience of studio-owner Cosimo Matassa, the date produced one of Elmore's more popular tunes, "Shake Your Moneymaker", which has sparked life on juke-boxes with no less than six different 45 releases.

In February 1963, Robinson held his last two Elmore sessions at A-1 Studios in Manhattan. "Herb [Abramson] was the engineer .... and Elmore brought two guys up with him from Mississippi." stated Robinson. "It was kind of a thrown together session, wasn't planned as much, you know?" he told blues researcher Dick Shurman. The sessions were more or less a greatest-hits run through for Elmore, with only a couple of memorable moments. "I would say he was a little below peak performance," cited Robinson, "maybe it was because we didn't have any real exciting new material...." Nevertheless, a couple of nice singles ensued—notably "It Hurts Me Too" (Enjoy 2015) which charted for eight weeks, peaking at #25 and #106 on the R&B and Pop charts, respectively.

Walter Devenne, chief engineer for Relic Records, reports that Robinson recorded virtually everything in stereo as early as 1958. By 1963, Robinson would commonly roll a four-track master, a two-track stereo, and a mono safety take simultaneously during recording. In 1992, Devenne found one of the original stereo reels from the 13 February 1963 session, marked "Reel One of Two." "Reel two," said Devenne, "has not been found." Unfortunately, the hopes of finding *all* the remaining stereo tapes have been exhausted by Devenne, who said they looked everywhere they could in New York for the multi-track tapes that Robinson evidently cut during his six Elmore sessions.

About This Discography

The subsequent session listings, arranged chronologically, all have one thing in common: Elmore James. Every session Elmore James ever played on as a leader or accompanying on guitar are included, no matter how obscure. Studio location information, when deemed reliable, is also included.

Almost all song titles appear exactly as they do on issue of first release, with major exceptions noted in the text. The list of single (45 and 78 rpm) and album (LP and CD) releases following each song title have been arranged in chronological order, with the first single or album listed being the first issued source of that song or take. Precedence is given to readability rather than absolute chronological order, however, so in cases where the list of releases is lengthy, the order should be considered generally chronological. Release dates for all known singles and virtually every album are published chronologically after the session information.

In an attempt to aid readability and ease of understanding, no record label names have been abbreviated, except where recognition is standard (i.e., "Checker" is not shortened to "Ckr" as is common in other discographies, but "P-Vine Special" is listed as the widely accepted, commonly understood "P-Vine").

I have tried to be as thorough as possible, which is sometimes difficult, given the relative short life span of some LPs and CDs, and in some cases, the record companies themselves. Almost all of the major, important Elmore James albums are included in the discography, and most of the significant compilations and "various artists" CDs. No cassettes are listed in the discography. In the case where an album has been issued simultaneously as a CD and an LP, the CD listing is given priority. This is not due to any inherent bias I might have against vinyl (which I do not), but because of the continued popularity of the disc format.

Equivalent issues. An album is considered to be a replacement when it exactly duplicates the songs from the original issue. For example, Arhoolie CD 310 is not considered to be an equivalent issue of Arhoolie LP 2020, because the CD contains bonus tracks the LP doesn't, even though a majority of the songs are the same. However, Arhoolie LP 2020 is itself an equivalent of Blues Classics LP 9, because the songs are exactly the same (the fact that the title and the cover are different does not matter). Equivalent issue LPs are not listed in the discography, and only a few CD equivalents have been left in the list (primarily because of their general availability as of this writing). For a complete list of equivalents, see the table that follows the chronological lists of singles and albums.

Other tables included, such as the *Chronological List of First Issue for LP / CD tracks & Alternate Takes* has been included to give an overview of how the body of Elmore James material evolved into the form we know it today. The *Authorship of Songs* will hopefully aid future research, as this seems to be a topic of wide dissension. For the latter, I have used the standard research methodology initiated by Rhino Records, which states whoever is credited on the first issued source of a song is who gets the credit. Since Rhino is in the music reissue business, I figure they ought to know.

Finally, I have printed a complete list of source material, lest anyone whose previous work that has contributed to the accuracy and thoroughness of this document go unheeded. An index of musicians rounds out the discography.

It is my sincere hope that this booklet aids your enjoyment and understanding of the late, fantastically great Elmore James!

Introduction to the 2003 edition

I assume that many readers of the previous version of my Elmore discography will have questions, either about old details or revisions that are present in this update. Here are a few that I thought might be of the greatest interest. In the meantime, all are encouraged to visit the online Elmore discography at Görgen Antonsson's website (http://www.novia.net/~cedmunds/elmore/index.html), which is not only much more likely to be updated more frequently than is possible with this discography, but which also goes into much greater depth into European issues than I have been able to do here. And now, on to the questions.

Q. How did you arrive at a date for Elmore's first session with Bobby Robinson?

A. Robinson has repeatedly stated over the years that it was raining "cats and dogs" that particular day—a kind of dreary, all day type of rain is the impression he's given. If his memory is correct about the course of events (and as far as this one minute detail is concerned, he has never really changed his story about it), then the most likely date for this rehearsal/session to have taken place was on Tuesday, 3 November 1959 or Wednesday, 4 November 1959, when close to two inches of rain fell on the Chicago-land area in a forty-eight hour period (0.68" and 1.18" respectively—which accounts for almost three quarters of Chicago's total precipitation for the entire month of November 1959). In my collection, I have a copy of Fire 1011 (the first 45 from this session to be released) on which a DJ/record industry type person noted that he received his copy on December 21, 1959. This information would tend to reinforce the idea of a 3 November/4 November session date as being believable. I would greatly appreciate it if someone out there, in possession of a copy of Fire 1011 with a "Delta Number" (a five digit number found in the dead wax of the 45 with a "Δ" preceding it), would contact me.

Q. How did you arrive at a date for Elmore's second session with Bobby Robinson?

A. Elmore's BMI contract (discussed earlier in the book) strongly suggests that the document was executed in New York. Since we can already place Elmore in New York City for May, 1960, for his recording session with Bobby Robinson, it makes sense to this author that Robinson would have used the opportunity to get Elmore's BMI contract executed *while* he was in town. Robinson was certainly no stranger to the idea of how hard it was to get a hold of and find Elmore James. Therefore, it suggests to me that registering with BMI was something that, perhaps, they did together before the session (I say before the session, because why only just the four songs? If the document had been executed *after* his May 1960 session with Robinson, they, perhaps, would have had additional tunes to register with BMI).

Other pieces of evidence that might place Elmore in New York City for the week of 23 May 1960 would be what was happening to Elmore down at his Local 208 union in Chicago. Things had not gone well for Elmore at the 21 April 1960 board meeting (they decided to suspend him and levied a fine of $300 against him). Elmore's first course of action about all this was to go down to the union headquarters one week later and pay $2 in taxes that he owed (to say the least, not exactly what the board had told him to do). The next entry in Elmore's union file, chronologically speaking, was on Friday, 20 May 1960, when the fine of $300 was officially entered as a debit on his account (for those who are curious, Elmore's union file is essentially a "balance sheet" relating to his musical activities—i.e., membership dues, taxes, fines, etc.—and lists debits in one column and credits in the other; all entries are date stamped). One has to wonder, given that the board had waited almost a month to "officially" register the fine against his account, if they weren't trying to give him some kind of a grace period to pay it off? If that was indeed the case, Elmore chose not to avail himself of it; perhaps he figured that if he couldn't work in Chicago because of his suspension, then maybe it was a good time to leave town and find work elsewhere, say, a nice faraway place like Cleveland. (Elmore's Chicago union file courtesy of Patrick LeBlanc and the Estate of Elmore James).

Q. Speaking of Bobby Robinson, how come Fire LP 102 isn't listed in this discography?

A. That's a good question, and I'm glad you asked. Throughout my course of research on Elmore James, I was never able to find any concrete evidence indicating that it ever actually existed, i.e., as a bona fide LP issued by Bobby Robinson while the Fire label was originally active, in the 1959 to 1962 time frame. I own a copy of Fire LP 102, and it is a Buster Brown album, *The New King of the Blues* (it was probably issued in 1960). Interestingly, while my copy states "Fire LP 102" on the outside jacket, the labels on the record give "Fire LP 101." To further confuse things, there are two different versions of the Buster Brown album—two identically titled albums with different track selections and different covers. Another primary piece of evidence pointing to the non-existence of Fire LP 102 as an Elmore James album is its failure to show up in *any* of the early Elmore James discographies from the 1960s. It isn't until we get into later discographies (from the 1980s, for instance) that we start seeing its name pop up occasionally.

My best guess is that if there ever was a Fire LP 102, it was probably a specialty LP reissue from the late 1970s or early 1980s—to illustrate my point, for example, P-Vine's Elmore James 3 LP box set comes to mind (*Something Inside of Me / The Complete Fire-Enjoy Sessions;* P-Vine LP 6005/6006/6007, 1984)—while it was P-Vine in Japan who issued the set, the actual record labels themselves bear reproductions of Robinson's distinctive "Fire" logo. Perhaps it was a similar case with an Elmore James version of Fire LP 102—as I said—if indeed it ever existed at all (As an additional note, Alan Balfour has recalled seeing, in the late 1970s or early 1980s, a series of bootleg Fire albums issued complete with facsimile covers).

With no significant evidence to verify its existence (a record review or advertisement would be nice, for instance), it has not been included in this discography.

Q. Why wasn't Enjoy 2015 listed for "Bleeding Heart" in your 1994 discography?

A. This was another case where I had some trouble proving its existence based on the research material I was using at the time. It wasn't until after the discography had come out (in February 1994) that I was actually able to find a copy, and then, lo and behold, it started showing up in earlier discographies when I was doing final research for my master's thesis later that fall. It's included in this update, and there's a label shot of it too.

Q. Does Syl Johnson really play guitar on Chief 7006?

A. Listen to the guitar solo on Billy Boy Arnold's "Prisoner's Plea" (Vee-Jay 260) and get back to me.

Q. What about the Sam Myers Fury single?

A. If you're referring to my first Elmore discography in the liner notes to Relic CD 7040, that was a mistake based on my misreading of Myers' comments in his *Living Blues* interview. Elmore James does NOT play guitar on it (It's still a great single, however).

Q. Does Elmore James really play guitar on "Have You Heard About The Farmer's Daughter?" that was issued on Acoustic Archives CD 701 in 1990?

A. There is an interesting controversy over that particular recording. For the whole story, see the "Letters to the Editor" pages of *Juke Blues* magazine, number 23 (Summer 1991), pages 21 and 23. There you will find a letter from Marc Ryan (compiler/producer of the Acoustic Archives Trumpet label series) offering his evidence, and responses from Mark Harris, Warren Wilson, and Cilla Huggins, who are convinced, on an aural basis, that it is indeed Elmore James playing guitar on this particular recording (you can also read Cilla Huggins' review of the disc, from *Juke Blues* 21 (Autumn 1990), on pages 33 and 34).

Q. Why all the fuss over the alternate take versus the original take of "Wild About You" that you mentioned in one of those footnotes of yours? Isn't the alternate just as good as the original 78/45 rpm version?

A. In my opinion, no it's not. The original version of "Wild About You" is one of my favorite Elmore records of all time, and deserves to be more widely known. While the alternate take is certainly a worthy effort, the original version is simply superb, and should not be relegated to its current obscure status.

Q. How come you didn't list the 4 December 1951 Sonny Boy Williamson session in your 1994 discography, where Elmore plays guitar on some of the titles?

A. Again, the research material I was relying on at the time did not indicate that this was the case. My primary source of information on the Trumpet sessions was Marc Ryan's and Bill Daniels' discography in *Trumpet Records: An Illustrated History with Discography.* Since Marc had had access to the Trumpet Archives at Ole Miss, as well as the opportunity to interview Lillian McMurry on numerous occasions, I felt he really ought to be in the best position to know all the gritty details.

However, if one goes strictly on the basis of aural evidence, there is an undeniable continuity in the sound of the guitar from Sonny Boy's 5 August 1951 session that is also present in four titles recorded at the 4 December 1951 session as well—"She Brought Life Back To The Dead" (Trumpet 215, both 78 and 45 rpm versions); "Stop Now Baby" and "Mr. Down Child" (Trumpet 168); and "Too Close Together" (Trumpet 212). For the sake of comparison, take three titles on which Elmore James does not appear, and notice how different the guitar sounds—i.e., "Eyesight To The Blind" and "Crazy About You Baby" (Trumpet 129) and "Nine Below Zero" (Trumpet 166), and I think you'll begin to see what I mean.

Okay, one last question, and then I'm outta here.

Q. How complete is this discography?

A. As complete as I can make it at this time. As much as I would like to own a copy of every record, tape, album, CD, 45 and 78 that Elmore ever played a lick on, it's just not economically feasible for me at this time. All things considered, though, I believe I have hit almost all the "high spots" that one is likely to run into, but sorry, how many run-of-the-mill blues compilations with "The Sky Is Crying" on it does one person really need to own? In the meantime, be sure to check out Görgen Antonsson's very thorough Elmore James discography online at «http://www.novia.net/~cedmunds/elmore/index.html». Fans of Chicago blues in general will also find quite helpful The Red Saunders Research Foundation website at «http://hubcap.clemson.edu/~campber/rsrf.html», which features painstakingly detailed discographical research about many of the important independent Chicago labels of the postwar era—such as Aristocrat, Chance, Checker, Chess, J.O.B., Parrot, and United/States—as well as numerous label shots, extensive session notes, and short biographies of the artists who recorded for them.

Key to Abbreviations:

alt	=	alternate
as	=	alto sax
b	=	bass
bar s	=	baritone sax
bass g	=	bass guitar
BM	=	Blues Masterworks
CD	=	Compact Disc
dm	=	drums
EP	=	Extended Play
g	=	guitar
gtrs	=	guitars
hca	=	harmonica
inst	=	instrumental
LP	=	Long Play Record Album
No	=	number
p	=	piano
poss	=	possibly
PR / PRO	=	Promotional (LP/CD)
prob	=	probably
tk	=	take
tks	=	takes
tmb	=	trombone
tp	=	trumpet
ts	=	tenor sax
vo	=	vocal / vocals
vsn	=	version

U.S. State Abbreviations :

CA	=	California
IL	=	Illinois
LA	=	Louisiana
MS	=	Mississippi
NY	=	New York
TN	=	Tennessee

I.S.O. Country Code Abbreviations :

AT	=	Austria
AU	=	Australia
BR	=	Brazil
CH	=	Switzerland
DE	=	Germany
FR	=	France
GB	=	Great Britain
IT	=	Italy
JP	=	Japan
NL	=	Netherlands
PT	=	Portugal
UK	=	United Kingdom

Jules Bihari Defendant in $1 Mil Action

HOLLYWOOD, Feb. 9.—Jules Bihari, of Modern Records, Inc., was served with notice of a $1,001,000 damages suit instituted by Mrs. W. F. McMurray, owner of Diamond Records, Jackson, Miss. Mrs. McMurray alleges that Jules Bihari infringed upon her artist's agreement with Leroy Holmes and His Darktown Boys. She asks for $1,000, alleging that this amount has been spent in promoting and cutting the ork, which she had signed previously, and asks the $1,000,000 alleging damages done to the group by Bihari, which she claims will make it impossible for her to utilize the group in the future.

Bihari told The Billboard that he recorded J. W. Walker, a member of the group, as soloist with another band eight months ago and has had Walker under contract since that time. The suit by Mrs. McMurray was filed in U. S. District Court in Mississippi.

Don't Miss These 5 Potential Hits!

FOLK

TR #177—"TRIFLIN' ON ME"—by JIMMY SWAN
45 x 177

NEW RELEASE! You've been waiting for this—ANOTHER HIT by Jimmy Swan.
"I Love You Too Much"

TR #192—"BY AND BY"—By "TAG" WILLIAMS
45 x 192

A NEW RELEASE by a new artist—and he's REALLY GOOD. Don't miss this.
"Island of Heartaches"

RHYTHM AND BLUES

TR #187—"STRANGE KINDA' FEELIN'"—By "TINY" KENNEDY. Already a NUMBER 1 HIT in NEW YORK, ATLANTA and NEW ORLEANS.

"Early in the Morning, Baby"—Tiny gives out on a real Sock blues with "Elmer" the famous disc jockey rooster crowing.

TR #166—"MIGHTY LONG TIME"—By "SONNY BOY" WILLIAMSON
45 x 166

This NEW RELEASE by "Sonny Boy" is terrific—different enough to change the whole rhythm and blues field. Back side is good, too—a fine combination.
"Nine Below Zero"—A real bar room jive side.

TR #146—"I BELIEVE (DUST MY BROOM)" THE ORIGINAL BY ELMORE JAMES! ORDER NOW!

Free samples to D.J.'s

TRUMPET RECORDS

DIAMOND RECORD CO. · BOX 2221 · JACKSON, MISS.

Some of Lillian McMurry's tangling with the Bihari brothers—legal and otherwise—involved them recording her artists, and capitalizing on material that she felt Trumpet Records had a copyright on, such as the "original" version of "Dust My Broom." On the left: 16 February 1952 Billboard; Right: 7 February 1953 Billboard.

Elmore James: An Illustrated Career Discography

4 January 1951 • Trumpet Records • Scott Radio Service • Jackson, MS
Sonny Boy Williamson (vo, hca) Elmore James, Joe Willie Wilkins (gtrs) Willie Love (p) Joe Dyson (dm)

DRC 15	**Eyesight To The Blind**	Trumpet 129[820]
DRC 16	**Crazy About You Baby**	Trumpet 129
DRC 17	Stop Crying	unissued
DRC 18	Do It If You Wanta	unissued
DRC 19	Cool, Cool Blues	unissued
DRC 20	Come On Back Home	unissued
DRC 21	I Cross My Heart	unissued
DRC 22	West Memphis Blues	unissued

10 July 1951 • Trumpet Records • Scott Radio Service • Jackson, MS
Sonny Boy Williamson (vo, hca) Elmore James (gtr) Henry Reed (b) Joe Dyson (dm)

DRC 17	Stop Crying	unissued
DRC 18	Do It If You Wanta	unissued
DRC 19	Cool, Cool Blues	unissued
DRC 20	Come On Back Home	unissued
DRC 21	I Cross My Heart	unissued
DRC 22	West Memphis Blues	unissued
DRC 45	Sonny Boy's Christmas Blues	unissued
DRC 46	Pontiac Blues	unissued

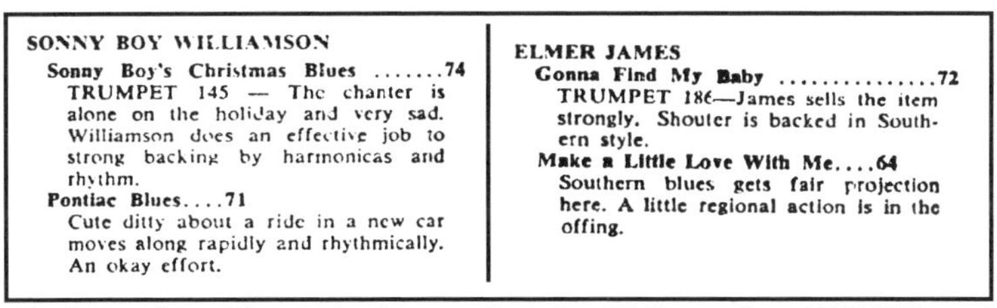
SONNY BOY WILLIAMSON
Sonny Boy's Christmas Blues 74
TRUMPET 145 — The chanter is alone on the holiday and very sad. Williamson does an effective job to strong backing by harmonicas and rhythm.
Pontiac Blues....71
Cute ditty about a ride in a new car moves along rapidly and rhythmically. An okay effort.

ELMER JAMES
Gonna Find My Baby 72
TRUMPET 186—James sells the item strongly. Shouter is backed in Southern style.
Make a Little Love With Me....64
Southern blues gets fair projection here. A little regional action is in the offing.

Reviews of two Trumpet releases, from the 20 December 1952 Billboard

[820] Note: Masters to DRC15 and DRC16 were lost in a fire. Williamson recut the titles (as DRC15-2 and DRC16-2) for Trumpet 129 on 12 March 1951 without Elmore James on guitar. No copies of the first pressing of Trumpet 129 have yet been recovered. See Ryan, *Trumpet Records: An Illustrated History with Discography,* 15, 17, 82.

25 July 1951 • Trumpet Records • Scott Radio Service • Jackson, MS

Willie Love (vo, p) Elmore James, Joe Willie Wilkins (gtrs; vo chorus -1) Otis Green (ts-2) prob Alex Wallace (dm)

DRC 48	**Everybody's Fishing**	-1	Trumpet 147; Oldie Blues LP 2825; Acoustic Archives CD 702; Collectables CD 5240; P-Vine CD 2184; Purple Pyramid CD 0832-2
DRC 50	**My Own Boogie**	-2	Trumpet 147; Oldie Blues LP 2825; Acoustic Archives CD 702; Collectables CD 5240; P-Vine CD 2184; Purple Pyramid CD 0832-2

NOTE: Either DRC 49 [unknown title] or DRC 51 [unaccounted for] might possibly have been an earlier waxing of "Nelson Street Blues." Little Milton Campbell has said that Willie Love recorded "Nelson Street Blues" on two different ocassions, and that the first recording was made in Jackson, MS with Elmore James on guitar. The second version of "Nelson Street Blues" was released as Trumpet 175, recorded on 1 December 1951, with Campbell on guitar. See "Little Milton: Living Blues *Interview" by Jim O'Neal and Patty Johnson,* Living Blues *114 (March/April 1994) pp 23-24, and Marc Ryan in* Trumpet Records: An Illustrated History with Discography, *p 86.*

5 August 1951 • Trumpet Records • Scott Radio Service • Jackson, MS

Sonny Boy Williamson (vo, hca) Elmore James, Joe Willie Wilkins (gtrs) Willie Love (p) Leonard Ware (b) unknown (poss Frock O'Dell) (dm)

DRC 17	**Stop Crying**	Trumpet 140; Blues Classics LP 9; Arhoolie CD 310
DRC 18	**Do It If You Wanta**	Trumpet 139; Blues Classics LP 9; Arhoolie CD 310
DRC 19	**Cool, Cool Blues**	Trumpet 139; Blues Classics LP 9; Arhoolie CD 310
DRC 20	**Come On Back Home**	Trumpet 140; Blues Classics LP 9; Arhoolie CD 310
DRC 21	**I Cross My Heart**	Trumpet 144; Blues Classics LP 9; Arhoolie CD 310
DRC 22	**West Memphis Blues**	Trumpet 144; Blues Classics LP 9; Arhoolie CD 310
DRC 45	**Sonny Boy's Christmas Blues**	Trumpet 145; Blues Classics LP 9; Arhoolie CD 310
DRC 46	**Pontiac Blues**	Trumpet 145; Blues Classics LP 9; Arhoolie CD 310, CD 102; Ace CD 590

Same Session

Elmore James (vo, g) Sonny Boy Williamson (hca) Leonard Ware (b) poss Frock O'Dell (dm)

DRC 53	**Dust My Broom** (I Believe My Time Ain't Long)	Trumpet 146[821]; Ace 508; Sue LP 921; Blues Classics LP 5; Jewel 764, LP 5015, CD 5015; Teem LP 5005; Up Front LP 122; Vivid Sound LP 1008; Ronn 96, CD 8016; Charly LP 1008, CDRED Box 4-1, CD DIG 3-1, CPBOX 301-1; RST/Blues Documents LP 1; Arhoolie CD 310; P-Vine CD 1883, CD 2108; Rhino CD 71190, CD 79803; Ace Box CD 4-1, CD 583; Opal CD 106; Blue Sun CD 2000

[821] Mike Leadbitter reported the following in the February 1966 issue of *Blues Unlimited:* "Bruce Bromberg has found a copy of Elmore's Trumpet on which 'Broom' has the issue number as 143 not 146! However, 'Catfish' is still 146." See Mike Leadbitter, "Post-War Discographical Comment," *Blues Unlimited* 30 (February 1966), 13.

22 October 1951 • Trumpet Records • WHBQ Radio Studios • Memphis, TN

Jesse Tiny Kennedy (vo) Elmore James (g) unknown (as, b, dr, p)

	Early In The Morning, Baby	unissued
	Strange Kinda Feeling	unissued
	Have You Heard About The Farmer's Daughter?	Acoustic Archives CD 701; Collectables CD 5242

Note: for more info surrounding the controversy over the details of this session, see Juke Blues *23 (Summer 1991): 21-23.*

4 December 1951 • Trumpet Records • Cedars of Lebanon Club • Jackson, MS

Sonny Boy Williamson (vo, hca) Cliff Givens (b vo)

DRC 88	**Mighty Long Time**	Trumpet 166; Blues Classics LP 9; Arhoolie CD 310; Blues Encore CD 52018; Deja Vu REDCD 25

Same session

Sonny Boy Williamson (vo, hca) Willie Love (p -1) Joe Willie Wilkins (gtr) Elmore James (gtr -2) Cliff Givens (b vo) Joe Dyson (dm -3)

DRC 89	**Nine Below Zero**	-1, -3	Trumpet 166; Blues Classics LP 9; Arhoolie CD 310; Deja Vu REDCD 25
DRC 90	**She Brought Life Back To The Dead**	-1, -2	Trumpet 215 (78 rpm issues only); Blues Classics LP 9; Arhoolie CD 310
45-DRC 90	**She Brought Life Back To The Dead** (alt tk)	-1, -2	Trumpet 215 (45 rpm issues only); Acoustic Archives CD 801
DRC 91	**Too Close Together**	-2, -3	Trumpet 212; Blues Classics LP 9; Arhoolie CD 310; Blue Sun CD 2000
DRC 92	**Stop Now Baby**	-2, -3	Trumpet 168; Blues Classics LP 9; Arhoolie CD 310; Deja Vu REDCD 25
DRC 93	**Mr. Down Child**	-2, -3	Trumpet 168; Blues Classics LP 9; Arhoolie CD 310; Deja Vu REDCD 25

25/26 January 1952 • Modern Records • prob Club Bizarre • Canton, MS
Elmore James (vo, g) Ike Turner (p) unknown (dm)

	Please Find My Baby (alt tk)(vsn 1)	Kent LP 9001; Vivid Sound/Globe LP 5004; Ace CD 258, Box CD 4-1
FL-147[822]	**Please Find My Baby**[823] (vsn 2)	Flair 1022; Blues Classics LP 15; Ace Box CD 4-1, CD 583, CD 813[824]; P-Vine CD 3038, CD 3742; Opal CD 106
(MR 5017)	Hawaiian Boogie (No 1)(inst)(without overdubs)[825]	unissued
	Take A Little Walk With Me	unissued (lost or destroyed)
	Dust My Broom	unissued (lost or destroyed)
FL-161	**Hand In Hand**	Flair 1031; Kent LP 9001; Vivid Sound/Globe LP 5004; Ace LP 112, Box CD 4-1, CD 583; P-Vine CD 1883, CD 2741, CD 3742; Opal CD 106

Note: See explanation under May 1953 session for FL-147 and MR 5017

prob Same Session
Elmore James (vo, g) Ike Turner (p) unknown (ts, b, dm)

MM 1783	**Long Tall Woman**	Ace Box CD 4-1, CD 813
	Rock My Baby Right (tk 1)	unissued (lost or destroyed)
FL-201	**Rock My Baby Right** (tk 2)	Flair 1048; Kent LP 9001; Ace LP 112, Box CD 4-1, CD 583; Deja Vu LP 2035[826]; Opal CD 106
	My Baby's Gone	Ace LP 68, Box CD 4-1
	One More Drink (tk 1)	Kent LP 9010; Ace Box CD 4-1
	One More Drink (tk 2)	Ace LP 68, Box CD 4-1

822 Also MM 1782 (see note under May 1953).

823 Guitar parts were spliced into Boyd Gilmore's "All In My Dreams" (Modern 872); later reissued in 1966 in the U.K. on pwb LP2, *Memphis...On Down;* in the U.S. on Kent LP 9009 and Kent LP 700; and finally on compact disc on P-Vine CD 3041). See Leadbitter & Slaven, *Blues Records 1943-1970,* 461-462.

824 As "My Baby's Gone."

825 Overdubbed with bass and additional drums May 1953. Overdubbed master was assigned matrix MR5017. The original version (without overdubbing) evidently has not survived.

826 As "Rock My Baby Tonight."

prob 22 November 1952 • Modern Records • Universal Recording Studios • Chicago, IL

Elmore James (vo, g) J.T. Brown (ts) Johnny Jones (p) Ransom Knowling (b) Odie Payne (dm)

MR 5000	**Baby, What's Wrong**	Meteor 5003; Flyright LP 4712; Ace LP 112, Box CD 4-1, CD 583; Deja Vu LP 2035; Route 16 CD 9007[827]; Opal CD 106
MR 5001	**I Believe**	Meteor 5000; Kent 508, LP 535, LP 9001; United LP 7754; Vivid Sound/Globe LP 5004; Ace LP 112, CD 192, Box CD 4-1, CD 583; Blues Encore CD 52006; Cascade Box CD 3-2; Rhino CD 71130; P-Vine CD 3742; Opal CD 106
MR 5002	**Sinful Women**[828]	Meteor 5003; Kent LP 9001; Vivid Sound/Globe LP 5004; Ace LP 112, Box CD 4-1, CD 583; Deja Vu LP 2035; Route 16 CD 9007; Cascade Box CD 3-1; P-Vine CD 1883, CD 3742; Opal CD 106
MR 5003	**I Held My Baby Last Night**	Meteor 5000; Kent LP 9001; Trip LP 9511; Vivid Sound/Globe LP 5004; Ace LP 112, Box CD 4-1, CD 583; Black Label CD 2001; P-Vine CD 1883, CD 3742; Opal CD 106

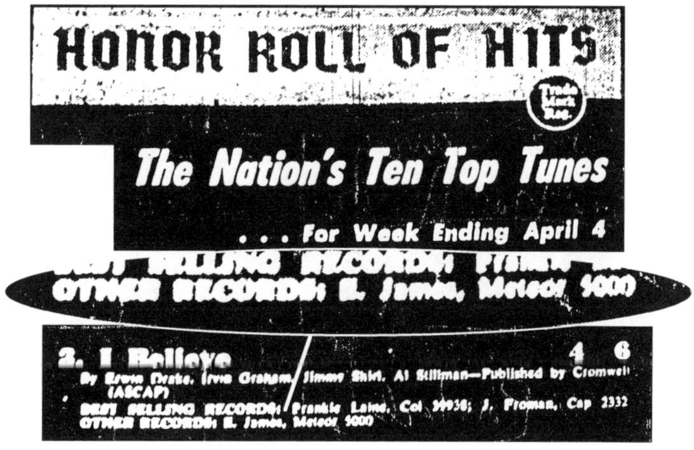

NEW RECORDS TO WATCH
Rhythm & Blues

ELMORE JAMES

I Believe—Meteor 5000—Initial release by label stacks up very strongly. James comes thru with a fine shout blues vocal over powerful ork backing.

ELMORE JAMES

I Believe 82
METEOR 5000 — Solid shouting by James of a powerful blues effort, to strong ork support. This is a potent side and coul'' crack thru as a big one for the warbler. A real coin-grabber.

I Held My Baby Last Night....77
James projects this slowly beat blues with great persuasive power for an impressive waxing. Side could stir up som- action.

I BELIEVE
Elmore James—Meteor 5000
On Chicago chart. Very strong in the South. Good actoin in New York and Philadelphia. Strong in St. Louis and beginning to build on Coast.

Various items about "I Believe." Above, Right: The "Honor Roll of Hits" page from 11 April 1953; Below, Left & Center: 3 January 1953; Below Right: 17 January 1953; all from Billboard.

---

827 Note: The outer tray cards identify this set as "That's Blues TB 201," however individual discs are actually labelled Route 16 CD 9005 (Disc 1) and Route 16 CD 9007 (Disc 2), respectively.

828 Often given as "Sinful Woman."

prob Same Session

J.T. Brown (vo -1, ts) Elmore James (g) Johnny Jones (p) Ransom Knowling (b) Odie Payne (dm)

MR 5004	**Round House Boogie** (inst)		Meteor 5001, 5024[829]; Flyright LP 4712; Krazy Kat LP 7420; Ace Box CD 4-1
MR 5005	**Kickin' The Blues Around** (inst)		Meteor 5001, 5024[830]; Flyright LP 4712; Krazy Kat LP 7420; Ace Box CD 4-1
MR 5006	**Sax-ony Boogie** (inst)		Meteor 5016; Flyright LP 4712; Krazy Kat LP 7420; Ace Box CD 4-1
MR 5007	**Dumb Woman Blues**	-1	Meteor 5016; Flyright LP 4712; Krazy Kat LP 7420; Ace Box CD 4-1

J.T. Brown: Meteor used a variety of pseudonyms on their releases.
The ad is from the 14 March 1953 Chicago Defender.

829 As "Sax Symphonic Boogie."

830 As "Flaming Blues."

Rhythm and Blues Tattler

Just about the time you think all the good disks are already on the market, up comes another good new release. Checker-777 is the new release you are going to hear about in the next few days. ELMO JAMES comes thru with two terrific sides on this one. The first, "Country Boogie," has that certain something you'll like—bounce. The second, "She Just Won't Do Right," is good coverage by James.

8 August 1953 Billboard

17 January 1953 • Chess Records • Universal Recording Studios • Chicago, IL
Elmore James (vo, g) J.T. Brown (ts) Johnny Jones (p) poss Ransom Knowling (b) Odie Payne (dm)

U 4321	**Country Boogie** (Tool Bag Boogie)(inst)	Checker 777; Chess LP 1537, LP 6641.125, CD 9114; Chess/Vogue CD 600119; Charly CDRED 36, CDRED Box 4-1
U 4322	**My Best Friend**	Blue Horizon LP 7-63204; Chess LP 1537, LP 6641.125, CD 9114; Chess/Vogue CD 600119; Charly CDRED 36, CDRED Box 4-1; Rhino CD 71190
U 4323	**I See My Baby**	Blue Horizon LP 7-63204; Chess LP 1537, LP 6641.125, LP 2-60012, CD 9114; Chess/Vogue CD 600119; Charly CDRED 36, CDRED Box 4 1
U 4324	**She Just Won't Do Right** (Dust My Broom)	Checker 777; Blue Horizon LP 7-63204[831]; Chess LP 1537, LP 6641.125, Chess LP 4010, LP 2-60012, CD 9114, CD 380 599-2[832]; Festival LP 1008; CBS LP 66278; Chess/Vogue CD 600048, CD 600119; Castle Communications CD 206[833]; Blues Collection CD 341; Charly CDRED 36, CDRED Box 4-1; Concept CD 0265; Marvel CD 725; MCA CD 140 069; LaserLight CD 12.336; The Hit Label CD 19
U 4325	**Whose Muddy Shoes**	Blue Horizon LP 7-63204; Chess LP 1537, LP 6641.125, CD 9114, CD 4-9340; Chess/Vogue CD 600048, CD 600119; Charly CDRED 36, CDRED Box 4-1; Blue Moon CD 4003

---

831 As "Going For Good."

832 Part of a 15 disc 1999 Italian box set numbered 3805962. Each disc of the set is individually numbered beginning with 380 597-2 and ending with 380 611-2.

833 Incorrectly labeled as recorded for the Fire label.

prob 1 April 1953 • Modern Records • Universal Recording Studios • Chicago, IL
Johnny Jones (vo, p) Elmore James (g) J.T. Brown (ts) Ransom Knowling (b) Odie Payne (dm)

FL-121	**Sweet Little Woman**	Flair 1010; Flyright LP 4712[834]; Ace LP 68, Box CD 4-1; Cascade LP 1010
FL-122	**I May Be Wrong**	Flair 1010; Flyright LP 4712; Ace LP 68, Box CD 4-1

prob Same Session • Modern Records • Universal Recording Studios • Chicago, IL
Elmore James (vo, g) Johnny Jones (p) J.T. Brown (ts) Ransom Knowling (b) Odie Payne (dm)

FL-123	**Early In The Morning**	Flair 1011; Modern 49; Kent LP 9010; Red Lightnin' LP 005; Ace LP 112, Box CD 4-2, CD 583; Deja Vu LP 2035; Route 16 CD 9007; P-Vine CD 3742; Opal CD 106
FL-124	**Hawaiian Boogie** (No 2)(inst)	Flair 1011; Kent LP 9010; Mamlish LP 3800; Red Lightnin' LP 005; Polydor LP 2383200; Ace LP 112, CD 192, CD 232, Box CD 4-2, CD 583; P-Vine CD 3003, CD 2741, CD 3742; Rhino CD 71190, CD 79803; Opal CD 106
FL-131	**Can't Stop Lovin**	Flair 1014; Kent LP 9010; Polydor LP 2383200; Ace LP 112, Box CD 4-2, CD 583; Deja Vu LP 2035; Route 16 CD 9007; P-Vine CD 1883; Pointblank PR CD 14171; Opal CD 106
FL-132	**Make A Little Love**	Flair 1014; Kent LP 9010; Ace LP 112, Box CD 4-2, CD 583; P-Vine CD 3742; Opal CD 106

May 1953 • Modern Records • Universal Recording Studios • Los Angeles, CA
unknown (dm, b) overdubbed onto MR 5017 & FL-147 [MM 1782], and the latter renumbered MR 5016

MR 5016	**Lost Woman Blues** (Please Find My Baby)(tk 1)	Ace LP 68, CD 276
	Lost Woman Blues (Please Find My Baby)(tk 2)(vsn 3)	Rhino CD 71190, CD 79803; Ace Box CD 4-1
MR 5017	**Hawaiian Boogie** (No 1)(inst)	Modern 49; Kent LP 9010; Ace Box CD 4-1; P-Vine CD 3038

Note: See details under 25/26 January 1952 session for original recording details.

Ray Topping reports in the discography notes to Ace Box CD 4:
"Master MM 1782[835] was slated for release on Modern in early 1952. It was withdrawn from production for legal reasons. In May 1953 the original master underwent bass and drums overdubbing and was retitled 'Lost Woman Blues'. This overdubbed version was given a Meteor master #MR5016 but was not released on Meteor because James was switched to the Flair label. The original version (no overdubs) was later released on Flair 1022." *(Topping, "Elmore James Discography," 29).*

---

834 As "Dirty By The Dozen."

835 Later renumbered FL-147 for release on Flair 1022.

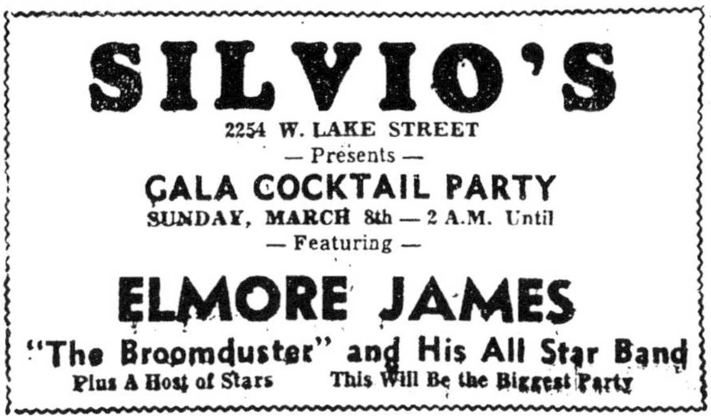

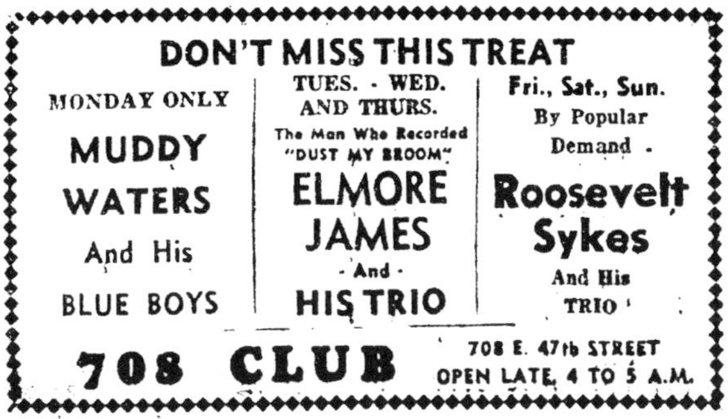

These ads appeared side-by-side in the 7 March 1953 Chicago Defender.

What the Cats Do While the Squares Sleep

Here are a couple of new ones for night lifers. On the Northwest side the FROST CORNER, 600 W. Scott street (one block North of Division) Where J. T. BROWN and his band plus sensational vocalist, TANGERINE and DIZZY ROGERS are featured nightly. BILL GARDNER, M. C. is starred every Wednesday and Sunday night over Station W. O. P. A.—1490 K.C. in a special broadcast from the Club 10-11 p.m. ELMO JAMES and his band take over the musical chores at the Sunday Matinee.

BLUES; BLUES; BLUES; is the slogan of the 708 CLUB, 708 E. 47th street. during the week there are three different blues artist appearing at the CLUB. Monday nite MUDDY WATERS, Tuesday, Wednesday and Thursday nite, ELMORE JAMES and Friday, Saturday and Sunday ROOSEVELT SYKES and his original honey drippers. These three great blues artist's are tops in the blues field. . .

The NEW: FABULOUS and GONE SAVANAH CLUB, 350 E. 51st. is the rave of Southside.

"What the Cats Do While the Squares Sleep," according to this article from the 21 March 1953 Chicago Defender, is to go hear Elmo James for the Sunday Matinee at Frost Corner (with J.T. Brown appearing nightly); and on Tuesday, Wednesday, or Thursday night, stop by the 708 Club to see Elmore James. "These... great blues artists are tops in the blues field," the article states.

8 June 1953 • United / States Records • Universal Recording Studios • Chicago, IL

Junior Wells (vo, hca) Elmore James, Louis Myers, David Myers (gtrs) Johnny Jones (p) Willie Dixon (b) prob Odie Payne (dm)

1325-4	**Cut That Out**	States 122; XX (UK) EP 715; Red Lightnin' LP 007; Delmark LP 640, CD 640
1326-5	**Ways Like An Angel**	Delmark LP 640, CD 640
1327-2	**Hoodoo Man** (Hodo Man/Somebody Hoodooed The Hoodoo Man)	States 134; Blues Classics LP 8; pwb LP 1; Delmark LP 640, CD 640
1328-4	**Tomorrow Night**	States 143; XX (UK) EP 715; Red Lightnin' LP 007; Delmark LP 640, CD 640
1329-4	**Eagle Rock** (alt tk)(inst)	Delmark LP 640, CD 640
1329-5	**Eagle Rock** (inst)	States 122; XX (UK) EP 715; Red Lightnin' LP 007; Delmark CD 640
1330-2	**Junior's Wail** (alt tk)(inst)	Delmark CD 640
1330-3	**Junior's Wail** (inst)	States 134; pwb LP 1; Red Lightnin' LP 007; Delmark LP 640, CD 640; Pulse Box 498/3

Note: It has been suggested that Elmore James plays guitar on "Hoodoo Man" only. Also, those readers expecting to see Fred Below's name at the top of the page along with Odie Payne's are directed to the explanatory footnote on page 61 of the text.

Rhythm and Blues Tattler

A recent release gaining strength every day for States label 118 is a "best effort" by JIMMY COE, "After Hour Joint." Will go great on juke boxes. Another State record (number 122) is cutting out after the big time, and that's JUNIOR WELLS' version of "Cut That Out." Junior proves himself a senior on this one. TAB SMITH comes thru with a definite seller with his waxing of "Cherry" on the United label number 153. How good can you get?

JUNIOR WELLS

Cut That Out 67

STATES 122—Wells delivers an okay vocal and harmonica interlude on a blues rocker of some interest. (Pamlee, BMI)

Eagle Rock....65

Harmonica instrumental is in the rocking-riff style. (Pamlee, BMI)

From Billboard. Left: "Rhythm & Blues Tattler" advertisement, 18 July 1953; Right: 1 August 1953

August 1953 • Modern Records • Universal Recording Studios • Chicago, IL
Elmore James (vo, g) Boyd Atkins (as, ts) J.T. Brown (ts) Johnny Jones (p) Ransom Knowling (b) Odie Payne (dm)

	Make My Dreams Come True (My Best Friend)(tk 1)	Polydor LP 2383200; Ace LP 68, Box CD 4-2
	Make My Dreams Come True (My Best Friend)(tk 2)	Kent LP 9010; Ace CD 192, Box CD 4-2; Blues Encore CD 52006
	Make My Dreams Come True (tk 3)(false start)	Ace Box CD 4-2
	Make My Dreams Come True (tk 4)	Ace Box CD 4-2
	Make My Dreams Come True (tks 5,6)	unissued
FL-162	**Make My Dreams Come True** (tk 7)	Flair 1031; Fire 1011; Sue LP 918; Sphere Sound LP 7008; Trip LP 9511; Charly LP 1017; Ace LP 112, Box CD 4-2, CD 583; Black Label CD 2001; P-Vine CD 3742; Collectables CD 8829-1; Opal CD 106; Camden CD 74321 523762
	Strange Kinda' Feeling (tk 1)	Ace Box CD 4-2
	Strange Kinda' Feeling (tk 2)	Ace LP 68, Box CD 4-2
	Strange Kinda' Feeling (tk 3)	Ace Box CD 4-2
	Strange Kinda' Feeling (tk 4)(false start)	Ace Box CD 4-2
	Strange Kinda' Feeling (tk 5)	Kent LP 9010; Polydor LP 2383200; Ace Box CD 4-2
FL-148	**Strange Kinda' Feeling** (tk 6)	Flair 1022; Ace LP 112, Box CD 4-2, CD 583; Deja Vu LP 2035; Route 16 CD 9007; Opal CD 106
	Dark And Dreary (tk 1)(false start)	Ace Box CD 4-2
	Dark And Dreary (tk 2)	Ace LP 68, Box CD 4-2
	Dark And Dreary (tk 3)	unissued
FL-200	**Dark And Dreary** (tk 4)	Flair 1048; Crown LP 5168; Kent LP 5022; Ace LP 31, CD 192, Box CD 4-2, CD 583; Deja Vu LP 2035; Cascade CD 1005; Blues Encore CD 52006; Route 16 CD 9007; Opal CD 106
	Dark And Dreary (tk 5)	unissued

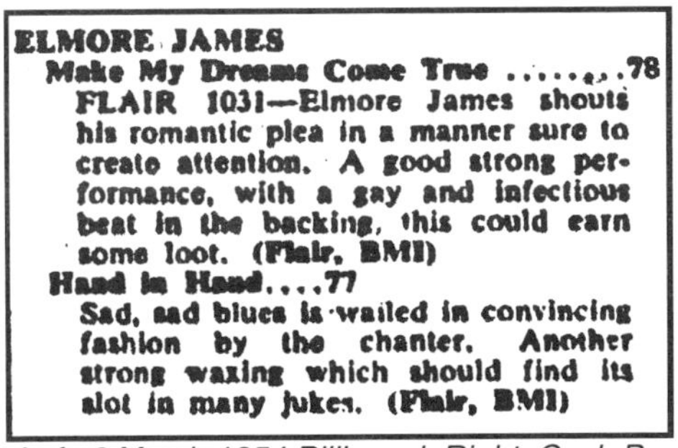
ELMORE JAMES
Make My Dreams Come True 78
FLAIR 1031—Elmore James shouts his romantic plea in a manner sure to create attention. A good strong performance, with a gay and infectious beat in the backing, this could earn some loot. (Flair, BMI)
Hand in Hand....77
Sad, sad blues is wailed in convincing fashion by the chanter. Another strong waxing which should find its slot in many jukes. (Flair, BMI)

Left: 6 March 1954 Billboard; Right: Cash Box, courtesy Bill Greensmith Collection

7 October 1953 • Atlantic Records • Universal Recording Studios • Chicago, IL

Big Joe Turner (vo) Elmore James (g) Johnny Jones (p) Sonny Cohn (tp) Grady Jackson (ts) Mack Easton (bar s) Jimmy Richardson (b) Theodore "Red" Saunders (dm)

A 1125	Love To Spare	unissued
A 1126	**Ti-Ri-Lee**	Atlantic 1053, LP 8033, LP 8081, CD 81663-2; Atlantic LP 332015; Charly LP 1070[836]; Blues Encore CD 52008; Rhino CD 71550
A 1127	**Oke-She-Moke-She-Pop**[837]	Atlantic 1016, CD 81696-2, CD; Atco LP 33-376; Charly LP 1070; Rhino CD 72968
A 1128	**TV Mama**	Atlantic 1016, EP 536, LP 8023, LP 8081, CD 81663-2, CD 81695-2; Atco LP 33-376; Charly LP 1070; Blues Encore CD 52008; Rhino CD 71190, CD 71550, CD 72968; Ace CD 773

9 November 1953 • Atlantic Records • prob Universal Recording Studios • Chicago, IL

Johnny Jones (vo, p) Elmore James (g) J.T. Brown (ts) Odie Payne (dm) unknown (poss Ransom Knowling)(b)

A 1335	**Wait Baby**	Atlantic LP 7227; Ace CD 773
A 1336	**Hoy Hoy**	Atlantic 1045; LP 81697-1[838]; Savage Kick LP 507; Rhino CD 71125; Ace CD 773
	Hoy Hoy (alt tk)	Atlantic LP 7227; Ace CD 773
A 1337	**Chicago Blues**	Atlantic LP 7227; CD 81697-2; Ace CD 773
A 1338	**Doin' The Best I Can** (Up The Line)	Atlantic 1045; Atlantic LP 7227; Ace CD 773

---

836 Incorrectly dated as from a later session in the liner notes.

837 Note: this track does not appear on Rhino CD 71550, contrary to the liner notes; rather, a version recorded on 12 May 1953 with other musicians was substituted. Other session information from the Rhino set (which claims Elmore plays guitar on three other tracks) is incorrect.

838 LP only track; deleted from the CD reissue.

(Early?) 1954 • Modern Records • Chicago, IL

Elmore James (vo, g) Ike Turner (p) Odie Payne (dm) unknown (b, two tenor saxes)

	Quarter Past Nine		Kent LP 9010; Polydor LP 2383200; Ace Box CD 4-2

Note: There is a possibility that "Quarter Past Nine" is actually one of the first three takes of "I Got A Strange Baby" (see below). Both songs have a similar opening lyric line and utilize a "Dust My Broom"-type format.

prob 5 April 1954 • Modern Records • Universal Recording Studios • Chicago, IL

Elmore James (vo, g) Johnny Jones (p) Ike Turner (g, lead g-1) Raymond Hill (ts) unknown (as, bar s, b) Odie Payne (dm)

	Where Can My Baby Be (tks 1-6)		unissued (thought to be destroyed)
	Where Can My Baby Be (tk 7)(false start)		Ace LP 68, Box CD 4-2
	Where Can My Baby Be (tk 8)		Ace LP 68, Box CD 4-2
	Where Can My Baby Be (tk 9)		Kent LP 9001; Vivid Sound/Globe LP 5004; Ace Box CD 4-2
	Sho Nuff I Do (Please Come Back To Me)(prob one of tks 1-4)		Ace LP 68, Box CD 4-2
	Sho Nuff I Do (Please Come Back To Me)(prob tk 5)(false start)		Ace Box CD 4-2
	Sho Nuff I Do (tk 6)(false start)		Ace LP 68, Box CD 4-2
	Sho Nuff I Do (tk 7)(prob incomplete or false start)		unissued
FL-182	**Sho Nuff I Do** (prob tk 8)		Flair 1039; Ace LP 112, Box CD 4-2, CD 583; Rhino CD 71190, CD 79803; P-Vine CD 3742; Opal CD 106
	Sho Nuff I Do (tk 9)(false start)		Ace LP 68, Box CD 4-2
	Sho Nuff I Do (tk 10)(false start)		Ace Box CD 4-2
	Sho Nuff I Do (prob tk 11)		Kent LP 5022, LP 9010; Polydor LP 2383200; Ace CD 192, Box CD 4-2; Blues Encore CD 52006; Cascade Box CD 3-3; P-Vine CD 1883
FL-183	**1839 Blues**		Flair 1039; Kent 508, LP 9001; Vivid Sound/Globe LP 5004; Ace LP 112, Box CD 4-2; Deja Vu LP 2035; Route 16 CD 9007; P-Vine CD 1883; Opal CD 106
	I Got A Strange Baby (tks 1-3)		unissued
	I Got A Strange Baby (tk 4)(fragment)		Kent LP 9001; Vivid Sound/Globe LP 5004; Ace CD 192, Box CD 4-2
	Canton, Mississippi Breakdown (inst)	-1	Kent LP 9001; Vivid Sound/Globe LP 5004; Ace CD 192, Box CD 4-2

Note: Görgen Antonsson adds "poss. Oliver Sain, alto/bar sax" to the above personnel, with this explanation: "Oliver Sain has claimed to have made recordings with Elmore James, Johnny Jones and J.T. Brown in Chicago (Bob Eagle, 'Elmore revisited!' *Jefferson* 27 (Winter 1974): 31). This session (or possibly the 4 Jan 1956 session) seems to match his description best."

August/September 1954 • Modern Records • Modern Records Studios • Culver City, CA

Elmore James (vo, g) James Parr (tp) Maxwell Davis (ts) Jewell Grant (bar s) Willard McDaniel (p) Ralph "Chuck" Hamilton (b) Jesse Sailes (dm) (Omit Brass -1)

FL-216	**Sunny Land**	-1	Flair 1057; Crown LP 5168; Kent 433, 465, LP 5022; Modern 55; Ace LP 31, CD 192, Box CD 4-3, CD 583; Cascade CD 1005; Blues Encore CD 52006; P-Vine CD 1883; Rhino CD 71190; Opal CD 106
FL-217	**Standing At The Crossroads**		Flair 1057; Crown LP 5168; Kent 433, LP 5022, LP 2030[839]; Modern 55; Custom LP 1; Ace LP 31, CD 192, CD 335, Box CD 4-3, CD 583; Vivid Sound/Globe LP 5004; Blues Encore CD 52006; Route 16 CD 9005[840]; P-Vine CD 3742; Opal CD 106
FL-225	**Late Hours At Midnight**		Flair 1062; Kent LP 9010; Polydor LP 2383200; Ace LP 31, Box CD 4-3, CD 583; Deja Vu LP 2035; Route 16 CD 9005; Opal CD 106
FL-226	**The Way You Treat Me** (Mean And Evil)		Flair 1062; Crown LP 5168; Kent LP 5022, LP 700[841]; Ace LP 31, CD 192, Box CD 4-3, CD 583; Blues Encore CD 52006; Opal CD 106
FL-240	**Happy Home**		Flair 1069; Kent 331, 394, LP 5022, LP 544; Crown LP 5168; Sue 335, LP 918; Modern 15; United LP 7718; Ace LP 31, CD 192, Box CD 4-3, CD 583; Vivid Sound/Globe LP 5004; Blues Encore CD 52006; Route 16 CD 9005; P-Vine CD 1883; Opal CD 106
FL-241	**No Love In My Heart** (For You)		Flair 1069; Crown LP 5168; Kent LP 5022; Ace LP 31, CD 192, Box CD 4-3, CD 583; Blues Encore CD 52006; P-Vine CD 3742; Opal CD 106

---

839 Kent LP 2030 and Custom LP 1 both have guitar intro and solo edited out.

840 Note: The outer tray cards identify this set as "That's Blues TB 201," however individual discs are actually labelled Route 16 CD 9005 (Disc 1) and Route 16 CD 9007 (Disc 2), respectively.

841 Crown and Kent issues as "Mean And Evil."

Summary 1955 • Modern Records • J & M Studios • New Orleans, LA

Elmore James (vo, g) Edward Frank (p) Frank Fields (b) Earl Palmer (dm) unknown vo group -1 (prob the Four Speeds)

	Dust My Blues (tks 1, 2)		unissued (tapes destroyed)
FL-250	**Dust My Blues** (tk 3)		Flair 1074; Kent 331, 394, LP 5022, LP 544, LP 5027, LP 700, LP 2030[842]; Crown LP 5168; Sue 335, LP 918; Modern 15; Custom LP 1; United LP 7718; Ace LP 31, CD 192, CD 232, Box CD 4-3, CD 964, CD 583, CD 784; Vivid Sound/Globe LP 5004; Blues Encore CD 52006; Rhino CD 70716; Evasound CD 019; Cascade Box CD 3-3; Broad Music CD 003[843]; P-Vine CD 2741; Europa Music CD 10046; Fat Boy CD 415/3
FL-260	**Blues Before Sunrise**		Flair 1079; Crown LP 5168; Kent LP 5022; Specialty LP 6009; Ace LP 31, CD 192, Box CD 4-3, CD 583, CD 784; Vivid Sound/Globe LP 5004; Deja Vu LP 2035, CD 5-115-2; Blues Encore CD 52006; Fat Boy CD 415/2; P-Vine CD 3742
FL-251	**I Was A Fool**		Flair 1074; Crown LP 5168; Kent LP 5022; Ace LP 31, CD 192, Box CD 4-3, CD 583; Deja Vu LP 2035; Blues Encore CD 52006; Route 16 CD 9007
FL-261	**Good Bye** (Baby)	-1	Flair 1079; Kent 465, LP 5022, LP 535; Crown LP 5168; United LP 7724, LP 7754; Ace LP 31, CD 192, Box CD 4-3, CD 583; Cascade CD 1001; Blues Encore CD 52006; P-Vine CD 2741; Fat Boy CD 415/4; P-Vine CD 3742

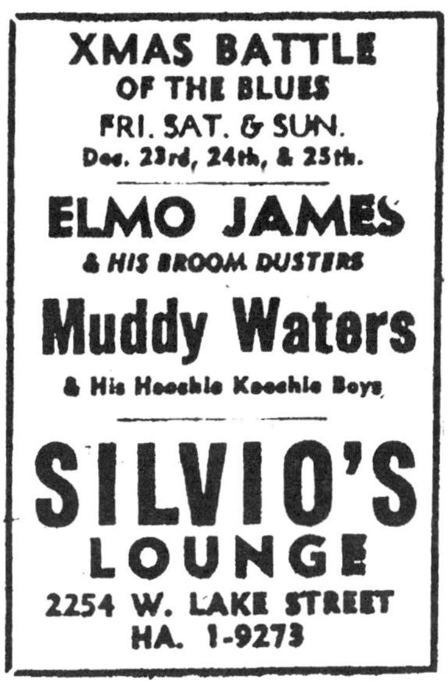

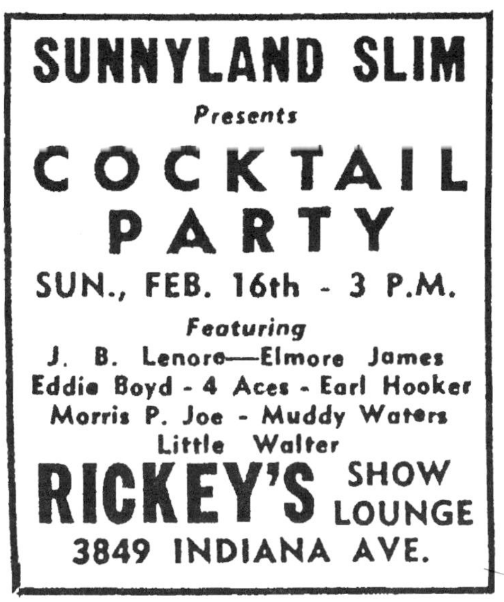

Left: 24 December 1955 Chicago Defender; Right: 15 February 1958 Defender

842 Kent LP 2030 and Custom LP 1 both have guitar solo edited out

843 Broad Music and Eurpoa Music issues as "Dust My Broom."

4 January 1956 • Modern Records • Universal Recording Studios • Chicago, IL

Elmore James (vo, g) Eddie Taylor (g) Johnny Jones (p) Raymond Hill (ts) Odie Payne (dm) unknown (poss J.T. Brown?)(ts) unknown (poss Ransom Knowling?)(b)

MR5614-1	**So Mean To Me** (tk 1)(false start)	Ace LP 68
	So Mean To Me (tk 2)	Ace LP 68, Box CD 4-3
	So Mean To Me (tk 3)	Ace Box CD 4-3; P-Vine CD 3742
	So Mean To Me (tk 4)	Kent LP 9001; Ace CD 192, Box CD 4-3; Blues Encore CD 52006
MR5614-2	**Wild About You** (Baby) (tks 1-3)(false starts)	Ace Box CD 4-3
	Wild About You Baby (tk 4)	Kent LP 5022, LP 9001; Ace LP 31, CD 192, Box CD 4-3, CD 583; Vivid Sound/Globe LP 5004; Blues Encore CD 52006; Route 16 CD 9005; P-Vine CD 3003, CD 1883, CD 3742; Sequel CD 185/1; Rhino CD 79803
	Wild About You (tks 5-8, 10, 11, 13, 15-18, 20, 21)(Incomplete or false starts)	unissued
	Wild About You (tks 9, 12, 14, 19)(rejected complete tks)	unissued
MM 2285	**Wild About You** (tk 22)	Modern 983; Ace LP 68, Box CD 4-3
	Elmo's Shuffle (tks 1 [false start], 2)(inst)	unissued
MR5614-3	**Elmo's Shuffle** (tk 3)(inst)	Ace Box CD 4-3
	Elmo's Shuffle (Part 2)(tk 4)(inst)	Ace LP 68, Box CD 4-3
	Elmo's Shuffle (tk 5)(inst)	Kent LP 9010; Polydor LP 2383200; Ace CD 232, Box CD 4-3
MR5614-4	**Long Tall Woman** (alt tk)	Kent LP 9001; Ace CD 192, Box CD 4-3; Blues Encore CD 52006; P-Vine CD 1883; Connoisseur Collection CD 205
MM 2286	**Long Tall Woman** (tk 2)	Modern 983; Ace LP 68, CD 216, Box CD 4-3, CD 583; Cascade LP 1010

Note: Görgen Antonsson gives the following personnel for this session: Elmore James (vo, g) Raymond Hill (ts) unknown (ts) Johnny Jones (p) Eddie Taylor (g) unknown (b) Odie Payne (dm), and adds the following note: To these ears neither of the tenor [sax] players sound like J.T. Brown, and a more likely candidate for the second tenor would be Oliver Sain; see comment to 5 April 1954 session.

Some of Elmore's last recordings for the Bihari brothers were also among his strongest, including "Wild About You," "Standing At The Crossroads," "Good Bye," and "Dust My Blues." All of these titles—except for "Wild About You"—were reissued as singles on a number of different occasions. The Advertisement is from the 19 November 1955 Chicago Defender, celebrating Elmore's return from Atlanta.

prob 12 April 1957 • Chief Records • Chicago, IL

Elmore James (vo, g) prob Eddie Taylor (g) prob Wayne Bennett (g -1) Johnny Jones (p)
J.T. Brown (ts) Homesick James (bass g) Odie Payne (dm)

C-2402	**The 12 Year Old Boy**	-1	Chief 7001; Vee-Jay 249, CD 711, CDBox 3-400; Sue LP 927; Cobblestone LP 9001; Charly LP 1008, CD 34, CDRED Box 4-1, CD DIG 3-2, CPBOX 301-1 Muse CD 5087; Blue City CD 2652712; P-Vine CD 1410, CD 5272; Zillion CD 2610272; Rhino CD 71190, CD 79803; Collectables CD 7271
C-2403	**Coming Home**		Chief 7001; Vee-Jay 249, LP 1020, CD 718; Sue LP 927; Columbia LP 1417; Cobblestone LP 9001; Joy LP 185; Charly LP 1008, CD 34, CD 1027[844], CDRED Box 4-1, CPBOX 301-1; Intermedia LP 5034; Topline LP 120; Deja Vu LP 2035; Muse CD 5087; Blue City CD 2652712; Blues Encore CD 52006; Instant CD 5030; Route 16 CD 9005; P-Vine CD 1410, CD 5271; Zillion CD 2610272; Masters CD 61046-2; Music Club CD 083; Pilz CD 449322-2; Eclipse CD 64739-2; Rhino CD 79803; Collectables CD 7271
C-2404	**It Hurts Me Too**		Chief 7004; Vee-Jay 259, CD 711, CDBox 3-400; Sue LP 927[845]; Mel 7011; Cobblestone LP 9001; Charly LP 1008, CD 34, CDRED Box 4-1, CPBOX 301-1; Topline LP 120; Muse CD 5087; Blue City CD 2652712; Instant CD 5030, CD 5071; Route 16 CD 9005; P-Vine CD 1410, CD 5271; Zillion CD 2610272, CD 2610232; Music Club CD 083; Rhino CD 71190, CD 79803; Collectables CD 7271
C-2405	**Knocking At Your Door**	-1	Chief 7020; Sue 392, LP 927; Storyville LP 176, Xtra LP 1047; Cobblestone LP 9001; Charly LP 1017, CD 34, CDRED Box 4-1, CPBOX 301-1; Muse CD 5087; P-Vine CD 1410, CD 1883, CD 5271
C-2406	**Elmore's Contribution To Jazz** (inst)		Chief 7004; Vee-Jay 259; Sue LP 927; Cobblestone LP 9001; Charly LP 1017, CD 34, CDRED Box 4-1, CPBOX 301-1; Muse CD 5087; P-Vine CD 1410, CD 5272; Collectables CD 7272

Note: An alternate school of thought has also suggested Willie Johnson as the guitarist instead of Wayne Bennett.

844 Note: No real label identity; however material was licensed from, compiled by, and marketed by Charly records, and listed as such.

845 As "It Hurts Me Too (Part 1)."

Review of Chief 7006 from the 30 December 1957 Billboard, and advertisement from the 4 January 1958 Chicago Defender. "It Hurts Me Too" courtesy Bill Greensmith Collection.

poss Fall 1957 • Chief Records • Chicago, IL

Elmore James (vo) prob Syl Johnson (g) Eddie Taylor (g) J.T. Brown (ts) Willie Dixon (b) Fred Below (dm)

25-117 **Cry For Me Baby** Chief 7006; Vee-Jay 269, CD 718; Sue LP 927; U.S.A. 815; S&M 101; M-Pac 7231; Mel 7011; Cobblestone LP 9001; Charly LP 1008, CD 34, CDRED Box 4-1, CPBOX 301-1; Muse CD 5087; Blue City CD 2652712, CD 2652322; Blues Encore CD 52006; Route 16 CD 9007; P-Vine CD 1410, CD 2346, CD 5271; Zillion CD 2610272, CD 2610232; Rhino CD 71190, CD 79803; Ronn CD 8016; Collectables CD 7272

25-118 **Take Me Where You Go** Chief 7006; Vee-Jay 269; Sue LP 927; U.S.A. 815; S&M 101; M-Pac 7231; Cobblestone LP 9001; Charly LP 1008, CD 34, CDRED Box 4-1, CPBOX 301-1; Muse CD 5087; Blue City CD 2652712; Blues Encore CD 52006; Ripete EP1031; Route 16 CD 9005; P-Vine CD 1410, CD 1883, CD 5271; Zillion CD 2610272; Ronn CD 8016; Collectables CD 7272

poss 3/4 November 1959 • Fire Records • Chicago, IL

Elmore James (vo, g) Johnny Jones (p) J.T. Brown (ts) poss Boyd Atkins (ts) Homesick James (bass g) Odie Payne (dm)

FM 124	**Bobby's Rock** (inst)	Fire 1011; Sue LP 918; Sphere Sound LP 7002[846]; Trip LP 9511; P-Vine LP 6005, CD 2180; Charly CD 180, BM CD 12, CDRED Box 4-1, CPBOX 301-1; Collectables CD 5184, CD 8829-1; Black Label CD 2002; Capricorn CD 42006-2; Relic CD 7040
FM 133	**The Sky Is Crying**	Fire 1016; Down Home 775[847]; Flashback 15; Mercury LP 20826; Sue LP 918; Sphere Sound LP 7002; Bell LP 6037; Pickwick LP 5014; Trip LP 9511; Charly LP 1008, CD 34, BM CD 12, BM CD 100, CD 1027, CDRED Box 4-1, CPBOX 301-1; Intermedia LP 5034; Topline LP 120; P-Vine LP 6005, CD 2180, CD 1883; Deja Vu LP 2035; Blue City CD 2652712; Collectables CD 5184, CD 8829-1; Tomato CD 70386, CD 70389; Blues Encore CD 52006; Instant CD 5030, CD 5071; Ripete CD 2390005; Route 16 CD 9005; Black Label CD 2001; Zillion CD 2610272, CD 2610242; Relic CD 7009, CD 7026; Masters CD 61046-2; Capricorn PRO CD 5831, CD 42006-2, CD 42009-2; Music Club CD 083; Rhino CD 71190, CD 75348, CD 79803; Smithsonian Box CD 101; Pilz CD 449322-2; Eclipse CD 64739-2; Camden CD 74321 523762; Buddah CD 99781-2

Over the years, Bobby Robinson has repeatedly stated that "Bobby's Rock" and "The Sky Is Crying" were paired together to make up the sides of Elmore's first Fire single. As the above labels show, that was not the case. "Make My Dreams Come True" is, quite curiously, a straight reissue of Flair 1031, complete with credits to Flair Publishing and authorship given as "James-Josea."

---

846 As "Bobbie's Rock."

847 Note: flip side has a different catalog number of 776 (see next entry).

"Stormy Monday Blues" courtesy Bill Greensmith Collection

poss 3/4 November 1959, cont'd

FM 134 **Held My Baby Last Night**
Fire 1016; Down Home 776[848]; Sue LP 918; Sphere Sound LP 7002[849]; Charly LP 1017, CD 34, BM CD 12, CDRED Box 4-1, CPBOX 301-1; P-Vine LP 6005, CD 2180; Blue City CD 2652712; Collectables CD 5184, CD 8829-1; Route 16 CD 9005; Tomato CD 70389; Zillion CD 2610272; Capricorn CD 42006-2; Relic CD 7040; Buddah CD 99781-2

6711 **Dust My Broom** (vsn 2)
Sphere Sound LP 7002, 712; Sue LP 927, LP 966; Bell LP 6037; Pickwick LP 5014; Charly EP126, LP 1017, CD 34, BM CD 12, CD 1027, CD 1050, CDRED Box 4-1, CPBOX 301-1, CDGR 216; Topline LP 120, CD 520; P-Vine LP 6005, CD 2180; Blue City CD 2652712, CD 2652322; Ripete CD 2390004; Collectables 3157, CD 5128, CD 5184, CD 8829-1; Instant CD 5017, CD 5030; Route 16 CD 9005; Blues Journey CD 897; Tomato CD 70389; Sire CD 26617-2; Music Club CD 026, CD 083; Zillion CD 2610272, CD 2610252; Relic CD 7009; CD 7026; Capricorn PRO CD 5831, CD 42006-2, CD 42009-2; Pilz CD 449322-2; Versailles CD 478308 2; Camden CD 74321 523762; Buddah CD 99781-2

Baby Please Set A Date
Sphere Sound LP 7008; Bell LP 104, LP 6037; Trip LP 9511; P-Vine LP 6005, CD 2180; Charly CD 34, BM CD 12, CDRED Box 4-1, CPBOX 301-1; Blue City CD 2652712; Collectables CD 5184, CD 8829-1; Route 16 CD 9005; Tomato CD 70389; Black Label CD 2002; Zillion CD 2610272; Relic CD 7026; Capricorn CD 42006-2; Camden CD 74321 523762

---

848 Note: flip side of Down Home 775.

849 As "I Held My Baby."

prob early April 1960 • Chess Records • Chess Records Studios • Chicago, IL

Elmore James (vo, g) Johnny Jones (p) J.T. Brown (ts) unknown (ts) Homesick James (g) Fred Below (dm)

10109	**I Can't Hold Out** (Talk To Me Baby)	Chess 1756, LP 1537, CD 9114, CD 2-9393, CD 380 605-2[850]; Blue Horizon LP 7-63204; Chess/Vogue CD 600119; Instant CD 5071; Charly CDRED 36, CDRED Box 4-2; Rhino CD 71190, CD 79803; Roots CD 33046
10110	**The Sun Is Shining**	Chess 1756, CD 9114; Rhino CD 71190, CD 79803
	The Sun Is Shining (alt tk)(vsn 2)	Blue Horizon LP 7-63204; Chess LP 1537; Trip LP 9511; Chess/Vogue CD 600119; Black Label CD 2001; Charly CDRED 36, CDRED Box 4-2, CD 1124
	The Sun Is Shining (alt tk)(vsn 3)	Argo LP 4034; Pye LP 28345, LP 0293; Marble Arch LP 804; Chess LP 4010, CD 9276, CD 4-9340; Sequel CD 47555/3; Instant CD 5034; Charly CDRED 36, CDRED Box 4-2; Marvel CD 722
10111	**Stormy Monday Blues**[851]	Blue Horizon LP 7-63204; Chess LP 1537, LP 4010, CD 9114; Down Home 800; Trip LP 9511; Chess/Vogue CD 600119; Black Label CD 2001; Charly CDRED 36, CDRED Box 4-2; MCA CD 20768
10112	**Madison Blues**	Blue Horizon LP 7-63204; Chess LP 1537, LP 26023, CD 31316, CD 9114, CD 9368; Down Home 800; Trip LP 9511; Chess/Vogue CD 600119; Connoisseur Collection LP 130; Ripete CD 2390005; Black Label CD 2002; Charly CDRED 36, CDRED Box 4-2; Rhino CD 71127, CD 71190, CD 79803; Ace CD 610

Three different label shots of Chess 1756. The one on the left bears a "Delta" number (a special identification number assigned by the pressing plant) in the dead wax.

850 Part of a 15 disc 1999 Italian box set numbered 3805962. Each disc of the set is individually numbered beginning with 380 597-2 and ending with 380 611-2.

851 Chess LP 1537 and MCA CD 20768 as "Call It Stormy Monday."

poss 23/24 May 1960 • Fire Records • Beltone Studios • New York, NY

Elmore James (vo, g) Homesick James (bass g) prob Jimmy Spruill (g) prob Belton Evans (dm) prob Johnny Acey (p) prob Paul "Hucklebuck" Williams (bar s) unknown (saxes / horns)

FM 151 **Rollin And Tumblin**[852] Fire 1024; Sue LP 918; Sphere Sound LP 7002, 712; Bell LP 6037; Trip LP 9511; Charly LP 1008, CD 34, BM CD 12, BM CD 102, CD 1027, CDRED Box 4-2, CPBOX 301-1; Intermedia LP 5034; Topline LP 120; P-Vine LP 6005, CD 2180, CD 1883; Deja Vu LP 2035; Blue City CD 2652712; Collectables CD 5184, CD 8829-1; Instant CD 5017, CD 5030; Route 16 CD 9007; Tomato CD 70389; Black Label CD 2002; Zillion CD 2610272; Masters CD 61046-2; Relic CD 7026; Capricorn PRO CD 5831, CD 42006-2; Music Club CD 083; Rhino CD 71190; Pilz CD 449322-2; Eclipse CD 64739-2; Camden CD 74321 523762; Buddah CD 99781-2

FM 152 **I'm Worried** Fire 1024; Sue LP 918; Sphere Sound LP 7002; Trip LP 9511; P-Vine LP 6005, CD 2180; Charly CD 180, BM CD 12, CDRED Box 4-2, CPBOX 301-1; Collectables CD 5184, CD 8829-1; Instant CD 5030; Black Label CD 2002; Capricorn CD 42006-2; Music Club CD 083; Relic CD 7040; Camden CD 74321 523762; Buddah CD 99781-2

FM 165 **Done Somebody Wrong**[853] Fire 1031; Sue LP 918; Sphere Sound LP 7002; Trip LP 9511; Charly EP126, LP 1017, CD 34, BM CD 12, CD 1027, CDRED Box 4-2, CPBOX 301-1; Intermedia LP 5034; Topline LP 120; P-Vine LP 6005, CD 2180, CD 1883; Deja Vu LP 2035; Blue City CD 2652712; Collectables CD 5184, CD 8829-1; Instant CD 5030; Route 16 CD 9005, CD 9007; Tomato CD 70389; Black Label CD 2002; Zillion CD 2610272; Masters CD 61046-2; Capricorn PRO CD 5831, CD 42006-2; Music Club CD 083; Relic CD 7040; Rhino CD 71190, CD 79803; Pilz CD 449322-2; Eclipse CD 64739-2; Camden CD 74321 523762; Buddah CD 99781-2

FM 166 **Fine Little Mama** Fire 1031, 5001; Sue LP 918; Sphere Sound LP 7002; Bell LP 6037; Trip LP 9511; Charly LP 1017, CD 34, BM CD 12, CD 1027, CDRED Box 4-2, CPBOX 301-1; Topline LP 120; P-Vine LP 6005, CD 2180; Blue City CD 2652712; Collectables CD 5184, CD 8829-1; Instant CD 5030; Route 16 CD 9005; Tomato CD 70389; Black Label CD 2001; Zillion CD 2610272; Relic CD 7026; Capricorn CD 42006-2; Music Club CD 083; Camden CD 74321 523762; Buddah CD 99781-2

---

852 Frequently listed as "Rollin' And Tumblin'" or "Rolling And Tumbling."

853 Shown as "I Done Somebody Wrong" on Black Label, Deja Vu, Intermedia, Masters, Music Club, Pilz, Sphere Sound, Topline, and Trip issues, on Charly CD 1027, and on Route 16 CD 9007.

poss 23/24 May 1960, cont'd

	I Can't Stop Lovin' You	Sphere Sound LP 7002; Sue LP 927; P-Vine LP 6005, CD 2180; Charly CD 180, BM CD 12, CDRED Box 4-2, CPBOX 301-1; Collectables CD 5184, CD 8829-1; Instant CD 5030; Capricorn CD 42006-2; Music Club CD 083; Relic CD 7040; Camden CD 74321 523762
	Early One Morning	Sphere Sound LP 7008; Bell LP 104; Charly LP 1017, BM CD 12, CD 180, CDRED Box 4-2, CPBOX 301-1; P-Vine LP 6005, CD 2180; Collectables CD 5184, CD 8829-1; Capricorn CD 42006-2; Music Club CD 083; Relic CD 7040; Camden CD 74321 523762; Buddah CD 99781-2
6517	**I Need You** (Baby) (edited vsn)	Sphere Sound 708, LP 7008; Bell LP 104, LP 6037; Trip LP 9511; Sue 4007; Charly LP 1008, CD 34, BM CD 12, CDRED Box 4-2; P-Vine LP 6005, CD 2180; Blue City CD 2652712; Collectables CD 5184; Route 16 CD 9005; Tomato CD 70389; Black Label CD 2001; Zillion CD 2610272, CD 2610252; Camden CD 74321 523762
	I Need You (Baby) (complete)	Relic CD 7026; Capricorn CD 42006-2; Rhino CD 71190; Collectables CD 8829-1; Charly CPBOX 301-1
	Strange Angels	Sphere Sound LP 7008; Bell LP 104; Charly LP 1017, CD 180, BM CD 12, CDRED Box 4-2, CPBOX 301-1; P-Vine LP 6005, CD 2180; Collectables CD 5184, CD 8829-1; Capricorn CD 42006-2; Relic CD 7040; Camden CD 74321 523762
8317	**She Done Move**(d) (inst)	Sphere Sound 713, LP 7008; Bell LP 104; P-Vine LP 6005, CD 2180; Charly CD 180, BM CD 12, CDRED Box 4-2, CPBOX 301-1; Collectables CD 5185, CD 8829-1; Capricorn CD 42006-2; Relic CD 7040; Camden CD 74321 523762
8316	**Something Inside Me** (edited vsn)	Sphere Sound 713
	Something Inside Of Me (complete)	Sphere Sound LP 7008; Bell LP 104, LP 6037; Trip LP 9511; Fire 5001; Charly LP 1008, CD 34, BM CD 12, CDRED Box 4-2, CPBOX 301-2; P-Vine LP 6005, CD 2180, CD 1883; Blue City CD 2652712; Collectables CD 5185, CD 8829-1; Route 16 CD 9005; Tomato CD 70389; Black Label CD 2001; Zillion CD 2610272[854]; Relic CD 7026; Capricorn CD 42006-2; Rhino CD 71130, CD 71190; Camden CD 74321 523762; Buddah CD 99781-2

[854] As "Something Inside."

SPHERE SOUND
RECORDS
RHINELANDER MUSIC
BMI 6327
SSR 702
TIME: 2:25
ONE WAY OUT
(SEHORN - JAMES)
ELMO JAMES
FROM SPHERE SOUND LP 7002
"THE SKY IS CRYING"
A PRODUCT OF BELL RECORDS, INC.
SPHERE SOUND
RECORDS
RHINELANDER MUSIC
BMI 6517
SSR 708
TIME: 2:54
I NEED YOU
(M. SEHORN - E. JAMES)
ELMORE JAMES
PRODUCT OF BELL RECORDS, INC. • NEW YORK
FLASHBACK
RECORDS
FLAIR PUBLISHING CO.
BMI 6432
FLB 15
TIME: 2:56
STANDING AT THE CROSSROADS
(JAMES - JOSEA)
ELMORE JAMES
A PRODUCT OF BELL RECORDS, INC. • NEW YORK
BELL
RECORDS
Rhinelander Music Co.
BMI
8606-BW
B - 719
Time: 3:05
PROMOTION COPY
PLUG SIDE
STRANGE BLUES
(E. James - M. Sehorn)
ELMORE JAMES
Prod. by Marshall E. Sehorn
AMY mala BELL N.Y.C.
ENJOY
RECORDS
Bob-Dan Music
BMI
Time: 2:37
45 RPM
ZTSP 98718
A Bobby Robinson Production
BLEEDING HEART
(Bobby Robinson)
ELMORE JAMES
2015
CHARLY
DONE SOMEBODY WRONG
(James)
Uncle Doris Music
Licensed from Sansu Enterprises
SIDE 1
45 RPM
CTD 126
AT 1011
MCPS
ELMORE JAMES
SPHERE SOUND
Rhinelander Music Co.
BMI
8317-BW
713
Time: 1:47
SHE DONE MOVE (Instrumental)
(M. Sehorn - E. James)
ELMORE JAMES
Produced by Marshall E. Sehorn
A PRODUCT OF BELL RECORDS, INC. • NEW YORK
SPHERE SOUND
Rhinelander Music Co.
BMI
8316-BW
713
Time: 3:21
PROMOTION COPY
PLUG SIDE
SOMETHING INSIDE ME
(M. Sehorn - E. James)
ELMORE JAMES
Produced by Marshall E. Sehorn
A PRODUCT OF BELL RECORDS, INC. • NEW YORK

poss c. late February or early March 1961 • Fire Records • Beltone Studios • New York, NY

Elmore James (vo, g) Danny Moore (tp) prob George Coleman (ts) Paul "Hucklebuck" Williams (bar s) Johnny Acey (p) Nehemiah "Riff" Ruffin (g) Johnny Williams (dm) unknown (b) Dickie Harris? (tmb?)[855]

FB 301	**Stranger Blues** [856]	Fire 1503; Sue LP 918; Trip LP 8007; P-Vine LP 6006, CD 2181; Charly CD 180, BM CD 12, BM CD 28, CDRED Box 4-2, CPBOX 301-2; Collectables CD 5185, CD 8829-1; Capricorn CD 42006-2; Music Club CD 083; Relic CD 7040; Camden CD 74321 523762
8606	**Strange**(r) **Blues** (alt tk)	Bell 719, LP 104; P-Vine LP 6005, CD 2180, CD 1883; Charly CD 180, CDRED Box 4-3, CPBOX 301-2; Collectables CD 5185, CD 8829-1; Instant CD 5030; Relic CD 7026; Buddah CD 99781-2
	Lee's Rock (inst)	unissued
FB 302	**Anna Lee** (edited vsn)	Fire 1503; Sue LP 918; Trip LP 8007, LP 1650; Pickwick LP 5014; P-Vine LP 6006, CD 2181; Charly CD 180, BM CD 28, CD 1027; Collectables CD 5185; Tomato CD 70389
8607	**Anna Lee** (complete)	Bell 719; Relic CD 7026; Capricorn CD 42006-2; Charly CDRED Box 4-3, CD 2007, CPBOX 301-2; P-Vine CD 1883; Camden CD 74321 523762; Buddah CD 99781-2
ZTSP98718	**Bleeding Heart** (edited vsn)	Enjoy 2015[857], 2020; Sue 383, LP 927; Up Front LP 122; Trip LP 8007; LP 1650; Pickwick LP 5014
6326	**My Bleeding Heart** (complete)	Sphere Sound LP 7002, 702; Bell LP 6037; Charly LP 1017, CD 180, BM CD 28, CDRED Box 4-3, CD 2007, CPBOX 301-2; P-Vine LP 6006, CD 2181; Collectables CD 5185, CD 8829-1; Instant CD 5030; Relic CD 7026; Capricorn CD 42006-2; Music Club CD 083; Camden CD 74321 523762; Buddah CD 99781-2
6432	**Standing At The Crossroads** (vsn 2)	Sphere Sound LP 7002; Sue LP 927; Flashback 15; Bell LP 6037; Trip LP 9511; Charly LP 1008, CD 180, BM CD 28, CD 1027, CDRED Box 4-3, CD 2007, CPBOX 301-2; Intermedia LP 5034; Topline LP 120; P-Vine LP 6006, CD 2181; Deja Vu LP 2035, CD 5-115-2; Collectables CD 5185, CD 8829-1; Instant CD 5017, CD 5030; Black Label CD 2001; Masters CD 61046-2; Relic CD 7026; Capricorn CD 42006-2; Music Club CD 083; Rhino CD 71190, CD 79803; Pilz CD 449322-2[858]; Eclipse CD 64739-2; Camden CD 74321 523762; Buddah CD 99781-2

855 Note: In his Elmore James discography, Görgen Antonsson deletes Dickie Harris from the personnel for this session, noting that a trombone is not aurally discernible among the recordings.

856 This was also used as the backing track (i.e., Elmore's vocal was rubbed out) for Wilbert Harrison's "Pretty Little Woman." It was released as a single on the SSS International label in 1971, and was later reissued on the album *Kansas City,* Relic CD 7035, 1992.

857 From the less common first issue of Enjoy 2015, with "It Hurts Me Too" on the reverse.

858 Incorrectly labeled as "I Believe."

poss c. late February or early March 1961, cont'd

6327	**One Way Out**	Sphere Sound LP 7002; 702; Sue LP 927; Bell LP 6037; Trip LP 9511; Charly LP 1008, CD 34, BM CD 28, BM CD 102, CD 1027, CDRED Box 4-3, CD 2007, CPBOX 301-2; P-Vine LP 6006, CD 2181, CD 1883; Blue City CD 2652712; Collectables CD 5185, CD 8829-1; Instant CD 5030; Tomato CD 70389; Black Label CD 2002; Zillion CD 2610272; Relic CD 7026; Capricorn PRO CD 5831, CD 42006-2; Camden CD 74321 523762
	Got To Move	Sphere Sound LP 7008; Bell LP 104; Charly LP 1017, CD 34, BM CD 28, BM CD 101, CD 1027, CDRED Box 4-3, CD 2007, CPBOX 301-2; P-Vine LP 6006, CD 2181; Blue City CD 2652712; Collectables CD 5185, CD 8829-2; Route 16 CD 9007; Concept CD 0265; Zillion CD 2610272; Capricorn CD 42006-2; Relic CD 7040
	Person To Person	Bell LP 104; Charly LP 1008, CD 34, BM CD 28, CDRED Box 4-3, CD 2007, CPBOX 301-2; P-Vine LP 6006, CD 2181; Blue City CD 2652712; Collectables CD 5185, CD 8829-2; Route 16 CD 9007; Tomato CD 70389; Zillion CD 2610272; Capricorn CD 42006-2; Relic CD 7040
	So Unkind	Bell LP 104; P-Vine LP 6006, CD 2181; Charly CD 180, BM CD 28, CDRED Box 4-3, CD 2007, CPBOX 301-2; Collectables CD 5185, CD 8829-2; Capricorn CD 42006-2; Relic CD 7040
	My Kind Of Woman	Bell LP 104; P-Vine LP 6006, CD 2181; Charly CD 180, BM CD 28, CDRED Box 4-3, CD 2007, CPBOX 301-2; Collectables CD 5185, CD 8829-2; Capricorn CD 42006-2; Relic CD 704

prob Summer 1961 • Fire Records • J & M Studios • New Orleans, LA
Elmore James (vo, g) Sam Myers (hca -1 / vo -2) Johnny "Big Moose" Walker (p, vo -3)
Sammy Lee Bully (bass g) King Mose Taylor (dm)

	Shake Your Moneymaker (tk 1)(false start)		Relic CD 7026; Capricorn PRO CD 5831, CD 42006-2, CD 42009-2; Charly CDRED Box 4-3, CD 2007, CD DIG 3-3, CPBOX 301-2; Collectables CD 8829-2
FM 194	**Shake Your Moneymaker** (tk 2)		Fire 504; Enjoy 2022; Sphere Sound 708, LP 7008; Burn 504; Sue LP 918; Bell LP 104, LP 6037; Up Front LP 122; Trip 102, LP 8007, LP 1650; Pickwick LP 5014; Charly LP 1008, CD 34, BM CD 28, CDRED Box 4-3, CD 2007, CD DIG 3-3, CPBOX 301-2; P-Vine LP 6006, CD 2181; Blue City CD 2652712; Ripete CD 2390004; Collectables 3157, CD 5186, CD 8829-2; Instant CD 5030; Route 16 CD 9005; Tomato CD 70389; Zillion CD 2610272, CD 2610262; Relic CD 7009, CD 7026; Capricorn PRO CD 5831, CD 42006-2, CD 42009-2; Music Club CD 083; Rhino CD 71190, CD 79803; Camden CD 74321 523762; Buddah CD 99781-2
FM 193	**Look On Yonder Wall** (tk 1)	-1	Fire 504; Enjoy 2022; Burn 504; Sue LP 918; Sphere Sound LP 7008; Bell LP 6037; Up Front LP 122; Trip LP 8007, LP 1650; Charly LP 1017, CD 26, CD 180, BM CD 28, CD 1027, CDRED Box 4-3, CD 2007, CPBOX 301-2; Intermedia LP 5034; Topline LP 120; P-Vine LP 6006, CD 2181, CD 1883; Deja Vu LP 2035; Collectables CD 5185, CD 8829-2; Blues Encore CD 52006; Instant CD 5030; Masters CD 61046-2; Relic CD 7026; Capricorn PRO CD 5831, CD 42006-2; Music Club CD 083; Rhino CD 71190; Pilz CD 449322-2; Eclipse CD 64739-2; Camden CD 74321 523762; Official CD 5254; Buddah CD 99781-2
	(Poor Little) **Angel Child** (tk 1)	-2	P-Vine LP 6101/02, CD 5461 Charly LP 1208; Relic CD 7040; Collectables CD 8829-2; Official CD 5254
	Little Girl	-2	P-Vine LP 6101/02, CD 5461; Charly LP 1208
	Mean Mistreatin' Mama (tk 1)(incomplete)		Blue Horizon LP 7-66230; P-Vine LP 6006, CD 2181; Collectables CD 5186, CD 8829-2; Charly BM CD 28, CDRED Box 4-3, CPBOX 301-2
	Mean Mistreatin' Mama (tk 2)		Blue Horizon LP 7-66230; Intermedia LP 5034; P-Vine LP 6006, CD 2181; Collectables CD 5129, CD 5186, CD 8829-2; Masters LP 5686, CD 61046-2; Blues Encore CD 52006; Route 16 CD 9007; Success CD 2122; Charly BM CD 28, CDRED Box 4-3, CPBOX 301-2, CD 2007; Relic CD 7040; Eclipse CD 64739-2

ZTSP105797	**Mean Mistreatin' Mama** (tk 3)		Enjoy 2020; Sue 4007; Blue Horizon LP 7-66230; Up Front LP 122; Trip LP 8007, LP 1650, LP 7503; DJM LP 8005; Mid South LP 15901; Topline LP 120; P-Vine LP 6006, CD 2181; Collectables 3351, CD 5112, CD 5186, CD 8829-2; Charly CD 180, BM CD 28, CD 1027, CDRED Box 4-3, CPBOX 301-2; Relic CD 7026; Capricorn CD 42006-2; Music Club CD 083; Pilz CD 449322-2; Camden CD 74321 523762
	Sunnyland (Train)(tk 1)		Blue Horizon LP 7-66230; CBS LP 66218; Trip LP 8007, LP 1650; Pickwick LP 5014; P-Vine LP 6006, CD 2181; Collectables CD 5112, CD 5186, CD 8829-2; Charly CD 180, BM CD 28, CD 1027, CDRED Box 4-3, CD 2007, CPBOX 301-2; Columbia CD 468992-2; Relic CD 7026; Capricorn CD 42006-2; Buddah CD 99781-2
	You Know You're Wrong (tk 1)(incomplete)		Collectables CD 8829-2
	You Know You're Wrong (tk 2)		Relic CD 7026; Capricorn CD 42006-2; Charly CDRED Box 4-3, CPBOX 301-2; Collectables CD 8829-2
	You Know You Done Me Wrong (tk 3)[859]		Collectables CD 5187, CD 8829-2; P-Vine CD 2182; Capricorn CD 42006-2; Charly CDRED Box 4-3, CD 2007, CPBOX 301-2; Relic CD 7040
	Go Back Home Again (tk 1)	-1	Relic CD 7026; Capricorn CD 42006-2; Charly CDRED Box 4-3, CD 2007, CPBOX 301-2; Collectables CD 8829-2[860]
	Footrace To A Resting Place	-3	Blue Horizon LP 7-66230

859 Note: The title of this song changed during the recording session (after the first two takes).

860 As "Going Back Home Again."

13 February 1963 • Enjoy Records • prob A-1 Studios • New York, NY

Elmore James (vo, g) unknown ([prob including Marshall Jones] b, dm)

Look On Yonder Wall (Look Up On The Wall)	Collectables CD 5187, CD 8829-2; P-Vine CD 2182; Charly CDRED Box 4-3, CD 2007, CPBOX 301-3; Relic CD 7040, CD 7097
Find My Kind Of Woman (tk 1)	Relic CD 7026, CD 7097; Capricorn CD 42006-2; Charly CDRED Box 4-3, CD 2007, CPBOX 301-2; Collectables CD 8829-2
Find My Kinda Woman (tk 2)	Trip LP 8007; P-Vine LP 6006, CD 2181; Charly CD 180, BM CD 28, CDRED Box 4-3, CPBOX 301-3; Collectables CD 5186, CD 8829-2; Capricorn CD 42006-2; Relic CD 7097
Dust My Broom (tks 1-3)	unissued
Dust My Broom (tk 4)(vsn 3)	Relic CD 7040, CD 7097; Collectables CD 8829-2; Charly CPBOX 301-3
My Baby's Gone (tks 1-3)	unissued
My Baby's Gone (tk 4)(vsn 2)	Trip LP 8007, LP 1650; P-Vine LP 6006, CD 2181; Charly CD 180, BM CD 28, CDRED Box 4-3, CD 2007, CPBOX 301-3; Collectables CD 5186, CD 8829-2; Relic CD 7026, CD 7097; Capricorn CD 42006-2

Same Session

Marshall Jones (vo) Elmore James (g) unknown ([prob including Marshall Jones] b, dm)

You Can Do It If You Want To	Capricorn CD 42009-2; Collectables CD 8829-2[861]
Woke Up Happy	Capricorn CD 42009-2; Collectables CD 8829-2[862]

---

861 As "Do It If You Wanna."

862 As "Woke Up Screamin' & Cryin'."

21 February 1963 • Enjoy Records • A-1 Studios • New York, NY
Elmore James (vo, g) prob Johnny "Big Moose" Walker (p, vo -1) unknown ([prob including Marshall Jones] b, dm)

	Hand In Hand (tk 1)	Blue Horizon LP 7-66230; P-Vine LP 6007, CD 2182; Collectables CD 5129, CD 5186, CD 8829-3; Charly CDRED Box 4-4, CPBOX 301-3
	Hand In Hand (tk 2)(incomplete)	Blue Horizon LP 7-66230
	Hand In Hand (tk 3)	Blue Horizon LP 7-66230; Charly CD 180, CDRED Box 4-4, CPBOX 301-3; Music Club CD 083; Collectables CD 8829-3
	Hand In Hand (tk 4)	Blue Horizon LP 7-66230, PR LP 46; Intermedia LP 5034; P-Vine LP 6007, CD 2182; Deja Vu LP 2035; Collectables CD 5112, CD 5187, CD 8829-3; Relic LP 1021, CD 7097; Blues Encore CD 52006; Route 16 CD 9007; Capricorn CD 42006-2; Charly CDRED Box 4-4, CPBOX 301-3; Pilz CD 449322-2
	I Have [I've Got] **A Right To Love My Baby**	Blue Horizon LP 7-66230; Trip LP 8007; Charly LP 1017, CD 180, CDRED Box 4-4, CPBOX 301-3; P-Vine LP 6007, CD 2182; Collectables 3350, CD 5112, CD 5128, CD 5186, CD 8829-3; Relic LP 1021, CD 7097; Capricorn CD 42006-2
EN 34578	**Everyday I Have The Blues** (tk 1)	Enjoy 2027; Blue Horizon LP 7-66230; Trip LP 8007, LP 1650; Fury 2000[863]; Pickwick LP 5014; Charly LP 1017, CD 180, CD 1027, CDRED Box 4-4, CD 2007, CPBOX 301-3; Topline LP 120; P-Vine LP 6007, CD 2182; Collectables 3350, CD 5112, CD 5127, CD 5186, CD 8829-3; Relic LP 1021, CD 7026, CD 7097; Capricorn CD 42006-2; Music Club CD 083
EN 34579	**Dust My Broom** (vsn 4)	Enjoy 2027; Blue Horizon LP 7-66230; Trip 102, LP 8007, LP 1650, LP 7503; DJM LP 8005; Intermedia LP 5034; P-Vine LP 6007, CD 2182; Deja Vu LP 2035, CD 5-115-2; Collectables CD 5112, CD 8829-3; Relic LP 1021, CD 7097; Blues Encore CD 52006; Masters CD 61046-2; Capricorn CD 42006-2; Charly CDRED Box 4-4, CD 2007, CPBOX 301-3; Rhino CD 71126; Eclipse CD 64739-2
ZTSP98719	**It Hurts Me Too** (tk 1)(vsn 2)	Enjoy 2015; Sue 383, LP 927[864], LP 5; Fire 2020, 5000; Blue Horizon LP 7-66230; Up Front LP 122; Trip 24, LP 8007, LP 1650, LP 7503; Pickwick LP 5014; DJM LP 8005; Charly LP 1017, CD 180, CD 1027, CDRED Box 4-4, CD DIG 3-3, CD LAB 104, CPBOX 301-3; Intermedia LP 5034; P-Vine LP 6007, CD 2182, CD 1883; Collectables CD 5112, CD 5186, CD 8829-3; Relic LP 1021, CD 7026, CD 7046, CD 7097; Blues Encore CD 52006; Masters CD 61046-2; Capricorn PRO CD 5831, CD 42006-2, CD 42009-2; Bullseye Blues CD 9533; Pilz CD 449322-2; Eclipse CD 64739-2

863 Fades at end.

864 As "It Hurts Me Too (Part 2)."

	Talk To Me Baby (I Can't Hold Out)(tk 1)	Blue Horizon LP 7-66230; Trip LP 8007, LP 1650; Charly LP 1008, CD 34, CDRED Box 4-4, CPBOX 301-3; P-Vine LP 6007, CD 2182; Collectables CD 5112, CD 5186, CD 8829-3; Blue City CD 2652712; Relic LP 1021, CD 7040, CD 7097; Route 16 CD 9005; Tomato CD 70389; Zillion CD 2610272; Capricorn CD 42006-2
	Can't Stop Loving My Baby	Blue Horizon LP 7-66230; Charly LP 1008, CD 34, CDRED Box 4-4, CPBOX 301-3; P-Vine LP 6007, CD 2182; Blue City CD 2652712; Relic LP 1021, CD 7097; Collectables CD 5186, CD 8829-3; Tomato CD 70389; Zillion CD 2610272; Capricorn CD 42006-2; Music Club CD 083
	Got To Move (She's Got To Go)[865]	Blue Horizon LP 7-66230; Trip LP 8007, LP 1650; P-Vine LP 6007, CD 2182; Relic LP 1021, CD 7097; Collectables CD 5187, CD 8829-3; Capricorn CD 42006-2; Charly CDRED Box 4-4, CPBOX 301-3
ZTSP104841	**Pickin' The Blues** (edited vsn)(inst)	Enjoy 2015[866]; Sue LP 927; Up Front LP 122; Fire 2020, 5000; Trip 24; Charly EP126, LP 1017, CD 1027; Intermedia LP 5034; Topline LP 120; Route 16 CD 9007; Eclipse CD 64739-2
	Manhattan Slide (Pickin' The Blues)(complete)(inst)	Blue Horizon LP 7-66230; Trip LP 8007, LP 1650; P-Vine LP 6007, CD 2182; Relic LP 1021, CD 7097; Collectables CD 5187, CD 8829-3; Capricorn CD 42006-2; Charly CDRED Box 4-4, CD 2007, CPBOX 301-3; Pilz CD 449322-2
	Twelve Year Old Boy	Blue Horizon LP 7-66230; Trip LP 8007, LP 1650; P-Vine LP 6007, CD 2182; Collectables 3351, CD 5112, CD 5127, CD 5187, CD 8829-3; Charly CD 180, CDRED Box 4-4, CPBOX 301-3; Relic LP 1021, CD 7040, CD 7097; Capricorn CD 42006-2

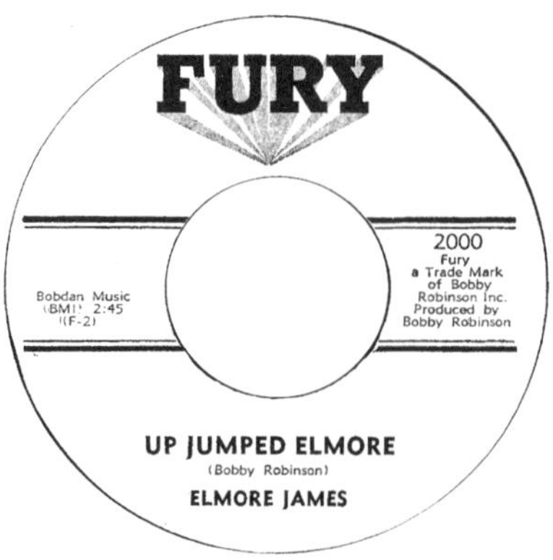

865 Shown as "She's Got To Go" on Black Label, Capricorn, Charly, Collectables, P-Vine, and Trip issues; and as "I Got To Move" on Relic LP1021.

866 From the (more common) second pressing of Enjoy 2015; "Pickin' The Blues" replaces "Bleeding Heart."

Elmore Jumps One (Up Jumped Elmore)(false starts)		Blue Horizon LP 7-66230; P-Vine LP 6007, CD 2182; Collectables CD 5187, CD 8829-3
Elmore Jumps One (Up Jumped Elmore)(complete)(inst)		Blue Horizon LP 7-66230; Trip LP 8007, LP 1650; P-Vine LP 6007, CD 2182; Relic LP 1021, CD 7097; Collectables CD 5187, CD 8829-3; Capricorn CD 42006-2; Charly CDRED Box 4-4, CPBOX 301-3
Up Jumped Elmore (Black Snake Slide [Blues])(inst)[867]		Fury 2000; Collectables CD 5187, CD 8829-3; P-Vine CD 2182; Capricorn CD 42006-2; Relic CD 7097
I Believe (tk 1)(vsn 2)		Blue Horizon LP 7-66230; Trip LP 8007, LP 1650; Pickwick LP 5014; Intermedia LP 5034; P-Vine LP 6007, CD 2182; Deja Vu LP 2035; Collectables CD 5112, CD 5187, CD 8829-3; Relic LP 1021, CD 7046, CD 7097; Route 16 CD 9007; Masters CD 61046-2; Capricorn CD 42006-2; Charly CDRED Box 4-4, CPBOX 301-3; Pilz CD 449322-2; Eclipse CD 64739-2
I Gotta Go Now		Blue Horizon LP 7-66230; P-Vine LP 6007, CD 2182; Collectables CD 5112, CD 5187, CD 8829-3; Relic LP 1021, CD 7040, CD 7097; Capricorn CD 42006-2; Charly CDRED Box 4-4, CPBOX 301-3
Make My Dreams Come True (false start)		Blue Horizon LP 7-66230; P-Vine LP 6007, CD 2182; Collectables CD 5112, CD 5187, CD 8829-3
Make My Dreams Come True (tk 3)(vsn 2)		Blue Horizon LP 7-66230; P-Vine LP 6007, CD 2182; Collectables CD 5112, CD 5187, CD 8829-3; Charly CD 180, CDRED Box 4-4, CPBOX 301-3; Relic LP 1021, CD 7040, CD 7097; Instant CD 5030; Capricorn CD 42006-2; Music Club CD 083
Second Fiddle Man (omit b)	-1	Blue Horizon LP 7-66230
Back In Mississippi (conversation)		Blue Horizon LP 7-66230; Trip LP 8007; P-Vine LP 6007, CD 2182; Collectables CD 5187, CD 8829-3; Capricorn CD 42006-2; Charly CDRED Box 4-4, CPBOX 301-3; Relic CD 7097

867 Note: These are not alternate takes, but simply "Up Jumped Elmore" ("Elmore Jumps One") with premature fade out. Collectables, P-Vine, and Relic issues as "Black Snake Slide." Capricorn as "Blacksnake Blues."

FILL IN WITH TYPEWRITER OR LEGIBLE PRINTING

ORIGINAL 572.

STATE OF ILLINOIS

STATE FILE NUMBER 63-609-2744

CORONER'S CERTIFICATE OF DEATH

DECEDENT'S BIRTH NO. | REGISTRATION DISTRICT NO. 16.10 | REGISTERED NUMBER 34744

1. PLACE OF DEATH a. STATE ILLINOIS | b. COUNTY COOK

c. [X] INSIDE corporate limits and in City, Village, or Incorporated Town: CHICAGO

d. [ ] OUTSIDE corporate limits and in Township name........ Road District No........

e. LENGTH OF STAY IN 1c or 1d: 10 YRS

f. NAME OF HOSPITAL OR INSTITUTION

g. LENGTH OF STAY IN 1f

h. If not in hospital or institution, give Street & No. or R.F.D. and Post Office: 1503 N. WIELAND STREET

2. USUAL RESIDENCE (Where deceased lived. If institution, residence before admission.) a. STATE Illinois | b. COUNTY COOK

c. [X] INSIDE corporate limits and in City, Village, or Incorporated Town: Chicago

d. [ ] OUTSIDE corporate limits and in Township name........ Road District No........

e. LENGTH of RESIDENCE AT 2c or 2d: 10 YRS

f. RESIDENCE ADDRESS (Street & No. or R.F.D. and Post Office): 1503 N. WIELAND STREET

g. Did decedent reside ON A FARM? YES [ ] NO [X]

3. NAME OF DECEASED a. (FIRST) ELMORE b. (MIDDLE) (JOE WILLIE) c. (LAST) JAMES

4. DATE OF DEATH (MONTH) (DAY) (YEAR) 5-24-63

5. SEX MALE | 6. RACE NEGRO | 7. MARRIED, NEVER MARRIED, WIDOWED, DIVORCED (specify) NEVER MARRIED

8. DATE OF BIRTH UNKNOWN | 9. AGE (in years last birthday) AT. 44 | if under 1 year MONTHS DAYS | if under 24 hrs. HOURS MIN.

10a. USUAL OCCUPATION MUSICIAN | 10b. KIND OF BUSINESS OR INDUSTRY SELF EMPLOYED

11. BIRTHPLACE (City and state or foreign country) LEXINGTON, MISSISSIPPI | 12. Citizen of what country? U.S.A.

13. FATHER'S FULL NAME JOE WILLIE JAMES

14. MOTHER'S FULL MAIDEN NAME LEARO BROOKS.

15. Was deceased ever in U. S. Armed Forces? (Yes, no, or unknown) YES | (Give war or dates of service) WW II

16. SOCIAL SECURITY NUMBER 419-36-8925

17. INFORMANT a. SIGNATURE Learo Randoll | b. ADDRESS 745 S. KEELER ST. | c. RELATIONSHIP TO DECEASED MOTHER

18. MEDICAL CAUSE OF DEATH

PART I. DEATH WAS CAUSED BY. [Enter only one cause per line for (A), (B) and (C).]

IMMEDIATE CAUSE (A) ORGANIC HEART DISEASE

Conditions, if any, which gave rise to the above IMMEDIATE CAUSE (A), stating the UNDERLYING cause last. due to (B) .... due to (C) ....

INTERVAL BETWEEN ONSET AND DEATH

PART II. OTHER SIGNIFICANT CONDITIONS CONTRIBUTING TO DEATH BUT NOT RELATED TO THE TERMINAL CONDITION GIVEN IN PART I(A).

19a. DATE OF OPERATION | 19b. MAJOR FINDINGS OF OPERATION

20. AUTOPSY? YES [ ] NO [X]

21a. ACCIDENT [ ] SUICIDE [ ] UNDETERMINED [ ] HOMICIDE [ ] | 21b. PLACE OF INJURY (e.g., in or about home, farm, factory, street, office bldg., etc.) | 21c. INJURED AT (CITY, TOWNSHIP, OR LOCATION) (COUNTY) (STATE)

21d. TIME OF INJURY (HOUR) (MONTH) (DAY) (YEAR) A.M. P.M. | 21e. INJURY OCCURRED WHILE AT WORK [ ] NOT WHILE AT WORK [ ] | 21f. HOW DID INJURY OCCUR?

22a. Upon medical investigation I find this death was caused as stated above. DATE: 5/25/63 SIGNED: Joel Kearney M.D. CORONER'S PHYSICIAN

22b. Upon official investigation I find the person described died as stated above. DATE: SIGNED: Andrew J. Toman M.D. COUNTY CORONER.

23. DISPOSITION: BURIAL, REMOVAL, CREMATION Date 5-28-63

CEMETERY LOCAL

LOCATION DURANT, MISSISSIPPI

24. FUNERAL DIRECTOR SIGNATURE Leo T. Johnson

ADDRESS 462 W. DIVISION ST. Chicago Illinois | License Number 3956

25. Received for filing on MAY 28 1963 (Signed) Samuel L. Andelman, M.D. LOCAL REGISTRAR

1960 revision based on the U. S. Standard Certificate of Death.

VS & R 202—BUREAU OF STATISTICS—ILLINOIS DEPARTMENT OF PUBLIC HEALTH

Complete List of Singles in Chronological Order

Note: Whenever possible, information has been taken directly from the original 78 or 45 rpm issue.

Matrix #	Artist, Label & Number	Title(s)	Writer's Credit	Release Date
	Elmo James:			
DRC 53	Trumpet 146	Dust My Broom	(Elmo James)	27 Nov 1951
DRC 52		Catfish Blues (by Bobo Thomas)	(Elmo James)	
	Elmore James:			
MM 1782	Modern Unissued	Please Find My Baby	n/a	
MM 1783		Long Tall Woman	n/a	

Note: Although scheduled for release in early 1952, it was withdrawn from production due to legal reasons. See the text or the explanatory note under May 1953 session for more details. MM 1782 was later released as Flair 1022 (and assigned matrix number FL-147). MM 1783 was first issued in October 1993 on the 3 CD Box Set, The Classic Early Recordings 1951-1956 *(Ace (UK) Box CD 4), and should not be confused with the version recorded on 4 January 1956 and released on Modern 983 that same year.*

Matrix #	Artist, Label & Number	Title(s)	Writer's Credit	Release Date
	Elmore James:			
MR 5001	Meteor 5000	I Believe	(James)	late Dec 1952
MR 5003		I Held My Baby Last Night	(James)	

Note: On some 78 rpm issues, "MR" prefix deleted in dead wax.

Matrix #	Artist, Label & Number	Title(s)	Writer's Credit	Release Date
	Elmore James:			
MR 5000	Meteor 5003	Baby, What's Wrong	(James-Taub)	April 1953
MR 5002		Sinful Women	(James-Taub)	
	Elmore James and the Broom Dusters:			
FL-123	Flair 1011	Early In The Morning	(James)	May 1953
FL-124		Hawaiian Boogie	(James)	
	Elmore James:			
MR 5016	Meteor Unissued	Lost Woman Blues	n/a	
MR 5017		Hawaiian Boogie	n/a	

Note: Production of Elmore's third Meteor single was stopped due to the fact that he was switched from Meteor to the Flair label in the spring of 1953. MR 5016 was first released on the album King Of The Slide Guitar *(Ace (UK) LP 68, 1983), while MR 5017 saw release as Modern 49 in mid to late 1968 (and assigned matrix number MX 49-B). It should not be confused with the version of "Hawaiian Boogie" that was released as Flair 1011 in 1953.*

Matrix #	Artist, Label & Number	Title(s)	Writer's Credit	Release Date
	Elmore James:			
U 4321	Checker 777	Country Boogie	(James)	late June/early July 1953
U 4324		She Just Won't Do Right	(James)	

Note: On 78 rpm issues, "U" prefix deleted in dead wax, while 45 rpm issues feature "45" prefix in dead wax.

Matrix #	Artist, Label & Number	Title(s)	Writer's Credit	Release Date
	Elmore James and His Broom Dusters:			
FL-131	Flair 1014	Can't Stop Lovin	(James)	August 1953
FL-132		Make A Little Love	(James)	
	Elmore James And The Broomdusters:			
FL-147	Flair 1022	Please Find My Baby	(James)	December 1953
FL-148		Strange Kinda' Feeling	(James)	

ELMORE JAMES
Baby, What's Wrong? 76
METEOR 5003—Routine jump blues is given a strong performance by James, with the ork selling all the way. Could attract some juke loot.
Sinful Women....73
James wails a sad weeper to Southern backing. He creates a mournful mood as he presents this tale of duplicity. Should sell some.

ELMORE JAMES
(Flair 1011)

C+ "HAWAIIAN BOOGIE" (2:41) [Flair] Elmore James etches an instrumental quick beat boogie. Item is a foottapper.

B "EARLY IN THE MORNING" (2:54) [Flair] James shouts out a rhythmic middle tempo bounce energetically. A smart bit of guitar support rounds out on ok deck.

ELMORE JAMES
(Flair 1011)

B+ "EARLY IN THE MORNING" (2:41) [Flair-BMI] Elmore James etches a strong middle tempo southern blues that should get powerful juke box action.

B "HAWAIIAN BOOGIE" (2:38) [Flair-BMI] Flip is a quick beat instrumental that drives.

Below, Left: 2 May 1953 Billboard; Below Right: Cash Box, 13 June and 11 July 1953, respectively.
(Cash Box reviews courtesy Simon Evans/Man In Japan Collection)

Matrix #	Artist, Label & Number	Title(s)	Writer's Credit	Release Date
	Elmore James and His Broomdusters:			
FL-161	Flair 1031	Hand In Hand	(James-Josea)	March 1954
FL-162		Make My Dreams Come True	(James-Josea)	

Note: On some 78 rpm issues, suffix "RE" added to FL-161 and FL-162 in the dead wax.

Matrix #	Artist, Label & Number	Title(s)	Writer's Credit	Release Date
	Elmore James and his "Broomdusters":			
FL-182	Flair 1039	Sho Nuff I Do	(James)	late May 1954
FL-183		1839 Blues	(James)	
	Elmore James and His Broomdusters:			
FL-200	Flair 1048	Dark And Dreary	(Josea)	August 1954
FL-201		Rock My Baby Right	(Josea)	
	Elmore James and His "Broomdusters":			
FL-216	Flair 1057	Sunny Land	(James-Josea)	October 1954
FL-217		Standing At The Crossroads	(James-Josea)	
	Elmore James and His "Broomdusters":			
FL-225	Flair 1062	Late Hours At Midnight	(James-Josea)	Jan / Feb 1955
FL-226		The Way You Treat Me	(James-Josea)	
	Elmore James and His "Broomdusters":			
FL-240	Flair 1069	Happy Home	(Josea)	May 1955
FL-241		No Love In My Heart	(Josea)	
	Elmore James and His "Broom Dusters":			
FL-250	Flair 1074	Dust My Blues	(James-Josea)	early August 1955
FL-251		I Was A Fool	(James-Josea)	

Matrix #	Artist, Label & Number	Title(s)	Writer's Credit	Release Date
	Elmore James:			
A-60	Ace 508	I Believe My Time Ain't Long	(E. James)	September 1955
A-61		I Wish I Was A Catfish	(E. James)	

Note: Reissue of Trumpet 146. On 78 rpm issues, the dead wax on A-60 states Ace-60 and DRC 53. On A-61, it states Ace-61 and DRC 52. 45 rpm issues bear simply 45-60 and 45-61 in the dead wax, respectively.

	Elmore James and His "Broom Dusters":			
FL-260	Flair 1079	Blues Before Sunrise	(James-Josea)	Nov 1955
FL-261		Good Bye	(James-Josea)	
	Elmore James and His "Broom Dusters":			
MM 2285	Modern 983	Wild About You	(James-Josea)	February 1956
MM 2286		Long Tall Woman	(James-Josea)	
	Elmore James and his Broom Dusters:			
C-2402	Chief 7001	The 12 Year Old Boy	(Nel Rondon)	May 1957
C-2403		Coming Home	(E. James)	
	Elmore James and His Broomdusters:			
C-2404	Chief 7004	It Hurts Me Too	(Mel London)	July 1957
C-2406		Elmore's Contribution To Jazz	(E. James)	
	Elmore James and his Broom Dusters:			
57-699	Vee-Jay 249	The 12 Year Old Boy	(Mel London)	prob early Aug 1957
57-700		Coming Home	(E. James)	

Note: On some copies, C-2402 and C-2403 are inscribed in the dead wax, while label states 57-699/57-700.

	Elmore James and His Broomdusters:			
57-740	Vee-Jay 259	Elmore's Contribution To Jazz	(E. James)	mid Oct 1957
57-741		It Hurts Me Too	(Mel London)	

Note: On some copies, C-2406 and C-2404 are inscribed in the dead wax, while label states 57-740/57-741; on other copies, both sets of matrix numbers are given. Some copies bear Delta numbers 18242 and 18243 in the dead wax. (See Warren Cook, "Disc Dating " Record Exchanger 9 (March 1972): 22-23, for moro information).

	Elmore James and His Broomdusters:			
25-117	Chief 7006	Cry For Me Baby	(London)	Dec 1957
25-118		Take Me Where You Go	(James)	
	Elmore James and His Broomdusters:			
25-117	Vee-Jay 269	Cry For Me Baby	(London)	mid-Dec 1957
25-118		Take Me Where You Go	(James)	

Note: Some copies bear Delta numbers 19206 and 19207 in the dead wax.

	Elmore James And His Broomdusters:			
FM 123	Fire 1011	Make My Dreams Come True	(James-Josea)	Dec 1959
FM 124		Bobby's Rock	(James)	

Note: "Dreams" is a reissue of Flair 1031 (FL-162), not a re-recording.

	Elmore James and The Broom Dusters:			
K-331-1	Kent 331	Dust My Blues (I Believe)	(James-Josea)	early 1960
K-331-2		Happy Home	(James-Josea)	

Matrix #	Artist, Label & Number	Title(s)	Writer's Credit	Release Date
	Elmo James And His Broomdusters:			
FM 133	Fire 1016	The Sky Is Crying	(E. James)	March 1960
FM 134		Held My Baby Last Night	(E. James)	
	Elmore James:			
10109	Chess 1756	I Can't Hold Out	(E. James)	May / June 1960
10110		The Sun Is Shining	(E. James)	
Note: Some copies bear Delta number 35261 in the dead wax.				
	Elmore James and His Broom Dusters:			
FM 151	Fire 1024	Rollin And Tumblin	(B. Robinson)	July 1960
FM 152		I'm Worried	(E. James)	
	Elmore James:			
25-154	Chief 7020	Knocking At Your Door	(James)	Dec 1960
Note: Although credited to James, the reverse, "Calling All Blues," is actually by Earl Hooker-Junior Wells.				
	Elmo James:			
FM 165	Fire 1031	Done Somebody Wrong	(E. James)	Dec 1960
FM 166		Fine Little Mama	(E. James)	
	Elmore James:			
FM 193	Fire 504	Look On Yonder Wall	(Elmore James)	late Dec 1961
FM 194		Shake Your Moneymaker	(Elmore James)	
Note: Some copies bear Delta number 41429 in the dead wax.				
	Elmore James:			
FB 301	Fire 1503	Stranger Blues	(Elmore James-Bobby Robinson)	late June 1962
FB 302		Anna Lee	(Elmore James)	
Note: Some copies bear Delta number 43894 in the dead wax.				
	Elmore James:			
W 317	Down Home 775	The Sky Is Crying	(Elmore James)	1962 / 1963?
W 318	Down Home 776	Held My Baby Last Night	(Elmore James)	
Note: Reissue of Fire 1016; appears to be dubbed from disc.				

Three different label shots of Fire 1503. Did Bobby Robinson have hopes that this would be a big hit? The copy on the left bears the Delta number, possibly indicating the first one to be pressed.

Matrix #	Artist, Label & Number	Title(s)	Writer's Credit	Release Date
	Elmore James and The Broom Dusters:			
K-394-1	Kent 394	Dust My Blues (I Believe)	(James-Josea)	Spring 1964
K-394-2		Happy Home	(James-Josea)	

Note: Reissue of Kent 331. In the dead wax, K-331-1 is scratched out, and K-394-1 written in instead. Flip side has identical markings in dead wax as well, with -2 as suffix.

Matrix #	Artist, Label & Number	Title(s)	Writer's Credit	Release Date
	Elmore James and The Broom Dusters:			
	Sue 335	Dust My Blues	(James-Josea)	Oct 1964
		Happy Home	(James-Josea)	

Note: Reissue of Kent 331.

Matrix #	Artist, Label & Number	Title(s)	Writer's Credit	Release Date
	Elmore James:			
ZTSP 98718	Enjoy 2015	Bleeding Heart	(Bobby Robinson)	early April 1965
ZTSP 98719	(1st pressing)	It Hurts Me Too	(Elmore James)	

Note: Numbers stamped in dead wax are ZTSP 98718-1A and ZTSP 98719-1A, respectively.

Matrix #	Artist, Label & Number	Title(s)	Writer's Credit	Release Date
	Elmore James:			
ZTSP 98719	Enjoy 2015	It Hurts Me Too	(Elmore James)	prob late Spring 1965
ZTSP 104841	(2nd pressing)	Pickin' The Blues	(Bobby Robinson)	

Note: Numbers stamped in dead wax are ZTSP 98719-1B and ZTSP 104841-1C, respectively. Another pressing with "Fire 1" for ZTSP 98719 and "Fire 2" for ZTSP 104841 (on both the label and dead wax) has also been seen.

Matrix #	Artist, Label & Number	Title(s)	Writer's Credit	Release Date
	Elmo James:			
6326	Sphere Sound 702	My Bleeding Heart	(Sehorn-James)	early June 1965
6327		One Way Out	(Sehorn-James)	
	Elmore James:			
	Sue 383	It Hurts Me Too	(Robinson)	July 1965
		Bleeding Heart	n/a	
	Elmore James:			
ZTSP 98718	Enjoy 2020	Bleeding Heart	(Bobby Robinson-Elmore James)	prob Aug 1965
ZTSP 105797		Mean Mistreatin' Mama	(Bobby Robincon)	
	Elmore James:			
	Sue 392	Knocking At Your Door	n/a	Sept 1965

Note: Reissue of Chief 7020

Matrix #	Artist, Label & Number	Title(s)	Writer's Credit	Release Date
	Elmore James:			
ZTSP 105800	Enjoy 2022	Look On Yonder Wall	(Elmore James)	
ZTSP 105801		Shake Your Moneymaker	(E. James-Bobby Robinson)	prob Fall 1965

Note: A different pressing (with blue and silver label instead of orange and black) with "EN" prefix instead of "ZTSP" has also been seen. Writers' credit on "Shake" also listed as "Elmore James-B. Robinson" on certain reissues.

Matrix #	Artist, Label & Number	Title(s)	Writer's Credit	Release Date
	Elmore James:			
6431	Flashback 15	The Sky Is Crying	(Robinson-James)	prob late Fall 1965
6432		Standing At The Crossroads (vsn 2)	(James-Josea)	
	Elmore James:			
K-433-1	Kent 433	Standing At The Crossroads	(Josea-Taub-Ling)	late 1965
K-433-2		Sunnyland	(Josea-Taub-Ling)	

Note: Reissue of Flair 1057

Matrix #	Artist, Label & Number	Title(s)	Writer's Credit	Release Date
	Elmore James:			
EN 34578	Enjoy 2027	Everyday I Have The Blues	(Peter Chatman)	late 1965
EN 34579		Dust My Broom (vsn 4)	(E. James)	

	Elmore James:			
M-4970-01A	U.S.A. 815	Cry For Me Baby	(London)	prob late 1965
M-4970-01B		Take Me Where You Go	(James)	

Note: On "Cry," the dead wax bears both 25-117 and M-4970-01A. On "Take," both 25-118 and M-4970-01B are given.

	Elmore James:			
M-4970-01A	S&M 101	Cry For Me	(London)	c. late 1965 / early 1966?
M-4970-01B		Take Me Where You Go	(London)	

Note: On "Cry," the dead wax bears both 25-117 and M-4970-01A. On "Take," both 25-118 and M-4970-01B are given.

	Elmore James:			
6516	Sphere Sound 708	Shake Your Money Maker	(Elmore James)	poss c. Jan 1966
6517		I Need You	(M. Sehorn-E. James)	
	Elmore James:			
25-117	M-Pac 7231	Cry For Me Baby	n/a	1966
25-118		Take Me Where You Go	n/a	
	Elmore James:			
	Sue 4007	I Need You	n/a	April 1966
		Mean Mistreatin' Mama	n/a	
	Elmo James:			
TM-1519	Jewel 764	Dust My Broom	(James)	Spring / Summer 1966

Note: Reissue of Trumpet 146 and Ace 508, but with Arthur Crudup's "Gotta Find My Baby" (Trumpet 186) on reverse instead of "Catfish Blues." A September 1980 repressing carries matrix number SL 2949.

	Elmo James:			
6711	Sphere Sound 712	Dust My Broom (vsn 2)	(Elmo James)	June 1966
6712		Rollin' And Tumblin'	(James-Robinson)	
	Elmore James:			
8316	Sphere Sound 713	Something Inside Me	(M. Sehorn-E. James)	prob 1966
8317		She Done Move [*sic*]	(M. Sehorn-E. James)	
	Elmore James:			
JJ-689	Burn 504	Look On Yonder Wall	(Elmore James)	1966/1967?
JJ-690		Shake Your Moneymaker	(Elmore James)	

Note: "Shake Your Moneymaker" has Burn 504A in dead wax; Reverse has Burn 504B in dead wax.

	Elmore James:			
K-465-1	Kent 465	Sunnyland	(Josea-Ling-Taub)	Summer 1967
K-465-2		Goodbye Baby	(Josea-Ling-Taub)	
	Elmore James:			
MX-15-A	Modern Oldies 15	Dust My Blues	(James)	1967
MX-15-B		Happy Home	(James)	

Note: Reissue of Kent 331. In the dead wax, K-331-1 and K-394-1 are both scratched out and MX-15-A is written in instead. Flip side has identical markings in dead wax as well, with -B as suffix.

Matrix #	Artist, Label & Number	Title(s)	Writer's Credit	Release Date
	Elmore James:			
8606	Bell 719	Strange [*sic*] Blues	(E. James-M. Sehorn)	early 1968
8607		Anna Lee	(E. James-M. Sehorn)	
	Elmore James:			
MX 49-A	Modern Oldies 49	Early In The Morning	(James/Josea)	mid / late 1968
MX 49-B		Hawaiian Boogie (No 1)	(James/Josea)	
	Elmore James:			
MX 55-A	Modern Oldies 55	Sunnyland	(James/Josea)	prob mid / late 1968
MX 55-B		Standing At The Crossroads	(Jmaes[*sic*]/Josea)	
Note: Reissue of Flair 1057				
	Elmore James:			
Fire-1	Fire 2020	It Hurts Me Too	(Elmore James-Bobby Robinson)	Spring/Summer 1969
Fire-2		Pickin' The Blues	(Bobby Robinson)	
	Elmore James:			
K 508-1	Kent 508	I Believe	(Ling-Josea-Taub)	1969
K 508-2		1839 Blues	(Ling-Josea-Taub)	
	Elmore James:			
24-A	Trip 24	It Hurts Me Too	[no writer's credit listed]	1970?
24-B		Pickin' The Blues	[no writer's credit listed]	
	Elmore James:			
SMX-00117	Trip 102	Shake Your Moneymaker	[no writer's credit listed]	May 1971
SMX-00118		Dust My Broom (vsn 4)	[no writer's credit listed]	
Note: Some pressings give label as "Trip Oldie" or "Trip Oldies." Date of 4-30-71 is inscribed in the dead wax.				
	Elmore James:			
F-1 & 1	Fury 2000	Everyday I Have The Blues	(Peter Chatman)	prob late 1971
F-2		Up Jumped Elmore	(Bobby Robinson)	
	Elmore James:			
379201-1	Mel 7011	Cry For Me Baby	(London)	1971/1972?
379201-2		It Hurts Me Too	(London)	
	Elmore James:			
DH-2000	Down Home 800	Stormy Monday Blues	(T-Bone Walker)	early 1970s?
DH-2001		Madison Blues	(Elmore James)	
	Elmore James and the Broom Dusters:			
FL-123	Flair 1011	Early In The Morning	(James)	1973
FL-124		Hawaiian Boogie	(James)	
	Elmore James:			
U 4321	Checker 777	Country Boogie	(James)	1973
U 4324		She Just Won't Do Right	(James)	

Matrix #	Artist, Label & Number	Title(s)	Writer's Credit	Release Date
	Elmore James:			
MR 5000	Meteor 5003	Baby, What's Wrong	(James-Taub)	1973
MR 5002		Sinful Women	(James-Taub)	
Note: Above three listings (for Flair 1011, Checker 777, and Meteor 5003) are all "bootleg reissues." On Flair 1011, both maroon and black label reproductions have been seen.				
	Elmore James:			
	Fire 5000	It Hurts Me Too	n/a	early 1976
		Pickin' The Blues	n/a	
	Elmore James:			
	Fire 5001	Something Inside Me	n/a	early 1976
		Fine Little Mama	n/a	
	Elmo James:			
SL 2949	Ronn 96	Dust My Broom	(James)	circa Sept 1980?
Note: Reissue of Jewel 764.				
	Elmore James:			
AT 1011	Charly EP126	Done Somebody Wrong	(James)	Mar 1981
AT 1012		Pickin' The Blues	(Robinson)	
AT 1013		Dust My Broom (vsn 2)	(James)	
	Elmore James:			
U-28341-M-B	Ripete EP 1031	Take Me Where You Go	(James)	1990
Note: Other artists featured are Jimmy Reed, George McCrae, Etta James, and Sugar Pie De Santo.				
	Elmore James:			
COL 3157-A	Collectables 3157	Dust My Broom (vsn 2)	(James)	1991/1992?
COL 3157-B		Shake Your Moneymaker	(Elmore James-B. Robinson)	
	Elmore James:			
COL 3350-A	Collectables 3350	Everyday I Have The Blues	(P. Chatman)	1991/1992?
COL 3350-B		I Have A Right To Love My Baby	(E. James)	
	Elmore James:			
COL 3351-A	Collectables 3351	Mean Mistreatin Mama	(Elmore James)	1991/1992?
COL 3351-B		Twelve Year Old Boy	(M. London)	

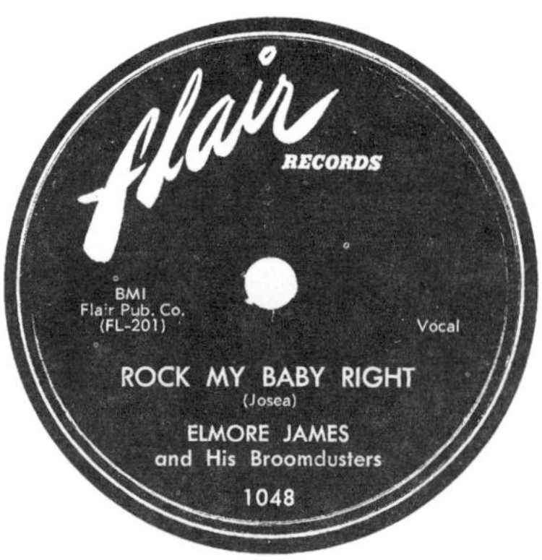

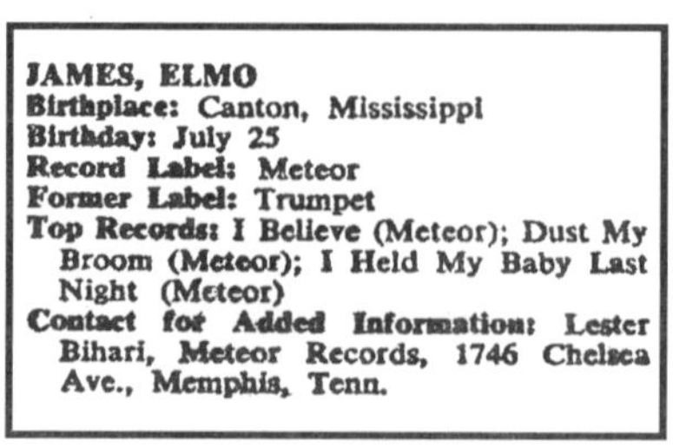

JAMES, ELMO
Birthplace: Canton, Mississippi
Birthday: July 25
Record Label: Meteor
Former Label: Trumpet
Top Records: I Believe (Meteor); Dust My Broom (Meteor); I Held My Baby Last Night (Meteor)
Contact for Added Information: Lester Bihari, Meteor Records, 1746 Chelsea Ave., Memphis, Tenn.

This small biographical detail, from Billboard's "1953 Artist Biography Section," was probably among the earliest personal info published about Elmore James. Curiously, both birth date and place are inaccurate (28 February 1953).

Singles Featuring Elmore James on Guitar

<table>
<tr><th>Matrix #</th><th>Artist, Label & Number</th><th>Title(s)</th><th>Writer's Credit</th><th>Release Date</th></tr>
<tr><td></td><td colspan="4">Sonny Boy Williamson:</td></tr>
<tr><td>DRC 15</td><td>Trumpet 129</td><td>Eyesight To The Blind</td><td>(Sonny Boy Williamson)</td><td>Feb/Mar 1951</td></tr>
<tr><td>DRC 16</td><td></td><td>Crazy About You Baby</td><td>(Sonny Boy Williamson)</td><td></td></tr>
<tr><td colspan="5">Note: No copies of DRC 15/16 have yet surfaced. On DRC 15-2/16-2, Elmore James does not play guitar. According to Marc Ryan and Bill Daniels, DRC 15/16 was issued (Ryan, Trumpet Records, 95).</td></tr>
<tr><td></td><td colspan="4">Sonny Boy Williamson:</td></tr>
<tr><td>DRC 18</td><td>Trumpet 139</td><td>Do It If You Wanta</td><td>(Sonny Boy Williamson)</td><td>Sept 1951</td></tr>
<tr><td>DRC 19</td><td></td><td>Cool, Cool Blues</td><td>(Sonny Boy Williamson)</td><td></td></tr>
<tr><td colspan="5">Note: On some copies, matrix number on label bears a typo of DRCI 18 and DRCI 19, respectively.</td></tr>
<tr><td></td><td colspan="4">Sonny Boy Williamson – His Harmonica and House Rockers:</td></tr>
<tr><td>DRC 17</td><td>Trumpet 140</td><td>Stop Crying</td><td>(Sonny Boy Williamson)</td><td>prob Oct 1951</td></tr>
<tr><td>DRC 20</td><td></td><td>Come On Back Home</td><td>(Sonny Boy Williamson)</td><td></td></tr>
<tr><td></td><td colspan="4">Sonny Boy Williamson – His Harmonica & House Rockers:</td></tr>
<tr><td>DRC 21</td><td>Trumpet 144</td><td>I Cross My Heart</td><td>(W. Williamson)</td><td>Nov 1951</td></tr>
<tr><td>DRC 22</td><td></td><td>West Memphis Blues</td><td>(W. Williamson)</td><td></td></tr>
<tr><td colspan="5">Note: On some copies, label credit is listed as "Sonny Boy" Williamson - His Harmonica & Houserockers</td></tr>
<tr><td></td><td colspan="4">Sonny Boy Williamson:</td></tr>
<tr><td>DRC 45</td><td>Trumpet 145</td><td>Sonny Boy's Christmas Blues</td><td>(Sonny Boy Williamson)</td><td>Nov 1951</td></tr>
<tr><td>DRC 46</td><td></td><td>Pontiac Blues</td><td>(Sonny Boy Williamson)</td><td></td></tr>
</table>

12 January 1952 Billboard

<table>
<tr><td></td><td colspan="4">Willie Love and His Three Aces:</td></tr>
<tr><td>DRC 48</td><td>Trumpet 147</td><td>Everybody's Fishing</td><td>(Willie Love)</td><td>Dec 1951</td></tr>
<tr><td>DRC 50</td><td></td><td>My Own Boogie</td><td>(Willie Love)</td><td></td></tr>
<tr><td></td><td colspan="4">Sonny Boy Williamson - His Harmonica and House Rockers</td></tr>
<tr><td>DRC 92</td><td>Trumpet 168</td><td>Stop Now Baby</td><td>(W. Williamson)</td><td>Apr/May 1952</td></tr>
<tr><td>DRC 93</td><td></td><td>Mr. Down Child</td><td>(W. Williamson)</td><td></td></tr>
<tr><td colspan="5">Note: On some 78 rpm issues, the dead wax bears both DRC 92 and ACA 2120 on "Stop Now Baby," and DRC 93 and ACA 2121 on the reverse.</td></tr>
</table>

Matrix #	Artist, Label & Number	Title(s)	Writer's Credit	Release Date
	Bep Brown Orchestra (a.k.a. J.T. Brown):			
MR 5004	Meteor 5001	Round House Boogie	(Brown)	late Dec 1952
MR 5005		Kickin' The Blues Around	(Brown)	
	Little Johnny Jones and the Chicago Hound Dogs:			
FL-121	Flair 1010	Sweet Little Woman	(Jones)	May 1953
FL-122		I May Be Wrong	(Jones)	

"Hodo Man" courtesy Bill Greensmith Collection

Matrix #	Artist, Label & Number	Title(s)	Writer's Credit	Release Date
	Junior Wells:			
1325	States 122	Cut That Out	(Wells)	late July 1953
1329		Eagle Rock	(Wells)	
	Joe Turner and his Blues Kings:			
A 1128	Atlantic 1016	TV Mama	(Lou Willie Turner)	Dec 1953
A 1127		Oke-She-Moke-She-Pop	(Lou Willie Turner)	
	Sonny Boy Williamson - His Harmonica & Houserockers			
DRC 91	Trumpet 212	Too Close Together	(W. Williamson)	Dec 1953
Note: On the reverse, "Cat Hop," Elmore James does not play guitar.				
	Sonny Boy Williamson & His Houserockers			
DRC 90	Trumpet 215	She Brought Life Back To The Dead	(W. Williamson?)	Jan/Feb 1954
Note: On the reverse, "Gettin' Out Of Town," Elmore James does not play guitar. DRC 90 was used for 78 rpm issue only. The 45 rpm issue features an alternate take, with matrix number 45-DRC 90.				
	Junior Wells and his Eagle Rockers			
1327	States 134	Hoodoo Man	(Wells)	Mar 1954
1330		Junior's Wail	(Wells)	
Note: "Hoodoo Man" given as "Hodo Man" or "Somebody Hoodooed The Hoodoo Man" on some copies of States 134.				
	Elmo James Broom Dusters Featuring Sax Man Brown:			
MR 5006-1	Meteor 5016	Sax-ony Boogie	(J.T. Brown)	Sept 1954
	Elmo James Broom Dusters Vocal By J.T. (Big Boy) Brown:			
MR 5007-2	(Meteor 5016 cont'd)	Dumb Woman Blues	(J.T. Brown)	
Note: Some copies of "Sax-ony Boogie" have MR 5006-1 in dead wax and MR 5006-2 on label, while other copies show MR 5006-2 on the label and *the dead wax.*				

Matrix #	Artist, Label & Number	Title(s)	Writer's Credit	Release Date
	Little Johnny Jones:			
A 1336	Atlantic 1045	Hoy Hoy	(Jones)	Nov 1954
A 1338		Doin' The Best I Can	(Jones)	

Note: On some 78 rpm issues, matrix numbers are reversed between the label and the dead wax, i.e., "Hoy Hoy" has A 1338 on label and A 1336-2 in dead wax, while "Doin' The Best I Can" has A 1336 on label and A 1338-1 in dead wax. Other issues have dead wax bearing A 1336-1 for "Hoy Hoy," and A 1338-2 for "Doin' The Best I Can." Dead wax of 45 rpm issue has 45-A-1336-1 for "Hoy Hoy," and 45-A-1338-1 for "Doin' The Best I Can."

Matrix #	Artist, Label & Number	Title(s)	Writer's Credit	Release Date
	Junior Wells:			
1328	States 143	Tomorrow Night	(Wells)	Dec 1954

Note: On the reverse, "So All Alone," Elmore James does not play guitar.

Matrix #	Artist, Label & Number	Title(s)	Writer's Credit	Release Date
	Joe Turner and His Blues Kings:			
A 1126	Atlantic 1053	Ti-Ri-Lee	(Turner-Nugetre-Gerald)	Mar 1955

Note: On some issues, matrix number A 1126-2 is given in the dead wax, while other copies bear A 1126-1. On the reverse, "Flip Flop And Fly," Elmore James does not play guitar.

Matrix #	Artist, Label & Number	Title(s)	Writer's Credit	Release Date
	Sax Man Brown with The Broomdusters:			
5004	Meteor 5024	Sax Symphonic Boogie	(L. Leslo)	Oct 1955
5005		Flaming Blues	(L. Leslo)	

Note: reissue of Meteor 5001.

Matrix #	Artist, Label & Number	Title(s)	Writer's Credit	Release Date
	Little Johnny Jones:			
A 1338	Atlantic 1045	Hoy Hoy	(Jones)	1974
A 1336		Doin' The Best I Can	(Jones)	

Note: Bootleg reissue. Matrix numbers as stated on label. Dead wax bears Atlantic 1045A and Atlantic 1045B, respectively.

Chronology of Elmore James LP & CD Releases

Label	Record#	Titles	Release Date
Crown	LP 5168	Blues After Hours	1961
Sue (GB)	LP 918	The Best of	Jan 1965
Sphere Sound	LP 7002	The Sky Is Crying	c. May 1965
Sue (GB)	LP 927	Memorial Album	Aug 27 1965
United	LP 716	The Blues In My Heart, The Rhythm In My Soul (re of Crown LP 5168)	late 1966
United	LP 7716	The Blues In My Heart, The Rhythm In My Soul (stereo of LP 716)	prob late 1966
Custom	LP 1054	The Blues In My Heart, The Rhythm In My Soul (re of Crown LP 5168)	1966/1967?
Custom	LP 2054	The Blues In My Heart, The Rhythm In My Soul (mono of LP 1054)	1966/1967?
Kent	LP 502	Original Folk Blues (mono/stereo issue)	Summer / Fall 1967
Kent	LP 5022	Original Folk Blues (mono issue)[868]	Summer / Fall 1967
Sphere Sound	LP 7008	I Need You	Fall 1967
Ember (GB)	LP 3397	The Late Fantastically Great (reissue of Crown LP 5168)	early 1968
Blue Horizon (GB)	LP 7-63204	Tough (Chess sides) (w/ John Brim)	Aug 1968
Bell (GB)	LP 104	Something Inside Of Me	Fall 1968
Kent	LP 9001	The Legend of Elmore James	mid-1969
Bell	LP 6037	Elmore James	mid-1969
Chess	LP 1537	Whose Muddy Shoes (w/ John Brim)	October 1969
Kent	LP 9010	The Resurrection of Elmore James	late 1969
Blue Horizon (GB)	LP 7-66230	To Know A Man (2 LPs)	Dec 1969
Up Front	LP 122	The Great Elmore James	early 1970
United Artists (GB)	LP 29109	The Legend of Elmore James (reissue of Kent LP 9001)	mid 1970
Blue Horizon (US)	LP 4601	Blues Masters Vol. 1 (first half of Blue Horizon LP 7-66230)	prob 1971
Musidisc (FR)	LP 5601	The Legend of Elmore James (reissue of Kent LP 9001)	early 70s?
Musidisc (FR)	LP 5610	The Resurrection of Elmore James (reissue of Kent LP 9010)	early 70s?
Bell (FR)	LP 062.90865	The Sky Is Crying (reissue of Bell LP 6037)	early 1970s?
Trip	LP 8007	History of Elmore James (2 LPs)	mid 1971
Pickwick	LP 5014	Screamin' Blues	prob 1972
Cobblestone	LP 9001	South Side Blues (w/ Eddie Taylor, Jimmy Reed)	Spring 1972
Polydor (GB)	LP 2383200	Cotton Patch Hotfoots (w/ Walter Horton)	Early/Mid 1973
United	LP 7743	Original Folk Blues (reissue of Kent LP 5022)	prob late 1974
Trip	LP 9511	History of Elmore James Volume 2	1973/74/75?
Byg (FR)	LP 529004	The Blues In My Heart (reissue of Crown LP 5168)	1970s?
Byg (FR)	LP 529503	The Blues In My Heart The Rhythm... (re of Crown LP 5168)	1970s?
Goody (FR)	LP 7000	The Blues In My Heart The Rhythm... (re of Crown LP 5168)	1970s?
United	LP 7778	The Legend of Elmore James (reissue of Kent LP 9001)	1975?
United	LP 7787	The Resurrection of Elmore James (reissue of Kent LP 9010)	1975?
DJM (UK)	LP 8008	All Them Blues (2 LPs)(reissue of Trip LP 8007)	Oct 1975
Muse	LP 5087	Street Talkin' (w/ Eddie Taylor, Jimmy Reed)	early 1976
Trip	LP 1650	16 Greatest Hits	1978
Vivid Sound/Globe (JP)	LP 5004	Dust My Blues	late 1979?
Charly (UK)	LP 1008	One Way Out	19 Sept 1980
Charly (UK)	LP 1017	Got To Move	Mar 1981
Ace (UK)	LP 31	The Best of Elmore James	Mar 1981
Audiofidelity (GB)	LP 1034	All Them Blues (2 LPs)	1981
Oxford (IT)	LP 3238	One Way Out (Italian reissue of Charly LP 1008)	1981

868 Numbered as 502/5022. This album was later reissued as Kent LP 522.

Oxford (IT)	LP 3242	Got To Move (Italian reissue of Charly LP 1017)	1981
Phoenix	LP 241-1	History of Elmore James (reissue of Trip LP 8007)	1981
Chess (IT)	LP 2016	Whose Muddy Shoes (reissue of Chess LP 1537)	1981
Chess/Vogue (FR)	LP 515006	Whose Muddy Shoes (w/ John Brim)(reissue of Chess LP 1537)	early 1982
Phoenix	LP 334	The Great Elmore James (reissue of Up Front LP 122)	1982
Ace (UK)	LP 68	King Of The Slide Guitar	April 1983
Intermedia	LP 5034	Red Hot Blues	Spring/Summer 1983
Blue Moon (GB)	LP 1008	Red Hot Blues (reissue of Intermedia LP 5034)	Nov 1983
Line/Outline (EEC)	LP 8018	To Know A Man (2 LPs • Reissue of Blue Horizon LP 7-66230)	late 1983
Chess	LP 9114	Whose Muddy Shoes (w/ John Brim)(reissue of Chess LP 1537)	1984
P-Vine (JP)	LP 6005/06/07	Something Inside of Me/The Complete Fire-Enjoy Sessions	1984
Chess/P-Vine (JP)	LP 823	Whose Muddy Shoes (w/ John Brim)(reissue of Chess LP 1537)	1984
Ace (UK)	LP 112	The Original Meteor/Flair Sides	Aug 1984
Topline (GB)	LP 120	Dust My Broom	Dec 1984
Deja Vu (IT)	LP 2035	The Elmore James Collection	1985
Cleo (NL)	LP 00271283	Greatest Hits (reissue of Intermedia LP 5034)	1985?
Kent	LP 4003	The Best of Elmore James (reissue of Ace LP 31)	1985
Kent	LP 4004	King Of The Slide Guitar (reissue of Ace LP 68)	1985
Crown/Gem (GB)	LP 003	King of the Bottleneck Blues	Feb 1986
Chess/Vogue (FR)	CD 600119	Elmore James-John Brim-Floyd Jones	1986
Castle Showcase (GB)	LP 140	Pickin' The Blues	1986
Charly (UK)	CD 34	Shake Your Moneymaker	Dec 1986
Ace (UK)	CD 192	"Let's Cut It"—The Very Best of Elmore James	March 1987
Collectables	CD 5112	Golden Classics—Guitars In Orbit	March 1988
Deja Vu (IT)	CD 2035	Collection: Elmore James/20 Blues Greats	July 1988
Muse	CD 5087	Street Talkin' (w/ Jimmy Reed and Eddie Taylor)	Fall 1988
Blue City (NL)	CD 2652712	20 Greatest Hits	1988
Chess Greenline	LP 8097	Whose Muddy Shoes (reissue of Chess LP 1537)	1989
Chess Greenline	CD 78097	Whose Muddy Shoes (reissue of Chess LP 1537)	1989
Charly (UK)	CD 180	Come Go With Me	May 1989
Deja Vu (IT)	CD 24	The Elmore James Story	May 1989
Relic	LP 1021	The Last Session	Fall 1989
Collectables	CD 5184	The Complete Fire And Enjoy Sessions Part 1	Dec 1989
Collectables	CD 5185	The Complete Fire And Enjoy Sessions Part 2	Dec 1989
Collectables	CD 5186	The Complete Fire And Enjoy Sessions Part 3	Dec 1989
Collectables	CD 5187	The Complete Fire And Enjoy Sessions Part 4	Dec 1989
Blues Encore (CH)	CD 52006	The Master of the Slide Guitar	early 1990
P-Vine (JP)	CD 2180/1/2	Something Inside of Me / The Complete Fire-Enjoy Sessions	1990
Instant (GB)	CD 5030	Dust My Broom	July 1990
Route 16[869]	CD 9005/9007	Greatest Hits	1991
Black Label	CD 2001	History of Elmore James Vol. 1	1991
Black Label	CD 2002	History of Elmore James Vol. 2	1991
Chess	CD 9114	Whose Muddy Shoes (w/ John Brim)[870]	April 1991
P-Vine (JP)	CD 1410	South Side Blues (w/ Eddie Taylor)	May/June 1991
Zillion (NL)	CD 2610272	Rolling And Tumbling	Summer/Fall 1991
Masters (DE)	CD 61046-2	Golden Hits	1991/1992?
Flair/Virgin	CD 2-91800[871]	"Let's Cut It"—The Very Best of E.J. (reissue of Ace CD 192)	Nov 1991

869 Note: The outer tray cards identify this set as "That's Blues TB 201," however individual discs are actually labelled Route 16 CD 9005 (Disc 1) and Route 16 CD 9007 (Disc 2), respectively.

870 Not a true reissue of Chess LP1537; "The Sun Is Shining" is a different take from the version on LP.

871 Reissued by Capitol Records as 86257.

Tomato	CD 70389	Dust My Broom	Nov 1991
Relic	CD 7026	Rollin' & Tumblin'—The Best of Elmore James	Mar 1992
Charly (UK)	BM CD 12	The Sky Is Crying (Blues Masterworks series)	May/June 1992
Capricorn	PRO CD 5831	King Of The Slide Guitar Sampler (Promotional Sampler)	Summer 1992
Capricorn	CD 42006-2	King Of The Slide Guitar (2 CD Box Set)	Aug 1992
Charly (UK)	BM CD 28	Standing At The Crossroads (Blues Masterworks series)	Fall 1992
Music Club (GB)	CD 083	The Immortal Elmore James King of the Bottleneck Blues	late Fall 1992
Charly (UK)	CD 1027	Dust My Broom	Nov 1992
Relic	CD 7040	Dust My Broom—The Best of Elmore James Part 2	3 Dec 1992
Charly (UK)	CDRED Box 4	King Of The Slide Guitar (4 CD Box Set)	late Dec 1992
Music Options/ARC	CD 3013	(NL)(equivalent or reissue(?) of Topline LP 120)	1992/1993?
P-Vine (JP)	CD 1883	The Very Best of Elmore James	Early 1993
Rhino	CD 71190	The Sky Is Crying: The History of Elmore James	late Mar 1993
Ace (UK)	Box CD 4	The Classic Early Recordings 1951-1956 (3 CD Box Set)	late Oct 1993
Pilz	CD 449322-2	Red Hot Blues	late 1993
Charly (UK)	CD 2007	Dust My Broom	late 1993?
Flair/Virgin	CD 39632/33/34	The Classic Early Recordings 1951-1956 (3 CD Box Set)	14 June 1994
Eclipse	CD 64739-2	King of the Slide Guitar	1994
Black Label	CD 2009	Every Day I Have the Blues (equiv of Trip LP 1650)	late 1994
Relic	CD 7097	The Last Sessions	1995
Ace (UK)	CD 583	The Best of Elmore James – The Early Years	Spring 1995
P-Vine (JP)	CD 3742	P-Vine Presents 21 Blues Giants, Vol. 2: Elmore James	Late July 1995
Collectables	CD 8829	The Complete Fire And Enjoy Recordings (3 CD Set)	1 Sept 1995
Opal (Spain)	CD 106	Elmore James and His Broom Dusters: Early Years 1951-1954	1995
P-Vine (JP)	CD 2889/90/91	The Sky Is Crying: The Legendary Fire/Enjoy Sessions	Late Nov (?) 1995
Ronn	CD 8016	Dust My Broom (w/ Homesick, Crudup, & Bobo Thomas)	26 Nov 1996
Camden	CD 74321 523762	The Sky Is Crying	1997
Charly (DE)	CPBOX 301	King of the Slide Guitar / The Complete Chief & Fire Sessions	1997
Recall (UK)	CD 231	Rollin' And Tumblin'	1999
Rhino	CD 79803	Blues Masters: The Very Best of Elmore James	14 Mar 2000
Buddah	CD 99781-2	Shake Your Moneymaker: The Best of the Fire Sessions	2001

Selected Compilation / Anthology LP & CD Releases

Vee-Jay	LP 1020	The Blues	1960
Mercury	LP 20826	Original Golden Hits of the Great Blues Singers (Mono)	1963
Mercury	LP 60826	Original Golden Hits of the Great Blues Singers (Stereo)	1963
Columbia (GB)	LP 1417	Blues	early 1960s (pre-1965)
Argo	LP 4034	The Blues Vol. 3	March 1964
Sue (GB)	LP 921	We Sing The Blues	Spring 1965
Blues Classics	LP 5	Country Blues Classics Vol. 1	late Summer 1965
Storyville (Denmark)	LP 176	Chicago - Rhythm & Blues Sounds (Blues Scene USA Vol. 1)	1965
Xtra (UK)	LP 1047	The Mike Raven Blues Show	late 1966
Blues Classics	LP 15	Memphis and the Delta—1950s	prob 1967
Custom	LP 1	20 Greatest Blues Hits by the Original Artists	mid-late '60s?
United	LP 7718	The Best of the Biggest *(poss reissue of Custom LP 1056?)*	prob 1967
Teem	LP 5005	The Kings Sing The Blues	1967 / 1968?
Kent	LP 535	Underground Blues	1968 / 1969
CBS (GB)	LP 66218	The Story of the Blues	prob Aug 1969

Blue Horizon (UK)	PR LP 45/46	How Blue Can We Get?	1970
Red Lightnin' (UK)	LP 005	Blues In D Natural	early 1970
Columbia	LP 30008	The Story of the Blues	early/mid 1970
Ember/Specialty	LP 6609	All The Blues – All The Time	Summer 1970
CBS (FR)	LP 66426	The Story of the Blues Vols. 1 & 2 (4 LP Box set)	1970
Mamlish	LP 3800	Black Cat Trail	Fall 1970
United	LP 7748	20 Greatest Blues Hits (reissue of Custom LP 1)	1970s
United	LP 7754	Underground Blues (reissue of Kent LP 535)	1970s
Kent	LP 700	Roots/Soul Sounds Of A Proud People[872]	1970s?
Chess	LP 6641.125	Genesis Vol. 2—Memphis to Chicago	Oct 1974
Trip	LP 7503	The Blues Vol. 1	1975
DJM (UK)	LP 8005	All Them Blues (2 LPs)	prob Fall 1975
Trip	LP 7504	The Blues Vol. 2	1976
Festival	LP 1008	America's Musical Roots—The Blues	1976
Jewel	LP 5015	Jewel Spotlights the Blues, Vol. 1	late summer 1978
Vivid Sound (JP)	LP 1008	The Kings Sing the Blues Vol. 1 (*not* a reissue of Teem LP 5005)	1979
Chess (GB)	LP 4010	Chess Masters (2 LP set)	1982
Cascade (UK)	LP 1010	20 Great Blues Recordings of the 50's & 60's Vol. 2	1984
Chess/Vogue (DE)	CD 600048	The Golden Age of Chicago Blues	prob 1986
Ace (UK)	CD 216	Juke Joint Blues	1987
Ace (UK)	CD 232	Blues Guitar Blasters	1988
Cascade (UK)	CD 1001	20 Great R&B Hits of the 50's	1988
Cascade (UK)	CD 1005	20 Great Blues Recordings of the 50s and 60s	1988
Chess	CD 9276	The Blues Vol. 3 (reissue of Argo LP 4034)	15 Aug 1988
Chess	CD 31316	The Best of Chess Blues Vol. 2	Oct 1988
Ace (UK)	CD 258	R&B Confidential No. 1/The Flair Label	Feb 1989
Collectables	CD 5127	The Collectables Blues Collection Vol. 1	1989
Collectables	CD 5128	The Collectables Blues Collection Vol. 2	1989
Collectables	CD 5129	The Collectables Blues Collection Vol. 3	1989
Chess Greenline	CD 1025	The Best of Chess Blues (both volumes on 1 CD)	1989
Ace (UK)	CD 276	Kings of the Blues	1989
RST/Blues Documents	LP 1	The Greatest In Country Blues (1927-1956)(3 LP box set)	1989
Castle Communications (AU)	CD 206	The Ultimate Blues Collection	1990
Rhino	CD 70716	Legends of Guitar – Electric Blues Vol. 1	1990
Sequel (GB)	CD 47555/3	The Blues Guitar Box (only disc three has Elmore)	1990
Sequel (GB)	CD 185/1	The Blues Guitar Box 2 (only disc one has Elmore)	1991
Evasound (AU)	CD 019	The History of the Blues & Soul	1991
Relic	CD 7009	Raging Harlem Hit Parade	1991
Blues Collection (AU)	CD 341	Blues! Blues! Blues!	1991
Charly (UK)	CDRED 36	Slidin' (w/ Hound Dog Taylor, Earl Hooker, John Littlejohn)	1991
P-Vine (JP)	CD 3003	Modern/Kent The Best of Blues Guitars	Summer 1991
Story Of Blues (AT)	CD 3523-2	The Greatest In Country Blues – Vol. 3 (1929-1956)	c. Aug 1991
Ace (UK)	CD 335	Jukebox R&B	1991
Sire	CD 26617-2	Music From The Film *A Rage In Harlem*	1991
Music Club (GB)	CD 026	Comin' Home To The Blues 2	1991
Columbia (GB)	CD 468992-2	The Story of the Blues (re of CBS LP 66218 / Columbia LP 30008)	1991
Concept (AU)	CD 0265	Blues Brothers Soul Sisters (2 CD set)	1990s
Success (AU)	CD 2122	Blues Collection – Vol. 2	1990s
P-Vine (JP)	CD 2346	Willie Dixon: Working On The Blues Vol. 1	Late Jan (?) 1992

[872] Note: Also contains Boyd Gilmore's "All In My Dreams."

Cascade (UK)	Box CD 3	60 Great Blues Recordings (3 disc set)	1992
Marvel (AU)	CD 722	Feelin' The Blues – Diggin' The Rhythm #2	1992
Marvel (AU)	CD 725	Feelin' The Blues – Diggin' The Rhythm #5	1992
Chess	CD 4-9340	Chess Blues (4 disc box set)	22 Dec 1992
Relic	CD 7046	Raging Harlem Hit Parade, Vol. 2	1993
Vee-Jay	CD 711	A Taste of the Blues—Vol. 1	1993
MCA (BR)	CD 140 069	Sho Got The Blues – Blues Classics 3	1993
Bullseye Blues	CD 9533	Slidin' ... Some Slide	1993
Roots	CD 33046	Willie Dixon's Blues Dixonary Vol. 2	1993
Rhino	CD 71127	Blues Masters, Vol. 6: Blues Originals	16 Feb 1993
Rhino	CD 71130	Blues Masters, Vol. 8: Mississippi Delta Blues	16 Feb 1993
Rhino	CD 71126	Blues Masters, Vol. 15: Slide Guitar Classics	Aug 1993
Broad Music (AU)	CD 003	Legendary Blues Men	1993
P-Vine (JP)	CD 2741	Jam Packed Blues Guitar • Vol. 1 Dynaflow Electric Style	Fall 1993
Charly (UK)	CD 1050	Kings of the Blues	c. Fall 1993
Charly (UK)	CD 1124	The Chess Story	late 1993
Vee-Jay	CD 718	A Taste of the Blues—Vol. 2	Dec 1993
MCA	CD 20768	Greatest Blues Legends	1994
LaserLight (DE)	CD 12.336	Guitar Blues	1994
The Hit Label (GB)	CD 19	The Chart Show Ultimate Blues	1994
Jewel	CD 5015	Jewel Spotlights the Blues, Vol. 1 (cf LP 5015/has bonus tracks)	Spring 1994
Pointblank	PR CD 14171	Pointblank Doggone Blues Sampler (Promotional Sampler)	1994
P-Vine (JP)	CD 3038	Anthology of the Blues – Blues From The Deep South	Summer 1994
Europa Music (BR)	CD 10046	Spotlight On Blues	1994
Connoisseur Collection	CD 205 (GB)	Born Under A Bad Sign	1994
Fat Boy (GB)	CD 415/2	Blues & Soul Vol. 2	1994
Fat Boy (GB)	CD 415/3	Blues & Soul Vol. 3	1994
Fat Boy (GB)	CD 415/4	Blues & Soul Vol. 4	1994
Versailles (FR)	CD 478308 2	La Route du Blues	1994
Broad Music (AU)	CD 019	History of the Blues & Soul Vol. 1 (reissue of Evasound CD 019)	1994
Charly (UK)	CD DIG 3	A Modern Blues Anthology – Ain't Times Hard (4 disc set)	1994
Ace (UK)	CD 610	House Rockin' Blues	prob Jan / Feb 1995
Blue Moon (Spain)	CD 4003	Rhythm & Blues Legends Vol. 1	1995
Ace (UK)	CD 964	Mojo Working: The Best of Ace Blues	1995
Charly (UK)	CD LAB 104	The Vee-Jay Story[873]	1996
Blue Sun	CD 2000	King Biscuit Blues—The Helena Blues Legacy	1996
Chess	CD 9368	Chess Blues Classics 1957-1967	25 Mar 1997
P-Vine (JP)	CD 5271/72/73/74	Vee-Jay, The Chicago Black Music (4 CD set)	Late Dec(?) 1997
Chess	CD 2-9393	Chess Blues Guitar/Two Decades of Killer Fretwork 1949-1969	13 Jan 1998
Charly (DE)	CDGR 216	Slide Guitar Masters	1998
Rhino	CD 75348	Blues Masters, Vol. 18: More Slide Guitar Classics	14 July 1998
Chess (IT)	CD 3805962.	The Chess Story 1947-1975 (15 discs)[874]	1999
Collectables	CD 7271	The Very Best of Vee-Jay Blues Vol. 3	17 Oct 2000
Collectables	CD 7272	The Very Best of Vee-Jay Blues Vol. 4	17 Oct 2000
Ace (UK)	CD 784	The Modern Records Story	2001
Ace (UK)	CD 813	Travelling Record Man: Historic Down South Recording Trips of Bihari & Turner	2001

873 Lists Vee-Jay 259 ("It Hurts Me Too"), but plays Enjoy 2015 instead.

874 Each disc of the set is individually numbered beginning with 380 597-2 and ending with 380 611-2.

Selected LP & CD Releases w/ Elmore James on Guitar

Atlantic	EP 536	Big Joe Turner/Joe Turner Sings	1955
Atlantic	LP 8023	Big Joe Turner/Rockin' The Blues	1958
Atlantic	LP 8033	Big Joe Turner/Big Joe Is Here	1960
Atlantic (FR)	LP 332015	Big Joe Turner/Blues No. 5 (10-inch LP issue)	prob 1960
Atlantic	LP 8081	Big Joe Turner/The Best of Joe Turner	1963
Blues Classics	LP 8	Various/Chicago Blues—The Early 1950's	1965
pwb (GB)	LP 1	Various/The Post-War Chicago Blues	c. May / June 1965
Blues Classics	LP 9	Sonny Boy Williamson/"The Original" Sonny Boy Williamson	mid / late1965
Atco	LP 33-376	Big Joe Turner/His Greatest Recordings	1971
XX (UK)	EP 715	Junior Wells (7" 6 song EP)	prob Spring 1972
Red Lightnin' (GB)	LP 007	Junior Wells/In My Younger Days	prob Summer 1972
Atlantic	LP 7227	Various/Blues Piano—Chicago, Plus	5 Oct 1972
Arhoolie	LP 2020	Sonny Boy Williamson /King Biscuit Time (reissue of Blues Classics LP 9)	late 1974
Flyright (GB)	LP 4712	J.T. Brown/Rockin With J.T.	1975
Delmark	LP 640	Junior Wells/Blues Hit Big Town	June / July 1977
Krazy Kat (GB)	LP 7420	J.T. Brown/Rockin With J.T. (similar to Flyright LP 4712)	1984
Charly (UK)	LP 1070	Big Joe Turner/Jumpin' With Joe	1984
Atlantic	CD 81663-2	Big Joe Turner/Rhythm & Blues Years	Nov 1986
Atlantic	CD 81695-2	Various/Atlantic Blues: Guitar	1986
Atlantic	CD 81696-2	Various/Atlantic Blues: Vocalists	1986
Atlantic	LP 81697-1	Various/Atlantic Blues: Chicago	1986
Atlantic	CD 81697-2	Various/Atlantic Blues: Chicago	1986
P-Vine (JP)	LP 6101/02	Various/Bobby's Harlem Rock Vol. 2: New York on Fire	1987 / 88?
Arhoolie	CD 310	Sonny Boy Williamson/King Biscuit Time (similar to Arhoolie LP 2020)	late 1989
Atlantic/P-Vine	LP 6187A	Various/Blues Piano—Chicago, Plus	late 1980s?
Acoustic Archives	CD 701	Various/Strange Kind Of Feelin'	Spring 1990
Acoustic Archives	CD 702	Various/Delta Blues—1951	1990
Blues Encore (GB)	CD 52008	Big Joe Turner/The Blues Boss	1990
P-Vine (JP)	CD 2184	Willie Love/Nelson Street Blues	1990
Acoustic Archives	CD 801	Sonny Boy Williamson, Crudup, et al/Goin' In Your Direction	1991
Collectables	CD 5240	Willie Love/Trumpet Masters Vol. 1 – Lonesome World Blues	1991
Collectables	CD 5242	Tiny Kennedy, et al/Trumpet Masters Vol. 3 – Red Hot Kisses	1991
Savage Kick	LP 507	Various/Savage Kick Vol. 7	1991/1992?
Rhino	CD 71125	Various/Blues Masters, Vol. 5: Jump Blues Classics	Nov 1992
Capricorn	CD 42009-2	Various / The Fire/Fury Records Story	23 Feb 1993
Alligator	CD 2701	Various/Strange Kind Of Feelin' (re of Acoustic Archives CD 701)	25 May 1993
Alligator	CD 2702	Various/Delta Blues—1951 (re of Acoustic Archives CD 702)	25 May 1993
Rhino	CD 71550	Big Joe Turner/Big, Bad & Blue	late Jan 1994
Alligator	CD 2803	Sonny Boy Williamson, et al/Goin' In Your Direction (re of A.A. CD 801)	1994
Ace (UK)	CD 590	Various/Let's Have A Blues Ball!	early(?) 1995
Arhoolie	CD 102	Various / 15 Down Home Urban Blues Classics/American Masters Vol. 2	5 Nov 1996
Rhino	CD 72968	Big Joe Turner/The Very Best of Big Joe Turner	3 Feb 1998
P-Vine (JP)	CD 5461	Various / N.Y. on Fire/Bobby's Harlem Rock Vol. 2	1998
Delmark	CD 640	Junior Wells/Blues Hit Big Town (w/ bonus tracks not on LP)	16 June 1998
Pulse (UK)	Box 498	Various/Nothin' But the Blues (4 CD Box Set)	1998
Official (Denmark)	CD 5254	Papa Lightfoot & Sammy Myers / Blues Harmonica Wizards	c. 1999?
Purple Pyramid	CD 0832-2	Willie Love & His Three Aces / Greenville Smokin'	2000
Ace (UK)	CD 773	Various / Messing With the Blues (Atlantic blues sides)	c. Sept 2000

Chronological List of First Issue for LP / CD Tracks & Alternate Takes (Only complete takes are listed; no false starts included)

Note: For those readers who like to collect Elmore James LPs and CDs, this guide is a handy reference to Elmore James' alternate takes and LP-or-CD-only tracks, and on which particular album they first appeared. Even though some of the songs listed below were later picked up for reissue as singles, all of the following items made their first appearance on either an LP or a CD.

Album **Song Title**	**Writer's Credit**	**Release Date**
Argo LP 4034:		
The Sun Is Shining (alt tk)(vsn 3)	(Elmore James)‡	March 1964
Sphere Sound LP 7002:		
Dust My Broom (vsn 2)	(Elmo James)	c. May 1965
I Can't Stop Lovin' You	(Elmo James)	
My Bleeding Heart (complete)	(Sehorn-James)	
Standing At The Crossroads (vsn 2)	(James-Josea)	
One Way Out	(Sehorn-James)	
Kent LP 5022:		
Sho Nuff I Do (prob tk 11)	(James)†/‡	Summer / Fall 1967
Wild About You (Baby) (tk 4)	(James-Josea-Taub-Ling)†/‡	
Sphere Sound LP 7008:		
Baby Please Set A Date	(Sehorn-James)	Fall 1967
Early One Morning	(Sehorn-James)	
Strange Angels	(Sehorn-James)	
Something Inside Of Me (complete)	(Sehorn-James)	
Got To Move	(Sehorn-James)	
Blue Horizon LP 7-63204:		
My Best Friend	(E. James)‡	Aug 1968
I See My Baby	(E. James)‡	
Whose Muddy Shoes	(E. James)	
The Sun Is Shining (alt tk)(vsn 2)	(E. James)	
Stormy Monday Blues	(T Bone Walker)	
Madison Blues	(E. James)	
Bell LP 104:		
Person To Person	(Sehorn-James)	Fall 1968
So Unkind	(Sehorn-James)	
My Kind Of Woman	(Sehorn-James)	
Kent LP 9001:		
Please Find My Baby (alt tk)(vsn 1)	(James-Josea-Taub-Ling)	mid-1969
Where Can My Baby Be (tk 9)	(James-Josea-Taub-Ling)	
Canton, Mississippi Breakdown (inst)	(James-Josea-Taub-Ling)	
So Mean To Me (tk 4)	(James-Josea-Taub-Ling)	
Long Tall Woman (alt tk)	(James-Josea-Taub-Ling)	

Kent LP 9010:

One More Drink (tk 1)	(E. James)†	late 1969
Make My Dreams Come True (My Best Friend)(tk 2)	(E. James)†	
Strange Kinda' Feeling (tk 5)	(Josea-James)†	
Quarter Past Nine	(E. James)†	
Elmo's Shuffle (inst)(tk 5)	(E. James)†	

Blue Horizon LP 7-66230:

Mean Mistreatin' Mama (tk 2)	(E. James)	Dec 1969
Sunnyland (Train)(tk 1)	(E. James)	
Hand In Hand (tk 1)	(E. James)	
Hand In Hand (tk 3)	(E. James)	
Hand In Hand (tk 4)	(E. James)	
I Have A Right To Love My Baby	(E. James)	
Talk To Me Baby (I Can't Hold Out)(tk 1)	(E. James)	
Can't Stop Loving My Baby	(E. James)	
Got To Move (She's Got To Go)	(J. Williamson)	
Manhattan Slide (Pickin' The Blues)(complete)(inst)	(E. James)	
Twelve Year Old Boy	(M. London)	
Elmore Jumps One (Up Jumped Elmore)(inst)(complete)	(E. James)	
I Believe (tk 1)(vsn 2)	(E. James)	
I Gotta Go Now	(E. James)	
Make My Dreams Come True (tk 3)(vsn 2)	(E. James)	
Back In Mississippi (conversation)		

Trip LP 8007:

Find My Kinda Woman	(E. James)†	mid 1971
My Baby's Gone (tk 4)(vsn 2)	(James)†/‡	

Polydor LP 2383200:

Make My Dreams Come True (My Best Friend)(tk 1)	(James)	Early / Mid 1973

Ace LP 68:

My Baby's Gone	(James)	April 1983
One More Drink (tk 2)	(James)	
Lost Woman Blues (tk 1)	(James-Josea-Taub-Ling)	
Strange Kinda' Feeling (tk 2)	(James)	
Dark And Dreary (tk 2)	(Bihari-James)	
Where Can My Baby Be (tk 8)	(James-Josea-Taub-Ling)	
Sho Nuff I Do[875] (prob one of tks 1-4)	(James)	
So Mean To Me (tk 2)	(James-Josea-Taub-Ling)	
Elmo's Shuffle (Part 2)(inst)(tk 4)	(James)	

Collectables CD 5187:

You Know You Done Me Wrong (tk 3)	(James)†/‡	Dec 1989
Look On Yonder Wall (Look Up On The Wall)	(Sehorn-James)†	

875 As "Please Come Back To Me" on Ace Box CD 4.

Relic CD 7026:

I Need You (Baby) (complete)	(E. James)	Mar 1992
You Know You're Wrong (tk 2)	(E. James)	
Go Back Home Again (tk 1)	(James)	
Find My Kind Of Woman (tk 1)	(James)	

Relic CD 7040:

Dust My Broom (tk 4)(vsn 3)	(James)	3 Dec 1992

Ace Box CD 4:

Long Tall Woman (1952 recording)	(E. James)	Nov 1993
Lost Woman Blues (tk 2)(vsn 3)	(Josea-James)	
Make My Dreams Come True (tk 4)	(E. James)	
Strange Kinda' Feeling (tks 1,3)	(Josea-James)	
So Mean To Me (tk 3)	(James-Ling)	
Elmo's Shuffle (inst)(tk 3)	(E. James)	

Notes: † First issued source gives no writer's credit information
‡ Information deemed reliable but not verified

with Elmore James on guitar:

Johnny "Big Moose" Walker (vo, p)			
	Footrace To A Resting Place	Blue Horizon LP 7-66230	Dec 1969
prob Johnny "Big Moose" Walker (vo, p)			
	Second Fiddle Man	Blue Horizon LP 7-66230	Dec 1969
Johnny Jones (vo, p)	Wait Baby	Atlantic LP 7227	5 Oct 1972
	Hoy Hoy (alt tk)	——	
	Chicago Blues	——	
Junior Wells (vo, hca)	Ways Like An Angel	Delmark LP 640	1977
	Eagle Rock (alt tk)(inst)	——	
Sam Myers (vo)	(Poor Little) Angel Child (tk 1)	P-Vine LP 6101/02	1987 / 88?
	Little Girl	——	
Jesse Tiny Kennedy (vo)			
	Have You Heard About The Farmer's Daughter?	Acoustic Archives CD 701	Spring 1990
Marshall Jones (vo, probably b or dm)			
	Woke Up Happy	Capricorn CD 42009-2	1993
	You Can Do It If You Want To	——	
Junior Wells (vo, hca)	Junior's Wail (alt tk)(inst)	Delmark CD 640	16 June 1998

Guide to Equivalent LP & CD Issues

Ace LP 31 (UK)	=	Kent LP 4003
Ace LP 68 (UK)	=	Kent LP 4004
Ace CD 192 (UK)	=	Flair Records/Virgin Records America 2-91800
Ace Box CD 4 (UK)	=	Flair/Virgin CD 39632/33/34; P-Vine CD 3023/24/25 (JP)
Bell LP 6037	=	Bell LP 062.90865 (FR)
Blue Horizon LP 7-66230	=	Blue Horizon LP 4601[876] (US); Line/Outline LP 8018 (DE)
Blues Classics LP 9	=	Arhoolie LP 2020
Charly LP 1008 (UK)	=	Oxford LP 3238 (IT)
Charly LP 1017 (UK)	=	Oxford LP 3242 (IT)
Charly CD 1027 (UK)	=	Carlton Home Entertainment CD 304012 (UK)
Chess LP 1537	=	Chess LP 9114 (1984 reissue); Chess/P-Vine LP 823 (JP) Chess LP 2016 (IT); Chess/Vogue LP 515006 (FR) Chess Greenline LP 8097, CD 78097 (GB)
Cobblestone LP 9001	=	Muse LP 5087, CD 5087
Crown LP 5168	=	United LP 716, LP 7716; Custom LP 1054; Ember LP 3397 (GB); Byg LP 529004, LP 529503 (FR); Goody LP 7000 (FR)
Intermedia LP 5034	=	Cleo LP 00271283 (NL); Blue Moon LP 1008 (GB)
Kent LP 502/LP 5022	=	Kent LP 522; United LP 7743
Kent LP 9001	=	United LP 7778; United Artists LP 29109 (GB); Musidisc LP 5601 (FR)
Kent LP 9010	=	United LP 7787; Musidisc LP 5610 (FR)
P-Vine CD 2180/81/82	=	P-Vine CD 2889/90/91
Topline LP 120 (GB)	=	Music Options/ARC CD 3013 (NL)
Trip LP 8007	=	DJM LP 8008 (GB); Audio Fidelity LP 1034 (GB); Phoenix LP 241-1
Trip LP 9511 (Record 1)	=	Black Label CD 2001
Trip LP 9511 (Record 2)	=	Black Label CD 2002
Trip LP 1650	=	Black Label CD 2009
Up Front LP 122	=	Phoenix LP 334

Anthology / Compilation Equivalents

Ace CD 216 (GB)	=	Flair/Virgin CDV2-86304 (US)
Ace CD 258 (GB)	=	Flair/Virgin CDV2-86303 (US)
Ace CD 335 (GB)	=	Flair/Virgin CDV2-86302 (US)
Acoustic Archives CD 701	=	Alligator CD 2701
Acoustic Archives CD 702	=	Alligator CD 2702
Acoustic Archives CD 801	=	Alligator CD 2803
Argo LP 4034	=	poss Cadet LP 4034 (1967); Chess CD 9276
Atlantic LP 7227	=	Atlantic/P-Vine LP 6187A (JP)
Chess CD 31316	=	Chess Greenline CD 1025 (Both volumes on 1 CD)
CBS (GB) LP 66218	=	Columbia LP 30008; Columbia CD 468992-2; Vol. 1 of CBS LP 66426 (4 LPs)
Custom LP 1	=	United LP 7748
Evasound CD 019 (AU)	=	AVM CD 019 (AU); Broad Music CD 019 (AU)
Kent LP 535	=	United LP 7754
Mercury LP 20826	=	Mercury LP 60826 (Stereo issue)
PAV CD 3PAV 002A (GB)	=	PSD 3-CD 3PSD 005A (Disc 1)(GB)
RST/Blues Documents LP 1	=	Story Of Blues CDs 3521-2/3522-2/3523-2 (AT)

[876] Equals vol 1 of the two-volume 66230 LP set.

Elmore James LP & CD Releases Alphabetical by Label

Label	Record#	Titles	Release Date
Ace (UK)	LP 31	The Best of Elmore James	Mar 1981
Ace (UK)	LP 68	King Of The Slide Guitar	April 1983
Ace (UK)	LP 112	The Original Meteor/Flair Sides	Aug 1984
Ace (UK)	CD 192	"Let's Cut It"—The Very Best of Elmore James	March 1987
Ace (UK)	Box CD 4	The Classic Early Recordings 1951-1956 (3 CD Box Set)	late Oct 1993
Ace (UK)	CD 583	The Best of Elmore James – The Early Years	Spring 1995
Audiofidelity (GB)	LP 1034	All Them Blues (2 LPs)	1981
Bell (GB)	LP 104	Something Inside Of Me	Fall 1968
Bell	LP 6037	Elmore James	mid-1969
Bell (FR)	LP 062.90865	The Sky Is Crying (reissue of Bell LP 6037)	early 1970s?
Black Label	CD 2001	History of Elmore James Vol. 1	1991
Black Label	CD 2002	History of Elmore James Vol. 2	1991
Black Label	CD 2009	Every Day I Have the Blues (equiv of Trip LP 1650)	late 1994
Blue City (NL)	CD 2652712	20 Greatest Hits	1988
Blue Horizon (GB)	LP 7-63204	Tough (Chess sides) (w/ John Brim)	Aug 1968
Blue Horizon (GB)	LP 7-66230	To Know A Man (2 LPs)	Dec 1969
Blue Horizon (US)	LP 4601	Blues Masters Vol. 1 (first half of Blue Horizon LP 7-66230)	prob 1971
Blue Moon (GB)	LP 1008	Red Hot Blues (reissue of Intermedia LP 5034)	Nov 1983
Blues Encore (CH)	CD 52006	The Master of the Slide Guitar	early 1990
Buddah	CD 99781-2	Shake Your Moneymaker: The Best of the Fire Sessions	2001
Byg (FR)	LP 529004	The Blues In My Heart (reissue of Crown LP 5168)	1970s?
Byg (FR)	LP 529503	The Blues In My Heart The Rhythm... (re of Crown LP 5168)	1970s?
Camden	CD 74321 523762	The Sky Is Crying	1997
Capricorn	PRO CD 5831	King Of The Slide Guitar Sampler (Promotional Sampler)	Summer 1992
Capricorn	CD 42006-2	King Of The Slide Guitar (2 CD Box Set)	Aug 1992
Castle Showcase (GB)	LP 140	Pickin' The Blues	1986
Charly (UK)	LP 1008	One Way Out	19 Sept 1980
Charly (UK)	LP 1017	Got To Move	Mar 1981
Charly (UK)	CD 34	Shake Your Moneymaker	Dec 1986
Charly (UK)	CD 180	Come Go With Me	May 1989
Charly (UK)	BM CD 12	The Sky Is Crying (Blues Masterworks series)	May/June 1992
Charly (UK)	BM CD 28	Standing At The Crossroads (Blues Masterworks series)	Fall 1992
Charly (UK)	CD 1027	Dust My Broom	Nov 1992
Charly (UK)	CDRED Box 4	King Of The Slide Guitar (4 CD Box Set)	late Dec 1992
Charly (UK)	CD 2007	Dust My Broom	late 1993?
Charly (DE)	CPBOX 301	King of the Slide Guitar / The Complete Chief & Fire Sessions	1997
Chess	LP 1537	Whose Muddy Shoes (w/ John Brim)	October 1969
Chess (IT)	LP 2016	Whose Muddy Shoes (reissue of Chess LP 1537)	1981
Chess	LP 9114	Whose Muddy Shoes (w/ John Brim)(reissue of Chess LP 1537)	1984
Chess	CD 9114	Whose Muddy Shoes (w/ John Brim)[877]	April 1991
Chess Greenline	LP 8097	Whose Muddy Shoes (reissue of Chess LP 1537)	1989
Chess Greenline	CD 78097	Whose Muddy Shoes (reissue of Chess LP 1537)	1989
Chess/P-Vine (JP)	LP 823	Whose Muddy Shoes (w/ John Brim)(reissue of Chess LP 1537)	1984

[877] Not a true reissue of Chess LP1537; "The Sun Is Shining" is a different take from the version on LP.

Chess/Vogue (FR)	LP 515006	Whose Muddy Shoes (w/ John Brim)(reissue of Chess LP 1537)	early 1982
Chess/Vogue (FR)	CD 600119	Elmore James-John Brim-Floyd Jones	1986
Cleo (NL)	LP 00271283	Greatest Hits (reissue of Intermedia LP 5034)	1985?
Cobblestone	LP 9001	South Side Blues (w/ Eddie Taylor, Jimmy Reed)	Spring 1972
Collectables	CD 5112	Golden Classics—Guitars In Orbit	March 1988
Collectables	CD 5184	The Complete Fire And Enjoy Sessions Part 1	Dec 1989
Collectables	CD 5185	The Complete Fire And Enjoy Sessions Part 2	Dec 1989
Collectables	CD 5186	The Complete Fire And Enjoy Sessions Part 3	Dec 1989
Collectables	CD 5187	The Complete Fire And Enjoy Sessions Part 4	Dec 1989
Collectables	CD 8829	The Complete Fire And Enjoy Recordings (3 CD Set)	1 Sept 1995
Crown	LP 5168	Blues After Hours	1961
Crown/Gem (GB)	LP 003	King of the Bottleneck Blues	Feb 1986
Custom	LP 1054	The Blues In My Heart, The Rhythm In My Soul (re of Crown LP 5168)	1966/1967?
Custom	LP 2054	The Blues In My Heart, The Rhythm In My Soul (mono of LP 1054)	1966/1967?
Deja Vu (IT)	LP 2035	The Elmore James Collection	1985
Deja Vu (IT)	CD 2035	Collection: Elmore James/20 Blues Greats	July 1988
Deja Vu (IT)	CD 24	The Elmore James Story	May 1989
DJM (UK)	LP 8008	All Them Blues (2 LPs)(reissue of Trip LP 8007)	Oct 1975
Eclipse	CD 64739-2	King of the Slide Guitar	1994
Ember (GB)	LP 3397	The Late Fantastically Great (reissue of Crown LP 5168)	early 1968
Flair/Virgin	CD 2-91800[878]	"Let's Cut It"—The Very Best of E.J. (reissue of Ace CD 192)	Nov 1991
Flair/Virgin	CD 39632/33/34	The Classic Early Recordings 1951-1956 (3 CD Box Set)	14 June 1994
Goody (FR)	LP 7000	The Blues In My Heart The Rhythm... (re of Crown LP 5168)	1970s?
Instant (GB)	CD 5030	Dust My Broom	July 1990
Intermedia	LP 5034	Red Hot Blues	Spring/Summer 1983
Kent	LP 502	Original Folk Blues (mono/stereo issue)	Summer / Fall 1967
Kent	LP 5022	Original Folk Blues (mono issue)[879]	Summer / Fall 1967
Kent	LP 9001	The Legend of Elmore James	mid-1969
Kent	LP 9010	The Resurrection of Elmore James	late 1969
Kent	LP 4003	The Best of Elmore James (reissue of Ace LP 31)	1985
Kent	LP 4004	King Of The Slide Guitar (reissue of Ace LP 68)	1985
Line/Outline (EEC)	LP 8018	To Know A Man (2 LPs • Reissue of Blue Horizon LP 7-66230)	late 1983
Masters (DE)	CD 61046-2	Golden Hits	1991/1992?
Muse	LP 5087	Street Talkin' (w/ Eddie Taylor, Jimmy Reed)	early 1976
Muse	CD 5087	Street Talkin' (w/ Jimmy Reed and Eddie Taylor)	Fall 1988
Music Club (GB)	CD 083	The Immortal Elmore James King of the Bottleneck Blues	late Fall 1992
Music Options/ARC	CD 3013	(NL)(equivalent or reissue(?) of Topline LP 120)	1992/1993?
Musidisc (FR)	LP 5601	The Legend of Elmore James (reissue of Kent LP 9001)	early 70s?
Musidisc (FR)	LP 5610	The Resurrection of Elmore James (reissue of Kent LP 9010)	early 70s?
Opal (Spain)	CD 106	Elmore James and His Broom Dusters: Early Years 1951-1954	1995

878 Reissued by Capitol Records as 86257.

879 Numbered as 502/5022. This album was later reissued as Kent LP 522.

Oxford (IT)	LP 3238	One Way Out (Italian reissue of Charly LP 1008)	1981
Oxford (IT)	LP 3242	Got To Move (Italian reissue of Charly LP 1017)	1981
Phoenix	LP 241-1	History of Elmore James (reissue of Trip LP 8007)	1981
Phoenix	LP 334	The Great Elmore James (reissue of Up Front LP 122)	1982
Pickwick	LP 5014	Screamin' Blues	prob 1972
Pilz	CD 449322-2	Red Hot Blues	late 1993
Polydor (GB)	LP 2383200	Cotton Patch Hotfoots (w/ Walter Horton)	Early/Mid 1973
P-Vine (JP)	LP 6005/06/07	Something Inside of Me / The Complete Fire-Enjoy Sessions	1984
P-Vine (JP)	CD 2180/81/82	Something Inside of Me / The Complete Fire-Enjoy Sessions	1990
P-Vine (JP)	CD 1410	South Side Blues (w/ Eddie Taylor)	May/June 1991
P-Vine (JP)	CD 1883	The Very Best of Elmore James	Early 1993
P-Vine (JP)	CD 3742	P-Vine Presents 21 Blues Giants, Vol. 2: Elmore James	Late July 1995
P-Vine (JP)	CD 2889/90/91	The Sky Is Crying: The Legendary Fire/Enjoy Sessions	Late Nov (?) 1995
Recall (UK)	CD 231	Rollin' And Tumblin'	1999
Relic	LP 1021	The Last Session	Fall 1989
Relic	CD 7026	Rollin' & Tumblin'—The Best of Elmore James	Mar 1992
Relic	CD 7040	Dust My Broom—The Best of Elmore James Part 2	3 Dec 1992
Relic	CD 7097	The Last Sessions	1995
Rhino	CD 71190	The Sky Is Crying: The History of Elmore James	late Mar 1993
Rhino	CD 79803	Blues Masters: The Very Best of Elmore James	14 Mar 2000
Ronn	CD 8016	Dust My Broom (w/ Homesick, Crudup, & Bobo Thomas)	26 Nov 1996
Route 16[880]	CD 9005 / 9007	Greatest Hits	1991
Sphere Sound	LP 7002	The Sky Is Crying	c. May 1965
Sphere Sound	LP 7008	I Need You	Fall 1967
Sue (GB)	LP 918	The Best of	Jan 1965
Sue (GB)	LP 927	Memorial Album	Aug 27 1965
Tomato	CD 70389	Dust My Broom	Nov 1991
Topline (GB)	LP 120	Dust My Broom	Dec 1984
Trip	LP 8007	History of Elmore James (2 LPs)	mid 1971
Trip	LP 9511	History of Elmore James Volume 2	1973/74/75?
Trip	LP 1650	16 Greatest Hits	1978
United	LP 716	The Blues In My Heart, The Rhythm In My Soul (re of Crown LP 5168)	late 1966
United	LP 7716	The Blues In My Heart, The Rhythm In My Soul (stereo of LP 716)	prob late 1966
United	LP 7743	Original Folk Blues (reissue of Kent LP 5022)	prob late 1974
United	LP 7778	The Legend of Elmore James (reissue of Kent LP 9001)	1975?
United	LP 7787	The Resurrection of Elmore James (reissue of Kent LP 9010)	1975?
United Artists (GB)	LP 29109	The Legend of Elmore James (reissue of Kent LP 9001)	mid 1970
Up Front	LP 122	The Great Elmore James	early 1970
Vivid Sound/Globe (JP)	LP 5004	Dust My Blues	late 1979?
Zillion (NL)	CD 2610272	Rolling And Tumbling	Summer/Fall 1991

---

880 Note: The outer tray cards identify this set as "That's Blues TB 201," however individual discs are actually labelled Route 16 CD 9005 (Disc 1) and Route 16 CD 9007 (Disc 2), respectively.

Compilation/Anthology Releases Alphabetical by Label

Ace (UK)	CD 216	Juke Joint Blues	1987
Ace (UK)	CD 232	Blues Guitar Blasters	1988
Ace (UK)	CD 258	R&B Confidential No. 1/The Flair Label	Feb 1989
Ace (UK)	CD 276	Kings of the Blues	1989
Ace (UK)	CD 335	Jukebox R&B	1991
Ace (UK)	CD 610	House Rockin' Blues	prob Jan / Feb 1995
Ace (UK)	CD 964	Mojo Working: The Best of Ace Blues	1995
Ace (UK)	CD 784	The Modern Records Story	2001
Ace (UK)	CD 813	Travelling Record Man: Historic Down South Recording Trips of Bihari & Turner	2001
Argo	LP 4034	The Blues Vol. 3	March 1964
Blue Horizon (UK)	PR LP 45/46	How Blue Can We Get?	1970
Blue Moon (Spain)	CD 4003	Rhythm & Blues Legends Vol. 1	1995
Blues Classics	LP 5	Country Blues Classics Vol. 1	late Summer 1965
Blues Classics	LP 15	Memphis and the Delta—1950s	prob 1967
Blues Collection (AU)	CD 341	Blues! Blues! Blues!	1991
Blue Sun	CD 2000	King Biscuit Blues—The Helena Blues Legacy	1996
Broad Music (AU)	CD 003	Legendary Blues Men	1993
Broad Music (AU)	CD 019	History of the Blues & Soul Vol. 1 (reissue of Evasound CD 019)	1994
Bullseye Blues	CD 9533	Slidin' ... Some Slide	1993
Cascade (UK)	LP 1010	20 Great Blues Recordings of the 50's & 60's Vol. 2	1984
Cascade (UK)	CD 1001	20 Great R&B Hits of the 50's	1988
Cascade (UK)	CD 1005	20 Great Blues Recordings of the 50s and 60s	1988
Cascade (UK)	Box CD 3	60 Great Blues Recordings (3 disc set)	early 1992
Castle Communications (AU)	CD 206	The Ultimate Blues Collection	1990
CBS (GB)	LP 66218	The Story of the Blues	prob Aug 1969
CBS (FR)	LP 66426	The Story of the Blues Vols. 1 & 2 (4 LP Box set)	1970
Charly (UK)	CDRED 36	Slidin' (w/ Hound Dog Taylor, Earl Hooker, John Littlejohn)	1991
Charly (UK)	CD 1050	Kings of the Blues	c. Fall 1993
Charly (UK)	CD 1124	The Chess Story	late 1993
Charly (UK)	CD DIG 3	A Modern Blues Anthology – Ain't Times Hard (4 disc set)	1994
Charly (UK)	CD LAB 104	The Vee-Jay Story[881]	1996
Charly (DE)	CDGR 216	Slide Guitar Masters	1998
Chess	LP 6641.125	Genesis Vol. 2—Memphis to Chicago	Oct 1974
Chess (GB)	LP 4010	Chess Masters (2 LP set)	1982
Chess	CD 9276	The Blues Vol. 3 (reissue of Argo LP 4034)	15 Aug 1988
Chess	CD 31316	The Best of Chess Blues Vol. 2	Oct 1988
Chess	CD 4-9340	Chess Blues (4 disc box set)	22 Dec 1992
Chess	CD 9368	Chess Blues Classics 1957-1967	25 Mar 1997
Chess	CD 2-9393	Chess Blues Guitar/Two Decades of Killer Fretwork 1949-1969	13 Jan 1998
Chess (IT)	CD 3805962.	The Chess Story 1947-1975 (15 discs)[882]	1999
Chess Greenline	CD 1025	The Best of Chess Blues (both volumes on 1 CD)	1989
Chess/Vogue (DE)	CD 600048	The Golden Age of Chicago Blues	prob 1986
Collectables	CD 5127	The Collectables Blues Collection Vol. 1	1989
Collectables	CD 5128	The Collectables Blues Collection Vol. 2	1989

881 Lists Vee-Jay 259 ("It Hurts Me Too"), but plays Enjoy 2015 instead.

882 Each disc of the set is individually numbered beginning with 380 597-2 and ending with 380 611-2.

Collectables	CD 5129	The Collectables Blues Collection Vol. 3	1989
Collectables	CD 7271	The Very Best of Vee-Jay Blues Vol. 3	17 Oct 2000
Collectables	CD 7272	The Very Best of Vee-Jay Blues Vol. 4	17 Oct 2000
Columbia (GB)	LP 1417	Blues	early 1960s (pre-1965)
Columbia	LP 30008	The Story of the Blues	early/mid 1970
Columbia (GB)	CD 468992-2	The Story of the Blues (re of CBS LP 66218 / Columbia LP 30008)	1991
Concept (AU)	CD 0265	Blues Brothers Soul Sisters (2 CD set)	1990s
Connoisseur Collection	CD 205 (GB)	Born Under A Bad Sign	1994
Custom	LP 1	20 Greatest Blues Hits by the Original Artists	mid-late '60s?
DJM (UK)	LP 8005	All Them Blues (2 LPs)	prob Fall 1975
Ember/Specialty	LP 6609	All The Blues – All The Time	Summer 1970
Europa Music (BR)	CD 10046	Spotlight On Blues	1994
Evasound (AU)	CD 019	The History of the Blues & Soul	1991
Fat Boy (GB)	CD 415/2	Blues & Soul Vol. 2	1994
Fat Boy (GB)	CD 415/3	Blues & Soul Vol. 3	1994
Fat Boy (GB)	CD 415/4	Blues & Soul Vol. 4	1994
Festival	LP 1008	America's Musical Roots—The Blues	1976
The Hit Label (GB)	CD 19	The Chart Show Ultimate Blues	1994
Jewel	LP 5015	Jewel Spotlights the Blues, Vol. 1	late summer 1978
Jewel	CD 5015	Jewel Spotlights the Blues, Vol. 1 (cf LP 5015/has bonus trax)	Spring 1994
Kent	LP 535	Underground Blues	1968 / 1969
Kent	LP 700	Roots/Soul Sounds Of A Proud People[883]	1970s?
LaserLight (DE)	CD 12.336	Guitar Blues	1994
Mamlish	LP 3800	Black Cat Trail	Fall 1970
Marvel (AU)	CD 722	Feelin' The Blues – Diggin' The Rhythm #2	1992
Marvel (AU)	CD 725	Feelin' The Blues – Diggin' The Rhythm #5	1992
MCA (BR)	CD 140 069	Sho Got The Blues – Blues Classics 3	1993
MCA	CD 20768	Greatest Blues Legends	1994
Mercury	LP 20826	Original Golden Hits of the Great Blues Singers (Mono)	1963
Mercury	LP 60826	Original Golden Hits of the Great Blues Singers (Stereo)	1963
Music Club (GB)	CD 026	Comin' Home To The Blues 2	1991
Pointblank	PR CD 14171	Pointblank Doggone Blues Sampler (Promotional Sampler)	1994
P-Vine (JP)	CD 3003	Modern/Kent The Best of Blues Guitars	Summer 1991
P-Vine (JP)	CD 2346	Willie Dixon: Working On The Blues Vol. 1	Late Jan (?) 1992
P-Vine (JP)	CD 2741	Jam Packed Blues Guitar • Vol. 1 Dynaflow Electric Style	Fall 1993
P-Vine (JP)	CD 3038	Anthology of the Blues – Blues From The Deep South	Summer 1994
P-Vine (JP)	CD 5271/72/73/74	Vee-Jay, The Chicago Black Music (4 CD set)	Late Dec(?) 1997
Red Lightnin' (UK)	LP 005	Blues In D Natural	early 1970
Relic	CD 7009	Raging Harlem Hit Parade	1991

[883] Note: Also contains Boyd Gilmore's "All In My Dreams."

Relic	CD 7046	Raging Harlem Hit Parade, Vol. 2	1993
Rhino	CD 70716	Legends of Guitar – Electric Blues Vol. 1	1990
Rhino	CD 71127	Blues Masters, Vol. 6: Blues Originals	16 Feb 1993
Rhino	CD 71130	Blues Masters, Vol. 8: Mississippi Delta Blues	16 Feb 1993
Rhino	CD 71126	Blues Masters, Vol. 15: Slide Guitar Classics	Aug 1993
Rhino	CD 75348	Blues Masters, Vol. 18: More Slide Guitar Classics	14 July 1998
Roots	CD 33046	Willie Dixon's Blues Dixonary Vol. 2	1993
RST/Blues Documents	LP 1	The Greatest In Country Blues (1927-1956)(3 LP box set)	1989
Sequel (GB)	CD 47555/3	The Blues Guitar Box (only disc three has Elmore)	1990
Sequel (GB)	CD 185/1	The Blues Guitar Box 2 (only disc one has Elmore)	1991
Sire	CD 26617-2	Music From The Film *A Rage In Harlem*	1991
Story Of Blues (AT)	CD 3523-2	The Greatest In Country Blues – Vol. 3 (1929-1956)	c. Aug 1991
Storyville (Denmark)	LP 176	Chicago - Rhythm & Blues Sounds (Blues Scene USA Vol. 1)	1965
Success (AU)	CD 2122	Blues Collection – Vol. 2	1990s
Sue (GB)	LP 921	We Sing The Blues	Spring 1965
Teem	LP 5005	The Kings Sing The Blues	1967 / 1968?
Trip	LP 7503	The Blues Vol. 1	1975
Trip	LP 7504	The Blues Vol. 2	1976
United	LP 7718	The Best of the Biggest *(poss reissue of Custom LP 1056?)*	prob 1967
United	LP 7748	20 Greatest Blues Hits (reissue of Custom LP 1)	1970s
United	LP 7754	Underground Blues (reissue of Kent LP 535)	1970s
Vee-Jay	LP 1020	The Blues	1960
Vee-Jay	CD 711	A Taste of the Blues—Vol. 1	1993
Vee-Jay	CD 718	A Taste of the Blues—Vol. 2	Dec 1993
Versailles (FR)	CD 478308 2	La Route du Blues	1994
Vivid Sound (JP)	LP 1008	The Kings Sing the Blues Vol. 1 (*not* a reissue of Teem LP 5005)	1979
Xtra (UK)	LP 1047	The Mike Raven Blues Show	late 1966

Selected LP & CD Releases w/ Elmore James on guitar

Ace (UK)	CD 590	Various/Let's Have A Blues Ball!	early(?) 1995
Ace (UK)	CD 773	Various / Messing With the Blues (Atlantic blues sides)	c. Sept 2000
Acoustic Archives	CD 701	Various/Strange Kind Of Feelin'	Spring 1990
Acoustic Archives	CD 702	Various/Delta Blues—1951	1990
Acoustic Archives	CD 801	Sonny Boy Williamson, Crudup, et al/Goin' In Your Direction	1991
Alligator	CD 2701	Various/Strange Kind Of Feelin' (re of Acoustic Archives CD 701)	25 May 1993
Alligator	CD 2702	Various/Delta Blues—1951 (re of Acoustic Archives CD 702)	25 May 1993
Arhoolie	LP 2020	Sonny Boy Williamson/King Biscuit Time (re Blues Classics LP 9)	late 1974
Arhoolie	CD 310	Sonny Boy Williamson/King Biscuit Time (similar to Arhoolie LP 2020)	late 1989
Arhoolie	CD 102	Various / 15 Down Home Urban Blues Classics/American Masters Vol. 2	5 Nov 1996
Atco	LP 33-376	Big Joe Turner/His Greatest Recordings	1971
Atlantic	EP 536	Big Joe Turner/Joe Turner Sings	1955
Atlantic	LP 8023	Big Joe Turner/Rockin' The Blues	1958

Atlantic	LP 8033	Big Joe Turner/Big Joe Is Here	1960
Atlantic (FR)	LP 332015	Big Joe Turner/Blues No. 5 (10-inch LP issue)	prob 1960
Atlantic	LP 8081	Big Joe Turner/The Best of Joe Turner	1963
Atlantic	LP 7227	Various/Blues Piano—Chicago, Plus	5 Oct 1972
Atlantic	CD 81663-2	Big Joe Turner/Rhythm & Blues Years	Nov 1986
Atlantic	CD 81695-2	Various/Atlantic Blues: Guitar	1986
Atlantic	CD 81696-2	Various/Atlantic Blues: Vocalists	1986
Atlantic	LP 81697-1	Various/Atlantic Blues: Chicago	1986
Atlantic	CD 81697-2	Various/Atlantic Blues: Chicago	1986
Atlantic/P-Vine	LP 6187A	Various/Blues Piano—Chicago, Plus	late 1980s?
Blues Classics	LP 8	Various/Chicago Blues—The Early 1950's	1965
Blues Classics	LP 9	Sonny Boy Williamson/"The Original" Sonny Boy Williamson	mid / late1965
Blues Encore (GB)	CD 52008	Big Joe Turner/The Blues Boss	1990
Capricorn	CD 42009-2	Various / The Fire/Fury Records Story	23 Feb 1993
Charly (UK)	LP 1070	Big Joe Turner/Jumpin' With Joe	1984
Collectables	CD 5240	Willie Love/Trumpet Masters Vol. 1 – Lonesome World Blues	1991
Collectables	CD 5242	Tiny Kennedy, et al/Trumpet Masters Vol. 3 – Red Hot Kisses	1991
Delmark	LP 640	Junior Wells/Blues Hit Big Town	June / July 1977
Delmark	CD 640	Junior Wells/Blues Hit Big Town (w/ bonus tracks not on LP)	16 June 1998
Flyright (GB)	LP 4712	J.T. Brown/Rockin With J.T.	1975
Krazy Kat (GB)	LP 7420	J.T. Brown/Rockin With J.T. (similar to Flyright LP 4712)	1984
Official (Denmark)	CD 5254	Papa Lightfoot & Sammy Myers / Blues Harmonica Wizards	c. 1999?
P-Vine (JP)	LP 6101/02	Various/Bobby's Harlem Rock Vol. 2: New York on Fire	1987 / 88?
P-Vine (JP)	CD 2184	Willie Love/Nelson Street Blues	1990
P-Vine (JP)	CD 5461	Various / N.Y. on Fire/Bobby's Harlem Rock Vol. 2	1998
pwb (GB)	LP 1	Various/The Post-War Chicago Blues	c. May / June 1965
Pulse (UK)	Box 498	Various/Nothin' But the Blues (4 CD Box Set)	1998
Purple Pyramid	CD 0832-2	Willie Love & His Three Aces / Greenville Smokin'	2000
Red Lightnin' (GB)	LP 007	Junior Wells/In My Younger Days	prob Summer 1972
Rhino	CD 71125	Various/Blues Masters, Vol. 5: Jump Blues Classics	Nov 1992
Rhino	CD 71550	Big Joe Turner/Big, Bad & Blue	late Jan 1994
Rhino	CD 72968	Big Joe Turner/The Very Best of Big Joe Turner	3 Feb 1998
Savage Kick	LP 507	Various/Savage Kick Vol. 7	1991/1992?
XX (UK)	EP 715	Junior Wells (7" 6 song EP)	prob Spring 1972

***LATE ADDITIONS**: The following albums, which are referred to at different points in the discography, were inadvertently left out of the LP and CD lists above, due to an unfortunate oversight.*

Chess	LP 2-60012	Chicago Blues Anthology (2 LPs)(also reissued in 1984 as LP 2-9213)	1972
Alligator	CD 2803	Sonny Boy Williamson, Crudup, et al/Goin' In Your Direction	31 Aug 1993
Vee-Jay	CD Box 3-400	Celebrating 40 Years of Classic Hits, 1953-1993 (3 CD Box Set)	1993

Carlton Home Entertainment (UK) CD 304012 • Elmore James / Crossroads (reissue of Charly CD 1027) 1996

Chart Appearances of Elmore James' Records

CB = Cash Box; **BB** = Billboard. Chart positions for "Dust My Broom" from Ryan, *Trumpet Records,* 101-102. Other *Cash Box* chart positions from *The Cashbox Black Contemporary Singles Charts, 1960-1984,* by George Albert and Frank Hoffman

Date	Source	Title & Record Number	Position	Location and/or Chart Name
12 Jan 1952	CB	Dust My Broom / Trumpet 146	#6	Dallas
19 Jan 1952	CB	Dust My Broom / Trumpet 146	#7	Dallas
2 Feb 1952	CB	Dust My Broom / Trumpet 146	#5	Dallas
23 Feb 1952	CB	Dust My Broom / Trumpet 146	#5	Pueblo, CO
1 Mar 1952	CB	Dust My Broom / Trumpet 146	#6	Denver
1 Mar 1952	CB	Dust My Broom / Trumpet 146	#8	Oxford, MS
29 Mar 1952	CB	Dust My Broom / Trumpet 146	#1	Oakland
29 Mar 1952	CB	Dust My Broom / Trumpet 146	#4	Los Angeles
29 Mar 1952	CB	Dust My Broom / Trumpet 146	#5	Monroe, LA
5 Apr 1952	BB	Dust My Broom / Trumpet 146	#9	Best Selling Retail Rhythm & Blues Records
12 Apr 1952	CB	Dust My Broom / Trumpet 146	#2	Los Angeles
19 Apr 1952	CB	Dust My Broom / Trumpet 146	#1	Los Angeles
19 Apr 1952	CB	Dust My Broom / Trumpet 146	#8	Dallas
19 Apr 1952	CB	Dust My Broom / Trumpet 146	#9	Somerset, KY
3 May 1952	CB	Dust My Broom / Trumpet 146	#8	New Orleans
3 May 1952	CB	Dust My Broom / Trumpet 146	#9	Chicago
10 May 1952	CB	Dust My Broom / Trumpet 146	#3	New Orleans
17 Jan 1953	BB	I Believe / Meteor 5000	#5	Chicago / Territorial Best Sellers
24 Jan 1953	BB	I Believe / Meteor 5000	#5	Chicago / Territorial Best Sellers
24 Jan 1953	BB	I Believe / Meteor 5000	#6	New York / Territorial Best Sellers
24 Jan 1953	BB	I Believe / Meteor 5000	#7	Saint Louis / Territorial Best Sellers
31 Jan 1953	BB	I Believe / Meteor 5000	#9	Chicago / Territorial Best Sellers
31 Jan 1953	BB	I Believe / Meteor 5000	#9	New York / Territorial Best Sellers
31 Jan 1953	BB	I Believe / Meteor 5000	#8	Saint Louis / Territorial Best Sellers
31 Jan 1953	BB	I Believe / Meteor 5000	#10	Cincinnati / Territorial Best Sellers
7 Feb 1953	BB	I Believe / Meteor 5000	#10	Chicago / Territorial Best Sellers
7 Feb 1953	BB	I Believe / Meteor 5000	#9	New York / Territorial Best Sellers
These following three all the same week:				
Feb? 1953	CB	I Believe / Meteor 5000	#2	San Francisco
Feb? 1953	CB	I Believe / Meteor 5000	#8	Newark
Feb? 1953	CB	I Believe / Meteor 5000	#4	Ft. Worth

Date	Source	Title & Record Number	Position	Location and/or Chart Name
14 Feb 1953	BB	I Believe / Meteor 5000	#10	National Best Sellers
14 Feb 1953	BB	I Believe / Meteor 5000	#6	New York / Territorial Best Sellers
14 Feb 1953	BB	I Believe / Meteor 5000	#8	Los Angeles / Territorial Best Sellers
21 Feb 1953	BB	I Believe / Meteor 5000	#9	National Best Sellers
21 Feb 1953	BB	I Believe / Meteor 5000	#10	New York / Territorial Best Sellers
21 Feb 1953	BB	I Believe / Meteor 5000	#8	Los Angeles / Territorial Best Sellers
21 Feb 1953	BB	I Believe / Meteor 5000	#5	Atlanta / Territorial Best Sellers
28 Feb 1953	BB	I Believe / Meteor 5000	#9	National Best Sellers
28 Feb 1953	BB	I Believe / Meteor 5000	#8	Los Angeles / Territorial Best Sellers
28 Feb 1953	BB	I Believe / Meteor 5000	#4	Atlanta / Territorial Best Sellers
7 Mar 1953	BB	I Believe / Meteor 5000	#8	Los Angeles / Territorial Best Sellers
7 Mar 1953	BB	I Believe / Meteor 5000	#5	Atlanta / Territorial Best Sellers
14 Mar 1953	BB	I Believe / Meteor 5000	#9	Los Angeles / Territorial Best Sellers
14 Mar 1953	BB	I Believe / Meteor 5000	#5	Atlanta / Territorial Best Sellers
21 Mar 1953	BB	I Believe / Meteor 5000	#9	Los Angeles / Territorial Best Sellers
21 Mar 1953	BB	I Believe / Meteor 5000	#5	Atlanta / Territorial Best Sellers
28 Mar 1953	BB	I Believe / Meteor 5000	#8	Atlanta / Territorial Best Sellers
4 Apr 1953	BB	I Believe / Meteor 5000	#8	Atlanta / Territorial Best Sellers
11 Apr 1953	BB	I Believe / Meteor 5000	#1	Philadelphia / Territorial Best Sellers
11 Apr 1953	BB	I Believe / Meteor 5000	#9	Atlanta / Territorial Best Sellers
25 Apr 1953	BB	I Believe / Meteor 5000	#10	Atlanta / Territorial Best Sellers

THIS WEEK'S BEST BUYS

Rhythm & Blues

I BELIEVE—Elmore James—Meteor 5000
Record building well in Chicago, Tennessee and Cincinnati. Heavy demand in New York. Top dealer pick this week.

10 January 1953 Billboard

2 May 1960	BB	The Sky Is Crying / Fire 1016	#22	Hot R&B Sides
9 May 1960	BB	The Sky Is Crying / Fire 1016	#15	Hot R&B Sides
16 May 1960	BB	The Sky Is Crying / Fire 1016	#21	Hot R&B Sides
23 May 1960	BB	The Sky Is Crying / Fire 1016	#21	Hot R&B Sides
30 May 1960	BB	The Sky Is Crying / Fire 1016	#27	Hot R&B Sides

Date	Source	Title & Record Number	Position	Chart Name
24 Apr 1965	BB	It Hurts Me Too / Enjoy 2015	#36	Hot Rhythm & Blues Singles
1 May 1965	BB	It Hurts Me Too / Enjoy 2015	#30	Hot Rhythm & Blues Singles
8 May 1965	BB	It Hurts Me Too / Enjoy 2015	#32	Hot Rhythm & Blues Singles
8 May 1965	CB	It Hurts Me Too / Enjoy 2015	#34	Top 50 In R&B Locations
15 May 1965	BB	It Hurts Me Too / Enjoy 2015	#32	Hot Rhythm & Blues Singles
15 May 1965	CB	It Hurts Me Too / Enjoy 2015	#20	Top 50 In R&B Locations
22 May 1965	BB	It Hurts Me Too / Enjoy 2015	#28	Hot Rhythm & Blues Singles
22 May 1965	BB	It Hurts Me Too / Enjoy 2015	#127	Bubbling Under The Hot 100
22 May 1965	CB	It Hurts Me Too / Enjoy 2015	#11	Top 50 In R&B Locations
29 May 1965	BB	It Hurts Me Too / Enjoy 2015	#32	Hot Rhythm & Blues Singles
29 May 1965	BB	It Hurts Me Too / Enjoy 2015	#106	Bubbling Under The Hot 100
29 May 1965	CB	It Hurts Me Too / Enjoy 2015	#9	Top 50 In R&B Locations
5 Jun 1965	BB	It Hurts Me Too / Enjoy 2015	#25	Top Selling Rhythm & Blues Singles
5 Jun 1965	BB	It Hurts Me Too / Enjoy 2015	#106	Bubbling Under The Hot 100
5 Jun 1965	CB	It Hurts Me Too / Enjoy 2015	#10	Top 50 In R&B Locations
12 Jun 1965	BB	It Hurts Me Too / Enjoy 2015	#28	Top Selling Rhythm & Blues Singles
12 Jun 1965	BB	It Hurts Me Too / Enjoy 2015	#106	Bubbling Under The Hot 100
12 Jun 1965	CB	It Hurts Me Too / Enjoy 2015	#19	Top 50 In R&B Locations
19 Jun 1965	CB	It Hurts Me Too / Enjoy 2015	#25	Top 50 In R&B Locations
26 Jun 1965	CB	It Hurts Me Too / Enjoy 2015	#43	Top 50 In R&B Locations

Notes:

• *During the time that "Dust My Broom" was making* Cash Box *regional chart appearances, there were no regional charts for Rhythm & Blues records in* The Billboard *(regional charts were given only for popular records at that time).*

• *At this time, a full reporting of regional* Cash Box *chart positions for "I Believe" is, unfortunately, not available.*

• *Between 12 March 1960 and 10 December 1960,* Cash Box *deleted its weekly R&B chart in favor of running the pop "Hot 100" chart. This probably accounts for why "The Sky Is Crying"—which enjoyed a five week run on the* Billboard *Top 30 R&B charts starting 2 May 1960—failed to be listed in the* Cash Box *charts.*

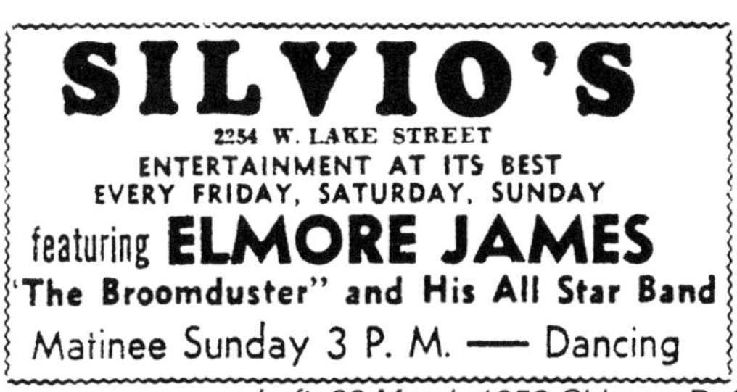

Left: 28 March 1953 Chicago Defender; Right: 15 November 1952 Defender

A few inspirations and influences. Advertisement from 28 March 1953 Billboard. "I Must Have Done Somebody Wrong" courtesy Bill Greensmith Collection.

Profiles of family members, musicians, and record labels (along with record label personnel) mentioned in the text.

The Family:

- **Leola Brooks – Elmore's mother**
  Born Holmes County, Mississippi, circa 1902 - 1904

Listed as "Leola" on Elmore's birth certificate, and "Leora" in the 1920 Census, she was known to use either name. Elmore supposedly was her only child, whom she outlived. Prior to Elmore's death, she evidently married and adopted the surname Randoll. Death information unknown.

- **Father – probably Joe Willie "Frost" James**

On Elmore's death certificate, Joe Willie James (a.k.a. Joe Willie "Frost" James) is listed as Elmore's father. Elmore would adopt the last name of "James" from this man—the one his mother had set up house with after Elmore had been born (Note that on Elmore's birth certificate, the entry for "father" is simply left blank, and has been crossed out with a big "X").

- **Robert Earl Holston – adopted step-brother to Elmore**
  Born Belzoni, Mississippi, 27 May 1918
  Died Carthage, Mississippi, 22 September 1989

Robert Earl played guitar and performed with Elmore in the 1930s.

- **Other Relations Include:**

- Wash (prob short for Washington) Brooks – Maternal Grandfather
  Born Mississippi, 16 October 1873
  Died Holmes County, Mississippi, 30 October 1925

- Sleata Brooks – Maternal Grandmother
  circa 1876 – ?

According to records kept by the U.S. Navy, Sleata Brooks was still living at the time of Elmore's death.

- Mac Willie James – Uncle
  Birth and death information unknown.

Elmore initially roomed with his uncle upon moving to Chicago in 1952. As of the July 1972 issue of *Blues Unlimited,* it was noted that his uncle Mac was still living at 4218 S. Cottage Grove, Apt. 205, in Chicago. According to Dick Shurman, one night at Turner's Lounge in January 1973, Chicago blues veteran Johnny Young introduced him to Mac Willie James. "We shared the front table for a very colorful night," Shurman recalled. "He said, 'All those good times Elmore and Sonny Boy had—I paid for 'em!'"[884]

---

884 Shurman, personal communication, 29 November 2001.

- Minnie Mae James née ? (maiden name unknown) – Elmore's wife
  Birth and death information unknown.

Elmore's marriage, in the 1940s, to a woman from Schlater, Mississippi, was something not previously known by researchers, until Pat LeBlanc and The Estate of Elmore James turned up evidence of her existence in the 1990s. Evidently the union of Elmore and Minnie Mae James produced numerous offspring. Although the marriage did not last, they were never formally divorced. She died shortly before Pat LeBlanc was able to find her.

The Musicians:

All musicians: vocals

- **"Homesick" James Williamson – guitar, bass guitar**
  Born Somerville, Tennessee, 30 April 1910 *or* 3 May 1914

A cousin and an early mentor for Elmore on guitar. Homesick was reunited with Elmore in Chicago in the 1950s, where they subsequently recorded and toured together. Homesick's two singles for Chicago's Chance label (in 1952-1953) are considered to be prime examples of the raw, electric country blues sound in the postwar era.

- **Boyd Gilmore – guitar**
  Born (probably Belzoni), Mississippi, 12 June 1910
  Died Fresno, California, 23 December 1976

Reportedly a childhood friend and cousin of Elmore James, Gilmore played in a similar, but more rudimentary style, and recorded for Modern Records around the same time as James. Dubbed a "latter-day phantom," researchers were unable to locate him for an interview prior to his death, in spite of worldwide interest and efforts.

- **Sonny Boy Williamson #2 (real name Alex or Aleck "Rice" Miller) – harmonica**
  Born Glendora, Mississippi, 5 December 1899? (dates/places vary widely)
  Died Helena, Arkansas, 25 May 1965

Prior to his 1951 recording debut on the Trumpet label, Williamson had enjoyed a widespread popularity in the mid-south via his *King Biscuit Time* radio show, broadcast from Helena, Arkansas each workday during the noon hour. Elmore and Sonny Boy played widely throughout the Delta in the late 1930s to early 1950s, and they recorded together at Trumpet Records. Williamson enjoyed a "second career" in Chicago, recording and performing until his death.

- **Robert Johnson – guitar**
  Born Hazlehurst, Mississippi, 8 May 1911
  Died Greenwood, Mississippi, 16 August 1938

The quintessential Mississippi Delta blues guitarist and songwriter of the pre-war era. Johnson was essentially a musical sponge, picking up musical ideas and phrases from varied sources, which he carefully crafted and edited into his magnificent recorded body of work. His innovations on guitar were influential not only to Elmore James, but to James' generation of blues guitar players as well. Elmore recorded three of his compositions.

- **Arthur "Big Boy" Crudup – guitar**
  Born Forest, Mississippi, 24 August 1905
  Died Nassawadox, Virginia, 28 March 1974

Although famous today for his song "That's All Right," with which Elvis Presley enjoyed his initial popularity, Crudup was—more importantly, perhaps—among the first of the Mississippi blues artists to feature an electric guitar on his records. He often worked with Elmore and Sonny Boy in the mid-south. Even though this powerful Delta trio never recorded as a group, James and Crudup would often (quite by chance) have competing singles out on the market—sometimes on the same record label—at the same time. In 1952, Crudup recorded for Trumpet as Elmer James.

- **Willie Love – piano**
  Born Duncan, Mississippi, 6 October 1906
  Died Jackson, Mississippi, 19 August 1953

Love was a popular figure over the airwaves, and in his hometown of Greenville, Mississippi as well. Love recorded with Sonny Boy Williamson and Elmore James while at Trumpet Records.

- **Ike Turner – guitar, piano**
  Born Clarksdale, Mississippi, 5 November 1931

Turner was employed as a talent scout for Modern Records in 1952 when Modern held its first recording session with James. The multi-talented Turner played both piano and guitar, and is the ex-husband of the world-famous Tina. Ike was present for three of Elmore's recording sessions.

- **James "Kokomo" Arnold – guitar**
  Born Lovejoy's Station, Georgia, 15 February 1901
  Died Chicago, Illinois, 8 November 1969

What Arnold lacked in technical proficiency as a musician, he made up for in feeling. His records, described as "zany" and "loud and exuberant," were atypical of the era, accompanied by his fast bottleneck guitar playing. He was one of the first blues singers to record the line "I believe I'll dust my broom" in a song.[885] James was obviously a spiritual cousin to Arnold—each man shared the mutual passions of

[885] In the song, "Sagefield Woman Blues" (Decca 7044, 1935). Other artists in this list include Carl Rafferty ("Mr. Carl's Blues." Bluebird B5429, 1934) and Big Joe Williams ("49 Highway Blues." Bluebird B5996, c. 1935).

A little bit of record sleuthing reveals that Rafferty's "Mr. Carl's Blues" was issued as Bluebird B5429 probably sometime in mid-1934. Kokomo Arnold was in the studio recording "Sagefield Woman Blues" in September 1934, with the title being issued as Decca 7044 circa January/February 1935. Whether or not songs recorded and issued this close together exhibit evidence of one having influenced the other—a few months is nothing, for instance, if your point of reference is the geological sense of time—is, decidedly, very hard to determine.

Also worth noting is that in "49 Highway Blues" (recorded 25 February 1935), Big Joe Williams sings the following couplet: "...I'm gonna get up in the mornin', I believe I'll dust my bed / I'm gwine down Highway 49, boys, I'm gon' be rockin' 'til my end." Not only is this an interesting theme and variation on the standard "Dust My Broom" lyric, but as Bob Groom points out, the last part of the couplet 'foreshadows' Robert Johnson's "Traveling Riverside Blues." "49 Highway Blues" was issued as Bluebird B5996 circa very late 1935, still almost a full year before Johnson entered a recording studio. Big Joe Williams would use the couplet again in "Highway 49," which he recorded on 12 December 1941, and later released as Bluebird B9025 during the summer of 1942 (Bob Groom, notes to Big Joe Williams, *Complete Recorded Works in Chronological Order, Vol. 1.* RST Records CD 6003, 1991; Oliver, *Screening the Blues,* 189; and Dixon, Godrich, and Rye, 476, 1039).

bootlegging and fishing, and the curious habit of humming or moaning during guitar solos. Arnold's "Milk Cow Blues" and "Old Original Kokomo Blues" was a huge two-sided hit in the mid 1930s; both songs have become standards (the latter would be adapted and recorded by Robert Johnson as "Sweet Home Chicago").

- **Tampa Red (real name Hudson Woodbridge) – guitar, kazoo**
  Born Smithville, Georgia, 8 January 1904
  Died Chicago, Illinois, 19 March 1981

Hugely popular and widely influential, Tampa Red enjoyed a recording career that lasted several decades and included hundreds of songs (some of them became standards), several of which James recorded. His advanced slide guitar style impressed blues guitarists of both the pre and postwar era Chicago blues, especially Robert Nighthawk and Elmore James.

- **Robert Nighthawk (real name Robert Lee McCollum) – guitar, harmonica**
  Born Helena, Arkansas, 30 November 1909
  Died Helena, Arkansas, 5 November 1967

An influential and vital—but often overlooked—link in the development of the modern electric slide guitar sound from Tampa Red to Elmore James. On 5 May 1937, he and John Lee "Sonny Boy" Williamson (#1) made their recording debut, accompanied by Big Joe Williams. This legendary recording session would be a harbinger of the small ensemble approach that would predominate postwar Chicago blues. After a noteworthy career as an artist for Bluebird, he would go on to record after World War II for Aristocrat, Chess, United, and States. In 1964, Nighthawk was captured in live performance on Maxwell Street for the film *And This Is Free;* these recordings are among the finest live blues ever committed to tape.

- **Odie Payne – drums**
  Born Chicago, Illinois, 27 August 1926
  Died Chicago, Illinois, 1 March 1989

Drummer with Tampa Red's band in the late 1940s and early 1950s. Played and recorded with Elmore James in Chicago during the early and mid 1950s in James' legendary group, "The Broomdusters." Considered to be one of Chicago's top blues drummers of the era.

- **"Little" Johnny Jones – piano**
  Born Jackson, Mississippi, 1 November 1924
  Died Chicago, Illinois, 19 November 1964

Pianist with Tampa Red's band during the same time frame as Payne. Played and recorded with Elmore James throughout the 1950s, and was another original member of "The Broomdusters." Considered to be one of the top blues pianists of the Chicago postwar era.

- **J.T. Brown – tenor sax**
  Born Mississippi (unknown location), 2 April 1910
  Died Chicago, Illinois, 24 November 1969

Famous for his "nanny goat" or down-home "honking" style of tenor saxophone playing. Brown was a fixture on the Chicago blues scene as early as 1945, and recorded with such artists as Eddie Boyd, Roosevelt Sykes, and Washboard Sam, before joining the Broomdusters in 1952.

- **Sam Myers – harmonica**
  Born Laurel, Mississippi, 19 February 1936

When James was blacklisted by the Chicago musician's union in 1960, he returned to Mississippi where he formed another group, which included Myers on harmonica. They often performed together, and recorded on one occasion. Myers enjoys a successful, award-winning blues career today, touring and recording with Anson Funderburgh and the Rockets.

The Record Labels:

- **Trumpet Records – Jackson, Mississippi**
  Proprietor: Lillian Shedd McMurry
  Born Purvis, Mississippi, 30 December 1921
  Died Jackson, Mississippi, 18 March 1999

Between 1951 and 1955, recorded some of the cream of the Mississippi Delta Blues, during a unique time when the music was in a transitional phase. Helped to foster the recording careers of Sonny Boy Williamson, Willie Love, Elmore James and others. "Dust My Broom" was one of Trumpet's biggest sellers. Marc Ryan's Acoustic Archives label reissued most of the extant Trumpet material on a series of albums between 1989 and 1991. Alligator Records later picked up the series for reissue. *Trumpet Records: An Illustrated History with Discography* by Marc Ryan is recommended for further reading.

- **Modern Records – Beverly Hills, California**
  • **President: Saul Bihari** – Born Saint Louis, Missouri, 8 March 1920
  Died probably Beverly Hills, California, March 1975
  • **Vice Presidents:**
  Jules Bihari – Born Philadelphia, Pennsylvania, 9 September 1913
  Died Los Angeles, California, 17 November 1984
  Joe Bihari – Born Memphis, Tennessee, 1925

The Bihari brothers—Joe, Jules, and Saul—started Modern Records in 1945 (their associated labels included at one time or another: Blues & Rhythm, Crown, Flair, Kent, and RPM). Although based on the west coast, their labels featured a surprising amount of Texas and Mississippi Delta blues—thanks to their field trips to the mid-south—and on one of these excursions they first recorded James. He was an artist for the Modern operation between 1952 and 1956. Ace Records (in the UK) and P-Vine (in Japan) have extensively reissued material from Modern—and their affiliated labels. Some of these CDs have been issued in the U.S. as well. Starting in 2001, Ace Records implemented a series of compact disc issues chronicling Modern Records' field trips in the early 1950s; the first volume also contains a capsule biography of Joe Bihari.

- **Meteor Records – Memphis, Tennessee**
  Proprietor: Lester Bihari – Born (Location unknown) 12 May 1912
  Died probably Los Angeles, California, September 1983

Not formally a Modern subsidiary, operations at Meteor Records were overseen by Lester Bihari, one of the four brothers. Elmore James' follow-up recording to "Dust My Broom" was released on Meteor (as their debut issue) and was a huge R&B hit. Included among the dozen or so blues singles released on Meteor between 1952 and 1958 were some of the most highly revered down-home blues of the era. Incidentally,

Meteor is also known—in rockabilly circles—for a string of records they issued in that vein between 1955 and 1958. Elmore's four Meteor sides (along with four more from the same session with J.T. Brown leading) can all be found on *The Classic Early Recordings 1951-1956* box set. A 1993 compact disc issued by Ace Records nicely surveyed the Meteor rockabilly material. According to Bez Turner in the Spring 2001 issue of *Juke Blues* magazine, work is currently underway on a CD collection of Meteor blues recordings.

- **Chess Records – Chicago, Illinois**
  Proprietors: Leonard Chess
  Born Lejzor Czyz in Motele, Poland, 12 March 1917
  Died Chicago, Illinois, 16 October 1969
  Phil Chess
  Born Fiszel Czyz in Motele, Poland, 1921 (specific dates vary)

Perhaps the most famous of the independent Chicago blues labels. Chess got its start in 1947 as Aristocrat Records, devoting a substantial portion of its output to the Mississippi Delta blues of Muddy Waters, Robert Nighthawk, Sunnyland Slim and others. In 1950 the name was changed to Chess. Such blues stalwarts as Howlin' Wolf, Little Walter Jacobs, Bo Diddley, the aforementioned Sonny Boy Williamson and Muddy Waters, and Chuck Berry enjoyed long careers at Chess, or their subsidiary label Checker. Elmore James recorded for Chess in 1953, and again in 1960. MCA Records has maintained an ongoing reissue program of the Chess catalog for more than fifteen years. Two books on Chess Records are now available: John Collis' *The Story of Chess Records;* and Nadine Cohodas' *Spinning Blues into Gold: The Chess Brothers and the Legendary Chess Records.* Readers interested in researching the Chess blues and R&B catalogs are directed to Les Fancourt's *Chess Blues Discography* and *Chess R & B Discography,* published in England in 1989 and 1991, respectively.

- **Chief Records – Chicago, Illinois**
  Proprietor: Mel London
  Born Mississippi (unknown location), 9 April 1932
  Died Chicago, Illinois, 16 May 1975

Founded by Mel London in 1957, Chief Records was a tiny outfit that released several memorable Elmore James records. Junior Wells, Earl Hooker and Magic Sam were among the Chicago blues artists that recorded for Chief, between 1957 and 1961. Six of Elmore's seven Chief sides were reissued by the Vee-Jay label. This material periodically pops up on reissue albums. Muse Records issued a CD with all seven sides in 1988. Bez Turner compiled a discography for the July/August 1977 issue of *Blues Unlimited* magazine that lists all of London's record labels, with a complete list of issues for each of his labels.

- **Fire / Fury / Enjoy Records – New York City**
  Proprietor: Bobby Robinson
  Born Union, South Carolina, 16 April 1917

Adept as a talent scout and producer, Robinson not only has a long string of record labels to his credit, but also a long string of R&B hits—such as "Fannie Mae" and "Kansas City"—as well. Elmore James recorded for Robinson's Fire label between 1959 and 1961, and for Enjoy in 1963. James' two biggest selling R&B hits were Robinson productions, "The Sky Is Crying" in 1960, and "It Hurts Me Too" in 1965. Relic Records has painstakingly researched Robinson's tape archives, and has implemented a first-rate reissue program of his artists and labels. Capricorn, a Time-Warner subsidiary, has also issued some of this material.

Adins, George. "A la recherche du blues perdu." *Soul Bag* 94 (May/June 1983): 24-27.

Albert, George, and Frank Hoffman, comps. *The Cash Box Black Contemporary Singles Charts, 1960-1984.* Metuchen, New Jersey: Scarecrow Press, 1986.

Altman, Billy. Notes to Sonny Boy Williamson and Big Joe Williams, *Throw a Boogie Woogie.* RCA CD 9599-2, 1989.

Anonymous [Name withheld by request]. Personal interview by Steve Franz. Helena, Arkansas, 12 October 1990.

Astbury, Ray. "Drink That Hadacol." *Blues & Rhythm* 53 (July 1990): 4-6.

"Back in Mississippi" [conversation]. From the album Elmore James, *To Know a Man.* Blue Horizon LP 7-66230, 1969.

Balfour, Alan. "Elmore James Story." *Soul Bag* 94 (May/June 1983): 19-21.

___. Notes to Tampa Red, *Complete Recorded Works in Chronological Order, Vol. 15.* Document CD 5215, 1993.

___. Electronic communication with Steve Franz. 21 May 2002.

Balfour, Alan, et al. "Sonny Boy Williamson Discography." *Soul Bag* 134 (Spring 1994): 12-17.

Barry, John. *Rising Tide: The Great Mississippi Flood of 1927 and How It Changed America.* New York: Simon & Schuster, 1997.

Bastin, Bruce, and Pete Lowry. "Blues from the Southeast (Part 7)." *Blues Unlimited* 73 (June 1970): 4-5.

Baum, Wolfie. "Elmore James Discography." *Jazz Statistics* 24 (December 1961): 8.

Berry, Chuck. *The Autobiography.* New York: Harmony Books, 1987.

Besnier, Christian. "Elmore James/Discographie." *Soul Bag* 94 (May/June 1983): 12-15.

Biehler, Chris. Notes to Al King, *Blues Master.* Forevermore CD 4601, 1996.

"Blues News." *Blues Unlimited* 26 (October 1965): 19.

"Blues News." *Living Blues* 4 (Winter 1970/1971): 26, et al.

"Blues News." *Living Blues* 10 (Autumn 1972): 40.

"Blues News Coast-to-Coast." *Blues Unlimited* 36 (September 1966): 23.

"Bobby's Top Sellers." *Record Exchanger* 12 (Winter 1972): 11.

Bonner, Brett J. Notes to James "Son" Thomas. *Beefsteak Blues.* Evidence CD 26095-2, 1998.

___. Notes to *Living Country Blues: An Anthology.* Evidence CD 26105-2, 1999.

Briggs, Keith. Notes to *Chicago Blues—The Chance Era.* Charly CD 146-2, 1997.

Brisbin, John Anthony. "Big Moose Walker: Playin' All Night Long." *Living Blues* 105 (September/October 1992): 34-41.

___. "Lester Davenport: It's All About Havin' a Good Time." *Living Blues* 107 (February 1993): 20-27.

___. "Robert Plunkett: I Think I Had a Little Magic." *Living Blues* 114 (March/April 1994): 40-51.

___. "The Lost American Bluesmen." *Living Blues* 134 (July/August 1997): 28-41.

___. "Pryor Arrangements." *Blues Access* 36 (Winter 1999): 52-54.

Bromberg, Bruce. Notes to Elmore James, *The Legend of Elmore James.* Kent LP 9001, 1969.

Bromberg, Michael. Notes to Elmore James, *The Resurrection of Elmore James.* Kent LP 9010, 1969.

Broven, John. "Elmore James on Record." *Blues Unlimited* 5 (October 1963): 6-7.

___. "Sonny Boy Williamson." *Blues Unlimited* 8 (January 1964): 3-4.

___. "J.B. Lenoir: Yet Another Forgotten Artist." *Blues Unlimited* 15 (September 1964): 5-6.

___. "Bobby's Happy House of Hits, part 1." *Juke Blues* 15 (Spring 1989): 6-11.

___. "Bobby's Happy House of Hits, part 2." *Juke Blues* 16 (Summer 1989): 10-15.

___. "I Found Lightnin' Hopkins!" *Juke Blues* 31 (Summer 1994): 23.

Broven, John, Mike Leadbitter, and Simon Napier. "The American Folk Blues Festival 1963: What They Said." *Blues Unlimited* 7 (December 1963): 7-9.

Broven, John, Kurt Mohr, Mike Rowe, et al. "Discography." *Collectors Classics* 7 (May 1965): 4-6.

Bruynoghe, Yannick. "Chicago: Home of the Blues," 67-76. In Sinclair Traill and Gerald Lascelles, eds., *Just Jazz No. 2.* London: Peter Davies, 1958.

___. "In Chicago with Big Bill & Friends: Chicago Scrapbook Excerpts." *Living Blues* 55 (Winter 1982/83): 7-16.

___. "25 Years Ago." *Soul Bag* 94 (May/June 1983): 27-28.

Burke, Tony. Notes to Juke Boy Bonner, *Things Ain't Right—The 1969 London Sessions.* Sequel CD 209, 1992.

___. "New Releases/Homesick James with the Hypnotics." *Blues & Rhythm* 78 (April 1993): 25.

Burke, Tony, and Chris Smith. "Moonshine and the Moose." *Blues & Rhythm* 69 (May 1992): 12-13.

Burke, Tony, and Norman Darwen. "'Who May Your Regular Be?'" *Blues & Rhythm* 156 (February 2001): 4-8.

Calt, Stephen. Notes to *The Roots of Robert Johnson.* Yazoo CD 1073, 1990 [reissue].

___. "The Idioms of Robert Johnson." *78 Quarterly* Vol. 1, No. 4 (1989): 53-60.

Calt, Stephen, and Gayle Dean Wardlow, "Robert Johnson." *78 Quarterly* Vol. 1, No. 4 (1989): 40-50.

Carlton, William Orten. "Hop Wilson." *Living Blues* 26 (March/April 1976): 8-9.

Carroll, Ted. Personal communication with Steve Franz. 13 November 1992.

Chapman, Robert, ed. *American Slang.* New York: Perennial Library, 1987 [reprint].

Charters, Samuel. *The Country Blues.* New York: Rinehart & Company, Inc., 1959.

___. *"Chicago/The Blues/Today!:* A Reminiscence," 11-24. In the notes to *Chicago/The Blues/Today!* Vanguard CD 172/74-2, 1999.

Chauvard, Marcel, and Jacques Demêtre. "Smokey Smothers," 97. In Mike Leadbitter, ed., *Nothing But the Blues.* London: Hanover Books, 1971.

Chauvard, Marcel, Kurt Mohr, John Broven, et al., "Discography." *Blues Unlimited* 5 (October 1963): 4-6.

"Chicago Blues News." *Living Blues* 22 (July/August 1975): 15.

The Chicago Defender [Advertisement]. (4 October 1952): 23.

The Chicago Defender [Advertisement]. (1 November 1952): 19.

The Chicago Defender [Advertisement]. (15 November 1952): 17.

The Chicago Defender [Advertisement]. (1 October 1953): Reprinted in the notes to Elmore James, *The Classic Early Recordings 1951-1956.* Ace BOXCD 4, 1993.

The Chicago Defender [Advertisement]. (16 January 1954): Reprinted in the notes to Elmore James, *The Classic Early Recordings 1951-1956.* Ace BOXCD 4, 1993.

The Chicago Defender [Advertisement]. (19 November 1955): 18.

The Chicago Defender [Advertisement]. (26 November 1955): 28.

Chisholm, Malcolm. Personal interview by Diana Reid Haig. In the notes to *The Cobra Records Story.* Capricorn CD 42012-2, 1993: 12-13.

Christgau, Robert. "Chuck Berry," 58-63. In Jim Miller, ed., *The Rolling Stone Illustrated History of Rock & Roll.* New York: Rolling Stone Press, 1976.

Clee, Ken. *The Directory of American 45 R.P.M. Records.* 4 vols. Philadelphia: Stak-O-Wax, 1997.

Clinco, Paul. *"Living Blues* Interview: Big Joe Turner." *Living Blues* 10 (Autumn 1972): 20-26.

Cohodas, Nadine. *Spinning Blues Into Gold: The Chess Brothers and the Legendary Chess Records.* New York: St. Martin's Press, 2000.

Cokliss, Harley, dir. *Chicago Blues.* Irit Films, 1970.

Coller, Derek, Jacques Demêtre, and Marcel Chauvard. "Elmore James." *Vintage Jazz Mart* 71 (January? 1960): 4.

Collins, Tony. "'On My Way:' The Al King Story." *Juke Blues* 27 (Autumn 1992): 9-13.

Cone, James H. *The Spirituals and the Blues: An Interpretation.* San Francisco: Harper & Row, 1972.

Connor, Anthony, and Robert Neff. *The Blues: In Images and Interviews.* New York: Cooper Square Press, 1999 [reprint].

Cook, Warren. "Disc Dating." *Record Exchanger* 9 (March 1972): 22-23.

Cushing, Steve. "Odie Payne: An Inward Feeling of an Expression." *Living Blues* 96 (March/April 1991): 52-63.

Cushing, Steve, and Justin O'Brien. "Behind the Beat of the Blues." *Living Blues* 96 (March/April 1991): 12-23.

Dahl, Bill. Notes to Morris Pejoe and Arthur "Big Boy" Spires, *Wrapped in My Baby.* Delmark CD 716, 1998.

Dallas, Karl. "Elmore James Jr., 100 Club, London." *Melody Maker* vol. 54 (17 February 1979): 50.

Danchin, Sebastian. "Introduction," 8-22. In Jacques Demêtre and Marcel Chauvard, *Land of the Blues.* Levallois-Perret, France: CLARB/Soul Bag, 1994.

___. *'Blues Boy:' The Life and Music of B.B. King.* Jackson, Mississippi: University Press of Mississippi, 1998.

Daniels, William, comp. *The American 45 and 78 RPM Record Dating Guide, 1940-1959.* Westport, Connecticut: Greenwood Press, 1985.

Darwen, Norman. "Hip Linkchain and Odie Payne." *Blues & Rhythm* 44 (May 1989): 17.

___. Notes to Robert Nighthawk and Forest City Joe, *Black Angel Blues.* Charly CD RED 29, 1991.

___. Notes to *Slidin'.* Charly CD RED 36, 1991.

Darwen, Norman and Tamara Shad. "Bob Shad – The Record Man: The *Sittin' In With* Story." *Blues & Rhythm* 100 (June/July 1995): 16-30.

Davis, Fred. "Joe Willie Wilkins," 144-145. In Mike Leadbitter, ed., *Nothing But the Blues.* London: Hanover Books, 1971.

Davis, Maxwell. American Federation of Musicians Local Number 47 contract 1525: 16 July 1954.

Dawkins, Jimmy. "Big Bill Hill's Story." *Blues Unlimited* 70 (February/March 1970): 18-19.

Dawkins, Jimmy, Dick Shurman, and Keith Tillman. "Willie Johnson: Boppin' the Blues." *Blues Unlimited* 93 (July 1972): 4-7.

DeKoster, Jim. "Records." *Living Blues* 3 (Autumn 1970): 28-29.

Demêtre, Jacques. "Rencontre avec Elmore James." Translated by Marty Champion. *Soul Bag* 94 (May/June 1983): 23-24.

Demêtre, Jacques, and Marcel Chauvard. *Land of the Blues.* Levallois-Perret, France: CLARB/Soul Bag, 1994.

Demêtre, Jacques, Marcel Chauvard, and Bob Koester. "Elmore James." *Collectors Classics* 7 (May 1965): 3-4.

Devenne, Walter. Telephone interview by Steve Franz, 16 June 1992.

Dirks, Scott. "Elmore James and the Musicians Union." *Living Blues* 162 (April 2002): 40-45.

Dixon, Robert, John Godrich, and Howard Rye, comps. *Blues and Gospel Records 1890-1943,* 4th Ed. Oxford: Clarendon Press, 1997.

Dixon, Willie, and Don Snowden. *I Am the Blues: The Willie Dixon Story.* London: Quartet Books, 1989.

Doggett, Peter. "Elmore James." *Record Collector* 161 (January 1993): 18-22.

Donoghue, William. *'Fessor Mojo's "Don't Start Me to Talkin."* Elliott & James Publishing: Seattle, 1997.

___. "Did Elmore James Know He Was Recording 'Dust My Broom'?" *Blues & Rhythm* 125 (Christmas 1997): 10-11.

___. "Obituaries: Lillian McMurry." *Blues & Rhythm* 139 (May 1999): 20-21.

"*'Do You Need a Good Artist?'* Elmore James's Phone Call to Lillian McMurry." *Living Blues* 67 (1986): 28.

Eagle, Bob. "Big Town Playboy: Johnnie Jones." *Living Blues* 12 (Spring 1973): 28-29.

Edwards, David Honeyboy. *The World Don't Owe Me Nothing,* as told to Janis Martinson and Michael Robert Frank. Chicago: Chicago Review Press, 1997.

"Enjoy Discography." *Record Exchanger* 12 (Winter 1972): 12.

Erlewine, Michael, et al., eds. *All Music Guide to the Blues,* 2nd ed. San Francisco: Miller Freeman Books, 1999.

Escott, Colin, and Martin Hawkins. *Sun Records: The Brief History of the Legendary Record Label.* New York: Quick Fox, 1980.

Escott, Colin, with George Merritt and William MacEwen. *Hank Williams: The Biography.* Boston: Little, Brown and Company, 1994.

Evans, David. "Trumpet Records for Sale!" *Blues Unlimited* 39 (December 1966): 21.

___. "Afro-American One-Stringed Instruments." *Western Folklore* 29 (1970): 229-245.

___. "Peck Curtis: Interview." *Blues Unlimited* 69 (January 1970): 10-13.

___. "Blues." Memphis State University, Memphis, Tennessee, 5 September 1989.

___. Notes to Johnnie Temple, *Complete Recorded Works in Chronological Order Vol. 1.* Document CD 5238, 1994.

___. Notes to *Bottleneck Blues.* Testament CD 5021, 1995.

Fancourt, Leslie. *Chess Blues Discography,* 3rd ed. Kent, England: [no publisher], 1989.

___. *Chess R & B Discography,* 2nd ed. Kent, England: [no publisher], 1991.

___. *B.B. King, Albert & Freddy, A Discography.* Kent, England: Retrack Books, 1993.

Fanzone, Carmen. Personal interview by Steve Franz. Hollywood, California, 15 November 1993.

Ferris, William. *Blues from the Delta.* New York: Da Capo Press, 1984 [reprint].

Field, Kim. *Harmonicas, Harps, and Heavy Breathers.* New York: Cooper Square Press, 2000.

Fileti, Donn. Telephone interview by Steve Franz, 6 June 1992.

Finch, Nigel, dir. *25 x 5: The Continuing Adventures of the Rolling Stones.* Promotour U.S., Inc./Andrew Solt Productions, 1989.

"Fire Discography," *Record Exchanger* 12 (Winter 1972): 12.

Fleetwood, Mick, and Stephen Davis. *Fleetwood: My Life and Adventures with Fleetwood Mac.* New York: William Morrow & Co., 1990.

Flerlage, Raeburn. *Chicago Blues—As Seen from the Inside: The Photographs of Raeburn Flerlage.* Toronto: ECW Press, 2000.

Ford, Robert. *A Blues Bibliography: The International Literature of an Afro-American Music Genre.* Kent, England: Paul Pelletier, 1999.

Forte, Dan. "J.B. Hutto," 189-192. In Jas Obrecht, ed., *Rollin' and Tumblin': The Postwar Blues Guitarists.* San Francisco: Miller Freeman, 2000.

Foulger, Byron. "King Biscuit Name in Jeopardy." *Blues & Rhythm* 152 (September 2000): 20.

Franz, Steve. "Cap'n Pete: Blues from the Beginning." WEVL FM 90 *Program Guide* (May 1988): 1.

___. "Elmore James: The Complete Fire & Enjoy Sessions, Parts 1-4." *Rock & Roll Disc* Vol. 4, No. 9 (September 1990): 9-10.

___. "Elmore James Discography." In the notes to Elmore James, *Dust My Broom—The Best of Elmore James Part 2.* Relic CD 7040, 1992.

___. "About the Recordings." In the notes to Elmore James, *The Sky Is Crying: The History of Elmore James.* Rhino CD 71190, 1993.

___, comp. "Dating Guide to Chief Records numbers 7000 through 7022." unpublished manuscript, 1994.

___, comp. "Dating Guide to Vee-Jay Records numbers 240 through 270." unpublished manuscript, 1994.

___, comp. and ed. *Elmore James: The Ultimate Guide to the Master of the Slide.* St. Louis: Primal Art, 1994.

___, comp. "Fire Records FM Series Numbering and Dating Guide." unpublished manuscript, 1994.

___. *Elmore James: Standing at the Crossroads.* Master's Thesis, The University of Memphis, 1994.

___. Notes to *Sounds Like "Dust My Broom:" Development and Transition of the Most Famous Guitar Riff in History, Volume 1 (1931-1953).* Compact disc (unissued), 2001.

Garon, Paul. *Blues and the Poetic Spirit.* New York: Da Capo Press, 1979 [reprint].

___. "Postwar Chicago and the North," 195-220. In Paul Oliver, ed., *The Blackwell Guide to Blues Records.* Cambridge, Massachusetts: Basil Blackwell Inc., 1989.

Garon, Paul, and Beth Garon. *Woman with Guitar: Memphis Minnie's Blues.* New York: Da Capo Press, 1992.

Gart, Galen. *The American Record Label Directory and Dating Guide, 1940-1959.* Milford, New Hampshire: Big Nickel Publications, 1989.

___, comp. and ed. *First Pressings—The History of Rhythm & Blues Volume 3: 1953.* Milford, New Hampshire: Big Nickel Publications, 1989.

___, comp. and ed. *First Pressings—The History of Rhythm & Blues Volume 4: 1954.* Milford, New Hampshire: Big Nickel Publications, 1990.

___, comp. and ed. *First Pressings—The History of Rhythm & Blues, Volume 5: 1955.* Milford, New Hampshire: Big Nickel Publications, 1990.

___, comp. and ed. *First Pressings—The History of Rhythm & Blues, Volume 6: 1956.* Milford, New Hampshire: Big Nickel Publications, 1991.

___, comp. and ed. *First Pressings—The History of Rhythm & Blues, Volume 1: 1951.* Milford, New Hampshire: Big Nickel Publications, 1991.

___, comp. and ed. *First Pressings—The History of Rhythm & Blues Volume 2: 1952.* Milford, New Hampshire: Big Nickel Publications, 1992.

___, comp. and ed. *First Pressings—The History of Rhythm & Blues, Volume 7: 1957.* Milford, New Hampshire: Big Nickel Publications, 1993.

___, comp. and ed. *First Pressings—The History of Rhythm & Blues, Special 1950 Volume.* Milford, New Hampshire: Big Nickel Publications, 1993.

___, comp. and ed. *First Pressings—The History of Rhythm & Blues, Volume 8: 1958.* Milford, New Hampshire: Big Nickel Publications, 1995.

Gordon, Gregg. "Beale Street *Can* Talk." *The Downtowner* Vol. 5, No. 4 (May 1995): 13-17.

Green, Jonathon. *The Slang Thesaurus.* London: Penguin Books, 1988 [reprint].

Greensmith, Bill. Personal communication with Steve Franz. 27 December 2001.

Gronda, Steve, and Bez Turner. "Eddie Kirkland Part 2: 'Eddie Kirk Is My Georgia Name.'" *Juke Blues* 5 (Summer 1986): 11-16.

Groom, Bob. *The Blues Revival.* London: Studio Vista, 1971.

___. "Standing at the Crossroads: Robert Johnson's Recordings. [Part 1]" *Blues Unlimited* 118 (March/April 1976): 17-20.

___. Notes to Big Joe Williams, *Complete Recorded Works in Chronological Order, Vol. 1.* RST Records CD 6003, 1991.

Groslier, Daniel. "J.T. Brown/Discographie." *Soul Bag* 94 (May/June 1983): 16.

Guralnick, Peter. *Feel Like Going Home.* New York: Outerbridge & Dienstfrey, 1971.

___. *Searching for Robert Johnson.* New York: Obelisk/E.P. Dutton, 1989.

Hannusch, Jeff. "Elmore James Grave Marker to Be Dedicated." *Goldmine* 325 (8 January 1993): 7.

Hansen, Barry. "Blues In Review." *Record Research* 33 (March 1961): 14.

Hansen, Terry. "Elmore James' CD Legacy." *Blues Access* 9 (Spring 1992): 3-5.

Hanson, Nils. "Elmore James Revisited." *Jefferson* 76 (Våren 1987): 2-9.

Harris, Mark. "Little Johnny Jones Discography." *Pickin' the Blues* 4 (April/May 1982): 8-9.

___. "Mark's Blues No. 1." *Pickin' the Blues* 24 (May 1984): 8-13.

___. "Mark's Blues No. 2." *Pickin' the Blues* 25 (1984): 5-13.

Harris, Sheldon. *Blues Who's Who.* New Rochelle, New York: Arlington House, 1979.

Harvey, Hank. "Growing Up With the Blues." *Living Blues* 71 (1986): 25-28.

Hawkins, Martin, Colin Escott, et al. "The Blues In Memphis/Artists' Biographies," 16-31. In the notes to *Sun Records—The Blues Years 1950-1958.* Charly CDSUNBOX 7, 1996.

Hearn, Gary. *Elmore James & Sonny Boy Williamson on Compact Disc.* St. Neots, England: Limited Edition, 1994.

Hill, Big Bill. "Chicago Blues Radio: Big Bill Hill." *Living Blues* 7 (Winter 1971/72): 14.

Hobus, André. "Joe Carter." *Blues Unlimited* 129 (March/April 1978): 33.

Hoffman, Larry. Notes to Homesick James, *Goin' Back in the Times.* Earwig CD 4929, 1994.

___. "Robert Lockwood, Jr.: *Living Blues* Interview." *Living Blues* 121 (May/June 1995): 12-29.

"Honor Roll of Hits." *The Billboard* (11 April 1953): 20.

Huggins, Cilla. "A Little More on Milton," *Blues Unlimited* 144 (Spring 1983): 30-34.

___. "Dusting off Elmore!" *Juke Blues* 28 (Spring 1993): 18-19.

___. "Ike Turner: In the Beginning." *Juke Blues* 37 (Spring 1997): 9-14.

Hyslop, Tom. Personal Communication with Steve Franz. 16 June 1994.

Iglauer, Bruce. Notes to Hound Dog Taylor and the Houserockers, *Beware of the Dog.* Alligator LP 4707, 1976.

___. Notes to Johnny Jones, *Johnnie Jones with Billy Boy Arnold.* Alligator LP 4717, 1979.

___. Notes to Hound Dog Taylor and the Houserockers, *Genuine Houserocking Music.* Alligator LP 4727, 1982.

___. Notes to *The Alligator Records 20th Anniversary Collection.* Alligator CD 105/106, 1991.

James, Elmore. Coroner's Certificate of Death. State of Illinois: State File number 63-609-2744, 1963.

___. Notice of Separation from the U.S. Naval Service. Naval Service Record 8439732. LeFlore County, Mississippi, 31 December 1945.

Jones, Malcolm. Notes to Elmore James, *"Let's Cut It"—The Very Best of Elmore James.* Ace LP 192, 1987.

Jordan, Gertrude. Personal interview by David Evans. Jackson, Mississippi, 8 September 1966.

___. Personal interview by David Evans. Jackson, Mississippi, 26 June 1989.

Jung, Maureen. "Sacramento Blues, Part One." *Living Blues* 114 (March/April 1994): 58-65.

Kent, Don. "A Note on Robert Nighthawk." *Blues Unlimited* 42 (March/April 1967): 8-9.

Kilzer, Jobie. Personal interview by Steve Franz. Memphis, Tennessee, 20 January 1991.

King, B.B. American Federation of Musicians Local Number 47 contract 1761: 18 August 1954.

Koda, Cub. Notes to *Blues Hangover/Excello Blues Rarities.* Excello CD 2002, 1995.

___. Notes to *Blues Masters, Vol. 18: More Slide Guitar Classics.* Rhino CD 75348, 1998.

Koester, Bob. Notes to Junior Wells, *Blues Hit Big Town.* Delmark LP 640, 1977.

___. "Putnam the Record Straight." *Blues Unlimited* 137/138 (Spring 1980): 25.

___. Personal interview by Steve Franz. Chicago, Illinois, 20 November 1989.

___. "Letters." *Juke Blues* 48 (Winter 2000/2001): 27.

Koester, Bob, and Sue Koester. Notes to J.B. Hutto & His Hawks, *Hawk Squat.* Delmark LP 617, 1969.

Kriss, Eric. "Blues Notes." *Living Blues* 21 (May/June 1975): 12.

Kudlacek, Kerry, and Dave Sax. "The Ike Turner Blues Story." *Blues Unlimited* 57 (November 1968): 4-6.

Küstner, Axel. Notes to *Living Country Blues: An Anthology.* Evidence CD 26105-2, 1999.

Lazar, Helen Doob. "*Living Blues* Interview: James Cotton." *Living Blues* 76 (1987): 22-33.

Leadbitter, Mike. "Little Johnny Jones—An Obituary." *Blues Unlimited* 18 (January 1965): 18.

___. "Elmore James." *R&B Scene* Vol. 1, No. 5 (February 1965): 12, 16.

—. "Call the Doctor—Information Received." *Blues Unlimited* 28 (December 1965): 10-11.

___. "Hound Dog Taylor." *Blues Unlimited* 48 (November/December 1967): 21.

___. *Delta Country Blues.* Bexhill-on-Sea, England: Blues Unlimited, 1968.

___. Notes to Elmore James, *Something Inside of Me.* Bell LP 104, 1968.

___. "Mike's Blues: Postwar Discography." *Blues Unlimited* 64 (July 1969): 15.

___. Notes to Elmore James, *To Know a Man.* Blue Horizon LP 7-66230, 1969.

___. "J. T. Brown." *Blues Unlimited* 70 (February/March 1970): 14.

___. "Big Boy Crudup." *Blues Unlimited* 75 (September 1970): 16-18.

___. "Big Boy Crudup, Part 2." *Blues Unlimited* 76 (October 1970): 18.

___. "An Interview with Juke Boy Bonner." *Blues Unlimited* 78 (December 1970): 18-19.

___, ed. *Nothing But the Blues.* London: Hanover Books, 1971.

___. "I Know Houston Can't Be Heaven," 167-170. In Mike Leadbitter, ed., *Nothing But the Blues.* London: Hanover Books, 1971.

___. "Notes." *Blues Unlimited* 88 (January 1972): 6.

___. Notes to Elmore James and Walter Horton, *Cotton Patch Hotfoots.* Polydor LP 2383200, 1973.

___. "Mike's Blues." *Blues Unlimited* 102 (June 1973): 20, 30.

___. "That Pinetop Man." *Blues Unlimited* 103 (August/September 1973): 7-8.

___. "Nelson Street Blues." *Blues Unlimited* 104 (October/November 1973): 13.

___. "Serving the South." *Blues Unlimited* 105 (December 1973/January 1974): 5-7.

___. "Canton, Mississippi Breakdown," 11-12. In the notes to *Genesis: The Beginnings of Rock Vol. 2.* Chess LP 6641.125, 1974.

___. "A Jumpin' and a Shufflin'," 13-15. In the notes to *Genesis: The Beginnings of Rock Vol. 2.* Chess LP 6641.125, 1974.

___. "Mike's Blues." *Blues Unlimited* 110 (October/November 1974): 19, 30.

___. "Mike's Blues." *Blues Unlimited* 111 (December 1974/January 1975): 5.

Leadbitter, Mike, and John Broven. "Behind the Sun." *Blues Unlimited* 78 (December 1970): 4-8.

___. "Behind The Sun—West Memphis." *Blues Unlimited* 79 (January 1971): 5-10.

Leadbitter, Mike, and Mike Nicholls. "Current U.S. & British Singles." *Blues Unlimited* 16 (October 1964): 16.

Leadbitter, Mike, and Chris Robinson. "Lazy Bill Called Me Homesick (I Wasn't Though)."*Blues Unlimited* 84 (September 1971): 4-6.

___. "Homesick James (Part 2)." *Blues Unlimited* 85 (October 1971): 7-10.

___. "Lazy Bill Called Me Homesick (I Wasn't Though)(Part 3)." *Blues Unlimited* 86 (November 1971): 9-11.

Leadbitter, Mike, and Neil Slaven. *Blues Records: 1943-1966.* London: Hanover Books, 1968.

___. *Blues Records 1943-1970, A Selective Discography.* Vol. 1, A-K. London: Record Information Services, 1987.

Leadbitter, Mike, and Gayle Dean Wardlow. "Canton Mis'sippi Breakdown." *Blues Unlimited* 91 (May 1972): 5-10.

___. "Canton Mis'sippi Breakdown" [reprint]. *Blues Unlimited* 144 (Spring 1983): 4-8.

Leadbitter, Mike, Leslie Fancourt, and Paul Pelletier. *Blues Records 1943-1970,* Vol. 2, L-Z. London: Record Information Services, 1994.

Leary, S.P. Personal interview by Steve Franz. Chicago, Illinois, 19 November 1989.

LeBlanc, Patrick. Telephone interview by Steve Franz. 11 January 1995.

___. Telephone interview by Steve Franz. 21 February 1995.

___. Notes to *Masters of Blues—Tribute to Elmore James.* Icehouse CD P2 50569, 1996.

___. Personal communication with Steve Franz. 29 May 1996.

___. Telephone interview by Steve Franz. 7 June 1996.

Lehtonen, Heikki. "Crawl?....Nobody Makes Me!" *Blues Unlimited* 87 (December 1971): 8-10.

"Lester Bihari Sets New Meteor Label." *The Billboard* (20 December 1952): 25.

Lewens, Alan, and Karen Walsh, prods. *Rock & Roll—Episode 5: Crossroads.* WGBH/BBC, 1995.

Lillard, Dick. "The Cash Box Charts, Part 2." *Blues & Rhythm* 81 (August 1993): 10-12.

Litweiler, John. "Elmore James/John Brim." *Down Beat* 36 (6 February 1969): 24-25.

"Live Chicago Blues." *Living Blues* 4 (Winter 1970/1971): 24.

Lodetti, Antonio. "Elmore James." *Il Blues* 43 (June 1993): 10-14.

Lomax, Joseph. "Hop Wilson." *Living Blues* 26 (March/April 1976): 8.

Love, Clayton. Personal interview by Steve Franz. St. Louis, Missouri, 16 February 2002.

Lowry, Pete. "Current Albums Reviewed." *Blues Unlimited* 48 (November/December 1967): 22.

Marsh, Dave. *Louie Louie.* New York: Hyperion, 1993.

Marsh, Dave, with John Swenson, eds. *The Rolling Stone Record Guide.* New York: Random House, 1979.

Maultsby, Portia M. "Selective Bibliography: U.S. Black Music." *Ethnomusicology* Vol. 19, No. 3 (September 1975): 421-449.

Mawhinney, Paul, ed. *MusicMaster: The 45 RPM Record Directory, 1947-1982.* 2 vols. Pittsburgh: Record-Rama, 1983.

Mazzolini, Tom. "*Living Blues* Interview: L.C. 'Good Rockin'' Robinson." *Living Blues* 22 (July/August 1975): 16-21.

McCarthy, Albert, Alun Morgan, Paul Oliver, et al. *Jazz On Record: A Critical Guide to the First 50 Years 1917-1967.* London: Hanover Books, 1968.

McEwan, Joe. "Jimmy 'Early' Bird." *Blues Unlimited* 83 (July 1971): 4-5.

McGrath, Bob. *The R&B Indies.* West Vancouver, Canada: Eyeball Productions, 2000.

McMurry, Lillian. Personal interview by David Evans and Marc Ryan. Jackson, Mississippi, 13 March 1989.

___. Telephone interview by Steve Franz, 27 November 1994.

McMurry, Vitrice, and Almost Slim. "Mrs. Lillian McMurry's Story." *Goldmine* 103 (6 July 1984): 8-24.

Meadows, Eddie S. "African World View in Blues: A Prefatory Analysis." *Blues Unlimited* 148/149 (Winter 1987): 18-20.

Mercer, Colin. "The Slide Is Crying." *Blues & Rhythm* 72 (September 1992): 12-15.

Meredith, James. *Three Years in Mississippi.* Bloomington, Indiana: Indiana University Press, 1966.

___. "Elmo' 1960: As A Negro Saw Him." *Blues Unlimited* 64 (July 1969): 8-9.

___. "Elmore Vu par un Noir." *Soul Bag* 94, (May/June 1983): 28.

Millar, Chris, and Mike Rainsford. "We Were Bad to the Bone!: Homesick James Interviewed." *Blues & Rhythm* 95 (January 1995): 4-8.

Moran, Tom. "Story of a Bluesman." *Living Blues* 38 (May/June 1978): 41 [reprint].

Moss, Les. Personal communication with Steve Franz, 11 December 1992.

Murray, Charles Shaar. *Boogie Man: The Adventures of John Lee Hooker in the American Twentieth Century.* New York: St. Martin's Press, 2000.

Myers, Sam. "Comments from Sam Myers." In the notes to Elmore James, *King of the Slide Guitar.* Capricorn CD 42006-2, 1992.

Napier, Simon. Notes to Elmore James, *Memorial Album.* Sue LP 927, 1965.

___. "Reviews." *Blues Unlimited* 58 (December 1968): 27.

___. "Michael Andrew Leadbitter." *Blues Unlimited* 111 (December 1974/January 1975): 3.

Napier, Simon, and Mike Leadbitter. "Introduction." *Collectors Classics* 7 (May 1965): 2.

___. "The Sixth American Folk Blues Festival – 1967." *Blues Unlimited* 48 (November/December 1967): 18, 20.

"News." *Blues Unlimited* 83 (July 1971): 15, 18.

"News." *Blues Unlimited* 94 (September 1972): 17.

"News." *Blues Unlimited* 109 (August/September 1974): 20, 30.

"New York Blues News." *Living Blues* 18 (Autumn 1974): 38.

Nicholson, Robert. *Mississippi: The Blues Today!* New York: Da Capo Press, 1999.

Obrecht, Jas. "Listening with Ry." *Guitar Player* (November 1992): 42-43.

___. "The Ballad of Elmore & Homesick James." *Guitar Player* 285 (September 1993): 69-84.

O'Brien, Justin. "All Around Man: Lee Jackson (Part Two)." *Living Blues* 34 (September/October 1977): 12-18.

___. "Odie Payne." *Living Blues* 87 (July/August 1989): 30-34.

Oliver, Paul. Notes to Sonny Boy Williamson, *"The Original" Sonny Boy Williamson.* Blues Classics LP 9, 1965.

___. *Blues Off the Record.* New York: Da Capo Press, 1984.

___. *Screening the Blues: Aspects of the Blues Tradition.* New York: Da Capo Press, 1989 [reprint].

___. *Conversation with the Blues,* 2nd ed. Cambridge: Cambridge University Press, 1997.

Oliver, Paul, and Jacques Demêtre. "Chicago Blues Singers." *Jazz Monthly* Vol. 6, No. 2 (April 1960): 12-13.

Olsson, Bengt. Notes to *On The Road Again: Country Blues 1969-1974.* Flyright CD 58, 1997.

O'Neal, Jim. "45's." *Living Blues* 2 (Summer 1970): 34.

___. "Atomic Blues." *Living Blues* 9 (Summer 1972): 8-15.

___. "Joe Willie Wilkins." *Living Blues* 11 (Winter 1972/1973): 13-17.

___. "Blues Questions and Answers." *Living Blues* 12 (Spring 1973): 37.

___. "*Living Blues* Interview: Houston Stackhouse." *Living Blues* 17 (Summer 1974): 20-36.

___. "Obituaries: Mel London." *Living Blues* 22 (July/August 1975): 4, 21.

___. Notes to Tampa Red, *Guitar Wizard.* RCA Bluebird LP 2-5501, 1975.

___. Notes to Homesick James, *Goin' Back Home.* Trix LP 3315, 1976.

___. Notes to J.T. Brown, *Windy City Boogie.* Pearl LP 9, 1978.

___. "Willie Nix: The Memphis Blues Boy in Mississippi." *Living Blues* 43 (Summer 1979): 9-13.

___. "In Session with Elmore and Bobby Robinson: Herb Abramson." *Living Blues* 54 (Autumn/Winter 1982): 11.

___. "Big Bill: Opening the Door to the Blues." *Living Blues* 55 (Winter 1982/83): 4-5.

___. Notes to Big Walter Horton and Alfred "Blues King" Harris, *Harmonica Blues Kings.* Pearl LP 12, 1986.

___. "*Living Blues* Interview: Lillian S. McMurry." *Living Blues* 67 (1986): 15-27.

___. "The ENDLESS LOOP BLUES Contest: I Win." *Stackhouse/Delta Record Mart Mail Order Catalogue and Rooster Blues Newsletter* 5 (March 1992): 2.

___. "I Once Was Lost, But Now I'm Found: The Blues Revival of the 1960s," 347-387. In Lawrence Cohn, ed., *Nothing But the Blues.* New York: Abbeville Press, 1993.

___. "Junior Wells: *Living Blues* Interview." *Living Blues* 119 (January/February 1995): 8-29.

___. Notes to Memphis Slim, *Memphis Slim U.S.A.* Delmark CD 710, 1998 [reissue].

O'Neal, Jim, and Cary Baker. "Chicago Blues Label Guide." *Living Blues* 12 (Spring 1973): 8-12.

O'Neal, Jim, and R.T. Cuniff. "Hound Dog Taylor." *Living Blues* 4 (Winter 1970/1971): 4-7.

O'Neal, Jim, and Bill Greensmith. "Discography." In the notes to *Meat & Gravy from Cadillac Baby—"Records was cheap to make then," Vol. 1.* Red Lightnin' LP 0019, 1978.

O'Neal, Jim, and Patty Johnson. "Little Milton: *Living Blues* Interview." *Living Blues* 114 (March/April 1994): 19-39.

O'Neal, Jim, and Peter Lee. "Sam Myers—Blowing it off the Top." *Living Blues* 85 (March/April 1989): 10-21.

O'Neal, Jim, and Amy O'Neal. "Sam Myers in Jackson." *Living Blues* 3 (Autumn 1970): 19, 21.

___. "*Living Blues* Interview. Eddie Boyd, Part 2." *Living Blues* 36 (January/February 1978): 14-23.

___. "Muddy Waters." *Living Blues* 64 (March/April 1985): 15-40.

O'Neal, Jim, and Amy van Singel. "J.B. Hutto." *Blues Unlimited* 71 (April 1970): 18-19.

Osborne, Jerry. *Rockin' Records,* 15th Ed. Jellyroll Publications (1993).

Paikos, Mike. *Rhythm & Blues Covers and Re-Recordings.* Moraga, California: [no publisher], 1998.

Palmer, Robert. *Deep Blues.* New York: Viking, 1981.

Paterson, Neil. "Obituary." *Blues Unlimited* 4 (August 1963): 9.

___. "Mel London," 50-52. In Mike Leadbitter, ed., *Nothing But the Blues.* London: Hanover Books, 1971.

Paulsen, Gary. "The Re-incarnation of Elmore James." *Blues Unlimited* 63 (June 1969): 17.

___. "Jules Bihari!" *Blues Unlimited* 68 (December 1969): 13-14.

Paulus, George. "Motor City Blues & Boogie." *Blues Unlimited* 85 (October 1971): 4-6.

___. Notes to Joe Carter and His Chicago Broomdusters, *Mean & Evil Blues.* Barrelhouse LP 07, 1976.

___. "Belzoni Broomduster 1938." *Blues & Rhythm* 120 (June 1997): 4-5.

Pearlin, Victor. Electronic communication with Steve Franz. January 8, 2002.

Pearson, Barry. "The Late Great Elmore James." *Keystone Folklore Quarterly* Vol. 17, No. 4 (Winter 1972): 162-172.

Perkins, Terry. "We Like Ike." *The Riverfront Times* (24 June 1992): 32.

Peters, Margey. "Wild Jimmy Spruill: You Got to Move the Soul First." *Living Blues* 115 (June 1994): 32.

Pierson, Leroy. Notes to Chicago Slickers 1948-1953. Nighthawk LP 102, 1976.

___. Notes to *Detroit Ghetto Blues 1948-1954.* Nighthawk LP 104, 1976.

___. Notes to *Lake Michigan Blues 1934-1941.* Nighthawk LP 105, 1980.

___. Notes to *Downhome Delta Blues 1949-1952.* Nighthawk LP 109, 1980.

___. Personal interview by Steve Franz. St. Louis, Missouri, 27 March 1990.

Pitchford, Lonnie. Notes to *All Around Man;* Jim O'Neal and Patty Johnson, comps. Rooster Blues CD 2629, 1994.

Pomposello, Tom. "The Bobby Robinson Tapes: Elmore James." *Living Blues* 54 (Autumn/Winter 1982): 9-11.

Pruter, Robert. "Famous Desk-Drawer Manuscripts, Part 2." *Juke Blues* 22 (Winter/Spring 1991): 26.

___. "The Syl Johnson Story." *Living Blues* 122 (July/August 1995): 23-33.

Pruter, Robert, and Jim O'Neal. "Leonard Allen and the United/States Story, Part 1." *Living Blues* 92 (July/August 1990): 37-40.

___. "Leonard Allen and the United/States Story, Part 2." *Living Blues* 93 (September/October 1990): 34-36.

___. "Leonard Allen and the United/States Story, Part 3." *Living Blues* 95 (January/February 1991): 41-46.

Pruter, Robert, Armin Büttner, and Robert L. Campbell. "The Chance Label." http://hubcap.clemson.edu/~campber/chance.html, May 2002.

"Questions and Answers." *Living Blues* 29 (September/October 1976): 41.

Race, Wesley. "Hound Dog Taylor." *Blues Unlimited* 93 (July 1972): 16-17.

Ramsey, Frederic, Jr. *Been Here and Gone.* Athens, Georgia: University of Georgia Press, 2000 [reprint].

"Reviews of This Week's New Records." *The Billboard* (3 January 1953): 24.

"Rhythm & Blues Record Reviews." *The Billboard* (13 June 1953): 22.

"Rhythm & Blues Record Reviews." *The Billboard* (6 March 1954): 102.

"Rhythm and Blues Tattler" [Advertisement]. *The Billboard* (18 July 1953): 57.

"Rhythm and Blues Tattler" [Advertisement]. *The Billboard* (8 August 1953): 36.

Robinson, Bobby. Notes to Elmore James, *History of Elmore James.* Trip LP 8007, 1971.

___. "Comments from Bobby Robinson." In the notes to Elmore James, *King of the Slide Guitar.* Capricorn CD 42006-2, 1992.

___. "Comments from Bobby Robinson." In the notes to *The Fire/Fury Records Story.* Capricorn CD 42009-2, 1993.

Rotante, Anthony. "Elmore James." *Vintage Jazz Mart* 68 (October 1959): 4, 34.

Rowe, Mike. "Mike Rowe's Review," 61-69. In Mike Leadbitter, ed., *Nothing But the Blues.* London: Hanover Books, 1971.

___. *Chicago Breakdown.* London: Eddison Press Ltd., 1973.

___. "'I Was Really Dedicated'—An Interview with Billy Boy Arnold, Part 2." *Blues Unlimited* 127 (November/December 1977): 10-12.

___. "Let's Cut It." *Blues Unlimited* 148/149 (Winter 1987): 26-27.

___. Notes to *Blues Is Killin' Me.* Flyright CD 28, 1990.

Ryan, Marc. Notes to Sonny Boy Williamson/Willie Love, *Clownin' with the World.* Acoustic Archives CD 700, 1989.

___. "Tracing the Trumpet Masters." *Blues & Rhythm* 48 (Christmas 1989): 5.

___. Personal interview by Steve Franz. Memphis, Tennessee, 3 July 1990.

___. Telephone interview by Steve Franz. 7 June 1992.

___. *Trumpet Records: An Illustrated History with Discography.* Milford, New Hampshire: Big Nickel Publications, 1992.

___. Telephone interview by Steve Franz. 2 November 1992.

___. Telephone interview by Steve Franz. 28 June 1994.

Sacré, Robert. "An Interview with Henry Gray." *Crazy Music* 11 (Dec 1977): 26-33.

Sain, Oliver. Personal interview by Steve Franz. St. Louis, Missouri, 16 February 2002.

Santelli, Robert. *The Big Book of Blues: A Biographical Encyclopedia.* New York: Penguin Books, 1993.

Schwartz, Julie Anne. "Did a Rhinoceros Step On These Acetates?" In the notes to Calvin Frazier, *This Old World's in a Tangle.* Laurie CD 7001, 1993.

Scott, Frank, and Gary Paulsen. "Joe and Jules Bihari! [Part 1]" *Blues Unlimited* 73 (June 1970): 9-12.

___. "Joe and Jules Bihari! [Part 2]" *Blues Unlimited* 74 (July 1970): 11-13.

___. "Joe and Jules Bihari! [Part 3]" *Blues Unlimited* 75 (September 1970): 11.

___. Electronic communication. 14 September 2002

Seeger, Pete. *The Incompleat Folksinger.* New York: Simon and Schuster, 1972.

Selvin, Joel. Notes to L.C. "Good Rockin'" Robinson, *Mojo in My Hand.* Arhoolie CD 453, 1996.

Shurman, Dick. "Billy Boy Arnold's Story," 71-76. In Mike Leadbitter, ed., *Nothing But the Blues.* London: Hanover Books, 1971.

___. "Never Seen a Slide." *Blues Unlimited* 92 (June 1972): 12-14.

___. "Voo Doo Dust." *Blues Unlimited* 107 (April/May 1974): 5.

___. Notes to Elmore James, *The Last Session.* Relic LP 1021, 1989.

___. Notes to *Cool Playing Blues.* Relic CD 7016, 1990.

___. "Dick Shurman's Chicago Scene." *Juke Blues* 47 (Summer 2000): 10.

___. Personal communication with Steve Franz. 4 July 2001.

___. Personal communication with Steve Franz. 29 November 2001.

Simmons, John. Notes to Big Joe Williams, *Nine String Guitar Blues.* Delmark CD 627, 1990 [reissue].

Skoller, Don. Personal Communication with Steve Franz. 22 August 1994.

Slaven, Neil. Notes to Elmore James and John Brim, *Tough.* Blue Horizon LP 7-63204, 1968.

___. Notes to *Chicago Calling.* Charly LP 1135, 1986.

___. Notes to Elmore James, *Rollin' and Tumblin'.* Recall CD 231, 1999.

___. Notes to *John Vincent Presents Genuine Mississippi Blues... Plus: The Ace (MS) Blues Masters Vol. 4.* West Side CD 579, 1999.

Smith, Chris. Notes to *East Coast Blues.* Krazy Kat LP 824, 1988.

___. Notes to Roosevelt Sykes, *Complete Recorded Works in Chronological Order, Vol. 10.* Document CD 6050, 1994.

Smith, Wayne. Personal communication with Steve Franz. 3 January 2001.

___. Personal communication with Steve Franz. 26 January 2001.

Spottswood, Richard. Notes to *The Slide Guitar—Bottles, Knives & Steel.* Columbia CD 46218, 1990.

Springer, Robert. "Juke Boy Bonner's (Last?) European Tour." *Blues Unlimited* 124 (March/June 1977): 32-33.

Spruill, Jimmy. "Comments from Jimmy Spruill." In the notes to Elmore James, *King of the Slide Guitar.* Capricorn CD 42006-2, 1992.

Stackhouse, Houston. Personal interview by David Evans. Crystal Springs, Mississippi, 3 September 1967.

Standish, Tony. "Elmore James." *Vintage Jazz Mart* 70 (December 1959): 4.

Stevens, Guy. "Elmore James: Classic Blues Singer." *Jazz Beat* 11 (November 1964): 13.

Stolper, Darryl. "It Was Very Rewarding: Trumpet Records History." *Blues Unlimited* 88 (January 1972): 4-6.

Strachwitz, Chris. Notes to *John Littlejohn's Chicago Blues Stars.* Arhoolie LP 1043, 1969.

___. "Lil' Son Jackson," 187-190. In Mike Leadbitter, ed., *Nothing But the Blues.* London: Hanover Books, 1971.

___. Notes to John Littlejohn, *Slidin' Home.* Arhoolie CD 9019, 2001.

Summers, Lynn, and Bob Scheir. "Little Milton." *Living Blues* 18 (Autumn 1974): 17-24.

Sunnyland Slim [r.n. Albert Luandrew]. Personal interview by Willie Dixon. In the notes to Sonny Boy Williamson, *The Real Folk Blues,* Chess LP 1503, 1966.

Sutherland, Sandy. "Uncle Johnny Now Rev. Williams." *Blues Unlimited* 100 (April 1973): 17-19.

___. "Blues for Florence." *Blues Unlimited* 106 (February/March 1974): 20-21.

Swedien, Bruce. Personal interview by Diana Reid Haig. In the notes to *The Cobra Records Story.* Capricorn CD 42012-2, 1993: 13-14.

Taylor, Eddie, and Frank Scott. Notes to Eddie Taylor, *I Feel So Bad.* Advent LP 2802, 1972.

Tefteller, John. Electronic communication with Steve Franz. January 8, 2002.

Templeton, Ray. Notes to Juke Boy Bonner, *Juke Boy Bonner 1960-1967.* Flyright CD 38, 1991.

Terkel, Studs. Notes to Big Bill Broonzy and Washboard Sam, *Big Bill Broonzy and Washboard Sam.* Chess LP 1468, 1962.

"Territorial Best Sellers." *The Billboard* (17 January 1953): 56.

"Territorial Best Sellers." *The Billboard* (11 April 1953): 40.

"This Week's Best Buys." *The Billboard* (10 January 1953): 26.

Tillman, Keith. "Current Singles." *Blues Unlimited* 55 (July 1968): 22.

Tooze, Sandra B. *Muddy Waters: The Mojo Man.* Toronto: ECW Press, 1997.

Topping, Ray. Notes to Elmore James, *King of the Slide Guitar.* Ace LP 68, 1983.

___. Notes to B.B. King, *Do the Boogie!* Ace CD 916, 1988.

___. "Canton Mississippi Breakthrough 1993," 18-23. In the notes to Elmore James, *The Classic Early Recordings 1951-1956.* Ace BOXCD 4, 1993.

___. "Elmore James Discography," 29-33. In the notes to Elmore James, *The Classic Early Recordings 1951-1956.* Ace BOXCD 4, 1993.

___. "The Legend," 4-9. In the notes to Elmore James, *The Classic Early Recordings 1951-1956.* Ace BOXCD 4, 1993.

___. "Ramblin' from Town to Town," 10-17. In the notes to Elmore James, *The Classic Early Recordings 1951-1956* Ace BOXCD 4, 1993.

___. "R.T. - On the Box!" 26-28. In the notes to Elmore James, *The Classic Early Recordings 1951-1956.* Ace BOXCD 4, 1993.

___. Notes to Hop Wilson & His Buddies, *Steel Guitar Flash!* Ace CD 240, 1994.

___. "Discography," 246-271. In Ike Turner with Nigel Cawthorne, *Takin' Back My Name.* London: Virgin Books, 1999.

Totten, Brennan. Telephone interview by Steve Franz. 22 July 1989.

Townsend, Henry. *A Blues Life,* as told to Bill Greensmith. Chicago: University of Illinois Press, 1999.

Tracy, Steven, ed. *Write Me a Few of Your Lines: A Blues Reader.* Amherst, Massachusetts: University of Massachusetts Press, 1999.

Tucker, Neely. "Bo Diddley." *Living Blues* 77 (December 1987): 17-20.

Turco, Art. "Interview: Bobby Robinson. [Part 2]" *Record Exchanger* 11 (Fall 1972), 4-11.

___. "Interview: Bobby Robinson. [Part 3]" *Record Exchanger* 12 (Winter 1973), 4-11.

Turco, Art, Sal Salzano, and Bob Turco. "Interview: Bobby Robinson. [Part 1]" *Record Exchanger* 10 (May 1972), 4-10.

Turner, Bez. "Mel London's Labels." *Blues Unlimited* 125 (July/ August 1977): 13-15.

___. "Three Mexicans, A Hillbilly and a Polock." *Blues Unlimited* 141 (Autumn/Winter 1981): 5-10.

Turner, Ike. American Federation of Musicians Local Number 47 contract 1001: 24 April 1954.

Turner, Ike, with Nigel Cawthorne. *Takin' Back My Name.* London: Virgin Books, 1999.

"Vee-Jay Records." *Blues Unlimited* 42 (March/April 1967): 24.

"Vee-Jay Stars Celebrate Rebirth of Their Music." *Rhythm & Blues Foundation News* Vol. 2 (January 1993): 4.

Vernon, Paul. *African-American Blues, Rhythm and Blues, Gospel and Zydeco on Film and Video, 1926-1997.* Brookfield, Vermont: Ashgate Publishing, 1999.

Vogler, Michel. "Elmore James Discography." *Jazz Statistics* 18 (1960): 3-4.

___. "Elmore James Discography." *Jazz Statistics* 22 (June 1961): 3.

Wardlow, Gayle Dean. "Highway 80 Blues." *Blues Unlimited* 66 (October 1969): 12-13.

___. "Greenville Smokin'." *Blues Unlimited* 99 (February/March1973): 12.

___. Telephone interview by Steve Franz. 27 November 1994.

___. *Chasin' that Devil Music: Searching for the Blues.* San Francisco: Miller Freeman Books, 1998.

Wayland, C.R. "Robert Johnson and Standards in Blues Criticism." *Jazz Journal* Vol. 16 No. 4 (April 1963): 25-26.

Weinstock, Ron. "Elmore James—A BRQ Profile." *Blues Review Quarterly* 12 (Spring 1994): 24-33.

Weld, Dave. "Interview with Bob Koester." *Living Blues* 30 (November/December 1976): 22-23.

___. "*Living Blues* Interview: J.B. Hutto." *Living Blues* 30 (November/December 1976): 14-24.

___. "J.B. Hutto." *Living Blues* 57 (Autumn 1983): 12-13.

Welding, Pete. Notes to Homesick James [Williamson], *Blues on the South Side.* Prestige LP 7388, 1965.

___. "Homesick James Williamson." *Collectors Classics* 7 (May 1965): 7-8.

___. "An Interview with Skip Layne." *Blues Unlimited* 92 (June 1972): 4-6.

___. Notes to Elmore James, Eddie Taylor, and Jimmy Reed, *South Side Blues.* Cobblestone LP 9001, 1972.

___. "Ramblin' Johnny Shines." *Living Blues* 22 (July/August 1975): 23-32.

Wexler, Jerry, and David Ritz. *Rhythm and the Blues.* New York: Alfred A. Knopf, 1993.

Whelan, Pete. "Sam Collins and the Gennett Madness." In the notes to *14 Rare Country Blues by Sam Collins & 2 Surprises by King Solomon Hill, Vintage 1927-1931.* Origin Jazz Library LP 10, c. 1965.

Whitburn, Joel. *Top R&B Singles 1942-1988.* Menomonee Falls, Wisconsin: Record Research, Inc., 1988.

___. *A Century of Pop Music.* Menomonee Falls, Wisconsin: Record Research, Inc., 1999.

White, George R. *The Complete Bo Diddley Sessions.* Bradford, England: George R. White Publications, 1993.

Whiteis, David. "Elmore James: The Sky Is Crying." *Goldmine* 304 (20 March 1992): 18-24.

___. "John Littlejohn." *Living Blues* 115 (June 1994): 60-61.

___. "Elmore James, The Broomduster." *Juke Blues* 48 (Winter 2000/2001): 56-62.

Whiteis, David, and Robert Pruter. "Elmore James Discography." *Goldmine* 304 (20 March 1992): 22-24.

White, Skippy. Telephone interview by Steve Franz. 6 September 2002.

Williams, Arthur. Personal interview by Steve Franz. St. Louis, Missouri, 9 February 2002.

Williams, Big Joe, Bob Koester, Marcel Chauvard, et al. "The Story of Elmore James." *Blues Unlimited* 5 (October 1963): 3-4.

Williams, Eliot. Electronic communication. 24 November 1995.

Williams, Martin. "The Recordings," 16-44. In the notes to *The Smithsonian Collection of Classic Jazz.* Smithsonian/ Columbia Special Products LP 11891, 1973.

Wilmer, Valerie. "Legend of the Back Streets." *Melody Maker* vol. 53 (18 November 1978): 47-48, 56.

Wolfe, Charles, and Kip Lornell. *The Life and Legend of Leadbelly.* New York: Harper Collins, 1992.

Wyman, Bill, with Richard Havers. *Bill Wyman's Blues Odyssey.* London: Dorling Kindersley, 2001.

The Legend of Elmore James

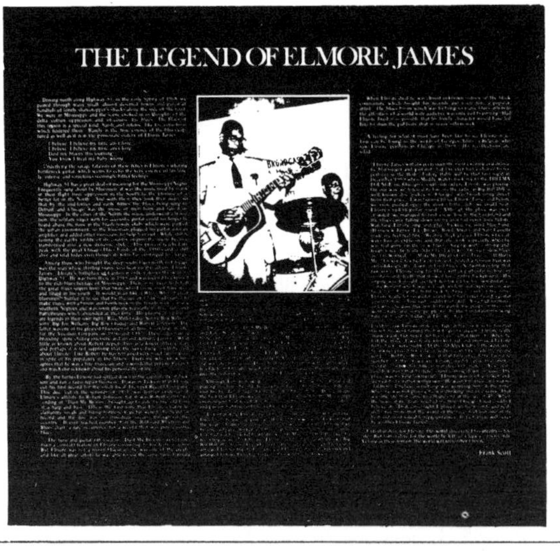

Regarded by many as the most important Blues album of the year.

Including tracks never before issued on record

UAS 29109

UNITED ARTISTS

Originally issued in 1969 in the U.S. as Kent LP 9001, The Legend of Elmore James *was one of two LPs resulting from Bruce Bromberg and Frank Scott's exploration of the Modern Records vaults for untapped Elmore James material. It featured George Adins' vivid recollection of seeing Elmore live in performance, and was reissued several different times, such as this ad for the U.K. version.*

Adams, Woodrow. "She's Done Come and Gone." Checker 757, 1952.

___. "Baby You Just Don't Know." Meteor 5018, 1955.

___. "The Train Is Coming." From the album *Sun—The Roots of Rock, Vol. 12: Union Avenue Breakdown.* Charly LP 30127, 1977.

Allen, Ricky. "You'd Better Be Sure." Age 29102, 1961.

Barbee, John Henry. "You'll Work Down To Me Someday." From the album *Giants of Country Blues – Vol. 1 (1927-1938).* Wolf CD 107, [no date].

Bell, Carey. "I Cry So Much." From the album Carey Bell, *Carey Bell's Blues Harp.* Delmark LP 622, 1970.

Berry, Chuck. "Childhood Sweetheart." Chess 1737, 1959.

___. "Blues for Hawaiians." From the album Chuck Berry, *Berry Is on Top.* Chess LP 1435, 1959.

___. "Run Around." From the album Chuck Berry, *New Juke Box Hits.* Chess LP 1456, 1961.

___. "Surfing Steel" (a.k.a. "Crying Steel"). From the album Chuck Berry, *Chuck Berry on Stage.* Chess LP 1480, 1963.

___. "It Hurts Me Too." Mercury 72748, 1967.

Bo Diddley. "Little Girl." From the album Bo Diddley, *Go Bo Diddley.* Checker LP 1436, 1959.

___. "Live My Life." From the album Bo Diddley, *In the Spotlight.* Checker LP 2976, 1960.

___. "Blues Blues." From the album Bo Diddley, *Rare & Well Done.* MCA/Chess CD 9331, 1991.

Boines, Houston. "Relation Blues." Blues & Rhythm 7001, 1952.

___. "Carry My Business On." From the album *Sun Records—The Blues Years 1950-1958.* Charly CDSUNBOX 7, 1996.

Bonner, Weldon "Juke Boy". "Life Is a Dirty Deal." From the EP *More Downhome Blues.* Jan & Dil EP 451, 1966.

___. *Juke Boy Bonner 1960-1967.* Flyright CD 38, 1991.

___. *Life Gave Me a Dirty Deal.* Arhoolie CD 375, 1992.

___. *Things Ain't Right—The 1969 London Sessions.* Sequel CD 209, 1992.

Booker, Charley [a.k.a. Chris]. "Walked All Night." From the album *Sun—The Roots of Rock, Vol. 12: Union Avenue Breakdown.* Charly LP 30127, 1977.

Boyd, Eddie. "Nothing But Trouble." Chess 1561, 1954.

Bradford, Walter. "Love for My Baby." From the album *Sun Records—The Blues Years 1950-1958.* Charly CDSUNBOX 7, 1996.

Brim, John & Grace. *Gary Stomp—The (Almost) Complete Singles 1950-1956.* Compact disc (unissued), 2001.

Brooks, Junior. "She's the Little Girl for Me." RPM 343, 1952.

Broonzy, Big Bill. "You Do Me Any Old Way." American Record Company 7-06-64, 1937.

Brown, Buster. "Fannie Mae." Fire 1008, 1959.

___. "When Things Go Wrong." From the album Buster Brown, *The New King of the Blues.* Fire LP 102, 1960.

Brown, Earl. "Dust My Broom." Swing Time 307, 1952.

Brown, J.T. *Windy City Boogie.* Delmark CD 714, 1998.

Butterfield Blues Band, The Paul. "Shake Your Money-Maker." From the album *Paul Butterfield Blues Band.* Elektra LP 7294, 1965.

Campbell, "Little" Milton. "If You Love Me." Sun 200, 1954.

Carr, Leroy. "Midnight Hour Blues." Vocalion 1703, 1932.

___. "Blues Before Sunrise." Vocalion 02657, 1934.

___. "Mean Mistreater Mama." Vocalion 02657, 1934.

Carter, Joe, and His Chicago Broomdusters. *Mean & Evil Blues.* P-Vine CD 5202, 1997 [reissue].

___. "Talk To Your Daughter." From the album *Chicago Blues 2.* JSP CD 405, 1998.

Clark, James "Beale Street". "Get Ready to Meet Your Man." Columbia 30005, 1945.

Cole, Ann. "Got My Mo-Jo Working (But it Just Won't Work on You)." Baton 237, 1957.

Collins Kids. "Hoy Hoy." Columbia 41087, 1958.

Crudup, Arthur "Big Boy". "Dust My Broom." RCA Victor 50-0074, 1949.

___. "Hand Me Down My Walking Cane." RCA Victor 22/50-0100, 1950.

___. "Do It If You Want To." RCA Victor 20/47-4933, 1952.

___ (as Elmer James). "Make a Little Love with Me." Trumpet 186, 1952.

Drane, Early. "Look on Yonders Wall." From the album *Blues Hangover/Excello Blues Rarities.* Excello CD 2002, 1995.

Edwards, David "Honeyboy". "Sweet Home Chicago." From the album *Sun Records—The Blues Years 1950-1958.* Charly CDSUNBOX 7, 1996.

Fleetwood Mac. "Shake Your Money Maker." From the album, *Fleetwood Mac.* Blue Horizon LP 7-63200, 1968.

___. "Evenin' Boogie." From the album Fleetwood Mac, *Mr. Wonderful.* Blue Horizon LP 7-63205, 1968.

___. *Fleetwood Mac in Chicago 1969.* Sire/Warner Bros./Blue Horizon CD 9 45283-2, 1994 [reissue].

Frazier, Calvin. "Highway 51." From the album *This Old World's in a Tangle.* Laurie CD 7001, 1993.

Fuller, Blind Boy. "Homesick and Lonesome Blues." Vocalion 03234, 1936.

Gillum, Jazz. "Look on Yonder Wall." RCA Victor 20-1974, 1946.

Gilmore, Boyd."Just an Army Boy." Modern 860, 1952.

___. "Ramblin' on My Mind." Modern 860, 1952.

___. "All in My Dreams." Modern 872, 1952.

Guitar Crusher [r.n.: Sidney Selby]. "I've Got to Know." T & S 102, 1968.

Guitar Slim [r.n.: Eddie Jones]. "The Things That I Used to Do." Specialty 482, 1953.

Harris, Ramblin' Hi. "Early One Morning." From the album *Louisiana Swamp Blues.* Flyright CD 09, 1989.

Hendrix, Jimi. "Bleeding Heart." From the album *Jimi Hendrix: Blues.* MCA CD 11060, 1998.

Hill, Raymond. "My Baby Left Me." From the album *Sun Records—The Blues Years 1950-1958.* Charly CDSUNBOX 7, 1996.

Hines, Earl. "Stormy Monday Blues." Bluebird B11567, 1942.

Hogg, Andrew "Smokey". "Long Tall Mama." Modern 20-574, 1948.

___. "Sure 'Nuff." Ebb 127, 1958.

Hooker, Earl. "Shake 'Em Up." From the album *John Lee Hooker Sings Blues.* King LP 727, 1961

___. "Alley Corn." From the album *Rockin' the Blues.* Rockin' CD 5502-2, 1998.

House, Son. "My Black Mama—Part 1." Paramount 13042, 1930.

Howlin' Wolf [r.n.: Chester Arthur Burnett]. "Riding in the Moonlight." RPM 333, 1951.

___. "No Place to Go." Chess 1566, 1954.

Hurt, Mississippi John. "Got the Blues Can't Be Satisfied." OKeh 8724,1929.

Hutto, J.B. "Combination Boogie." Chance 1155, 1954.

___. "Now She's Gone." Chance 1155, 1954.

___. "Lovin' You." Chance 1160, 1954.

___. "Pet Cream Man." Chance 1160, 1954.

___. "Dim Lights." Chance 1165, 1954.

___. "Things Are So Slow." Chance 1165, 1954.

___. "Hip Shakin'." From the album J.B. Hutto & His Hawks, *Hawk Squat.* Delmark LP 617, 1969.

___. "Price of Love." From the album *Chicago Blues After Midnight 1952-1957.* Delta Swing LP 379, c. 1977.

___. *J.B. Hutto and the Houserockers Live 1977.* Wolf CD 120.289, 1991 [reissue of Baron LP 101, 1978].

___. *J.B. Hutto and the New Hawks: Keeper of the Flame.* Wolf CD 120.292, 1991.

___. *J.B. Hutto and the New Hawks: Live at the Shaboo Inn, Conn., 1979.* Fan Club CD 085, 1991.

___. "Price of Love." From the album *Chicago Blues—The Chance Era.* Charly CD 146-2, 1997.

Jackson, Melvin "Little Son". "Thrill Me Baby." Imperial 5267, 1954.

___. "I Wish to Go Home." Imperial 5319, 1954.

___. *The Complete Imperial Recordings.* Capitol CD 31744, 1995.

James, Elmore. "Dust My Broom." Trumpet 146, 1951.

___. "I Believe." Meteor 5000, 1952.

___. "I Held My Baby Last Night." Meteor 5000, 1952.

___. "Baby, What's Wrong." Meteor 5003, 1953.

___. "Early in the Morning." Flair 1011, 1953.

___. "Hawaiian Boogie." Flair 1011, 1953.

___. "Country Boogie." Checker 777, 1953.

___. "She Just Won't Do Right." Checker 777, 1953.

___. "Can't Stop Lovin." Flair 1014, 1953.

___. "Make a Little Love." Flair 1014, 1953.

___. "Please Find My Baby." Flair 1022, 1953.

___. "Strange Kinda' Feeling." Flair 1022, 1953.

___. "Hand in Hand." Flair 1031, 1954.

___. "Make My Dreams Come True." Flair 1031, 1954.

___. "1839 Blues." Flair 1039, 1954.

___. "Sho Nuff I Do." Flair 1039, 1954.

___. "Dark and Dreary." Flair 1048, 1954.

___. "Rock My Baby Right." Flair 1048, 1954.

___. "Standing at the Crossroads." Flair 1057, 1954.

___. "Sunny Land." Flair 1057, 1954.

___. "The Way You Treat Me." Flair 1062, 1955.

___. "Happy Home." Flair 1069, 1955.

___. "No Love in My Heart." Flair 1069, 1955.

___. "Dust My Blues." Flair 1074, 1955.

___. "I Was a Fool." Flair 1074, 1955.

___. "Blues Before Sunrise." Flair 1079, 1955.

___. "Good Bye." Flair 1079, 1955.

___. "Wild about You." Modern 983, 1956.

___. "Long Tall Woman." Modern 983, 1956.

___. "Coming Home." Chief 7001, 1957.

___. "The 12 Year Old Boy." Chief 7001, 1957.

___. "Elmore's Contribution to Jazz." Chief 7004, 1957.

___. "It Hurts Me Too." Chief 7004, 1957.

___. "Cry for Me Baby." Chief 7006, 1957.
___. "Bobby's Rock." Fire 1011, 1959.
___. "Held My Baby Last Night." Fire 1016, 1960.
___. "The Sky Is Crying." Fire 1016, 1960.
___. "I Can't Hold Out." Chess 1756, 1960.
___. "The Sun Is Shining." Chess 1756, 1960.
___. "Rollin and Tumblin." Fire 1024, 1960.
___. "I'm Worried." Fire 1024, 1960.
___. "Done Somebody Wrong." Fire 1031, 1960.
___. "Look on Yonder Wall." Fire 504, 1961.
___. "Shake Your Moneymaker." Fire 504, 1961.
___. "Anna Lee." Fire 1503, 1962.
___. "Stranger Blues." Fire 1503, 1962.
___. "Sho Nuff I Do" [alternate take]. From the album Elmore James, *Original Folk Blues.* Kent LP 522, 1964.
___. "Bleeding Heart." Enjoy 2015, 1965.
___. "It Hurts Me Too." Enjoy 2015, 1965.
___. "Pickin' the Blues." Enjoy 2015 [2nd pressing], 1965.
___. "Mean Mistreatin' Mama." Enjoy 2020, 1965.
___. "Everyday I Have the Blues." Enjoy 2027, 1965.
___. "One Way Out." Sphere Sound 702, 1965.
___. "Dust My Broom." From the album Elmore James, *The Sky Is Crying.* Sphere Sound LP 7002, 1965.
___. "I Can't Stop Lovin' You." From the album Elmore James, *The Sky Is Crying.* Sphere Sound LP 7002, 1965.
___. "Standing at the Crossroads." From the album Elmore James, *The Sky Is Crying.* Sphere Sound LP 7002, 1965.
___. *The Sky Is Crying.* Sphere Sound LP 7002, 1965.
___. *The Best of Elmore James.* Sue LP 918, 1965.
___. *Memorial Album.* Sue LP 927, 1965.
___. "I Need You." Sphere Sound 708, 1966.
___. "Early One Morning." From the album Elmore James, *I Need You.* Sphere Sound LP 7008, 1967.
___. "Something Inside of Me." From the album Elmore James, *I Need You.* Sphere Sound LP 7008, 1967.
___. "Strange Angels." From the album Elmore James, *I Need You.* Sphere Sound LP 7008, 1967.
___. *I Need You.* Sphere Sound LP 7008, 1967.
___. "Hawaiian Boogie." Modern Oldies 49, 1968.
___. "My Kind of Woman." From the album Elmore James, *Something Inside of Me.* Bell LP 104, 1968.
___. "So Unkind." From the album Elmore James, *Something Inside of Me.* Bell LP 104, 1968.
___. "I See My Baby." From the album Elmore James and John Brim, *Tough.* Blue Horizon LP 7-63204, 1968.
___. "Madison Blues." From the album Elmore James and John Brim, *Tough.* Blue Horizon LP 7-63204, 1968.
___. "My Best Friend." From the album Elmore James and John Brim, *Tough.* Blue Horizon LP 7-63204, 1968.
___. "Stormy Monday Blues." From the album Elmore James and John Brim, *Tough.* Blue Horizon LP 7-63204, 1968.
___. "Whose Muddy Shoes." From the album Elmore James and John Brim, *Tough.* Blue Horizon LP 7-63204, 1968.
___. "Canton, Mississippi Breakdown." From the album Elmore James, *The Legend of Elmore James.* Kent LP 9001, 1969.
___. "So Mean to Me." From the album Elmore James, *The Legend of Elmore James.* Kent LP 9001, 1969.

___. "Where Can My Baby Be." From the album Elmore James, *The Legend of Elmore James.* Kent LP 9001, 1969.

___. *The Legend of Elmore James.* Kent LP 9001, 1969.

___. "Elmo's Shuffle." From the album Elmore James, *The Resurrection of Elmore James.* Kent LP 9010, 1969.

___. *The Resurrection of Elmore James.* Kent LP 9010, 1969.

___. "Make My Dreams Come True." From the album Elmore James, *To Know a Man.* Blue Horizon LP 7-66230, 1969.

___. "Sunnyland." From the album Elmore James, *To Know a Man.* Blue Horizon LP 7-66230, 1969.

___. *To Know a Man.* Blue Horizon LP 7-66230, 1969.

___. "Find My Kinda Woman." From the album Elmore James, *History of Elmore James.* Trip LP 8007, 1971.

___. "My Baby's Gone." From the album Elmore James, *History of Elmore James.* Trip LP 8007, 1971.

___. *History of Elmore James.* Trip LP 8007, 1971.

___. "Up Jumped Elmore." Fury 2000, 1972.

___. *King of the Slide Guitar.* Ace LP 68, 1983.

___. "Look on Yonder Wall." From the album Elmore James, *The Complete Fire and Enjoy Sessions, Part 4.* Collectables CD 5187, 1989.

___. "You Know You Done Me Wrong." From the album Elmore James, *The Complete Fire and Enjoy Sessions, Part 4.* Collectables CD 5187, 1989.

___. *The Complete Fire and Enjoy Sessions, Part 4.* Collectables CD 5187, 1989.

___. "Go Back Home Again." From the album Elmore James, *Rollin' & Tumblin'—The Best of Elmore James.* Relic CD 7026, 1992.

___. "I Need You Baby" [complete version]. From the album Elmore James, *Rollin' & Tumblin'—The Best of Elmore James.* Relic CD 7026, 1992.

___. *Rollin' & Tumblin'—The Best of Elmore James.* Relic CD 7026, 1992.

___. *King of the Slide Guitar.* Capricorn CD 42006-2, 1992.

___. "Dust My Broom." From the album Elmore James, *Dust My Broom—The Best of Elmore James Part 2.* Relic CD 7040, 1992.

___. *Dust My Broom—The Best of Elmore James Part 2.* Relic CD 7040, 1992.

___. "Long Tall Woman." From the album Elmore James, *The Classic Early Recordings 1951-1956.* Ace BOXCD 4, 1993.

___. *The Classic Early Recordings 1951-1956.* Ace BOXCD 4, 1993.

James, Elmore, and John Brim. *Tough.* Blue Horizon LP 7 63204, 1968.

James, Elmore, and Walter Horton. *Cotton Patch Hotfoots.* Polydor LP 2383200, 1973.

Jenkins, Bobo. "Baby Don't You Want to Go." Fortune 838, 1957.

Johnson, Robert. "I Believe I'll Dust My Broom." Vocalion 03475, 1937.

___. "Cross Road Blues." Vocalion 03519, 1937.

___. "Rambling on My Mind." Vocalion 03519, 1937.

___. "Love in Vain." Vocalion 04630, 1939.

Jones, (Little) Johnny. "Big Town Playboy." Aristocrat 405, 1950.

___. "Sweet Little Woman." Flair 1010, 1953.

___. "Doin' the Best I Can." Atlantic 1045, 1954.

___. "Hoy Hoy." Atlantic 1045, 1954.

___. "Chicago Blues." From the album *Blues Piano—Chicago, Plus.* Atlantic LP 7227, 1972.

___. "Hoy Hoy" [alternate take]. From the album *Blues Piano—Chicago, Plus.* Atlantic LP 7227, 1972.

___. *Johnnie Jones with Billy Boy Arnold.* Alligator LP 4717, 1979.

___. "Prison Bound Blues." Rooster Blues 23, 1980.

Kennedy, Jesse "Tiny." "Strange Kind of Feeling." Trumpet 187, 1952.

King, B.B. "Woke Up This Morning." RPM 380, 1953.

___. "Please Love Me." RPM 386, 1953.

___. "Got a Right to Love My Baby." Kent 333, 1960.

King, Freddy. "Bossa Nova Blues." From the album Freddy King, *Bossa Nova & Blues.* King LP 821, 1963.

___. "King-A-Ling." Federal 12515, 1964.

Kirk, Andy, and His 12 Clouds of Joy. "Floyd's Guitar Blues." Decca 2483, 1939.

Kirkland, Eddie. "I Must Have Done Somebody Wrong." Fortune 848, 1959.

Leavy, Calvin. "It Hurts Me Too." Soul Beat 110, 1973.

Lenoir, J.B. "The Mojo." J.O.B. 1012, 1953.

___. "Louise." J.O.B. 1102, 1954.

___. "Lou Ella." Shad 5012, 1959.

Little Walter [Jacobs]. "Blue and Lonesome." Checker 1117, 1965.

Littlejohn, John. "What in the World." Margaret 997, 1968.

___. *John Littlejohn's Chicago Blues Stars.* Arhoolie LP 1043, 1969 [reissued as *Slidin' Home;* Arhoolie CD 9019, 2001].

___. "Slidin' Home." From the album John Littlejohn, *John Littlejohn's Chicago Blues Stars.* Arhoolie LP 1043, 1969.

___. "Dust My Broom." From the album The Bob Riedy Chicago Blues Band, *Lake Michigan Ain't No River.* Rounder LP 2005, 1973.

___. "Reconsider Baby." From the album The Bob Riedy Chicago Blues Band, *Lake Michigan Ain't No River.* Rounder LP 2005, 1973.

___. *Dream.* Storyville CD 8034, 1995.

___. "Dust My Broom." From the album *Bottleneck Blues.* Testament CD 5021, 1995.

___. *Slidin' Home.* Arhoolie CD 9019, 2001 [reissue of Arhoolie LP 1043, 1969].

Littlejohn, John, and Carey Bell. *The Blues Show! Live at Pit Inn.* Yupiteru LP 23-4004, 1982.

Lockwood, Robert Jr. "Dust My Broom." Mercury 8260, 1951.

Louis, Joe Hill. "Jealous Man." Rockin' 517, 1953.

___. *Gotta Boogie Baby.* P-Vine Club CD 22002, 1995.

Love, Willie. "Nelson Street Blues." Trumpet 175, 1952.

Mayall & the Bluesbreakers, John. "Mr. James." Decca (U.K.) 11900, 1964.

___. "It Hurts Me Too." Decca (U.K.) 12621, 1967.

McClennan, Tommy. "My Baby's Gone." Bluebird B8669, 1941.

McGhee, Brownie. "Evil, But Kindhearted." Alert 409, c. 1947.

Memphis Minnie. "Please Set a Date." Columbia 36895, 1945.

Memphis Slim. "Angel Child." Miracle 145, 1949.

___. "Sassy Mae." United 176, 1954.

Milton, Roy. "Hop, Skip and Jump." Specialty 314, 1948.

Muddy Waters [r.n.: McKinley Morganfield]. "Screaming and Crying." Aristocrat 406, 1950.

___. "Gone to Main Street." Chess 1526, 1952.

___. "Mad Love" (a.k.a. "I Want You to Love Me"). Chess 1550, 1953.

Myers, Sam. "Sad, Sad Lonesome Day." Fury 1035, 1960.

Nighthawk, Robert. "Annie Lee Blues." Aristocrat 2301, 1949.

___. "Six Three O." Aristocrat 413, 1950.

Papa Too Sweet. "Big Fat Mama." OKeh 8651, 1929.

Parker, Junior. "Yonder's Wall." Duke 367, 1963.

Pejoe, Morris. "Hurt My Feelings." Vee-Jay 148, 1955.

___. "Let's Get High." From the album Morris Pejoe and Arthur "Big Boy" Spires, *Wrapped in My Baby.* Delmark CD 716, 1998.

Peppermint Harris [r.n.: Harrison Nelson]. "Raining in My Heart." Sittin' In With 543, 1950.

Pitchford, Lonnie. "One String Boogie." From the album *American Folk Blues Festival '83.* L+R CD 2063, 1984.

___. *All Around Man.* Rooster Blues CD 2629, 1994.

___. "Shake Your Money Maker." From the album *Living Country Blues: An Anthology.* Evidence CD 26105-2, 1999.

Pryor, Snooky. "Going Back on the Road." J.O.B. 115, 1952.

___. *Snooky Pryor and the Country Blues.* Today LP 1012, 1973.

Ravens, The. "She's Got to Go." Mercury 70119, 1953.

Ray, Harmon. "Working Man." Decca 48107, 1949.

Robinson, L.C. "Good Rockin'". "Why Don't You Write to Me." Rhythm 1772, 1954.

___. *Mojo in My Hand.* Arhoolie CD 453, 1996.

Rush, Otis. "So Many Roads, So Many Trains." Chess 1751, 1960.

Shakey Jake [r.n.: James Harris]. "Roll Your Moneymaker." Artistic 1502, 1958.

Smith, Alvin. "On My Way." Music City 744, 1954.

Smoke Daddy Band featuring Billy Flynn, The. "Chicago Blues." From the album *The Smoke Daddy Band featuring Billy Flynn.* Easy Baby CD 400, 2000.

Sykes, Roosevelt. "Sweet Old Chicago." Imperial 5347, 1955.

Tampa Red [r.n.: Hudson Whittaker or Hudson Woodbridge]. "Mean Mistreater Blues." Bluebird B5546, 1934.

___ "It Hurts Me Too." Bluebird B8635, 1941.

___. "Annie Lou Blues." Bluebird B8654, 1941.

___. "Sure Enough I Do." Bluebird 34-0731, 1945.

___. "When Things Go Wrong with You." RCA Victor 22-0035, 1949.

___. *The Guitar Wizard.* Columbia/Legacy CD 53235, 1994.

Taylor, Eddie. *I Feel So Bad.* Advent LP 2802, 1972.

___. "My Heart Is Bleeding." From the album *My Heart Is Bleeding.* Evidence CD 26054-2, 1994 [reissue].

___. "Leave This Neighborhood." From the album Eddie Taylor, *Big Town Playboy.* P-Vine CD 5259, 1997.

Taylor, Hound Dog. "Baby Is Coming Home." Bea & Baby 112, c. 1960.

___. "Take Five." Bea & Baby 112, c. 1960.

___. "Alley Music." Firma 626, c. 1962;

___. "Christine." Firma 626, c. 1962;

___. "Christine" [instrumental version]. From the album *C.J.'s Roots of Chicago Blues, Vol. 1.* Blue Flame LP 101, c. 1970.

___. "It Hurts Me, Too." From the album Hound Dog Taylor and the Houserockers, *Hound Dog Taylor and the Houserockers.* Alligator LP 4701, 1971.

___. "Hawaiian Boogie." From the album Hound Dog Taylor and the Houserockers, *Natural Boogie.* Alligator LP 4704, 1974.

___. "The Sky Is Crying." From the album *American Folk Blues Festival '67.* L+R CD 2070, 1990.

___. *Live at Joe's Place.* Fan Club CD 100, 1992.

Taylor, Hound Dog, and the Houserockers. *Hound Dog Taylor and the Houserockers.* Alligator LP 4701, 1971.

___. *Natural Boogie.* Alligator LP 4704, 1974.

___. *Beware of the Dog.* Alligator LP 4707, 1976.

___. *Genuine Houserocking Music.* Alligator LP 4727, 1982.

Temple, Johnny. "Lead Pencil Blues." Vocalion 03068, 1936.

Terry, Sonny. "Screamin' and Cryin' Blues." Capitol 40061, 1947.

Tharpe, Sister Rosetta. "Strange Things Happening Every Day." Decca 8669, 1945.

Thomas, James "Son". *Beefsteak Blues.* Evidence CD 26095-2, 1998.

___. *Hard Times.* Black & Blue CD 440.2, 2000.

Turner, Baby Face. "Blue Serenade." Modern 882, 1952.

Turner, Big Joe. "Oke-She-Moke-She-Pop." Atlantic 1016, 1953.

___. "TV Mama." Atlantic 1016, 1953.

___. "The Sun Is Shining." Bayou 015, 1953.

Turner, B.K. "Whiskey and Women." Decca 7340, 1938.

Turner, Ike. "All the Blues All the Time." From the album Ike Turner & the Kings of Rhythm, *Rocks the Blues.* P-Vine CD 3031/3032, 1993 [reissue].

Unknown. "Where Have You Been So Long." From the album *Blues Is Killin' Me.* Flyright CD 28, 1990.

Various Artists. *The Blues.* Vee-Jay LP 1020, 1960.

___. *Chicago/The Blues/Today!, Vol. 1.* Vanguard LP 9216, 1966.

___. *Chicago/The Blues/Today!, Vol. 2.* Vanguard LP 9217, 1966.

___. *Chicago Blues at Home.* Advent LP 2806, 1977.

___. *Delta Blues—1951.* Acoustic Archives CD 702, 1990.

___. *Slidin'.* Charly CD RED 36, 1991.

___. *Willie Dixon: Working on the Blues Vol. 2/Chef Willie Cooks Up the Blues.* P-Vine CD 2347, 1992.

___. *The Fire/Fury Records Story.* Capricorn CD 42009-2, 1993.

___. *N.Y. on Fire: Bobby's Harlem Rock Vol. 2.* P-Vine CD 5461, 1998.

___. *Chicago Ain't Nothin' But a Blues Band.* Delmark CD 624, 1999.

___. *The Cream of Chicago Blues: The Guitarists, Vol. 1, 1946-1952.* Compact disc (unissued), 2001.

Vinson, Eddie "Cleanhead." "Person to Person." King 4582, 1952.

Walker, T-Bone. "Call it Stormy Monday." Black & White 122, 1947.

___. "Goodbye Blues." Black & White 123, 1948.

Weldon, Casey Bill. "What's the Matter with My Milk Cow?" Vocalion 03078, 1936.

Weldon, Casey Bill, and Kokomo Arnold. *Bottleneck Guitar Trendsetters of the 1930s,* Yazoo CD 1049, 1992 [reissue].

Wells, Junior. "Hoodoo Man." States 134, 1954.

___. "It Hurts Me Too." Chief 7035, 1961.

___. "It Hurts Me Too (When Things Go Wrong)." From the album *Chicago/The Blues/Today! Vol. 1.* Vanguard LP 9216, 1966.

White, Bukka. "Pinebluff Arkansas." Vocalion 03711, 1937.

Williams, Jody. "Groan My Blues Away." From the album *Cool Playing Blues.* Relic CD 7016, 1990.

Williamson, Homesick James. "Farmer's Blues." Chance 1121, 1952.

___. "Lonesome Ole Train." Chance 1121, 1952.

___. "Homesick." Chance 1131, 1953.

___. "The Woman I Love." Chance 1131, 1953.

___. "Crossroads." U.S.A. 746, 1963.

___. "Set a Date." Colt 632, 1964.

___. *Blues on the South Side.* Prestige LP 7388, 1965.

___. "Somebody's Been Talkin'." From the album *Encore for the Chicago Blues.* Spivey LP 1009, c. 1965/1966.

___. "I Got to Move." From the album *Spivey's Blues Cavalcade.* Spivey LP 1015, 1975.

___. *Goin' Back Home.* Trix LP 3315, 1976.

___. "Williamson Shuffle." From the album Homesick James, *Chance Vintage Blues/R&B Crops Vol. 2.* P-Vine LP 706, 1977.

___. "My Baby's Gone." From the album *Meat & Gravy from Cadillac Baby—"Records was cheap to make then," Vol. 1.* Red Lightnin' LP 0019, 1978.

___. "Homesick Sunnyland Special." From the album *Meat & Gravy from Cadillac Baby—Hits that Missed Vol. 2.* Red Lightnin' LP 0020, 1978.

___. *Goin' Back in the Times.* Earwig CD 4929, 1994.

___. *Chicago Slide Guitar Legend.* Official CD 5253, 1998.

Williamson, Homesick James, and Snooky Pryor. *Sad and Lonesome.* Wolf LP 120.409, 1980.

Williamson, Sonny Boy. "Sunny Land." Bluebird B7500, 1938.

___. "Alcohol Blues." Victor 20-2893, 1948.

Williamson (#2), Sonny Boy. "Mighty Long Time." Trumpet 166, 1952.

___. "One Way Out." Checker 1003, 1961.

___. "309." From the album Sonny Boy Williamson and Willie Love, *Clownin' with the World.* Acoustic Archives CD 700, 1989.

___. *King Biscuit Time.* Arhoolie CD 310, 1989.

Willis, Ruth Mary. "Low Down Blues." OKeh 8921, 1931.

Wilson, Hop. "My Woman Has a Black Cat Bone." Ivory 127, c. 1961.

___ "Rocking in the Cocanut Top." Goldband 1246, 1973.

___. *Steel Guitar Flash!* Ace CD 240, 1994.

Wilson, Jimmy. "Strangest Blues." Rhythm 1765, 1954.

VISIT

HENRY'S BEEFBURGERS

For the best American-style take-away food in Sydney (just ask Hound Dog Taylor and the HouseRockers, seen below with manager Bruce Iglauer and Henry's genial proprietor Arne Saeter and his wife Mary following one of the HouseRockers' highly successful Bondi Lifesaver gigs during their recent Australian tour) you really should make it along to HENRY'S BEEFBURGERS, 13 Albion Street, Waverly (also at Big Bear Plaza, Neutral Bay).

HENRY'S is open Monday to Thursday 11am to 2am, Fridays and Saturdays 11am to 4am, Sundays 11am to 1am.

HENRY'S BEEFBURGERS is the only take-away food emporium in Sydney run by blues fans (even the cook is an ABS member).

1975 Advertisement from Crazy Music (The Journal of the Australian Blues Society).

Note: Page numbers appearing in italics indicate that the entry refers to a footnote.

ABOUT THE AUTHOR

Steve Franz has had a lifelong interest in music. He received a Bachelor of Arts degree in Liberal Arts from Hanover College, and a Master of Arts degree in Musicology (Regional Studies) from The University of Memphis. He has hosted several blues radio shows, was founding editor of *Hawaiian Boogie Disease,* a short-lived blues newsletter, and served as program director for a Community Radio station. He has written various articles and liner notes, including projects for *Living Blues* magazine, *Rock & Roll Disc,* and the Relic and Rhino Record groups.

The British Institute of Jazz Studies

An archive of 20th Century writings on jazz, blues and related musics

The British Institute of Jazz Studies was the U.K.'s first jazz archive. Founded in the mid-1960s, and inspired by the Institute of Jazz Studies now based at Rutgers, the aim was to set up a resource centre for students, writers, discographers and enthusiasts. Concentrating on the written word, The British Institute of Jazz Studies has built an extensive library of books, periodicals, festival/concert brochures, newscuttings and ephemeral material.

Donations are gratefully accepted. For more information, please contact:

Graham Langley
The British Institute of Jazz Studies
17 The Chase, Crowthorne, Berkshire, RG45 6HT, England

Telephone: 01344 775669
Fax: 01344 780947

Registered Charity No.: 250388

Praise for ***ELMORE JAMES: The Ultimate Guide to the Master of the Slide***

"*Obviously A Labor of Love...*
This excellent booklet provides everything you ever wanted to know about old Elmo's recordings and then some, and belongs in the library of every self-respecting Elmoholic."

—*Scott Dirks,* Blues Revue Quarterly

"Highly recommended. Steve Franz is to be commended for the diligent research he has put into this booklet which all Elmore James enthusiasts will have to have."

—*Phil Wight,* Blues & Rhythm *magazine*

"...the most comprehensive discography of Elmore James... It's all completely indexed and cross-referenced as it should. The perfect resource for the serious fan." —*R. Seth Friedman,* Factsheet Five

"...extensive and *painstakingly* detailed.... You can lose yourself for long periods of time in this little book... [and] can learn more than you ever hoped to know about your Elmore collection. I hope Mr. Franz earned himself at least a Master's Degree for this piece of work." —Lucille's BluesLetter

"This is a labor of love.... Neatly laid out with session details, reprints of record labels, and dates, I'm constantly picking this up to check out facts and taking notes of songs I'm missing."

—*Chip Lamey, editor,* Juke Joint Notes *and WLFR Blues Radio Programmer*

"With your little book, I hope to get all the Elmore material in the Blues Archive nailed down."

—*Edward Komara, Music Librarian/Blues Archivist, the University of Mississippi*

"It is going to be extremely useful and makes a valuable addition to our archive."

—*Graham Langley, The British Institute of Jazz Studies*

"Exhaustive and excellently structured... It's a pleasure to see someone in the U.S. produce a scholarly effort equal to the oversea's stellar products." —*Jim Herbert, Maryland*

"I love the music of Elmore James. When you issue a discography on the man, heaven can only be a couple weeks away." —*Max Sievert, Sweden*

"Thanks for making such a valuable resource available to Elmore fans!" —*John Pearson, California*

"remarkable....this work should remain handy..." —*Bob Rusch,* Cadence *Magazine*

"Franz's scholarship is first-rate..." —*T.J. McGrath,* Dirty Linen *Magazine*

"An impressive piece of work." —*Alan Balfour, Blues researcher / writer*

"It's great." —*Peter Guralnick, noted author*

ORDER FORM

YES! PLEASE SEND ME __________ COPIES OF ***THE AMAZING SECRET HISTORY OF ELMORE JAMES.*** I HAVE ENCLOSED **U.S. FUNDS** (Check, Money Order, International Postal Money Order **made payable to STEVE FRANZ)** FOR:

_______ **$40.00 FOR EACH COPY** shipped to the UNITED STATES, CANADA or MEXICO; *or*

_______ **$45.00 FOR EACH COPY TO ANY INTERNATIONAL / OVERSEAS ADDRESS.**

(Note: Prices include all shipping and handling fees)

SEND TO:

STEVE FRANZ
BLUESOURCE PUBLICATIONS
PO BOX 20074
SAINT LOUIS, MO 63144-0074 USA

SHIPPING INFORMATION (PRINT CLEARLY!):

NAME: ____

ADDRESS: ____

ADDRESS: ____

CITY: ____

STATE: ____

ZIP: ______________________ COUNTRY: ______________________